THE
UNITED STATES

Conquering a Continent

Volume I

Winthrop D. Jordan
University of Mississippi

Leon F. Litwack
University of California, Berkeley

North
West
Publishing LLC

PHOTO RESEARCHER: Turi Robertson

COMPOSITION: Archetype Book Composition

ILLUSTRATIONS: JoAnn Gibson, John Harman, Nathaniel Levine, and Peggi Rodgers

ISBN 1-931910-07-3

Copyright © 2002 by North West Publishing, LLC

Printed in the United States of America

CONTENTS

CHAPTER 1

MIGRANTS TO THE NEW WORLD   I

CHAPTER 2

AN OVERSEAS EMPIRE   19

CHAPTER 3

THE COLONIAL PEOPLE   45

CHAPTER 4

NEW WAYS OF THOUGHT   67

CHAPTER 5

THE MAKINGS OF REVOLT   87

CHAPTER 6

THE AMERICAN REVOLUTION   109

CHAPTER 7

PROBLEMS OF GOVERNMENT   129

CHAPTER 8

THE FEDERALIST ERA 151

CHAPTER 9

JEFFERSON, THE CONTINENT, AND WAR 171

CHAPTER 10

INTERNAL DEVELOPMENT 193

CHAPTER 11

NEW POLITICS FOR A NEW AGE   219

CHAPTER 12

THE SPIRIT OF ANTEBELLUM AMERICA   241

CHAPTER 13

SOCIETY IN THE NORTH   265

CHAPTER 14

A SOUTHERN NATION   287

CHAPTER 15

MANIFEST DESTINY AND SLAVERY   307

CHAPTER 16

THE UNION COMES APART   327

CHAPTER 17

CIVIL WAR   349

CHAPTER 18

AFTER THE WAR: RECONSTRUCTION AND RESTORATION   377

CONTENTS

MAPS AND CHARTS

WORDS AND NAMES
IN AMERICAN HISTORY

A NOTE OF INTRODUCTION

A word about history. The word *history* has a double meaning. It refers to what did in fact take place in the past. It also refers to our study and understanding of those events and how we talk and write about them.

These two meanings are often confused. We all have met such expressions as "history tells us . . . ," "history shows . . . ," and "the lessons of history are. . . ." These expressions assume that the actual events of the past can themselves teach us about the present and perhaps even the future. However, past events cannot themselves speak, let alone teach. But we can and do learn from what has been said and written about them. We learn from what other people today are saying about what went on in the past, as well as from what people in *our* past said about *their* past.

Here things get tricky, simply because historians are people. No two historians look at past events in exactly the same manner. They draw differing conclusions about the meaning of what went on and sometimes about what actually did go on. They also disagree about what was important enough to bother discussing. For example, historians still disagree as to exactly when President Woodrow Wilson suffered his first stroke. At a different level of inquiry, they disagree about the causes and consequences of the American Civil War and the Cold War. Today, much more than they used to, historians are learning and writing about the lives of ordinary men and women. Whether Joe and Josephine Smith went to the supermarket on October 4, 1958, is in itself obviously not of great importance, but the fact that millions of Americans were getting their food in such a manner obviously is, especially since we know that the Smiths' parents could not have fed themselves or their families in that manner.

Why bother with the past in any form? The most basic answer is that we cannot do without it. As individuals, we use it all the time. Each of us lives in the present, but our immediate experiences, thoughts, and perceptions are shaped by our previous ones. We are what we have been—and what we think we have been. An important part of our present is our awareness of our past. Similarly, an entire society is shaped by its past and by its consciousness of that past. As individuals and as a nation, we cannot tell where we are (much less where we are going) without knowing where we have been. And because the United States is a vast and profoundly complex entity, including over the years more than half a billion individual lives and millions of groups, the task of understanding this nation is not an easy one. But it can be very rewarding and even fun.

This book has a number of thematic chapters, such as those dealing with important intellectual and literary developments. Nonetheless we have adhered to a fundamentally chronological structure, an approach that is dictated by the unfolding of events. We are convinced that anyone who thinks that the U.S. Constitution was adopted before the American Revolution is not going to be able to understand either of those two major developments. The same may be said of the Vietnam War and World War II, or of the invention of the atomic bomb and the creation of the steam engine.

A few words about this substantially revised edition of *The United States*. We have tried to convey both the personalities and importance of such public leaders as George Whitefield, John

Calhoun, and Dorothea Dix; of Franklin Roosevelt, Martin Luther King, Jr., and Ronald Reagan. We have also emphasized the history of less powerful people. The ordinary folk who have made up the great bulk of American society expressed themselves in various ways in the past, as they still do today. We have stressed their experiences and their voices—the lives of Indians, blacks, Hispanic Americans, and dozens of immigrant groups from Europe and Asia, as well as working people in the fields, boats, shops, factories, mines, and homes of the nation.

This edition has much more about women because a solid body of scholarship in women's history has emerged in very recent years. We have dealt with women in such various roles as young daughters and child laborers, mothers and grandmothers, factory and office workers, farmers and westward pioneers, reformers, intellectuals, professionals, and politicians. As we have with ethnic, racial, and religious groups, we have dealt with the record of women's achievements and with the record of the obstacles and defeats that barred their way.

This edition also includes a unique feature—a series of boxes entitled "Words and Names in American History." These are miniature essays about the specifically American background of words that are in common use today, or were until quite recently. Some are political, such as *lobby, logrolling, gerrymander,* and *platform;* others are geographical, such as *Mississippi, Wall Street,* and the *Mason-Dixon line;* still others defy classification, such as *Uncle Sam, cafeteria, deadline, lynch,* and *hazing.* All of them cast small shafts of light on the American past.

Finally, we have tried to set American history into the context of global history, to convey American developments as they related to the ongoing development of the rapidly modernizing society in which the inhabitants of the world are participants, whether they wish to be or not.

This book derives from one first published in 1957 by Richard Hofstadter, William Miller, and Daniel Aaron. Since then it has been successively revised, after 1976 by the present two authors. As with the previous edition, the text of the chapters through the Civil War is by Winthrop Jordan; those from Reconstruction and Restoration to the present, by Leon Litwack.

Both of us hope that readers of this book will gain more than a formal knowledge of American history. We hope they will also gain an appreciation of the richness and diversity of American cultural expression, and a deeper, more subtle sense of what it means to live in this somewhat ambiguous, ever-changing nation.

A number of teaching and learning aids are available with the text. These include a **Two-Volume Study Guide,** prepared by Elizabeth Neumeyer of Kellogg Community College, Battle Creek, Michigan. An **Instructor's Manual,** authored by Robert Tomes of St. John's University, Staten Island, New York and a **Test Item File** by Paul Harvey of the University of California at Berkeley provide, respectively, teaching suggestions, chapter outlines, and film lists, and over one thousand objective-test and essay questions. The material in the **Test Item File** is also available on CD.

Many instructors read the manuscript of the text and offered helpful suggestions for improvement. They include William C. Hine, South Carolina State College; Roger L. Nichols, University of Arizona; George H. Skau, Bergen Community College; Alwyn Barr, Texas Tech University; Robert Haws, University of Mississippi; Robert D. Cross, University of Virginia; Leonard L. Richards, University of Massachusetts; Peyton McCrary, University of South Alabama; Richard Wightman Fox, Yale University; Robert G. Pope, State University of New York at Buffalo; Joseph C. Morton, Northeastern Illinois University; Thomas A. Drueger, University of Illinois at Urbana; John Mayfield, University of Kentucky; Linda Dudik Guerrero, Palomar College; Bradley R. Rice, Clayton Junior College; David C. Hammack, Princeton University; Alasdair Macphail, Connecticut College; Harvey H. Jackson, Clayton Junior College; Jerry Rodnitzky, University of Texas at Arlington; Michael L. Lanza, University of New Orleans; Clarence F. Walker, University of California at Davis; and Ray White, Ball State University. We would especially like to thank our editors at Northwest Publishing, as well as the many others whose hard work is reflected in this new edition.

Winthrop D. Jordan

Leon F. Litwack

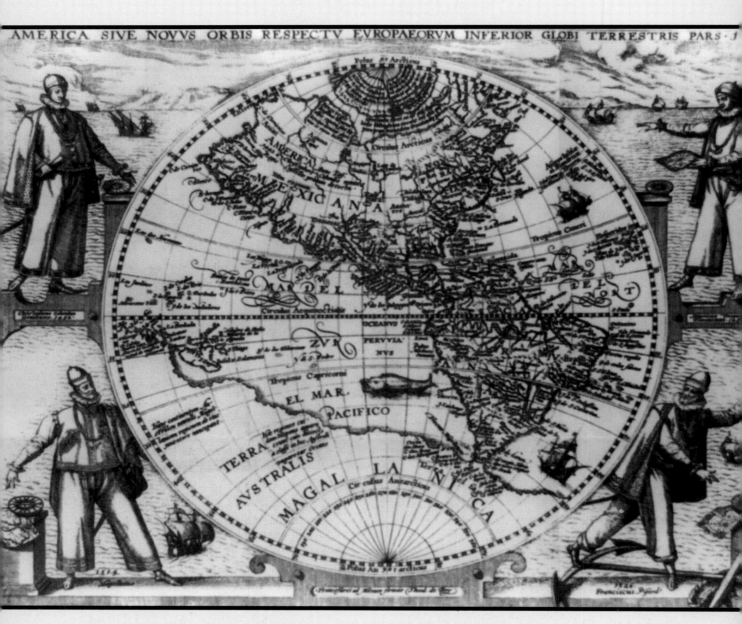

Replica map of the Americas with portraits of Christopher Columbus, Amerigo Vespucci, Ferdinand Magellan, and Francisco Pizarro around border. *(Library of Congress)*

CHAPTER 1

MIGRANTS TO THE NEW WORLD

The first people who migrated to this part of the world came from Asia. They made this adventurous journey, probably hunting large animals, somewhere between ten and forty thousand years ago. They came on foot in small groups at several different periods when lower sea levels exposed an ancient land bridge between Asia and Alaska at what is now the Bering Strait. As thousands of years went by, they fanned out over North, Central, and South America. This scattering resulted in the development of hundreds of different languages and a wide variety of physical characteristics, social organization, and levels of technology. For thousands of years these various peoples remained isolated from one another because the land was so vast, and from their Asian homeland because melting ice caps drowned the ancient land bridge under three hundred feet of water.

Much later, only five hundred years ago, came a remarkably sudden burst of immigration by sea from western Europe and western Africa. This was the beginning of the explosion of western European culture that has so profoundly shaped the entire world today. At first that immigration to the Americas was largely Spanish, but then other Atlantic-European nations began to

take an interest in what Europeans called the New World. People from Portugal, France, the Netherlands, the British Isles, and even Germany migrated across the Atlantic Ocean. These western Europeans forced people from many nations in West Africa to migrate as slaves, especially to tropical regions of the Western Hemisphere.

From about 1500, therefore, the history of the American continents and islands was no longer isolated from developments in the Old World. And of course developments in the New World were beginning to change what went on in the Old.

At that time western Europe was developing a new, dynamic economic system: commercial capitalism. The Atlantic nations of western Europe were becoming more centralized than before, usually under newly powerful monarchs. They developed strong international rivalries that greatly affected events in the Americas, Europe, and even Africa and Asia. At the same time, the great Western Christian church was split by the Reformation; for several centuries the deep-seated hostility between Roman Catholics and Protestants caused friction and sometimes war among nations.

The Europeans who migrated to the New World had a profound and usually disastrous impact on the descendants of the original settlers—the "Indians," as the Europeans called them. Some of this impact was cultural and technological. But the most important result was that European diseases took an appalling toll among the Indians. In its early phases, European migration to America resulted in one of the most drastic drops in population over a large area that humankind has ever experienced.

In turn, however, the Indians influenced the European and African immigrants in various ways. They did a great deal to reshape Old World agricultural practices, patterns of settlement, and military tactics. So did the New World environment, especially the climate and such natural resources as precious metals, timber, fish, fur, and plants.

Historians have used a good many terms to describe this sudden burst of migration from the Old World to the New. It was called a "discovery" by Europeans, even though Cristoforo Colombo died in the stubborn conviction that the lands he had seen on his voyages lay just off the coasts of China and Japan, and even though other Europeans had touched American shores five hundred years earlier. Recent writers have referred to the "invention" of America, assuming that Europeans needed to find a different sort of world in order to understand their own. The coming of the Europeans has also been called an "invasion" of the Indians' lands. Finally, it should be borne in mind that Indian America was settled not just by Europeans, but by Africans as well.

THE FIRST AMERICANS

Little is known about the long history of the original American immigrants. Much of the available evidence is *archaeological* and has literally been dug up. Some is *geological;* it is known, for example, that when Indians were spearing mammoths in New Mexico, northern New England was covered with ice. There are written materials from a few Indian cultures, including the famous calendar of the Aztecs in Mexico, but most Indian peoples used oral tradition rather than writing. Much of what is known about these people comes from the early reports of European explorers and conquerors. These reports have to be treated with great caution because of the prejudices and lack of comprehension of the observers.

Five hundred years ago, the peoples of the New World were as various as those of the Old. They spoke some twelve hundred different dialects and languages, and they varied enormously in appearance, dress, customs, technology, and political organization. Some went about nearly naked, clad only around the waist with animal skin, and used stones and shells as tools. Some produced stunning works of art in gold or silver, constructed highways, and built enormous pyramids of stone. Some lived on nuts and berries; others cooked food in baskets of reeds or bark, or in clay pots. Some lived in cities as large as those

in Europe; others were nomadic hunters. Some were governed by "divine" kings; others knew no greater authority than their own family. Traditionally, historians have concentrated on the "high civilizations" of Mexico and Peru—the Aztec, Maya, and Inca—but for the history of the *early* United States, it seems more appropriate to concentrate on the peoples who lived along the North Atlantic coast.

Technology in the Eastern Woodlands

Indians arrived along the Atlantic seaboard relatively late in the long process of settling the American continents. Those who populated the wooded region stretching from what is now Georgia to Maine shared many characteristics, although with considerable variation. Anthropologists usually divide them into three large groups, principally on the basis of language. The Algonquian tribes, who extended all the way from Canada to North Carolina and as far west as the Great Lakes, became for the early English migrants the "typical" Indians. Farther south and west were several large groups who spoke Muskogean languages: the Choctaw, Chickasaw, Creek, and Seminole. The Cherokee in Georgia were similar in living habits but had probably arrived more recently; they spoke a dialect of a

Algonquian village on the Pamlico River estuary showing Native structures, agriculture, and spiritual life. *(Library of Congress)*

Although they had several technological skills not known to Europeans, their lack of other skills put them at a severe disadvantage when they met the new immigrants from across the Atlantic. The Iroquois and Algonquian had developed a highly efficient means of transportation at a time when roads in most parts of the world were inferior to the highways of ancient Rome. Their elm- and birch-bark canoes were brittle, but they had the great advantage of light weight for portages between lakes and streams. Hollowed-out logs were also used, but more often on coastal waters. Many of the coastal Indians fished with great efficiency, using nets and weirs. They did not, however, venture far onto deep water, for they had not developed sails.

All the eastern woodland Indians grew corn (maize) and various kinds of squash, pumpkins, and beans. They hunted deer and bears, which provided clothing as well as food, and they trapped and hunted a variety of smaller animals unknown in the Old World, such as beaver, opossum, and raccoon. Hunting was done with bows and arrows, which in skillful hands were as accurate as European muskets and much more rapid-firing. These men also used tomahawks in warfare. The Muskogean carried, in addition, spears and shields woven from bark and vines.

Their housing usually consisted of bent poles covered with thatch or hides; the word *wigwam* is the Algonquian term for "house." Stones and shells served for weapons and tools. All these peoples lacked three technological advantages widely used by Europeans: the wheel, the plow, and draft animals such as oxen and horses.

Nature and Society

Eastern woodland Indians lived closer to nature than Europeans did, though of course Europeans

third language, Iroquoian, which prevailed in the area around the eastern Great Lakes. Those Iroquoian peoples were probably also relative newcomers, having come from the Mississippi Valley into what is now upstate New York and neighboring parts of Canada.

All these people shared common cultural characteristics, but climate plus available food and housing made for important differences.

WORDS AND NAMES IN AMERICAN HISTORY

Succotash is a mixture of boiled corn and lima or butter beans. The dish, still commonly served in New England, is actually much older than the first arrival of English Puritans there. It was a staple of the New England Indians, and the word itself comes directly from the Algonquian word for the mixture. For the Indians there it was an obvious combination, since they planted both beans and squash in their cornfields. It is now realized what a clever agricultural practice this was, for the leaves of the bean and squash plants shaded out the growth of weeds, and the cornstalks provided natural poles on which the bean plants could climb. The succotash mixture provided a nutritious dietary base. One can even buy frozen succotash in some markets today, although not nationwide.

then lived much closer to the natural world than we do now. They kept time by the sun or moon or walking distances, in an age when Europeans were increasingly using clocks and calendars. The Indians had a close psychological rapport with animals and even with trees and mountains; many tribes believed that animals had souls. Their religious faiths reflected their strong ties with their natural surroundings. Most—perhaps all—believed in a high god, a single deity superior to all other deities. The less powerful spirits were often associated with specific animals, vegetation, or parts of the landscape.

This affinity with nature was reflected in the way these people thought about their societies. Many tribes considered themselves to be divided into clans, or groups of people regarded as being related to one another. These clans were often identified by such names as wolf, bear, deer, and beaver.

The Indians were strongly attached to their land, which they felt was theirs by reason of tradition and use, not because they "owned" it. The land almost seemed to own them. This way of thinking was very different from the one that prevailed in western Europe, where various groups of people staked out their own turf by means of national boundaries and carved up those spaces among individuals who "owned" land as "real estate." The gap between these concepts about land was to prove an enduring source of conflict between Indians and Europeans in America.

The social and political organization of the tribes varied considerably. Today, it is impossible to describe them accurately, largely because early Europeans tended to talk about Indian societies in terms based on their own experiences. European observers expected to find kings, nobles, and commoners, and they became confused when they discovered that such categories did not fit. There was similar confusion about the different Indian groups, which the English variously called "nations," "tribes," or simply "sorts." It is clear, however, that there were at least a hundred Algonquian tribes. Sometimes, groups of them were shaped into confederacies by forceful leaders, but more often they were hostile to their neighbors, in much the same way the various European and West African peoples were.

The famous League of the Iroquois in upstate New York came about when five tribes fashioned a sophisticated, powerful, and remarkably enduring political alliance. Each tribe sent a specific number of representatives to a central council for decisions about war and diplomacy. The Iroquois fascinate historians and anthropologists because of the unusual strength of this confederation and also because of other distinguishing aspects of their society: their "longhouses," huge wigwams occupied by four to six families; their reputation as fierce warriors; their reliance on communal interpretation of individual dreams; and the powerful influence of Iroquois women, who farmed while their men hunted and warred and who chose which men would lead them in both war and peace.

Among all eastern Indians, political leadership depended on maturity, wisdom, and forcefulness much more than on heredity or the accumulation of wealth.

The division of labor between these Indian men and woman was even more rigid than it was in Europe at the time. Men hunted, trapped, and fished; in short, they concentrated on taking animal resources. Women cleaned and processed animals and did almost all the farming and preparation of food. Men went to war, but women did more than half the labor that provided food, clothing, and shelter.

The woodland Indians were no more peaceful than Europeans: They fought frequently against each other, more for sport and manhood than for territory. By European standards, casualties were low. Silence and surprise were the usual methods of attack. Many tribes practiced ritual torture of captives and/or formal tribal adoption. Their style of peace resembled their style of war; Europeans were struck by their quiet dignity in diplomatic negotiations. They spoke with brief eloquence, weighing their remarks with confident assurance that those few words would seal whatever agreement was being made.

THE OLD WORLD MEETS THE NEW

People from the western part of the Old World discovered Indian America at least twice, but the first discovery had little effect. The impact of the second was momentous, in Europe as well as America. In both instances, "America" was not discovered as a whole; rather, European navigators stumbled onto particular landfalls without the slightest notion that they had found two "new" continents.

The Norsemen

The Norse contacts with America took place about one thousand years ago. Bold Norwegians had long since settled in Iceland; from there they pushed westward along the stepping-stone islands of the North Atlantic. In about 980 they established tiny settlements near the southern tip of Greenland. In the thirteenth century some four thousand Norse were living there, but for unknown reasons they lost contact with Europe in the second half of the fifteenth century and died out for lack of food and supplies.

Yet that thrust westward had gone farther. In 986 Biarni Heriulfson set sail from Iceland to join his father, Heriulf, in Greenland. By mistake his course was too far south. He missed that island and ended up cruising along a shore he was sure could not be Greenland because it was "a fiat and wooded country" and had no mountains of ice. He was, in fact, running along the coasts of Baffin Island and Labrador, but he did not land because he was aiming for Greenland.

Although Biarni was the first European we know of who saw American shores, Leif Ericson was the first to set foot on American soil. Sailing westward from Greenland in the same boat Biarni had used, he landed on Baffin Island and then made his way south down the coast of Labrador. At last the voyagers came ashore at a place they called Vinland "in accordance with all the good things they found in it."

There has been much conjecture about the location of this spot; some people have claimed that Leif got as far south as Massachusetts or even Virginia. But the site has recently been pinpointed to be L'Anse aux Meadows on the northern tip of Newfoundland. Archaeological evidence there shows conclusively that Norwegians established a fishing colony that lasted for several years.

This original European discovery of America remained unknown except in some obscure old Norse sagas, until the nineteenth century. Some people—the ancient Phoenicians from the Mediterranean, black Africans, and even Pacific Islanders—have made claims of earlier contact with Indian America. None of these claims are totally improbable, but all are very far from firmly established. Much more to the point, if such contacts did occur, they had no widespread effect. The voyages of Christopher Columbus did.

European Expansion

There is no easy explanation for the sudden wanderlust of western Europeans in the fifteenth century. Various factors—which we might label

The world known to Europeans in 1492

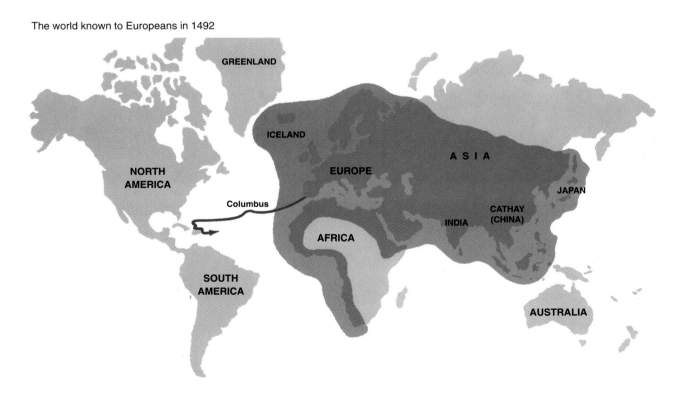

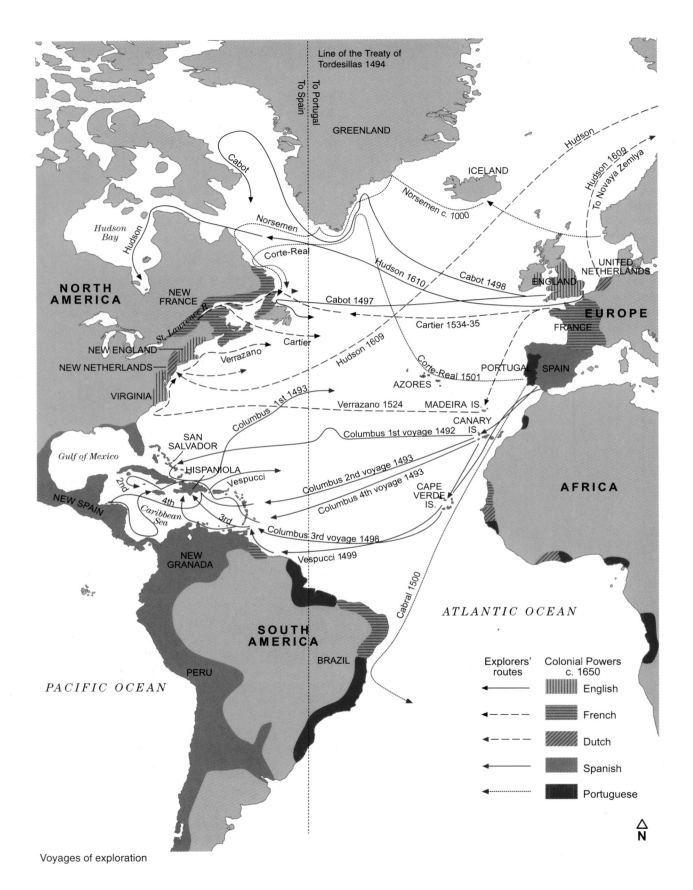

Voyages of exploration

6

economic, political, technological, and demographic—contributed to their thrust overseas.

For centuries Europeans had traded with the peoples of southeastern Asia for highly valued commodities that could not be found or grown in Europe, among them jewels, silk, and spices. (Spices improved the flavor of food and, in an age without refrigeration, preserved meat and disguised its taste when rotten.) That trade was carried on over thousands of miles across the Indian Ocean, through the Middle East, over the Mediterranean Sea to the ports of southern Europe, and then overland to the north and west. At the western ports of entry, the trade was controlled by the merchants of Venice and other city-states in what is now Italy.

As time went on, merchants in the western parts of Europe grew more and more discontented with the problems of this trade: high prices, piracy, too many middlemen, and lack of reliability. At the same time, new financial practices that developed in Italy were beginning to spread north and west: double-entry bookkeeping of financial records, pooling of capital among several individuals or families, rudimentary banks, and the use of arabic rather than roman numerals in account books.

Politically, the monarchs of western Europe were becoming more successful in their struggles with powerful feudal warlords. Geographic areas that are now single countries, such as France, Portugal, and Spain, were then collections of separate provinces and dukedoms. During the fifteenth century, monarchs consolidated their authority over larger territories, and it was these powerful new monarchies that became the modern countries of western Europe. Many historians summarize these developments as *the rise of nation-states.*

A third development in European society was just as complicated but much less dramatic. Trade with the Far East had resulted in knowledge of both gunpowder and the compass. Although neither of these Chinese inventions had an immediate impact on methods of warfare and navigation, in the long run they helped give Europeans a sense of mastery over other peoples and the sea. Also important to overseas expansion were hundreds of small improvements in ship design. Taken together, these improvements enabled Europeans to build vessels that could handle ocean swells without capsizing, be steered by workable rudders, and be propelled entirely by sails, without the need for oars.

The demographic change that helped set off expansion was the result of a disaster. In the fourteenth century Europe was struck by bubonic plague, a deadly infection carried by infected fleas on rats. The Black Death swept away about a third of western Europe's population. Even though it damaged the economy, the tragedy raised the economic and social status of the agricultural laborers (serfs) who survived, because it meant that their labor was in great demand. The old idea that people were bound to the land began to break down. People grew restless and no longer assumed they had to remain where they had been born.

Portugal in the Van

These four factors interacted in various ways in different parts of western Europe, but together they produced a mood of adventure. Early in the fourteenth century, Italian, Spanish, and French sailors began to explore the west coast of Africa in search of a way around that continent. They came upon and occupied the Canary Islands, then the Madeiras, and then the Azores, all in the eastern Atlantic Ocean. But it was the Portuguese, after 1420, who began the systematic collection of geographic information that enabled them to transform the Atlantic into a pathway of adventure and commerce. And it was they who first brought enslaved blacks back by sea from Africa to Europe, in 1442.

In 1420, Prince Henry the Navigator set up his great maritime research institute at Sagres on Portugal's southwestern tip, "where the two seas, the Mediterranean and the Great Ocean, fight together." There, until his death in 1460, he conducted a laboratory in astronomy, cosmography, mapmaking, ship and sail design, and instruments of navigation. Some of his most valuable information came from returning sailors and ship captains who were making longer and longer voyages down the western coast of Africa. Prince Henry's work was crowned in 1488, many years after he died, when Bartholomeu Dias at last rounded the Cabo Tormentoso (Cape of Storms) at Africa's southernmost tip, opening the first all-water route from Europe to the Indies. The king of Portugal was so impressed by this feat that he renamed that treacherous neck of land the Cape of Good Hope.

Nine years after Dias's voyages, a flotilla of four Portuguese ships under Vasco da Gama sailed for India from Lisbon and returned in triumph in 1499, laden with spices and jewels. Vasco da Gama's voyage meant the end of Levantine (Middle East) supremacy in the Oriental trade, the eclipse of the Italian merchants, and the decline of the Mediterranean. The Portuguese, moreover, soon drove Muslim merchants and pirates from the Indian Ocean itself, reduced their strongholds at the sources of supply for Oriental goods, and established a Far Eastern empire of their own that lasted, at least in fragments, almost to our day.

THE SPANISH AND FRENCH IN AMERICA

While the Portuguese were attempting to reach Asia by sailing south and east, a singleminded mariner decided to approach the same goal by sailing directly west. He came upon a puzzling barrier on that route, and died dejected because he had not found Japan and China. By his own standards Columbus failed, but in doing so he laid the foundation for an enormous and extremely profitable Spanish empire in America. Through his exploits, Spain claimed control over most of the two American continents. Other European nations refused to accept that claim, so soon European rivalries found a new field of battle in the Americas.

Cristoforo Colombo

The son of a tailor, Cristoforo Colombo was born in Genoa, one of the major maritime Italian city-states. At an early age he turned to the sea and became an experienced navigator and shipmaster. His private dream was to reach the Orient by sailing westward. Like most educated people, he believed that the world was round, but he grossly underestimated the size of the globe by discounting the quite accurate estimates of ancient Greek scholars. For five years, he pleaded for financial backing at the courts of the monarchs of Spain, England, France, and Portugal. He was turned down everywhere.

In 1492, a dramatic event changed the minds of the jointly reigning Spanish monarchs, King Ferdinand and Queen Isabella. For centuries the Spanish had struggled to expel the Moors, the Muslim conquerors who had invaded their land from North Africa. They finally succeeded in 1492. Immediately they moved to expel other non-Catholics, particularly the Jews, whose

Columbus's belief that he could reach the Orient by sailing westward was backed up by Paolo Toscanelli, a scholar who sent Columbus this map of the world in 1481. *(Windsor, History of America, Vol. 2 [1886])*.

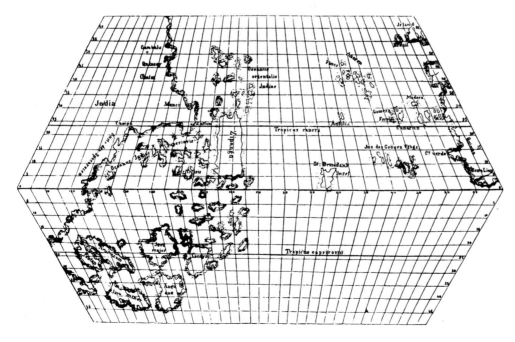

Cristoforo Colombo. *(Library of Congress)*

wealth had helped finance the long wars against the Moors.

The Spanish had conducted their campaigns as a religious crusade, and now Ferdinand and Isabella were willing to help spread Christianity elsewhere, as Columbus promised to do. They were also eager for profits from trade with "the lands of India," or the "Indies," as the Far East was called. So they agreed to back the eccentric sailor who insisted he could reach the Indies by sailing west. Columbus was given the title (as he carefully noted) of "Admiral-in-Chief of the Ocean Sea and Viceroy and Perpetual Governor of all the lands and mainlands that I should discover."

On August 3, 1492, Columbus's expedition set sail from the little Spanish port of Palos aboard three vessels, the *Nina*, the *Pinta*, and the *Santa Maria*. After stopping at the Canary Islands off the coast of West Africa, Columbus set a course due west. He had calculated that he was on the same latitude as Cipangu (Japan), which was regarded as the richest part of "the lands of India." The crewmen, mostly Spanish, did not fully trust their Italian captain. He, in turn, doctored the ship's log by understating the daily mileage of his little fleet.

Having doubled all records for ocean sailing beyond sight of shore, *Santa Maria*'s crew mutinied. The boredom of an endless voyage strained the nerves of sailors made idle by the easy passage. Columbus managed to quiet the crew by promising to turn back if no land was sighted within three days. Then, just past 2 A.M. on October 12, *Pinta*'s lookout called, "Tierra! Tierra!"

"To the first island which I found," Columbus later wrote to Ferdinand and Isabella, "I gave the name San Salvador, in remembrance of the Divine Majesty, Who had marvelously bestowed all this." The inhabitants of the island called it Guanahani. Columbus called them "Indians" on the assumption that he was on the outskirts of the Indies. Soon, "I found very many [other] islands," Columbus added in his letter to Ferdinand and Isabella, "filled with innumerable people, and I have taken possession of them all for their Highnesses, done by proclamation and with the royal standard unfurled, and no opposition was offered to me."

After a few months of exploring the Caribbean, Columbus left some of his men behind on the large island of Hispaniola and set out for Spain with a few gold nuggets and several "Indians" to prove the success of his venture. None of the Indians survived the voyage. Columbus made three more trips to the New World. His search on these visits was for a passageway through the barrier beyond which, he remained certain, must lie Japan. He found no such passage. Not until Ferdinand Magellan's men sailed around the world in the service of Spain (1519–1522) did the truth become known about the enormous distance of the westward passage to the Far East.

Upon learning of Columbus's great discoveries, the pope proceeded to divide up the newly discovered world between the Catholic Spanish and the Portuguese. In 1494, in the Treaty of Tordesillas, Spain and Portugal agreed on the specific boundary separating their territories. In effect, Portugal received the Orient and Spain the New World, except for the eastern part of South America. In 1500, on a voyage around Africa to the Orient, a Portuguese captain, Cabral, was blown off course and found himself on a New World shore that he promptly claimed for his native land. Cabral's discovery became known as Brazil, but the Portuguese took little interest in the New World for another half century.

Soon after Columbus's first triumphant return, Spain encouraged other mariners to occupy her

New World claim, search out its limits, convert its inhabitants, and seize its wealth. One of the first to sail under Spanish colors was Amerigo Vespucci, a native of the Italian city of Florence. In 1497 he began a series of voyages on which he explored the coastline southeast from Mexico all the way to Brazil. Ten years later, a German geographer first called the New World "America" in his honor.

The Spanish and the Indians

Before other Atlantic nations offered a challenge, Spain had established a vast empire in the New World. Small numbers of Spaniards occupied the largest Caribbean islands: Cuba, Hispaniola, Puerto Rico, and Jamaica. Led by Hernando Cortés, the Spanish went on to conquer the Indian civilizations in Mexico. Francisco Pizarro began the occupation of Peru in 1528. In both regions the Spanish found fabulous sources of gold and silver. Other Spanish explorers pushed through Florida, the lower Mississippi Valley, and the North American Southwest, but they were discouraged by not finding precious metals in those regions.

Francisco Pizarro. *(Library of Congress)*

The Indians of the Caribbean islands—the Arawaks and Caribs—were relatively primitive in technology and political organization, although they had mastered the art of interisland

THE AZTEC VIEW OF THE SPANIARDS

Spanish soldiers, under command of Francisco Pizarro, burning a Peruvian to make him tell where the gold is located. *(Library of Congress)*

One of the few Indian texts about early contact with Europeans described the reaction of the Spanish conquerors to gifts of gold sent by Montezuma, king of the Aztecs:

Then Motecuhzoma dispatched various chiefs. Tzihuacpopocatzin was at their head, and he took with him a great many of his representatives. They went out to meet the Spaniards in the vicinity of Popocatepetl and Iztactepetl, there in the Eagle Pass.

They gave the "gods" ensigns of gold, and ensigns of quetzal feathers, and golden necklaces. And when they were given these presents, the Spaniards burst into smiles; their eyes shone with pleasure; they were delighted by them. They picked up the gold and fingered it like monkeys; they seemed to be transported by joy, as if their hearts were illumined and made new.

The truth is that they longed and lusted for gold. Their bodies swelled with greed, and their hunger was ravenous; they hungered like pigs for that gold. They snatched at the golden ensigns, waved them from side to side, and examined every inch of them. They were like one who speaks a barbarous tongue: everything they said was in a barbarous tongue.

boating. The first European drawings of these Indians showed them eating human flesh. They may or may not have been cannibals; what is certain is that the Arawaks told the Spanish that the Caribs, their enemies, were. On the mainland of Mexico, the Yucatán Peninsula, and Peru, the Spanish found densely populated, advanced civilizations, genuine empires with powerful kings, highway systems, enormous temples, and stunning works of art in silver and gold.

Until recently, the success of the small numbers of Spanish explorers has been explained largely in terms of their superior boldness and technology. The Spanish conquerors were indeed brutal, but the Aztecs in Mexico were themselves conquerors of earlier peoples and practiced ritual human sacrifice and perhaps cannibalism as well. The Spanish advantage was mainly psychological. Many more Indians were overawed by Spanish firearms than were killed by them. And the Indians also were amazed by the sight of men on horseback, who they thought were single animals.

In recent years, however, it has become clear that the Spanish had one enormous advantage of which neither they nor the Indians were aware. Over hundreds of centuries, most of the peoples of the Old World had developed partial immunity to certain diseases that were unknown in the New World. Within fifty years of first contact with the Spanish, the Indians of Hispaniola had nearly died out. In Mexico the Indian population appears to have dropped to along the lines of 10 percent of its previous level. Measles and especially smallpox were probably the two chief killers. Whatever the diseases, it is clear that no society can survive when it loses 90 percent of its people in two or three generations. Unwittingly the Indians had their revenge, for

Columbus's sailors introduced syphilis into Europe. But that disease did not kill masses of people in a short period.

In the New World, the political and social consequences of disease were profound. Many Indian societies were virtually destroyed. Depopulation was largely responsible for the demand for slaves from the Old World to work the fields and mines of the New. Starting about 1522, the Spanish began importing slaves from Africa. Although they too died in large numbers, the Africans had had sufficient contact with Europeans across the Sahara Desert to have acquired partial immunity themselves, so they did not suffer the drastic mortality rates of the Indians. But they too had a measure of revenge, for many European slave traders died from tropical diseases. The dimensions of this human tragedy, then, were enormous and bitterly ironic.

The French

Except in Brazil, the Spanish claimed a monopoly on the entire New World, one that was endorsed by the pope. Yet other Christian nations refused to recognize Spain's exclusive jurisdiction. The French were the first to challenge it. In 1524 another Florentine, Giovanni da Verrazano, sailed westward in the service of the French king along the coast of North America. He was looking for a passageway to the Far East.

Ten years later, the French monarch sent Jacques Cartier on a similar mission in search of what had become known as the Northwest Passage—not because it was expected to run northwest, but because it was supposed to be in the north and to run directly westward to the Indies. Cartier hit upon the mouth of the St. Lawrence

River, and he was able to sail so far up that stream he was convinced that he had found the route to the Orient. But then, at the site of modern Montreal, he came up against rapids that prevented further progress to the west. Despite his disappointment, he was impressed by "the immense numbers of people in Hochelga" and by "their kindness and peacefulness."

The Spanish showed little interest in the northern voyages, but they were deeply concerned by a French settlement in Florida that was uncomfortably close to the shipping lanes of their treasure ships from Peru and Mexico. They wiped it out and confidently built Fort Augustine on the northeast coast of that region. From there they sent missionaries farther north, but established no permanent settlements. Although by the 1540s Vásquez de Coronado had explored as far north as present-day Kansas, it was the French and not the Spanish who gained control in North America.

In the early seventeenth century, under the leadership of Samuel de Champlain, French explorers established outposts at Quebec, Montreal, and various other points along the St. Lawrence River, the great gateway to the interior of the continent. Then they passed on through the regions of the Great Lakes and the Ohio and Mississippi valleys. The French also established settlements at New Orleans and Biloxi on the Gulf of Mexico, and at St. Domingue, the western end of the island of Hispaniola.

Most French settlements in the Midwest were forts and trading stations, aimed primarily at serving the fur trade. Many French fur traders married Indian women and adopted Indian ways. French farmers were widely scattered and remained sufficiently few to take very little land from the Indians. Thus the French avoided conflict with the native inhabitants, unlike the Spanish and the English.

THE ENGLISH IN THE NEW WORLD

Among the Atlantic nations of Europe, England, and the Netherlands lagged behind Portugal, Spain, and France in taking an interest in the New World. In the sixteenth century, the Dutch were still fighting for national unity and independence from the Spanish. They established no claims in North America until 1609, when Henry Hudson, an Englishman in the employ of a Dutch trading company, sailed up the river that he was

to name for himself. The first English claim was established much earlier along the northern coast by two voyages sponsored by King Henry VII in 1497 and 1498. But those expeditions, led by John and Sebastian Cabot, provoked little interest among the English, and for more than seventy-five years the only Englishmen to see American shores were summertime fishermen.

This delay had two important consequences. During the latter half of the sixteenth century, the economies of England and the Netherlands were becoming committed to commercial capitalism, much more so than the economies of the other Atlantic nations of western Europe. Thus the English and Dutch settlements in America in the early seventeenth century were financed largely by private merchants rather than by royal wealth. Fully as important, by the time they attempted to establish colonies in America, the Dutch and the English had become Protestants and were locked in bitter opposition to the supporters of the Roman Catholic church.

The Reformation

The Protestant Reformation began in Germany in 1517 when Martin Luther publicly denounced the Catholic church for selling pardons for sins. Luther contended that people could be saved "by faith alone," not by outward observances, charity, and good behavior—mere "good works." He went on to claim that Christians must acquire faith directly from the Bible, the Word of God. Luther's assault on Catholic hierarchy and doctrine triggered more than a century of religious warfare in Europe. Eventually religious divisions came to coincide roughly with national boundaries. Spain, Portugal, and most of Ireland remained Roman Catholic, as did France, except for a strong minority of Protestants called Huguenots. England, Wales, Scotland, the Netherlands, and the Scandinavian countries became Protestant. The German states were divided.

The reformers were not a united group. Protestants in France, the Netherlands, and Scotland followed the doctrines of John Calvin, a French refugee who established a religious government in Geneva, Switzerland. Calvin stressed human helplessness in the face of an all-powerful God. He also emphasized humankind's original sin and the doctrine of *predestination*, the idea that God, from the beginning of time, had decided the eternal fate of every individual—whether he or she was to be saved or damned. Calvin also sought to eliminate from Protestant services the forms and ceremonies of Roman Catholic ritual, and he insisted that all members of the religious community must constantly examine the condition of their souls. Although people could not earn their way to heaven by good deeds, diligent labor in their job or "calling," Calvin taught, was often a sign of redemption. It seemed to Calvinists that God would favor communities committed to His ways.

Calvinist ideas began to seep into England in the middle of the sixteenth century. By then, however, the English nation had already broken away from the Roman Catholic church. In the 1530s Henry VIII had become entangled in marital problems that involved both the pope and Spain, whose monarch was rapidly becoming the international defender of Catholicism. Henry established a national English church with himself as "supreme governor" and confiscated the vast landholdings of the monasteries. Two short reigns followed Henry's death—one Protestant, the next Catholic. Then Queen Elizabeth, monarch from 1558 to 1603, tried to achieve a compromise between the nationalized Protestant

Church of England, still partly Catholic in ceremony and doctrine, and the growing number of English Calvinists who demanded further reform of the national church.

England versus Spain

Queen Elizabeth became the champion of Protestantism against the Catholic Counter-Reformation being mounted by Spain. She secretly financed Dutch Protestants in their wars against the Spanish and eventually sent English troops into the Netherlands to help them. She also quietly invested in voyages of English captains who wanted to raid the Spanish treasure ships bringing back gold and silver from Mexico and Peru.

In 1577, even though her nation and Spain were supposedly at peace, Elizabeth backed a brilliantly successful expedition led by Francis Drake. Drake sailed through the Strait of Magellan, raided Spanish ships and settlements along the western coast of South America, touched at California, which he claimed for England as "Nova Albion," and returned to England in 1580, having circled the world. In Plymouth harbor Elizabeth knighted Drake on the deck of his ship, the *Golden Hind.* Elizabeth then rather deviously assured the Spanish ambassador that she had no hostile intentions toward his country. Drake's exploits helped establish a tradition among European nations, which lasted until the middle of the eighteenth century, whereby they could war against each other in the New World while remaining at peace in the Old. As the common phrase went, "No peace beyond the Line."

For a generation England and Spain held onto a shaky peace, but in 1588 the Spanish mounted a massive attempt to invade England. The famous Spanish Armada was probably the largest naval force ever assembled up to that time. But the Spanish fleet was hit by gale winds and the guns of the English ships. The result, for the Spanish, was a disastrous defeat. For England, whose population was less than half of Spain's, it was a glorious victory for the cause of Protestantism and the English nation. The war with Spain dragged on until 1604, but the defeat of the Armada established England as a major power. As such, it began to think more seriously about challenging its international rivals in the New World.

Queen Elizabeth. *(Library of Congress)*

Frobisher and Gilbert

English interest in America was not merely a matter of challenging Catholic Spain. In the 1550s London merchants began to organize joint-stock companies for trading overseas with Russia, Africa, and the Levant (the Middle East). In the 1570s a new Cathay (China) Company financed three voyages led by Martin Frobisher to find the Northwest Passage.

Frobisher sailed directly west below the southern tip of Greenland and then northwest until he came on the enormous, forbidding island of Baffin not far below the Arctic Circle. Finding further passage blocked by ice and barren land, Frobisher brought back to England several tons of ore that glittered with specks of gold. When tested it proved to be pyrite, or fool's gold, and for years piles of the ore lay blocking one of the interior gates of the Tower of London.

Another Englishman was dreaming about a more promising destiny for his country in America. Sir Humphrey Gilbert was the first Englishman to see the New World as a place where profit could be made by permanent settlement rather than by setting up trading posts. He organized two expeditions. Virtually nothing is known about the first one (1578), but in the summer of 1583 he set sail with five ships and reached Newfoundland with four.

There he found a little community of European fishermen who for years had been drying fish in the summer. He took possession of the land in the name of Elizabeth, and then sailed south in search of a more favorable climate. But winter was beginning to close in, and his ships (now reduced to two) were running short of supplies. On the return voyage they ran into a storm, and one of the vessels was lost. Sir Humphrey Gilbert was last seen sitting in the stern of a ten-ton fishing boat reading a copy of Thomas More's *Utopia*.

Raleigh's Roanoke

Gilbert's mantle fell to his half brother, Sir Walter Raleigh, a dashing, impulsive favorite of Elizabeth. Raleigh had no trouble in getting a royal charter to found a colony in America. In 1584 he sent out an expedition with instructions to explore much farther south along the coast. His men came back with glowing descriptions of the land around Chesapeake Bay, which Raleigh named Virginia after the unmarried queen. The next year he equipped an expedition that included an artist, John White, who made superb paintings of the Indians, and Thomas Cavendish, who later became the third European to sail around the world.

They settled on Roanoke Island in Albermarle Sound. The men were frustrated in their search for gold and for a water passage to the Pacific, so when Sir Francis Drake stopped at the colony the next year on his way back from robbing Spanish gold in the West Indies, the Roanoke settlers returned with him to London.

Raleigh was as persistent as he was impulsive: In 1587 he sent out a large expedition of 120 people, which for the first time included women. Virginia Dare, the first English child born in America, was the granddaughter of the group's leader, John White. Leaving his family in the colony, White returned to England to help arrange for supplies. But because of the Spanish Armada and the war with Spain, every English vessel was pressed into service. When a supply ship finally reached the colony in 1590, all the settlers were gone. To this day, no one knows what happened to them.

Sir Walter Raleigh. *(Library of Congress)*

A Carolina Indian dance, painted around 1585 by John White. *(Library of Congress)*

Marked by bad luck, unrealistic expectations, lack of financial resources, and the ongoing war with Spain, English colonizing efforts seemed to be going nowhere. Yet in the closing decades of the sixteenth century there were significant changes in England that may in the long run have been more important than all these early expeditions. More and more capital was accumulating in the hands of English merchants. The transfers of land that began with Henry VIII's seizure of the monasteries helped trigger a process by which some people were gaining great wealth and others were being thrown off the land and becoming the roving "beggars" of Elizabethan England.

The mood of the English people was becoming nationalistic. Defeating the Armada did nothing to diminish this feeling. One man captured this mood so well that he became known as the "trumpet" of English colonization. Richard Hakluyt was a friend of Gilbert and Raleigh, a clergyman, and a propagandist for overseas expansion. In 1584 he set forth a comprehensive case for English settlement in the New World. In the 1590s he captivated a wide audience with his *Principal Navigations, Voyages, Traffiques, and Discoveries of the English Nation.*

Yet clearly it would require more than this kind of pleading to make English colonization in America a success. The necessary ingredients for successful "planting" in America did not become obvious until the English found them in the next century by a process of trial and error, greed and faith.

SUMMARY

European voyages of exploration and discovery had by the late fifteenth century reached the Americas, which until then had known only Asian immigrants. This expansionism was motivated by desire for the trade and wealth on which the new economic system of commercial capitalism was based, as well as by political rivalries. The latter, in turn, were based on the religious conflicts that had grown out of the Protestant Reformation.

The most important immediate effect of this "invasion" by Europeans of the New World was the destruction of the native populations, who died by the thousands of diseases to which they had no resistance. These "Indians," as the Europeans called them, varied greatly in language, culture, and appearance. Their societies and political organizations ranged from the sophisticated empires of the Aztecs, Incas, and Mayas to simple family or tribal groupings of nomadic hunters.

The woodland Indians of the Atlantic seacoast lived primarily by hunting, fishing, trapping, and simple agriculture. Political organization was based on tribes or nations, and sometimes on confederations of tribes. These societies were remarkably "classless"; there were leaders, but leadership was based on age and merit, not birth.

Although we say Christopher Columbus "discovered" America, it had actually been known to Europeans much earlier. The tenth-century Scandinavians who found and settled Iceland and Greenland also made their way to Labrador and Newfoundland. But it was not until late in the fifteenth century that economic, political, and technological developments made long sea voyages and large-scale colonization both possible and desirable.

Portuguese navigators were the first to venture out in search of an ocean route to India and the Far East. They sailed south and east around the southern tip of Africa to find the "Indies." Then Spanish and later French and English explorers tried to reach the "east" by sailing west. When Columbus landed in the Caribbean, he thought he was near Japan.

The pope divided the world between the Spanish and the Portuguese in the Treaty of Tordesillas. The Spanish claimed all the New World except for Brazil; the Portuguese got Brazil and the entire Orient. By the time the English, the French, and the Dutch realized the potential of Spain's new possessions, the Spanish had built a huge overseas empire and extracted from it enormous amounts of gold and silver. It was not until 1534 that Cartier found the St. Lawrence River and Canada for the French, and even then the French settlements were trading outposts that did not greatly disturb the Indians. The Dutch did not arrive until 1609, when Henry Hudson discovered the river

TIME LINE

40,000–15,000 B.C.	First human migration from Asia to North America	1522	First Spanish importation of slaves from Africa to America
A.D. 1001	Probable date, Norse site at L'Anse aux Meadows, Newfoundland	1535	Cartier lays French claim to St. Lawrence River valley
1442	Portuguese bring black African slaves to Europe	1583	Unsuccessful attempt by Gilbert to establish permanent settlement in America
1492	Columbus's "discovery" of America	1584	Hakluyt advocates "western planting" by the English
1492	Old World diseases begin devastation of Indian populations	1587	Raleigh's Roanoke colony established; it vanishes some time within the next three years
1494	Treaty of Tordesillas		
1497–1498	Cabot voyages establish English claim in North America	1588	Spanish Armada defeated in attempt to conquer England
1499	Vasco da Gama returns to Portugal from sea voyage to India	1590	Drake knighted after spectacular voyage around the globe
1500	Cabral's voyage lays Portuguese claim to Brazil	1603	Death of Queen Elizabeth; peace between England and Spain
1517	Beginning of Protestant Reformation	1609	Hudson establishes Dutch claim in North America
1519	Cortés begins Spanish conquest of Mexico		

that bears his name. The English had actually come earlier, in 1497 and 1498, but it was seventy-five years before they attempted to establish a settlement.

Martin Luther's challenge in 1517 to the supreme authority of the Catholic church started centuries of religious conflict in Europe. As a result, Spain, Portugal, and France became loyal supporters of the pope; England, Scotland, the Netherlands, and Scandinavia were split among various Protestant denominations.

The defeat of the Spanish Armada in 1588 made England a major maritime power. Its merchants were by this time eager to share in the rewards of overseas trade. But the first attempts to establish English settlements in North America—in Newfoundland in 1578 and 1583, and at Roanoke in the huge area called Virginia, in 1584 and 1587—all failed. It would take much trial and error before the English found the right formula for empire in North America.

Suggested Readings

The best book on the original American peoples is B. Fagan, *The Great Journey: The Peopling of Ancient America* (1987). (There is controversy as to when the migrants came from Asia.) Among many studies, the following are useful: R. Hurt, *Indian Agriculture in America: Prehistory to the Present* (1987); and J. Bradley, *Evolution of the Onondaga Iroquois: Accommodating Change, 1500–1655* (1987).

The thrust of Europeans overseas is discussed in R. Reynolds, *Europe Emerges: Transition toward an Industrial World-Wide Society, 1660–1750* (1961); L. McAlister, *Spain and Portugal in the New World, 1492–1700* (1984); and the fine study by I. Clendinnen, *Ambivalent Conquests: Maya and Spaniard in Yucatan, 1517–1570* (1987).

C. Verlinden, *Beginnings of Modern Colonization* (1970), emphasizes the medieval antecedents to European expansion. There is extremely interesting material in C. Cipolla, *European Culture and Overseas Expansion* (1970); and R. Davis, *The Rise of the Atlantic Economies* (1973), covers the fifteenth through the eighteenth centuries.

The Norse voyages have been controversial. Perhaps the best start is with W. Washburn (ed.), *Proceedings of the Vinland Map Conference* (1971); C. Sauer, *Northern Mists* (1968); and F. Pohl, *The Viking Settlements of North America* (1972).

C. Gibson, *Spain in America* (1966), is the best survey of that subject, and contains a good bibliography. J. Hardoy, *Pre-Columbian Cities* (1973), has an informative text and magnificent pictures. A complex subject is dealt with by M. Morner, *Race Mixture in the History of Latin America* (1967). J. Parry, *The Spanish Seaborne Empire* (1966), is a vivid account.

As for other European nations in the New World, there are two works by C. Boxer: *Race Relations in the Portuguese Colonial Empire, 1415–1825* (1963), and *The Dutch Seaborne Empire, 1600–1800* (1965). For the French, see W. Eccles, *France in America* (1972). Numerous works on the Amerindians have been published since the mid-1960s, most of them great improvements over older studies. Probably the best survey is still H. Driver, *Indians of North America* (2nd ed., 1970), supplemented by G. Willey, *An Introduction to American Archaeology*, Vol. 1, *North and Middle America* (1966), and R. Underhill, *Red Man's America: A History of Indians in the United States* (rev. ed., 1971). A useful collaboration between anthropologists and historians is E. Leacock and N. Lurie (eds.), *North American Indians in Historical Perspective* (1971). For more references, see the splendid bibliographical essay in W. Washburn, *The Indian in America* (1975).

The discovery of the New World by European voyagers has received loving attention from several distinguished historians. S. Morison's *Admiral of the Ocean Sea* (2 vols., 1942) remains one of the great biographies of American history. Morison, who was both a sailor and a superb stylist, capped his long historical career with *The European Discovery of America: The Northern Voyages*, A.D. *500–1600* (1971) and *The European Discovery of America: The Southern Voyages*, A.D. *1492–1616* (1974). Especially good on ship design is J. Parry, *The Age of Reconnaissance* (1963). Several other books have titles that explain themselves: D. Quinn, *England and the Discovery of America, 1481–1620* (1974); J. Axtell (ed.), *The Indian Peoples of Eastern America: A Documentary History of the Sexes* (1981); A. Rowse, *The Expansion of Elizabethan England* (1955); and H. Baudet, *Paradise on Earth: Thoughts on European Images of Non-Europeans* (1965). A different perspective is offered in R. Brown, *Historical Geography of the United States* (1948); and D. Meinig, *The Shaping of America*, Vol.1 (1986).

There is an enormous body of works on the Reformation in England and in western Europe. Partly because of differing religious perspectives, no single study stands out as the place to begin. A bibliography that focuses on the English Reformation may be found in R. Lockyer, *Tudor and Stuart Britain, 1471–1714* (1964).

Portrait of the children of King Charles I of England: The future Charles II of England (right), and Princess Mary (center).
(Library of Congress)

CHAPTER 2

AN OVERSEAS EMPIRE

Between 1600 and 1700, England acquired a permanent empire in the New World, and the New World acquired a new society. The colonies that grew up on the eastern coast of North America became linked with one another and with England in a mercantile system of empire. It was an economy based on the exchange and sale of goods in a pattern designed to build the prosperity and power of England as the center. Founding and running an overseas empire was a new venture for England; making a new life was a new venture for the colonists. Problems were inevitable, particularly because England sent colonists rather than warriors to North America. The colonies themselves differed from one another because they were established for different reasons.

By the end of the century, government officials in England began to realize that they had the makings of an overseas empire. In actuality, that empire consisted of nearly twenty different settlements stretching from the Caribbean to New England. English officials knew what they wanted the colonies to become, but enforcing their wishes was difficult at a time when it took London at least three months to get an answer to the simplest question about what was going on in America. But none of this was apparent in 1603–1604, when events in England made permanent settlement on the Atlantic coast a real possibility.

CHANGES IN ENGLAND

Several factors combined to make many English people decide to emigrate to the forbidding wilderness in America. The war between Spain and England came to an end in 1604, and peace encouraged merchants to invest their capital in overseas enterprises. James I, who had succeeded Elizabeth, tried to support some of these efforts, but the royal treasury lacked funds. James was hostile to the growing number of Calvinists in his church. Many of these Puritans, as they were called, decided that truly godly communities could be more easily established in America than in England. Many of them also thought James was undermining the traditional English freedoms of representative government, free speech, taxation by consent, and trial by due process. In addition, economic dislocations led to a widespread belief that England was overpopulated; there seemed to be too many "beggars" roaming the countryside and flooding into London. Finally, a sense of exhilaration and expansive power was sweeping the nation after its victories over Catholic Spain.

A learned and well-intentioned man, James I was also tactless and opinionated. It was a bad combination for a ruler who had to deal with an unruly Parliament and a growing Puritan party within the national church. Although he willingly presided over the great English translation of the Bible, the King James version, he came into conflict with the Puritans, who thought the Church of England was still too much like the Catholic church of Rome. He also clashed with Parliament over taxation and free speech. At the bottom of these and other issues was that of parliamentary versus royal power.

James I died in 1625, but his son Charles I took a hard line on taxation and the privileges of Parliament. After a major constitutional crisis in the late 1620s, Charles I tried for more than a decade to rule without Parliament. When forced by financial necessity to call Parliament together in 1639, he became involved in a civil war that resulted in his execution in 1649. This was followed by the Puritan dictatorship of Oliver Cromwell and his "saints." After Cromwell's death, the monarchy was "restored" in 1660.

The Restoration of Charles II marked a turning point in English history that had a great impact on the colonies, just as the outbreak of the civil war had in 1640. Whereas the latter event ended the Great Migration of the 1630s and threatened the colonies with economic disaster, the Restoration helped make possible the establishment of more colonies and a system for supervising them. Yet the religious issue in England was only partially settled. Most people still belonged to the Church of England, but a large minority still clung to Puritan principles in the face of some persecution. The constitutional issue remained less clear. It was not until another revolution in 1689 that the primacy of Parliament over the Crown was firmly established.

VIRGINIA

When James I assumed the throne in 1603, he was quite willing to issue land grants in America. James gave his backing to the Virginia Company, which had two branches, one in London and the other in the little port city of Plymouth. He awarded Sir Ferdinando Gorges's Plymouth branch an enormous territory on the northern portion of the Atlantic coast, and in the spring of 1607 Sir Ferdinando sent an expedition to Sagadahoc on the Kennebec River in Maine. The settlement lasted barely one winter. After an "extreme, unseasonable, and frosty" season, the men simply quit. It was the Jamestown settlement that finally succeeded.

This first permanent English settlement in the New World came very close to failure; only an accident of timing saved it from going the way of Roanoke. At first it was an all-male enterprise, but gradually a few women braved the hardships of the Atlantic voyage and the crude conditions in the struggling colony. In order to survive, an overseas colony needed a reliable source of income, and this first successful settlement found one in a new crop, tobacco. The early English settlers also had to deal with the fact that the land was already occupied. The Indian residents of the area could easily have wiped out the tiny settlement, and they came quite close to doing so.

In December 1606 the *Susan Constant*, *Godspeed*, and *Discovery*, with 160 men under the command of Captain Christopher Newport, weighed anchor in the name of the Virginia Company of London and set sail across the Atlantic. Four months later they sighted "the Bay of Chesupiac," or Chesapeake. The three tiny ships sailed up a broad river the settlers tactfully named the James and chose an island they called Jamestown, a site well situated for defense—and also, as it turned out, for the spread of disease.

Here, after the most terrible experiences, England won its first permanent foothold in America.

During the bleak winter of 1608–1609, the "starving time," the colony was held together by the efforts of Captain John Smith, an energetic and iron-willed war veteran. Smith was aided by Powhatan, a chief who had forged a powerful confederacy of Indian tribes in the area. Powhatan at first regarded the English as pawns in his power game and befriended them with food supplies, as he would any local tribe whose loyalty he wished to cultivate.

The English undertaking in Virginia had three principal objectives: to find a northwest water passage to the wealth of Asia, to exploit the gold and silver of America, and to find suitable lands for producing crops such as silk, grapes, dyes, and oranges. All three efforts failed. The James River did not go very far west. Smith's explorations aroused the hostility of Powhatan's people, who soon realized that the English had come not merely to trade metal for corn, but to take Indian land. Powhatan's daughter Matoaka, whom the English called Pocahontas, voiced this resentment when she said: "Many do inform me that your coming is not for trade but to invade my people and possess my country."

In addition to meeting growing hostility from the Indians, the settlers failed to find the gold that the Spanish experience in Mexico told them ought to be lying about for the taking. But that did not stop the "gentlemen" the Virginia Company had sent out from spending their time looking for treasure instead of providing shelter and food or establishing plantations.

By late 1608, more colonists had arrived. Smith tried to force Powhatan to trade, but Powhatan chose to let the English starve. When Smith was injured in 1609 and left Virginia permanently, the settlement remained, as he accurately described it, "a miserie, a ruin, a death, a Hell." By 1610, although Christopher Newport on successive visits had brought almost two hundred newcomers, only sixty settlers lived in Jamestown. The Virginia Company struggled to support its overseas enterprise, but met with little success. By 1624, when James I revoked the colony's charter and made Virginia a royal province, it had only 1200 people. About 6000 had set out for Jamestown, but 4000 had perished on the ocean voyage or in the New World, and hundreds of others had given up and gone home.

The Colony Takes Hold

By then, however, conditions had begun to improve. The first settlers had been mere servants of the promoters, men who had signed contracts called *indentures*, by which they agreed to work for a certain number of years in exchange for their passage across the ocean. Once they reached Virginia, these servants became very hard to control. Many ran off to seek gold, and those who fulfilled their contracts had little incentive to work. In 1619, the promoters gave each of the "ancient planters" one hundred acres of his own and instituted the *head right* system, under which any settler received fifty acres for every servant he induced to come to America. The government of the colony was liberalized by the creation of a House of Burgesses. This first legislature of elected representatives in America held its first meeting in 1619. By that time, a few women had arrived in the colony. Their presence helped change Virginia from a military outpost to a permanent settlement.

King James the 1st. *(Library of Congress)*

A SERVANT IN VIRGINIA

In 1623, the year after the great Indian massacre in Virginia, a young English servant owned by the Virginia Company wrote his parents in hopes that they would arrange to buy his freedom.

Loveing and kind father and mother my most humble duty remembered to you hopeing in God of your good health, as I my selfe am at the makeing hereof, this is to let you understand that I your Child am in a most heavie Case by reason of the nature of the Country is such that it Causeth much sicknes, as the scurvie and the bloody flux and divers other diseases, wch maketh the bodie very poore, and Weake, and when wee are sicke there is nothing to Comfort us: for since I came out of the ship, I never at[e] anie thing but pease, and loblollie (that is water gruell) as for deare or venison I never saw anie since I came into this land, ther is indeed some

foule, but Wee are not allowed to goe, and get it, but must Worke hard both earelie, and late for a messe of water gruell, and a mouthfull of bread, and beife, a mouthfull of bread for a pennie loafe must serve for 4 men wch is most pitifull. . . .

Living as he was on an isolated plantation, Richard Frethorne also referred to the continuing danger from Indians: "Wee are but 32 to fight against 3000 if they should Come, and the nighest helpe that Wee have is ten miles of us." He had been befriended by a kindly freeman, he said, who "much marvailed that you would send me a servaunt to the Companie, he saith I had beene better knockd on the head, and Indeede so I find it now to my great greife and miserie, and saith, that if you love me you will redeeme me suddenlie, for wch I doe Intreate and begg. . . ."

Fully as important was the discovery in 1612 that tobacco could be grown successfully. A market for this product had been growing in Europe since the middle of the sixteenth century. In 1618, Virginia shipped 30,000 pounds to England, mostly for reexport to the Continent. By 1627, the colony was exporting more than 500,000 pounds a year. Not until sugar in the Caribbean a generation later, or until the invention of the cotton gin nearly two centuries later, would a New World crop take off in such spectacular fashion.

This explosion of tobacco production had important social and political effects. Tobacco rapidly depleted the fertility of the soil: Four years on the same ground was the usual limit. In their search for more and more land, the great planters gradually pushed small farmers back from good water transportation in the Tidewater, the rich coastal plain. Some of these farmers ventured west into the upland area called the Piedmont.

These developments resulted in the concentration of economic and political power in the hands of a relatively small ruling class. Daughters of wealthy planters began to marry the sons of wealthy planters—even their first cousins. The planting class became a network of interrelated families. The ruling "heads" of these households translated their economic and familial positions into political power by restricting voting and rep-

resentation in the House of Burgesses, both financially (with a property requirement) and geographically (by overrepresenting the Tidewater). The tobacco planters mercilessly exploited their indentured servants—but they could not always prevent them from moving on after their terms had expired. What they needed was a labor force they could control for life.

Bacon's Rebellion

The one-crop system became the source of some of the grievances that led in 1676 to Bacon's Rebellion. In 1622, several years after tobacco culture had begun to push settlers into Indian territory, Powhatan's successor led an attack on the English settlements and killed nearly a third of the inhabitants. The English response was bitter and violent. All Indians, whether friendly or not, were now enemies. Instructions from London directed settlers "to root out [the Indians] from being any longer a people."

There was another conflict in the 1640s. When the fighting was over, in 1646, leaders on both sides agreed to occupy separate territories. The Indians and the English lived in relative peace for the next three decades, until a new wave of settlers began spreading onto the Indian lands. In the 1670s these settlers complained of Indian raids on their hogs and demanded official permission to push the Indians out of the lands near white settlements. Virginia's governor, William Berkeley, was reluctant, so the frontiersmen took matters into their own hands and attacked a group of about 400 Susquehannocks living in an abandoned fort. Weakened by European diseases and warfare, the Susquehannocks and several other local tribes were extremely vulnerable. In the war of extermination that followed, revenge was taken on both sides. When Governor Berkeley failed to provide a force that could remove or destroy the Indians, Nathaniel Bacon had his chance.

An aristocrat with a shady past, Bacon was in his twenties when he arrived in Virginia and set himself up on more than one thousand acres in the interior. The elderly governor was his cousin by marriage, and within a year of his arrival Bacon was given a seat on the governor's council. Bacon, however, remained an outsider. The Virginia country, he said, wanted dead Indians, not friendly ones, and he demanded that Berkeley grant him a military commission to do the job. When Berkeley refused, Bacon set himself up as the leader of an anti-Berkeley party. He gathered a force of volunteers and led them in successful raids against the Indians and then against Jamestown itself. They burned the capital.

News reached England in September 1676, and the king shipped out 1100 soldiers to restore order. But by that time Nathaniel Bacon had died of "swamp fever," and his followers had scattered into the woods. Probably less than a hundred Englishmen died in the rebellion, but Governor Berkeley—a man of vengeance—had twenty-three of the rebels hanged.

PURITANS IN NEW ENGLAND

The Puritans who migrated to New England were very different from the settlers of the tobacco colonies. They were committed to dynamic religious beliefs that had profound and lasting effects on the settlement of the region and later on much of English America as well. They were not seeking religious liberty. Rather, they intended to set up their own Puritan churches, and they expected all settlers to follow Puritan principles and leadership. In order to do this, Puritan leaders tried to control the pattern of settlement; they wanted compact village communities rather than scattered farms. And the Puritans migrated as families rather than as individuals. Thus, from the beginning there were more women and children in New England than in the other English colonies.

Puritan Ideology

Much nonsense has been written about the Puritans. They did not all wear tall black hats and drab clothing. They drank liquor, but not to excess. "Wine is from God," one of them wrote, "but drunkenness is from the devil." Far from denouncing sex, they declared that it should be enjoyed by both women and men. But they firmly believed that sex ought to take place only between husband and wife. Not only that, they insisted that a husband and wife *ought* to love each other both physically and spiritually. On this score they had only one reservation—that married love should not distract the partners from the higher love of God.

These English Calvinists kept God at the center of their attention. As Calvin himself had taught, they were certain that from the beginning of creation God had either saved or damned every single person for all eternity. Yet this conviction did not make Puritans give up trying to lead good and moral lives. Both God and His word, the Bible, required good behavior on the part of the individual and the community as a whole. Puritans knew that God would see fit to punish violations of His laws both in this world and in the next; surely He would punish an individual sinner. It was also entirely within His power to show His displeasure with entire communities by means of storms, disease, and other natural disasters.

What could a person do to be saved? Strictly speaking, the answer was nothing, because the decision was predetermined by God. At the same time, Puritans believed they should watch for signs of God's pleasure with them. They should prepare their hearts to receive salvation. Through Christ, people should try to gain assurance that they were saved.

The problem was that a person could never be absolutely certain about God's decision. In daily life, therefore, Puritans were constantly examining themselves for signs about their eternal life. Puritans also watched their neighbors. They believed they had excellent reasons for doing so, since God, speaking through the Bible, required good behavior of everyone. So the Puritans looked for sinful words and deeds in their communities. They expected to find them, and of course they did, for they regarded all people as sinful by nature. They kept a watchful eye out for such sins as swearing, drunkenness, unlawful sex, theft, assault, murder, and idleness.

Puritans included idleness in the catalog of sins because they believed God required everyone to be busy at his or her work. God "called" men and women to their jobs—minister, farmer, mother, servant, seamstress, or carpenter. Whatever the job, or "calling," God required that men and women work long and hard at it. Thus the members of the wealthiest merchant's family shared the same obligations that those in the household of the humblest farmer did.

As we look back now, we can easily see that these requirements produced men and women of great faith and little tolerance. In the early years of New England settlement, this world view resulted in impatience toward anyone who stood in the Puritans' way, whether it was an English king and his bishops, the Atlantic Ocean, or the Indians who already lived on land the Puritans decided ought to be their own.

Pilgrims in Plymouth

The first Puritans who migrated to New England were a small and somewhat peculiar group. Though today we know them as Pilgrims, at the time they were called Separatists because they wished to break completely from the Church of England. The Separatists regarded the English church as hopelessly corrupt. King James and the church authorities responded by harassing their ministers and little congregations. In 1614 one of these congregations fled to Holland, where the authorities were more tolerant. After several years there, however, some of them grew worried about the condition of their own piety and particularly about the behavior of their children. They finally decided to attempt to go to America, where they could "live as a distinct body by themselves."

After obtaining financial backing from some London businessmen, thirty-five Pilgrims set out aboard the *Mayflower* in the autumn of 1620. Also in the ship's company were some sixty "strangers"—artisans, soldiers, and indentured servants. The entire group was led by William Bradford and Captain Miles Standish, the military commander. Finding themselves off Cape Cod in November 1620, they decided not to seek Virginia, where they had been given a land grant. Rather, they would find a suitable harbor in the region where God's winds had sent them.

A month later their search was rewarded by discovery of the place they called Plymouth, on the inner shoreline of Massachusetts Bay. Anchored offshore, forty-one adult men signed a written compact of government: "solemnly and mutually in the presence of God and one of another, [we] Covenant and Combine ourselves together into a Civil Body Politic, for our better ordering and preservation." In effect, the Mayflower Compact established a government based on the consent of the governed. The governor of

---

THE HARDSHIPS OF LIFE IN PLYMOUTH

William Bradford described the early trials of the Pilgrims with an eloquence that made plain the importance of the Pilgrims' religious faith. Early in his history *Of Plymouth Plantation*, Bradford conceded that the Indians

showed them no small kindness in refreshing them, but these savage barbarians, when they met with them (as after will appear) were readier to fill their sides full of arrows than otherwise. And for the season it was winter, and they that know the winters of that country know them to be sharp and violent, and subject to cruel and fierce storms, dangerous to travel

to known places, much more to search an unknown coast. Besides, what could they see but a hideous and desolate wilderness, full of wild beasts and wild men—and what multitudes there might be of them they knew not. . . . For summer being done, all things stand upon them with a weather-beaten face, and the whole country, full of woods and thickets, represented a wild and savage hue. If they looked behind them, there was the mighty ocean which they had passed and was now as a main bar and gulf to separate them from all the civil parts of the world. . . . What could now sustain them but the Spirit of God and His grace?

the settlement would be elected annually by free adult males. In a world of hereditary monarchies, this was a radical step.

The Pilgrims knew very little about fishing and hunting and not much more about farming in the extreme New England climate. The tiny settlement barely survived the "starving time" of that first winter, when half the group died. Yet eventually it grew by means of luck, fortitude, and faith.

Only a few years before, a plague carried by European fishermen had wiped out many Indians in southeastern New England. Those the English met were wary but not unfriendly. The new settlers were greatly aided by Squanto, an Indian who had been to England. He and several other Indians showed the Pilgrims how to plant corn. Squanto also served as a translator between the Pilgrims and Massasoit, the chief sachem of the region. Characteristically, Bradford described Squanto as "a special instrument sent by God" for the good of the English settlers.

Six years after they landed, the Pilgrims were able to buy out their financial backers with shipments of lumber and furs. That purchase virtually cut their connection with England. After ten years on their own, with new towns scattering southward and onto Cape Cod, the Pilgrims adopted a system of elective, representative government, very much in the spirit of the original Mayflower Compact. Each town sent representatives to the central government at Plymouth. Still, only those orthodox in religion and wealthy enough to rank as "freemen" were given the vote. Until 1691, when their little towns were absorbed into the Massachusetts Bay Colony, the Pilgrims led an independent existence, sustained by fish, fur, lumber, and religious faith. They were, as one of their friends in England wrote, "the instruments to break the ice for others."

The Commonwealth of Massachusetts Bay

Unlike the Separatist Pilgrims, most English Puritans wanted to remain within the Church of England. By the late 1620s, however, many had grown discouraged about the future of their movement. The new king, Charles I, tried to suppress their preachers. This harassment made some Puritans toy with the idea of emigrating to America in order to establish a holy commonwealth of their own. In 1629 a well-to-do Puritan

John Winthrop (1588–1649). His strength and determination are reflected in this portrait, painted before he migrated to America. *(Library of Congress)*

lawyer, John Winthrop, led a successful effort to establish a company with rights of settlement in New England. Winthrop became the first governor of the Massachusetts Bay Company.

The company's charter from the king resembled those granted to other trading companies, except that it did not specify the company's official residence or place of administration. This was an unusual omission and may well have been deliberate on the part of Winthrop and his friends. In any event, when these Puritans migrated in 1630 they took their charter with them, thereby transferring the entire enterprise to New England. As the Reverend Cotton Mather later explained, "We would have our posterity settled under the pure and full dispensation of the gospel; defended by rulers who should be ourselves."

The Great Migration began in 1630. By the end of that year, a thousand selected settlers had landed in Massachusetts. Moving outward from Boston, these Puritan families laid out other little towns. Migrants kept coming, and by the end of the decade, about 15,000 persons had crossed the Atlantic.

This large migration sustained the prosperity of the colony; there was no "starving time" in Massachusetts. Few of the Puritan settlers were very wealthy, but many of them were able to pay for their own passage, with enough savings left over to support themselves for the first few months. The earlier settlers prospered by selling food and other articles to the newcomers.

The arrangement worked very well as long as immigration lasted. But about 1640 the Great Migration came to a halt when civil war broke out in England. Massachusetts faced its first economic depression. Yet the colony escaped disaster because, as Winthrop wrote, "the Lord was pleased to open up a trade with the West Indies." After only a dozen years of settlement, Massachusetts found its economic prosperity resting not on any single crop, but on overseas trade with other colonies and with England.

The quest for a suitable form of government proved more difficult. The colony had control over its own charter and thus was able to act like an independent republic while acknowledging allegiance to the king. But it was not at all clear which settlers should control that government. Winthrop and other Puritan leaders, convinced that most settlers were not truly godly persons, struggled to keep control in the hands of the Puritan elite. They never thought Puritan ministers should rule the holy commonwealth, although they often turned to them for advice and support. They simply assumed that any truly godly community should be governed by thoroughly orthodox Puritan men.

This leadership was challenged from two directions. The leaders were, as a group, wealthier than the other settlers. Thus, their control of the colony was resented for both religious and economic reasons. Men of lesser religious and economic status began grumbling about their rights. As freeborn Englishmen, they argued, they had the right to participate in government. After all, they had done so at home in England, if only by being allowed to vote. They had no wish to allow servants or the poor to vote, and they agreed that the wicked and irreligious should be excluded. But they balked at being governed by a handful of self-appointed gentlemen on the governor's council.

There was a quiet but very real struggle for power between these two groups. After about fifteen years, a series of compromises was hammered out. Most adult male members of the churches would be allowed to vote. A representative legislature—the General Court—would be divided into two houses. The smaller upper house would be made up of relatively wealthy men. The larger lower house would consist of humbler representatives, with each town able to send two of its own. The governorship would remain an annually contested elective office. This workable compromise was possible because so many of the settlers shared a common belief in English liberties and Puritan values. The firmness of that ground is apparent in the fact that John Winthrop was elected governor almost every year until his death in 1649.

The Dissidents of Rhode Island

The rule of orthodox Puritans in Massachusetts was also challenged by two outstanding but very different individuals: Roger Williams and Anne Hutchinson. Roger Williams was a Separatist minister who migrated to Massachusetts in 1631. He was greatly admired for his piety and talents, but he soon began to irritate the authorities with alarming ideas. Williams announced that the settlers had no just claim to land unless they *purchased* it from the Indians. He also insisted that the government had no right to interfere in religious matters, not even the right to punish violations of the Sabbath. Most Puritans thought such proposals both absurd and dangerous. And much as they liked him, Massachusetts authorities were unwilling to tolerate his preaching. So in 1636, Roger Williams was banished from the colony.

In the dead of winter, Williams tramped southward through the snow to the headwaters of Narragansett Bay. For a time he lived with Narragansett Indians and even took the trouble to learn their language—one of the few English leaders ever to do so. Soon he was joined by sympathizers from Massachusetts. They established the town of Providence, which became the center of a new colony, Rhode Island. In 1644, during the English civil war, Williams went back to England and successfully obtained a charter for his new settlement from a sympathetic Puritan Parliament.

Rhode Island's charter provided for a government similar to that of Massachusetts, but it contained unusual provisions that reflected Williams's personal views. All Christian groups were allowed to worship as they pleased, without any interference from the government. Even men who were not members of any church were permitted to vote. In these matters, Rhode Island remained unique among the colonies for many years.

The other early challenger of the authorities in Massachusetts, Anne Hutchinson, was a quick-witted and forceful person who jolted that colony even more than Williams had. She began discussing Sunday sermons with an ever-widening circle of admirers and announced that most ministers in the colony were wrong about the process of salvation. She publicly claimed the ministers were erroneously preaching that proper outward behavior could be a sign of salvation. She also announced that saints who had been saved were under no obligation to obey the outward laws of God.

These unorthodox views, known to theologians as Antinomianism, attracted a considerable following in the colony. The authorities were alarmed by the threat she posed to the social order, and they brought her to trial in 1638. At first she defended herself skillfully before a frustrated court, but then she made one fatal mistake. When asked where she obtained her unorthodox ideas, she replied that she had heard from God "by an immediate voice." Most Puritans believed that God no longer spoke directly to individuals but only through His holy word, the Bible, and that the only proper interpreters of the Bible were educated ministers.

The court banished Anne Hutchinson from Massachusetts. She moved with her family and numerous supporters to Rhode Island. Several years later she migrated westward, where she was killed by Indians—a brutal end that several Massachusetts leaders interpreted as a positive sign of God's providence.

Connecticut, New Hampshire, and Maine

In the meantime, orthodox Puritan settlers were venturing far from the cluster of towns around Boston. Some moved northward onto land between the Merrimack and Kennebec rivers claimed by Massachusetts and also by several wealthy individuals in England. After considerable confusion about boundaries and land titles, New Hampshire emerged in 1679 as a separate Puritan colony with a governor appointed by the king. The coastal land to the northeast, known as the Province of Maine, remained part of Massachusetts.

Other Puritans left Massachusetts in favor of the fertile lands of the lower Connecticut Valley. The Reverend Thomas Hooker led the first sizable migration and established the town of Hartford in 1636. More settlers from Massachusetts

Migrations from England before 1640

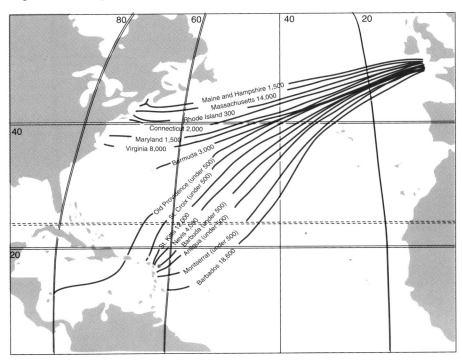

arrived and set up towns of their own. Puritans from England migrated to the Connecticut coast, where they founded New Haven. Eventually these towns banded together, applied for a charter much like those of Massachusetts and Rhode Island, and emerged in 1662 as the colony of Connecticut.

Thus five separate colonies had been established in New England. Of the five, Massachusetts was by far the most populous. All were thoroughly Puritan in their origins, and only Rhode Island was wayward and unorthodox. Yet Rhode Island was Puritan too. Religious tolerance in that colony demonstrated that orthodox Puritanism contained the seeds of disagreement and of change.

Puritans and Indians

The Puritans in Massachusetts, like the Pilgrims in Plymouth, had at first encountered small and sparsely settled Indian tribes who usually were peaceful and even generous to them. The colonists were not as generous in return. Although the Puritans talked about an obligation to convert the Indians to Christianity, they did little about it. The first missionary activity did not take place until thirteen years after the Puritans' arrival, and even then only a few ministers took any interest. Puritan governments forbade the sale of firearms to Indians and barred them from entering English settlements.

The Indians were puzzled and angered by the English encroachment on their lands. For their part, the Puritans wished the Indians would become civilized or simply go away. Intent on establishing their holy commonwealths, the English settlers regarded the Indians with a combination of hostility, contempt, and indifference. When smallpox killed several thousand Indians in eastern Massachusetts, for example, Governor John Winthrop explained the tragedy by saying: "The Lord hathe cleared our title to what we possess."

Given these attitudes, conflict was unavoidable. Usually the Puritans took advantage of old hostilities between Indian tribes. In 1637 the Pequots chose to resist the English by force. In May of that year, the English and their allies, the Narragansetts, set fire to the last Pequot stronghold, a fort on the Mystic River. They slaughtered or captured nearly the entire nation. Plymouth's governor, William Bradford, wrote of the massacre:

It was a fearful sight to see them thus frying in the fire and the streams of blood quenching the same, . . . but the victory seemed a sweet sacrifice, and they [the Puritans] gave the praise thereof to God, who had wrought so wonderfully for them . . . and given them a speedy victory over so proud and insulting an enemy.

The Narragansetts, shocked at this savagery, thought that the warfare of their English allies "is too furious and slays too many men."

A generation later, one tribe, the Wampanoags, organized a last-ditch offensive to oust the white invaders. The alliance was led by Metacom (or King Philip, as the Puritans called him), who won support from tribes whose lands and livelihood had been taken by the whites. These Indians had become dependent on English trade goods but could no longer supply beaver pelts in exchange, since the animals had been hunted out of their eastern territories.

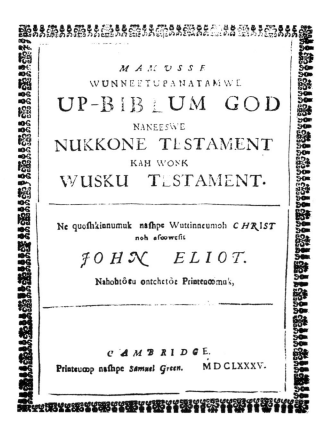

Title page of the Bible translated awkwardly but lovingly by the Reverend Mr. John Eliot into an Algonquian dialect spoken by several Indian groups in eastern New England. Published in the Massachusetts Bay Colony in 1685. *(Rare Book Division, The New York Public Library, Astor, Lenox, and Tilden Foundation)*

Successful guerrilla raids on outlying Puritan villages attracted more and more tribes (including the Narragansetts) to the Wampanoags' cause. During the winter of 1675–1676 the Indians devastated the New England frontier. By March they were attacking towns twenty miles west of Boston. In response, the Puritans followed the usual policy of extermination, massacring both friendly and hostile tribes.

Food shortages and disease finally halted Metacom's forces. Of some ninety Puritan towns, fifty-two had been attacked and twelve destroyed, and the English frontier had been moved back. A higher proportion of the white New England population had died than in any American war before or since. Many of the surviving Indians were placed in "praying villages" (so-called Christianized reservations) or shipped off to the West Indies as slaves. They had gone the way of the coastal tribes in Virginia in the face of European pressure for their land.

New England's Economy

The geography and climate of New England did a great deal to shape the life of the new arrivals. In Maine and New Hampshire, the colder weather restricted farming for the English as it had for the Indians. Except for the Connecticut and Merrimack valleys, New England was much more hilly and far less fertile than the Chesapeake region. Small farms were the rule. Farming families settled in villages where the houses clustered around the church and the village green instead of being scattered over the countryside.

When a group of colonists wished to establish a new town, they obtained permission from the colonial legislature to settle a block of land of approximately six square miles, usually adjoining an older town. All freemen were eligible to draw for the town lots and to use the woods and meadows. The richer settlers sometimes got additional lots, but even they never received more than two

King Philip's War, 1675–1676

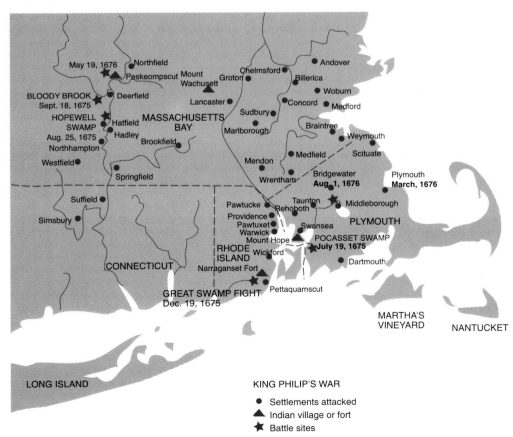

or three times as much land as the poorest. The system had certain disadvantages: By keeping control of the undivided land, the original owners could discriminate against newcomers, who often formed a deprived majority, along with landless and voteless tenants and laborers. Disputes between old and new settlers frequently ended with the newcomers moving west or north to areas beyond the town's control. Eventually the system of planned expansion broke down. During most of the seventeenth century, however, the system worked, and Puritan culture was carried to new frontiers.

Most settlers in this period lived by farming and home industry, with relatively little hired help or indentured labor. As early as 1644, iron was being smelted commercially in Massachusetts, rum was being made from West Indian molasses, and cider pressed from local fruits had become available for sale locally and overseas. New England craftsmen also made many of the commodities needed in the colony, such as furniture, pottery, hardware, and tools. Three vital products were made primarily by women: clothing, soap, and candles. Since New Englanders did not have an export staple such as tobacco, they could not easily pay to import such articles from abroad.

Some New Englanders turned to the sea for a living. Fishing off the banks of Newfoundland became so important in Massachusetts that the cod became the symbol of the colony. Enough fish were caught for export to the West Indies and elsewhere, along with foodstuffs, horses, lumber, rum, and even captive Indians to be sold as slaves.

Puritan trading in black slaves began in 1638, when the Salem ship *Desire* brought Africans from the West Indies. Blacks were imported in small numbers; by 1700 the region's population of 90,000 included about one thousand blacks, most of them slaves. It was the traffic *to* the West Indies, not from it, that soon dominated the slave trade. Early in the 1640s, Puritan captains began voyaging to the West African coast. Before the end of the century, Massachusetts and Rhode Island merchants were involved in the trade, with their main customers being in the Caribbean sugar islands. Gradually they developed markets for slaves in the mainland colonies as well.

Overseas commerce, like fishing, stimulated shipbuilding. New England ships were so seaworthy and so inexpensive that they were soon being built for foreign as well as domestic merchants and captains. Once on the sea, Puritan ships, like those of other maritime nations, sought out all kinds of cargoes and sailed to any port, legal or illegal. By the end of the seventeenth century Boston had become an international port through which goods of many nations were transshipped. Boston merchants and traders were becoming as rich and powerful as the planters of the Tidewater. They also had interests that extended beyond their ties with England.

THE DUTCH BEACHHEAD

While the English were establishing themselves in the Chesapeake and New England areas, the Dutch suddenly snatched one of the most strategic portions of the eastern seaboard. The Netherlands had established its credentials as a Protestant nation during Elizabeth's reign by fighting for independence against a Catholic Spanish monarch. It became a commercial and naval power strong enough to rival England during the first half of the seventeenth century.

The Dutch organized trading companies and naval flotillas, much like the English, and successfully challenged the Spanish in the Caribbean and the Portuguese in Brazil, in the East Indies, and in West Africa. Almost incidentally, a Dutch trading company sent Henry Hudson (an Englishman) in the *Half Moon* to scout the northern coast of America. He found the Hudson River, the major seaway into the interior. On the southern tip of a little island at its mouth, the Dutch set up a fort and a town they called New Amsterdam.

To the north they then established Fort Orange (later renamed Albany) at the critical junction of the Mohawk and Hudson rivers. From there they extended their influence westward to the most powerful and politically sophisticated group of Indians in northeastern America, the Iroquois Confederacy. By the 1630s, the Dutch had established enormous landed estates along the Hudson. They traded for furs with the Iroquois and probed east to the Connecticut River and south to the Delaware, where there was a tiny settlement of Swedes and Finns. The English were not yet fully aware that the three major water-level routes into the interior of the continent—the St. Lawrence, the Mississippi, and the Hudson—were in the hands of foreign powers.

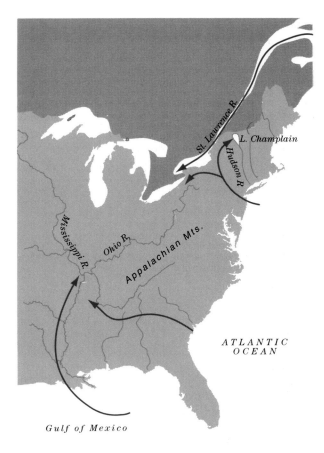

Routes to the interior

During the first half of the seventeenth century, the Dutch dominated the slave trade in West Africa, the international carrying trade (what we would call the merchant marine), the East Indies and trade with India, and the sugar industry in Brazil. But almost as soon as it began, the bubble of success collapsed. England and the Netherlands engaged in three naval wars in the mid-seventeenth century, and the English won. New Netherland, which was what the Dutch colony in North America was called, changed hands several times, but ended up as New York. Because of its half century of Dutch settlement and government, New York remained for many years the most culturally varied province among the English continental colonies.

THE PROPRIETARY COLONIES

Most of the early English colonies, except Rhode Island and Connecticut, were founded by joint-stock trading companies. By the 1630s, however, the English Crown had begun to take a more direct interest in controlling land grants. King Charles I granted a portion of the American coast—Maryland—to a single individual and his heirs. Then, after the Restoration of 1660, his son Charles II gave out enormous tracts of land to various wealthy individuals. Recipients of these grants were called *proprietors* because they literally owned the land. Yet in the long run the proprietary colonies developed along much the same lines as the earlier settlements, largely because the settlers insisted on having representative legislatures of their own.

Maryland

King Charles I was married to a Roman Catholic. One of the major figures in his court, Sir George Calvert, was also a Catholic—and one who wanted to found a colony in America. Partly he hoped to profit financially from such a venture; partly too, Calvert wanted to establish a haven for English Catholics, who remained a small and unhappy minority in England. The king was well aware that the settlements around Jamestown did not occupy all the land of Virginia. He was thus happy to respond to Calvert's request for a land grant.

Charles simply gave Calvert the area of Virginia that surrounded the northern part of Chesapeake Bay. The gift was personal. Calvert and his heirs were to be the proprietors of an entire colony. The royal charter provided that the Calvert family would actually own the land and collect rents from people who settled on it. The charter gave Calvert broad powers of government in the colony, but it did provide for a representative assembly. Calvert and his son gratefully named the colony Maryland in honor of Charles's Catholic queen.

George Calvert died while the charter was still being processed by royal bureaucrats. His son Lord Baltimore organized the expedition that set out for the Chesapeake in 1634 and first settled on an island in the upper part of the bay. There was no starving time in Maryland; the settlers had learned from the sad experiences at Jamestown. They brought plenty of provisions, and they were able to trade for supplies with the other colonies. They soon discovered that tobacco grew as well in Maryland as in Virginia. Economically, the two colonies became almost twins.

The Calvert–Baltimore family realized from the start that the Protestant settlers might outnumber the Catholics in Maryland, even though the early leaders of the settlement were Catholic. The Baltimores had no desire to persecute Protestants, and as things turned out, they had little opportunity. When Protestants settled in large numbers in Maryland, Lord Baltimore began to fear that Catholics in the colony might themselves become victims of religious persecution.

In 1649 he requested the Maryland assembly to pass his Toleration Act, and the assembly did so. This landmark act provided for freedom of worship for all Christians except those few who did not believe in the Holy Trinity. For a time there was political friction between Protestants and Catholics in Maryland. But the important principle of religious toleration was firmly established, largely out of necessity.

Carolina

Carolina, which extended from the southern boundary of Virginia to the borders of Spanish Florida and supposedly as far westward as the continent itself, was the first colony established after the Restoration of Charles II. This enormous territory was granted by Charles II in 1663 to eight friends who had helped place him on the throne. The first permanent settlement began in 1670. Some colonists sailed directly from England; others came from the West Indian island of Barbados, where several of the Carolina proprietors had made large fortunes. The growth of large sugar plantations there had squeezed many men off the land, and they were eager to seek new opportunities. From the beginning Carolina was something of an offshoot of Barbados.

The new colony grew slowly, but without starvation. In 1680 the capital of Charles Town was moved to its present site at the junction of two rivers about three miles from the ocean. Charles Town (later spelled Charleston) became a thriving commercial center. The colonists traded with the Indians for deer hides; they also established a thriving cattle industry. They experimented with a variety of crops, but the weather proved too warm for tobacco and too cold for tropical fruits.

Finally they found a crop that could be profitably exported—rice. It became the staple crop of Carolina and the source of great wealth for successful planters. Some African slaves had been brought in at the very beginning, and it was they who probably introduced the cultivation of rice—a crop not grown in England but well known in parts of West Africa.

Rice came to dominate the low-country lands near Charles Town in the same way that tobacco dominated the Virginia and Maryland tidewater. Since rice cultivation required much labor, planters imported more and more Africans and enslaved large numbers of Indians as well. By the early decades of the eighteenth century, the majority of settlers in southern Carolina were black.

The northern part of the Carolina land grant had already been partly settled by people from Virginia. The area was handicapped by lack of good ports, and for many years it remained a land of small farms, with fewer slaves than in Virginia or the southern part of the colony. The Carolina proprietors placed a deputy governor over this territory and provided for separate elected assemblies for the two areas. As the years went by, settlers in both parts of Carolina grew increasingly unhappy about proprietary rule. That rule was in fact inefficient because of the large number of proprietors, and the situation grew more confused as some of them died

King Charles the II of Great Britain. *(Library of Congress)*

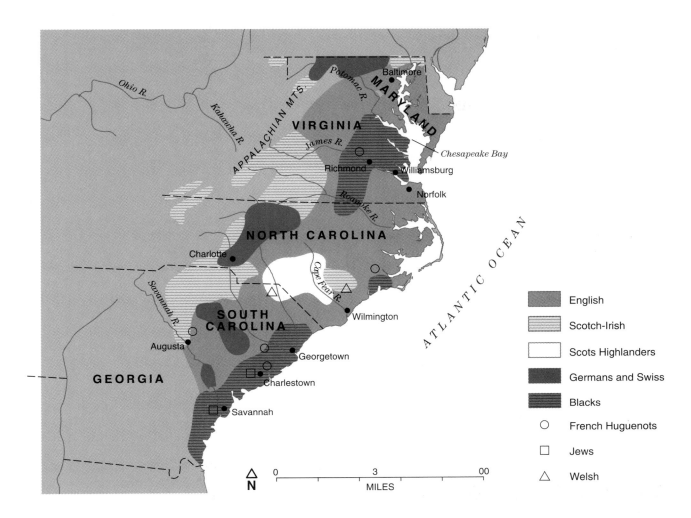

Early settlements in the South

and willed their rights to their heirs. In 1721 the king made South Carolina a royal colony; henceforth the governor was appointed. A few years later, North Carolina was also made a royal colony. Both kept their representative assemblies, for by this time assemblies were regarded as normal and essential parts of English colonial governments.

New Jersey

King Charles II had been generous to the Carolina proprietors, and he was even more so to his younger brother James, the Duke of York. He turned over to James all the territory captured from the Dutch. Partly because the Dutch settlers were foreigners, no provision was made for a representative assembly. James simply sent over a royal governor to rule the colony, which was renamed New York. James also granted the southern portion of this vaguely defined territory to two of his friends. This area eventually became the colony of New Jersey, but only after a series of events produced great confusion.

A large group of Puritan New Englanders moved into northeastern New Jersey. They were encouraged to do so by the royal governor of New York, who expected to collect rents from them. In the meantime, the two proprietors were also encouraging settlements in the same area, also in the hope of collecting rents. The inevitable result of this situation was widespread uncertainty about who owned what land. Residents of East Jersey were still quarreling about land titles a century later.

There was further confusion about government. The two proprietors had no authority to appoint a governor or permit a legislative assembly, yet they went ahead and did so. Then the proprietors split the colony into East and West Jersey, and sold West Jersey to a group of English Quakers.

The situation was finally resolved in 1702, when the two halves were joined into the single colony of New Jersey. The Quaker proprietors retained some land rights, but none in government. From then on the governor was to be appointed by the king, and there was to be a representative assembly. Yet the confusion could not be ended at once. For more than thirty years, New Jersey's royal governor was the royal governor of New York. Yet the colony's economy rested on a solid basis of small farming, which provided food for two growing cities in neighboring colonies, New York and Philadelphia.

Pennsylvania and Delaware

Only one section of the Atlantic seaboard remained to be given away, and Charles II gave it to a most unlikely person. William Penn was the son of an admiral and was raised as a conventional gentleman. He learned some Latin, some law, how to duel with a sword, and at the age of sixteen was introduced to the king at court. Years later, in 1681, King Charles gave him a huge tract of land that ran north and west from the Delaware River and its bay. The king owed Admiral Penn both gratitude and money, and he decided to repay the son. But rather than naming his colony after a member of the royal family, William Penn chose to call it Penn's Woods, or Pennsylvania.

The younger Penn had become a Quaker. He remained a gentleman, but his Quaker ideas were regarded by many people as radical, foolish, and dangerous. The Quakers (who called themselves Friends) had emerged from the turmoil of the English civil war as a religiously and socially radical group of Protestant Christians. They pressed certain Christian beliefs to extremes. All Christians, for example, believed in good will toward others; Quakers acted upon this principle. They believed that love for God could be shown by love for every man and woman, and they believed that everyone could be saved.

Quakers insisted that there was an Inner Light in every person that enabled him or her to learn God's will. Accordingly, Quakers had no distinct class of ministers, for they felt that every person was both a minister and a child of God. Quakers insisted on a life of simplicity, and for this reason dressed plainly. They refused to honor customary social distinctions. They called everyone "thee" or "thou" in an age when most people used the plural "you" when speaking to people of high station. They refused to swear legal oaths because they believed there should not be two standards of Truth. In addition, Quakers were firm pacifists.

To most Christians, Quakerism was Christianity gone mad. When Quakers tried to gain converts, not only in England but in the West Indies and the continental colonies, they met outraged resistance. In Massachusetts, the Puritan authorities hanged two Quakers who returned after being banished. In England, many Quakers were jailed for holding religious meetings. As time went on, however, the group became somewhat more conventional and conservative. People began to realize that Quakers were not trying to undermine all good government. It was in this changing atmosphere that William Penn received the charter for his colony in 1681.

Penn provided a liberal plan of government for his colony. He kept his own authority at a minimum, and gave the right to vote to all adult male landowners and taxpayers. All Christians of whatever sort were to have complete freedom of worship. Penn had every reason to think his plan would work, so he grew puzzled and discouraged when he met opposition. He had given the smaller upper house of the assembly the power to introduce legislation. Members of the lower house wanted that power. Characteristically, Penn told the legislators to draft a plan of their own.

The result was the Charter of Liberties of 1701, which provided for a single-house legislature. It was the only such legislature in all the English colonies, and the only one to depart from the model of the two houses of Parliament in England. The Charter of Liberties also provided for a separate assembly for the three southern counties along Delaware Bay. Delaware gained a somewhat separate existence, but it continued to have the same governors Penn and his heirs appointed for Pennsylvania.

The colony proved to be a great success. Its liberal government and its policy of religious freedom attracted large numbers of settlers. At first most of the colonists were English and Welsh Quakers, and they continued to dominate

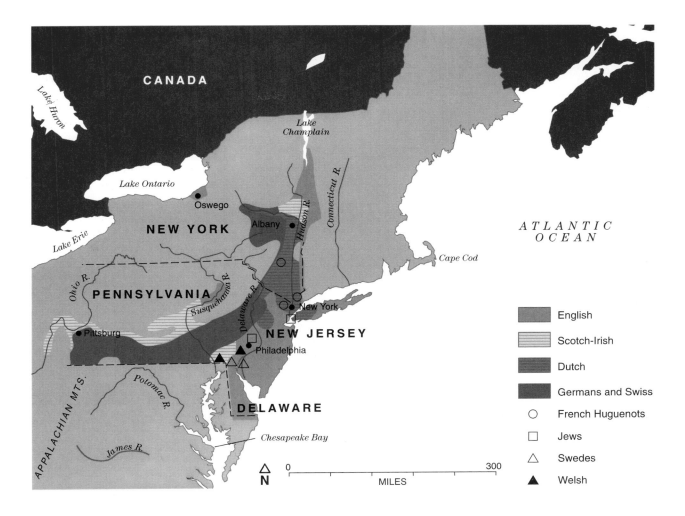

Early settlements in the Middle Colonies

the government of the colony. But Penn's policies attracted many other groups. When he sent agents to western Germany to advertise the virtues of his colony, large numbers of German Protestants emigrated, drawn by promises of religious freedom and cheap land.

The immediate success of Pennsylvania showed how much the colonists had learned since Jamestown and Plymouth. Penn carefully selected the site for Philadelphia before the first settlers arrived, and he laid out his city with foresight. His province turned out to be highly fertile. As in New England, a flourishing trade quickly sprang up with the West Indies, where pork, beef, and flour were in great demand.

A unique feature of this colony was the Quaker policy of nonviolence and peaceful coexistence with the Indians. Penn was one of the few English leaders to learn an Indian language. He recognized Indian ownership of the land and allowed colonists to settle on tracts he had purchased from tribal chiefs. Contact between the Delawares (the largest tribe in the area) and the settlers was limited in the early years because there was little trade in furs. That enterprise had been monopolized much earlier by the Susquehannocks and the Dutch.

The situation began to change at the end of the seventeenth century, when non-Quakers came to the colony in large numbers. They did not share Quaker convictions about Indians' rights to the land, and treaties with the Delawares were broken. Alcohol became a bargaining tool. The Indians eventually migrated westward, but the resentment they felt would be unleashed a generation later.

William Penn's Treaty with the Indians in 1681, as depicted nearly a century later (1771) by Benjamin West (1738–1820), one of the first noted American-born artists. Historians came to question if such a conference actually took place, but the legend persisted and West no doubt prolonged it with his persuasive and much-reproduced painting. The painting did capture the spirit of peaceful relations that Penn sought to establish with the Delaware tribe inhabiting his colony, and it reflects his recognition of the Indians as the lawful owners of the land included in his grant. *(Library of Congress)*

William Penn's colony became the most populous and the richest in North America. But he did not share in its good fortune. After returning to England in 1701 to keep the Crown from taking his charter, Penn had financial difficulties. He spent a short time in debtor's prison and died in 1718. More than any other proprietor, Penn had sought to establish a good society, what he called a ""holy experiment." As things turned out, the experiment worked very well.

BUILDING AN EMPIRE

The permanent settlement of the mainland colonies—their economic growth, political maturity, and territorial expansion—all took place within the framework of an emerging imperial system. The English government struggled to bring the colonies under its control so that they would

benefit the mother country. But England was far from stable in the second half of the seventeenth century. In fact, there was another revolution in 1689, and it had important consequences in the colonies. Once that revolution was over, however, England began to consolidate its empire.

The Mercantile System in Theory and Practice

The English had a theory of empire long before they had an empire. That theory, known as *mercantilism*, was simple, and was not only used by England. It was the way in which all the Atlantic European nations operated their economies and their overseas empires. In that age, people saw two main sources of national strength: wealth and military power. National leaders were well aware that the two were closely related, and they spent much time and energy trying to enlarge their own and diminish that of their rivals.

Mercantilists in the home country assumed that economic activity should be regulated by the government for the sake of the nation as a whole. They thought of the "nation" as including both the mother country and its overseas settlements. They also thought the colonies should contribute to the nation's wealth and power by providing products not found or grown or made in the mother country. In particular, they assumed colonies should provide raw materials for manufacturing. The making of finished goods, or manufacturing, should take place in the mother country, which would then sell these items in the colonies or to foreign countries. National wealth could best be increased by selling more goods to other nations than were purchased from them. Today we would call this simply a favorable balance of trade.

Mercantilists were also very much concerned about military strength, which for the English meant naval power. The ships of His Majesty's navy had to be built and supplied and manned. The vessels could be built in England, but trees for masts and spars had to be imported. Before the English colonies were settled, pine trees were bought from Sweden and other Scandinavian countries. Such imports violated mercantilist principles in two ways. They cost the nation money, and they made England dependent on foreign powers for a vital article of defense. So English authorities turned to the colonies, where after 1729 the largest pines in northern New England were reserved for masts for His Majesty's navy.

At that time there was no clear dividing line between naval warships and the civilian merchant marine. Many merchant ships were armed with cannon, and in wartime were given written licenses to prey on enemy shipping. For this reason, the English government encouraged the construction of ships of all sorts. Although authorities in London agreed that manufacturing should normally be done in England, in this case the importance of defense overrode the economic principle. The English government thus encouraged one kind of manufacturing in the colonies—shipbuilding.

Ships needed sailors. Here was another reason to encourage shipbuilding and a large merchant marine. Skilled seamen on merchant vessels could be pressed into service during wartime. The government encouraged the fishing industry for the same reason. The "fisheries," it was said, were "nurseries for seamen." The government even tried to retain the old Roman Catholic tradition of not eating meat on Fridays. By eating fish instead, the English people would help build England's maritime power.

The twin aspects of mercantilism—financial and naval—usually worked well together. In the seventeenth century and even later, these principles were in the best interests of the colonies. The colonies did not have enough people for large-scale manufacturing. The colonists produced raw materials that sold well in England, and English manufacturers could in turn supply them with a broad range of finished goods. Yet the fit between mercantilist principles and the interests of the colonies was not a perfect one. Left to themselves, the colonists might prefer to buy cloth from French or Dutch manufacturers. They might prefer to sell masts, pitch, and tar to outfitters of Dutch ships rather than English ones. To work well, the mercantilist system required supervision by the home government.

The royal government never doubted that it had the right to undertake such supervision. Nor did the colonists—although they sometimes found it convenient to evade regulations that hurt their interests. Obviously, the colonists had no desire to weaken England's naval power or to lessen its wealth. But what if the choice was filling colonists' pockets or those of London merchants? The colonists would have been less than human if they had not chosen their own.

And although the need for supervision was clear, setting up an effective system was not easy. The colonies were three thousand miles and many weeks away from London. English bureaucrats had no experience or training in administering overseas lands. They did have experience in regulating economic activity at home, and they had little doubt that they could do the same abroad. But if they knew what sort of activity *ought* to be going on in the colonies, they often found it difficult to discover what actually *was* going on. And sometimes the colonists were less than helpful in letting them know.

The mercantilist system worked best when the colonies produced agricultural staples, such as the tobacco of Virginia and Maryland, the rice of South Carolina, and the sugar of the West Indies. Planters found a protected market for their products in the mother country, and were granted credit for the manufactures they bought.

British exporters, assured of payment in marketable crops each year, encouraged the colonial planters to live well—indeed, well beyond their means.

The system had fewer attractions for Middle Colony merchants and fewest of all for those of New England, who had no true staple crops that were marketable in England. The northern colonies developed an extensive trade with the West Indies and looked for other means of profiting from overseas trade. Meanwhile, England was still battling the Dutch for maritime supremacy.

The struggle included three naval wars and the capture of New Netherland. It also included several important acts of Parliament aimed at regulating the trade of the American colonies as well as weakening the Dutch merchant marine. These were the Navigation Acts, which were intended to encourage English shipping and trade at the expense especially of the Dutch.

The Navigation Acts

The Navigation Acts of 1660 and 1663 set up certain basic regulations that were later enlarged and tinkered with, but never abandoned. The various Navigation Acts embodied both the naval and the economic principles of mercantilism. First, they banned all trade with the colonies except in colonial or English-built ships. These vessels had to be manned by crews at least three-quarters English or colonial. Second, the acts required that certain colonial products be exported only to England or another colony. The list included such important items as sugar and tobacco. Third, most European goods imported by the colonies had to be shipped by way of England.

The system was tightened up and extended over many years with four important modifications. First, certain rules and paperwork were imposed on ship captains to prevent evasion of the acts. Second, the list of goods was enlarged to include important colonial crops such as rice and the wood products known as naval stores (masts, smaller spars, pitch, tar, and turpentine). Indigo, a plant that produced a purple-blue dye, was also added to the list, partly because it was used for sailors' uniforms. Third, the English government began to pay bounties, or cash supplements, to colonial exporters of naval stores and indigo. Fourth, the government restricted certain colonial manufacturing enterprises that developed in the eighteenth century. These included woolen cloth, hats, and finished iron products. The Iron Act of 1750, for example, encouraged the colonists to make iron in bulk bars or sheets for export to England, but it prohibited them from making such finished iron products as nails and tools.

These regulations were intended to benefit English subjects everywhere. But some subjects benefited more than others. For example, the Iron Act of 1750 helped English makers of finished iron products by banning colonial competition, but English producers of bulk iron were hurt. One part of the English iron industry had won out over the other. Similar differences of economic interest existed in the various colonies, and sometimes they appeared within a single colony. In Pennsylvania, for example, producers of bulk iron were happy with the Iron Act, while manufacturers of finished iron products were not.

There were also important differences among the colonies. These differences were especially clear in the case of the Molasses Act of 1733, which placed a high tax on molasses imported from the colonies of other countries. Designed to protect the interests of the British sugar-island colonies by making foreign molasses more expensive, the act was a blow to New England merchants who imported molasses for making rum. If these merchants had observed the Molasses Act, they would have had to buy high-priced molasses from the English islands. Instead, they preferred to pay lower prices in the French islands. In short, they smuggled.

Problems of Enforcement

Somehow all these laws had to be enforced. But even while the Navigation Acts were being passed, Charles II was giving away powers of government in the colonies. He gave huge territories to individual colonies, to proprietors, and to colonial assemblies. He authorized new charters for Rhode Island and Connecticut that gave those colonies almost complete control over their own affairs, including the right to elect their own governors. Except in New York, Charles's proprietary grants provided for representative assemblies. Because the men who sat in these assemblies usually took a different view of colonial interests than bureaucrats in London, there was bound to be friction between the assemblies and the appointed agents of the Crown.

Within the English government, a small group of bureaucrats were responsible for colonial affairs. They were commonly known as the Lords of Trade, but the group's powers were not clear. In 1664 the Lords of Trade sent a royal commission to the colonies to find out what was going on and to remind the colonists of their obligations under the new Navigation Acts. The commissioners decided to investigate New England. Both Virginia and Maryland were exporting large quantities of tobacco, on which the royal government was collecting handsome taxes, but New England did not seem to fit into the system nearly so well. These colonies were exporting masts and spars, but otherwise were not contributing to the wealth and power of the mother country.

The royal commissioners were suspicious of the New Englanders for still another reason. Most were Puritans, and both Charles II and the royal commissioners hated Puritans. After all, English Puritans had chopped off the head of Charles's father only fifteen years before. The commissioners suspected that the Puritan authorities in New England wanted as much independence from the Crown as they could manage. Their suspicions were correct.

When the commissioners arrived in Boston, the leaders of Massachusetts did their best to ignore them and then questioned their authority to make inquiries. Accustomed to having their own way for thirty-five years, leaders of the Bay Colony did not take kindly to the agents of a monarch who was persecuting Puritans in England. The frustrated commissioners reported back that Massachusetts was a nest of arrogant "independency." They recommended that the colony be compelled to observe the Navigation Acts and that its charter be recalled and canceled. But nothing was done about this first imperial inspection of an American colony; Massachusetts went on as it had before.

Eventually, however, authorities in London managed to bring the colony into line. The Board of Trade sent Edmund Randolph, an able and energetic young bureaucrat, to the colonies several times. On each visit Randolph collected more damaging information about violations of the Navigation Acts. Randolph also discovered that Massachusetts had been passing laws contrary to the laws of England—something specifically forbidden by its original charter.

Over the years, Randolph and other royal officials repeated the same recommendation: The Massachusetts charter ought to be revoked. Charles II was finally convinced. Canceling a royal charter was not easy, but it could be done. Randolph presented his evidence to an English court, which in 1684 declared the charter null and void. The most populous English colony in America no longer had any legal basis.

THE "GLORIOUS REVOLUTION"

Very shortly afterward, a great and general crisis shook the English-speaking world. At first it had nothing to do with Massachusetts. When Charles II died in 1685 he was succeeded by his brother,

---

WORDS AND NAMES IN AMERICAN HISTORY

Many people today use the expression *to keel over* without any awareness of its origins. We all know what is meant by such a sentence as, "Well, Joe looked perfectly all right when he was telling me about his trip, but then he suddenly just keeled over, and it took us quite a while to get an ambulance." Actually, the term is nautical, from the days of sailing vessels. The keel of a sailing ship was originally the main beam running fore and aft at the bottom of the hull. To achieve greater stability and better sailing qualities, ship designers extended wooden plates downward from that beam. Modern recreational sailboats have keels, or sometimes a centerboard—a board or plate that is raised and lowered from inside the cockpit of the boat. For such a boat to keel over is obviously disastrous. It means that the boat has capsized, with its keel showing horizontally on the surface of the water or sticking straight up in the air; in the latter case the boat's mast(s) is underwater, pointing straight at the bottom.

the Duke of York, who became James II. As king, James remained the proprietor of New York. Far more important, he had become a Roman Catholic. At the time, he had no children and therefore no Roman Catholic heir, but he was still young and might yet produce one. His Protestant subjects were appalled by this possibility. In addition, James was determined to rule with an iron hand. A stubborn and tactless man, he had little idea how much his subjects valued their Protestantism and the privileges of their Parliament.

The king took sweeping and drastic action to settle the Massachusetts problem. With a stroke of his pen he created a single vast colony called the Dominion of New England, a new administrative unit that included all the New England colonies, as well as New York and East and West Jersey. This huge territory was to be administered from Boston by a royal governor and by a deputy governor in New York. A governor's council was to be appointed by the Crown, and there were to be no representative assemblies in any part of the dominion.

This sweeping reorganization sent a shudder through the colonies. Virginia was already a royal colony, but what did the future hold for Pennsylvania, Maryland, and Carolina? What would government be like without the protections provided by elected assemblies? The man James II appointed governor of the Dominion of New England did nothing to calm these fears. Edmund Andros was an able administrator, but he was arrogant and highhanded. Within a few weeks of arriving in Boston, Andros managed to make thousands of enemies.

Traditional political leaders found themselves out in the cold because the assemblies had been abolished. When Andros and his counselors took it upon themselves to levy taxes, Puritan leaders pointed out that such taxes violated their rights as Englishmen. Andros replied that such rights did not necessarily exist in the Dominion of New England. He went further. He announced that the town governments established under the old Massachusetts charter were illegal; therefore, the land grants these towns had made to individuals were void. Landowners would have to reconfirm their titles with dominion authorities and pay rents to the dominion as well. As if this were not enough, Andros questioned the lawfulness of the Puritan churches. The proper church for English colonists, he said, was the established Church of England. He also made it clear

that the Navigation Acts would be enforced, and he brought in customs officers to do so.

The colonists were outraged. In one way or another, Andros had stepped on the toes of just about everyone in the colony. In 1687 Massachusetts sent its most prominent minister, Increase Mather, to London. Mather's task was to get the old charter revived and Andros recalled. But just as Mather was putting his diplomatic skills to work, the entire political picture was changed by a bloodless revolution.

During his brief reign, James II managed to produce almost as much resentment in England as Andros had in Massachusetts. James knew better than to try to rule without Parliament, but he did his best to get around Parliament's laws. He openly favored English Roman Catholics and began tinkering with the organization of the army. People began to wonder if he meant to use the army at home rather than abroad. Worst of all, James fathered a baby, and England was faced with a continued line of Roman Catholic monarchs.

A group of parliamentary leaders boldly invited William of Orange to become their new king. William was Dutch, but he was Protestant and married to James's Protestant daughter Mary. He accepted and landed in England with an army that met no opposition. James fled abroad, and William and Mary were installed as joint monarchs. Parliament proceeded to pass a series of laws that set forth the rights of Englishmen, enlarged parliamentary powers, and restricted the power of the monarch. An Act of Toleration gave religious freedom to Dissenters—that is, to English Puritans. Roman Catholics were forever excluded from the English throne. Ever afterward, the English described all these events as their Glorious Revolution.

When Puritan leaders in Massachusetts learned that William had landed in England, they decided to attempt a revolution of their own. Without waiting to hear whether William had gained the throne, a group of armed citizens marched on Andros's house in Boston and forced him to take refuge in an island fort in Boston harbor. Later, in London, Increase Mather succeeded in gaining the official recall of Andros and the abolition of the Dominion of New England. The northern colonies were returned to their previous status. But Massachusetts still had no charter. Mather tried but failed to restore the old one.

In 1691, however, a new charter was issued that incorporated the old Plymouth colony into Massachusetts. It combined features of royal government with features from the old colony form. A royal governor was to be appointed. But the governor did not have the power to appoint members of his council, as he did in other royal colonies. The council would serve as the upper house of the assembly, just as in all the royal colonies. But in Massachusetts the council was to be elected by the lower house. The charter of 1691 also provided for religious toleration; Puritans would no longer be able to persecute such groups as Quakers and members of the Church of England. Puritan leaders were not altogether happy with the new charter, but they could live with it. And more and more, they were turning away from religious concerns and toward the more worldly path of trade.

In New York, Andros's deputy, Francis Nicholson, resigned. In May 1689, Jacob Leisler, a German trader in Manhattan since its Dutch days, took advantage of Nicholson's absence to call on neighboring counties and towns to set up a representative government. With the support of those alarmed by rumors of a French invasion and a Catholic conspiracy, Leisler managed civil affairs for several months.

But by disregarding a message he had intercepted from the Crown ordering Nicholson to conduct colonial affairs until new authorities took over, he gave support to the charges that he was a revolutionary. When in March 1691 Leisler resisted the deputy sent by William III, he was captured, tried, and sentenced to death along with seven of his men. Leisler and his son-in-law, his closest follower, were hanged in May. The others were pardoned by the king, who then established royal and representative government in New York. But the rebellion poisoned the atmosphere of New York politics for years afterward.

New Imperial Regulations

William III brought with him to England his rivalry with the Catholic French, which was intensified by Louis XIV's hospitality to James II. As early as 1689, this rivalry led to war. And as things turned out, the conflict was the beginning of a series of world wars in the eighteenth century.

To bolster his position in the New World, William III in 1696 established a new committee for governing the colonies and strengthened the administration of the navigation system. The old Lords of Trade were replaced by a group known as the Board of Trade, a committee made up of high royal officials, private gentlemen, and merchants who had business interests in the colonies. The Board of Trade had no power to make or enforce regulations for the colonies. Nor could it appoint royal governors or other officials. But the board could offer its advice on such matters, and its advice was usually taken, because the Board of Trade was the only government agency that knew much about the colonies.

New navigation acts strengthened the board's hand. Customs offices were set up in each colony. These offices enjoyed the same powers as their counterparts in England, including access to writs of assistance, by which officials could use police power to search private premises. Offenders against the new navigation code were to be tried in admiralty courts, which were staffed by royal judges and had no juries. Admiralty courts became one of the most detested of all English institutions in the colonies. The navigation code itself was strengthened by the enumeration of more commodities to be shipped exclusively to England.

Yet the colonies prospered, and the richness of America's natural resources contributed heavily to their success. Smuggling and other kinds of evasion continued to go largely unpunished. American as well as English merchants benefited from the exclusion of other nations from their trade and from protection against enemies at sea. With all these benefits, the colonists took pride in their roles as overseas subjects of the English ("British" after 1707) crown. They were not yet conscious that they were developing a distinctively American way of life.

SUMMARY

The pattern of English colonization and the push to establish permanent settlements in North America were the result of several conditions in England and Europe at the turn of the seventeenth century: religious and political discontent, economic changes that uprooted people, and a sense of power and opportunity in England after its victory over Spain.

The first permanent English settlement in North America was at Jamestown in Virginia. It survived early hardships and began to prosper with the discovery of a valuable export crop: tobacco. Another factor in the growth of Virginia and all the agricultural southern colonies was the discovery of a new system of cheap labor: black slaves imported from West and western central Africa.

The Jamestown settlement was followed by the Puritan migration to New England, which grew into the Commonwealth of Massachusetts Bay and set another colonial economic pattern: shipping and trade. By the middle of the seventeenth century, New England included Connecticut, Rhode Island, New Hampshire, Plymouth, and Massachusetts.

What were to become the Middle Colonies—New York, New Jersey, Pennsylvania, and Delaware—began with the Dutch settlement of New Netherland after the voyage of Henry Hudson. Except for New York, all the Middle Colonies, as well as Maryland and Carolina, began as proprietary colonies—huge grants of land to wealthy individuals—rather than as grants to joint-stock companies.

Although the colonies were settled by different types of people and for different reasons, they developed in similar ways. One factor underlying this similarity was the colonists' attachment to representative government. By the time the English king and the government in London became aware of the role the colonies could play in the new mercantile system of world empire, certain patterns of independence and self-government were already set.

The close supervision by governors and agents sent from London was not always welcome in America. Nor were the Navigation Acts, a series of laws passed by Parliament to regulate the commerce and defense of the empire.

Open discontent with these ideas began when James II, in an effort to tighten control, lumped New York, New Jersey, and the New England colonies into the Dominion of New England, a new entity that was to be ruled by a royal governor without any colonial assemblies. The Glorious Revolution of 1688–1689 in England cancelled this experiment, but authorities in London remained interested in controlling their imperial possessions. William III established a new committee to govern the colonies, the Board of Trade, and pressed Parliament to pass new acts strengthening the mercantile system; these included lists of items that could be shipped only to England, and admiralty courts staffed by royal judges to try offenders. Despite these restrictions, by the beginning of the eighteenth century the colonies were flourishing under the mercantile system.

TIME LINE

1607	Jamestown founded	1660	The first of the Navigation Acts
1612	First growth of tobacco in Virginia	1660	Restoration of Charles II
1619	First Africans arrive in Virginia	1662	Colony of Connecticut receives charter
1619	Virginia receives representative assembly	1670	First permanent English settlement in Carolina
1620	Pilgrims sail on *Mayflower* to Plymouth	1674	New Netherland permanently taken by English as New York
1622	Indians kill one-third of the English settlers in Virginia	1675–1676	King Philip's War
1624	Dutch settle New Netherland	1676	Bacon's Rebellion
1630	Puritans found Massachusetts Bay Colony	1681	William Penn receives charter for his own colony
1634	English settle in Maryland	1685	James II establishes Dominion of New England
1636	Roger Williams banished to Rhode Island		
1638	Anne Hutchinson tried for heresy	1689	Glorious Revolution
1640	Outbreak of English Civil War	1696	Establishment of the Board of Trade

Suggested Readings

For the course of events in England, see R. Lockyer, *Tudor and Stuart Britain, 1471–1714* (1964). Two works focus specifically on settlement in America: C. Bridenbaugh, *Vexed and Troubled Englishmen, 1590–1642* (1968), and W. Notestein, *The English People on the Eve of Colonization* (1954). For a subtle Marxist appreciation of English society, there is C. Hill, *Society and Puritanism in Pre-Revolutionary England* (1964).

R. Simmons, *The American Colonies: From Settlement to Independence* (1976), provides an overview and has a good bibliography. W. Craven, *The Southern Colonies in the Seventeenth Century, 1607–1689* (1949), remains outstanding. A. Vaughn's *American Genesis: Captain John Smith and the Founding of Virginia* (1975) discusses a man who has fascinated historians ever since he undertook to write a history of his own career. Bacon's Rebellion in Virginia has received such partisan treatment from historians that it is safest to begin with R. Middlekauff's edited collection of documents, *Bacon's Rebellion* (1964).

The New England colonies have received much attention because settlers there preserved so many original records. The two best introductions to Puritan thought and society are E. Morgan, *The Puritan Dilemma: The Story of John Winthrop* (1958), a superb example of the way in which biography can be enlarged to become broad history; and C. Haskins, *Law and Authority in Massachusetts* (1960).

Puritan theology is complex. Perry Miller's brilliant studies are essential but not easy reading. Crucial are his *Errand into Wilderness* (1964); *The New England Mind: The Seventeenth Century* (1939); and *The New England Mind: From Colony to Province* (1953). Some of Miller's contentions have since been modified by first-rate studies such as E. Morgan's *Visible Saints: The History of a Puritan Idea* (1966); D. Hall, *The Faithful Shepherd: A History of the New England Ministry in the Seventeenth Century* (1972); and R. Dunn, *Puritans and Yankees: The Winthrop Dynasty of New England, 1630–1717* (1962).

By far the most important modifications of Miller's studies are in R. Middlekauff, *The Mathers: Three Generations of Puritan Intellectuals, 1596–1728* (1971). A recent work lays bare many biblical and personal aspects of Puritanism: C. Cohen, *God's Caress: The Psychology of Puritan Religious Experience* (1986). See also H. Stout, *The New England Soul: Preaching and Religious Culture in Colonial New England* (1986).

New England's history has been greatly enriched by local studies. Two of the most widely read are K. Lockridge, *A New England Town, The First Hundred Years: Dedham, Massachusetts, 1636–1736* (1970); and P. Greven, Jr., *Four Generations: Population, Land, and Family in Colonial Andover, Massachusetts* (1970). S. Powell, *Puritan Village: The Formation of a New England Town* (1963), does much more with the migration of English customs and institutions.

A very small colony gets interesting treatment in G. Langdon, *Pilgrim Colony: A History of New Plymouth, 1620–1691* (1966). A much more controversial work is J. Demos, *A Little Commonwealth: Family Life in Plymouth Colony* (1970), which, like several of the books cited in the two previous paragraphs, deals with family relationships. In this connection, the best place to start is E. Morgan, *The Puritan Family* (1966). The great original account of Plymouth is William Bradford's *Of Plymouth Plantation, 1620–1647*, best read in S. Morison's 1952 edition.

A new approach to history is W. Cronon, *Changes in the Land: Indians, Colonists, and the Ecology of New England* (1983). Probably the most interesting studies of the various offshoots of the bay colony focus on Rhode Island. O. Winslow, *Master Roger Williams* (1957), is a traditional biography. S. James, *Colonial Rhode Island: A History* (1975), deals with what was called the "sinkhole" of New England.

The early years of the Restoration colonies have received less attention from historians. A. Trelease, *Indian Affairs in Colonial New York: The Seventeenth Century* (1960), and L. Leder, *Robert Livingston, 1654–1728, and the Politics of Colonial New York* (1961), deal with the turmoil that followed the transition from Dutch to English rule. For Pennsylvania, see G. Nash, *Quakers and Politics: Pennsylvania, 1681–1726* (1968), and M. Dunn, *William Penn: Politics and Conscience* (1967). Although there are several specialized studies on the Carolinas, the best beginning is W. Craven, *The Colonies in Transition, 1660–1713* (1969), which has much information in other Restoration colonies and a good bibliography.

Several of the most interesting books on the seventeenth and eighteenth centuries deal with intercultural contacts and cultures. See G. Nash, *Red, White, and Black: The Peoples of Early America* (1974); A. Wallace, *The Death and Rebirth of the Seneca* (1969); K. Kupperman, *Settling with the Indians: The Meeting of English and Indian Cultures in America, 1580–1640* (1980); and J. Axtell, *The Invasion Within: The Contest of Cultures in Colonial North America* (1985).

D. Lovejoy, *The Glorious Revolution in America* (1972), is the best place to start on that subject. An old account of the first colonial system still stands up very well: C. Andrews, *The Colonial Period of American History*, Vol. 4 (1938). Also see S. Webb, *The Governors General: The English Army and the Definition of the Empire, 1569–1681* (1979).

Williamsburg, Virginia. *(Library of Congress)*

THE COLONIAL PEOPLE

Before the American Revolution, the Anglo-American colonies grew more rapidly in population than any other portion of the world. This growth stimulated geographical expansion, and it had important social and economic consequences. Many new settlers in the English colonies were not English at all, and outside New England ethnic diversity became the rule rather than the exception.

As the colonies grew, distinct social patterns emerged in various regions. Along the southern part of the Atlantic coast, slavery transformed the English settlements; after about 1720 it begins to make sense to speak of southern and northern colonies. To the west, in all the colonies, we can begin to talk about a frontier culture. In the east, with the rapid growth of towns, it is possible to detect the emergence of an urban way of life.

Yet it is important to bear in mind that the single most common experience of the colonists was life on a family farm. This dominance of rural over urban life is of course exactly opposite the situation in the United States and much of the world today. Rural ways and values did a great deal to shape the structure and practices of colonial politics. Yet political life in the colonies was shaped by other factors as well. Among them were the continuing ties with the mother country, the reign of English common law, the nature of the colonial economy, and the prevailing idea that government should represent the people but should remain in the hands of the rich, the well born, and the able.

PATTERNS OF POPULATION

In many ways the population of the English colonies in America was unique. The number of people grew faster than anywhere else in the world. This rapid growth had a profound impact on the colonial economy and the nature of colonial society. In addition, the English colonies attracted a great many non-English peoples. By the time of the American Revolution, colonists of *English* descent made up only slightly more than half the entire population.

The Population Explosion

At the end of New England's Great Migration in 1640, the non-Indian population of all the English continental colonies was about 27,000. This figure includes all the English colonies along the Atlantic seaboard, as well as New Netherland, but not the English colonies in the West Indies. It does not include Indians, because no one knew or knows how many Indians there were. Today, 27,000 people would make a very small town; modern football stadiums hold about three times that number.

By 1700 the non-Indian population in these colonies was nearly ten times as large, about 250,000. This rapid growth continued during the eighteenth century. No other European settlements in the New World grew nearly so fast. Although this increase was remarkable, we still need to bear in mind that 250,000 is about the population of a medium-sized city in the United States today. Put another way, the town that Roger Williams founded—Providence, in Rhode Island—today with its suburbs has nearly as many people as lived in all the English continental colonies in 1700.

There were several reasons for the rapid increase. One, of course, was the founding of new colonies; each new colony offered more land, and more land attracted more settlers. Another was the continued migration from England to the older colonies. Some of these people returned to England, but most stayed in America. In addition, the birth rate was considerably higher in the colonies than in England. Probably this was owing largely to the relative ease of obtaining land, which enabled couples to marry younger and therefore to have more children. Parents on farms found children useful, since they could be put to work at an early age. Most parents assumed that their children would obtain land of their own when they grew up, so a large family—five or six children was the average—seemed a welcome advantage.

The spurt in population also reflected a relatively low death rate. After the early years of settlement, the mortality rate in the American colonies became far lower than that in England. This difference was caused partly by the presence in England of large cities, especially London. Two and three hundred years ago, large cities killed off people much faster than they produced them. Crowding encouraged the spread of disease, especially because the drinking water in almost all cities was badly polluted by garbage and sewage. In 1700 London was probably the largest city in the world. By comparison, Boston, New York, and Philadelphia were tiny towns. And because they were so much smaller, they had far fewer urban problems.

Even though the death rate in the colonies was lower than in Europe and in Asia, it was far higher than it is today, especially among infants and young children. There were no effective cures for diseases, and no one knew that germs even existed, let alone how to kill them. The American colonists suffered a higher death rate in the early years of settlement than later on. Virginia remained a particularly unhealthy place for fifty years. Overwork, malnutrition, and harsh treatment shortened the lives of Virginia laborers. Two diseases took the greatest toll: malaria (from mosquitoes) and typhoid fever (from polluted drinking water). After about 1650 the health of the Virginia colonists improved dramatically. The reasons for this change are not entirely clear, but the death rate dropped and population began to increase rapidly.

By contrast, the New England colonies were healthier from the beginning. It was largely for this reason that early Massachusetts had a far larger population than Virginia. New England, and later the Middle Colonies of New York, New Jersey, and Pennsylvania, had one of the lowest death rates in the entire world.

Another brake on population growth in the colonies was the proportion of women and men. In early Virginia, most settlers were male. Since the number of children in any society depends upon the number of young women, not the number of men, Virginia's early growth was far slower than New England's. The English migration to all the northern colonies usually involved entire families. Single settlers were more common in the southern colonies. As the years went by, children born in America became a larger and larger part of the population. Because males and females were born in about equal numbers, the proportion of men and women in the population gradually evened out and fewer men remained unmarried. This was an important development, for married men tend to settle down and to think more about security and less about adventure. The American colonies were becoming settled in more ways than one.

Specialization of Labor

The population explosion in the American colonies had several important effects. It stimulated continued growth and helped raise the standard of living, since a growing population meant more mouths to feed and a growing market for farmers. A small settlement could afford only to cultivate food and make clothes and shelter. A larger one could support a greater variety of jobs.

As an example, let us take John, a young shoemaker who arrived in Massachusetts as part of the Great Migration of the 1630s. He had little money, but was a skilled bootmaker. He settled in the little town of Hingham outside Boston. With the help of his neighbors, he built a glorified hut that he called a house. In turn he helped his neighbors at the same task, and together they constructed a meetinghouse to serve as a church and as a meeting place for the voters of the town. But John had to eat; so he had to farm. His neighbors, including the minister, did the same.

Yet John remained a shoemaker at heart, for he was better at his craft than at raising squash and corn. He used his little remaining cash to buy some leather. In his spare time, our shoemaker lovingly made some boots, which he sold to his neighbors. There were more and more of them as time went by. They paid him in food and firewood more often than in cash, but eventually he was able to stop farming, sell his land, and move to Boston.

Once in town, John bought a small house and hung out his sign—a piece of wood in the shape of a boot. One room in his two-room house was his place of work and his retail store. Boston was growing from a village into a real town, and could no longer feed itself. Nearby farmers drove their wagons into town with food and firewood

A shoemaker prospering in his trade. *(American Antiquarian Society)*

to sell, and they were happy to have the chance to buy John's boots. There were more and more of them every year. John died at his workbench of a heart attack, reasonably secure in the knowledge that he had labored hard at his calling. That, at least, is the way he would have looked at the matter. We would call it increasing specialization of labor, fueled by population growth.

The Young and the Old

The high birth rate also shaped early American society by making it very youthful. Today, fewer than half the people of the United States are under the age of thirty. In the seventeenth and eighteenth centuries, half the people were under the age of sixteen. This youthfulness had several important effects. Obviously, only a relatively small number of men could take part in politics and government, since the voting age was the traditional twenty-one. It also meant that the military power of the colonies was relatively small. The colonists did their best to meet the latter situation by setting the age for service in the colonial militias at sixteen to sixty. People often referred to the "men and boys" of colonial armies, as is reflected in the song "Yankee Doodle" from the Revolution.

The youthfulness of the colonial population had an even more important result: the absence of a large group of people who were too old to work. Some people lived to be seventy or eighty, but not many. Elderly people assumed they should work until they died or became too feeble. The age of sixty-five had no special meaning, and no one thought about "retirement." Most people did a full day's work from about age twelve on, unless they were disabled.

In sharp contrast, the United States today has a very large group of old people who either do not or cannot work. They are supported partly by savings from their working years and partly by the social security and welfare systems. But as a group they are not self-supporting; they are supported by younger people who can and do work.

The colonists did have large numbers of dependent children. But we do too today, despite a lower birth rate. This is because many people today do not do much productive work until they are eighteen, or even thirty, and the law supposedly prevents them from working before the age of sixteen. In the colonies, a much higher proportion of the population engaged in productive labor, and the group of nonworking dependents was relatively small. So many people working made for economic growth and a rising standard of living for everyone.

NON-ENGLISH IMMIGRANTS

In the early years of the eighteenth century, miserable social and economic conditions in western Germany and northern Ireland created a large pool of discontented people who were eager to migrate overseas. The Palatines (as Americans called most Germans) and the Scotch-Irish (as those from the province of Ulster in northern Ireland were called) made up by far the largest groups of European newcomers. However, by far the largest group of non-English immigrants came from West Africa, and of course they came against their wills.

The Germans

Continual German immigration began in 1683, when small groups of Mennonites and Quakers established Germantown, near Philadelphia. During the next three decades other radical German Protestants founded such biblically named Pennsylvania towns as Bethlehem and Nazareth. These early immigrants were mainly well-educated people who paid their own passage, brought property from the Old World, and bought land on their arrival. They built substantial communities, in which many original buildings still stand. All the radical sects were opposed to domination of the church by the state, a position that took its most extreme form in their refusal to bear arms. They also refused to swear oaths, an aberration that annoyed British administrators of the Navigation Acts but appealed to the dominant Quakers.

Along with these sects, many German Lutherans and German Reformed Calvinists also settled in Pennsylvania early in the eighteenth century. These denominations, with the Lutherans predominant, were by far the most numerous of the German-speaking immigrants to America. As members of large and well-established Protestant groups, they were usually called "church people." Most of them, too poor to pay their way to America, came as *redemptioners*, one of the several forms of white servitude.

The indentured servants who were first shipped to Virginia and Maryland early in the seventeenth century had made contracts with the joint-stock companies or proprietary agents abroad. They agreed to work in the colonies in exchange for passage across the Atlantic. Redemptioners of the eighteenth century sold themselves to ship captains or "soul brokers" in European ports.

In 1750, Gottlieb Mittelberger warned Germans about the voyage to America: "There is on board these ships terrible misery . . . stench, fumes, horror, vomiting . . . fever, dysentery . . . heat, constipation, boils, scurvy, cancer, mouth-rot . . . from old and sharply salted food and . . . foul water, so that many die miserably." On one ship arriving in Philadelphia in 1745, only forty of four hundred passengers survived. As many as a third of the redemptioners may have died at sea. Sometimes the survivors were forced into extra years of servitude to pay back the cost of the passage of their dead relatives.

Once in America, the redemptioners' contracts were sold to the highest bidders. Since the

From the old to the new world—German emigrants for New York embarking on a Hamburg steamer. *(Library of Congress)*

healthiest were sold first, ship captains kept the sick and old on board until their contracts were sold or they died. Parents were often forced to sell their children into service. The usual term was from four to seven years, at the end of which the servant was to receive "freedom dues," usually fifty acres of land, tools, and clothing. These dues were often withheld; when granted, the servant commonly sold off the land for a small amount of cash. Not surprisingly, runaways were frequent.

German immigration reached its high point between 1749 and 1754, when over five thousand Germans arrived in American ports each year, most in Philadelphia. Although many of the church people tried to learn English ways, others held to their own language and traditions. The Pennsylvania Germans became celebrated throughout the country for their rich gardens and orchards, their sturdy barns and well-tended livestock. German artisans developed the

famous long rifle, first manufactured in Lancaster and later adopted and improved by frontiersmen everywhere. Yet many English Pennsylvanians became concerned that the colony might be becoming a New Germany—and, in fact, some 40 percent of Pennsylvanians in the mid-eighteenth century were of German ancestry.

The Scotch-Irish

The large number of German immigrants in the eighteenth century was exceeded by the so-called Scotch-Irish. Their ancestors were the lowland Scottish Calvinists who migrated to the province of Ulster in northern Ireland early in the seventeenth century. James I deliberately encouraged this migration in order to strengthen Protestantism in Ireland. At first they prospered as farmers and artisans. After 1696, however, new Navigation Acts hurt the Irish economy.

Then, in the early years of the eighteenth century, British absentee landlords started doubling rents. The people of Ulster began leaving in thousands.

Poverty in Ireland, as in England, helped fill the prisons with debtors. In time of war, male prisoners were often forced into the army. But when poverty and unemployment spread during periods of peace, as it did starting in 1713, after the cessation of a quarter century of hostilities between England and France, something was needed to empty the jails. The common penalties of "burning the hand and whipping" seemed inadequate to the authorities. As a substitute, thousands of English and Scotch-Irish convicts were shipped to Virginia and especially to Maryland to sweat in the tobacco fields. A Treasury decision in 1716 to pay merchants for transporting them overseas created a powerful special interest in the practice.

Paying passengers probably accounted for no more than one in ten of the Scotch-Irish immigrants. The rest, like most of the Germans, obtained their passage by signing indentures. Many landed in Philadelphia or in nearby Newcastle, Delaware. They continued to arrive by the thousands each year, and as their indentures expired they moved beyond the Germans and Philadelphia's western frontier, across the Susquehanna River to the Cumberland Valley. From there, mountain passes led southwest to Maryland, western Virginia, and North Carolina. These routes took them along the outer rim of a smaller number of Germans who had earlier moved in the same direction.

The West Africans

The first Africans brought to the English colonies were sold by a Dutch shipmaster at Virginia in 1619, the same year the first legislative body met in America. Whether these early arrivals were treated as slaves for life or servants for term is uncertain, but they were never regarded as just another kind of settler. After 1640 in Virginia and Maryland, some of the Africans and their children were being enslaved for life. By 1660, a pattern had clearly emerged: *Negroes* (a term borrowed from the Portuguese-Spanish word for "black") customarily would be lifetime, hereditary slaves. They were forbidden to bear arms, and—a crucial, enduring, and often over-

looked distinction—Negro women were routinely put to work "in the fields." White women generally were not, nor would they ever be on a regular, routine basis.

At the same time, about 1660, the legislatures of Virginia and Maryland began to enact laws to permit, and even require, the status of slavery for Africans, and Africans only. The irony was that the English, who prided themselves on being the freest people of all Europe, hammered out in the New World legal frameworks for slavery. By the early 1670s, complex slave codes had been enacted in the Chesapeake colonies. Yet the system was not watertight. At least a few Negroes were "free," no matter how much they might otherwise be degraded. From the beginning, race and slavery never matched completely.

The general pattern, however, rapidly became clear. There were not a great many blacks in the Chesapeake colonies until about 1700. From then until the Revolution, they were imported in huge numbers into the tobacco colonies and into South Carolina. A relative trickle reached the Middle Colonies and New England. From 1720 to the American Revolution, Africans and Americans of African descent constituted some 20 percent of the mainland non-Indian population, a far higher proportion than before or since.

The West African migration to the British mainland colonies was a very small part of the slave trade to the New World. Between 9 and 12 million slaves were dragged to the Americas during the 350 years of the slave trade. Ninety

African origins of the slave trade

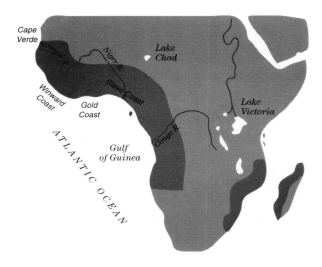

The *banjo*—the musical instrument and the word itself—came to the United States and to other parts of the New World from West Africa. A few banjos may perhaps have been brought across the Atlantic aboard slave ships, but knowledge of the instrument and the skill to construct it most certainly did. There are many references to the *banjo* (variously spelled) as early as the mid-eighteenth century. Thomas Jefferson referred to it in 1784: "The instrument proper to them [the blacks] is the Banjor, which they brought hither from Africa." The original version had five strings (as most still do) and depended on a small drum for its resonance, unlike the wooden box of the European guitar. Since West African music made such extensive use of drumming, the combination of strings with a drum was a natural development. After generations of homemade construction and strumming on slave plantations, the banjo was taken up by whites in their blackface minstrel shows in the 1830s. Throughout American history, and probably in Africa, the instrument has customarily been played by men rather than women.

percent went to tropical America; according to the best current assessment, only some 350,000, or 5 percent, arrived in the area that is now the United States.

The cruelty of this forced migration has usually and perhaps rightly drawn attention away from its enormous significance Brutality began with wartime capture or kidnapping or conviction for a crime. Warfare among various African tribes was the most common cause of enslavement, but sometimes European raiding parties attacked Africans directly. During the marches to the sea, which often covered hundreds of miles, many died or were killed. On the coast, survivors were chained, herded into open stockades, branded, and segregated by age and sex. The greatest shock of all was perhaps the sudden, enforced separation from familiar surroundings, the awful sight of the great pounding ocean, and the tall-masted vessels that rolled offshore with such seeming grace and confidence. (It seems small compensation for anyone then or since that mortality was even higher among the European sailors involved in the slave trade than among the victims.)

Despite the careful organization of the trade on the African coast, vessels frequently rode offshore for weeks before gathering a full load of human beings or finding a favorable wind. Slaves most often rebelled during these periods, sometimes with complete success. On the high seas some captives threw themselves into shark-infested waters. What Europeans saw as suicide was actually a thoroughly rational action, since many West Africans believed that Europeans were cannibals and that only through death and spiritual remigration could they return to their homeland.

Britain was one of the last of the Western powers to enter the slave trade on a commercial basis, but the British came to dominate the trade in the eighteenth century. Of the relatively small number of slaves who were sold to the mainland colonies, at least 85 percent came directly from Africa. The remainder came from the Caribbean islands, usually after staying there for only a few weeks. Because males were in greater demand, they greatly outnumbered the female slaves. In addition, like servants from the British Isles, the African migrants tended to be young, many of them in their teens.

We will never know the exact nature of the early cultural contact between the English colonists and their slaves. Africans and their immediate descendants learned English manners and language rapidly—because they had to. The English who had day-to-day contact with them also became to some extent bicultural. Africans and their children learned to accommodate themselves to powerlessness. English slaveholders and their children learned new roles of unrestrained personal power.

For obvious reasons, historians know more about the white side of this equation than the black. We know that whites saw blacks as enemies, and there is nothing to suppose that the reverse was not the case. The tyranny that resulted was self-reinforcing. As the slave system developed in the early years of the eighteenth century, it tightened the restrictions on the personal freedom of blacks, and whites too. But it was blacks who suffered the chains of slavery.

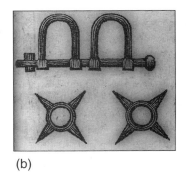

(a)

(b)

(c)

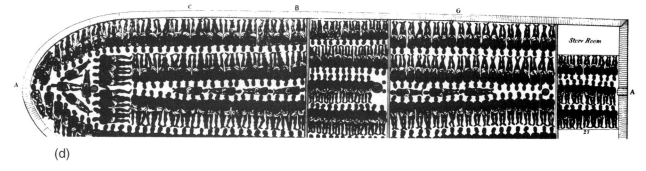

(d)

Treatment of African slaves, as illustrated in an eighteenth-century treatise on "Methods of Procuring Slaves": (a) mouthpiece and neck brace with hooks, to prevent escape; (b) leg shackles and spurs used to restrict slaves; (c) Iron mask; (d) plan for stowing slaves below decks for the long sea voyage on the British slave ship *Brookes* under the regulated slave trade act of 1788. *(Library of Congress)*

Slaves waiting for sale in Virginia. *(Library of Congress)*

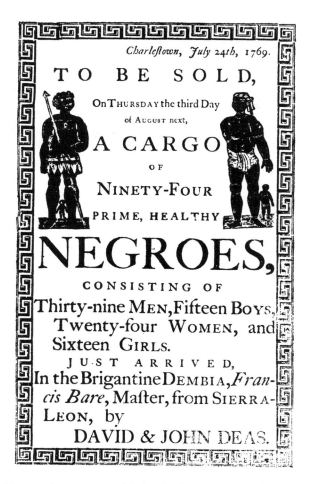

Slave traders announced their sales in newspaper advertisements and broadsides such as this one, from South Carolina. Note the imbalanced sex ratio among the slaves in the cargo. *(American Antiquarian Society)*

In Virginia and Maryland, "new Negroes" from Africa were normally put to work in the fields ("into the ground") on a "quarter" of some sixteen people, under a young male overseer, far from the larger home plantation of the actual owner. In the Chesapeake colonies, many African American men of the second and third generations were trained or permitted to practice as "tradesmen" (skilled craftsmen) on the home plantations, which served as commercial and manufacturing centers because there were no large towns. In South Carolina and Georgia, the rice plantations contained larger numbers of Africans and fewer whites. This heavy concentration in the coastal low country of South Carolina and Georgia meant that Africans were able there, as nowhere else in the English

continental colonies, to preserve many of the customs and languages they had known in West Africa. Those styles and their own creolized language (known usually as Gullah) survive there to this day.

CLASSES AND LIFESTYLES

During the eighteenth century the English settlements were becoming more complex and less and less like mere outposts of the British Isles. They became much more diverse in terms of ethnic makeup, and differences in their economies made for differences in social organization. Although most colonists still farmed, or forced servants and slaves to farm for them, an increasing number moved to urban areas. In all the colonies, everyone assumed that there would always be distinctions of social rank among people, an arrangement that seemed perfectly ordinary and proper at the time.

Tidewater Gentry

Throughout the colonial period, most of the white population of tidewater Virginia and Maryland and of adjacent parts of North Carolina was of English extraction. Here, although corn and other food crops continued to be grown, the production and export of tobacco was the main focus of economic activity, along with land speculation.

Led by a small elite group, the Chesapeake planters kept close ties with Britain and copied the manners of its aristocracy. The Carters, Lees, Byrds, Randolphs, and Fitzhughs of Virginia, the Carrolls, Dulaneys, and Galloways of Maryland lived in great Georgian mansions. They filled the well-proportioned rooms with the finest imported furniture or hired artisans to carry out the designs of foreign cabinetmakers. Contemporary artists painted the Chesapeake gentry in all their imported finery.

A few planters owned large libraries with books in several languages, although learning and schools were not emphasized. In 1693 William and Mary College, endowed by the established Anglican church, opened in Williamsburg, Virginia, which was soon to become the provincial capital. But few students spent more than a year there. Some planters sent their sons to England for education, but those who profited from the opportunity often did not come back. The Chesapeake gentry were an outdoor people, fonder of fox hunting, horse racing, and partying than of learning.

The Chesapeake planters had to take the management of their plantations seriously. But they seemed driven to keep up the good life, or at least the appearance of it. Land, which represented their greatest wealth, was also their downfall. "Such amazing property," observed Philip Fithian, a tutor to the Carter children, "no matter how deeply it is involved in debt, blows up the owners to an imagination which is visible to all." They "live up their suppositions," a Londoner remarked, "without providing against calamities and accidents."

From the 1730s to the 1750s, when the price of Virginia tobacco soared, rising profits made the planters' land more valuable. The Chesapeake gentry enjoyed a golden age. Yet few could long keep up the high life, the expenditures for clothes, carriages, body slaves, mansions, parks, and wine. Eventually, the debts for imported goods grew too high. To those who crashed, the West became a refuge or a new springboard to success. It also fed ideas of empire among such Virginians as young George Washington.

Of all the mainland settlements, tidewater South Carolina, extending inland about sixty miles and southward to the Savannah River, was closest to the West Indian sugar islands in character. Eighteenth-century South Carolina was the only mainland colony where blacks outnumbered whites, as they did in the islands. The whites below the two-thousand leading families, moreover, were among the poorest on the continent. They had the lowest literacy rate and some of the strongest antagonisms toward the ruling elite.

Carolina rice proved to be the single most profitable staple in all the mainland colonies, and the rice barons of South Carolina became the wealthiest of American planters. By midcentury, they were being encouraged to grow indigo, heavily in demand as the source of a dye for the booming English textile industry. Indigo and rice were less subject than tobacco to price fluctuations and other market hazards, so the Carolina planters, unlike the Chesapeake gentry, had stable incomes and fewer problems with debt.

A scene of Williamsburg, Virginia, with soldiers and a wagon train. *(Library of Congress)*

CHAPTER 3   THE COLONIAL PEOPLE

GROWING UP IN VIRGINIA

Devereaux Jarrett, an Anglican minister, was born in tidewater Virginia, where simplicity and frugality characterized his upbringing during the years before the American Revolution:

Our food was altogether the produce of the farm, or plantation, except a little sugar, which was rarely used; and our raiment was altogether my mother's manufacture, except our hats and shoes, the latter of which we never put on, but in the winter season. We made no use of tea or coffee for breakfast, or at any other time; nor did I know a single family that made any use of them. Meat, bread and milk was the ordinary food of all my acquaintance. I suppose the richer sort might make use of those and other luxuries, but to such people I had no access. We were accustomed to look upon, what were called gentle folks, as beings of a superior order. For my part, I was quite shy of them, and kept off to a humble dis-

tance. A periwig, in those days, was a distinguishing badge of gentle folk—and when I saw a man riding the road, near our house, with a wig on, it would so alarm my fears, and give me such a disagreeable feeling, that, I dare say, I would run off, as for my life. Such ideas of the difference between gentle and simple, were, I believe, universal among all of my rank and age. . . .

My parents neither sought nor expected any titles, honors, or great things, either for themselves or children. Their highest ambition was to teach their children to read, write, and understand the fundamental rules of arithmetic. I remember also, they taught us short prayers, and made us very perfect in repeating the Church Catechism. They wished us all to be brought up in some honest calling, that we might earn our bread, by the sweat of our brow, as they did. . . .

Carolina rivers were not deep enough for seagoing vessels to sail directly to the plantations, as they did in the Chesapeake region, so the colony's produce was brought to Charles Town for transshipment abroad. Although the Chesapeake region remained virtually without towns for generations, Charleston by the 1750s had become the fourth largest colonial town. Its midcentury population of 10,000 was almost equally divided as to race, with a sizable proportion of the blacks serving as household and personal slaves to planters who maintained homes there. The masters, living much of the year far from the heat and disease of the rice fields, left to overseers and blacks the labors and hazards of producing the crops.

The Southern Backcountry

Although the entire southern backcountry at first was a paradise for hunters and trappers, European settlers there developed a mixed subsistence agriculture of cereals, potatoes, fruits, meat, flax, and hemp. In the Chesapeake, small market centers grew up along the main routes and at ferry crossings. Even before midcentury there were such tiny thriving crossroads communities as Fredericksburg and Hagerstown in

Maryland (dominated by German newcomers), Berkeley Court House (modern Martinsburg) and Winchester in Virginia, and Charlotte in North Carolina (where the Scotch-Irish prevailed).

Yet tough conditions continued to breed rough manners. The back parts of the Carolina country were more isolated than those of the Chesapeake region. Settlers fresh from Ulster or German villages found it hard to spend lonely years in such a wild, disease-ridden country. But the major difficulty was the unending labor of clearing the land. Many settlers soon fell into a seminomadic life. Some became herdsmen of wild swine and cattle often stolen from the Indians. Itinerant clergymen reported with dismay how the people in the backcountry dwelt together in "Concubinage, swapping their wives as Cattle, and living in a State of Nature, more irregularly and unchastely than the Indians." A few made fortunes out of meat, skins, and tallow, forming a backcountry gentry living on great cattle ranges.

Gradually, tidewater institutions, both legal and political, were imposed on the Maryland and Virginia backcountry, although not without resistance. Antagonism to Charles Town's domination in South Carolina was even stronger. Throughout the eighteenth century, farmers in the interior complained frequently about the

Philadelphia landowners kept elaborate carriages to carry them from town to their country estates, like this one belonging to Isaac Norris. *(From a 1717 drawing; the Historical Society of Pennsylvania)*

lack of courts and the "parasites" who came from Charles Town to collect taxes.

The Middle Colonies

During the eighteenth century, the Middle Colonies formed the most culturally varied part of British North America. Pennsylvania, the newest, quickly became the largest and most diversified of these colonies. By 1755, Philadelphia was the largest city in the colonies, with about 18,000 people. Although Quakers were no longer a majority, Quaker merchants made up Philadelphia's wealthiest group and dominated the entire colony. Quaker religious beliefs, like those of the Puritans, inspired the thrift, industry, and reliability that proved so conducive to business success.

Persecution in Europe and America had scattered Friends all over the Atlantic world, a situation they used to advantage by establishing business contacts with Friends in other colonies. The industrious farmers Penn had brought to his colony supplied Philadelphia merchants with excellent grain and other staples for export and a thriving market for imported goods.

Travelers passing through New Jersey in the eighteenth century sometimes stopped long enough to comment on its natural beauty, its prosperity, or its wonderful oysters, but there was little more to detain the curious traveler. Jerseyites often felt the same way about their settlements. In the 1750s many of them looked upon their colony as a "keg tapped at both ends," for its surplus hemp, grain, flax, hay, and Indian corn was transported to New York or Philadelphia to feed those cities or to be shipped overseas.

Nature had endowed New York with the finest harbor in the Atlantic world, yet the growth of that colony was far slower than that of New England, Pennsylvania, or the southern colonies.

Tilling the soil on a farm in Pennsylvania. *(Library of Congress)*

Huge landed estates along the Hudson River valley and Iroquois control of the interior were partly responsible. From the start of the eighteenth century, British governors of New York, copying the Dutch, had rewarded their favorites with land grants ranging from 50,000 to 1 million acres along the Hudson Valley. These patroons, as they were called, sometimes paid nothing but a token tax and thus had little incentive to sell or rent their property. German, Scotch-Irish, and other squatters, however, took advantage of the unused land. When the patroons eventually tried to collect rents from families that had squatted there for generations, they met armed resistance.

At midcentury, New York City had 13,000 inhabitants, many of them living in houses built, as a visitor reported, "after the Dutch model." But the city had begun to lose many of its Dutch features, and the Dutch language itself was dying out. Dutch influence persisted in the Hudson Valley, in towns such as Albany, where the Dutch language remained predominant as late as the 1740s. Exposed to Indian raiders from French Canada until the British defeated the French in 1763, colonial Albany kept the look of a frontier outpost. Wooden walls enclosed the town, and at its center stood a square stone fortress.

New England

Connecticut, like all New England, was dominated by family farms and Puritan churches; it became known as "the land of steady habits." The same could have been said of rural New Hampshire, Rhode Island, and Massachusetts, except that the latter two colonies each boasted a large town. Newport, Rhode Island, was a favorite summer vacation spot for southern planters. That town also thrived on the slave trade and the distilling of molasses into "rumbullion"—a beverage now called rum.

The city of Boston was the heart of Massachusetts, as Massachusetts was the heart of New England. North of Boston such ports as Salem, Marblehead, and Gloucester, which much later were to supply many of the "proper Bostonians" of the Victorian era, were already trading centers. But the capital of the commonwealth, with over 15,000 people in 1750, a fine harbor, and the biggest inland markets, dwarfed the other New England towns.

In the seventeenth century, Boston's merchants had been quick to take advantage of England's wars with the Dutch, which had diverted the ships of those two powerful commercial and maritime nations from their regular trading routes. Early in the eighteenth century, peace boosted Boston's prosperity. In the West Indies, a growing demand for necessities sent prices and profits soaring. By the terms of the Peace of Utrecht (1713), Britain took Newfoundland and Nova Scotia from France and opened the vast fisheries off their coasts to New Englanders. At the same time, Nantucket whalers began to sail to the Arctic Ocean and to Brazil.

Throughout New England, the demand for more and better ships promoted such land-based businesses as rope manufacture and sailmaking. These enterprises drew artisans from nearby towns and from abroad. Their growing number brought new home and business construction, as well as prosperity to the surrounding countryside.

As in Pennsylvania and the South, in Massachusetts wealth brought a change in social style. Although Calvin had warned the Saints against "all superfluities" and luxuries, by the eighteenth century many of the richest Puritans, like the richest Quakers, had shifted to the less austere Anglican church. Boston's "codfish aristocracy" and its imitators in nearby ports now sported swords, satins, and English broadcloths and dwelled in elegant houses.

New England merchants, like those elsewhere, often installed their brothers, sons, and in-laws as agents in foreign lands. In Britain itself they turned to relatives. If there were no family connections, they, like the Quakers, sought out other Puritans. As a last resource in foreign ports, they employed their own countrymen to look after their interests. Family businesses were enlarged, and family ties multiplied by marriages among the merchant group.

North, south, and west of Boston, new settlements grew up everywhere during the eighteenth century. To outsiders, rural New England villages were remarkable for two qualities that seemed contradictory: proper social order and a "democratic" style. One visitor commented on the relative lack of social distinctions: "they seem to be a good substantial Kind of Farmers, but there is no break in their Society; their Government, Religion, and Manners all tend to support an equality. Whoever brings in your Victuals sits down and chats to you." Here were the makings of a more democratic society than prevailed in many of the other colonies and in Europe.

Family Farms

From Pennsylvania northward the typical way of life was that of the family farm. Even in the southern colonies, the majority of whites were farmers. Anyone who has ever lived on a family farm knows that such a life involves long hours and hard work for everyone. Children worked at least some of the time from the age when they could be shown how to shell peas, shuck corn, or fetch firewood. Older girls and women had an unending round of tasks. They cooked in metal pots hung over the open fireplace, and they baked in the hollow compartment in the chimney that served as an oven. Many of them spun and wove rough cloth and sewed it into clothing for the family. They washed clothes and bedding in wooden tubs, with soap they made themselves, and then hung it out to dry on a fence or anything else that was handy.

Mothers fed their babies at the breast. They used a nursing can with cow's milk only if they

A colonial housewife spinning wool. *(American Antiquarian Society)*

had to. When the baby was old enough, he or she was fed a mixture of potatoes or cornmeal or wheatmeal, and seasonally with vegetables or fruit. Meat was sometimes available for the family, but not every day. Stringy chicken meat was fresh when available, but pork and beef were usually salted or smoked. In winter, some foods could be kept cold in an underground compartment; the warmer months were more of a problem because food tended to spoil.

For the most part, a woman's work outdoors was confined to "lighter" jobs such as feeding livestock and slopping the hogs (which ate most of the family's garbage). Only at harvest time did women join in the heavier jobs; even then, these were regarded as necessary tasks rather than as normal and desirable work. There was an important exception to this assumption: Widows worked in the fields because they had to—which was one reason widows so often remarried as soon as they could.

The men of farming families did most of the heavy outdoor work. They cleared the fields. They prepared the fields with a horse or ox or mule, steering the plow around boulders and tree stumps. They set the seed, prayed for rain, chopped the weeds, and prayed for clear skies at harvest time. After harvest, they had time to build a shed, cut fence rails, mend the harnesses, trap raccoons, fix the chimney, and help the women teach the children to obey, to work, to read, and to pray.

For all the members of farming families, life was busy but not rushed. Certain things had to be done. If you did not chop firewood, you went hungry and in the winter you froze. As always and everywhere, there were emergencies and sudden strokes of bad luck. If the new baby died, a little grave had to be dug. If lightning struck the house, another had to be built. If Indians gave trouble, they had to be talked to or shot at. If the field just planted for corn was washed out by a thunderstorm, it had to be re-seeded. If the planks over the creek on the way to town washed out, they had to be replaced.

In many ways this was a simple life by modern standards. There was very little paperwork—or paper of any kind. There were practically no bills to pay, for exchanges of goods and services were usually done on the spot, often without any cash. Credit normally depended on one's reputation with a peddler or the owner of a tiny general store or with a neighbor. As time went on, however, rents became a problem for

THE EXPLOITATION OF THE LAND

Peter Kalm, a Swedish naturalist who traveled extensively in the colonies, was one of the few commentators of that time who even glimpsed the connections among rapid population growth, the availability of land, and wasteful exploitation of natural resources. As for population, Kalm wrote:

It does not seem difficult to find out the reasons, why the people multiply more here than in Europe. As soon as a person is old enough, he may marry in these provinces, without any fear of poverty; for there is such a tract of good ground yet uncultivated, that a new-married man can, without difficulty, get a spot of ground, where he may sufficiently subsist with his wife and children. The taxes are very low, and he need not be under any concern on their account. The liberties he enjoys are so great, that he considers himself as a prince in his possessions.

Yet these "possessions" were exploited with little eye to their future value:

The Europeans coming to America found a rich and fine soil before them, lying as loose between the trees as the best bed in a garden. They had nothing to do but to cut down the wood, put it up in heaps, and to clear the dead leaves away. They could then immediately proceed to ploughing, which in such loose ground is very easy; and having sown their corn, they got a most plentiful harvest. This easy method of getting a rich crop has spoiled the English and other European inhabitants, and induced them to adopt the same method of agriculture which the Indians make use of; that is, to sow uncultivated grounds, as long as they will produce a crop without manuring, but to turn them into pastures as soon as they can bear no more, and to take in hand new spots of ground, covered since time immemorial with woods, which have been spared by the fire or the hatchet ever since the creation. This is likewise the reason why agriculture, and the knowledge of this useful branch, is so imperfect here. . . .

the minority of family farmers who did not own their own land.

Taxes, whether from the town, the county, or the colony's government, could also become a problem. But the purpose of such taxes was obvious. The farmer who voted on the local tax rate had a very good idea of what he was paying for. His taxes would go toward support for a couple of widows and several orphans, toward the minister's salary, and to pay the travel costs of the town's or county's representatives in the colonial assembly. Taxes also went for maintenance of the meetinghouse, and to pay minor expenses for several neighbors who were helping to clear a road to a nearby settlement.

There were dozens of such local expenses, plus taxes to the colony as well. But many farmers voted annually for representatives to the colonial assembly, and they therefore had a sense of control, or at least of participation, in the process of taxation and government.

These farmers were not well off by modern standards; they lived with more hardship and far less leisure than modern Americans. Compared with the farmers of Europe, however, they were prosperous. They had a far better chance of owning land of their own. Because land was easy to get, American farmers wasted what they had. They knew it would be easy to move on, so

Patrick Lyon, who suffered three months severe imprisonment on merely a vague suspicion for the internal robbery of the Bank of Pennsylvania. He was a locksmith and blacksmith who had manufactured the iron doors and locks for the vault of the Bank of Pennsylvania. *(Library of Congress)*

they often simply abandoned fields that had been worn out. Many farming families moved from one place to another, from old land to new. Family farming was a hard life, but one could always hope to start again on better soil.

Colonial Cities

All the colonies remained closely tied to the Atlantic Ocean. The sea had its dangers, but it was the great highway of trade and migration. Water transportation was crucial. As settlers moved inland, they settled the river valleys first, partly because the soil was more fertile, but also because river transportation was easier and cheaper than trying to move things overland. Even the best roads consisted of twin ruts worn by the wheels of wagons.

All the important urban centers in the English colonies were Atlantic ports. In 1740 Boston was still the largest colonial city, with a population of 17,000. But the size of Boston was limited because it was confined to a small neck of land, so Philadelphia and New York soon grew to be larger. Charles Town and Newport remained the fourth and fifth largest towns in the colonies. By the time of the American Revolution, Philadelphia had about 35,000 inhabitants. London was more than ten times as large, but Philadelphia was by then one of the two or three largest cities in the English-speaking world.

To the country farmers of eighteenth-century America, the city was an impressive place. Many of the streets were actually paved with stones, and later some of them were even lit by oil lamps. Many country people never saw a city in their entire lives. Those who did were astounded by the crowding and the bustle. The farmer's wagon was only one of many that creaked and rattled through the narrow streets, piled high with corn or wheat, vegetables and fruits, boards or firewood. Now and then a brightly painted gentleman's carriage made its way through the traffic. Dogs yapped and nipped at the horses and oxen, and pigs and an occasional goat jostled for the garbage in the streets. Sheep and cattle were herded along to slaughterhouses, while hundreds of screaming sea gulls circled overhead, waiting to feed on the refuse. Hundreds more circled the masts of the sailing vessels tied up at the wharves or lying at anchor in the harbor, watching for more garbage from the ships.

Hundreds of doorways beckoned the curious visitor. The visitor could tell a good deal about what went on behind these doors by peering through the windows on either side, or merely by watching what sort of person went in and out. Gentlemen wearing wigs and their well-dressed ladies shopped at the silversmith's and the cloth merchant's. Ship captains came by the chandler's shop to purchase clocks, telescopes, and ship fittings of all kinds. Weatherbeaten sailors clambered ashore from longboats on their way to the sailmakers and rope makers, who worked in buildings far larger than the meetinghouse in the farmer's village.

There seemed to be taverns everywhere. Some obviously were for gentlemen or at least men of middling wealth. The windows of these taverns were filled with printed political and commercial notices. There were other taverns of a different sort. Sailors headed into them on their sea legs and staggered out on legs weakened by rum. Next to some of these taverns were little houses with the wooden shutters closed over the windows even in the daytime. Sailors and fishermen went in and out, as did an occasional farmer. A visitor knew what sort of women were behind that door.

The visitor was also tempted by all the things for sale. The grand merchants sold goods just off the ships from England. Some of these articles might find their way to crossroads stores in the country, but here in the city there was a far greater variety of things to buy. There were bells, buckles, brass buttons, and books. There were copper kettles, iron nails, and steel knives. There were heads for axes and heads for hoes. A man could buy hinges, pulleys, almanacs, and harness fittings, medicines in glass bottles, a nursing can for his baby, and a whalebone corset for his wife. He could empty his pocket without any difficulty.

The inhabitants of the cities saw these surroundings rather differently. A small group was wealthy enough to live a comfortable life. But the majority of people, even the wealthy, worked hard. Prosperous merchants worked long hours supervising their account books. With quill pens they wrote instructions for their shipmasters and letters to their agents in other colonies, in the West Indies, and in London.

Already there were urban problems that did not exist in the countryside. All the cities had exhausted their local supplies of firewood. This

actively in government. Most people also assumed that it was right for government to be in the hands of men of wealth, refinement, and education. Most farmers, whether literate or not, could think of no worse experience than having to address public meetings or sit in legislative bodies.

City artisans, shopkeepers, and laborers shared these feelings. By and large, most voters were still proud to be represented by the great men of their neighborhood. Thus they returned to office generation after generation of gentlemen from the same distinguished families.

Even in Massachusetts, where the voting qualifications were not as strict and educational levels and literacy were higher than elsewhere, members of the same families were repeatedly returned to office. Social and political deference was still the cement that held the various colonial societies together. The word *gentleman* was not yet a sign meaning merely that "ladies" should use the other door.

This is not to suggest that colonial politics were free from conflict. In many colonies, rival factions in the assemblies sometimes struggled for power. In New York, for example, the factions were shaped by family rivalries, religious differences, and the poisonous legacy of Leisler's Rebellion. In Pennsylvania, Quakers and non-Quakers battled for control. In Rhode Island, two factions grew from political rivalry between Newport and Providence. In some colonies, however, politics remained remarkably free from such conflict. In Virginia, especially, a stable group of elite families remained in control. They strengthened and harmonized their rule with a complicated network of marriages among leading families.

The most important source of political conflict was money. Farmers were often in debt; urban merchants were usually their creditors. The normal scarcity of cash in the colonies was aggravated by the mercantile system, which drained gold and silver to the mother country. It became common for debtors to demand more and more paper money. Out of necessity, all the colonies issued paper money at one time or another. But since paper money had a tendency to be overissued and to decline in value, easy-money policies usually were reversed during economic down-swings. At such times, taxes, interest, rents, and loans went unpaid; creditors who tried to collect might be chased from the debtor's door at gunpoint.

Conflicts over the money supply, taxation, and debt were not necessarily sectional, although farmers in frontier regions were more likely to fall into debt than those close to water transportation. Other political conflicts *were* sectional. One of the most persistent arose over the complaints of new settlers on the frontier that the government failed to protect them from the Indians, the French, and the Spanish. Failure to provide passable roads to markets was a second source of sectional conflict. A third was the failure of some assemblies to establish courts in the backcountry and thus save farmers the time and cost of several days' travel. A fourth was the collection of tithes for the established churches, which had few ministers and few members in the wilderness. It was these issues that made backcountry people begin to take an interest in representation in the assemblies.

As important as these issues were, other matters seem to have concerned the settlers more. New ways of thought were sweeping the colonies. The new sciences presented a novel view of humankind's proper relationship to the natural world. Many people found a more traditional concern more important: their relationship with God. Simple farming folk worried about their children, their debts, the condition of their souls, and the proper allotment of firewood for their minister.

SUMMARY

As the colonies grew, they developed new forms of politics and also new kinds of societies. The population exploded because of easy access to land, and this growth speeded up the economy and raised the standard of living. No longer was it necessary for everyone to farm; artisans and merchants could support themselves in the new urban centers. And since most of the population was young, and almost everyone, young or old, worked, productivity was high. The new settlers were no longer exclusively English. Immigrants began to come from western Germany and northern Ireland; there were the Dutch in New York and the numerous West Africans in the South.

Distinctions were drawn between social classes in all the colonies. In the South, the Tidewater gentry copied the lifestyle and manners of the English aristocracy; in the North, wealthy Quaker and Puritan merchants lived in elegant homes filled with fine furnishings. But poor whites in the South lived in misery. The Middle Colonies and New England had a more varied social structure; there were prosperous artisans and farmers among the variety of people and classes that lived in the thriving new cities—Boston, Philadelphia, New York, Newport. Most people, however, lived on family farms, where everyone worked long and hard and almost everything the family needed was made at home. Only about 5 percent of the population actually lived in urban centers.

English colonial politics were marked by both unity and diversity. The colonies were certainly different from one another, but common interests, such as trade, language, and legal and political traditions, drew them together. The American colonists shared a commitment to representative government as embodied in the colonial assemblies. Eventually, the struggle for power between royal governors and the colonial assemblies was won by the colonists. Voting qualifications kept voting power in the hands of a small and wealthy group of men. Yet there was little objection to this arrangement, since most people thought this was the way things ought to be. While there was some conflict between sections and classes over such issues as money and debt, taxation, and government protection on the frontier, these issues remained less troublesome and more local than they would later become.

TIME LINE

1660	Tobacco colonies begin legal establishment of slavery	1720	Blacks begin to outnumber whites in South Carolina
1700	Beginning of large-scale slave importations from Africa	1730s–1750s	Tobacco profits reach their peak decades
1700	Population of English continental colonies reaches 250,000	1730s	Emergence of colonial newspapers
1713	Peace of Utrecht temporarily ends Anglo-French wars	1730s	Charles Town emerges as fourth-largest English colonial town
1716	Rise in immigration of Scotch-Irish	1749–1754	German immigration peaks
1720s–1760s	Blacks constitute 20 percent of the population—more than ever before or since	1755	Philadelphia overtakes Boston to become largest colonial urban center
		1760s	Colonial assemblies clearly triumphant over governors

Suggested Readings

The best demographic study of the colonial era is R. Wells, *The Population of the British Colonies in America before 1776: A Survey of Census Data* (1975). P. Curtin, *The African Slave Trade: A Census* (1969), somewhat underestimates the number of people forced from Africa to the New World. A. Smith, *Colonists in Bondage* (1947), deals with the servant trade from England. Also see B. Bailyn, *The Peopling of America: An Introduction* (1986). J. Greene, *Pursuits of Happiness: The Social Development of Early Modern British Colonies and the Formation of American Culture* (1988), emphasizes the importance of colonies outside New England.

Non-English immigrants have been dealt with by R. Dickson, *Ulster Emigration to Colonial America, 1718–1775* (1966); J. Leyburn, *The Scotch-Irish: A*

Social History (1962); and D. Rothermund, *The Layman's Progress: Religious and Political Experience in Colonial Pennsylvania, 1740–1770* (1961). One of the best studies of ethnic pluralism in colonial America is J. Lemon, *The Best Poor Man's Country: A Geographical Study of Early Southeastern Pennsylvania* (1972). See also M. Rediker, *Between the Devil and the Deep Blue Sea: Merchant Seamen, Pirates, and the Anglo-American Maritime World, 1700–1750* (1987).

For the early years of slavery in this country: G. Mullin, *Flight and Rebellion: Slave Resistance in Eighteenth-Century Virginia* (1972); P. Wood, *Black Majority: Negroes in Colonial South Carolina from 1670 through the Stono Rebellion* (1974); T. Tate, Jr., *The Negro in Eighteenth-Century Williamsburg* (1965); B. Wood, *Slavery in Colonial Georgia, 1730–1775* (1984); L. Greene, *The Negro in Colonial New England* (1942); A. Kullikoff, *Tobacco and*

Slaves: The Development of Southern Cultures in the Chesapeake, 1680–1800 (1986); and M. Sobel, *The World They Made Together: Black and White Values in Eighteenth-Century Virginia* (1987).

Several other books on eighteenth-century American society are especially rewarding. R. Hooker's edition of *The Carolina Backcountry on the Eve of the Revolution: The Journal of Charles Woodmason* (1953) is highly readable because the Reverend Mr. Woodmason was such a crusty chap. C. Bridenbaugh's *The Colonial Craftsman* (1950) is broader than the title suggests, as are J. Blake, *Public Health in the Town of Boston, 1630–1822* (1959), and R. Bushman, *From Puritan to Yankee: Character and Social Order in Connecticut, 1690–1765* (1967). O. Winslow, *Meetinghouse Hill, 1630–1783* (1952), is a fine social history of New England. C. Bridenbaugh's *Myths and Realities* (1952) gives a useful introduction to eighteenth-century southern society. In this connection: R. Weir, *Colonial South Carolina: A History* (1983); D. and A. Rutman, *A Place in Time: Middlesex County, Virginia, 1650–1750* (1984); T. Breen, *Tobacco Culture: The Mentality of the Great Tidewater Planters on the Eve of the Revolution* (1985).

J. Spruill, *Women's Life and Work in the Southern Colonies* (1938), still remains very useful. There is much information (polemically presented) in M. Ryan, *Womanhood in America: From Colonial Times to the Present* (1975).

Social history emerges in some works on eighteenth century politics: L. Labaree, *Royal Government in America: A Study of the British Colonial System before 1783* (1930); and J. Greene, *The Quest for Power: The Lower Houses of Assembly in the Southern Royal Colonies, 1689–1763* (1963). B. Bailyn's short interpretive essay *The Origins of American Politics* (1965) has been very influential. Another important study is C. Sydnor, *Gentlemen Freeholders: Political Practices in Washington's Virginia* (1952), a vivid account of the politics of deference. Different styles are described in F. Tolles, *James Logan and the Culture of Provincial America* (1957); and P. Bonomi, *A Factious People: Politics and Society in Colonial New York* (1971), which emphasizes ethnic tensions. A nearly anthropological view is that of R. Isaac in *The Transformation of Virginia* (1982).

Two important books on the eighteenth-century British empire are M. Kammen, *Empire and Interest: The American Colonies and the Politics of Mercantilism* (1970); and J. Henretta, *"Salutary Neglect": Colonial Administration under the Duke of Newcastle* (1972).

Sir Isaac Newton, 1642–1727. *(Library of Congress)*

CHAPTER 4

NEW WAYS
OF THOUGHT

When we speak of the "mind" of an entire society, we are talking about a concept that we use as an organizing principle. There were, of course, as many actual minds in the English colonies as there were colonists from Europe and Africa, and Native Americans. But because so many of the dominant people shared so many ideas and assumptions, it seems both fair and useful to treat them as a unit, even though there was radical dissent among many people. In doing this we are doing what historians always do: We generalize about the past, and select from it, because we cannot possibly re-create it in all its infinite detail and complexity.

During the first half of the eighteenth century, religious concerns were still primary for a great many Americans. Yet concern about religion could take many different forms. Individuals might worry about their own souls—and large numbers of people did. Ministers and congregations might argue about their proper relationship. Different denominations might fret about their relative status and about proper church organization. And many people might grow concerned about the state of religion in general, and ask themselves about the general health of society as a whole. Americans still ask this question today.

These were not new questions, nor have they ever been fully answered. But they were framed in new ways largely because of the impact of other ideas. These eighteenth-century ideas, which may perhaps be better described as a mental posture, originated in Europe, especially but not exclusively in France, England, and Scotland. They have become known as the Enlightenment.

Enlightened thinkers deliberately chose science over superstition, thought over feeling, order over chaos, and the powers of the individual as opposed to those of the state. The very term *Enlightenment* captures much of the new mood: If human beings would only cast the light of reason on nature and society, they would see the world with a new clarity. And by doing so they would be able to improve and perhaps even perfect the human condition.

All attitudes are adopted under specific circumstances. The Enlightenment in the colonies was strongly shaped by Calvinist convictions and by the seemingly boundless opportunities the new land offered. The colonists tended to see their own prosperity and political freedom as the cutting edges of human progress. If other people stood in their way, such as the French, the Spanish, and the Indians, they would have to be removed—by force if necessary.

RELIGIOUS CONVICTIONS

The English colonists were slow to give up the assumption that there could be only one true and lawful church in a Christian society. Yet eventually they had to face the fact that competing religious denominations existed in the colonies. They also had to deal with a general consensus that religion was in a state of decline. Then suddenly, in 1740, a fire storm of religious enthusiasm swept their settlements. Afterwards they had to deal with its consequences, most of which they had not foreseen at all.

Established Churches

Since England had a national church, the Anglican church, it should logically have been the church of the English colonies as well. But the Church of England was established only in the southern colonies and in parts of New York. Those Anglican churches were supported by taxes assessed on all colonists, whether or not they belonged or attended. Yet there were no Anglican bishops in the colonies, and Anglican ministers had to go all the way to London to be ordained. Thus, ministers were scarce and parishes enormous. Effective control of the affairs of these churches was in the hands of vestrymen, who were usually wealthy, slaveholding planters.

Elsewhere the situation was different. In Pennsylvania, New Jersey, and Rhode Island, there were no established churches. In the three remaining New England colonies, the Puritan churches, now often called Congregational, were established by law and supported by public taxes. The Massachusetts charter of 1691 prevented the Puritans from persecuting other denominations, but groups such as Baptists, Quakers, and Anglicans had to support their churches by voluntary contributions rather than with money from the government. And they were still taxed for the support of the local Congregational minister.

The Great Awakening

The early decades of the eighteenth century saw a decline in church membership. Many people seemed to be doing so well in this world that they paid less attention to the next, and many preachers seemed to lack spiritual warmth and enthusiasm. There was a general feeling that religion was in a state of decline.

Certain ministers tried to promote "revivals" in their churches. Theodore Frelinghuysen led several such revivals among the Dutch Reformed (Calvinist) churches of New Jersey in the 1720s. In the next decade William Tennent and his son Gilbert stirred up the Presbyterians of Pennsylvania. In 1735 there was a successful revival in the Congregational church of Northampton in

Theodore Frelinghuysen, who was nominated for Vice President of the United States. *(Library of Congress)*

western Massachusetts led by the local minister, Jonathan Edwards.

Edwards was perhaps the most profound philosopher and theologian ever to live in America. His writings dealt with fundamental and very difficult questions about human existence. In his *Freedom of the Will* (1754), for example, Edwards struggled with the following problem: Is a person ever free not to do what he actually does do? Edwards reemphasized Calvin's original insistence that humankind was helpless in the hands of an all-powerful God. He declared that people must do more than recognize their own sinfulness. They must *feel* it, and they must *feel* the necessity of opening themselves to God. Unless they did so, they were doomed. Edwards saw conversion as a profoundly emotional experience of the heart rather than the head. It was this view that led him to active and successful preaching.

It took a different sort of person, however, to bring about a more widespread revival. This revival began in the colonies in 1740, and it produced such excitement that it soon became known as the Great Awakening. The man who sparked it was a remarkable young Englishman named George Whitefield (pronounced Whitfield). When he arrived in the colonies, Whitefield had already gained fame as a popular preacher. Technically, he was a minister of the Church of England, but he had no special attachment to any particular church. When he arrived in America, he was persuaded to a Calvinist view by Gilbert Tennent. But it was not *what* Whitefield preached that drew the crowds—it was *how*.

No building in all the colonies could hold the astonishing numbers of people who flocked to hear him, so he often preached outdoors. In Philadelphia, Benjamin Franklin made a very careful estimate and concluded that 30,000 people could hear him at the same time. (This sounds like an absurdly high number for someone without a microphone, but Franklin was not a man to exaggerate). Whitefield traveled from one colony to another, and everywhere he drew huge crowds.

His fame spread as the newspapers reported his progress. He was aided, it has recently been discovered, by a friend who planted newspaper stories on Whitefield's behalf. At the end of 1740 he returned to England, leaving the colonies in a state of general excitement and turmoil. In later years he made more trips to the colonies, but these visits failed to cause the great stir of 1740. As we look back on this famous preacher,

The charismatic George Whitefield preaching. *(Library of Congress)*

however, we can see a significance the colonists could not: Whitefield was the first person known to almost everyone in every colony.

Effects of the Great Revival

Much controversy developed in the wake of Whitefield's passage through the colonies. Some ministers, including the Tennents and Edwards, saw his preaching as the work of God and tried to do the same themselves. Thousands of people, especially young women, flocked to join the churches. But some ministers got carried away. In Connecticut, James Davenport made a specialty of torchlit evening meetings where he stripped to the waist and did imitations of the devil. More conservative ministers thought this sort of behavior was more the devil's work than God's. Jonathan Edwards was not disturbed when his own preaching caused members of the congregation to fall on the floor and scream aloud for mercy. But some ministers were profoundly shocked.

They were also disturbed that uneducated, unqualified men were wandering about preaching to anyone who would listen. Charles Chauncy of

Boston referred to these itinerant preachers as "Men who, though they have no Learning, and but small Capacities, yet imagine they are able, and without Study too, to speak to the spiritual Profit of such as are willing to hear them." Chauncy especially attacked the Great Revival's "bitter Shriekings and Screaming; Convulsion-like Tremblings and Agitations, Struggling and Tumblings." None of this turmoil, Chauncy declared, was evidence of genuine conversion. In turn, Chauncy and other conservatives found themselves called cold, lifeless men of letters, "dead at heart" and lacking God's saving grace.

Church members began to take sides. Individual congregations split over the proper qualifications of their minister. By 1742 the two largest Calvinist groups, the Congregationalists and the Presbyterians, were divided into two camps, which became known as New Lights and Old Lights.

As the names implied, Old Lights emphasized the need for learned preaching and a thoroughly educated ministry; New Lights stressed the importance of emotional experience. There were arguments over doctrine and church organization. In New England especially, many people left the Congregational churches and founded independent Baptist churches.

The general excitement of the Great Awakening was pretty well over by the end of 1742. Yet it never really died out completely, for local revivals kept breaking out from time to time. The southern colonies had been less affected by the Awakening. But over the course of the next generation, Presbyterians, Baptists, and Methodists began organizing churches there. This process was not confined to the South; in fact, it has gone on everywhere in this country ever since. Yet the process has not always worked to multiply churches, for sometimes churches have united or reunited. Both the Presbyterians and the Congregationalists managed to reunite within fifteen years of the splits. In general, New Light views prevailed; revivalism was here to stay in American culture.

The Great Awakening had two other results. First, the prestige of ministers was undermined. People were evaluating religious leaders as never before. Members of individual congregations even felt free to debate whether their minister was saved or damned. Second, the multiplication of churches gave people more choices. If they did not like one church and its minister, they could always choose another. The Great Awakening worked in the direction of spiritual democracy, planting an idea that could easily be applied to politics as well.

Another development was the revival meeting. The huge crowds that came to hear Whitefield and the other preachers yearned for social contact. At the vast outdoor meetings that were to become a common feature of revivals, women, men, and children found release for their emotions and meaning for their lives. Despite the excesses accompanying the Great Awakening and the backsliding that followed, a new social form had been created in America. It was one especially suited to a spiritually and socially lonely rural people.

Although many revivalists mistrusted an educated clergy, the Great Awakening led to the founding of a number of educational institutions. William Tennent's Log College at Neshaminy,

NEWS FROM HEAVEN

Nathan Cole, a simple Connecticut farmer, described the impact of George Whitefield's arrival:

Now it pleased God to send Mr. Whitefield into this land; and my hearing of his preaching at Philadelphia . . . and many thousands flocking to hear him . . . and great numbers . . . converted to Christ; I felt the Spirit of God drawing me . . . I longed to see and hear him, and wished he would come this way. . . . [T]hen on a Sudden, in the morning . . . there came a messenger and said Mr. Whitefield . . . is to preach at Middletown this morning . . . I was in my field at Work,

I dropt my tool that I had in my hand and ran home to my wife telling her to make ready quickly. . . . [W]hen we came within about half a mile . . . of the Road that comes down from Hartford . . . to Middletown . . . I saw before me a Cloud or fogg rising . . . [and] I heard a noise something like a low rumbling thunder and . . . found it was the noise of Horses feet. . . . [A]nd as I drew nearer it seemed like a steady Stream of horses and their riders . . . all of a Lather and foam with sweat . . . every horse seemed to go with all his might to carry his rider to hear news from heaven.

Pennsylvania, founded in 1736, was the first of similar schools for the preparation of Presbyterian ministers. The Baptists lagged behind the Presbyterians, but they established their own schools, such as Hopewell Academy, and later the College of Rhode Island (Brown) in 1764. Other colleges, such as Princeton (Presbyterian), Rutgers (Dutch Reformed), and Dartmouth (Congregational), all started with the encouragement of the revival movement. At first their main purpose was to train ministers. In time, however, some of the new colleges dropped that original purpose and became institutions for the study of science, the arts, and literature.

The Awakening, Blacks, and Slavery

The Great Awakening also quickened the humanitarian spirit of the eighteenth century. When Jonathan Edwards defined virtue as "love of Being in general," he was suggesting that there was a divine element in everyone. Orphans, paupers, Indians, and even slaves shared in this Being and were thus the objects of Christian concern. Whitefield's original purpose in coming to America was to establish an orphanage.

Revivalists did not challenge slavery as an institution. But they preached that every person, no matter what his or her color, was "conceived and born in sin." Thus the Great Awakening strongly implied the spiritual equality of blacks. Indeed the Great Revival marked the beginning of the slow but effective Christianization of African Americans. Blacks began attending revival meetings, and joining various churches, especially Baptist churches. The religious egalitarianism of the Awakening permitted and even encouraged the rise of preaching by blacks themselves. Eventually this meant the growth of a leadership class within black communities. Finally, by becoming Christians in increasing numbers, blacks were becoming more like whites. In turn, whites sought other grounds for distinguishing themselves from blacks, emphasizing especially physical differences.

Although the Quakers did not participate in the Great Awakening, the Society of Friends underwent its own revival in the mid-1750s and in the process became increasingly hostile to slavery. Quakers were led to adopt this view by John Woolman, a determined humanitarian who never ceased to admonish that

placing on men the ignominious Title, Slave, dressing them in uncomely Garments, keeping them to servile Labour, in which they are often dirty, tends gradually to fix a notion in the Mind, that they are a sort of people below us in Nature, and leads us to consider them as such in all our Conclusions about them.

It was Woolman who first clearly realized that whites were "prejudiced" against blacks and that slavery and prejudice were intertwined. The term *prejudice* itself, as it concerned attitudes toward racial groups, was first used in America about 1760. Woolman was joined in the antislavery cause by the Quaker pamphleteer and teacher Anthony Benezet. By speaking to the world at large as well as to other Quakers, Benezet helped broaden the issue. Yet antislavery action remained largely confined to the Society of Friends, which took an increasingly hard line on slaveholding among its members. By the time of the American Revolution, the Society had nearly rid its membership of the moral taint of slaveholding and had raised the fundamental issue for everyone.

Many Protestant Denominations

Despite all these developments, at the time of the Revolution a majority of Americans had no church affiliation. Yet the spirit of Protestantism, especially in its Calvinist forms, remained strong, perhaps stronger than in most parts of Europe. It took on a new energy as denominations splintered and new sects sprang up, and it affected many people who were not members of a particular church. The great number of religious denominations promoted practical tolerance and a growing acceptance of what finally came to be the American principle of the separation of church and state.

Despite the variety of sects and the ethnic and geographical divisions among the denominations, the following generalizations about colonial religion in the 1750s seem valid. First, it was overwhelmingly Protestant. Although the colonies provided a refuge for the persecuted of all religions, only about 25,000 Catholics and 2000 Jews were living in America on the eve of the Revolution.

Protestant colonists, in a real sense children of the Reformation, differed among themselves in creed and doctrine, yet stood united in their

WORDS AND NAMES IN AMERICAN HISTORY

Many American surnames—"last" names—originally came from occupations that thrived in the colonies but are now nearly extinct. Some names came from other sources, such as names ending in -son—John(son) and Jack(son) in the British Isles and Scandinavia—names beginning with O'— O'Riley (of the Rileys') in Ireland—and names beginning with Mc—McNeil (of the Neil family) in Scotland. American names have come from dozens of countries and several continents. But even if one confines oneself to a survey of English names in the New York City telephone book, there are numerous entries that once were the names of particular callings or occupations. We can start with the name *Smith*. Originally it meant someone who worked with iron, but that original meaning has

been broadened (as in Tinsmith, Goldsmith), and in some cases the "Smith" has been dropped, as in the name Black(smith). Some such names are obvious and common, such as Carpenter; others are equally obvious but less common, as with the jockey Willie Shoemaker. Taylors made clothes. Wheelwrights made wheels. Chandlers made candles and branched out into retailing, specializing in equipping ships. Fullers processed wool and Tanners leather. Other such names (picked from the telephone book for a small American town) scarcely need explanation: Boatwright, Brewer, Walker, Weaver, Miller, Mason, Marshall, Shepard, Marchbanks, Fisher, and (without further comment) Lovelady.

---

opposition to the Roman church. Catholics were not physically molested in eighteenth-century America, but they were the targets of propaganda spread by ministers, educators, editors, and publishers of popular almanacs. England's wars with Catholic France partly explain this anti-Catholic feeling, but the hostility went far deeper because it was embedded in the original English Reformation.

Second, much of American Protestantism was strongly colored by its strongly Calvinist heritage. That is, the great majority of churches shared, in varying degree, certain common emphases. They tended to favor simple ceremony that was grounded in biblical theology, and they emphasized individual piety rather than control by a strong clergy.

Third, the doctrine and organization of American churches reflected, in a very rough way, the social background of their members. The wealthiest denominations in the colonies were the New England Congregationalists, the Presbyterians, and the Anglicans. These churches numbered among their members many poorer people in addition to most of the merchant and landed families. A higher proportion of those of modest means was found in the Baptist churches, among the Methodists, who emerged in the late 1760s, and in various small sects. By their frankly evangelical appeals, these two denominations reached elements in the colonial population neglected by the elite churches. Especially because of their successes in the South and on the frontier, these

two groups eventually emerged as the two largest Protestant denominations.

Fourth, although the churches of the non-English-speaking settlers in the eighteenth century had little influence on the main currents of colonial religion, they served as vital social organizations. It took some time for European immigrants to adjust to American ways, and they often looked to religious leaders for guidance. The German churches survived best, although they faced a continual problem about whether English should be substituted for their congregations' native tongue.

Fifth, the tendency throughout the eighteenth century was toward greater religious freedom. Even in orthodox New England, the persecution of Quakers and Baptists had ceased by 1700. A minister such as John Wise of Ipswich could almost singlehandedly stop an organized group of ministers from centralizing church government and destroying the independence of its congregations. In defending the congregational principle and church democracy, Wise introduced arguments that were later adopted in defense of political democracy. All men are born free, he said; "Democracy is Christ's government in Church and State."

As eighteenth-century Americans became more humanitarian, secular, and liberal, and turned their attention away from God in heaven and toward people on earth, their God also seemed to grow more tractable, less demanding, more involved with the happiness of His children. By

1755, John Adams could speak of "the frigid John Calvin" and turn elsewhere for peace of mind.

THE ENLIGHTENMENT

Religious belief continued to be of great importance to many Americans of the eighteenth century; yet new ideas were in the air. These ideas were closely connected with the beginnings of modern science. Since we have inherited many of these ideas, they now usually seem simply normal and reasonable. At the time, however, they were revolutionary.

The End of Witchcraft

A dramatic example of this kind of change can be found in the witchcraft crisis in Salem, Massachusetts, in 1692. Several girls accused certain townspeople of bewitching them. There were official trials and more accusations. Before the crisis was over, twenty people had been executed for witchcraft and another one hundred had been jailed on the same charge. The excite-ment began to die down when prominent people were accused. Some ministers finally convinced the court not to accept evidence from the supposed victims. But the episode has fascinated Americans ever since.

Historians have recently discovered that personal hostility between two groups of townspeople had a good deal to do with what happened in Salem. But it is impossible to understand the episode without recognizing one important fact. Everyone involved, including the ministers, believed that witches and witchcraft really existed. In Europe in the seventeenth century, thousands of people were executed for this crime. Yet the Salem trials were the last witchcraft prosecutions in the colonies, for soon thereafter people began to doubt the reality of witches. William Penn dismissed a case against a woman charged with riding a broomstick by saying: "There is no law in Pennsylvania against riding on broomsticks."

The World of Isaac Newton

The relationship between the earth and the sun seems to be a simple matter. Everyday

The trial of George Jacobs of Salem for witchcraft, Essex Institute, Salem, Massachusetts. *(Library of Congress)*

Nicolaus Copernicus, 1473–1543. (*Library of Congress*)

observation clearly suggests that the sun goes around the earth, since the sun rises in the morning, moves through the sky, and disappears on the other side of the earth at night. By ordinary observation, we cannot see or feel the earth rotate. The obvious conclusion is that the sun moves around a stationary earth. Western Europeans took this very sensible view of the matter until the sixteenth century.

In 1543 the Polish scholar Copernicus proposed a completely opposite view—that the earth moves once a year around the sun and that the earth itself does one full rotation every twenty-four hours. Copernicus saw things in a new way, partly because he looked at more bits of information and because he handled data mathematically. His discovery had important implications for the way people looked at God's universe: Now the earth was no longer at the center.

During the next few centuries scientists made many other advances in understanding the natural world. One man in particular dominated the thinking of the eighteenth century. The work of Sir Isaac Newton suggested that the universe was not governed by chance or miracles, but rather was a perfect machine governed by fixed

mathematical laws. The universal force of gravity, for example, governed both the falling of an apple and the movement of planets around the sun. Newton showed that apparently unrelated facts and events were part of a unified plan. Many other scientists set out to follow his example in hopes of discovering all the laws of the natural world.

But there were dangers in this new way of thinking. Perhaps God was merely a great watchmaker who had wound up the universe and left it to run by itself forever. By the end of the eighteenth century, a few Americans had adopted this view, although most still saw God in a more traditional way. Some ministers took an active interest in scientific matters, proceeding with full assurance that God wanted them to understand His works.

John Locke: Social Scientist

Human reason seemed to be the key to unlocking the secrets of the natural world. It also seemed to be the key to an understanding of human beings and society. Another great English thinker dominated eighteenth-century views on these subjects. John Locke argued that human beings were born with blank minds. They learned things, Locke said, by using their senses to accumulate experience. The mind had the ability to organize this experience into true understanding.

This view of human knowledge had important implications. It was experience that counted, not previous ideas. People could learn about the world through experiments. Reason was the process of ordering the information the senses provided, and proper order was the goal. This was what Newton had shown for the natural world.

Locke also spread new and important ideas about society and government. People, he declared, had originally existed in a "state of nature," totally without laws or government. In order to gain protection, human beings agreed to come together in an organized society. In this new condition they retained certain "natural" rights God had originally given them. There were three such rights: life, liberty, and property.

In order to protect themselves, people made a contract with a ruler. In return for the ruler's protection, they agreed to obey him. If the ruler protected their natural rights, they owed obedience, but if the ruler violated these rights, the people no longer had any obligation to obey. Indeed, the people could replace such a tyrant with a ruler who would respect their natural rights.

Locke's influence in the colonies was powerful but often indirect. Probably more widely read were certain English "Commonwealth writers" of the early eighteenth century, especially John Trenchard and Thomas Gordon. They were themselves much indebted to Locke, but they wrote as critics of the British monarchy. Their strongest theme was that the English court and crown tended toward dissipation, extravagance, and corruption. Their writings were widely read and struck a responsive chord in the colonies.

Other beliefs strengthened the natural rights philosophy. The common-law rights of freeborn Englishmen, for example, were closely identified with the natural rights of all people. And these legal rights were sustained by two English authorities who were immensely influential in America: Sir William Blackstone, known through his *Commentaries on the Laws of England* (1765–1769), and Sir Edward Coke (pronounced Cook), the seventeenth-century lawyer and scholar. The colonists quoted Blackstone to the effect that a person's first allegiance was to a God whose will was the universal law of nature, and that human laws in conflict with natural law were clearly invalid.

All these ideas seemed to fit perfectly with the colonists' own experiences. Because so many people owned property in the colonies, property did indeed seem like a natural right. And all these ideas supported political freedom. Locke himself wrote in support of religious toleration, and others called for a free press and free speech. Most Englishmen at home and in the colonies prided themselves on having the freest government in the world, and they sneered at what they often called "Oriental despotism," which they thought oppressed such peoples as the Turks and the Chinese.

Benjamin Franklin: The Enlightened American

One Anglo-American became a living example of the ideals of the Enlightenment. Benjamin Franklin was born in Boston, where his father owned a tannery, and at age twelve was apprenticed to his older brother as a printer's assistant. They did not get along together, so the younger Franklin took off for Philadelphia, where he soon set himself up as a printer. This was the beginning of the most varied and successful career in early American history. By the age of forty Franklin had made a small fortune and was able to retire from business. Then he began a half dozen careers at once, all of them distinguished.

In Philadelphia, Franklin founded the first American public library, the first American volunteer fire company, and the first American scientific society. He made many useful inventions—a fuel-efficient stove, bifocal eyeglasses, improved carriage wheels, a musical instrument, an improved watering trough for horses, and a fan for his chair to keep off the flies. He worked out accurate ideas about the paths of hurricanes, and he showed ship captains how to shorten the voyage to Europe by taking advantage of the Gulf Stream.

He achieved international fame as a scientist by his work with electricity. Most of that work was a good deal more sophisticated (and less dangerous) than flying a kite in a thunderstorm. He was the first to propose the concept of positive and negative electrical currents. His famous kite experiment was helpful, however, for it showed that lightning and electricity (which was then regarded as a toy) were in fact the same

Benjamin Franklin. *(Library of Congress)*

thing. Characteristically, Franklin gave his discovery a practical application—the lightning rod.

Franklin refused to take out patents on his inventions because he felt that the benefits of science should be available to everyone. He explained this attitude by saying: "As we enjoy great advantages from the inventions of others, we should be glad of an opportunity to serve others by any invention of ours." In the same quiet and open spirit, he kept his own newspaper open to a wide variety of opinions.

When he was an elderly man, Franklin became the American ambassador to France. By then he was internationally famous. At the extremely formal court of the French king, Franklin stood out in his simple clothes. He wore a long-haired wig, as all gentlemen did, but no one else walked the streets of Paris wearing a fur cap. At age seventy-five, he charmed the ladies and greatly impressed the gentlemen by his direct, modest, and reasonable manner. They saw him as a Pennsylvanian, as an American, and as a man who applied reason and good will to the problems of the natural and the human world.

Science in the Colonies

The brilliance of Franklin's career, including his important work on electricity, has tended to make us forget the achievements of his contemporaries. They shared his reliance on Enlightenment thought and, like him, believed that "natural philosophy" could be put to practical use. They were also motivated by curiosity and a desire for recognition. Indeed, they sensed very keenly their colonial status in the international realm of science. Living in a society without a distinct group of scholars, they looked to Europe for encouragement and support.

European scholars were keenly interested in the New World, and they encouraged Americans to report their findings on plant and animal life, Indians, medicines, and earthquakes. By collecting unknown plants, for example, Americans helped the great Swedish scholar Carl Linnaeus to complete his encyclopedic classifications of what he thought (incorrectly) were most of the the species of living things. By the middle of the eighteenth century, European and American scientists had developed a system of communication that kept them informed about one another's findings. Through the efforts of Peter Collinson, a Quaker merchant of London and an influential member of the Royal Society, the reports of the Americans were transmitted to interested Europeans. To have an article published in the Royal Society's *Transactions* was an honor most American scientists yearned for.

In the early years, New England was the leader in scientific investigation. Many of its leaders and professional men had been trained at English universities, and several Harvard teachers and graduates had been elected to the Royal Society before 1700. John Winthrop, Jr., of Connecticut, a charter member of the society, donated a telescope to Harvard in 1672. It enabled Thomas Brattle to observe the comet of 1676. Newton used Brattle's observations in his *Principia Mathematica* to illustrate how the orbits of comets are fixed by gravitational force.

No less important were the eighty-two letters Cotton Mather sent to the Royal Society's *Transactions* between 1712 and 1724. Among them were reports on inoculation against smallpox, about which Mather learned from his African slave, Onesimus, who reported on the practice in West Africa. Equally characteristic of Mather's contributions, although rather less useful and scientifically impressive, was his article on a "snake" (perhaps some sort of worm) growing in a horse's eye.

By 1750, however, Philadelphia had clearly become the capital of colonial science. Commercial

Cotton Mather. *(Library of Congress)*

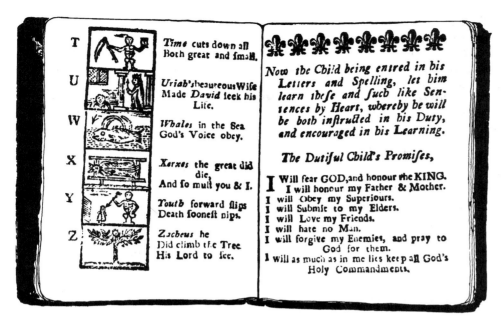

Pages from a 1727 textbook. *(New York Public Library Picture Collection)*

prosperity was partly responsible for the willingness of Philadelphians to support scientific enterprises. Equally important was the Quaker connection with co-religionist intellectuals abroad. It was the English merchant Collinson who put the self-taught naturalist John Bartram in touch with Linnaeus, who was regarded at the time as the Newton of the natural world. When Peter Kalm, a pupil of Linnaeus, visited America in 1748, he came straight to Philadelphia to see Bartram. According to Kalm, their discussions ranged from silk culture, vineyards, stalactites, and truffles to Indian pottery, hummingbirds, and cures for snakebite. Bartram had a genius for collecting specimens and a knack for communicating his enthusiasm to others.

In 1743 Franklin and Bartram tried unsuccessfully to establish a scientific society. Twenty-five years later their plan took form in the American Philosophical Society, today the oldest learned society in the United States. The 1771 *Transactions* of the society carried reports by a number of colonial scientists on a transit of Venus across the sun that had occurred in 1769. In Philadelphia, where the astronomical observations took on the proportions of a community enterprise, David Rittenhouse, an ingenious clockmaker and builder of the celebrated orrery (a planetarium), was the principal contributor. European scientists hailed the Society's *Transactions* as evidence that American science had attained maturity.

Formal Education

Benjamin Franklin was never a good public speaker; in fact, he admired his friend George Whitefield for that ability. In small groups or in private conversation, Franklin was enormously persuasive, partly because he was so quietly logical and partly because he was so careful to offer his deepest convictions as merely sensible possibilities. In order to reach a large number of people, Franklin relied on the printed word. Although he had fewer years of formal education than most readers of this book, he made himself a master of words by reading. And he wrote largely for an American public that was more literate than people anywhere else in the world.

The proportion of people who knew how to read was highest in New England. Even more than most Protestants, the Puritans insisted that members of a godly community know how to read the Word of God. That principle applied to both sexes, although in application boys were given preference over girls. The New England pattern of orderly settlement by towns made it possible to set up arrangements for formal schooling. From the 1640s, Massachusetts law required all towns with more than fifty families to support a schoolmaster. In effect, all children were supposed to be taught to read at public expense.

The New England ideal set very high standards. A later law in Massachusetts required that towns with over one hundred families support a schoolmaster who knew both Latin and Greek. Other New England colonies passed somewhat similar laws. Often, however, these laws were not observed, especially in small towns or in those exposed to attack by Indians. None of the townspeople liked the expense, but in general they believed in the ideal. Many children were taught to read by their parents without benefit of formal schooling. Yet by the 1720s many New England towns found they could maintain schools that remained open from the end of harvest until spring planting. In the eighteenth century, more than 90 percent of New Englanders could read and write, at least on a very simple level.

In the Middle Colonies, the literacy rate was lower. There were no laws requiring public support of schools, and farms were more scattered. Yet various Calvinist churches provided the same incentive the New England churches did. The situation in the southern colonies was more complicated. More than 40 percent of the people were slaves, and virtually no slaves knew how to read. Few people lived in towns, and there was little formal schooling. Yet Anglicans shared in the general Protestant insistence on reading the Bible. The literacy rate among southern whites was probably about 50 percent, which was about the same as that for adult males in old England.

In all the colonies, women were not excluded from education, but they were left behind. Many girls learned to read English, a few learned

French, but practically none were taught Latin and Greek. Sometimes girls were taught the piano and fancy sewing, rather than the fundamentals of arithmetic. Despite these disadvantages, however, the level of women's education was considerably higher in the colonies than in the mother country.

No women attended college, and in comparison with today, very few men did either. The first American college was Harvard, founded in 1636 as a training ground for ministers. From the beginning, however, students there studied the subjects that were traditional at English universities. These included Latin and Greek, mathematics, some sciences, and the philosophy of morals. After about 1700, more than half the graduates of Harvard went into occupations other than the ministry. By that time two other colleges had been established: William and Mary (1693) and Yale (1703). Later, as we have seen, at least five more colleges were founded as a result of the Great Awakening. Most of these remained connected to some church group, although enrollment was not restricted to church members.

The largest colleges were smaller than most high schools today. Usually the students came from well-to-do families, but there were bright farm boys at all of them. Only one of these little colleges (William and Mary) was located in a southern colony. As time went on, the liberal and rational influences of the age began to affect all the colleges. In mid century, King's College (later to become Columbia University) advertised that

An early view of the campus of Harvard College. *(Library of Congress)*

while the teaching of religion was its principal objective, "it is further the Design of this College to instruct and perfect the Youth in . . . the Arts of Numbering and Measuring, of Surveying and Navigation, of Geography and History, of Husbandry, Commerce and Government."

The colleges also became important centers of the new science. None of the college professors matched Benjamin Franklin or John Bartram in originality. But America's most competent astronomer, John Winthrop, IV, taught at Harvard, and David Rittenhouse, clockmaker, astronomer, model maker, and mathematician, lectured at the College of Philadelphia (later the University of Pennsylvania), as did Benjamin Rush, the first professor of chemistry in America and later the new nation's most prominent physician.

A People of the Printed Word

When Benjamin Franklin became a printer—and hence an editor and author—he also became head of an important educational institution. Today we tend to contrast our various mass media, such as television, radio, newspapers, and magazines, with formal learning in school. Such a distinction made much less sense in the colonies, where transmission of knowledge and information was by face-to-face contact or through print. A wide assortment of books was imported from England, and others were printed in the northern colonies. Until the political controversies of the 1760s, the most widely printed works were sermons. On many farms they were the only books in the house except the Bible.

Annual almanacs were popular; pocket-sized and paperbound, they served as calendars, astrological guides, recipe books, and children's schoolbooks. Sandwiched between bits of practical information were jokes, poems, and sayings. The better almanacs offered simplified summaries of the new science, and presented selections from the best British authors. Franklin's *Poor Richard's Almanack*, first published in 1732, soon was selling ten thousand copies a year.

Newspapers were even more widely read— and read aloud. The first colonial newspaper appeared in Boston at the beginning of the eighteenth century. By 1765, twenty-five newspapers were being published in the colonies. When Franklin was postmaster of the continental colonies, he managed to reduce mailing rates for

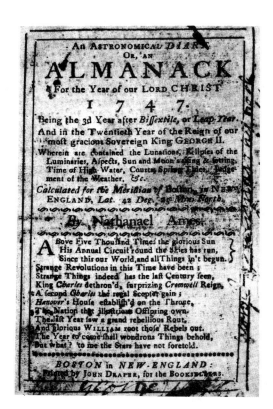

Title page of Nathaniel Ames's *Almanack,* published in Boston in 1747. *(Library of Congress)*

newspapers and speed their circulation. The papers appeared once a week, with only four pages, the last two mostly devoted to advertisements in very small print. The only illustrations were a few small woodcuts showing the outline of a ship (just arrived) or a runaway (servant or slave). There were no other drawings and of course no photographs. The news was known as "latest advices." Much of it was copied directly from English and other European newspapers. This news usually occupied the front page. On the second page one might find "advices" copied from newspapers published in other colonies.

Sometimes the newspapers carried accounts about the latest activities of the colony's governor and assembly, and from time to time there were letters from readers. Often there were brief stories and poems. But newspapers gave very little local news, since everyone knew what was going on in his or her own town.

Colonial newspapers served as the most important public tie among the colonies. Their circulations were small by modern standards. Many backwoods farmers rarely saw one, even if they knew how to read. Yet newspapers were passed from hand to hand and read aloud at crossroads stores. They served as a vital network of communication among a relatively literate people. And as time went on, that communication link became more and more vital to peoples' interests.

THE STRUGGLE FOR A PROTESTANT AMERICA

The ideas of the Enlightenment were downright intoxicating. They suggested to many Americans that they had only to continue what they were already doing in order to achieve a better society. Yet Protestant Americans saw their future in rather special terms, ones as dependent on religious traditions as on European Enlightenment ideas.

The Threat of New France

As time went on, the English-dominated settlements occupied more and more territory. Indians east of the Appalachians were drastically reduced in numbers and in power as they moved westward or succumbed to disease. To the north and west lay the French settlements, forts along the St. Lawrence Valley, the southern Great Lakes, and the Mississippi River all the way to New Orleans, as well as at Mobile on the Gulf Coast. French Catholic missionaries and fur traders had established friendly relations with the Indians, for the fur traders did not take the Indians' land. They often lived in Indian villages and had children by Indian wives. They placed young cadets with Indian groups in order to learn various Indian languages and to report on tribal affairs. French royal officials tried to encourage settlement by farmers, but they were not very successful. In 1760 there were only about 60,000 French people in all the huge territory of New France; the British colonists numbered nearly 1.5 million.

English numerical superiority was partly balanced by the weight of Indian power. Whenever there was war between England and France, the colonial French encouraged their Indian friends to raid English settlements. The balance of power between the French and British in North America was also affected by the fact that a large proportion of the French colonists were males of fighting age. In contrast, the British colonies had many more women and children.

New York became the most crucial battleground because it included the only water-level passage through the Appalachian mountain chain. Fortunately for the English, the Iroquois Confederacy controlled the Mohawk Valley. To the north and west of the Iroquois were the Hurons. The French had long ago befriended the Hurons, without knowing that they were traditional enemies of the Iroquois. Thus the English were able to make alliances with the Iroquois against their common enemies, the Hurons and the French.

When the Dutch William of Orange came to the English throne in 1689, he brought with him an old feud against Louis XIV of France. From 1689 to 1713 there was continual warfare between England and France, which by this time were the two most powerful nations in Europe. Europe remained the main scene of the conflict, and neither country sent troops to its colonies in America. But the English and French settlers in America sent raiding expeditions against each other, and Indians became involved in most of this fighting. By and large, the English won.

The wars finally ended in 1713, and the Peace of Utrecht gave important new American territories to the British. The French ceded the rich sugar island of St. Christopher (St. Kitt's) in the West Indies, and recognized British claims to the territory around Hudson Bay. The British also acquired the peninsula of Nova Scotia (previously known as Acadia), which New Englanders had captured. The French acknowledged the Iroquois as British subjects and their territory as British domain.

The Founding of Georgia

For twenty-five years after the Peace of Utrecht there was no further warfare between Great Britain and France. But the southern border of the mainland colonies remained in dispute with Spain, and the British moved to strengthen their position in that region. They did so by founding a new colony, the last of the thirteen that later became the United States.

In 1732 General James Oglethorpe and several other English gentlemen obtained a royal charter for a new colony to be located south of the Savannah River. The charter gave Oglethorpe and the other "trustees" the right to govern the colony for twenty-one years. Thereafter the colony of Georgia would have a royal gover-

nor. Two reasons prompted the establishment of the new colony. One, the British government wanted a military outpost for defense against the Spanish in Florida. Second, Oglethorpe was interested in setting up a place of refuge for people (mostly male) who had been imprisoned for debt. The Georgia trustees laid down certain rules they hoped would help further both aims: Landholdings were limited to five hundred acres; rum and brandy were banned, since farmers and militiamen ought to be sober; and slavery was prohibited, not because it was wrong but because it would weaken the colony as a military outpost.

Most of these plans for the new colony fell through. The trustees did support the settlement of some debtors from England, but they were soon outnumbered by land-hungry men from South Carolina and other established colonies. The trustees withdrew their ban on rum in the face of thirsty protests. Planters from South Carolina brought in slaves, bought up large tracts of land in the low country, and began planting rice. By the time Georgia became a royal colony in 1752, it was a small offshoot of its neighbor to the north. The Georgia assembly simply copied many of South Carolina's laws. Rice and slaves dominated the colony. Still, at the time of the American Revolution, Georgia had fewer people than any of the other British continental colonies.

Louisburg as Citadel and Symbol

Shortly after the founding of Georgia, war broke out again in Europe. From 1739 to 1748 Britain was at war, first with Spain and then with France. At the outset of this conflict, there was little action in the American colonies. Rumors about possible invasion swept some cities, such as New York, but they all proved false. Then, in 1745, something truly amazing happened. For years, the famous fort of Louisburg had stood on Cape Breton Island as the sentry for the St. Lawrence River. Louisburg was the gateway to New France, and it was heavily fortified. That year, Massachusetts and other New England colonies sent militia and sailors to assault Louisburg, with some aid from the British navy. To almost everyone's surprise, the expedition succeeded.

The victory fired the colonists' imagination. They had proved their own strength. Colonial

Map labels:

VIRGINIA

Jamestown

INDIAN COUNTRY

ROANOKE ISLAND

Albemarle Sound

NORTH CAROLINA

New Bern

ATLANTIC OCEAN

Cape Fear

SOUTH CAROLINA

GEORGIA · Charleston

· Savannah

Added to Georgia 1763

SPANISH FLORIDA

leaders (especially in Massachusetts) began to think in grander terms. Some began to predict that all of New France would eventually fall to Anglo-American power. Here would be a stunning triumph for British Americans and for the cause of Protestantism as well. Perhaps the entire continent might become a citadel of enlightened government and true religion.

Peace came three years later, in 1748. The Treaty of Aix-la-Chapelle ended the conflict known in the colonies as King George's War. One of the provisions rather casually handed Louisburg back to the French. That concession produced resentment in the colonies, especially in Massachusetts.

Yet it was widely believed that the treaty was merely a temporary truce. King George's War had been a sideshow to the main conflict in Europe. France itself remained more populous and perhaps more powerful than Great Britain. No one was sure on the latter point—but it was clear in London and Paris and the colonial capitals that a showdown was coming. It seemed possible that North America might become an important scene of the fighting. No one thought of another possibility—that such a conflict might set off a chain of events that would lead to war *within* the British empire. And no one realized that revivalism and the Enlightenment might contribute to such a development.

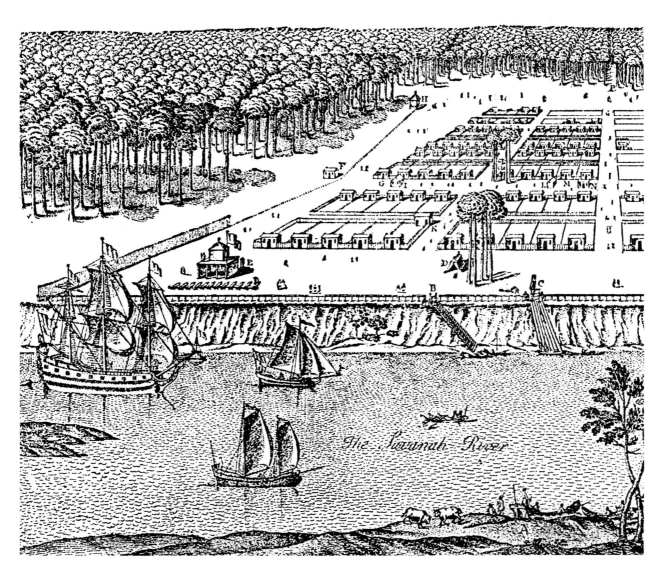

The first printed plan of Savannah, 1734, reveals English hopes for rigid order in the wilderness. *(Bettmann Archives)*

In the eighteenth century the concern about religion that had brought so many people to America remained very important. But it was affected by a whole new set of ideas called the Enlightenment—the belief in human reason and science.

Because at the beginning of the eighteenth century many Americans thought religion was in decline, some ministers began to promote revivalism. The most widespread revival, the Great Awakening in 1740, was led and preached by a popular young English preacher, George Whitefield. Thousands came to hear him, and the effects of his work lasted long after he returned from the colonies to England. Many ministers followed Whitefield's example, and the outdoor meeting at which emotion could be freely expressed became an American institution. Congregations split over the new and the old types of worship, and new denominations were formed. People had more choices. This new spiritual democracy was eventually to be transferred to other areas of life.

New educational institutions were set up, among them Princeton, Rutgers, and Dartmouth. Quakers began to question the morality of slaveholding. And although Americans were overwhelmingly Protestant, the many sects and denominations promoted ideas of toleration, religious freedom, and the separation of church and state.

These trends away from rigid belief and strict doctrine were encouraged by Enlightenment ideas of rationality and the power of human reason. Trials of witches came to an end, and magic and witchcraft came to seem ridiculous. New discoveries about the workings of the natural world changed people's world view and increased their confidence in their ability to understand and therefore control the world of nature.

The same was true for politics and philosophy. John Locke's ideas were particularly influential. Benjamin Franklin became a living example of Enlightenment ideas in America through his public service, his inventions, and his interest in science. With Franklin's help, a community of American scientists began to develop. Public education was the rule in New England, and literacy rates were high. Colleges began to expand their teaching to subjects other than religion and to become centers for the new science. Almanacs and newspapers were widely circulated and read. Weekly newspapers became an important link among the colonies. All these trends made Americans open to and eager for new ideas.

Political events fostered a spirit of optimism and expansionism. English colonists, moving west, began to encounter French settlements near the eastern Great Lakes. After a series of wars between England and France from 1689 to 1713, the English gained new territories in America by the Peace of Utrecht. In the south, Georgia was established as a buffer colony against the Spanish presence in Florida. Still another war in Europe was ended by treaty in 1748. But by then it was clear a showdown was coming, which this time might well involve the overseas colonies as well as the mother countries.

TIME LINE

1687	Isaac Newton's *Principia*
1690	John Locke's *Essay Concerning Human Understanding*
1692	Salem witchcraft trials
1693	College of William and Mary founded in Virginia
1703	Establishment of Yale College
1712	Mather's first paper in Royal Society's *Transactions*
1720	Inoculation against smallpox in Boston
1732	Colony of Georgia chartered
1732	First publication of Franklin's *Poor Richard's Almanack*
1739	George Whitefield arrives in the American colonies
1740	Beginning of Great Awakening
1742	Split between Old Lights and New Lights
1743	Franklin lays base for American Philosophical Society
1745	Anglo-colonial forces capture Fort Louisburg
1746	Franklin begins experiments with electricity
1748	Treaty of Aix-la-Chapelle ends King George's War, but is widely seen as only a temporary truce
1750s	Quakers begin to denounce slavery
1754	Jonathan Edward's *Freedom of the Will*
1765	First publication of Blackstone's legal *Commentaries*
1769	Colonial scientists observe transit of Venus across the sun

Suggested Readings

Two fine sweeping studies are S. Ahlstrom, *A Religious History of the American People* (1972), which has a fine bibliography; and R. Handy, *A History of the Churches of the United States and Canada* (1977). A good place to start is J. Bumsted and J. Van de Wetering, *What Must I Do to Be Saved? The Great Awakening in Colonial America* (1976). Several very different biographies are probably more useful than the regional studies: O. Winslow's straightforward *Jonathan Edwards* (1940); P. Miller's subtle but difficult *Jonathan Edwards* (1949); S. Henry's *George Whitefield: Wayfaring Witness* (1957); and M. Coalter, Jr., *Gilbert Tennent, Son of Thunder: A Case Study of Continental Pietism's Impact on the First Great Awakening in the Middle Colonies* (1986). Especially good on the continuing reverberations of the Awakening is W. McLoughlin's short biography *Isaac Backus and the American Pietistic Tradition* (1967); and P. Bonomi, *Under the Cope of Heaven: Religion, Society, and Politics in Colonial America* (1986). A. Heimert and P. Miller (eds.), *The Great Awakening: Documents Illustrating the Crisis and Its Consequences* (1967), provides fascinating contemporary accounts. D. Lovejoy, *Religious Enthusiasm in the New World: Heresy to Revolution* (1985), is a superb survey. A sweeping indictment is F. Wood, *The Arrogance of Faith: Christianity and Race in America from the Colonial Era to the Twentieth Century* (1990).

The best place to start on the Salem witchcraft episode is J. Demos, *Entertaining Satan* (1982). P. Miller, *The New England Mind: The Seventeenth Century* (1939), and R. Middlekauff, *The Mathers: Three Generations of Puritan Intellectuals, 1596–1728* (1971), deal with that crisis. K. Thomas, *Religion and the Decline of Magic* (1971), sets witchcraft in a much broader context. But probably the best thing to do is look up *Salem* or *Witchcraft* in the subject part of the library catalog or ask your reference librarian. The latter person is usually the most helpful resource of all.

S. James, *A People among Peoples: Quaker Benevolence in Eighteenth-Century America* (1963), deals with antislavery sentiment. The complex relationship between religion and the growth of humanitarianism is also discussed in D. Davis, *The Problem of Slavery in Western Culture* (1964), and W. Jordan, *White over Black: American Attitudes toward the Negro, 1550–1812* (1968).

Many of these books deal with the American Enlightenment (as do many cited in Chapter 3). A. Tourtellot's *Benjamin Franklin: The Shaping of Genius, The Boston Years* (1977), and R. Clark *Benjamin Franklin: A Biography* (1983), try to deal with an incredible man. Franklin headed off historians by writing his own *Autobiography*, available in many editions. S. Bedini, *Thinkers and Tinkers: Early American Men of Science* (1975), is encyclopedic. John Locke's *Two Treatises* is an eighteenth-century political tract much more closely connected with "science" than would at first appear. For a subtle interpretation of Enlightenment thinkers (both European and American) and their impact on American religious thought, see H. May, *The Enlightenment in America* (1976). D. Boorstin's cultural history *The Americans: The Colonial Experience* (1958) emphasizes the practical bent of the American mind.

L. Cremin, *American Education: The Colonial Experience, 1607–1783* (1970), discusses both formal and informal educational agencies. R. Middlekauff, *Ancients and Axioms: Secondary Education in Eighteenth-Century New England* (1963), is the best single monograph. There is a fine but dated bibliographical essay in the latter half of B. Bailyn, *Education in the Forming of American Society* (1960), which also deals with the family.

The March 5, 1770 massacre between British soldiers and the citizens of Boston. *(Library of Congress)*

CHAPTER 5

THE MAKINGS OF REVOLT

When war is expected, it usually comes. France and Great Britain slipped into war almost as if they had scheduled the conflict in advance. This time North America became a main theater in a worldwide war that also included fighting in Europe. Africa, India, and the West Indies. British victories resulted in a stunning enlargement of the British empire. In North America, all of New France came under British rule.

Officials in London quite naturally thought that an enlarged empire needed better administration and firmer control. Since Great Britain had piled up a huge debt for the war, they also felt the colonies ought to pay a fair share of the costs of running such an empire. Anglo-American colonists had been paying taxes for years. A few of these were part of the navigation laws, but most were levied by the colonial assemblies to support colonial governments. Parliament's decision to raise revenue in the colonies brought howls of protest, even though most of that revenue was earmarked for the defense of the colonists themselves.

For a dozen years the colonies and the mother country pushed and shoved each other on the matter. Other issues arose, and self-interest and high principles became so entangled that no one could tell them apart. The two sides staggered from crisis to crisis, each one never knowing exactly what to expect from the other. At some point they stepped onto the slippery slope of no return. Grievances on both sides finally exploded in armed conflict—a conflict neither wanted and both had tried to avoid.

Some of the British colonies did not revolt. Canada and Nova Scotia remained within the empire, as did Jamaica, Barbados, and the other British islands in the West Indies. Thirteen continental colonies took up arms against their lawful government. From the beginning, a major issue was whether these colonies would act separately or together, and in the long run this problem proved as difficult as making the break with Britain. Ideas about self-government helped support the thirteen colonies; so did the values of the Enlightenment and the emotions of the Great Awakening. Yet the colonists had little to guide them concerning the question of unity—little, that is, except the powerful force of necessity.

VICTORY OVER THE FRENCH

Before the ink was dry on the Treaty of Aix-la-Chapelle, both sides began to prepare for a showdown. The French refortified Louisburg and constructed a long string of forts from Lake Erie south to the "forks of the Ohio." There, where the Allegheny and Monongahela rivers join to form the Ohio, they built Fort Duquesne.

The Ohio Country

The westward pressure of Anglo-American settlement soon spilled against the line of French forts. In 1747 a group of wealthy Virginia planters formed the Ohio Company in hopes of acquiring land in the Ohio Valley. Two years later, the Virginia government gave the company 200,000 acres west of the Monongahela River in an area claimed not only by France and Virginia, but by Pennsylvania. Authorities in London approved the grant in hopes of encouraging further settlement. In 1751 Robert Dinwiddie arrived in Virginia as the new royal governor and was induced to join the Ohio Company. His appointment meant that the interests of imperial officials in London were interlocked with those of Virginia's ruling aristocrats.

Both as a British patriot and as a land speculator, Dinwiddie took a keen interest in the Ohio country. In 1753 he sent out a small group of Virginians to find out what the French were doing in the area, and they returned with news of the construction of Fort Duquesne. The next year, in 1754, he asked the leader of the previous expedition to lead a force of Virginia militiamen to get rid of the French intruders.

George Washington was then twenty-two years old, a young man with excellent connections including two brothers in the Ohio Company and an appointment as colonel in the Virginia militia. Washington led his small force toward the forks of the Ohio. When he learned that the fort was heavily fortified, he and his men built a stockade some fifty miles to the south, naming it Fort Necessity. The French attacked, and the badly outnumbered Virginians surrendered.

Because the two nations were not officially at war, the French released the Virginians so that they might return with word that the Ohio country was firmly in the hands of France. The skirmish at Fort Necessity was, in fact, the opening battle of a great war that lasted until 1763.

Anglo-Americans called it the French and Indian War. But since the worldwide conflict was not officially declared until 1756, it became known in Europe as the Seven Years' War.

The Albany Congress

While Washington and his men were returning from Fort Necessity, an important meeting was taking place in Albany, New York. The London government had summoned delegates from all the colonies from Virginia northward to meet with leaders of the Iroquois Confederacy. Officials in London knew that the various colonies would have to cooperate if there was renewed conflict with the French. They also regarded the Iroquois as crucial allies in any such war.

In Albany, the Iroquois leaders listened solemnly to the customary speeches of welcome and high regard and gravely accepted the usual gifts, which on this occasion were particularly generous. But they refused to make promises of support. They were aware of growing French power in the west and had no desire to back a losing cause.

At the Albany Congress, Benjamin Franklin and other delegates proposed a general "plan of union" that provided for a grand council of representatives from all the mainland colonies. The powers of the council would cover western lands and settlement, joint defense, and relations with the Indians. The council would have the power to raise taxes on its own. The presiding officer

This cartoon compared the squabbles of the colonies to the separated parts of a snake, warning that they must "join or die." *(Library of Congress)*

would be appointed by the king and have veto power over actions by the council.

The Albany delegates sent the plan to the various colonies for their approval. In every colony, it was rejected or ignored. The plan aimed to please all parties and ended up pleasing none. Authorities in London were relieved, for they had no desire to see the colonies united on a permanent basis. The various assemblies had no wish to share their taxation power, and many of them wanted to press their own claims in the west.

Fruits of Victory

After the Albany Congress, the government in London decided for the first time to send regular troops to the colonies. In the spring of 1755 General Edward Braddock arrived at the head of an impressive army of 1400 redcoats. Dinwiddie and Braddock planned a major expedition to destroy Fort Duquesne and drive the French from the Ohio country. The British troops were joined by 1000 colonial militiamen, but only 8 Indian guides could be found. Together they marched off through western Maryland and then north into Pennsylvania toward the forks of the Ohio. It was the same route Washington had taken a year before.

Only eight miles south of the fort, they were ambushed and badly mauled by a combined force of French and Indians. Braddock was mortally wounded, and his army suffered nearly a thousand casualties. This stunning defeat shook the reputation of the British redcoats, and it also badly weakened the prestige of the British among the western Indians.

By 1756 the war that had started in the American wilderness had spread over Europe. At first it went very badly for the British, both in Europe and America. Important forts in northern and western New York fell to French and Indian attacks. In 1758, however, a new chief minister took charge in London, and within a year he had turned the conflict completely around. William Pitt subsidized German armies on the European continent, leaving Britain free to pursue the war on the sea and in America. For Pitt, the central objective was the conquest of Canada and the American interior. He used British superiority at sea to strike hardest at two focal points of French power: Louisburg and Quebec.

In 1758 the British recaptured Louisburg. The event was celebrated with great bonfires in London, Philadelphia, Boston, and New York. In the same year, George Washington had the satisfaction of taking part in the capture of Fort Duquesne. The climax of the fighting came in

General James Wolfe, surrounded by soldiers and an Indian while lying mortally wounded on a field.
(Library of Congress)

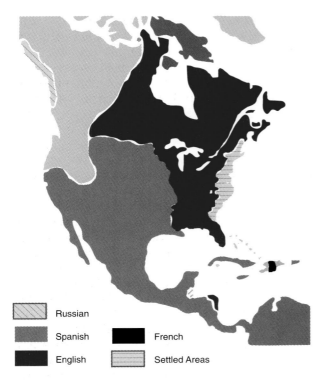

Russian

Spanish   French

English   Settled Areas

North America after the Treaty of Paris (1763)

1759, when the brilliant young general James Wolfe, after bringing a large army up the St. Lawrence from Louisburg, stormed the Heights of Abraham outside Quebec and took the city from a smaller force under General Montcalm. Both Wolfe and Montcalm were killed in the battle, but Wolfe lived long enough to know that he had won Canada for the empire.

The next year, British troops captured Montreal. They continued a long string of victories at sea, in the West Indies, in India, and in the American West. "Some time ago," said Pitt in the middle of all these triumphs, "I would have been content to bring France to her knees, now I will not rest till I have laid her on her back." The war dragged on, but Britain's new young monarch, George III, was determined to bring it to an end. He fired Pitt in 1761 and found ministers who were willing to make peace.

The Treaty of Paris (1763) was a general settlement of what had become a world war. France ceded to Britain all of Canada and all the great interior east of the Mississippi River except the crucial port of New Orleans. Britain returned to France two captured islands in the West Indies—Martinique and Guadeloupe. France retained

fishing rights and two small islands off the coast of Newfoundland. Spain surrendered East and West Florida to the British in exchange for Cuba, which the British had captured the year before. Finally, by a separate treaty, France ceded to Spain all its territories west of the Mississippi, as well as the port of New Orleans.

During the negotiations there was much discussion in Britain about whether to demand Canada or the rich sugar island of Guadeloupe. It was clear that France would continue to fight rather than give up both. That such a choice should even have been considered was evidence of the great value of the sugar plantations. The decision to ask for Canada resulted in large part from pressure by British owners of sugar plantations in colonies such as Jamaica and Barbados. They had no wish for more competition. In addition, British merchants were beginning to realize that the colonies on the North American continent provided a growing market for their manufactured goods.

During the arguments over the proposed treaty, several British politicians suggested that someday Canada might revolt and win its independence from Great Britain. They also pointed out that if the French were expelled from Canada, the American colonists would no longer feel as dependent on Britain for protection. Benjamin Franklin, then in London as an agent for Pennsylvania, wrote a pamphlet on the subject in which he argued for retaining Canada as part of the British empire. Franklin brushed aside the idea of independence. If the North American colonists could not unite against the French and Indians, he asked, could they unite against "their own nation," which "they love much more than they love one another?" A union among the colonies, he went on, "is not merely improbable, it is impossible." But Franklin went on to say: "When I say such a union is impossible, I mean without the most grievous tyranny and oppression."

Few people knew it at the time, but some British officials were already considering new regulations for the American colonies. Whether these regulations would constitute "grievous tyranny and oppression" was, of course, a matter of opinion.

NEW IMPERIAL MEASURES

After the French and Indian War, Great Britain adopted certain policies toward the colonies that aroused great resentment. The colonists' major grievance was taxes—direct taxes laid upon them by Parliament. But other imperial policies angered various segments of the colonial population. Westerners and land speculators resented London's ideas about how to handle the Indians. Merchants were troubled by enforcement of the Navigation Acts and by new currency regulations. And when the British government decided to station regular troops in the colonies, many Americans grew suspicious about the intentions of the king's ministers.

Two factors added to the deepening sense of alienation many Americans felt. One was the instability of the English government. In the early years of his reign, beginning in 1760, George III could not find a chief minister who really satisfied him. The king was intensely patriotic and intelligent, but so unsure of himself that he dismissed ministers almost as fast as he named them. (The young monarch showed no signs yet of the insanity that surfaced some twenty-five years later, when he clambered down from his carriage in a London park and began an animated conversation with an oak tree.) At that time, the king had the right to choose a first minister, who then chose other members of Parliament to form a "ministry." For ten years various ministries came and went, and with them Britain's policies toward the colonies. No one could be sure whether today's policy would be in effect tomorrow.

Second, many colonists were extraordinarily suspicious about British intentions. When officials in London proposed efficiency, officials in the colonies smelled attack. They had grown so attached to self-government that they were inclined, as a British statesman told the House of Commons, to "sniff the approach of tyranny in every tainted breeze."

Writs of Assistance

Rumblings of serious trouble in America were heard even before the end of the French and Indian War. From the start of the war, colonial merchants, with characteristic disregard for British policy, had traded with the enemy in Canada and in the West Indies. In 1760 Pitt's ministry ordered colonial governors to make greater efforts to enforce customs regulations. In Massachusetts, the center of illegal trade, royal customs collectors needed help to search the premises of merchants suspected of smuggling. They applied to the Supreme Court of the colony for *writs of assistance*, which would allow them to use police constables.

Writs of assistance had been in common use for a long time, both in Britain and America. Authorized by acts of Parliament, they had to be renewed each time a new sovereign came to the throne. When George II died in 1760, new writs had to be authorized in the name of George III. Some Massachusetts merchants took this opportunity to criticize the whole practice. They hired as counsel a brilliant but eccentric young Boston lawyer named James Otis.

Early in 1761, Otis appeared in court and delivered an astounding attack on these writs. John Adams, who was there, recalled years later: "Otis was a flame of fire! . . . he hurried away everything before him." Although the speech itself has been lost, we know that Otis rested his case on broad principles derived from John Locke and the Commonwealth writers. He claimed that the writs violated the people's rights of property, and that an act of Parliament contrary to natural law must be regarded as void. Parliament had no legal right, he said, to violate natural law either in Britain or in America.

Otis lost his case, and the writs were issued. But men in other colonies soon joined in the protest against their legality. And despite the pleas and threats of imperial customs officials, colonial judges often refused to grant them. Otis had established an important precedent, moreover, by basing his argument on the bedrock of natural rights.

Problems in the West

So long as France owned Canada, Americans were forced to rely on Britain for protection. The defeat of France removed one menace, but it failed to settle the colonists' relationship with the Indians.

Established fur traders in the thirteen colonies and in Canada wanted the West permanently reserved for Indian hunters and trappers. Newly influential land speculators, on the other hand, were urging settlers to go west; they wanted the Indians cleared out or "pacified." Both sides had powerful friends in Britain.

Colonial land speculators were particularly active in Pennsylvania and Virginia, and their claims often conflicted with one another, as well as with those of rivals abroad. Benjamin Franklin

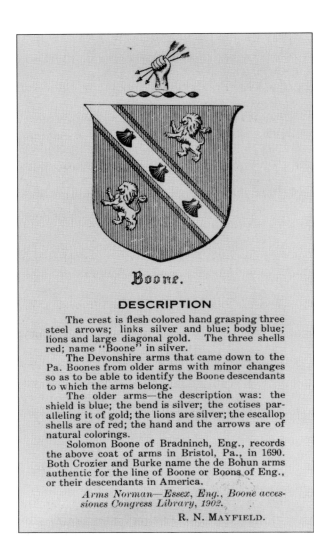

DESCRIPTION

The crest is flesh colored hand grasping three steel arrows; links silver and blue; body blue; lions and large diagonal gold. The three shells red; name "Boone" in silver.

The Devonshire arms that came down to the Pa. Boones from older arms with minor changes so as to be able to identify the Boone descendants to which the arms belong.

The older arms—the description was: the shield is blue; the bend is silver; the cotises paralleling it of gold; the lions are silver; the escallop shells are of red; the hand and the arrows are of natural colorings.

Solomon Boone of Bradninch, Eng., records the above coat of arms in Bristol, Pa., in 1690. Both Crozier and Burke name the de Bohun arms authentic for the line of Boone or Boons of Eng., or their descendants in America.

Arms Norman—Essex, Eng., Boone accessiones Congress Library, 1902.

R. N. MAYFIELD.

The Boone family coat of arms. *(Library of Congress)*

represented a group of wealthy Pennsylvanians interested in lands along the Ohio. One of the Virginia enterprises was promoted by George Washington, whose Mississippi Company, formed as a successor to the old Ohio Company, had its eye on thousands of acres at the junction of the Ohio and Mississippi rivers.

During the war, fearful of British expansionism, most of the northwestern Indian tribes had chosen to ally themselves with the French. The victory of the British renewed their anxiety. Goaded by French traders who talked of the return of French power to North America, Indians in New York and Pennsylvania launched an attack on British forts. They were led by the Ottawa chief Pontiac. With the objective of sweeping the entire white population into the sea, Pontiac's

followers destroyed seven of the nine British garrisons west of Niagara.

Soon after news of these attacks reached London, the government issued the royal Proclamation of 1763. It set boundaries for three new royal colonies: Quebec, East Florida, and West Florida. Most other western territory—from the Alleghenies to the Mississippi and from Florida to 50° north latitude—was reserved for the Indians. The proclamation excluded all white fur traders, land speculators, and settlers. It was intended as a temporary measure to give Britain time to work out a permanent western policy, but it aroused the anger of the colonists.

No proclamation issued thousands of miles away could keep speculators and frontiersmen out. Many colonists agreed with George Washington when he urged that the Proclamation of 1763 be disobeyed: "I can never look upon that proclamation in any other light . . . than as a temporary expedient to quiet the minds of Indians. . . . Any person, therefore, who neglects the present opportunity of hunting out good lands, and in some measure marking and distinguishing them for his own, will never regain it." Washington practiced what he preached. He and other land speculators sent agents into the Ohio Valley to stake out claims.

Opposition to the Proclamation of 1763 grew so strong that within a few years the British revised their western policy. They made a series of treaties with the Indians to give the speculators room. In each case the treaties pushed the map of English control farther westward, and before long the paper fence was in shreds. Every extension of the boundary line touched off new bursts of speculation. In 1768 the first settlers to penetrate the Blue Ridge barrier occupied the Watauga Valley of North Carolina. In 1769, having made his first trip west two years before, Daniel Boone crossed the future Wilderness Road through the Cumberland Gap into Kentucky. In 1775, he guided the first group of permanent settlers to the bluegrass region. As Americans moved deeper into the West, away from older centers of power, they became more and more determined to control their own destinies.

Discontent in Virginia

Britain's new policies caused strong resentment in Virginia, one of the most populous of all the colonies. By concentrating on one money-making

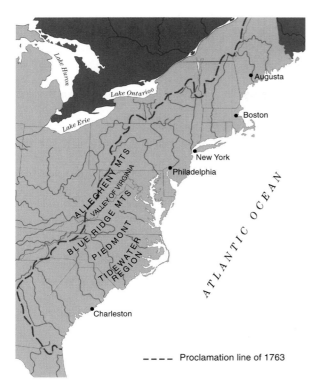

The Proclamation of 1763

crop, tobacco planters had depleted their best soil; cheap lands in the West seemed their only salvation. But land policy was only one source of planter discontent. British merchants served as middlemen for everything the planters bought or sold abroad, and British shipowners charged high rates for carrying the planters' produce and purchases across the ocean.

As the return from their lands dwindled, the planters' debts mounted. Thomas Jefferson once estimated that Virginia planters owed at least £2 million to British merchants and observed that these debts "had become hereditary from father to son, for many generations." Many planters grew concerned about their inability to finance their own agricultural expansion.

Troops and Taxation

The worst problem raised by the French and Indian War was taxation. Britain's long, costly struggles for empire had boosted tax rates so much that by 1763 British landowners were turning over about a third of their income to the government. Now the British had to face the cost of protecting their expanded possessions. Several bureaucrats estimated that ten thousand troops were needed for the colonies, and Parliament felt that the colonists should share the cost of their own protection.

There was also a more sinister motive behind the British plan to station regular troops in America. War veterans could be taken care of and a large army maintained without the distrust that would come if it were on home soil. As things turned out, colonial Americans had strong suspicions about what was then known as "a standing army at home."

The colonists had long since learned to manage their finances without British interference. They began to demand that the British solve their own financial crisis. For one thing, the colonies had piled up a war debt of £2.5 million. In addition, by Pitt's estimate, British merchants were making profits of at least £2 million a year on colonial commerce. Such profits seemed to Americans, and to Pitt himself, to be "tax" enough. The very prosperity that made the colonists fair game for the British had given them the self-assurance to stand up against Parliament.

The Sugar, Currency, and Quartering Acts

The task of handling postwar problems of imperial government and finance fell upon the ministry of George Grenville, who got his appointment chiefly because of his reputation as a fiscal expert. Grenville discovered that the American customs service cost four times as much as it was collecting. The Molasses Act of 1733 had imposed a duty of sixpence per gallon on foreign-made molasses. Everyone knew that New England merchants were importing vast quantities of relatively cheap molasses from the French sugar islands without paying any duties. Grenville thought he saw a way of stopping the smuggling and increasing revenue. His instrument was the Sugar Act, which he pushed through Parliament in 1764.

The Sugar Act actually reduced the duty on foreign molasses, from sixpence to threepence. Previously merchants had been bribing customs officials at about onepence per gallon. Now bribery would be less profitable. In addition, the Sugar Act placed duties on many other essential imports. Finally, it provided new mechanisms of enforcement. Violations of the Sugar Act would be tried in admiralty courts.

Previously the colonists had successfully steered most smuggling cases into colonial courts with juries. The local people on those juries had been understanding, and acquittals were easy to obtain. Now violators would have to deal with courts presided over by unfriendly judges sent from England.

The Sugar Act provisions alarmed colonial merchants, and they and other colonists found the title and preamble downright ominous. Its official title was the Revenue Act, and the preamble stated that its purpose was to raise money in the colonies. Previously all taxes laid by Parliament had been passed for the purpose of regulating trade. The Revenue Act would serve that aim, but it introduced the new and important principle that Parliament had the right to tax the colonies directly for the benefit of the British treasury.

George Grenville was a determined, precise, and energetic man, and he regarded the Sugar Act merely as one of several steps necessary to set colonial financial affairs in order. The next year he came up with still another means of getting the colonists to help pay for the cost of supporting British troops in America. The Quartering Act required any colony where troops were stationed to provide living quarters, certain supplies, and traditional rations of cider, beer, or rum. English law had many precedents for such requirements, but the colonists had never before been asked to support a standing army in their midst.

As part of his American revenue package, Grenville persuaded Parliament to pass the Currency Act of 1764. Although this act attracted little attention at the time, it was actually a serious blow to merchants outside New England. In 1750 the New England colonies had been told not to issue paper money not backed by gold or silver; in 1764 all the colonies were prohibited from printing such money. Because these two metals were scarce in the colonies, merchants everywhere found it difficult to pay their debts to English businessmen.

Grenville's measures had different effects in different colonies. The Quartering Act affected only those places where British troops were actually stationed. As things turned out, most of the troops were stationed in New York. The Currency Act probably had the greatest impact on the colonial economy, but its effects were slow and not easy to detect. The Sugar Act received the most attention, since it seemed the most radical departure from previous practices and struck directly at the influential merchants' pocketbooks. It affected Boston more than any other colonial city, and the Boston town meeting reacted accordingly.

In written instructions to its representatives in the General Court, the town asked an ominous question: "If taxes are laid upon us in any shape without ever having a legal representation where they are laid, are we not reduced from the character of free subjects to the miserable state of tributary slaves?" James Otis wrote a pamphlet that declared flatly: "No parts of his Majesty's dominions can be taxed without their consent." The Massachusetts General Court appointed a "committee of correspondence" to write to other provinces about the Sugar Act.

The Stamp Act Crisis

When Grenville announced the Sugar Act, he also announced that his ministry was preparing still another revenue measure. This was the Stamp Act, passed by Parliament in March 1765. The act required that a tax stamp (ranging in value from a halfpenny to £10) be purchased and placed on all legal documents, licenses, newspapers, pamphlets, almanacs, playing cards, and dice. The Stamp Act also provided that violators be tried in admiralty courts. To provide time for printing the stamps and shipping them to special distributors in the colonies, the new duties were scheduled to take effect on November 1. A few members of Parliament warned that the colonists would resist such a tax. But similar duties had been levied before in England, and the Stamp Act passed overwhelmingly. Grenville settled back to wait for the money to come in.

He never got any: No stamps were ever bought or used in the colonies. The moment word of the Stamp Act arrived, there was an outburst of protest and defiance. The colonial assemblies took the first steps. In Virginia, a fiery young lawyer named Patrick Henry took the floor of the assembly to offer a set of resolutions. The house adopted several which declared that Virginians could be taxed only by the Virginia assembly, but it rejected others that called for outright disobedience. Newspapers picked up both sets of resolutions and printed them as if they had all been passed. Other colonial assemblies rejected the more radical position and modeled their own resolutions on Virginia's more moderate ones. They simply denied the right of Parliament to tax the colonists.

The assemblies took a truly crucial step by deciding on joint protest. In June, the Massachusetts General Court called upon the other assemblies to name delegates to a congress to meet in New York City for the purpose of asserting the rights of British Americans. Delegates from nine colonies met there in October. (Several colonies had been prevented by their royal governors from selecting delegates.) The Stamp Act Congress quickly agreed on a Declaration of Rights and Grievances.

It began by acknowledging "all due subordination" to the Crown and Parliament, but went on to claim that the people of the colonies could be taxed only by their elected representatives. Only people chosen by themselves could represent the colonists, and "the people of these colonies are not, and from their local circumstances cannot be, represented in the House of Commons in Great Britain." No taxes could every be rightly imposed on the colonies by Parliament. Nor could Parliament expand the jurisdiction of admiralty courts beyond their traditional limits. The declaration closed by demanding repeal of both the Sugar Act and the Stamp Act.

The colonists' position was clear and consistent. For them, the matter was one of rights, principles, and common sense. To tax a man was to take away his property, to which he had a natural right. It could be rightly taken from him only if he consented, and the only way he could give his consent was to elect his own representatives. The colonial assemblies were the only bodies that represented the people of the colonies, and therefore they were the only bodies that could rightfully tax them. All this was simple and obvious. The phrase "no taxation without representation" was therefore more than a slogan. So far as the colonists were concerned, it described the heart of the relationship between government and the people.

The British rejected the American position by advancing the old idea of "virtual representation." The colonists, they argued, were represented in Parliament because members of Parliament were elected to represent all English people everywhere. The people of such large English cities as Birmingham and Manchester, they pointed out, sent no representatives to Parliament but were represented by members elected by other localities. So too with the colonists, who elected no one to Parliament but were "virtually" represented there by its current membership.

As far as most Americans were concerned, virtual representation was no representation at all. If some English cities were not permitted to elect anyone to Parliament, they should be. A representative, the colonists claimed, had to be elected by the people he represented. He should live among his constituents and be responsive to their interests.

The colonial argument had one flaw. Even before the Stamp Act crisis, it had been suggested that the colonists elect representatives to Parliament, but the idea got nowhere. Both sides recognized that the Atlantic was a real barrier to effective representation. The British were not anxious to press the matter because they sensed that any discussion might well open the whole question of the lack of representation *within* England. The Americans were even less anxious to open the question. They knew that any fair representation of the colonies in Parliament

THE IMPORTANCE OF INFORMATION

One astute observer of the prerevolutionary crisis was profoundly impressed by the impact and importance of the printed word. As be described it, he saw

a spectacle never before displayed among man, and even yet without a parallel on earth. It is the spectacle, not of the learned and the wealthy only, but of the great body of the people; even a large portion of that class of the community which is destined to daily labor, having free and

constant access to public prints, receiving regular information of every occurrence, attending to the course of political affairs, discussing public measures, and having thus presented to them constant excitement to the acquisition of knowledge, and continual means of obtaining it. Never, it may be safely asserted, was the number of political journals so great in proportion to the population of a country as at present in ours. Never were they, all things considered, so cheap, so universally diffused, so easy of access.

would be very small in comparison with all the English members. The colonists would probably always be outvoted. They sensed that their own interests were much better served by the local assemblies.

By the time of the Stamp Act Congress in October, some colonists were willing to go far beyond passing resolutions. That summer, secret organizations began forming in the port cities. Calling themselves Sons of Liberty, these self-appointed groups were composed largely of shopkeepers, artisans, and laborers, but they were often led by gentlemen of property and social standing. They aimed at defending American liberties by making sure that no stamps were distributed.

In August a shouting mob of Bostonians burned the records of the admiralty court, ransacked the house of stamp distributor Andrew Oliver, and called for his resignation or his head. The next day Oliver was forced to read his resignation aloud before a jeering, cheering crowd. Similar mobs assembled in other cities, and they proved remarkably effective without actually killing anyone. By the fateful day of November 1, every stamp agent in the colonies had been forced to resign or to promise not to issue any stamps.

Rioting in colonial cities was not altogether new; there had been riots against British navy press gangs during the wars against the French. But the Stamp Act riots were a new kind of demonstration: They were well organized, were frequently led by citizens of wealth and standing, and aimed at a clear political objective. Here was a new form of politics. Like the crowds of the Great Awakening, the crowds of the 1760s worked outside traditional institutions. In doing so, they established a new mode of public expression that was to surface again and again at times of crisis in American history.

This development coincided with and was connected to a similar development in England. There, mob action swirled about the person and name of John Wilkes, a clever, unstable agitator. In 1763 Wilkes came crashing onto the public stage by criticizing Lord Bute, an intimate friend of George III who pressed through the Treaty of Paris. Wilkes's remarks were published in number 45 of a magazine called *North Briton*, and he was arrested for libel. His career turned into a dizzying round of trials, jailings, flight abroad, election to Parliament, and later the post of lord mayor of London. Wilkes successfully equated himself with the cause of liberty at home and in the colonies, and the colonists made him a popular hero. "Wilkes and Liberty" became a common rallying cry in America, and the number 45 an almost sacred symbol.

After the Stamp Act Congress, hundreds of merchants signed agreements not to buy British goods until the act was repealed. When the Stamp Act went into force on November 1, 1765, merchants suspended business in protest. They resumed trading at the end of the year, but without using stamps. By then, Grenville had been fired after a quarrel with George III about the king's mother. The new ministry under the marquis of Rockingham faced opposition not only in America, but from merchants at home who were feeling the pinch of the American boycott.

Parliament reluctantly repealed the Stamp Act on March 17, 1766. Rockingham realized it was both unwise and unenforceable. William Pitt was one of the few members of Parliament to think that it was, as he put it, "founded on an erroneous principle." Most members regarded taxation of the colonists as entirely fair. On the day of repeal they voted overwhelmingly for a Declaratory Act asserting that Parliament had the full right to make laws "to bind the colonies and people of America in all cases whatsoever." In the colonies, news of repeal was greeted with the tolling of bells and joyous celebrations. The colonists were so jubilant about their victory that they scarcely noticed the Declaratory Act.

The Townshend Acts

Several months after repeal of the Stamp Act, Rockingham's ministry went the way of Grenville's. The king recalled William Pitt, now the earl of Chatham, to form a new ministry. But Pitt, by far the ablest among his contemporaries in Britain, soon became so ill with gout that he was forced to retire temporarily. Control of the government fell into the hands of the chancellor of the exchequer, Charles Townshend, a dashing man of great energy and little sense.

During the Stamp Act crisis Townshend had been led by American arguments to believe the colonists would accept revenue-raising acts if they were presented as traditional "external" trade regulation, rather than as "internal" taxes. In 1767, on his recommendation, Parliament passed the Townshend Acts, imposing new import duties on glass, lead, paints, paper, and tea. These duties were labeled regulations of trade, but in fact they violated traditional mercantilist principles because they taxed manufactured goods sent to the colonies from the mother country.

In addition, the Townshend Acts reasserted the legitimacy of writs of assistance and placed enforcement in the hands of admiralty courts. They also provided for a new means of enforcement, a Board of Customs Commissioners to be located in Boston, a city that by this time had the reputation of being the principal nest of smuggling and tax resistance in the colonies. The Townshend Acts also provided that customs officials would be paid out of fines levied by the admiralty courts—a sure recipe for official corruption.

And as part of his entire program, Townshend included an act to settle the disputes over the Quartering Act. Because New York's assembly had refused to vote supplies for British troops, the act voided all the assembly's new laws until it provided suitable quarters and rations.

The American response to the Townshend Acts followed a somewhat different pattern than the Stamp Act crisis in 1765. The new duties lacked the symbolic impact of the hated tax stamps. And this time merchants were more directly affected than anyone else. They revived the technique of boycotting imports from England. The nonimportation movement gathered strength month after month. As with all boycotts, however, there was great difficulty in gaining everyone's cooperation. If merchants in one port agreed on nonimportation, other merchants in neighboring ports were tempted to continue business as usual.

The Sons of Liberty made a three-pronged attack on this problem. They visited offending merchants and talked persuasively about the rights of the colonies. They also pointed out the dangers of not going along. In addition, the Sons of Liberty mounted a campaign in the newspapers to persuade the public to give up British-made luxuries. They sang the virtues of homespun cloth and the life of domestic simplicity. In doing so they touched the feelings of the populace as a whole. Simplicity and hard work had long been regarded as virtues by a people with a Calvinist outlook on life; now these traditional virtues could serve the cause of liberty.

As nonimportation grew more and more effective, some colonists grew busy with their pens. Pennsylvania's John Dickinson published a series of *Letters from a Farmer in Pennsylvania*, which gained a wide audience through the newspapers. Dickinson denounced the Townshend duties as a violation of the unwritten constitution of the British empire. He admitted that Parliament had the right to regulate trade with taxes. These taxes might even result in some revenue. But taxes imposed for the purpose of raising money for the English treasury were another matter. They were no more acceptable in the form of import duties than in the form of stamps. Dickinson also pointed out that if Parliament could shut down the New York assembly, it could shut down others.

DEEPENING CRISIS

In Boston a clever agitator took advantage of the Townshend Acts. Samuel Adams was a Bostonian who had failed in the brewery business but then turned with great success to local politics. Adams saw every new British measure as evidence of tyranny. For several years he sustained a high level of public indignation, and he even established a network of cooperation among the thirteen colonies. In the early 1770s, however, British policies seemed to most Americans much less oppressive than during the previous decade.

Trouble In Massachusetts

Not long after publication of Dickinson's *Letters*, the Massachusetts General Court sent a circular letter to the other colonial assemblies. The actual author was Sam Adams. Using the Boston town meeting as his power base, Adams was rapidly building a career as a professional patriot and popular agitator. With the Massachusetts circular letter, Adams played his cards beautifully. The tone of the letter angered the British, who ordered all colonial governors to dissolve their assemblies if they attempted to endorse it. This was exactly what Adams hoped would happen.

By the time these orders were received, three other colonies had endorsed the Massachusetts letter, and Virginia's assembly had produced one of its own. The ministry had specifically instructed

Governor Francis Bernard of Massachusetts to dissolve the General Court if it failed to repeal the letter. On June 30, 1768, the General Court voted 92 to 17 not to rescind. The next day Bernard dissolved that body, and the numbers 92 and 17 promptly joined 45 in the colonists' vocabulary of liberty.

The atmosphere in Boston was further heated by the activities of the new customs commissioners. They would have been resented whatever they did, for neither smugglers nor legitimate merchants liked to pay taxes, and few people welcomed the arrival of a swarm of bureaucrats. Here were men who came with power to line their own pockets by prosecutions in admiralty courts.

And the customs officials proved to be far from saintly. The provisions of the Sugar Act and the Townshend duties furnished them with perfect tools for trapping the most innocent merchants in a snare of red tape. Shippers had to post bonds and fill out long forms concerning their cargoes and destinations. It was easy to file the wrong form or to file the right form in the wrong way; many "violations" were possible. Some were punishable by seizure of the entire cargo and the ship as well.

Abuse by customs officials were numerous, but one incident became notorious. The sloop *Liberty*, belonging to a wealthy merchant named John Hancock, was tied up at one of the Boston wharves, and word got out that Madeira wine was aboard. Hancock thought he owed no duty, but some customs officials decided he did. They ordered the *Liberty* seized and towed out to anchor beside a British warship in the harbor. Crowds assembled on the wharf and outside the commissioners' homes. As things turned out there was no real violence, but the incident had important results. For his part, John Hancock's feeling for American liberty deepened considerably; he became something of a popular hero in Massachusetts. The commissioners were badly shaken and went to Castle William on an island in Boston harbor. From there they wrote London requesting (not for the first time) that troops be sent for their protection.

The Boston Massacre

Rumors about the possible arrival of British troops ran through Boston during that summer of 1768, and Sam Adams and other Sons of Liberty talked up the idea of active resistance. Two well-equipped regiments did finally arrive in late September, headed by General Thomas Gage. As the redcoats marched in, the townspeople watched with apprehension and resentment. But there was no violence. A Boston silversmith and engraver sat down to sketch the arrival of British soldiers in a peaceful Anglo-American town. His name was Paul Revere.

In looking back, one can easily see that the arrival of British soldiers in Boston was a turning point in relations between the American colonies and Great Britain. For more than a century, Englishmen in England and elsewhere had regarded a standing army at home in peacetime as a threat to their liberties. They almost automatically thought of the dictatorship of Oliver Cromwell after the English civil wars and the threat of oppression by James II before the Glorious Revolution. All the history they knew gave evidence that troops were the spearheads of tyranny.

It seems remarkable that British redcoats lived in Boston for eighteen months before a serious incident occurred. They found the town both dull and hostile. A major cause of friction was competition for jobs between local laborers and redcoats looking for work in off-duty hours. On the afternoon of March 5, 1770, a fistfight

Paul Revere was a silversmith and craftsman. He cast cannon for the army and designed the state seal used by Massachusetts. *(Library of Congress)*

Samuel Adams. *(Library of Congress)*

all been artisans or seamen, and one of them, Crispus Attucks, was a black man.

Adams's plea won acquittal on the murder charge. Two soldiers, found guilty of manslaughter, were released after minor punishment. But the "massacre" itself became a favorite theme for oratory and pamphleteering and was the subject of another famous engraving by Paul Revere. At the same time, the nonimportation movement proved increasingly effective as colonial trade with Britain fell off by a third.

Relative Quiet

In the meantime, events in England were moving in a more peaceful direction. When Charles Townshend died, George III finally found a chief minister he could get along with. The ministry of Lord North began in January 1770 and lasted for twelve years. King George and Lord North understood each other largely because they were rather alike. Both were hardworking English patriots but lacking in imagination.

North realized that the Townshend Acts were costing much more to enforce than they would ever bring in. English merchants were complaining loudly about the colonial boycott of their goods. So Lord North called upon Parliament to repeal all the duties except the one on tea. He saw two obvious reasons for retaining this one tax. Americans drank a lot of tea and seemed willing to pay a good price for it. More important, continuation of this tax would maintain the principle of Parliament's power to tax the colonists. Parliament did as North asked, in April 1770.

When word reached the colonies, the nonimportation movement collapsed. Sam Adams and the Sons of Liberty in other cities tried unsuccessfully to keep the boycott alive. In the early days of the boycott, many merchants had found that nonimportation permitted them to sell off goods from already well-stocked warehouses. At first, profit and patriotism had dovetailed very nicely. As time went on, however, and stocks ran low, merchants found it increasingly costly to support their political principles. They therefore happily abandoned nonimportation when they learned of Lord North's concessions. Business boomed. The political atmosphere became more relaxed than at any time since word of the Sugar Act had arrived in 1764.

broke out over this issue. That evening a mob gathered in front of the customhouse, where ten armed British soldiers stood guard outside. Someone threw something at the soldiers, and soon the air was filled with snowballs, garbage, and pieces of manure. For a while, the frustrated soldiers simply stood their ground, but finally they sent a volley of musket fire into the crowd. Five of the rioters were killed and six others wounded. To head off further clashes, Lieutenant Governor Thomas Hutchinson ordered the troops to islands in the harbor. They remained there for the next four years.

Samuel Adams immediately labeled this incident a "massacre" and made certain that it received wide publicity throughout the colonies. John Adams defended the soldiers in court. The civilian dead, he said later, were among "the most obscure and inconsiderable [men] . . . upon this continent." Adams contended they were not even genuine Bostonians, but outsiders looking for trouble. In fact, the five victims had

This relative quiet lasted for three years, even though there were incidents that Sam Adams and other agitators tried to take advantage of. In 1772, for example, word arrived that the salaries of Massachusetts judges would now be paid by the Crown rather than by the colony. Adams also made the most of a more dramatic incident that year in Rhode Island. For months the British customs schooner *Gaspee* had been harassing colonial vessels on Narragansett Bay, boarding them to see if they were smuggling goods. Sailors from the *Gaspee* went ashore and cut down fruit trees for firewood and stole pigs and chickens. On June 9 the *Gaspee* ran around while pursuing a local vessel. That night eight boatloads of men rowed out from Providence to the stranded schooner, boarded the vessel, wounded its captain, removed its crew, and burned it.

Several of the attackers were prominent merchants, but their identities were not known to British authorities. When word reached London, Lord North's ministers quite correctly concluded that no convictions could be obtained from local juries in Rhode Island courts. The king named a special commission to seek out the guilty and bring them back to England for trial.

The plan to drag colonial Americans to England for trial aroused widespread suspicion and hostility in the colonies. Rather than call a congress, as the assemblies had done at the time of the Stamp Act, they set up more permanent machinery for cooperation. The assemblies of Massachusetts and Virginia were the first to appoint "committees of correspondence" to communicate with other colonies about threats to American liberties. By February 1774 most colonies had established such committees. They were unofficial in the sense that the governors had nothing to do with their formation; the various assemblies simply appointed several members to serve as a committee. By doing so the assemblies established a network among the colonies entirely outside the framework of imperial government.

TOWARD CONCORD AND LEXINGTON

In the early months of 1773, very few American colonists realized they were on the verge of war with Great Britain. Only a handful had the faintest idea about the possibility of American

independence. But as often happens, a single and apparently trivial decision in one place started a chain of events that led to outright conflict in another. People in the thirteen colonies rapidly came to realize that they had to establish a united front against Great Britain. In doing so they fell back upon their previous experience at the time of the Stamp Act, on their representative assemblies, and on their commitment to ideas about English liberties and natural rights.

Tea and the Intolerable Acts

In those same months, Lord North found himself dealing with a problem that arose halfway around the world from the American colonies. The East India Company was teetering on the brink of bankruptcy. The company was a gigantic private business to which the British government had given a monopoly on trade with India and the responsibility for governing English territories there. Largely because the company had become riddled with corruption and mismanagement, its warehouses were bulging with 17 million pounds of unsold tea. North had to save the East India Company or watch Britain's imperial ambitions in India go down the drain.

He chose to push the Tea Act through Parliament in an attempt to save the company by helping it to get rid of its surplus in the American colonies. He had no idea that the act would arouse a storm of protest. Previously tea had been purchased at auction in London and then sold through a series of middlemen in the colonies. North's new act gave the East India Company a monopoly on the colonial tea market and thus would provide the colonists with cheaper tea by eliminating the middlemen's profits. So far so good. But North forgot about the possible reaction of established tea merchants in the colonies and the fact that the colonists might not like a quasi-governmental monopoly on a highly valued import.

When news of the Tea Act arrived in the colonies, mass protest meetings were held in most colonial ports. Tea agents of the East India Company were persuaded to resign, much like the Stamp Act commissioners nearly eight years before. Tea ships were turned back or the tea unloaded and placed in warehouses unsold. In Boston, however, Governor Thomas Hutchinson

The word *boss*, which is of course both a noun and a verb, comes originally from the Dutch *baas*, which was the rough equivalent of the English word *master*. Over the years in the American colonies and states the word underwent some interesting transformations, aside from the change in spelling. The term took on stronger suggestions of social and political and even physical power than the English *master*. Thus one could master the skill of carpentry but not boss it; on the other hand, factory managers could boss their workers but not necessarily master them. The term *master* is closely associated with *mastery*, with a skill, whereas the word *boss* suggests personal power. Thus we have political bosses, and even prison bosses—the term carries a faint whiff of illegitimacy. In the army, we have master sergeants, not boss sergeants, although master sergeants boss privates around. And the American system of higher education commonly offers the M.A., which stands for master of arts, and the B.A., which does *not* stand for boss of arts, no matter how well deserved.

decided the act would have to be obeyed. He refused to let the tea ships clear the harbor without first discharging their cargoes. (Hutchinson, a high-minded, aristocratic native of Massachusetts, was devoted to the cause of established authority. This commitment had made him enormously unpopular; in this case his position was weakened by the fact that two of his sons and a nephew were newly appointed tea agents). On the evening of December 16, 1773, a well-organized group of Bostonians disguised themselves as Indians, boarded the tea ships, broke open the tea boxes with hatchets, and tossed them into the murky waters of Boston harbor.

Many colonists thought the Boston men had gone too far. After all, those "Indians" had destroyed private property, and Americans had been busy defending property rights for ten years. Their minds changed very rapidly, however, when they learned of Lord North's reaction to the "Boston Tea Party."

Lord North and the king took aim at Boston and Massachusetts. North easily got Parliament to pass a series of measures that came to be known in the colonies as the Intolerable (or Coercive Acts). The Port of Boston was closed until the East India Company and the customs service were paid for their losses. Royal officials charged with a capital crime would be tried in England rather than in the colonies. The Massachusetts council was to be appointed by the crown rather than elected by the General Court. Judges and sheriffs who had previously been elected by the people were now to be appointed

by the royal governor. Town meetings were to be held only when called by the governor.

Finally, a new Quartering Act authorized military commanders to house their men in private homes as well as in barracks. The Quartering Act applied to all the colonies, but British authorities made clear where it was aimed. The troops stationed on islands in Boston harbor were reinforced and brought into the city itself. General Thomas Gage, commander of all British troops in the colonies, was appointed the new governor of Massachusetts.

While pressing through this legislation, Parliament also passed the Quebec Act, a law that had nothing to do with the situation in Boston. But in its timing and provisions, the Quebec Act seemed as "intolerable" and "coercive" to the colonists as any of the other measures. The Quebec Act provided the first civilian government for the conquered French province of Canada. As a concession to the traditions of the French inhabitants, the new government was to have no representative assembly, and court cases were to be tried by judges rather than juries. The Roman Catholic church was given a privileged position.

In London, all these provisions seemed like a generous way of treating a conquered people. In the thirteen colonies, however, they appeared as an ominous new form of colonial government and a cowardly concession to followers of the pope. Worse still, the Quebec Act enlarged that province to include all the territory north of the Ohio River, ignoring the land claims of Virginia, Pennsylvania, and other colonies.

The First Continental Congress

The reaction of the colonists to the Intolerable Acts was very different from what Lord North and the king expected. They had hoped to isolate Massachusetts by singling it out for special punishment. Instead, their actions drove the colonies together. People in other cities collected supplies to send to the suffering residents of Boston. Illegal conventions met in one colony after another. For the most part these conventions were composed of men who a few weeks before had been sitting as members of the colony's legislative assembly. They debated whether to try the strategy of nonimportation again, but most of them felt that events had moved beyond such measures.

The various committees of correspondence worked at keeping each other informed and at coordinating some kind of joint effort. At the urging of the Massachusetts General Court, they agreed at last that each colonial convention should name delegates to a "continental" congress in Philadelphia in September 1774. The congress that assembled on September 5 in Philadelphia represented only twelve colonies, for the royal governor of Georgia, James Wright, had outmaneuvered all attempts to send delegates.

At the outset, the delegates made a crucial decision: They decided that they represented individual colonies rather than the colonists in general. As a result, they agreed to count their votes by colony rather than by individuals. The delegates from Rhode Island and North Carolina would have equal voting power with those from far more populous colonies such as Massachusetts, Pennsylvania, and Virginia.

The First Continental Congress then agreed to endorse several resolutions that had been adopted by a meeting of town delegates in Suffolk County in eastern Massachusetts. The Suffolk Resolves denounced the Intolerable Acts and asked the colonies to raise troops and suspend trade with the rest of the empire. After this show of support for Massachusetts, the delegates considered a plan of union proposed by one of their most cautious and conservative members, Joseph Galloway of Pennsylvania.

The Galloway Plan was for a grand council of all the colonies to share power with Parliament. Each body would be able to veto the actions of the other concerning colonial matters. Galloway's plan ran into heavy opposition, especially from New England delegates, who objected to any arrangement that might curtail the

---

THE FARMINGTON RESOLVES

The following revealing news item was datelined Farmington, Connecticut, May 19, 1774:

A very numerous and respectable body were assembled, of near one thousand people, when a huge pole, just forty-five feet high was erected, and consecrated to the shrine of Liberty, after which the Act of Parliament for blocking up the Boston harbour was read aloud; sentenced to the flames, and executed by the hands of the common hangman; then the following Resolves were passed, . . .

1st. That it is the greatest dignity, interest, and happiness of every American to be united with our parent State, while our liberties are duly secured, maintained, and supported by our rightful Sovereign, whose person we greatly revere; whose Government while duly administered, we are ready with our lives and properties to support.

2d. That the present Ministry, being instigated by the Devil, and led on by their wicked and corrupt hearts, have a design to take away our liberties and properties, and to enslave us for ever.

3d. That the late Act which their malice hath caused to be passed in Parliament, for blocking up the port of Boston, is unjust, illegal, and oppressive; and that we, and every American, are sharers in the insults offered to the town of Boston.

4th. That those pimps and parasites who dared to advise their master to such detestable measures, be held in utter abhorrence by us and every American, and their names loaded with the curses of all succeeding generations.

5th. That we scorn the chains of slavery; we despise every attempt to rivet them upon us; we are the sons of freedom, and . . . that god-like virtue shall blazon our hemisphere.

powers of the colonial assemblies, and it was voted down.

Defeat of the Galloway Plan showed how far the thinking of many colonists had shifted since the Stamp Act crisis of 1765. The colonists began by denying Parliament's right to tax them. Now a majority of those at the First Continental Congress denied that Parliament had the right to pass any sort of laws for the colonies. The congress did admit, however, that Parliament could regulate trade by means of moderate customs duties. In effect, its members asked that the clock be turned back eleven years to the situation that had prevailed until 1763.

Yet the delegates were well aware that they were dealing with a new kind of political crisis. They were determined to establish mechanisms for combating the Intolerable Acts. They set up a Continental Association to enforce a real boycott of British imported goods; the Association would enforce not only nonimportation, but nonexportation as well. With that aim in mind, the Congress called upon every colonial assembly to appoint local committees that would publish the names of all violators of the boycott as "enemies of American liberty." Within months, local "committees of safety" were in operation in most of the colonies.

Before adjourning on October 26, the Continental Congress agreed to meet again in May 1775 unless American grievances were fully met. As they cast their ballots, the delegates were well aware that the countryside around Boston was becoming a powder keg that could explode at any moment.

War

Many people in the towns of eastern New England felt encouraged by the Continental Congress to proceed with military preparations. Special units of their militias prepared to assemble at a minute's notice, and these "minutemen" began stockpiling firearms and gunpowder. In Boston, General Gage found out about these activities and began writing London for more men. On April 14 he received a letter (dated January 27) ordering him to attack the rebellious minutemen with the soldiers he had. He immediately prepared to strike at Concord, twenty-one miles northwest of Boston, where, informants told him, there was a large collection of arms.

General Thomas Gage wearing uniform. *(Library of Congress)*

General Gage realized he could not conceal his preparations; in order to ferry his men across the Charles River, he had to gather longboats from warships anchored in the harbor. On the night of April 18, seven hundred British soldiers set out for Concord. Paul Revere and two other American riders rode off to spread word of the intended destination. The countryside rang with church bells and gunshots—prearranged signals sent from one town to the next.

The first British troops reached Lexington, five miles short of Concord, at dawn. There they found about seventy minutemen drawn up on the village green. The commanding British officer ordered them to lay down their guns and disperse. The Americans began to do so but without putting down their arms. Someone fired a shot—no one knows who—and the redcoats sent a volley into the dispersing militiamen. Eight were killed.

The British troops then pressed on to Concord, which they reached at about 8 A.M. There they drove off a small group of minutemen and searched for the supposed store of arms, but all that remained were a few gun carriages, digging tools, some flour, and a stripped tree—a "liberty pole" the Americans had erected to celebrate their cause. After burning this disappointing collection of objects, the redcoats regrouped in a thin column for the march back to Boston. They knew they had still another twenty miles to go with their heavy packs and muskets, but they did not know they were about to become involved in a kind of battle none of them had ever experienced.

The entire day's march was a disaster. The road to Boston seemed to be lined with riflemen who fired from behind trees and stone walls. In fact, some three to four thousand armed New England farmers had assembled in about twelve hours. The redcoats fell by the dozens, and only the arrival of reinforcements from Boston saved them from complete defeat. As it was, they suffered nearly four times as many casualties as the farmers they had always held in such contempt. Exhausted, humiliated, and bewildered, the British soldiers struggled back into Boston that night. They were probably too tired to notice that the surrounding hills were dotted with the campfires of the colonial Englishmen who had somehow become their enemies.

SUMMARY

The American Revolution had its seeds in the long war between France and England from 1756 to 1763. This conflict began in America and then spread to Europe, unlike those that had preceded it. American militia fought in this war, alongside regular British troops sent to the colonies. The Treaty of Paris (1763), which settled what had been a world war, gave Britain all of Canada and the interior lands east of the Mississippi River except for New Orleans, plus Florida. Spain received from France all the lands west of the Mississippi River, plus the port of New Orleans.

The Seven Years' War changed the balance of power in America. The British were now in command—but they were also in debt. The war had been expensive. Royal officials thought the colonists should help pay at least some of the costs of empire—in particular, those of their own defense. London's solution was new taxes, which Americans very much resented. The colonials also objected to the policy on western land established by the Proclamation of 1763, the use of writs of assistance to enforce the Navigation Acts, the new currency regulations, and the stationing of British troops in the colonies at the colonists' expense.

American leaders began to talk to one another about these developments, and a new network of communication—the committees of correspondence—came into being. The colonists focused on the question of taxation without representation. The first serious crisis came with the Stamp Act of 1765, which the colonists refused outright to obey. No stamps were ever bought or used in the colonies. At the Stamp Act Congress in October 1765, delegates from nine colonies drew up a Declaration of Rights and Grievances demanding repeal. Groups called Sons of Liberty began to enforce the protest by mob action and riots.

The Stamp Act was in fact repealed in March 1766. This brought the colonists joy, but within a few months the king's new chief minister, Charles Townshend, managed to enrage them once again. The Townshend Acts, passed by Parliament in 1767, imposed new import duties on manufactured goods sent to the colonies from the mother country, reaffirmed the use of writs of assistance, and put enforcement in the hands of admiralty courts. A Board of Customs Commissioners was to be sent to Boston, the center of resistance. Assemblies that refused to pay for British troops stationed in their colonies had their laws declared null and void. The American response to Townshend's program was nonimportation—a boycott of British goods—and a widespread, effective propaganda campaign.

For three years after the so-called Boston Massacre of March 1770, there was relative quiet. The Townshend Acts were repealed, except for the tax on tea, and the colonists relaxed their suspicions about what the British really meant to do. But then in 1773 a new crisis arose concerning—of all things—tea. Passage of the Tea Act, followed by the Boston Tea Party, brought retaliation in the form of the Intolerable Acts. But to the surprise of the British—and perhaps of the colonists themselves—instead of isolating the troublemakers in Massachusetts, the new laws united the colonists.

The First Continental Congress met in September 1774 to find effective ways to combat British policies. Other colonists, especially in New England, began to stockpile firearms and train militia. In the spring of 1775, British troops quartered in Boston had their first skirmishes with colonial minutemen. Without anyone quite realizing it, and with the colonists never intending it, the American Revolution had begun.

TIME LINE

1754	Washington surrenders at Fort Necessity	1767	Townshend duties and revival of nonimportation
1754	Franklin offers plan of union at Albany Congress	1768	British troops arrive in Boston
1755	Braddock defeated by French and Indians	1770	Boston Massacre
1758	William Pitt takes over war against French	1770	Lord North repeals Townshend duties except on tea
1759	British capture Quebec	1770	Nonimportation agreements collapse
1761	James Otis attacks writs of assistance	1772	Burning of the *Gaspee* in Narragansett Bay
1763	Treaty of Paris ends Seven Years' War	1773	Boston Tea Party
1763	Royal proclamation draws line of western settlement	1774	Intolerable or Coercive Acts
1764	Sugar and Currency Acts	1774	First Continental Congress meets in Philadelphia
1765	Stamp Act crisis	1775	War breaks out at Lexington and Concord
1766	Rockingham replaces Grenville and repeals Stamp Act		

Suggested Readings

For the great international conflict called by Americans the French and Indian War, try J. Schutz, *William Shirley: King's Governor of Massachusetts* (1961). H. Peckman, *The Colonial Wars, 1689–1762* (1964), is succinct. The thirteen volumes of L. Gibson, *The British Empire before the American Revolution (1936–67)*, have a great deal of interesting information. The perspective of the Indians during that war is in G. Nash, *Red, White, and Black* (1974); and F. Jennings, *Empire of Fortune: Crowns, Colonies, and Tribes in the Seven Years War in America* (1988). A fresh approach is by F. Anderson, *A People's Army: Massachusetts Soldiers and Society in the Seven Years' War* (1984).

A number of works deal with the Revolution as a whole. E. Morgan, *The Birth of the Republic, 1763–1789* (1956), gives a propatriot view. H. Aptheker, *The American Revolution, 1763–1783* (1960), gives a Marxist interpretation. The best place to gain a sense of the wide variety of historical interpretations of the subject is J. Greene, *The Reinterpretation of the American Revolution, 1763–1783* (1960). The most recent synthesis is grounded in a wide variety of sources: R. Middlekauff, *The Glorious Cause: The American Revolution* (1982), which is especially useful also for the next two chapters. Two

other good studies with differing points of view are M. Jensen, *The Founding of a Nation: A History of the American Revolution, 1763–1776* (1968); and E. Robson, *The American Revolution, 1763–1783* (1955). R. Palmer, *The Age of Democratic Revolution: A Political History of Europe and America, 1760–1800* (1959), places the American revolt in an international perspective.

Some of the very best books about the Revolution have been concerned with ideology: See E. Morgan, *Inventing the People: The Rise of Popular Sovereignty in England and America* (1988). B. Bailyn, *The Ideological Origins of the American Revolution* (1967), stresses the colonists' near paranoia about what they regarded as Britain's conspiratorial intentions. R. Merritt, *Symbols of American Community, 1735–1775* (1966), an intriguing analysis of the press during this period, attempts to discover when Americans began to think of themselves as such. A superb original study is R. Bloch, *Visionary Republic: Millennial Themes in American Thought, 1756–1800* (1986).

Many other books focus on political events. A. Schlesinger, *Colonial Merchants and the American Revolution, 1763–1776* (1918), emphasizes the conflict between wealthy conservatives and the more radical common folk. C. Bridenbaugh, *Cities in Revolt: Urban Life in America, 1743–1776* (1955), catalogs material and cultural life in those little towns. E. and

H. Morgan, *The Stamp Act Crisis: Prologue to Revolution* (1953), and B. Labaree, *The Boston Tea Party* (1964), focus on two key crises. For the maneuvering on the British side of the Stamp Act, see P. Thomas, *British Politics and the Stamp Act Crisis: The First Phase of the American Revolution, 1763–1767* (1975). The course of political events in the various colonies is charted by J. Main in *The Upper House in Revolutionary America, 1763–1788* (1967). A. Jones, *American Colonial Wealth: Documents and Methods* (3 vols., 1977), is a statistical study of wealth and its distribution. P. Maier, *From Resistance to Revolution: Colonial Radicals and the Development of American Opposition to Britain, 1756–1776* (1972), probes the organization of "mob" action in the cities.

I. Hutson and S. Kurtz, *Essays on the American Revolution* (1973), is a good collection, especially on social history. R. Brown, *The South Carolina Regulators: The Story of the First American Vigilante Movement* (1963), makes clear why there was so much guerrilla warfare in the lower South. For the west, see J. Sosin, *The Revolutionary Frontier, 1763–1783* (1967); and F. Philbrick, *The Rise of the West, 1754–1830* (1965). The context of the Revolution is clarified in D. Robson, *Educating Republicans: The College in the Era of the American Revolution, 1750–1800* (1985).

For a comprehensive account of the Revolution as a whole that is solidly grounded in economics, see F. Ferguson, *The American Revolution: A General History, 1763–1790* (1974). Another general history, which is both balanced and imaginative, is N. Risjord, *Forging an American Republic, 1760–1815* (1973).

Battle of Bunker Hill. *(Library of Congress)*

CHAPTER 6

THE AMERICAN REVOLUTION

The American Revolution was one of the major events in the history of the modern world. It was the first major rebellion by overseas European emigrants against a mother country. It set an example that was widely followed, especially in Latin America. It also set an example for other major political upheavals: the French Revolution and the much later colonial revolutions in Africa, the Middle East, India, Indonesia, the Philippines, Vietnam, and elsewhere. The American Revolution was the first in modern times to be based on ideas about equal rights for "all men." American revolutionaries claimed that their principles applied to people everywhere, not just to themselves.

They saw themselves, self-consciously, as leaders in a universal struggle for liberty, and they hoped and often assumed that others would follow their lead. A similar mode of thinking has prevailed in the other great revolutions of modern times, including those in Russia, China, and more recently in the Middle East and in Eastern Europe.

Yet the American Revolution was full of contradictions and inconsistencies. It was many things at once, and historians have never agreed on its exact nature. In two respects it was a civil war: It was a struggle between the British in Great Britain and the British Americans in the colonies, and it was also a conflict between colonists who supported independence and those who did not. The American Revolution has been called a simple war for independence. Yet the fighting went on for a year before more than a handful of colonists accepted independence as a goal. The struggle was carried on in the name of liberty by men who owned slaves. The armies in this major revolution rarely numbered more than a few thousand men. The Americans could not have won the war without the aid of the French, whom they had been fighting for years. The revolution was made by fourteen separate governments, one of which was a shaky union of the others.

Finally, one of its major leaders claimed it was over before it began. Looking back many years afterward, John Adams asked: "What do we mean by the Revolution? The War? That was no part of the Revolution. It was only an effect and consequence of it. The Revolution was in the minds of the people, and this was effected from 1760 to 1775, in the course of fifteen years before a drop of blood was drawn at Lexington." It is very possible that John Adams was right, that the "real" revolution was one of human consciousness.

TOWARD INDEPENDENCE

There were many people on both sides who refused to realize that a real war had begun. Actual revolt began before the actual revolution; that is why twentieth-century Americans celebrate 1776 rather than 1775. As news of the fighting spread, many colonists looked anxiously to a small gathering of men in Philadelphia for leadership. Very few Americans thought about the possibility of independence; for more than a year they insisted on their loyalty to the king. Finally, when they broke that tie and declared their independence, they met considerable opposition from other colonists.

The Second Continental Congress

The Second Continental Congress met in Philadelphia in May 1775. An atmosphere of crisis hovered over the meeting, since everyone knew that blood had already been shed. The delegates from the thirteen colonies made up a distinguished if divided group; three of them were later to become presidents of the United States. None of these men imagined that the Congress would remain in session almost continuously for fourteen years.

It was clear at the outset that the Congress would support the action Massachusetts had taken. Yet there was no formal resolution that the Continental Congress create an army. The existence of an intercolonial fighting force was recognized only in an offhand announcement that the Congress would "adopt" the army then gathering around Boston, for "the general defense of the rights of America." At the urging of John Adams, the delegates selected George Washington, a Virginian, as commander in chief of the army. Adams was well aware that his home colony of Massachusetts needed outside support.

On July 6, 1775, the Congress voted a Declaration of the Causes and Necessity of Taking up Arms: "Our cause is just," they confidently declared: "Our union is perfect." Then came an open threat: "Our internal resources are great, and, if necessary, foreign assistance is undoubtedly attainable. . . . The arms we have been compelled by our enemies to assume, we will . . . employ for the preservation of our liberties, being with one mind resolved to die free men rather than live slaves." But there was also a note of hope: "We have not raised armies with ambitious designs of separating from Great Britain, and establishing independent States."

Nearly at the same time, the Congress adopted the Olive Branch Petition, the work of its most cautious members. This document begged King George to keep Parliament from passing further measures so that a plan of reconciliation could be worked out. On receiving it in August, however, the king brushed it aside. In a

---

ABIGAIL AND JOHN ADAMS ON THE STATUS OF WOMEN

In March 1776, when John Adams was away from home at the Second Continental Congress in Philadelphia, his wife Abigail sent him some unusual thoughts that have since become famous:

I long to hear that you have declared an independency—and by the way in the new Code of Laws which I suppose it will be necessary for you to make I desire you would Remember the Ladies, and be more generous and favourable to them than your ancestors. Do not put such unlimited power into the hands of the Husbands. Remember all Men would be tyrants if they could. If perticular care and attention is not paid to the Ladies we are determined to foment a Rebellion, and will not hold ourselves bound by any Laws in which we have no voice, or Representation.

That your Sex are Naturally Tyrannical is a Truth so thoroughly established as to admit of no dispute, but such of you as wish to be happy willingly give up the harsh title of Master for the more tender and endearing one of Friend. Why then, not put it out of the power of the vicious and the Lawless to use us with cruelty and indiginity with impunity. Men of Sense in all Ages abhor those customs which treat us only as the vassals of your Sex. Regard us then as Beings placed by providence under your protection and in immitation of the Supreem Being make use of that power only for our happiness.

John Adams was somewhat taken aback; he protested to his beloved wife that men "have only the Name of Masters," and that "in Practice you know We are the subjects."

---

royal proclamation, he called the Americans rebels and warned all loyal persons not to help them. Still, there were peacemakers in Britain. Edmund Burke, in one of his great speeches, urged Parliament to meet American demands and surrender the right to tax. "An Englishman," he exclaimed, "is the unfittest person on earth to argue another Englishman into slavery." Lord North himself persuaded Parliament to offer concessions, but although these measures might have helped in 1765, by 1775 they were too late.

Early Fighting

By the time North's concessions reached Philadelphia, the two sides had met at the Battle of Bunker Hill, the bloodiest engagement of the entire war. The main battle actually took place on nearby Breed's Hill, overlooking Boston, where American militiamen had gathered soon after the British had returned from Concord. On June 17, 1775, General Gage, with fresh troops, decided to drive the Americans off. His troops finally managed to dislodge them, but at great cost. The Americans lost almost four hundred men; Gage lost more than a thousand—over 40 percent of those he had ordered into battle. Two weeks later, Washington arrived at Cambridge, outside Boston, to take command.

By this time too, fighting had begun farther north. In May, in an effort to gain control of Canada, Ethan Allen captured the British posts at Crown Point and Ticonderoga in New York. Congress approved an address to "fellow-sufferers" in Canada, inviting them to join the rebellion. But the Canadians' "sufferings" had been taken care of by the Quebec Act of 1774, and they remained

John Adams. *(Library of Congress)*

loyal to the British crown. Washington decided upon an invasion of Canada. He ordered Benedict Arnold to set out for Quebec from Cambridge with about one thousand men. Arnold was joined below the Canadian city by a smaller group of Americans under Richard Montgomery. On New Year's Eve 1775, Arnold and Montgomery made an unsuccessful assault that ended with Montgomery's death and Arnold's humiliation.

Elsewhere American arms proved more successful. A British fleet was forced from the harbor of Charles Town, South Carolina. In Virginia the royal governor, Lord Dunmore, took refuge on a British warship. When he publicly invited Virginia slaves to join the British cause several hundred answered his call, but there was no general slave uprising. Dunmore's action horrified white Virginians and united them in their conviction that blacks should have no part in a white man's war.

In Massachusetts, the Americans were finally able to bring about the liberation of Boston. The Americans obtained heavy cannons by hauling them on sleds hundreds of miles overland from Fort Ticonderoga in New York. Once set in place on Dorchester Heights just south of Boston, they commanded the city and much of the harbor. On March 17, 1776, British troops evacuated the city and sailed for Nova Scotia.

Boston and vicinity, 1775

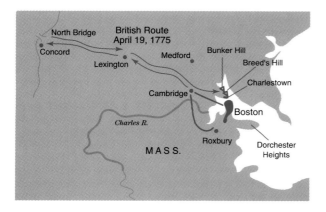

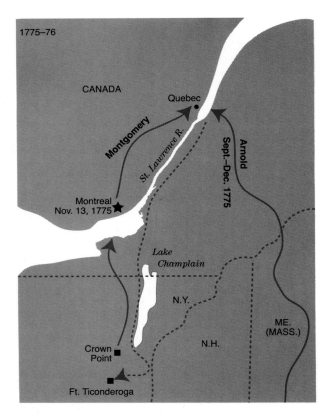

Canadian campaigns, 1775–1776

The Question of Loyalty

In the meantime, the Continental Congress was acting more and more like an independent government. It issued paper money to pay the army and established a committee for negotiating with foreign countries. It set up a postal department with Benjamin Franklin as Postmaster General and authorized the creation of a navy.

All these actions were undertaken while the Congress was still expressing its loyalty to the king. Most Americans felt such loyalty very deeply. Rather than blaming George III, they insisted that their difficulties were the fault of his corrupt and misguided ministers. As commander in chief, Washington was always careful to refer to the enemy as the "ministerial army." Americans remained loyal to the king in the face of royal proclamations declaring them to be in a state of rebellion. They protested that they were merely defending their rights and that they would stop fighting as soon as those rights were restored.

It was an English writer newly arrived in America who broke the logjam of public sentiment. In *Common Sense*, published anonymously in January 1776, Thomas Paine attacked the monarchy, not merely the king's ministers, and called for establishment of an independent republic. Having assailed "the Royal brute of Britain," he went on to declare: "There is something very absurd in supposing a Continent to be perpetually governed by an island." Paine's *Common Sense* was widely read and widely acclaimed; it was, in fact, one of the most immediately influential political pamphlets ever written.

Public opinion shifted rapidly. On April 6, 1776, the Congress opened American ports to the commerce of all nations except Britain. This measure in itself made America independent, as many delegates realized. A month later, the Congress advised all colonies to form new state governments if they had not already done so.

RUN away from *Hampton,* on *Sunday* laſt, a luſty Mulatto Fellow named ARGYLE, well known about the Country, has a Scar on one of his Wriſts, and has loſt one or more of his fore Teeth; he is a very handy Fellow by Water, or about the Houſe, &c. loves Drink, and is very bold in his Cups, but daſtardly when ſober. Whether he will go for a Man of War's Man, or not, I cannot ſay; but I will give 40 s. to have him brought to me. He can read and write.
NOVEMBER 2, 1775.   JACOB WRAY.

An advertisement for a runaway slave suspected of joining Lord Dunmore—a common sight in Virginia and Maryland newspapers during the fall and winter of 1775–1776. *(The Virginia State Library)*

Thomas Paine, by George Romney. *(Library of Congress)*

Nine hours of debate on July 1 helped to bring some reluctant delegates around; on July 2, 1776, Congress adopted Richard Henry Lee's Resolution of Independence:

RESOLVED, That these United Colonies are, and of right ought to be, free and independent States, that they are absolved from allegiance to the British Crown, and that all political connection between them and the State of Great Britain is, and ought to be, totally dissolved.

Adoption of this resolution was crucial, but the delegates also wanted to set forth their position with a formal declaration of principles. They decided to issue a statement with the broadest possible appeal: to British Americans in the colonies, to Englishmen at home, and to the people of the "world," meaning especially those in western Europe, with an eye particularly on potential allies in France.

The Declaration of Independence

The Congress appointed a committee to draft this public declaration. The committee in turn asked

Thomas Jefferson of Virginia to draw up a draft. Jefferson's draft, somewhat modified by John Adams and Benjamin Franklin, was then debated by Congress. One major change was made: Jefferson's attack on King George for promoting the slave trade was deleted. The charge was unfair, but it was removed for a different reason. South Carolina and Georgia, the two colonies most dependent on slaves, objected to Jefferson's description of the slave trade as "war upon humanity itself. " In order to gain the votes of those two colonies, the offending passage was deleted. The amended declaration was "authenticated and printed" on July 4, though it was not signed by all the members until November.

The Declaration of Independence was a masterpiece of political writing. The famous words of the preamble remain far better known than the long list of accusations aimed at George III. For people at the time, however, that list summarized the "long train of abuses" of the preceding

A facsimile of the Declaration of Independence in an ornamental oval frame containing medallions of seals of the thirteen original colonies, and medallion portraits of John Hancock, George Washington, and Thomas Jefferson. *(Library of Congress)*

dozen years. The accusations were not entirely fair, since George III did not bear personal responsibility for many of the actions the declaration condemned. But Americans were finally breaking their one remaining tie with Britain—the king—and so Jefferson aimed his propaganda at that last link.

Many years later, John Adams belittled Jefferson's achievement in the preamble by claiming that it merely repeated what everyone had been saying all along. But Jefferson replied that this was exactly what he had intended: The declaration, he said, was "to be an expression of the American mind." In framing it, he had "turned to neither book nor pamphlet." He had simply given expression to common ideas about natural rights and the right of the people to rebel.

In fact, these ideas no longer belonged just to John Locke or the Commonwealth writers, or even to the Scottish philosophers who had influenced Jefferson. They were simply the way most Americans thought about government. It was "self-evident" that the powers of government derived from the people, who could rightly take them back if they were abused; and in any such revolution, the people should then establish governments that would protect their natural rights.

When Jefferson came to naming those rights, he changed the traditional trinity of "life, liberty, and property" to "life, liberty, and the pursuit of happiness." His rewording has prompted the joke that the declaration gives everyone the right to pursue happiness, but not the right to catch up with it. But the point of this remark rests on a thorough misunderstanding of Jefferson's use of the word *pursuit*. He used it not in the sense of a chase, but in the older meaning of "practice" or "cultivation." To *pursue* something was to cultivate it, to learn and perfect it by practicing it repeatedly, by improving it with attention and care.

Jefferson regarded property as a means to happiness, as a way of leading the good life, rather than as a goal in itself. He had in mind the typical American farmer, who led a life of "happiness" precisely because he was so much more likely to own property than the typical farmer in Europe.

The Declaration of Independence stated flatly that "all men are created equal." This idea has

The signing of the Declaration of Independence, by John Trumbull. *(Library of Congress)*

proved in the long run to be the most enduring of all. At the time, though, it merely expressed the common assumption that free citizens were politically equal. It was not intended to include women or blacks, or to exclude them. It was not meant to suggest that all people were the same in ability or ought to be the same in wealth. It obviously did not apply to slaves. Later, however, the declaration's principle of equality took on a life of its own. The phrase "all men" could very easily be interpreted as meaning all human beings, not just the white men of America in 1776. It might even be extended—and eventually was—to include blacks and women.

The Loyalists

Some Americans opposed independence and the war. These *Loyalists*—or *Tories*, as the patriots called them—varied in number from place to place and also from time to time. The best modern estimates suggest that they never numbered more than a fifth of the white population. But numbers alone do not tell why some people chose to remain loyal to the British crown. For many, the decision was a crisis of conscience; for others, it was a matter of self-interest. Men who had held positions as royal officials, for example, found it easy to remain loyal. Some Loyalists had a distaste for popular rule. Certain ethnic groups in certain places tended to become Loyalist because other ethnic groups in the same area were becoming patriots. Quakers and German pacifists could not become active patriots because their principles prevented them from supporting war.

Probably the most important factor in pushing people toward a decision was the presence of armed men in the immediate neighborhood. The presence of British troops in an area could work in two ways: It could make Loyalists out of those who wished to pick the winning side, or it could make patriots out of outraged farmers who watched helplessly as redcoats made off with their corn and livestock. As the major fighting moved from one part of the colonies to another, more and more Americans had to make a choice. This pattern placed the Loyalists at a tremendous disadvantage; British troops came and went, while their armed American opponents remained. The patriot majority remained a majority mostly through its long-term control of the countryside.

Committees of patriots, backed with bayonets, drove many Loyalists from their homes and communities. The new states provided legal machinery for seizing Loyalist property. There were brutalities on both sides, but few principled Loyalists lost their lives except in open battle. Throughout the war, the British constantly overestimated the number of Loyalists, yet at the same time they failed to take full advantage of Loyalist support. Professional British army officers often treated these potential allies with the same contempt they had for all colonials.

One basic fact about the domestic opposition to the American Revolution has often been overlooked. Many of the Loyalists could simply leave without going permanently into exile. They could return "home" to England or move to another part of the British empire. Many did so. When British troops evacuated Boston, some one thousand Loyalists left with them for Nova Scotia. The same pattern was repeated whenever the British evacuated an American port. For many Loyalists, these journeys were heart-wrenching departures from their homes. But they were moving to places where people spoke English and had similar loyalties to the British crown. Many even received financial compensation from the British government for their losses. Few exiled refugees from a major revolution have had the same opportunity.

The departure of so many Loyalists had an important impact on the future of the new country. It meant that the most determined opponents of the revolution were no longer on the scene when victory was won. After the war, Americans were able to deal with the problems of nation building without having to worry about a large group of people who opposed the entire enterprise.

WAR—AND PEACE

The war had begun in Massachusetts, but the arena of conflict shifted to the Middle Colonies when the British decided to isolate New England by capturing New York. For several years, most of the fighting took place in New York, New Jersey, and Pennsylvania. During the final years, the theater of war shifted to the southern colonies. All in all, the Americans lost more battles than they won, but eventually they achieved a final victory. That triumph would have been impossible without the aid of their old enemies, the French.

Strengths and Weaknesses

The colonists faced enormous military disadvantages. They had a population of about 2.5 million, of whom perhaps nearly 20 percent became Loyalists; another 20 percent were slaves. The population of Great Britain was four times as large. The British could put far more troops on the field, and these were veteran soldiers who had been trained and seasoned during the Seven Years' War. The British navy was the largest and reputedly the most efficient in the world. In addition, Great Britain could afford to buy manpower. Early in the war it did so by hiring 30,000 Germans. The largest number came from the state of Hesse-Cassel in western Germany, which was why all German mercenaries came to be called Hessians by resentful Americans.

Yet the British also faced disadvantages. Chief among them was the Atlantic Ocean. In addition, they had to fight on unfamiliar, badly mapped stretches of territory that seemed to be crawling with hostile farmers. British troops and generals were accustomed to the better roads and more open country of Europe. Any army requires good transportation for cannon, troops, and supplies, and American roads proved disastrous. One British officer complained after the war that transportation difficulties "absolutely prevented us this whole war from going fifteen miles from a navigable river."

The Americans were fighting on their own ground. But they lacked a sizable navy, for Congress was able to find funds for only a few vessels. Even the successful efforts of John Paul Jones, who with one ship raided British shipping in the English Channel, did nothing to change the fact that for most of the war the British controlled the sea lanes and the American coastline. The Americans also had great difficulty keeping an army together. In any given place, the colonists would turn out in large numbers to fight. But staying in the army and marching off to other colonies was not an attractive prospect; long service in the army meant low pay, rigid discipline, cold, hunger, and disease. There were no pensions for soldiers disabled by wounds, no insurance payments for their widows if they died. So it is scarcely any wonder that many American farmers enlisted for three months and then went back home to their crops.

George Washington's great achievement was that he managed to keep something resembling an army in the field for eight years. He commanded two varieties of soldiers: militiamen from the various states, and the men of the Continental Army, so called because they were drawn from all the states and because they were paid (or supposed to be paid) by the Continental Congress. The Continental soldiers served longer periods and therefore became better trained and much more reliable in battle. As the war went on, the Continentals began to take pride in themselves both as professional soldiers and as the truest of patriots. They grew intensely loyal to their tall, somewhat aloof, but always devoted commander.

For his part, Washington was a firm yet fair administrator of military discipline. He was

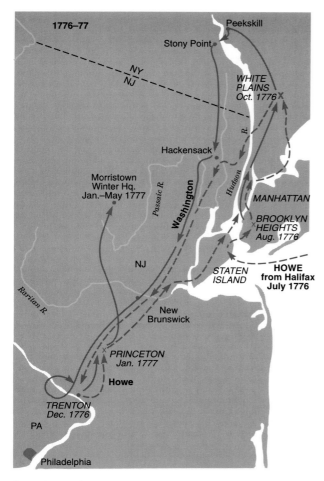

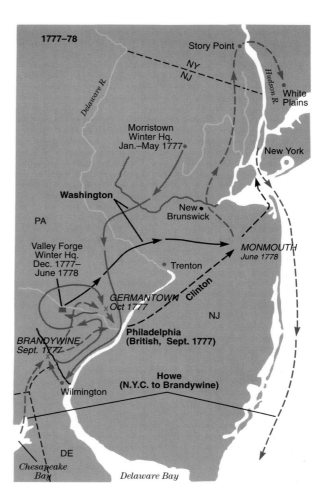

Central campaigns, 1776–1778

deeply committed to his new country, and he spent much of his time dealing with military problems that arose from the weaknesses of the civilian government. He constantly had to plead with the Congress for men, money, and supplies. The Congress, in turn, could and did print paper money, which quickly depreciated, but it had to beg the states to furnish men and supplies. It had no authority to raise taxes.

Fighting in the Middle Colonies

The British pulled out of Boston in March 1776. During the next fifteen months, American forces suffered one defeat after another and lost control of their two largest cities, New York and Philadelphia. The British, having won all these victories, then proceeded to lose an entire army in a confrontation that proved to be a turning point of the war.

In the spring of 1776, the British decided to seize New York as their headquarters. Two brothers, General Sir William Howe and Admiral Richard Howe, were sent in command of an awesome military and naval force, which arrived at New York harbor that summer. The Howes had instructions to discuss peace terms, but they also had 32,000 soldiers and 10,000 seamen to back their words.

When Washington learned about these plans, he ordered the American army, then numbering some 23,000 men, to march to the city's defense. Not only was his army outnumbered, but the great majority were inexperienced militia. Under great pressure from the British, the Americans retreated with heavy losses, first from the Brooklyn end of Long Island, then from Manhattan Island northward to White Plains, and from there across the Hudson River into New Jersey.

Following their first victory on Long Island, the Howe brothers invited the Americans to

LIFE, LIBERTY, AND THE PURSUIT OF HAPPINESS: EIGHT MASSACHUSETTS SOLDIERS

Early in the war, eight Massachusetts soldiers petitioned the provincial congress, the wartime successor of the Massachusetts General Court, for redress of their grievances. Their spelling was somewhat shaky, but they had a firm grip on certain ideological aspects of the Revolution. Addressing their words to the "Jentlemen Representatives of this province," they wrote:

Know dout it is a truth achnowlidged among men that god [has] placd men in greater and Lower Stations in life, and that Inferiours are moraly Bound to obay their Superiours in all their lawfvl Commands, But altho our king is our Superiour, yet his Commands are unlawful. Therefore we are not bound to obay, but are in providence Cald to rise up against Such tiranical usurpations, and our province at this difficult Day is Necessiated to Chuse Representitives and officers to Rule as king over us. To which we Cheerfully Submit in all things lawful or just and Count it our hapiness, but if their laws are greavious to bare, then the agreaved is by the

Same Rule authorized to Rise up in oppisition to Said laws. . . .

Having made their point, they went on to complain about scarcities in camp, even though many men had already gone back to their farms:

[by those men] that Remain Here are much Deuty Required, to which we, animated from a Spirit of Liberty, would Chearfully Submit, provided we had a Sufficient Support from day to day. we many times have drawn Such Roten Stinkin meat that the Smell is Sufficient to make us lothe the Same. . . . their is a large Nomber of men in verious Ragements that Rsents Their treatment with Regard to provision So fare that they have Sworn by the god that made them that, if the[y] Cannot have a Sufficient Support, they will Either Raise a mob and go to the general and Demand provision and obtain it that way, or they will Swing their packs Emediately and go home boldly throu all the Guards.

---

send delegates to a peace conference. Washington doubted that anything would come of it, but both he and the Congress were willing to try. The Congress appointed a geographically balanced negotiating team of John Adams of Massachusetts, Benjamin Franklin of Pennsylvania, and Edward Rutledge of Virginia. The talks broke off almost as soon as they began because the Howes demanded that the Declaration of Independence be rescinded immediately.

By the late fall of 1776, Washington's army had been pushed across New Jersey into Pennsylvania. By then, only about eight thousand men remained under his command; the rest had deserted to their farms, died of disease, or been killed or captured. The Howes had men to spare. They sent an expedition that captured the city of Newport, Rhode Island, early in December. Then, leaving a few garrisons in some New Jersey towns, the brothers settled back to sit out the winter in New York.

Washington was desperate for some sort of victory to revive morale. Most of his men had enlisted only until the end of December, and he faced the prospect of seeing his army dissolve

before his eyes. He decided to risk everything on one bold stroke. On Christmas night, in icy weather, he led 2400 men in boats back across the Delaware River into New Jersey. By eight o'clock the next morning they had marched nine miles to Trenton, where they surprised a large group of Hessians, most of whom were still asleep. They took 900 captives at the cost of only 5 casualties. The victory was so stunning that many of the Americans promptly reenlisted. They were further cheered by another smashing victory at Princeton on January 5. Washington then ordered his little army into winter camp near Morristown in northern New Jersey, where the troops suffered miserably in unusually cold weather.

When spring came, General Howe decided to occupy another major American city. His troops left New York by sea, sailed up the Delaware River, and landed near Philadelphia. Washington's Continentals tried to block the way at Brandywine Creek, but once again the Americans lost the pitched battle. British redcoats occupied Philadelphia in September, and the pleasure-loving General Howe settled back by

The Battlefield of Brandywine. *(Library of Congress)*

his fireside to enjoy the hospitality of the city's Loyalists. A week later, Washington's little army mounted an attack on the major British encampment outside the city at Germantown. At first things went well for the Americans, but patches of dense fog created so much confusion that at one point they were firing on each other. Once again, the British won.

Saratoga and the French Alliance

In the meantime, one of Howe's fellow generals was marching straight into the jaws of disaster. General John Burgoyne had persuaded the high command in London to let him lead a major army down the route of lakes from Canada to Albany, where he intended to link up with Howe's troops coming north from New York City. This strategy aimed at cutting off the New England

colonies, which British authorities regarded as the hotbed of rebellion.

When Burgoyne set out from Canada he did not know that Howe had gone off to Philadelphia. "Gentleman Johnny" Burgoyne also had little idea how to mount an expedition through trackless forest with 4000 British regulars, 3000 Hessians, and some 1400 Indians. He had 138 pieces of artillery, a good supply of wine and fine clothes, camp-following women for his men, his own mistress, and a four-poster bed. The farther he penetrated south of Lake Champlain, the more resistance he met. Local farmers cut trees to slow his progress. His food supplies ran low.

Although he did not know it, American militiamen and Continentals were gathering from all over New York and New England. One skirmish followed another, and every time the two sides clashed, Burgoyne lost several hundred men. The massed Americans finally brought Burgoyne's army to a standstill at Saratoga, New York, and the dashing British general surrendered his battered army on October 17, 1777. The importance of Saratoga was more psychological than military. Americans now had proof that they could defeat British regulars. The real impact of the battle came in London and Paris.

From the start, European governments had watched the conflict in America with mixed feelings. The French and Spanish governments had hoped to see the British humbled. Yet the monarchs of Spain and France were not at all anxious to encourage revolutions, for they had no desire to have ideas about popular government and natural rights spread among their subjects. Within the French government, however, hopes for humiliation of Great Britain eventually won out over fears of revolution.

Even before the French knew the Americans had declared independence, they decided to send aid to them secretly. Early in 1776, the Congress sent Silas Deane as its agent to Paris. When he arrived, Deane received a favorable response, and soon the Americans were importing about 80 percent of their gunpowder from France. A few months later, the Congress sent Benjamin Franklin to help Deane push the French into a formal alliance. But even Franklin's charm failed to move the French government into risking open aid to the Americans. When New York City fell to British forces the French decided not to back a hopeless cause, since to do so would surely bring another war with Great Britain.

For the Americans, victory at Saratoga brought concessions from London and a triumph at the negotiating table in Paris. Lord North's ministry was so shaken that it offered to suspend all laws concerning America passed since 1763. Two years earlier, the Americans probably would have ceased fire on such terms. Now they refused. American agents in Paris used the news of North's offer to prod the French into making an open alliance with the Congress of the United States. The French were now more than willing, for they smelled revenge in the news from Saratoga.

A formal treaty of alliance between France and the United States was concluded in March 1778. The stated aim of the treaty was the independence of the United States. The new nation would be permitted to keep all North American territories conquered from the British. The French and Americans also agreed that in the event of war between France and England, neither ally was to make peace without the consent of the other. When the British government learned about the treaty, it immediately declared war on France. The American war for independence was now transformed into still another European struggle for dominance in North America. In 1779 Spain joined the war as France's ally.

War In the South

The French alliance of 1778 was followed by three years of deep discouragement for the Americans. While the American negotiators were at work in Paris, Washington's Continentals were in winter camp at Valley Forge. There they suffered from cold, hunger, and desertions while General Howe reclined comfortably on his couch in Philadelphia only twenty miles away. In the spring of 1778, Lord North and the king decided to replace Howe with Sir Henry Clinton.

General Clinton turned out to be more imaginative, but even less capable of making up his mind about when and where to attack. Rumors about a French assault on New York City caused Clinton to order British troops to leave Philadelphia, cross New Jersey, and return to New York. Washington's forces pursued them but were unable to prevent their reaching their destination.

Northern campaigns, 1777

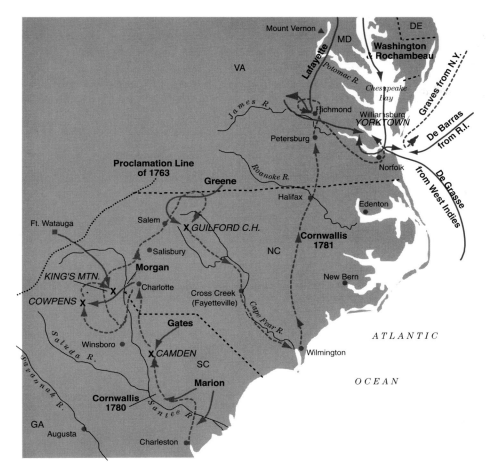

Southern campaigns, 1780–1781

The Americans then camped outside the British-occupied city, and there the two armies sat facing each other for three long years.

That same summer of 1778, the British high command in London decided to shift major military efforts to the southern colonies. They did this because they thought most people in the South remained loyal. They were wrong, but a British expedition captured Savannah at the end of that year. After months of hesitation, Clinton combined all his forces for a major assault on Charles Town, South Carolina. There the British won their greatest victory of the war. They captured not only the city but the entire force of American defenders, some 5500 men. Thoroughly satisfied, Clinton retired to New York, leaving General Lord Cornwallis in charge of mopping up the Carolinas.

At first Cornwallis was successful. At Camden, South Carolina, he smashed the American forces. As his army advanced into North Car-

olina, however, he was hit by a series of reverses. Several times his troops were outfought by southern militiamen and by Continentals commanded by Washington's ablest general, Nathaniel Greene of Rhode Island. Cornwallis concluded that he might do better by moving north into Virginia. Greene elected not to pursue him, but to mop up the remaining British units farther south.

Cornwallis then made the fateful mistake of leading his army out onto the peninsula between the James and the York rivers. His troops camped at Yorktown, not many miles from the original English settlement at Jamestown.

Very suddenly, in 1781, a combination of good luck and well-timed decisions favored the American cause. A major French army had assembled at Newport, Rhode Island. Two French fleets, one from Newport and the other from the West Indies, appeared within sight of the Yorktown peninsula. Upon learning of Cornwallis's exposed position,

Washington ordered his army to march for Virginia from outside New York City. On the peninsula the combined French and American armies laid siege to Cornwallis's seven thousand British regulars.

In New York, Clinton decided to save the situation by sending a fleet of warships to the York River. Usually the British navy ruled the seas, but for just a moment the British fleet was outnumbered and outgunned. The jaws of the trap closed rapidly. For the first time, the British could not escape by sea. On land, they were badly outnumbered. Cut off from reinforcements, Cornwallis agreed to have his men lay down their arms, but to French officers rather than to the despised Americans. As the redcoats marched forward to stack their arms, the British army band played a popular song. "The World Turned Upside Down."

The world was. When Lord North heard of the surrender at Yorktown he cried out again and again, "Oh God! It is all over." He resigned to make way for a ministry that could make peace with an independent American republic.

The Treaty of Paris

Negotiating a peace treaty proved to be a delicate and difficult business. Four nations were involved—the United States, Great Britain, France, and Spain—and each had different interests. Spain had no formal ties with the United States and indeed was hostile to the new nation's hopes for independence and a western boundary on the Mississippi River. The French-American treaty of 1778 required the Americans to consult with the French and obtain their consent before signing any treaty with Great Britain.

One of the American negotiators, John Jay of New York, described France's position very accurately: "We can depend upon the French only to see that we are separated from England, but it is not in their interest that we should become a great and formidable people, and therefore they will not help us to become so."

The Congress sent an extremely able team of negotiators to Paris. John Jay, Benjamin Franklin, and John Adams soon found out that the French were secretly encouraging the English to insist on a boundary well to the east of the Mississippi. They decided to ignore the French for the moment and to deal directly with the British delegation. The British and Americans

worked out a tentative agreement that included a western boundary at the Mississippi and the surrender of American claims to Canada.

By agreeing to this western boundary, the British hoped to drive a wedge between the Americans and the French. The Americans laid this agreement before the French as an accomplished fact. Vergennes, the French foreign minister, was greatly annoyed by this behind-the-back dealing, but Franklin managed to soothe him and even to extract another fat loan for the United States.

The Treaty of Paris between the United States and Great Britain was signed in September 1783 and ratified in Philadelphia in January 1784. Britain formally acknowledged American independence. The boundaries of the new nation were established at Florida in the south, the Mississippi in the west, and a border with Canada much like the present one. The British recognized American fishing rights off Newfoundland.

North America in 1783

The Americans agreed that private British creditors would be free to collect any debts owed by citizens of the United States. Finally, the Congress was to "earnestly recommend" to the various states that they return property taken from Loyalists. By a separate treaty, the British granted Florida back to Spain.

The treaty was highly favorable to the United States. George Washington watched the last British troops board their transports in New York harbor, bade farewell to his assembled officers, and then rode off to present to the Congress his resignation as commander in chief. He told the assembly he was leaving "all the employments of public life."

SOCIAL CHANGES

Historians have often asked an obvious question about the American Revolution. How much change did it produce in American society? We usually think of revolutions as being periods of great and rapid social change. Certainly the French Revolution of 1789 and the more recent Russian and Chinese revolutions produced profound changes in those societies. Was the American Revolution, in this sense, really revolutionary? The answer to this apparently simple question is, in fact, a complicated one.

It is clear that the American Revolution produced considerably less social change that almost any major modern revolution. The main reason for this is obvious. A great deal of change had already taken place during the century before the Revolution. The great majority of white people already had some property and good hopes of getting more. So there were few demands for taking property from the wealthy. There was no widespread cry for freedom of religious worship, because that freedom already existed. There were no calls for changing the economic system, because that system seemed to be working rather well. By and large, Americans were well off, and prosperous people do not like to rock the foundations of their prosperity.

Slavery

One group of Americans had no share in this freedom and prosperity. Black slaves and slavery itself stood out as the one great exception to

the principles of the ⟨...⟩ war itself changed th⟨...⟩ number of slaves, for s⟨...⟩ the armed forces of bo⟨...⟩ their freedom by doi⟨...⟩ cruited a battalion of ⟨...⟩ men served in the tiny ⟨...⟩ privateering vessels ha⟨...⟩ the South, however, m⟨...⟩ the idea of placing fire⟨...⟩ tentially dangerous bla⟨...⟩ blacks.

Thousands of slaves were carried off by the British when they left Georgia and South Carolina. Some of them were taken to freedom in Nova Scotia and eventually to Sierre Leone in Africa. Others, however, were transported to the West Indies, where they remained slaves. For the great majority of American blacks, though, the war meant continued toil in the fields.

Yet the ideas of the Revolution brought into question the entire institution of slavery, for it was obvious to many white Americans that their claims about "liberty" and the rights of "all men" meant that holding slaves was wrong. There were major barriers to freeing the slaves. First, slaves were property, and for years white Americans had argued that no government could deprive people of their property without their consent. In this case, one principle of the Revolution, the owner's natural right of property, collided directly with another, the slave's natural right of liberty.

Second, many white Americans thought that freed slaves would become a drain on society, a hostile group of people who would either rob and kill or starve. And many whites simply did not want to live with free blacks; they would have been happy to see them free if they would somehow go away. Many slave owners opposed emancipation simply because they were profiting from slave labor.

The net result of these feelings was that some states took steps toward abolishing slavery and others did not. From Pennsylvania northward, where there were few slaves, it was relatively easy to bring the practice to an end. In Massachusetts, court decisions found that slavery violated that state constitution's preamble that asserted "all men are born free and equal."

Elsewhere in the North, the states passed gradual emancipation laws. These acts did not abolish slavery outright; rather, they provided that slaves born after passage of the act would a certain age, such as twenty-one ... ght. Many of the laws were written ... effect on July 4. That date itself ... to the force of revolutionary principles. ... 02 all northern states had provided for the ... adual end of slavery.

In the southern states, the principles were the same but the number of slaves was much greater. In Virginia and Maryland, slavery was less profitable than farther south, and in those two states there was much discussion about getting rid of it. The major difficulty was that most whites wanted to get rid of blacks if they were freed, and there was no realistic way of doing this. A number of masters went ahead and privately freed some or all of their slaves. In doing so they often cited the principles of the revolution, but just as frequently they referred to principles of Christian brotherhood. In many cases they referred to both. In those states there had always been free blacks, but now their numbers increased considerably.

Farther south there was little discussion and no action. In South Carolina and Georgia, slavery was highly profitable and slaves were far more numerous in proportion to the white population. Thus white Americans succeeded in living up to their principles where it was easy to do so, but failed where it was difficult. The author of the Declaration of Independence continued to own slaves.

The revolution had still another important impact on the pattern of American slavery. The coming of the war brought the importation of slaves from Africa to a halt. Several factors worked to make this change nearly permanent. A majority of white Americans had begun to recognize the outrageous cruelty and injustice of the Atlantic slave trade. Slaves were in great demand only in South Carolina and Georgia; elsewhere in the South, planters had more slaves than they could use. And most whites also thought there was a surplus of black people. They feared and disliked the ones they already had, whether slave or free, and they wanted no more. The great majority of white Americans wanted the new nation to be a white man's country.

Churches, Property, and Women

The Revolution gave Americans a chance to make certain changes in the relationship between church and state. In New York and the southern states, the established church lost its privileged position. Yet most states continued to tax their citizens for the support of the churches. Usually the taxpayer could name the church he wanted to support. The Congregational churches in Massachusetts and Connecticut kept certain special privileges until the nineteenth century. Only Virginia provided for the complete separation of church and state. Virginia's advanced position was due largely to Thomas Jefferson, James Madison, and Baptists who refused to pay taxes for a state-supported church.

Although the principles of the American Revolution strongly supported the idea of private property, the war itself resulted in a slightly more equal distribution of property among white Americans. We do not know exactly how great this change actually was. Widespread printing of paper money resulted in its depreciation, a process that favored poorer people who borrowed money, because they were able to repay their debts with inflated currency. Many wealthy merchants suffered great losses during the war. Some farmers profited by selling food supplies to one army or the other and sometimes to both. Others lost most of what they had. The seizure of Loyalist lands by the states resulted in somewhat broader landholding, since the states usually sold these lands at public auction. However, many of these estates were purchased by large speculators who then made money by reselling to small farmers. The Revolution thus resulted in somewhat wider possession of land—an unexpected outcome that supported a growing conviction among Americans that ownership of land gave them special virtues.

One important group of Americans may have benefited from the Revolution, but it is very hard to say how widely and how much. Many white women were left completely in charge of the family farm for the first time in their lives. With their husbands in the army they had to tackle heavy jobs that they had never done before, such as plowing. Perhaps more important, they had to take responsibility for crucial farming decisions, such as when to plant and when to begin harvesting. Thus the Revolution thrust on many women a degree of independence they had never before experienced. Though their legal and political rights remained untouched by the Revolution, these experiences on the part of tens of thousands of American women may have had subtle but important effects not only on the wives themselves but on their daughters.

In addition, a much smaller number of women actually accompanied their husbands and boyfriends as part of the Continental Army. They were usually poor, but these "camp followers" were not all prostitutes. Many of them received army rations. In return they cooked, washed and mended, cared for the sick and wounded, and even helped bury the dead. Though Washington never really liked these arrangements, he put up with them for fear that if he threw the women out of his army, many of the men would follow them. All told, it is estimated that about one-sixteenth of the patriot army was female. Many of them suffered greatly, like the soldiers, but few of them could have been unaffected by the travel and widening of horizons that such an experience involved.

The Challenges Ahead

The winning of independence and the establishment of new governments caused Americans to examine their society more closely than ever before. By and large, they liked what they saw. Yet there were obvious flaws. Especially in the northern states, efforts were made to make punishments for crime more humane. Many states ended the practice of putting debtors in jail until they had paid their debts. New private schools and colleges were established because Americans thought they needed better educated citizens for the new republic. These and other reforms were stimulated by the Revolution. Yet they probably would have been undertaken even without it. Most of the constructive energies of the nation's leaders were going into problems of government. Independence raised pressing political problems that had somehow to be solved. It was in the realm of politics that the American Revolution turned out to be truly revolutionary.

SUMMARY

The American Revolution, the war for independence, was a long process. It was also the first major, successful rebellion by overseas Europeans against a mother country. Other events also made this revolution distinct. One was that armed rebellion began before formal independence was declared. When the Second Continental Congress met in May 1775, there were still hopes for settling the dispute, both in the colonies and in England. Most Americans, including those at the Congress, were still loyal to King George, if not to his ministers. Some continued that loyalty and never agreed to the idea of independence. Many of these Loyalists left the colonies at some point during the long struggle, so that the rebels—or patriots, as they called themselves—had the advantage of controlling the American countryside.

It was Thomas Paine's widely read pamphlet *Common Sense* that pushed the colonists past the point of no return. About a year after the fighting began, the Congress began opening American ports to commerce with all nations except Britain, told the colonies to form state governments, and declared American independence. The Declaration of Independence, a masterpiece of political writing to this day, embodied the principles on which the colonists based their revolt. But masterful as the declaration was, it did not solve the rebels' military and financial problems. The British had trained men, money, and supplies; the colonists did not.

The British navy controlled the seas; the Americans had just a few small ships. And American militiamen were ordinary citizens who left their farms to fight.

Despite all these problems—and military defeats—Washington managed to keep something resembling an army in the field for eight years. The American victory over the British at Saratoga in New York in the autumn of 1777 brought a major advantage: a formal alliance with the French, who up to then had kept their support secret.

As the war went on, the scene of the fighting shifted from New England to the Middle Colonies and then to the South. The British moved their forces by sea in hopes of winning a decisive victory. In 1781 Cornwallis, in command of the British forces in the South, made the mistake of marching his army to Yorktown, Virginia, located on a peninsula. The Americans, with the help of the French, took advantage of the momentary British vulnerability to force a surrender that ended the war by cutting Cornwallis off on land and on sea.

Four nations were involved in the Treaty of Paris, which ended the war—the United States, Britain, France, and Spain. Signed in 1783, that treaty was highly favorable to the United States. Its two most important provisions were that Great Britain recognized American independence, and that the new nation's western boundary was to be the Mississippi River.

In military and political terms, the American Revolution was indeed revolutionary. But in social and economic terms, change was more limited. More than half the newly independent states began the gradual abolition of slavery. Yet slavery continued in the southern areas where it was most profitable, although the Atlantic slave trade nearly ended. The lives of a great many American women were drastically changed by the war, though the long-term effects of their experiences are hard to gauge.

Tens of thousands of women had to supervise farms for the first time in their lives. Thousands of others served with the patriot armies. The idea of established churches began to fade, although in a few states citizens still paid taxes for church support. Land ownership was somewhat broadened as lands taken from the Loyalists were redistributed. But the economic system remained the same. Americans were mainly well off and were conscious of their country as a land of opportunity.

TIME LINE

1775	Battle of Bunker Hill
1775	Second Continental Congress justifies taking up arms
1775	Colonial troops fail to take Quebec and Canada
1776	Paine anonymously publishes *Common Sense*
1776	British evacuate troops from Boston
1776	Howes capture New York City
1776	Adoption of Declaration of Independence
1776–1777	Washington recrosses Delaware and wins two victories
1777	American army suffers through winter at Morristown
1777	Burgoyne surrenders a British army at Saratoga
1777	British win two battles and occupy Philadelphia
1778	Americans seal formal alliance with France
1779	Spain declares war on great Britain
1780	Massachusetts and Pennsylvania abolish slavery
1780	British capture Charles Town and an American army
1780–1781	Shifting warfare in the Carolinas
1781	Cornwallis surrenders to French and Americans at Yorktown
1782	Lord North resigns and peace talks begin
1783	Treaty of Paris signed
1783	Loyalists leave New York City

Suggested Readings

C. Becker, *The Declaration of Independence* (1922), offers now-outmoded but brilliant conclusions about that document's intellectual origins; his discussion of its style remains unsurpassed, as does his own style. See also J. Marston, *King and Congress: The Transfer of Political Legitimacy, 1774–1776* (1987). G. Wood, *The Creation of the American Republic, 1776–1787* (1969), is central to an understanding of the political philosophies of the founders. The extraordinarily influential pamphlet *Common Sense* by Tom Paine (1776) is available in many editions. For the continuing development of political events, the Main book cited in Chapter 5 is pertinent, along with his *The Sovereign States, 1775–1783* (1973). In fact, many of the works cited in Chapter 5 are relevant to the material discussed in Chapter 6. B. Graymont, *The Iroquois in the American Revolution* (1972), tells

how British and Americans both abandoned the Iroquois. The standard account on African Americans is B. Quarles, *The Negro in the American Revolution* (1967). Economic change is discussed in T. Doerilinger, *A Vigorous Spirit of Enterprise: Merchants and Economic Development in Revolutionary Philadelphia* (1986).

For slavery in this period: D. MacLeod, *Slavery, Race and the American Revolution* (1972); W. Jordan, *White over Black: American Attitudes toward the Negro, 1550–1812* (1968). See also D. Davis, *The Problem of Slavery in the Age of Revolution, 1770–1823* (1975); D. Robinson, *Slavery in the Structure of American Politics, 1765–1820* (1971); and R. McColley, *Slavery and Jeffersonian Virginia* (1964).

There are several studies on the American opponents of the Revolution: W. Nelson, *The American Tory* (1961); W. Brown, *The Good Americans: The Loyalists in the American Revolution* (1969); and

R. Calhoun, *The Loyalists in Revolutionary America* (1973). J. Ferling, *The Loyalist Mind: Joseph Galloway and the American Revolution* (1977); 5. Skemp, *William Franklin: A Man in the Middle* (1990); and B. Bailyn, *The Ordeal of Thomas Hutchinson* (1974), analyze three important loyalists. M. Norton, *The British-Americans: The Loyalist Exiles in England, 1774-1789* (1975), is a fine study. Finally, the four essays in E. Wright (ed.), *A Tug of Loyalties: Anglo-American Relations, 1765–1785* (1975), compare the mind-sets of the rebels and Loyalists.

Recently, historians have become interested in the relationship between armies and the larger societies from which they are drawn. See D. Higgenbotharn, *The War of American Independence: Military Attitudes, Policies, and Practices, 1763–1789* (1971); J. Martin and M. Lender, *A Respectable Army: The Military Origins of the Republic, 1763–1789* (1971); L. Cress, *Citizens in Arms: The Army and Militia in American Society to the War of 1812* (1982); R.

Wright, *The Continental Army* (1983); C. Royster, *A Revolutionary People at War: The Continental Army and American Character, 1775–1783* (1979); and E. Carp, *To Starve the Army at Pleasure: Continental Army Administration and American Political Culture, 1775–1783* (1984).

Naval action during the Revolution is explained in S. Morison, *John Paul Jones: A Sailor's Biography* (1959). G. Sheer (ed.), *Private Yankee Doodle* (1962), is an interesting memoir by a common soldier. The best account of the central American figure who lost so many battles but won the war is J. Flexnor, *George Washington in the American Revolution, 1775–1783* (1968). An important aspect of the conflict is dealt with by J. Dull in *A Diplomatic History of the American Revolution* (1985).

For women's status and roles in revolutionary America, see M. Norton, *Liberty's Daughters* (1980); and L. Kerber, *Women of the Republic* (1980).

Portrait of John Adams. *(Library of Congress)*

CHAPTER 7

PROBLEMS OF GOVERNMENT

In many ways the American revolutionaries were lucky when it came to dealing with problems of government. The idea of natural rights gave them a very clear idea of how governments ought to work. They already shared strong ideas about such matters as representation, taxation, and the dangers of standing armies, courts without juries, and public officials over whom they had no control. And the American rebels had one thing most other revolutionaries lacked. They already possessed certain institutions that embodied their ideas about government. These institutions—notably the courts and representative assemblies—provided a foundation for carrying on the work of change. No other single fact does more to explain the character of the American Revolution.

Yet old institutions and practices can create problems as well. Americans were accustomed to having their forms of government set down in writing. The governments of the colonies had been based on royal charters issued to a joint-stock company, to proprietors, or to an individual colony. Once the king had been rejected, the question arose as to who should write and issue new frames of government. Theory suggested that "the people" should draw up the fundamental framework, but here there were obvious difficulties. Exactly how did "the people" go about drafting and approving a charter of government, a constitution? Given their experience with Great Britain, Americans were anxious to write down not only what their governments could do, but what they could not do.

A related problem was the relationship of the various states. At first the Continental Congress called them the United Colonies and then the United States, but it was not at all clear what the "United States" actually was—or were. If the "United States" was to be anything more than a temporary alliance, there had to be some agreement about what it could and could not do.

As the war ended, the touchiest question remained the same one that had dominated politics in the 1760s: taxation. Other problems also came to the surface. A major one was how to deal with the vast territory won in the West. Another was the relationships of the new country (or thirteen countries) with foreign powers; Spain and Britain remained hostile, and France not overly friendly to American interests. Could Americans solve these problems and still remain faithful to the principles of the Revolution? In the modern world, most former colonies have ended up as dictatorships. Thanks to their own historical experience, however, Americans were able to find another way.

THE STATE CONSTITUTIONS

In 1776 the states were governed by provincial congresses composed mostly of men who had served in the colonial assemblies. Indeed, at first the old assemblies simply transformed themselves into the governing bodies of the new states. Everyone assumed that more permanent arrangements needed to be made and written down in a state constitution. Despite wartime difficulties, every state adopted a written document of fundamental law long before the war ended.

Power to the Legislatures

For the most part, the new constitutions continued old forms and practices. Rhode Island and Connecticut simply kept their old charters after eliminating references to Great Britain and the king. All the states retained their assemblies. Only Pennsylvania had lacked a governor's council to serve as the upper house of the legislature, and Pennsylvania was the only state to adopt a unicameral legislature; all the other states provided for two houses.

But they made important changes in the upper one. Rather than being appointed by the governor, the upper houses were now elected by the people or by the lower house. In addition, the upper houses lost their role of advising the governor and serving as the high court. As things turned out, the members tended to be the same sort of people who sat in the lower house.

Most of the new constitutions also broadened the suffrage somewhat by lowering property requirements for voting. Yet Americans did not abandon the old idea that a man ought to possess at least some property in order to vote, and they continued the practice of having higher qualifications for those seeking public office. In contrast with Europe, however, the suffrage was so broad that the United States seemed really to be ruled by the people.

Fundamental Power of the People

In most states, the revolutionary provincial congresses drew up and adopted new constitutions without consulting the voters. Massachusetts, however, set a different example that was later followed by the others when they rewrote their basic law, and by the Republic itself when the Great Convention of 1787 wrote the fundamental law of the entire nation. This new procedure emphasized one of the American Revolution's most important contributions to modern democratic government—the idea that constitutions are derived directly from the will of the people.

In Massachusetts, when the provincial congress asked the towns for power to draw up the new state constitution, the majority agreed but Concord objected. The Concord town meeting asked: If the provincial legislature makes the constitution, what is to prevent it from unmaking it? If the fundamental law has no standing above ordinary legislation, what will protect our liberties? Concord demanded that a special "Convention . . . be immediately Chosen, to form & establish a Constitution."

The Massachusetts provincial government ignored Concord's proposal and drafted a new constitution. But the Concord notion spread, and when the provincial congress presented its work to the people in 1778, they rejected it by a five-to-one majority. Recognizing that the principal objection to the constitution was its authorship, the provincial congress voted in June 1779 to follow the Concord idea. By March 1780, under the leadership of John Adams, a specially elected convention completed a new framework of government, which the voters approved in June.

Bill of Rights

Most state constitutions set forth at the outset a "bill" or "declaration" of "unalienable" or "natural" or "inherent" rights. These rights included "acquiring, possessing, and protecting property"; freedom of worship, speech, and assembly; moderate bail, prompt hearings, trial by jury, and punishment to fit the crime; and protection from general search warrants and from liability to serve in, or support, standing armies.

Above all, "when any government shall be found inadequate or contrary to [the people's wishes] a majority of the community hath an indubitable, unalienable and indefeasible right to reform, alter or abolish it." To reduce the likelihood of revolutions, elections must be "free, . . . frequent, certain, and regular." And in such elections, all "men having sufficient evidence to permanent common interest with, and attachment to the community, have the right of suffrage."

For some time conservatives found it easy enough to live with these generalizations. Yet the "bills of rights" gave the people, in the language of the times, "a standing law to live by." Without the promise of a bill of rights they almost certainly would have rejected the new federal constitution of 1787. Eventually, reformers used the liberal language of these bills to abolish imprisonment for debt, provide free schools, prohibit the use of public funds for favored religious sects, promote free expression in the press, reform the courts, improve the jails, liberalize qualifications for officeholding, and broaden the franchise.

THE ARTICLES OF CONFEDERATION

It took the Second Continental Congress more than two years to draft an instrument that its members would agree to submit to the states. John Dickinson of Pennsylvania, the principal author of the new document, tried to establish a national government without weakening the individual commonwealths. Dickinson's name for his government, "a firm league of friendship,"

ADAMS ON GOVERNMENT

Even before the Declaration of Independence, John Adams was thinking about long-range plans for a new government. His sense of optimism is clear in this letter of January 1776:

As politics is the art of securing human happiness, and the prosperity of societies depends upon the constitution of government under which they live, there cannot be a more agreeable employment to a benevolent mind than the study of the best kinds of government.

It has been the will of Heaven that we should be thrown into existence at a period when the greatest philosophers and lawgivers of antiquity would have wished to live. A period when a coincidence of circumstances without example, has afforded to thirteen Colonies, at once, an opportunity of beginning government anew from the foundation, and building as they choose. How few of the human race have ever had any opportunity of choosing a system of government for themselves and their children! How few have ever had any thing more of choice in government than in climate! These Colonies have now their election; and it is much to be wished that it may not prove to be like a prize in the hands of a man who has no heart to improve it.

Portrait of John Adams, the second president of the United States of America. *(Library of Congress)*

strongly suggested that where conflict of authority arose, the states, not the new central government, would triumph. The Congress was aware of defects in its proposal. In its request to the states for formal approval, it apologized for the "uncommon embarrassment and delay" in framing the document.

Strengths and Weaknesses

Under the proposed Articles of Confederation, each state elected and paid the salaries of its delegates and reserved the right to recall them. In the single-chamber legislature voting was to be by state. Each state had only one vote, no matter what its population and wealth or how many delegates it sent. Important legislation required a two-thirds majority, or nine of the thirteen states, a margin made more difficult to reach by the provision nullifying a state's vote if its delegates were evenly split. The administration of laws was made difficult by the provision making the executive a "committee of the states" consisting of one delegate from each state. The weakest link of all was that the Articles could be amended only with the *unanimous* consent of the states.

Yet the Articles gave the new central government considerable powers. It could make war and treaties of alliance and of peace. It could establish the amounts of men and money the states should provide for national purposes. It could settle disputes between states, admit new ones, borrow money, set standards for coins and weights and measures, establish a postal service, deal with Indians, appoint naval and military officers, and otherwise support national armed forces. But the new government was denied the power of levying taxes, raising troops, and regulating commerce, all of which were basic to sovereignty.

In retrospect it is clear that the Articles proposed a very new kind of government. They divided the fundamental *powers* of government between two *levels* of government. Many people had long thought such an arrangement impossible. Most people had previously assumed that the supreme or sovereign power of any government could not be shared. Out of wartime necessity, the Congress was proposing that sovereignty be divided between the states and the national government. For this reason, they naturally described their union as a *confederation*, a term that literally means "with trust."

The Problem of Land Claims

The framers of the Articles, having made every concession they could to the states' freedom of action, expected quick approval by the state governments. One last concession to Virginia, however, aroused the suspicions of Maryland and other "landless" states and delayed ratification for almost four years. This concession was that "no state should be deprived of territory for the benefit of the United States."

Seven "landed" states, on the basis of their original charters or on other grounds, had laid claim to territory extending either to the Ohio or Mississippi rivers or all the way to the Pacific Ocean. By the Quebec Act of 1774, Britain had overridden these claims. Maryland, a state without claims to western lands, now argued that since the Revolutionary War was a common effort, the territories claimed by the landed states should be "considered as common property." New Jersey and Delaware agreed with Maryland.

As the costs of the war mounted, the landless states became alarmed at the high taxes they would be forced to levy. The landed states would be able to pay their costs out of land sales. The landless states were also troubled by the probable growth in population and power of the landed ones. Their own people, they said, would be lured by low taxes to the western territories of the landed states, making such states too influential in any central government. Speculators added their voices to those of their representatives. Before the Revolution, these speculators had purchased millions of acres from Indians in areas claimed especially by Virginia. If Virginia's claims were allowed, their own would not be.

The deadlock over ratification of the Articles lasted until February 1780, when New York, a "landed" state, proposed to offer its lands to Congress to cement "the federal alliance." Connecticut followed suit. When Virginia at last yielded in January 1781, Maryland withdrew its objections. In February, Congress named March 1 as the day to proclaim the start of the new government. The Second Continental Congress then became the formal ruling body of "The United States of America."

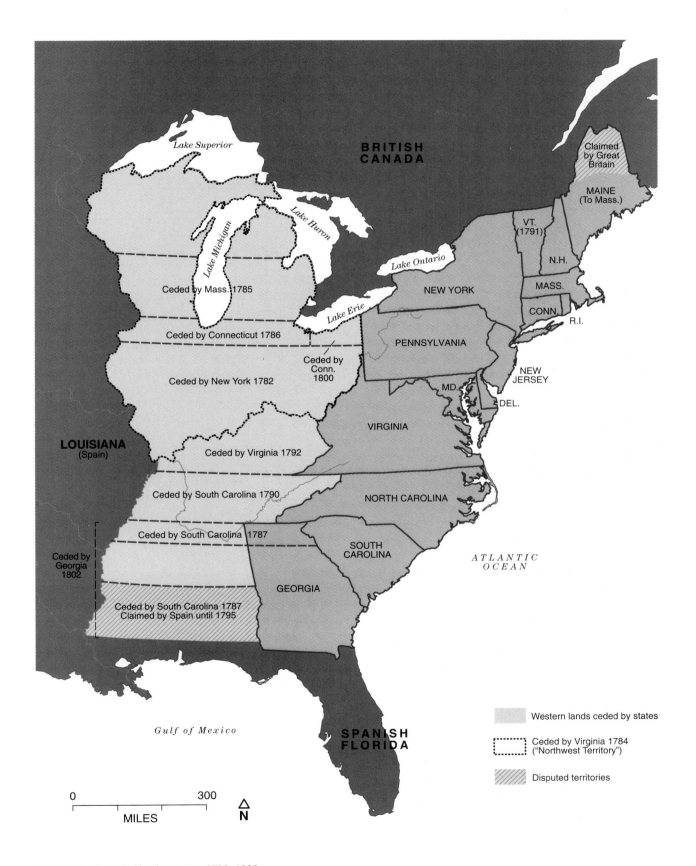

Western lands ceded by the states, 1782–1802

Foreign Affairs

At the close of the Revolution, an Englishman predicted that the Americans would be "a disunited people till the end of time, suspicious and distrustful of each other . . . divided and subdivided into little commonwealths or principalities . . . with no center of union and no common interest." In 1783 there was real justification for such a view. For several months, Congress lacked enough members to form a quorum. It proved impossible to gather enough delegates to ratify the peace treaty before the specified six-month time limit ran out; as it turned out, the British permitted the treaty to go into effect two months late. Charles Thomson, the "secretary" of Congress, admitted that "a government without a visible head must appear a strange phenomenon to European politicians."

According to the peace treaty, the British were to surrender their military and fur-trading posts in the Northwest with "all convenient speed." But the British held onto the posts in order to protect the rich Canadian fur trade until, as they hoped, the new nation collapsed. They stirred up Indians against American settlers, and they used force to deny Americans use of the Great Lakes.

Spain, an ally of France in the Revolutionary War, proved to be as much an enemy to the Americans as Britain. In 1783 the Spanish had received East and West Florida from the British. They established forts there and proceeded to make treaties with the Indians of the region. The treaties obligated the Indians to join in the harassment of American settlers. Congress was unable to force Spain to stop, and this weakness cost it support in the South and Southwest, just as weakness against the British angered Americans in the Northwest.

British and Spanish stubbornness over the West was hardened by American failures on other international issues. The peace treaty, for example, declared that no legal barriers should prevent creditors on either side from collecting old debts. Actually the great bulk of the debts were owed by the former colonists. Although Congress urged the new states to honor the treaty provision, it had no power to prevent their passing laws to frustrate collection. Not until 1802 did the United States settle private debts incurred by Americans before the Revolution by agreeing to pay the sum of £600,000 to British creditors.

In accordance with the terms of the peace treaty, Congress also made "earnest recommendation" to the states to restore confiscated property to former Loyalist owners. Most states chose to ignore this recommendation; even after the war, patriots continued to confiscate Loyalist lands without being punished by the courts.

Financial Problems

With no power to levy taxes, Congress had to face its problems without a sound financial base. With no money to pay the troops, Congress was physically menaced by its own army. Sharing the almost universal lack of confidence in the government, several units of the army refused to disband without being paid. In June 1783, told that the Philadelphia militia would not raise a single musket against mutinous Pennsylvania regiments and having no force of their own to use, the few delegates in attendance removed themselves to the hamlet of Princeton, New Jersey. One Pennsylvania officer called Congress "a jest."

Many other claims arising from the war poured in. There was the back interest, not to speak of the principal, to be paid on the public debt. Robert Morris, named secretary of finance in 1781, urged Congress to establish a national tariff so that it would no longer have to beg states for funds. He also proposed a land tax, a poll tax, and an excise tax on distilled liquors. But the delegates refused all these proposals. When Congress in 1782 requested $10 million from the states for the next year, it received less than $1.5 million.

When Morris finally left his post in 1784, the Treasury was empty as usual. Yet his efforts had not been wholly in vain. In 1781, at his suggestion, Congress chartered the Bank of North America, the first commercial bank in the nation. It was to be located in Philadelphia. The bank eventually lent millions to the government and saw it through some critical situations. But most of the bank's business was with private businessmen. Like other American institutions under the Confederation, this bank—and others modeled after it in New York and Massachusetts in 1784—performed more effectively than the central government.

Congress and the Private Economy

There were other postwar economic problems. American shipowners were especially hard hit by

The word *logrolling* is an almost perfect example of the way the meaning of words can reflect the workings of American history. Originally, *logrolling* meant something rather simple. It came into use when the earliest settlers, both European and African, had to cut down trees in the heavily forested lands along the Atlantic coast. These settles cut wood for several purposes: for fuel, for housing, for export, for shipbuilding, and (in many cases) to get it out of the way so they could grow crops. Moving trees that had been cut down required a great deal of power, and no elephants or bulldozers were available. So the logs had to be rolled by people in groups. Since logrolling always took place on one person's property, with the cooperation of others who did not own that land, the job and the term always suggested that services were being exchanged: "If you'll roll my log, I'll roll yours." The same feeling eventually spilled over into American politics. In the national Congress and in the state legislatures, *logrolling* came to describe exactly the same ethic that the original effort had: "You help me with mine, I'll help you with yours. I'll vote for your favorite bill if you'll vote for mine."

the loss of their favored trading position with Britain and the British West Indies. When the Americans tried to get Britain to reopen the West Indian trade to American ships, they were laughed out of court. The loss of British trade was only partially offset by the new trade opened with China in 1784 and by increased trade with France and other European countries.

American importers grew as discontented as American shipowners. Just after the war, importers had a taste of prosperity when the former colonists went on a buying splurge. But the market for luxuries was small, and the splurge was quickly over. American manufacturers and artisans, who had the American market for coarse goods largely to themselves during the war, also suffered from the foreign competition. They demanded protective tariffs to keep foreign goods out and subsidies to support their own industrial expansion—neither of which Congress could provide.

There was a brighter side. Most Americans were subsistence farmers who did not depend on Congress for their well-being. Even the loudest critics of Congress often found ways to help themselves. Philadelphia, New York, and Baltimore merchants profited from illegal West Indian trade. Public creditors, though unpaid by Congress, apparently still had enough money to sponsor new business ventures. Immediately following the war there was unprecedented activity in river and road improvements, house building, land transactions, and banking. The resumption of immigration from the British Isles and from Europe also helped the basic soundness of the economy.

Congress and the Frontier

In writings about American history, *frontier* usually describes the West in an early phase of its development. But this use of the word ignores the opening of the northern frontier of Vermont, New Hampshire, and Maine.

Vermont was the last part of the northern frontier to be entered by white settlers. Both New York and New Hampshire claimed the territory. After Ethan Allen's victory for the rebel states at Fort Ticonderoga in 1775, he and his brother Levi tried to get the governor of Canada to guarantee Vermont's independence in exchange for neutrality in the war. Failing in this effort, the Allens set up an independent government in 1777, when about 30,000 persons had settled in Vermont. Not until 1791 did Vermont become a state—the fourteenth.

Far to the southwest, other adventurers were staking out land for independent settlements. During the 1770s, James Robertson and John Sevier, two Virginia speculators, led settlers into the region of the Watauga and Holston rivers. In 1784, when North Carolina ceded its claims in this region to Congress, the Wataugans, now 10,000 strong and aware that Congress could do nothing for them that they could not do better themselves, set up the independent state of Franklin. Eventually, however, Franklin was absorbed into the sixteenth state, Tennessee.

Much the same pattern occurred beyond the Virginia mountains in the regions that became Kentucky in 1792. It was a pattern repeated in many frontier areas where settlement outran the reach of eastern governments. In the long run, what was most striking was the ease with which these little, supposedly independent "republics" were absorbed into the larger one. The key to the matter was, of course, that the federal union was itself, from the beginning, a union of little republics.

The Northwest Ordinance

Settlement of the vast area northwest of the Ohio River was somewhat more orderly, partly because of the New England tradition of controlled settlement and partly because of Thomas Jefferson's liking for planning. Jefferson wrote much of the Northwest Ordinance of 1785, which set the basic pattern. It established the crucial principle that the settled portions of the West would be admitted to the Union on an equal basis with the original provinces. Jefferson's original ordinance was modified two years later by the addition of provisions for the transition from organized territories to full-fledged states.

This Northwest Ordinance of 1787 was probably the Confederation Congress's most important piece of legislation. Under it, the Northwest Territory became a single unit with a governor appointed by Congress. When five thousand free adult male inhabitants had settled in the territory, those men owning at least fifty acres were to elect a territorial legislature whose acts would be subject only to the governor's veto. The voters would also send a nonvoting delegate to Congress. No less than three and no more than five states were to be carved out of the territory. The boundaries of three future states were laid out. When a potential state had sixty thousand free inhabitants, it was to be admitted to the Union on an equal footing with the original states. The ordinance also prohibited slavery in the territory and in all the states to be carved from it.

Following adoption of the ordinance, there was a rush of settlement. The Ohio Company sent out a small group of pioneers and established the village of Marietta at the junction of the Ohio and Muskingum rivers. A second group, sent out by a New Jersey speculator, laid the foundations of Cincinnati in 1788. Eight years later, Moses Cleaveland led a band of pioneers to build a town on the shores of Lake Erie.

Shays's Rebellion

Apart from the Northwest Ordinance, Congress had few successes during the postwar years. Even in the Northwest, pioneers were left almost entirely to their own resources in dealing with the Indians and the British. Frontier violence and threats of violence weakened the demand for land and left speculators a great deal less than happy.

Other postwar developments aroused the anger of the largest single economic class in the new nation, the farmers. The war had piled up what appeared to be monstrous debts for the states. As a result, the men who were owed money by state governments stood in conflict with the general mass of taxpayers, many of whom were debtors. In addition, as in any inflationary situation, private debtors were happy to pay off their debts in currency of reduced value, to the dismay of their creditors. Debtors demanded abundant paper money, lower taxes and "stay laws" that would delay mortgage foreclosures. Creditors wanted heavy taxes in gold or silver and swift and rigid enforcement of legal contracts.

Seven states issued some form of paper money, often with good effect. But in New England in particular, creditors and merchants in the coastal commercial towns usually managed to avoid paper money and also to shift much of the tax burden onto inland farmers. By 1786, conditions had grown so bad in New Hampshire that the militia had to be called out to disperse a mob of farmers who surrounded the legislative meeting house in an effort to force the members to issue paper money. It was in Massachusetts, however, where farmers appear to have been taxed as much as one-third of their income, that conservatives received their greatest shock. In 1785, Massachusetts farmers in the western part of the state decided to take the same sort of action Boston merchants had thought legitimate ten years earlier—domestic rebellion.

Daniel Shays was not very different from the thousand men who became his followers. He had seen action at Bunker Hill. "A brave and good soldier," as a subordinate described him, he waited four years for a promised commission to captain. In 1780 he returned home to await payment for his long service to his country. His farming went badly, his army compensation was delayed, his financial obligations accumulated, and he faced being jailed for debt.

His neighbors shared his bitterness. Many western towns were too poor to send delegates to the legislature in Boston. Without any voice in the state government, the debtor leaders resorted to the now familiar device of county conventions. Men from neighboring towns gathered at county seats to voice their political sentiments by means of resolutions and petitions to the legislature.

After the Massachusetts General Court adjourned in July 1786, having ignored these petitions, more and more county conventions met. Shays and other leaders warned the members to "abstain from all mobs and unlawful assemblies until a constitutional method of redress can be obtained." But popular discontent overrode such advice, and mobs began to threaten civil courts where foreclosure proceedings were scheduled. After forcing the suspension of many civil court sessions, the mobs attacked the criminal courts to prevent trials of the rioters. Finally, when armed mobs of farmers threatened federal arsenals, the government took action.

By October 1786, Shays had somehow become the focus of the whole movement, and the rebels who followed him soon became the tar-

Daniel Shays and Joe Shattuck. (National Portrait Gallery, Smithsonian Institution)

gets of state forces gathered by General Benjamin Lincoln at the request of Governor James Bowdoin. Fighting between the Shays forces and Lincoln's continued from mid-January to the end of February 1787, when the rebellion finally was crushed.

Shays fled to Vermont. A number of his followers, captured during the fighting, were freed by the legislature in June. The bitterness that followed this uprising emerged in the subsequent elections, when Governor Bowdoin was

JOHN JAY ON GOVERNMENT

Late in October 1786, John Jay wrote from New York the following gloomy assessment to Ambassador Thomas Jefferson in Paris. His sentiments echoed those of most nationalists throughout the states.

The inefficacy of our Government becomes daily more and more apparent. Our Credit and our Treasury are in a sad Situation, and it is probable that either the Wisdom or the Passions of the People will produce Changes.

A Spirit of Licentiousness has infected Massachusetts, which appears more formidable than some at first apprehended; whether similar Symptoms will soon mark a like Disease in several other States, is very problematical.

The public Papers herewith sent contain everything generally known about these Matters. A Reluctance to Taxes, an Impatience of Government,

a Rage for Property, and little Regard to the Means of acquiring it, together with a Desire of Equality in all Things, seem to actuate the Mass of those who are uneasy in their Circumstances; to these may be added the influence of ambitious Adventurers, and the Speculations of the many Characters who prefer private to public good, and of others who expect to gain more from Wrecks made by Tempests, than from the Produce of patient and honest Industry. . . .

In short, my Dr. Sir; we are in a very unpleasant Situation. Changes are Necessary, but what they ought to be, what they will be, and how and when to be produced, are arduous Questions. I feel for the Cause of Liberty and for the Honor of my Countrymen who have so nobly asserted it, and who at present so abuse its Blessings. If it should not take Root in this Soil little Pains will be taken to cultivate it in any other.

voted out of office. No real punishment was imposed on Shays or his followers. The Massachusetts legislature eased off on taxes and passed laws exempting household goods and workmen's tools from confiscation for debt.

News of Shays's Rebellion shocked many propertied Americans. They were already alarmed by the weakness of Congress, the discontent of the army, and the vulnerability of government to mob action. Washington himself described Congress as "a half-starved, limping" body "always moving upon crutches and tottering at every step."

THE CONSTITUTION

The movement for a stronger central government was sparked by a small group of energetic and dedicated nationalists. We know now that they succeeded with the Constitution of the United States. At the time, however, they faced enormous obstacles and came extremely close to failure. In the early 1780s many of the new nation's leaders had grown severely discouraged about the whole experiment; some even thought it should be abandoned. "Some of our more enlightened men," wrote Benjamin Rush in 1786, "have secretly proposed an Eastern, Middle, and Southern Confederacy, to be united by an alliance." Others spoke of the possibility of preserving the Union by means of a monarchy. "What a triumph for our enemies," exclaimed Washington, "to verify their predictions! What a triumph for the advocates of despotism to find we are incapable of governing ourselves."

Washington, steadfast in his nationalism and republicanism, would not tolerate monarchy, despotism, or disunion. Even before the Articles of Confederation had been ratified, he and other nationalists were advocating their improvement to strengthen the Union. They carried the day, but only by taking revolutionary steps of their own.

The Constitutional Convention

A strong movement for a new form of government emerged from the efforts of practical men to achieve what the Articles could not—a more satisfactory regulation of interstate commerce. Early in 1785, delegates from Maryland and Virginia met at Alexandria in an attempt to settle their differences over navigation of the Potomac River and Chesapeake Bay. The delegates decided to move to Washington's home at Mount Vernon, where they extended their sessions so that delegates from neighboring Delaware and Pennsylvania could attend. These discussions finally resulted in a recommendation to the Virginia legislature that it call a general meeting of all the states at Annapolis in September 1786.

In addition to the four states just mentioned, only New York responded. Among its delegates was Alexander Hamilton, whose ideas about government went far beyond commercial matters. To attempt much more in the way of change with only five states, however, seemed impractical. At Hamilton's and James Madison's suggestion, the Annapolis Convention adjourned with a call for a new convention to meet in Philadelphia the following May to amend the Articles. Owing largely to the concern generated by the recently suppressed Shays's Rebellion, the state legislatures responded far more positively than they had to Virginia's call a few months earlier. All except Rhode Island eventually sent representatives to Philadelphia.

The men the states chose were a remarkably able group. Some prominent political leaders were not available: John Adams and Thomas Jefferson were abroad on diplomatic missions; Sam Adams was not named a delegate; Patrick Henry, appointed by Virginia, refused to attend. Otherwise the famous names of the country were there: men such as Benjamin Franklin and James Wilson from Pennsylvania; James Madison, Edmund Randolph, and George Washington from Virginia; and Alexander Hamilton from New York.

Of the seventy-four men named to the convention, only fifty-five actually attended. Their average age was forty-two. Many had been army officers in the war, and twenty-seven belonged to the Society of the Cincinnati, a group formed to look after the interests of former army officers. Only eight had been signers of the Declaration of Independence. In an age when few Americans went to college, a majority of the delegates were college graduates. For the most part they were lawyers, merchants, and planters.

The convention was supposed to assemble on May 14, but delegates from the required minimum of seven states did not arrive in Philadelphia until May 25. On that day twenty-nine delegates unanimously elected Washington presiding officer. Next, uneasy about local rumors and the press, they voted to keep their discussions secret. Debate then took place on their purpose in coming together. Some maintained that they must follow their instructions to "amend" the Articles. But others, led by Hamilton, argued that they must not "let slip the golden opportunity." The convention decided to replace, not amend, the Articles. It adopted Edmund Randolph's resolution

that a national government ought to be established consisting of a supreme legislature, executive, and judiciary.

Fundamental Assumptions

Although the delegates had many disagreements, most of them shared certain basic assumptions about the nature of people and of government. They agreed that people were basically driven by self-interest and that the structure of any government had to deal with this fact. If people were, as Hamilton said, "ambitious, vindictive, and rapacious," how did one go about controlling them without establishing a tyranny? Most delegates agreed with Madison that vice could not be stopped by virtue; vice must be kept in check by vice: "Ambition must be made to counteract ambition."

The delegates wholeheartedly agreed that the people ought to have a voice in government. But they felt they knew from both history and recent experience that the people could be stampeded into following demagogues and dictators. So the people's role must be limited. Although most of the delegates were men of property who distrusted excessive democracy, they had no illusions about the benevolence of the rich. Even a wealthy aristocrat such as Gouverneur Morris of Pennsylvania acknowledged that "wealth tends to corrupt the mind," and that rich men as well as poor would use power to their own advantage if given the opportunity. Thus the greed and pride of the rich, like the gullibility and passions of the poor, must be held in check.

The delegates were as reluctant to entrust power to special interests as to individuals or social classes. They believed that a landed interest, a slaveholding interest, a creditor interest, a debtor interest, a commercial interest, or a religious interest would tyrannize the rest of society if given the opportunity. And the danger would be even greater if several interests were to join forces. To meet this problem, the advocates of a strong constitution turned to a variety of arrangements, including the division of sovereignty in a federal republic. But they also had in mind balancing powers within the fundamental units of government. Political selfishness among the parts would offset attempts to monopolize power by various interests working together.

The concept of offsetting competing interests was as old as Aristotle. It had been elaborately set forth by Montesquieu, one of the major *philosophes* of the French Enlightenment. He had argued that the various parts of the government should check and balance one another. In a book widely read by the delegates, John Adams gave the best statement of the idea of checks and balances:

A legislative, an executive, and a judicial power comprehend the whole of what is meant and understood by government. It is by balancing each of these powers against the other two, that the efforts of human nature toward tyranny can alone be checked and restrained, and any degree of freedom preserved in the constitution.

James Madison, the fourth president of the United States. *(Library of Congress)*

Traditional American political practices gave the delegates an opportunity to introduce such balancing into the new national government. In the provincial and state legislatures, the lower house usually served as the "democratical branch," elected by a broad suffrage. In the new national legislature, most delegates agreed, there must also be two houses, the democratic one to check and in turn be checked by a chamber representing the wealthier and more powerful members of society.

John Adams had written that there could be "no free government without a democratical branch in the constitution." A few delegates thought that a two-house legislature, by pulling in opposite directions, would be incapable of effective action. But advocates of bicameralism pointed out that a strong and independent executive could prevent this.

Naturally the convention could not agree unanimously even on these general principles. Some delegates were concerned about state power. Others earned reputations as obstructionists because they were so certain that the establishment of a sovereign national government would swallow up traditional personal liberties. Hamilton himself stood on the extreme conservative side, believing that concessions to the people made the proposed constitution "a frail and worthless fabric," though he later urged ratification of the document. Elsewhere, John Adams expressed the spirit of the Founding Fathers and the spirit of the age when he observed that "the blessings of society depend entirely on the constitutions of government." Leaning on that faith, the delegates at the convention managed to balance out contending claims and complete the instrument that has proved so durable.

Two Compromises

The first of the two most divisive controversies was that of the relative power to be granted large and small states. Once the delegates had agreed to go beyond the idea of amending the Articles, they took up Edmund Randolph's so-called Virginia Plan for a new government structure. Randolph proposed a two-house National Legislature with membership in both houses allotted among the states in proportion to their free population. Members of the upper house were to be elected by the members of the lower,

who were themselves to be elected by the people. The whole National Legislature was then to elect the National Judiciary.

This proposal obviously violated the principle of balancing separate powers within the government, and it aroused considerable opposition. It particularly alarmed the small-state delegates, who feared that their commonwealths would be overwhelmed in the popularly elected house and that some states might have no representatives at all in the upper chamber.

As a counterproposal, the small states offered a plan of their own, presented to the convention by William Paterson of New Jersey and known since as the New Jersey Plan. It proposed to have Congress remain a single house, as under the Articles, with each state having one vote. The delegates quickly rejected this suggestion because it continued the current situation and because it based representation on states rather than people. The convention returned to the Virginia Plan as the preliminary model from which to construct the final document.

Rejection of Randolph's proposals for the makeup of the new national legislature brought the issue of large- and small-state representation to a head. At one point the small-state delegations threatened, as a Delaware member put it, to "find some foreign ally, of more honor and good faith" than his large-state colleagues. They were on the verge of going home.

Disaster was avoided by the appointment of a special committee to restudy the whole issue of representation. Early in July this committee brought in a compromise devised largely by Benjamin Franklin: There would be a two-house legislature, with membership in the lower house based on population, thus satisfying the large states, and membership in the upper house equal for all states, thus satisfying the small ones. This arrangement, adopted after a great deal of debate, provided the basis for the Great Compromise of the Constitution. It determined the general character of what were to become the House of Representatives and the Senate.

The two-house plan enabled the delegates to establish the lower house as the people's branch. Members of this house were to be elected by all voters in each state who were eligible to vote for "the most numerous branch of the State Legislature." The matter of suffrage requirements was left to the states. The upper house, whose members were to be chosen by state legislatures, was expected to be more friendly to propertied classes and generally more conservative.

The Great Compromise raised several issues that divided the delegates along completely different lines—sectional ones that concerned slavery. None of the delegates seemed to have expected this line of division. The delegates clearly were nervous about the matter, and they succeeded in keeping the words *slave* and *slavery* out of the Constitution. When southern members insisted upon their right to recover fugitive slaves, there was not much debate, but the clause that emerged referred euphemistically to a "person held to service or labor."

The first issue raised by the Great Compromise concerned the "direct taxes" the new government could levy. The convention agreed that such taxes should be apportioned among the states according to population, just as representation was to be apportioned in the lower house. But the slave states wanted their blacks, if they were counted at all in apportioning taxes, to be given less weight than free men. The North wanted blacks to be given less weight only for congressional representation. In the debate, the proportion of three-fifths was proposed many times. But Wilson of Pennsylvania "did not well see on what principle the admission of blacks in the proportion of three-fifths could be explained. Are they admitted as Citizens? Are they admitted as property? Then why is not other property admitted into the computation?" Wilson nevertheless admitted "the necessity of compromise," and the others yielded on the three-fifths rule. For both direct taxes and representation, five blacks were to be counted as equivalent to three whites.

Another issue that split the states along sectional lines was foreign commerce. Delegates from the commercial North urged that the new government be granted full power to regulate interstate and foreign commerce and to make treaties the states must obey. The convention easily agreed on these points. But delegates from the southern states, fearful of being outvoted in the new Congress, demanded that commercial regulations and all treaties require the consent of two-thirds of the Senate rather than a simple majority. Southerners, whose constituents depended so heavily on agricultural exports, were concerned about export taxes and possible treaties requiring them. They were dependent on selling tobacco and rice in competitive world markets.

The Lower South was even more concerned about the slave trade. If Congress had control over commerce, it could ban the slave trade or tax it out of existence. Delegates from South Carolina and Georgia warned that their states would never approve the proposed constitution if their supply of slaves was threatened. From North Carolina and Virginia northward there was no demand for slave imports, and a great many people had begun to see the slave trade as unjust and inhumane. To placate South Carolina and Georgia, the majority of delegates reluctantly agreed on a compromise: Congress would be prohibited from interfering with the slave trade for a period of twenty years. The convention also compromised by prohibiting all taxes on exports. Finally, the South won the provision requiring a two-thirds vote in the Senate for the ratification of treaties. In exchange for these concessions, the northerners won their point on a simple congressional majority for acts regulating commerce, both among the states and with foreign nations.

The Executive

The convention next turned to the problem of the executive branch. The delegates discussed whether it should be composed of one or several men, how long he or they should serve, whether its holder(s) could serve for another term, and what name to give him or them. Discussion of these matters took far longer than others that now seem more important. Yet at the time it was not at all obvious, for example, how long the executive(s) should hold office. Seven years was the term most commonly suggested. Eventually the delegates settled on an arrangement that prevails to this day (with one exception, concerning reelection): a single executive, elected for four renewable years, called a president.

The method of the president's election presented one last test. Strong nationalists wanted the president elected directly by the people; state-sovereignty men wanted him chosen by state legislatures. After many arguments, the convention devised the elaborate electoral college plan (Article II, Section 1). Each state was to have as many electors as it had representatives and senators, and the method of choosing these electors was left up to the state legislatures.

Almost all the delegates assumed that the presidential electors in each state would usually vote for men from their own state. They expected that no candidate would receive the majority required for election. In that case, or in case two candidates, were tied with the most votes, the election would be decided in the House of Representatives, where each state, regardless of population, would cast one vote. This arrangement appeared to give the small states equal standing with the large ones in the ultimate choice of the president. The members of the convention assumed that, in effect, the president would be nominated by the large states in the electoral college, but actually elected by all the states in the House of Representatives.

This complex scheme was based on the assumption that each state would constitute its own party. The emergence of national political parties only a few years later made this elaborate machinery superfluous. The two-party system eventually made it possible for voters throughout the country to choose electors pledged to one of a few leading candidates. Yet constitutionally electors retained the privilege of exercising personal choice in the electoral college.

Toward Sovereign Power

Among the flaws of government under the Confederation, two were fatal: Congress had neither the power of the purse nor the power of the sword. Although distracted at the outset by problems of apportioning power to the states and the people, most delegates had come to Philadelphia mainly to address these two shortcomings by giving a new national government such sovereign strength.

Every delegate but Elbridge Gerry of Massachusetts voted to give the new national government power to levy and collect taxes and tariffs. The clause permitting Congress to pay the debts of the United States passed unanimously. No one opposed giving Congress the power to coin money and "regulate the value thereof" or the power to borrow money on the credit of the United States, or the power to regulate commerce among the states and foreign nations, or to deal with Indian tribes.

Madison complained about certain state laws, particularly those that made credit risky, investment hazardous, and long-term business planning uncertain. The big problem was paper money. The delegates agreed with Madison's position, and they almost unanimously forbade the states to issue "bills of credit" (paper money); to make anything but gold and silver legal tender for the payment of private or public debts; to interfere with the obligations of contracts; or to tax imports or exports in commercial wars with one another.

The Constitution's provisions for a military establishment also shifted power from the states to the national government. The new government alone was enabled to "provide for the common defense"; "to declare war" "to raise and support armies"; "to provide and maintain a navy"; "to provide for calling forth the militia to execute the laws of the Union, suppress insurrections and repel invasions"; and more broadly, to provide for the "general welfare of the United States." To ensure that national sovereignty would not be impaired by technicalities, the framers added what later became known as the elastic clause, enabling Congress "to make all laws which shall be necessary and proper for carrying into execution the foregoing powers."

A third flaw in the Confederation had been the absence of an independent executive. In remedying this defect, the Constitution made the president commander in chief of the army and navy and of the state militias when called into federal service. His power of appointing federal officers was extensive, and he was required to obtain the consent of the Senate only for his highest aides. The president could make treaties with foreign nations with the consent of two-thirds of the Senate. He could call Congress into extraordinary session and could veto acts of Congress, although his veto could be overridden by a two-thirds vote in both houses.

For protection against possible wrongdoing, the convention provided that the president could be impeached by majority vote in the House and then convicted by a two-thirds vote after a trial in the Senate, with the chief justice presiding.

A fourth flaw of the Confederation was its lack of a judiciary independent of state courts. The Constitution provided for a national judicial system. At the head of the system stood the Supreme Court of the United States: It could decide cases on appeal from lower federal courts, which Congress was empowered to establish, and from state courts in cases involving the Constitution, the laws of the United States, or treaties with other nations. The Constitution made no specific provision for *judicial review* of federal legislation—the power of federal courts to declare acts of Congress unconstitutional and void. But the Supreme Court later clarified this issue. Article III, Section 2, of the Constitution made possible the conclusion that any state actions or laws that encroached on the supreme powers of the federal government must be found unconstitutional by the federal courts. It was a short step for the Supreme Court to decide that it also had the power to declare acts of the federal Congress and president to be unconstitutional.

A Lasting Government

The Philadelphia convention proposed a government that could act with speed, strength, and dignity. The Constitution radically shifted sovereign power away from the states and toward a truly national government. No one knew at the time whether the arrangement would work. It took Americans about forty years before they began to regard the federal government as truly permanent. They were helped by the flexibility of the Constitution, and by the fact that its framers built into it their convictions about the fallibility—and the long-range bedrock importance—of "the people."

While the framers wanted mainly to substitute a strong central government for the weak Articles of Confederation, they also hoped to create a government, as Madison put it, "for the ages." Their success rested in part on features they introduced and on others unforeseen but ultimately at least as important.

From the framers' point of view, the Constitution's built-in checks and balances were the best safeguards of the Republic. No chief executive could become a dictator. And no temporary surge of popular feeling, reflected in the "democratical branch" of the legislature, could unseat the president or overturn the courts.

A second source of the Constitution's lasting strength was its amending process. Trying to amend the Articles by unanimous consent of the states had proved impossible. The easier amending process in the Constitution was at first used sparingly—but only after the first ten amendments, the much-desired federal Bill of Rights, had been adopted.

A third source of the Constitution's long life lay in the brevity of its wording. The framers avoided going into great detail because they assumed that the principles of good government were universal. They left important powers to the states, but they spelled out the powers of the national government so broadly that these powers could later be expanded.

Several later developments unexpectedly added to the strength of the Constitution. These included the two-party system and the cabinet, both of which developed within ten years of the Constitution's adoption. Two other innovations came much later: the committee system in the House and Senate, and the civil service.

The Constitutional Convention, for all its conservatism, set up what was by world standards a radical government. Under the Constitution, said John Marshall, who rose as a new leader during the ratification controversy in Virginia, "it is the people that give power, and can take it back. What shall restrain them? They are the masters who give it, and of whom their servants hold it."

For all its stress on private property, which in the eighteenth century was thought to be the best foundation for public responsibility, the Constitution required no property qualification for office, not even that of president. It also required "a compensation . . . , to be ascertained by law, and paid out of the Treasury of the United States," for all elective posts, so that the poor as well as the rich might hold them. The Constitution itself, before the Bill of Rights was added, forbade religious tests for any federal post. It provided that "for any speech or debate in either House," senators and representatives "shall not be questioned in any other place," thereby ensuring their fullest freedom of expression. It also guaranteed trial by jury for all crimes, "except in cases of impeachment," and forbade suspension of "the privilege of the writ of habeas corpus" except in times of invasion or rebellion. These provisions, which were similar to freedoms won in England in the seventeenth century, were important protections for legislative debate and individual liberty.

RATIFICATION

The Constitutional Convention was in session from May 25 to September 16, 1787. Of the fifty-five delegates who took part, forty-two stayed to the end and thirty-nine signed the document. The other three—Gerry of Massachusetts and

Randolph and Mason of Virginia—refused to go along. Their refusals gave warning of the storm ahead when the Constitution would be brought to the people for approval.

Antifederalist Arguments

The day after the convention adopted the Constitution, a copy was sent to Congress, largely out of courtesy, with a letter that did not mince words. "In all our deliberations on this subject," said the signers, "we kept steadily in our view that which appeared to us the greatest interest of every true American—the consolidation of the Union—in which is involved our prosperity, felicity, safety, perhaps our national existence." They did not ask Congress for a vote of approval. Nor would they ask the state legislatures for confirmation; in the Constitution itself they called for the consent of nine special state conventions like their own.

While the election of delegates to these conventions was in progress, the Constitution was discussed and debated throughout the country. Rufus King, a member of the Massachusetts ratifying convention, summed up the feelings of the opposition, though he did not share them, when he wrote to Madison in January 1788: "An apprehension that the liberties of the people are in danger, and a distrust of men of property and education have a more powerful effect upon the minds of our opponents than any specific objections against the Constitution."

But the Constitution's critics, named Antifederalists by the Constitution's friends, did in fact offer many specific objections. There was no Bill of Rights; state sovereignty would be destroyed; the president might become king; the standing national army would threaten personal freedoms; only the rich could afford to hold office; tax collectors would swarm over the countryside; the people could not bear to be taxed by both state and national governments; commercial treaties would hurt the particular needs of the West and the South; debtors would no longer be able to defend themselves through recourse to state paper money and state stay laws; the proposed federal capital district would become a nesting ground for tyranny.

Many state politicians feared that a stronger national government would mean the loss of their influence. More important, many ordinary citizens worried about so drastic an innovation in government and about centralized political power.

The First Ratifications

At first, ratification went smoothly. In December and January 1787–1788, five states approved the Constitution. The conventions of Delaware, New Jersey, and Georgia did so without a single opposing vote. Connecticut ratified by 123 to 40. Only in Pennsylvania, among the first five, was there serious divisiveness. By staying away, opponents of the Constitution tried to prevent the legislature from forming the quorum necessary for it to vote to call a ratifying convention. Federalists seized enough of their opponents and pushed them into the chamber to make a quorum. Pennsylvania voted to ratify, 46 to 23.

In the key state of Massachusetts, the next to ratify, the contest was extremely close; a shift in voting by only 10 of 355 delegates would have doomed ratification. The Massachusetts special convention debated for a month, but Federalist leaders maneuvered to win over opponents such as John Hancock and Sam Adams. They won over others by promising to support amendments guaranteeing popular liberties, namely some sort of bill of rights. In the end, Massachusetts voted for the Constitution, 187 to 168.

In the less crucial states of Maryland and South Carolina, ratification won easily. In New Hampshire, there was strong opposition. After a first convention failed to reach a vote, a second convention narrowly ratified on June 21, 1788. Technically speaking, the new government could now go into effect, for nine states had accepted it. But no one believed it could function without Virginia and New York, and in these two states the outcome remained doubtful.

Virginia and New York

In Virginia, an extraordinarily thorough and brilliant review of the issues took place, with the opposition led by George Mason and Patrick Henry. Washington's influence and the certain knowledge that he would consent to serve as the first president were responsible for the unexpected conversion of Edmund Randolph, who had refused to sign the Constitution. The promised

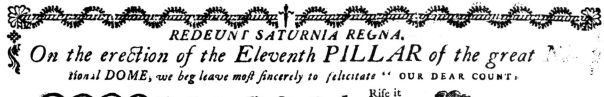

REDEUNT SATURNIA REGNA.

On the erection of the Eleventh PILLAR of the great
tional DOME, we beg leave moft fincerely to felicitate " OUR DEAR COUNTR

Rife it
will.

☞ *The foundation*
good—it may yet
be SAVED.

The FEDERAL EDIFICE.

ELEVEN STARS, in quick fucceffion rife—
ELEVEN COLUMNS ftrike our wond'ring eyes,
Soon o'er the *whole*, fhall fwell the beauteous DOME,
COLUMBIA's boaft—and FREEDOM's hallow'd home.
Here fhall the ARTS in glorious fplendour fhine !
And AGRICULTURE give her ftores divine !
COMMERCE refin'd, difpenfe us more than gold,
And this new world, teach WISDOM to the old—
RELIGION here fhall fix her bleft abode,
Array'd in *mildnefs*, like its parent GOD !
JUSTICE and LAW, fhall endlefs PEACE maintain,
And *the* " SATURNIAN AGE," *return again.*

North Carolina and Rhode Island were needed to help the other "pillars" support the new nation. *(Library of Congress)*

addition of a Bill of Rights further softened the opposition. Four days after New Hampshire had ratified, Virginia voted in favor, 89 to 79. By arrangement between Madison and Hamilton, couriers were quickly dispatched with the news to New York, where a tense struggle was in process.

In New York, Hamilton led the Federalist fight in support of ratification; Governor Clinton led the opposition. Well aware of Clinton's strength, Hamilton, John Jay, and James Madison had undertaken a series of anonymous newspaper articles supporting the Constitution. Later published as *The Federalist*, these articles provide the best commentary on the Constitution by contemporary advocates. More important for the voting in New York was the news of Federalist successes in New Hampshire and Virginia. Once again, the promise of a Bill of Rights overcame opposition. Having agreed to support such amendments, Federalists in New York finally won by a very narrow margin.

Rhode Island and North Carolina initially rejected the Constitution. But when the new national government got under way, they had little choice but to join. North Carolina, by a wide margin, decided to join in November 1789. Rhode Island held out for a few more months, and Congress considered a bill placing it on the footing of a foreign nation. Even then, Rhode Island decided to enter by the narrowest of margins.

Ratification: An Appraisal

Among historians there has long been controversy about all these events, and even today there is no complete agreement. Interpretations have varied all the way from a coup d'état by conservative counterrevolutionaries to the divinely inspired work of intellectual giants bent upon fulfilling the aims of the Revolution. The truth lies not exactly in between, but somewhere off center between these two poles.

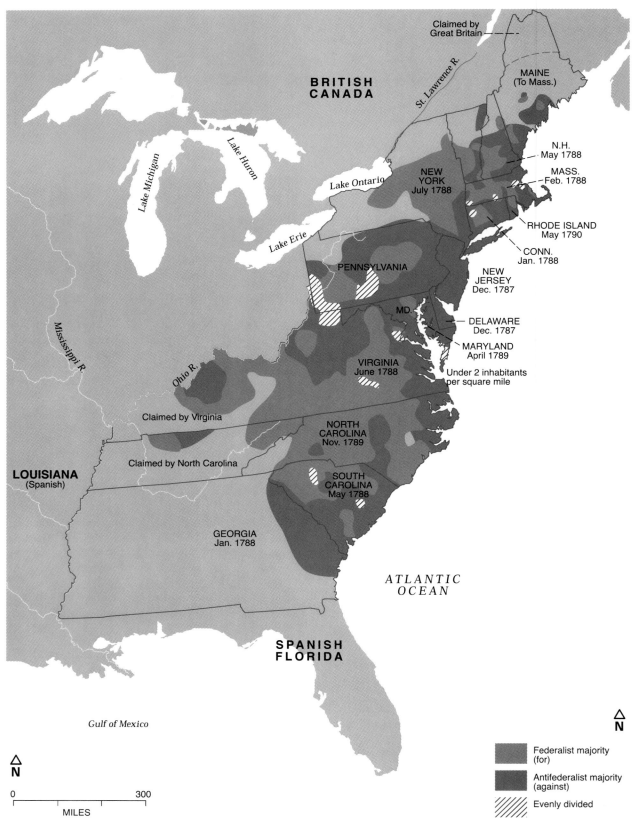

Claimed by
Great Britain

BRITISH
CANADA

St. Lawrence R.

MAINE
(To Mass.)

Lake Michigan

Lake Huron

Lake Ontario

N.H.
May 1788

NEW
YORK
July 1788

MASS.
Feb. 1788

Lake Erie

RHODE ISLAND
May 1790

PENNSYLVANIA

CONN.
Jan. 1788

NEW
JERSEY
Dec. 1787

MD.

DELAWARE
Dec. 1787

Mississippi R.

Ohio R.

MARYLAND
April 1789

VIRGINIA
June 1788

Under 2 inhabitants
per square mile

Claimed by Virginia

NORTH
CAROLINA
Nov. 1789

Claimed by North Carolina

LOUISIANA
(Spanish)

SOUTH
CAROLINA
May 1788

GEORGIA
Jan. 1788

*ATLANTIC
OCEAN*

SPANISH
FLORIDA

N

Gulf of Mexico

N

0   300

MILES

Federalist majority
(for)

Antifederalist majority
(against)

Evenly divided

Vote on ratification of the Constitution

At the national level it is clear that leaders who favored the new Constitution had the edge in talent. Men who previously participated in politics outside their own state tended to favor adoption. Wealthy persons were inclined toward adoption, and some who favored the Constitution knew they would gain financially from a stronger central government. Within each state, politics were important, especially the influence of popular local leaders such as John Hancock (who wanted ratification) and Patrick Henry (who did not). Cities and towns and regions of commercial activity tended to be Federalist; small farmers in more isolated areas tended to be Antifederalist. Representation in the ratifying conventions greatly favored the commercial regions, and because of this fact and elected delegates changing their minds it is quite clear that a majority of actual voters on the popular level *opposed* the Constitution.

Finally, had George Washington not favored it, the Federalist cause would have been doomed. It was almost universally assumed that he would be the first president under the new government. He was widely admired and trusted—but it remained to be seen whether a victorious general would make a good president, and whether the new system would work.

SUMMARY

The United States had become an independent nation so far as the world was concerned. But Americans had yet to establish the most important institution of all—a firm national government. New state governments, with written constitutions, had been created during the war. These documents gave governing power to legislatures elected by the people. Fundamental power was reserved to the people themselves, who were in some cases protected by bills of rights guaranteeing individual liberties.

The great problem was the national government. The Articles of Confederation, drawn up by the Second Continental Congress, provided for a loose association of states to be governed by a one-house legislature in which voting was by state. Each state had one vote, no matter how many delegates it sent. A two-thirds majority was required for important legislation, and a unanimous vote for amendments. The government could declare war and make treaties; could settle disputes between states and admit new ones; could borrow money, establish a postal service, and appoint military officers. But it could not levy taxes, raise troops, or regulate commerce among the states.

More difficulties came with disputes between the "landed" states (those with claims to western lands) and those without such resources. The question of how to keep the landless states from paying a greater share of the cost of the war, in fact, delayed ratification and the start of the new government until March 1781. The new nation ran into problems with foreign relations and with money. Neither the British nor the Spanish wanted the new nation to succeed, so they did their best to encourage Indians in Florida and the Northwest to harass the Anglo-Americans. In the meantime, Congress could not depend on its own army, which it did not have the money to pay. Nor did it have the authority to force the states to supply funds to pay back the national debt and to operate the government.

The most significant accomplishment of the government under the Articles of Confederation was the Northwest Ordinance of 1787, which established the terms for the settlement of the vast area northwest of the Ohio River. The ordinance unified the whole Northwest territory under a governor, laid out tentative boundaries for new states, and set the terms for their admission. It also prohibited slavery in the territory and in the states to be carved from it.

The worst problem for the government was money and credit. Farmers, who were taxpayers and often also debtors, wanted paper money to ease the pressure of their money payments. Creditors wanted payment in specie—gold or silver coin—so that they would not be paid back with devalued currency. The agitation and discontent over this issue reached a peak in western Massachusetts in the autumn of 1786 in Shays's Rebellion, which state authorities finally managed to put down in early 1787.

By that year it was clear something had to be done. The Articles had framed a government that was simply too weak. Work on a new and stronger central government actually began in 1785, when delegates from Maryland, Virginia, Delaware, and Pennsylvania met to discuss problems of interstate commerce. The result was a call for a general meeting of all the states at Annapolis in September 1786. Only five sent delegates, but the convention did recommend a new gathering to meet in Philadelphia in May 1787.

It was this convention that eventually replaced the Articles with a new federal constitution. This document set up not only a strong federal government, but a new kind of national structure. By means of checks and balances, power was divided among three branches of government—executive, legislative, and judicial—so that no one class, interest group, or faction could dominate for any length of time. The balance of power between large and small states was solved by the two-house legislature. The sectional division caused by slavery was handled by several compromises. And the new federal government had two powers the Confederation Congress had lacked: the power to tax and the power to raise an army. It also had an independent executive in the form of a single person—the president—and an independent judiciary.

The new Constitution of the United States was ratified only after a long and difficult campaign in the states, and only after immediate amendment by a bill of rights was promised. By June 1788 nine states had ratified. But Virginia and New York had strong opposition groups. Ratification, especially in New York, came late and by a narrow margin. But by the end of 1788, all the states except Rhode Island and North Carolina had ratified. The new government, with George Washington as first president, was ready to go to work.

TIME LINE

1776–1777	New state constitutions
1777	Congress adopts the Articles of Confederation
1780	Massachusetts adopts its constitution by popular vote
1781	Articles of Confederation finally ratified
1783	Congress flees Philadelphia
1785	First Northwest Ordinance provides for land surveys
1785	Mt. Vernon conference on commercial problems
1786	Annapolis Convention
1786–1787	Shays's Rebellion
1787	Northwest Ordinance provides for government of new states
1787	Philadelphia convention adopts U.S. Constitution
1787	Three states ratify Constitution
1788	New Hampshire becomes the ninth state to ratify; Constitution goes into effect
1789	New government meets in New York City
1789	North Carolina finally ratifies Constitution
1790	Rhode Island becomes last of original thirteen states to ratify

Suggested Readings

M. Jensen, *The New Nation: A History of the United States during the Confederation, 1781–1789* (1950), argues that postwar economic and political conditions were not chaotic. Other fine general studies include: M. Yazawa, *From Colonies to Commonwealths: Familial Ideology and the Beginnings of the American Republic* (1985); R. Morris, *The Forging of the Union, 1781–1787* (1987); and J. Reid, *Constitutional History of the American Revolution: The Authority of Rights* (1986). Several state studies illuminate various issues. See V. Hall, *Politics without Parties; Massachusetts, 1780–1791* (1972) I. Polisbook, *Rhode Island and the Union, 1774–1795* (1969); and S. Lynd, *Anti-Federalism in Duchess County, New York* (1962). R. Beeman, *The Old Dominion and the New Nation, 1788–1801* (1972), has a fine discussion of antifederalism in Virginia.

A fine biography of the "father of the Constitution" is I. Brant, *James Madison* (6 vols., 1941–1961). Hamilton's political views and his role in the adoption process are covered by C. Rossiter, *Alexander Hamilton and the Constitution* (1950). E. Ferguson, *The Power of the Purse: A History of American Public Finance, 1776–1790* (1961), is complex but crucial to a full understanding of the adoption of the Constitution. Much recent writing on that subject still revolves around Charles Beard's claim in *An Economic Interpretation of the Constitution of the United States* (1913) that the Constitution was written by, and in the interest of, wealthy public-securities holders and landowners. Beard's views were challenged by F. McDonald, *We the People: The Economic Origins of the Constitution* (1958), and *E Pluribus Unum: The Formation of the American Republic, 1776–1790* (1965). An alternative picture is presented by J. Main, *The Anti-Federalists: Critics of the Constitution, 1781–1788* (1961), who stresses that the commercial areas of the new nation were most favorable to the Constitution. See also G. Billias, *Elbridge Gerry: Founding Father and Republican Statesman* (1976).

R. Morris discusses reverberations elsewhere in *The Emerging Nations and the American Revolution*

(1970). For economic developments, see the Ferguson volume just cited; R. East, *Business Enterprise in the American Revolutionary Era* (1938); and C. Nettels, *The Emergence of a National Economy, 1775–1815* (1962). On the issue of slavery, see the works cited in Chapter 6. In addition, S. Lynd, *Class, Conflict, Slavery and the United States Constitution* (1967), offers an economic interpretation. See also D. Szatmary, *Shays' Rebellion: The Making of an Agrarian Insurrection* (1980).

Easily the best discussion of the political thought of the Founding Fathers is that of Wood cited in Chapter 6. But see also A. O. Lovejoy, *Reflections on Human Nature* (1961). More directly focused on the instrument itself are L. Levy (ed.), *Essays on the Making of the Constitution* (1969); and M. Jensen, *The Making of the American Constitution* (1964). The best text of the Constitution, with an analysis of each clause and summaries of Supreme Court interpretations, is E. S. Corwin, *The Constitution of the United States of America* (1953). The classic commentary on the Constitution is *The Federalist*, written 1787–1788 by Hamilton, Madison, and Jay. The definitive modern edition is J. E. Cooke's (1961). C. Kenyon (ed.), *The Antifederalists* (1966), is an outstanding anthology. There is no substitute for reading the original records of the fascinating debates; see M. Farrand (ed.), *Records of the Federal Convention* (4 vols., 1911–1937).

The Washington family, by Edward Savage. *(Library of Congress)*

THE FEDERALIST ERA

The new national government faced grave problems. For one thing, it had to create parts of itself. At first there were only two members of the executive branch—the president and vice-president—and no judicial system at all. The government was badly in debt. In the West, Spain claimed a huge portion of United States territory, and the British still occupied forts on American soil. Various Indian tribes regarded most of the eastern lands as their own. The monarchs of Europe hoped to see the new nation fall apart. Before long a major war broke out in Europe in the wake of the French Revolution, and the United States found itself involved in bitter battles on the high seas.

President Washington hoped for a spirit of unity in the national government. He disliked political factionalism, which he regarded as poisonous. But he soon discovered that the American people and their leaders disagreed on such critical matters as the powers of the new federal government, its fiscal policies, and the best way to deal with the war in Europe. Despite Washington's intentions, by the time he left office in 1797 two political parties had come into existence: the Federalists and the Republicans (the latter party was completely different from the modern one of the same name).

The president was not alone in his dislike for political parties; no one expected or welcomed the development of a system that has proved to be a basic feature of American political life. At the time, members of each party regarded the other as a troublemaking and even dangerous faction made up of the enemies of the nation. And John Adams, who succeeded Washington as president, discovered that deep divisions could take place within a party. A long time passed before Americans came to believe that political parties were a legitimate and useful means of working out differences about public policy.

THE NEW GOVERNMENT AT WORK

The president and the new Congress were acutely aware of the pitfalls and importance of their first actions. At the start of his administration, Washington wrote: "My station is new, and, if I may use the expression, I walk on untrodden ground. . . . There is scarcely any part of my conduct which may not hereafter be drawn into precedent." As the emerging leader of Congress, James Madison used much the same metaphor: "We are in a wilderness," he wrote, "without a single footstep to guide us." The president and Congress had to establish executive offices and a judicial system. They also had to find ways of raising money for operating expenses and for paying off the debts inherited from the Confederation government. But they dealt first with amendments to the constitution, amendments widely demanded (and promised) during the campaigns for ratification in the states.

The Bill of Rights

Almost everyone agreed the Congress's first business should be to adopt a set of amendments that would constitute a bill of rights. Members of the Philadelphia convention had considered including such a list in the Constitution. They had rejected the idea because the powers of the new federal government were carefully enumerated, and they assumed such enumeration would prevent the national government from doing anything it was not specifically authorized to do. Yet many Americans wanted to set specific restrictions on the powers of the new government. As things turned out during the ratification process, the nationalists in Philadelphia may have been lucky in their omission. Promises of a bill of rights won over many votes in the state ratifying conventions. Nearly half the states proposed such amendments during ratification.

The first ten amendments to the Constitution—the Bill of Rights—were ratified by the states in December 1791. Even a quick reading of them gives a good glimpse into the distrust of government that prevailed at the time. This first group of amendments protects freedom of religion, freedom of speech and of the press, the right to assemble peacefully with other persons, and the right to petition the federal government to correct wrongs. It requires federal officials to obtain search warrants from a court before searching a person's home. The Bill of Rights also provides for trial by jury in criminal cases and prohibits excessive bail and "cruel and unusual punishments." The Fifth Amendment gives individuals the right not to testify against themselves in court. The Ninth and Tenth Amendments limit the powers of the federal government to those specifically named in the Constitution. All other powers were, in a phrase that was both clear and ambiguous, "reserved to the States respectively, or to the people."

Like many provisions of the Constitution, the various provisions of the Bill of Rights have undergone considerable interpretation and re-interpretation by the courts. Though the Founding Fathers thought they were writing for the ages, changing circumstances have raised (and will continue to raise) such questions as whether a person is free to advocate overthrow of the government; whether police may search a person's automobile without a warrant; whether the death penalty is a "cruel and unusual punishment"; and whether "the right of the people to keep and bear arms" makes gun control laws unconstitutional. Yet the Constitution wisely provided mechanisms for dealing with changes in its interpretation: the amendment process and the federal courts.

The Judiciary

The Judiciary Act of 1789 did a great deal to cement the federal system. The first Congress spelled out the procedure by which federal courts could review—and if necessary declare void—state laws and state court decisions involving powers and duties the Constitution delegated to the federal government. It also specified that the Supreme Court be staffed by a chief justice and five associate justices. (Congress retains the power of numbering the members of the Supreme Court; it could change the present number of nine today without violating the Constitution.)

In 1789 the system of federal courts was completed by creation of three circuit courts and thirteen district courts. Attached to each district court were United States prosecuting attorneys, as well as marshals and deputies to serve as federal police. It was the duty of these marshals to supervise the taking of the first federal census in 1790, as required by the Constitution.

The Executive

The executive had been one of the weakest elements in the old Confederation. Nonetheless, Congress was slow in creating executive departments. In the summer of 1789 it created a Department of State to manage foreign relations, a War Department, and a Department of the Treasury. In 1792 Congress stipulated that there should be "one Postmaster General," but this official remained within the Treasury Department until 1829. The Judiciary Act of 1789 created the office of attorney general, but a separate Department of Justice was not established until 1870.

While Congress busied itself with these measures, the president gave his attention to appointments. Washington wanted to surround himself with the best men available, but he had other things in mind as well. He was acutely aware of the thinness of the thread that held the states together and of the need not to offend local people in filling even minor posts. "A single disgust excited in a particular state," he wrote, "might perhaps raise the flame of opposition that could not easily, if ever, be extinguished."

At the same time, Washington was reluctant to appoint any opponent of the Constitution to office. He also had in mind sectional considerations, and when he could he chose men he had known personally during the war. He appointed General Henry Knox of Massachusetts, his old chief of artillery and one of the army's most outspoken opponents of the old Congress, as the first secretary of war. He named Edmund Randolph of Virginia, one of his wartime aides-de-camp, as attorney general. The Treasury Department went to Hamilton, another of his military aides. John Jay, also of New York, had been in charge of foreign affairs for the old Congress and had continued to direct them until 1790. Then Thomas Jefferson of Virginia took over as secretary of state, and Jay became the first chief justice of the Supreme Court.

The Constitution made no provision for a presidential cabinet, but early in his administration Washington established the practice of taking action only on matters that had been referred to him by the secretaries of his three departments and the attorney general. Gradually he began to consult these men on questions outside their departments. In the spring of 1791, before a journey to the South that would keep him away for an extended period, Washington instructed the three secretaries that they should consult together if "any serious and important cases arise during my absence." While holding himself ready to return to the capital in an emergency, he told them to take whatever "measures . . . may be legally and properly pursued without the immediate agency of the President," and "I will approve and ratify" them. Thereafter, the secretaries began to meet periodically. After a crisis in foreign affairs in 1793 arising from the wars of the French Revolution, these meetings became regular. The cabinet thus became a permanent feature of the federal machinery.

PROBLEMS OF FINANCE

Hamilton was the driving force behind the solution of the new nation's financial difficulties. He supported a tariff for national revenue. His goals were political as well as fiscal. He was determined to win the support of wealthy financiers for the new government by giving them a personal stake in its success. In doing so, however, he aroused great opposition, especially from southerners who were not in a position to benefit from his measures. Yet he was largely successful in solving the financial problems that had so badly weakened the old Confederation government.

Hamilton's Funding Plan

At thirty-four years of age, Alexander Hamilton was a vigorous, ambitious, and extraordinarily able young man, and he proposed a bold financial program. Not content merely to propose, he worked closely with members of Congress; one senator declared that "nothing is done without him."

The government of the old Confederation had piled up a huge debt. Hamilton argued that the new United States government was obligated to take responsibility for it. No one really disagreed with his claim that "the debt of the United States . . . was the price of liberty. The faith of America has been repeatedly pledged for it." About one-fifth of the money was owed to foreigners. The remainder was in the form of various public securities or government bonds, which the Confederation government had sold to patriots during and after the war and had used to pay soldiers. Hamilton proposed to "fund" this foreign and domestic debt by exchanging new government securities for the old ones. He wanted to issue new bonds at the same face value as the old ones, plus any unpaid interest.

Hamilton's plan ran into opposition in Congress because the old bonds had dropped in value and because many of these securities had been bought up by wealthy speculators. During and shortly after the war, United States securities had fallen in value to a point where they were worth only 25 percent of their face value. This lower value reflected widespread doubts about the government's ability to pay interest or buy back the bonds. Many war veterans sold their bonds for less to speculators. Adoption of the new, stronger form of government increased confidence in the government's ability to pay, and the value of the bonds began rising.

In the early months of the new government there was an orgy of speculation. Wealthy speculators sent agents into the backcountry to buy up as many bonds as they could find, at the lowest possible price. In such a situation, there was great profit in knowing about Hamilton's proposals ahead of time. His subordinates in the Treasury Department leaked word of his plan to their friends. By the time the proposal became public, the old securities had risen to 80 percent of their face value; if passed, their value would rise to 100 percent.

Most of the speculators were northern capitalists. Few landholders in the South could compete with the northerners, since southern money was tied up in land and slaves. What really made the situation politically explosive, however, was that many northern speculators sat in Congress. They were in a superb position to vote in favor of their own pocketbooks.

Far from being horrified by the situation, Hamilton had planned it. He was deeply committed to the success of the new government. In his view, the way to strengthen the new nation was to involve the personal interests of powerful men in its continued success. Thus he deliberately set out to gain backing for the government from those who had a personal interest in maintaining its ability to pay its debts. Hamilton had neither the time nor inclination to profit personally from the situation; he had little interest in making money for himself But he was interested in power—both for himself and for the new government.

Madison's Discrimination

James Madison had opposite inclinations. Not a particularly wealthy man, he was in no position to profit personally in public securities, nor would he have done so even if able. He saw the situation as basically unfair to the war veterans and other original owners of the securities. He was shocked by the scramble for personal profit by those who would gain at the expense of ordinary soldiers and citizens. He and his friend and neighbor Thomas Jefferson (who was just taking over as secretary of state) grew increasingly opposed to Hamilton's policies.

Madison introduced a counterproposal in the House of Representatives. He conceded the need to pay off the foreign debt at face value in order to establish the new government's credit with other nations. There was no argument on that matter. But Madison proposed to "discriminate" between original holders of public securities and those who had bought them later for speculative purposes. He suggested that possessors of bonds that had not been resold should be offered new ones at face value. Those holding securities they had bought from someone other than the government—that is, speculators—should fall into a separate group that would receive half the original face value. He, and Jefferson even more, began to see the matter as one of justice to ordinary soldiers and farmers as against the interests of the northern merchants.

Madison's proposal lost for two reasons: One was the voting weight of those in Congress who were actively engaged in speculation; the other was that "discrimination" among holders of public securities was impractical, since some securities had changed hands five or six times. It was therefore virtually impossible to work out a plan that would be fair to everyone. The proposal failed in the House of Representatives by a wide margin.

Plan of the new center of the federal government, 1792. The government remained in Philadelphia until 1800. *(New York Public Library)*

Assumption

Hamilton also proposed that the federal government assume responsibility for paying the debts of the individual states, an amount that added up to nearly half the national debt. This "assumption" plan ran into greater opposition than the "funding" one. Speculators were involved in state securities, so there was bound to be opposition. More important, some states had almost paid off their debts, but others had not. A majority of the states that had done so were in the South. Virginians, for example, were unhappy with the prospect of being taxed to help pay for the unpaid debts of Massachusetts. Madison was able to gather enough opposition to defeat the proposal on a test vote.

Yet assumption eventually passed. The speculators in Congress threatened to vote against funding unless they could have assumption as well. Madison and his followers were unwilling to oppose the principle of funding because they knew it was essential for establishing the government's credit. Furthermore, Hamilton held out a suggestion that was particularly attractive to southern representatives. Rather than locate the capital in New York or Philadelphia, why not build a new city on the banks of the Potomac? So Congress passed both parts of Hamilton's program, plus a bill to establish a new "federal city" that would become the capital in 1800. It was soon named Washington, after the first president.

The National Bank

Hamilton made yet another financial proposal that stirred up sectional strife. He called for a Bank of the United States, modeled on the Bank of England. One-fifth of the capital was to be subscribed by the government, the rest by private investors. The Federalists, opposed on principle to government paper money, planned to have the Treasury issue only minted gold and silver. Hamilton argued that a commercial bank was needed to supply notes that would serve as currency in business transactions. This bank would also assist the government by lending it money to meet its short-term obligations and by serving as a depository for government funds. Finally, by providing personal loans, the bank would make it easier for individuals to pay taxes.

"This plan for a national bank," objected Representative James Jackson of Georgia, "is calculated to benefit a small part of the United States, the mercantilist interests only; the farmers, the yeomanry, will derive no advantage from it." But Hamilton's bill passed the House because the commercial North was able to outvote the agrarian South. In 1791 the Bank of the United States was chartered for twenty years, with headquarters in Philadelphia. Ultimately eight branches were established in port cities from Boston to New Orleans.

In the House debate, Madison had argued that a national bank would be unconstitutional. The 1787 convention, he insisted, had rejected the proposition that the federal government be given power to charter companies. When the bank bill was sent to Washington, the president asked Jefferson, Hamilton, and Attorney General Randolph for their opinions. Jefferson supported Madison. Hamilton argued that since the government had been given the power to regulate currency, it had the "implied power" to establish a bank to issue currency.

Randolph could not decide on the constitutional problem, and Washington himself never resolved it. He rejected Jefferson's and Madison's "strict interpretation" of the Constitution in favor of Hamilton's "broad interpretation." But his decision was based more on instinct than on constitutional reasoning. When in doubt on an issue, Washington ordinarily gave his support to the cabinet member whose office was most closely involved. On these grounds Hamilton won his bank. Yet he did not win the broader constitutional issue, and it remained unresolved for years.

Early Crises

Hamilton's second proposal for raising money was an excise tax on various commodities, including distilled liquor. It was enacted quietly in 1791, but it soon raised a storm that tested the inexperienced government. Opposition was especially strong in the West, because whiskey was the most easily transported grain product. The most violent resistance to Hamilton's measure occurred in western Pennsylvania, where resistance to tax collection gained such strong support that it became known as the Whiskey Rebellion. Here, as on other frontiers not close to water transportation, whiskey was regarded as an important means of raising cash. It was also thought of as a personal right and necessity. In addition, the new tax added to a general resentment of government meddling. Opponents of the excise, meeting in Pittsburgh, resolved that "it is insulting to the feelings of the people to have their vessels marked, houses . . . ransacked, to be subject to informers."

In 1794, the federal court in Philadelphia issued writs against seventy-five western Pennsylvania distillers, who would have to travel across the state to answer them in Philadelphia. When federal marshals came west with the writs, a mob attacked them. Hamilton interpreted the uprising against federal collectors as a rebellion against the United States. He prevailed upon Washington to order the mobilization of thirteen thousand militiamen to crush the farmers. Characteristically, Hamilton rode west with the troops. Although they found no organized opposition, the militia rounded up about a hundred men. Two were later convicted of treason and sentenced to death, but Washington eventually pardoned them.

While the Federalist administration aroused opposition with its financial measures, it managed to appear ridiculous in its dealings with the Indians and with foreign powers. Spain continued to claim much of the Southwest and to keep the Mississippi River closed at New Orleans to American shipping. In the Northwest Territory, Britain persisted in using military power to help Canadian fur trappers. British forts on American soil were deeply resented by settlers who looked

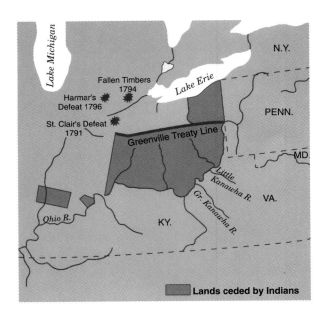

Treaty of Greenville (1795)

to a strong central government for protection against Indian raids.

Yet the new government failed them. In 1791 most of Governor St. Clair's two-thousand ill-equipped and untrained men deserted before they even met the Indians against whom they had been mobilized. The rest were trapped and forced to flee for their lives. Washington stormed: "Here in this very room, I warned General St. Clair against being surprised." Not until 1794, in the Battle of Fallen Timbers, did General "Mad Anthony" Wayne subdue the northwestern tribes. And not until 1795, by the Treaty of Fort Greenville, did these tribes yield most of their Ohio land to the United States. But the Treaty of Fort Greenville came too late for the Federalists to retrieve the political support that earlier failures on the northwestern frontier had cost them.

The awareness that a substantial opposition party was beginning to form only served to intensify a sense of crisis in Federalist ranks. In 1792 Daniel Carroll, one of the commissioners for the development of the federal city, explained that Congress's delay in making appropriations for the new capital arose from suspicions that the government was about to dissolved. In 1793, Oliver Wolcott of Connecticut, who was to succeed Hamilton at the Treasury two years later, observed that if the funding and assumption policies did break up the Union, "the separation ought to be eternal." In 1795 another commentator, observing the new state capitol at Hartford, Connecticut, wrote that it "excites the suspicion . . . that it is contemplated by some to make this a Capitol [for New England], should there be a division of the Northern from the Southern States."

PARTY POLITICS

No specific dates can be given for the beginnings of political parties in the United States. During the colonial period, factions came and went with little continuity. In the new government Washington regarded factions as unpatriotic. He was appalled as he watched opponents of his administration develop into a well-organized, permanent political party. He was unaware of his own contribution to this process, even as he became increasingly influenced by Hamilton. As Jefferson and Madison organized their political forces, he grew more and more upset. He could not know it, but a strange, four-handed game was shaping the course of the nation's politics.

Four Politicians

It was their differing visions of the proper future for the new country that separated Hamilton from Madison and Jefferson. Hamilton envisioned a powerful nation resting on a balanced economy of agriculture, trade, finance, and manufacturing. Agriculture, he thought, needed no special encouragement. After all, the country was predominantly agricultural, and other branches of the economy were more in need of help from the government. Hamilton saw finance as the major weakness of the old government. An elitist by temperament, Hamilton distrusted "the people." This view reflected his own background. Born illegitimate in the West Indies, he had made his way by marriage into the highest financial circles in New York. An outsider, he liked men of wealth and power.

Jefferson, on the other hand, thought farmers would always be the chief supporters of the Republic and the eternal guardians of public virtue. More than Madison, he distrusted the world of cities, commerce, and finance. He thought of them as breeding grounds for moral and political corruption, and he described urban workers as

The Washington family, by Edward Savage. *(Library of Congress)*

"debased by ignorance, indigence, and oppression." Born to the life of a Virginia slave-holding country gentleman, Jefferson felt deep attachment to the land and had an unquestioning trust in the common people who tilled it. He was neither the first nor the last public person to hate privilege because he had it himself.

Madison also owned a plantation (very near Jefferson's), but his interest was concentrated on the art and practice of politics. Deeply committed to balance and moderation, he thrived on the give and take of political horse trading. But now he saw his own goal of strengthening the national government being pushed too far by Hamilton's program. It was natural that he should ally with his Virginian friend in the executive branch.

For his part, Washington remained deeply attached to country and to duty. Convinced that his proper role was to stand at the head of the new nation, he felt he should take no part in quarreling over details of public policy. Although he was one of the wealthiest planters in the South, he never shared Jefferson's distrust of commercial interests. Unfamiliar with the complications of fiscal matters, he was happy to leave them to Hamilton. He tried evenhandedly to soothe the mounting hostility between Hamilton and Jefferson in the cabinet. He intervened more in foreign than in domestic affairs because he thought himself obligated and more competent to do so. When Hamilton assured him that no members of Congress were speculating in government securities, Washington believed him. The patriotic old general found it hard to recognize that some men might place their own interests above the government's.

Organizing

As tension mounted over Hamilton's financial program in 1791–1792, Madison and Jefferson set out to gain support for their position in the country at large as well as in Congress. They toured several New England states and especially New York to express their views to political leaders there. In New York they won over Governor George Clinton. Clinton had long been a rival of Hamilton's wealthy father-in-law, and he still had personal reasons for supporting state power since he held state office.

Jefferson and Madison also backed a new newspaper, the *National Gazette*, as a vehicle for criticizing Hamilton's policies. Madison wrote several articles for this newspaper supporting his position, and he referred to those who backed his views as "the Republican party, as it may be termed." Many readers responded enthusiastically.

Hamilton was not a man to sit by while his opponents organized. He and his allies, taking the name Federalists, backed a newspaper of their own. Like the Republicans, the Federalists began organizing local clubs. The Federalists had several important advantages. They had a well-thought-out, positive program. The great majority of newspaper editors and clergy supported Federalist ideas, and so did a majority of wealthy men. In addition, Federalists in government were able to reward party workers with government jobs.

At the time of the 1792 national election, the Republicans were not well enough organized to run a candidate for president. Furthermore, Washington had reluctantly agreed to serve again, and it would have been futile and perhaps self-destructive to oppose him. John Adams, who had been elected vice-president in the first election, was again the vice-presidential candidate. The Republicans organized behind George Clinton for vice-president. Washington and Adams were both reelected. But the election returns showed that the Republicans were a new force in American politics. During the next few years, voting in Congress did not take place according to firm party lines. Yet by 1795 certain developments in foreign affairs had further clarified the two national political parties and deepened the division between them.

FOREIGN AFFAIRS UNDER WASHINGTON

During Washington's first administration, party lines had been drawn over financial issues. In his second administration problems of foreign policy, as a contemporary said, "not merely divided parties, but molded them," and "gave them . . . their bitterness." Some of these problems were carryovers from the war with Britain. But the French Revolution, which began just a few

The name *Mississippi* was originally an Algonkian Indian term meaning "big river." Algonkian-speaking Indians ranged from the northern Atlantic coast westward through the Great Lakes region. Western Algonkian tribes gave that name to the northern part of a large river without knowing anything about the southern region through which it flowed to the Gulf of Mexico. French explorers first heard the name "Messipi" in 1666 as they pressed westward from the St. Lawrence river valley through and beyond the Great Lakes. Farther south, different Indian groups, speaking different languages, each had their own name for the great river. Hernando de Soto, the Spanish explorer who was buried in the southern part of the river, piously named it *Espiritu Santo*, or Holy Spirit. But as French adventurers pressed southward they used the northern Algonkian name for the entire waterway. In 1798 Congress created a U.S. territory in what was then the southwestern frontier and named it after the river. Later, in 1817, part of that territory was admitted to the Union as the state of Mississippi.

weeks after Washington first took office in 1789, was the source of most of the trouble.

Citizen Genêt and the Neutrality Proclamation

At first, most Americans welcomed the French Revolution. They felt their own revolutionary principles were spreading to Europe. In 1790, when Lafayette sent Washington the key to the fortress-prison known as the Bastille, the president acknowledged it as a "token of victory gained by liberty over despotism." Within a year, however, the Hamiltonians had aligned themselves against the French Revolution, while the Jeffersonians still praised it.

The execution of Louis XVI in January 1793 alarmed American conservatives, and the Jacobin reign of terror that followed confirmed their misgivings about excessive democracy. In the meantime, the French wars against the continental monarchs, who had combined to end the threat of republicanism, had begun in1792.

For weeks, westerly gales kept news of the executions and the wars from reaching America. When all the news flooded in at once, in April 1793, it strengthened the Hamiltonians in their opposition to France. The Jeffersonians, on the other hand, remained distrustful of monarchy and confident about the people of the French republic.

It was not long before the conflict of opinion was deepened by specific issues of foreign policy. The French treaty of 1778 obligated the United States to defend the French West Indies in case of an attack on France itself. It also provided that French privateers and men-of-war could bring captured ships to American ports. In 1792 the group of revolutionaries ruling France assumed that this treaty remained in force—as indeed it did under international law. They sent "Citizen" Edmond Genêt as envoy to America to see that it was carried out.

Genêt had other instructions. He was to organize expeditions from the United States to seize Louisiana and Florida from Spain, and outfit American ships to prey on British shipping. These enterprises were to be financed with American funds made available by a speedup in American payments on the old French loan. Genêt had one more project: to organize Jacobin clubs in America, to advance the cause of "Liberty, Equality, and Fraternity." This happened just when Jefferson himself had begun to sponsor Republican political clubs of his own.

Genêt, an attractive and enterprising young man, landed in Charleston, South Carolina, in 1793. After a warm welcome he went to work without even bothering to present his credentials to the government in Philadelphia. By the time he finally arrived at the capital, the president, after consulting Jefferson and Hamilton, had issued a Neutrality Proclamation making it clear that the United States would not participate in the French wars.

Jefferson defended the position of the Moderate Girondist faction in France that the treaty of 1778 was with the French nation, no matter what its government might be. He also argued that since only Congress could declare war, only Congress could proclaim neutrality. Jefferson also felt that if such a proclamation were issued, Britain should be forced to make certain concessions in return. Hamilton held that the French treaty had died with the French king, and that neutrality in any case was the only possible American policy. Jefferson, having made his arguments, did not persist in opposing the practical step: Washington's proclamation followed.

By this time, Genêt had already commissioned enthusiastic Charleston ship captains as French privateers to prey on British shipping. He had also organized a South Carolina military adventure against Spain in Florida and had persuaded a group of Kentuckians to float down the Mississippi and dislodge the Spanish from New Orleans. The warmth of Genêt's reception had convinced him that the American people were with him, whatever the government might do. When Washington received Genêt with forbidding coldness and gave him to understand that the government would no longer tolerate his operations, let alone support them, Genêt decided to ignore the president.

Even Jefferson was put off by this persistence, and when Genêt, contrary to Washington's express warnings, permitted *Little Democrat*, a prize ship converted into an armed vessel, to sail as a privateer, Jefferson voted with the president and the rest of the cabinet to ask for Genêt's recall. By then, Genêt's group had fallen out of favor at home. Fearing for his life, the young envoy remained in America, married Governor Clinton's daughter, and retired to a country estate on the Hudson.

The repercussions of this affair were less romantic. Washington's Neutrality Proclamation had reflected the president's determination to keep the nation at peace. Jefferson shared this hope, but his apparent sympathy with Genêt's early activities led the president to read the most sinister meaning into the conduct of his secretary of state and of those "self-constituted societies," as Washington called the new Republican clubs Jefferson sponsored. "It is not the cause of France, nor I believe of liberty, which they regard," he wrote in 1793, but only the "disgrace" of the new nation under Federalist rule. By the end of the year, Washington had accepted Jefferson's resignation from the cabinet. As for Jefferson himself, his nerves were frayed by political battling; he longed only to retire to his beloved Monticello.

Neutrality: Profits and Problems

The war in Europe opened the way for a shipping boom in the neutral nations. As a leading maritime nation, the United States was among the greatest gainers. Since the French had a relatively small merchant fleet that was vulnerable to British attack, they desperately needed neutral assistance. Early in the war, France at last surrendered its monopoly of the French West Indian trade and opened its island ports to American ships and produce. American ships began a brisk trade with the French sugar islands, supplying them with foodstuffs and barrels and returning with sugar and molasses.

The British retaliated. They resurrected their "rule of the War of 1756," which held that trade barred to a nation in peacetime could not be opened to it during hostilities. This applied with special force to the French West Indian trade. In 1793 they announced that all shipping to or from the French colonies would be subject to British seizure. American ships by then had swarmed into the Caribbean to trade with the French islands. The British seized about three hundred United States vessels, abused their passengers, and forced many of their sailors into the British navy.

Even so, American trade thrived. Many ships were captured, but many more slipped through. These losses served as an additional stimulus to the shipbuilding industry. By 1794, however, the British had become so brazen that even Federalists expected war. The United States insisted that "neutral ships made neutral goods," but the British enforced their self-proclaimed right to search for enemy supplies anywhere on any ship. The United States insisted that a blockade must be enforced by actual patrols of the closed ports. But the British simply announced "paper blockades" and undertook to enforce them whenever they found a vessel presumably bound for a forbidden harbor. The United States insisted that foodstuffs could not be classified as contraband, but the British did not hesitate to capture ships carrying food for France and its allies.

In addition, British authorities in Canada continued to encourage Indians to resist American settlers moving west. The British government made clear that it still had no intention of giving up its armed posts in northwestern American territory. It based this refusal to evacuate on the fact that the United States had not lived up to the provisions of the peace treaty of 1783, especially concerning Loyalist property and American debts.

Jay's Treaty

President Washington decided to try diplomatic negotiation in order to meet these problems. He named John Jay his special envoy, with instructions to get the British to surrender their military posts in the Northwest, to pay for American ships that had been captured illegally, and to respect the American position on the rights and privileges of neutrals. Jay was also to negotiate the best commercial treaty he could. If he could not get the British to agree on all these points, Jay was to try to get the northern countries of Europe to agree jointly with the United States to enforce neutral rights.

Jay had a good case, and the embattled British needed American friendship. But Hamilton undercut these advantages. As early as 1789, he had told Major Beckwith, his secret British contact reporting on American affairs: "I have always preferred a connexion with you, to that of any other country. We think in English, and have a similarity of prejudices and predilections."

In 1794, while Jay was still on his way to England, Washington received a proposal from Sweden and Denmark, two of the northern neutrals Jay was to consult if he failed to gain British concessions. They suggested just what Jay was instructed to suggest to them—that all three nations unite to combat British assaults on neutral shipping. Washington was favorably inclined. But Hamilton managed to stop him, arguing that far from strengthening Jay's hand, such action would only make the British more difficult to deal with. Hamilton, moreover, promptly told George Hammond, the British minister in New York, of Washington's decision. Hammond lost little time in sending this information to the British negotiators. The result was an uphill fight for Jay and a very unsatisfactory agreement.

By the Treaty of London (completed in November 1794 and known in America as Jay's Treaty), the British agreed again to evacuate their Northwest posts. By 1796 they had done so, but Jay had to barter away a great deal in return. The British could still carry on the fur trade on the American side of the Canadian border with Indians hostile to advancing American settlement. This concession almost canceled out the surrender of the posts and deeply angered westerners.

As for the British paying for captured ships, settlement of this issue was left to a future joint commission that would determine what, if anything, was owed. On the rights of neutrals, Jay failed altogether. His efforts to gain commercial concessions also fell completely flat.

Jay's whole agreement was so unsatisfactory that Washington hesitated a long time before sending it to the Senate. The Senate, in turn, made every effort to hide the terms from the people. But there were leaks. When the Senate on June 25, 1795, by the slenderest possible two-thirds majority ratified the treaty, the public outcry was as violent as expected. In the months following, "Sir John Jay" was hanged in effigy throughout the country. One person chalked up in large letters on a Boston street wall: "DAMN JOHN JAY! DAMN EVERY ONE WHO WON'T DAMN JOHN JAY!! DAMN EVERY ONE WHO WON'T SIT UP ALL NIGHT DAMNING JOHN JAY!!!"

By the time of Jay's Treaty, even the great wartime leader was being denounced in the opposition press. The following "Political CREED of a Western American" was copied in several newspapers:

I believe that the treaty formed by Jay and the British king is the offspring of a vile aristocratic few who have too long governed in America, and who are enemies to the equality of men, friends to no government but that whose funds they can convert to their private employment.

I do not believe that Hamilton, Jay or King and their minions, are devils incarnate: but I do believe them so filled with pride, and so fattened on the spoils of America, that they abhor every thing which partakes of Democracy, and that they most ardently desire the swinish multitude humbled in dust and ashes.

I believe the period is at hand when the inhabitants of America will cease to admire or approve the conduct of the Federal executive, because they esteem the man who fills the chair of state. . . .

I believe that the political dotage of our good old American chief, has arrived, and that while we record his virtues in letters of gold, we should consign his person to the tender offices due to virtuous age, and transfer him from the chair of state to the chair of domestic ease. . . .

Albert Gallatin, the congressman from Pennsylvania, 1795–1801. Gallatin argued that by withholding appropriations, the House of Representatives could, in effect, veto the Jay Treaty and thus "stop the wheels of government." *(Library of Congress)*

In the Congress that met in December 1795, the question was asked whether the House of Representatives, by failing to vote appropriations required under the agreement, could in effect reject the treaty, even though the Senate had accepted it. The House voted 57 to 35 that it had the constitutional right to reject treaties by withholding funds, but it went on to approve the appropriations by a narrow vote of 51 to 48.

Pinckney's Treaty

In June 1795, while the Senate was considering Jay's Treaty with Britain, Spain withdrew from the British coalition against France and made peace with the revolutionary government there. This step made Spain fearful of British reprisals, which might take the form of attacks on its empire in America. It also feared attacks from American frontiersmen. When Britain and America concluded Jay's Treaty, Spain's fears for its empire grew.

The Spanish decided to try to win American friendship. After several proposals failed to lure Thomas Pinckney, the American minister who had gone to Madrid on Spain's invitation in 1794, Pinckney wrote home that the king of Spain was now prepared "to sacrifice something of what he considered as his right, to testify to his good will to us."

Pinckney proceeded to negotiate the Treaty of San Lorenzo, usually called Pinckney's Treaty, which the Spanish signed in 1795 and the United

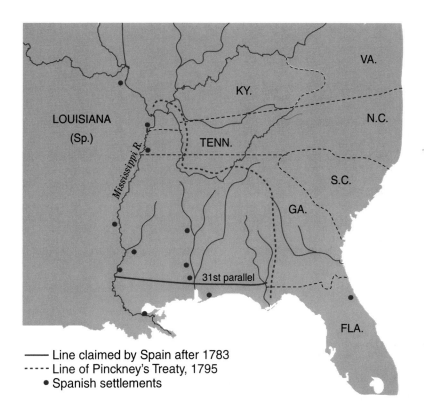

Louisiana (Sp.), VA., KY., N.C., Mississippi R., TENN., S.C., GA., 31st parallel, FLA.

—— Line claimed by Spain after 1783
----- Line of Pinckney's Treaty, 1795
• Spanish settlements

Pinckney's Treaty (1795)

States Senate unanimously approved in 1796. This agreement settled the northern boundary of Florida at the latitude of 31°. Much more important, Spain opened the Mississippi "in its whole length from its source to the ocean" to American river traffic and allowed Americans use of the port of New Orleans for three years, after which time the arrangement could be renewed.

The Election of 1796

Washington had felt so strongly about not running for a second term in 1792 that he had asked Madison and others to draw up ideas for his "valedictory" to the nation. Early in 1796 he turned these old papers over to Hamilton for a new draft. This time he was utterly determined not to serve again. He looked with deepest dismay, he said, on the "baneful effects of the spirit of party." But at the same time he took keen satisfaction in many of his accomplishments.

Washington did not deliver his Farewell Address in person; he simply published it in the newspapers on September 17, 1796. That date was so close to the presidential elections that it stirred resentment among opposition leaders, who felt that his delay in announcing his decision handicapped them in mounting an effective campaign. They also felt his warnings on party spirit were attacks on them and not on the Federalist party.

The party strife Washington hated was nearing its peak when he retired. Debate in the House over Jay's Treaty had continued well into 1796, and Washington's own decision intensified the conflict by opening up the highest office to the rising political machines. The Federalists brought out a ticket of John Adams of Massachusetts and Thomas Pinckney of South Carolina. The Republicans named Jefferson and Aaron Burr of New York.

Hamilton and Adams had long since grown cool toward each other, and Hamilton went to great pains to maneuver Pinckney into the presidency. His elaborate scheme backfired. Adams won with 71 votes. Jefferson, with 68 votes, was second in the balloting and defeated Pinckney for the vice-presidency. Thus the president and the vice-president represented two different political parties.

CHAPTER 8 THE FEDERALIST ERA   **163**

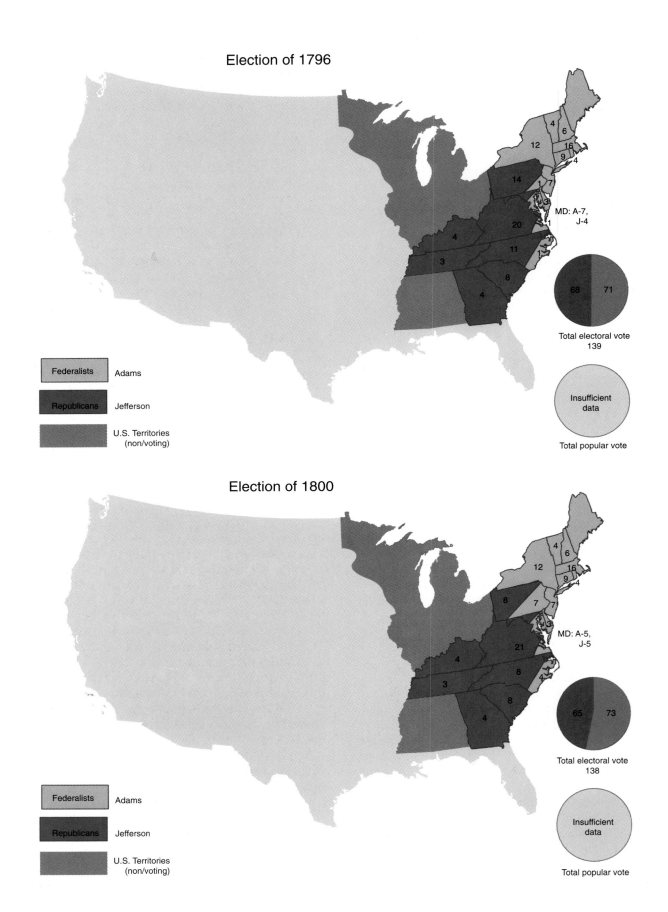

Election of 1796

MD: A-7, J-4

Total electoral vote
139

Insufficient data

Total popular vote

Federalists — Adams

Republicans — Jefferson

U.S. Territories (non/voting)

Election of 1800

MD: A-5, J-5

Total electoral vote
138

Insufficient data

Total popular vote

Federalists — Adams

Republicans — Jefferson

U.S. Territories (non/voting)

THE ADAMS ADMINISTRATION

Americans now take the transition from one presidential administration to another as a matter of course. In 1796 the public was experiencing the first transfer of presidential power from one man to another. Anxiety was deepened by the fact that a leader of Washington's stature was about to retire. The president, writes one historian, "had already determined to demonstrate to the world the supreme achievement of democratic government—the peaceful and orderly change of the head of the state in accordance with the voice of the people." John Adams himself was moved by the historic event to write to his wife about his inauguration: "All agree that . . . it was the sublimest thing ever exhibited in America."

Foreign Policy

During John Adams's presidency, the new government nearly lost control over its own foreign policy. No statesman in the United States had written more than John Adams about human nature. But Jefferson shrewdly observed that in practice Adams was "a bad calculator" of the "motives of men." He made the mistake of retaining in his cabinet second-rate Hamiltonians, such as Secretary of State Timothy Pickering and Secretary of the Treasury Oliver Wolcott, who had surrounded Washington toward the end. Worse, Adams spent a great deal of time at home in Massachusetts. In later years, after his retirement, Adams counted it as one of his major accomplishments that he, like Washington, had kept the United States at peace with revolutionary France. Yet Hamilton's anti-French friends in Adams's virtually independent cabinet managed to carry the administration to the brink of all-out hostilities.

The French government interpreted Jay's Treaty as a British diplomatic victory. They had already begun attacking American ships bound for British ports, and now they intensified their efforts. By the time of Adams's inauguration in March 1797, the French had captured about three hundred American vessels and had manhandled their crews.

In the meantime, Washington had recalled his minister to France, James Monroe, and sent Charles C. Pinckney to replace him. After he had been in France the two months allowed to

foreigners, the French police notified Pinckney that unless he got a permit to remain, they would arrest him. Pinckney fled to Amsterdam in a rage. When news of Pinckney's treatment reached Philadelphia, Adams (now president) had to deal with Federalist demands for war with the French.

Adams refused to give in. Without asking the French government, he decided to send a three-man mission to Paris to persuade the French to end their raids on American shipping. When Talleyrand, then foreign minister of France, refused to negotiate unless the Americans gave a bribe of $250,000 to three subordinates, the mission collapsed. In their reports home, the American envoys referred to Talleyrand's three subordinates as X, Y, and Z. When the reports became public, an uproar broke out among both parties over the so-called XYZ dispatches, during which someone is said to have cried, "Millions for defense, but not one cent for tribute!" Congress did vote millions for the expansion of the army and navy in 1798 and 1799; it also created a separate Navy Department and repealed all treaties with France.

To the disappointment of Hamilton, who wanted to lead it into battle, the new army grew very slowly. Adams himself saw little use for land forces in fighting for freedom of the seas. He was also reluctant to burden the country with needless expense. The new Navy Department, on the other hand, promptly pushed to completion three well-armed frigates then under construction, produced twenty other ships of war, and sent hundreds of American privateers to prey on the French. In 1798 and 1799, an undeclared naval war raged with France. American ships, operating mainly in the Caribbean, took almost a hundred French vessels and suffered serious losses themselves.

Hamilton's friends in the cabinet and Congress, meanwhile, were pushing the expansion of the army so hard that many people suspected a plan to use it against domestic as well as foreign enemies. Their suspicions were confirmed in February 1799, when troops were sent once more to western Pennsylvania to put down a rebellion led by John Fries against the collection of the new taxes to pay for the army.

The Hamiltonians even persuaded Washington, only a few months before his death, to take nominal command of the army once again. This step helped push Adams, much against his inclination, to put Hamilton next in command and effectively in charge. But Adams would go no further; he refused to ask Congress to make an official declaration of war against France.

The Alien and Sedition Acts

At the time of Adams's election, Madison had written to Jefferson: "You know the temper of Mr. A. better than I do, but I have always conceived it to be rather a ticklish one." One thing Adams quickly became ticklish about was the Republican taunt that he was "president by three votes." Other attacks on him and his administration aroused him, early in the summer of 1798, to lash back at his opponents.

Many of the most vocal were recent immigrants, including Albert Gallatin, the Swiss banker who became Republican leader of the House when Madison retired from that post. The English radical Thomas Cooper, who had come to America in 1794 and soon proved himself a vigorous Republican pamphleteer, was another. Adams suspected a number of recently arrived French intellectuals of engaging in espionage. Most offensive of all, perhaps, were the defeated fighters for Irish freedom who brought to the United States their hatred of Britain. Nor did Adams forget American-born Republican journalists.

Adams might easily have gotten over his anger if extremists in his party, in 1798, had not pushed through Congress four laws known as the Alien and Sedition Acts. The first was a Naturalization Act that raised the residence requirement for American citizenship from five to fourteen years. The second, the Alien Act, empowered the president even in peacetime to order any alien from the country and to imprison any who refused to leave. The third, the Alien Enemies Act, permitted the president to jail enemy aliens in wartime. No arrests were made under either alien act, but they did frighten hundreds of foreigners from the country.

The fourth measure was the Sedition Act. Its key clause provided severe fines and jail penalties for anyone speaking, writing, or publishing "with intent to defame ... or bring into contempt or disrepute" the president or other members of the government. That its purpose was to gag the Republican opposition until after the next presidential election was evident in the provision keeping the act "in force until March 3, 1801, and no longer."

A number of Republican editors were actually jailed, and some Republican papers were forced to shut down. The trials were travesties of justice dominated by judges who saw treason everywhere. Juries were handpicked by Federalist United States marshals in defiance of statutes prescribing orderly procedures. The presiding judges often ridiculed the defendants' lawyers and interrupted their presentations, prompting many to walk out and leave their client to the mercy of the court.

The Virginia and Kentucky Resolutions

The entire collection of acts aroused indignant opposition. Madison called the Sedition Act "a monster that must forever disgrace its parents." He and Jefferson both recognized it as the beginning of the Federalist campaign for the election of 1800. They moved quickly to a broad attack on the whole Federalist philosophy. Their offensive took the form of a series of resolutions for which their allies won the approval of the legislatures of Kentucky and Virginia in 1798. The resolutions were then circulated among the other states.

Jefferson wrote the Kentucky resolutions; Madison wrote those adopted in Virginia. Both sets attacked the broad interpretation of the Constitution and developed the states'-rights position later used to justify nullification and secession. In Jefferson's words, "the several states composing the United States of America, are not united on the principle of unlimited submission to their general government." That government, in Madison's terms, is but a "compact to which the states are parties." The Kentucky Resolutions held that the states, as parties to the compact, had the right to declare which measures went beyond their agreement and were "unauthoritative, void, and of no force," and to decide which remedies were appropriate. Madison, in the Virginia Resolutions, said that the states together might "interpose" to check the exercise of unauthorized federal powers. Jefferson went further; he held that the legislature of each state had this right.

No interpretation of the intent or action of the Great Convention of 1787 could have been more farfetched than that expressed in these resolutions. But in pressing their argument this far, Madison and Jefferson at least had a liberalizing goal that was not part of later states'-rights movements. In the Kentucky Resolutions, Jefferson said that the Alien and Sedition Acts, by employing the loosest construction of the Constitution to impose the tightest tyranny, soured "the mild spirit of our country and its laws."

In both states the resolutions asked other state legislatures to adopt the same position. None did so. Federalists in several northern states passed resolutions denouncing Virginia and Kentucky for misinterpreting the nature of the Constitution. They argued that the Constitution was much more than an agreement among independent states and that only the federal courts could decide whether actions of the other two branches violated it. So the Virginia and Kentucky Resolutions had little effect at the time, except to remind Americans that the relationship of the states to the national government was not a settled one. No one at the time realized how often the question would arise again.

The Election of 1800

Although the XYZ affair and other actions by France had cost the Republicans some strength in the country, their prospects for the presidential campaign of 1800 were brightened by the sharp split in Federalist ranks between the Adams men and the Hamiltonians.

For the campaign of 1800, the Republican caucus named Jefferson and Aaron Burr of New York. The badly divided Federalists finally brought out a ticket of Adams and C. C. Pinckney. After the election, the electoral college voted 65 for Adams and 64 for Pinckney, but Jefferson and Burr each received 73 votes.

The Republicans had won, but they faced an unexpected difficulty because of the tie between the Republican candidates for president and vice-president. Burr had no ambitions to be president at this time, but many Federalists, especially those from commercial New England and New York, saw his tie vote with Jefferson as an opportunity to keep Jefferson out.

The *Washington Federalist* described Burr as "a friend of the Constitution . . . a friend of the commercial interests . . . the firm and decided friend of the navy." The newspaper went on to argue for geographical balance: "The Eastern States [New England] have had a President and Vice President; So have the Southern. It is proper that the middle states should also be respected."

According to the Constitution, the House would have to decide between the two Republicans. There the voting was to be by states, and nine states (out of the sixteen) were needed to win. The first ballot was taken on February 11, with the results that Jefferson had foreseen: He carried eight states, Burr six, and two were undecided. And so it went for a feverish week, during which thirty-five ballots were taken. The deadlock was broken on the thirty-sixth ballot. Certain Federalist congressmen took their states out of Burr's camp by voting blanks.

The next Congress put an end to this kind of problem by writing the Twelfth Amendment, ratified by the states in 1804. This amendment provided that henceforth, "the electors . . . shall name in their ballots the person voted for as President and in distinct ballots the person voted for as Vice-President."

Despite the viciousness of the election campaign, the transfer of power from the Federalists to the Republicans had been accomplished peaceably. Americans were beginning to realize that an organized political opposition had to be permitted its own free voice and its hopes for power.

Although the Republicans captured the presidency and control of both the House and the Senate, the country's first great shift in political power was not quite complete. Just before adjourning in March 1801, the retiring Federalist Congress gave Adams a new Judiciary Act. It relieved Supreme Court justices, as well as district court justices, from the burden of riding to the circuit courts, created a whole new group of circuit court judges, and increased the number of district court judges. Adams proceeded to place Federalist sympathizers in these lifetime jobs and other new judicial posts. Most important, he named his interim secretary of state, John Marshall, as chief justice of the Supreme Court. Adams was the last Federalist president. After him, as the country became more Republican and expansive, his party became more sectional and narrow. Yet for more than thirty years of Republican political rule, Chief Justice Marshall handed down Federalist, nationalist interpretations of the law despite continual crises generated by wars in Europe and an expanding economy.

SUMMARY

The new Constitution described the United States government, but its leaders had to fill in the framework. The first item on the new Congress's agenda was the passage of the federal Bill of Rights—the first ten amendments to the Constitution. They were ratified by the states late in 1791. The Judiciary Act of 1789 set up the federal court system and spelled out its powers. The building of the executive branch was begun with three departments—State, War, and Treasury. Washington appointed secretaries for each, a chief justice, and an attorney general. The secretaries and the attorney general became the basis for a presidential cabinet.

Congress, meanwhile, turned to the urgent money problems that had caused so much trouble under the Articles and passed the first money-raising law, a tariff. Hamilton was the driving force behind longer-range solutions to the nation's financial difficulties. He proposed a variety of plans to deal with the public debt and to tie the fate of the new nation to the fortunes of the merchants and the wealthy, whom he saw as its most important citizens. He succeeded in establishing a national bank modeled on the Bank of England. But he had less success with an excise tax on commodities. Opposition to the tax resulted in the so-called Whiskey Rebellion in western Pennsylvania in 1794. The fact that the new government was not immediately able to deal firmly with the Indians, the British, and the Spanish on the frontiers also added to its troubles.

All these controversies helped to build factions, and eventually political parties. Four men—Hamilton, Madison, Jefferson, and Washington—were the country's leading figures. But they were not in agreement, and

from their opposing views of how government should work and where power should reside—whether with the national government or with the states—came political parties. The Federalists, led by Hamilton, favored a strong, wealthy nation led by commercial and financial interests. The Republicans, led by Jefferson and Madison, trusted the farmer and the common people far more than they did the urban merchant. Washington was a patriot, firmly against parties and factionalism. As president, he saw it as his duty not to take sides.

Washington's agreeing to serve for a second term meant there was no presidential contest in 1792. But the parties were already active in the vice-presidential race and would run presidential candidates in 1796.

Washington's second term was occupied with foreign affairs, mostly because of the French Revolution. It had begun in 1789, but within a few years its effects had spread beyond French borders and caused war between England and France. The subversive activities of Citizen Genêt, the problems of neutrality on the seas, and the unpopularity of the treaty John Jay negotiated with the British in 1795 all caused discontent in the United States. Pinckney's treaty with Spain in 1795 had a better reception, primarily because the United States gained access to the Mississippi and to the port of New Orleans.

The election of 1796, the first peaceful transfer of power, was won by the Federalist John Adams. Much of his attention was devoted to avoiding war with France and to battling political enemies at home. It was also in his administration that Congress passed the first laws abridging individual freedoms—the Alien and Sedition Acts. The Republican reaction to these measures was

TIME LINE

Year	Event	Year	Event
1789	Inauguration of George Washington in New York City	1795	Ratification of Jay's Treaty
1789	Outbreak of the French Revolution	1795	Pinckney's Treaty; ratified in 1796
1789	Judiciary Act	1796	Election of Federalist John Adams as president
1789	Adoption of the Bill of Rights; ratified in 1791	1797	XYZ Affair
1790	Congress adopts Hamilton's fiscal program	1798–1799	Undeclared naval war against France
1791	Establishment of a national bank	1798	Alien and Sedition Acts
1792	Open split between Hamilton and Jefferson	1798	Virginia and Kentucky Resolutions
1793	Arrival of Citizen Genêt	1799	Fries Rebellion
1793	Washington's Neutrality Proclamation	1800	Election of Thomas Jefferson after initial tie with Burr
1794	Whiskey Rebellion	1801	Adam's last-minute judicial appointments

sharp. Madison and Jefferson, through the Virginia and Kentucky Resolutions, began a debate over states' rights and federal power that would become part of American politics for many years.

With the Republican capture of the presidency in 1800, the Federalist party faded. But before Adams left office, he appointed a new chief justice of the Supreme Court, John Marshall. The decisions of this Federalist in favor of a broad, nationalist interpretation of the Constitution were to have a permanent influence on the new nation and to turn it in a direction opposite to what the Republicans intended.

Suggested Readings

J. Miller, *The Federalist Era, 1789–1801* (1960), a well-balanced survey, has an extensive bibliography. An interesting, sweeping approach is taken by J. Fliegelman, *Prodigals and Pilgrims: The American Revolution against Patriarchal Authority, 1750–1800* (1982).

Hamilton was, of course, a central figure in this period, and he remains almost as controversial now as he was then. The best approach to his thinking lies through his *Papers*, edited by H. Syrett and J. Cooke. J. Miller, *Alexander Hamilton* (1959), is probably the most balanced biography, though there is much more information in B. Mitchell, *Alexander Hamilton* (2 vols., 1957, 1962). J. Boyd, the Sherlock Holmes of modern historians, has unraveled Hamilton's machinations in *Number 7: Alexander Hamilton's Secret Attempts to Control American Foreign Policy* (1964). Hamilton's economic program has received impressive analysis by Mitchell (above) and Ferguson (cited in Chapter 7).

Washington is brought to life in the third and fourth volumes of the biography by J. Flexner, *George Washington and the New Nation, 1783–1793* (1969) and *George Washington: Angaish and Farewell, 1793–1799* (1972). D. Freeman, *George Washington* (7 vols., 1948–1957), provides more detail and is itself a monument to monumental biography. For Madison, see Brant's biography, cited in Chapter 7. For Jefferson, see the citations in Chapter 9.

Partly because the Founding Fathers disliked the very notion of political parties, historians have been fascinated by the parties' rapid emergence. See J. Chambers, *Political Parties in a New Nation: The American Experience, 1776–1809* (1963); N. Cunningham, Jr., *The Jeffersonian Republicans: The Formation of Party Organization, 1789–1801* (1957); and M. Borden, *Parties and Politics in the Early Republic, 1789–1815* (1967). J. Banner, *To the Hartford Convention: The Federalists and the Origins of Party Politics in Massachusetts* (1970), gives a sensible discussion at the state level. An important incident is covered in T. Slaughter, *The Whiskey Rebellion: Frontier Epilogue to the American Revolution* (1986).

Foreign affairs in the Federalist period and their impact on party development are dealt with by A. De Conde, *Entangling Alliance: Politics and Diplomacy under George Washington* (1958) and *The Quasi-War: The Politics and Diplomacy of the Undeclared War with France, 1797–1801* (1966); P. Varg, *Foreign Policies of the Founding Fathers* (1963); and J. Combs, *The Jay Treaty: Political Battleground of the Founding Fathers* (1970). See W. Fowler's interesting *Jack Tars and Commodores: The American Navy, 1783–1815* (1984). Perhaps the best writer on foreign policy for this and later periods is B. Perkins, *The First Rapprochement: England and the United States, 1795–1805* (1955).

The new nation's foreign policy in this period was intertwined with westward expansion. On this matter, see F. Philbrick, *The Rise of the West, 1754–1830* (1965); R. Horseman, *The Frontier in the Formative Years, 1783–1815* (1970); and M. Rohrbough, *Land Office Business: Public Lands, 1789–1837* (1968). Western policy and several of the key characters receive attention in J. Daniels, *Ordeal of Ambition: Jefferson, Hamilton, Burr* (1970).

There is no fully adequate biography of John Adams. C. Chinard, *Honest John Adams* (1933), is brief but out of date. Z. Haraszti, *John Adams and the Prophets of Progress* (1952), takes advantage of Adams's habit of filling the margins of the books he read with biting criticisms. No study has yet caught the fundamentally Puritan nature of Adams's thought and feeling. The best route to this puzzling man is through his *Diary and Autobiography*, ed. L. Butterfield et al. (4 vols., 1961); and L. Butterfield et al., *The Book of Abigail and John: Selected Letters of the Adams Family, 1762–1784* (1975). There are, however, two good political studies: M. Daner, *The Adams Federalists* (1953); and S. Kurtz, *The Presidency of John Adams: The Collapse of Federalism, 1795–1800* (1958).

A free press was not taken for granted during these years. On early repression, see J. Miller, *Crisis in Freedom; The Alien and Sedition Acts* (1951); J. Smith, *Freedom's Fetters* (1956); and D. Stewart, *The Opposition Press of the Federal Period, 1789–1800* (1969). R. Buel, *Securing the Revolution: Ideology in American Politics, 1789–1815* (1972), offers a brand of psychohistory while examining certain political leaders during the period of the Alien and Sedition Acts. An interesting overview is J. Appleby, *Capitalism and a New Social Order: The Republican Vision of the 1790s* (1984).

Sketch from the journal of Sergeant Patrick Gass, who accompanied Lewis and Clark in their travels; (Clark and his men hunt bears. *(Library of Congress)*

JEFFERSON, THE CONTINENT, AND WAR

Of all the great figures among the Founding Fathers, Thomas Jefferson was both the most approachable and the most aloof. He dressed casually and informally, even on solemn public occasions. A Pennsylvania senator described him critically when Jefferson took up his duties as secretary of state in 1790: "His clothes seem too small for him. He sits in a lounging manner, on his hip commonly, and with one of his shoulders elevated much above the other. . . . His whole figure has a loose, shackling air." The senator went on to refer to Jefferson's "rambling vacant look," which had "nothing of that firm collected deportment which I expected." The senator "looked for gravity," but found "rather the air of stiffness in his manner." But Thomas Jefferson did not slouch; he was both distant and tough in several ways. "The people," writes one of Jefferson's biographers, "could have quite taken him to their hearts if they had not felt, as everyone felt in his presence, that he was always graciously but firmly holding them off."

Thomas Jefferson called the Republican victory that brought him to office "the revolution of 1800." Never a man to see much

shading between good and evil, he wrote: "The Federalists wished for everything which would approach our new government to a monarchy; the Republicans to preserve it essentially republican."

Few historians today would agree with Jefferson. His election was followed by change, but not as much as he had hoped for. Jefferson thought that the great majority of Federalists had been led astray by a few wealthy, power-hungry men, and he wanted to gather the bulk of them into his own party. He was partially successful, for Federalists never again controlled the presidency. Yet they continued for at least fifteen years to sustain an active political organization. And they held control of the courts. Jefferson's "revolution" was in fact a completely peaceful transfer of political power from one political group to another; few countries at that (or any) time have had such good fortune.

Jefferson and his handpicked successors, James Madison and James Monroe, sought to avoid further entanglement with European conflicts. Jefferson's eyes were on what he called America's "continental destiny." He used that phrase even though much of the continent was still claimed by Spain, Great Britain, France, and Russia, and actually occupied by several hundred Indian nations. As things turned out, Jefferson doubled the size of the United States. But then James Madison allowed the country to drift into involvement in European wars. Only after those wars were over in 1815 was the United States free to concentrate on internal expansion.

JEFFERSON IN POWER

The new president immediately set out to correct what he regarded as the injustices of the previous administration. He cut the federal budget. He struggled against Federalists in the judiciary, but with very little success. His greatest interest, however, was more positive. Most of the North American continent, he thought, was destined to fall into the hands of the young Republic. He gave "destiny" a helping hand by sending out explorers and by approving the purchase of a territory so large that it doubled the size of the United States.

A New Broom

Jefferson's inaugural address extended the hand of peace to his political opponents. "We are all Republicans; we are all Federalists," he declared in a statement that was more hopeful than accurate. Jefferson also announced his faith that enemies of the Republic should be allowed to "stand undisturbed as monuments of the safety with which error of opinion may be tolerated where reason is left free to combat it." When Jefferson spoke these words at his inauguration, the previous president, John Adams, was already jostling homeward to Massachusetts in a coach.

The new administration did indeed seem very different from the previous Federalist ones. Jefferson's inauguration was the first to take place in the new federal city on the Potomac. Grand plans had been made for the city. A French architect, Pierre L'Enfant, had been hired to draw up an elegant plan of streets.

In 1800, however, the city was anything but imposing. The streets were ruts of dust and mud, except when they were frozen. Pennsylvania Avenue ran from the Capitol toward the president's house through a swamp. The few public buildings were still under construction. The rest of the city consisted of one stationery shop, one grocer, one shoemaker, one printer, one washerwoman, one tailor shop, one dry goods shop, and one oyster house. Elected and appointed officials lived in seven or eight crammed boardinghouses, seeing too much of each other in quarters far too close for privacy or comfort. Members of Congress spent as little time as possible in Washington. Philadelphia had been far more attractive, a real city with paved and lighted streets, established taverns, social life with ladies, and even a theater.

Upon taking office, Jefferson and the Republicans immediately set about to nullify the Alien and Sedition Acts. Since these laws were due to expire within a few months, their only positive action was to change the period of naturalization back from fourteen to five years. As a matter of personal and symbolic justice, the men convicted under the Sedition Act were pardoned and their fines returned with interest.

Jefferson's first appointments to his cabinet indirectly showed how important the first president's example had been. He named Republicans, men who basically agreed with him, but like Washington kept a careful eye on geographical balance. His most influential appointees were trusted comrades from the days when the Republicans had been a minority in Congress. James Madison became secretary of state and Albert Gallatin secretary of the Treasury. Gallatin agreed with Jefferson's instructions to cut the cost of government. He supervised one of the few reductions of the federal bureaucracy that has ever taken place. The new administration reduced the size of the army, halted the scheduled expansion of the navy, shrank the diplomatic corps, and cut expenses for government social functions.

Such reductions were easier than they could be today, for the federal bureaucracy was tiny. When Jefferson took office, the State Department had nine employees. Today it has some twenty-five thousand. Yet even then, the new president characteristically asked Gallatin to

BELKNAP ON THE GOOD SOCIETY

At the end of the eighteenth century a New England intellectual, Jeremy Belknap, described his ideal community in Jeffersonian terms:

Were I to form a picture of happy society, it would be a town consisting of a due mixture of hills, valleys, and streams of water: The land well fenced and cultivated; the roads and bridges in good repair; a decent inn for the refreshment of travellers, and for public entertainments: The inhabitants mostly husbandmen; their wives and daughters domestic manufacturers; a suitable proportion of handicraft workmen and two or three traders; a physician and lawyer, each of whom should have a farm for his support. A

clergyman of any denomination, which should be agreeable to the majority, a man of good understanding, of a candid disposition and exemplary morals; not a metaphysical, nor a polemic, but a serious and practical preacher. A school master who should understand his business and teach his pupils to govern themselves. A social library, annually increasing, and under good regulation. A club of sensible men, seeking mutual improvement. A decent musical society. No intriguing politician, horse jockey, gambler or sot; but all such characters treated with contempt. Such a situation may be considered as the most favourable to social happiness of any which this world can afford.

---

undertake the nearly impossible job of making the government's financial affairs so simple "that every member of Congress and every man of any mind in the Union should be able to comprehend them." Jefferson yearned to achieve a simple style appropriate for a republic. He graciously greeted foreign envoys while wearing bedroom slippers. Rather than give his first annual State of the Union address in person, he sent it to Congress by messenger.

Jefferson hoped that financial economies and a simple style of government would have several happy results. Taxes could be reduced. The national debt could be paid off and speculators kept out. Government could be made simple, inexpensive, and responsive to the needs of the people.

When he was forced to deal with challenges from foreign countries, Jefferson proved to be a strong nationalist. To the surprise and delight of Federalist leaders, he determined to face down the men who for years had been raiding American vessels off the coast of North Africa. The rulers of several Muslim states on the southwest shores of the Mediterranean (then known as the Barbary Coast; now western Libya, Tunisia, Algeria, and Morocco) had been extorting money and manpower from the ships of other countries. The United States, Britain, and other European nations had been paying "tribute" to these rulers. At times these Islamic rulers had seized American ships and enslaved their crews.

In 1801, when one of the North African states demanded more money, Jefferson responded by

sending a naval squadron to bottle up the "Algerian pirates" in their own ports. The undeclared "Barbary War" dragged on until 1805. The United States "won" only the right to make lower payments than other nations, payments that did not end for another ten years.

The President versus the Judiciary and *Marbury v. Madison*

Jefferson also set out to correct what he regarded as injustices at home. He was deeply angered by the judicial appointments that Adams had slipped through just before leaving office. The new president persuaded Congress to pass another Judiciary Act (1802), which reduced the number of federal judgeships. This was the opening gun of Jefferson's "war" on the Federalist judiciary.

A minor incident in this struggle was transformed into a major constitutional case by Chief Justice John Marshall. The case arose out of Adams's last-minute appointment of William Marbury to a five-year term as a federal justice of the peace in the District of Columbia. Marbury's commission was signed and sealed so late that it could not be sent to him before Jefferson took office. Secretary of State James Madison thereupon refused to deliver it. (The secretary of state in those days was charged with certain domestic duties as well as the conduct of foreign affairs).

Marbury asked the Supreme Court to issue a writ ordering Madison to deliver his commission.

Bombardment of Tripoli in North Africa, August 1804. *(Library of Congress)*

The Court, by the Judiciary Act of 1789, had the power to do as Marbury asked. But John Marshall, in *Marbury v. Madison* (1803), refused to use it. Writing for a unanimous Court, he held that the Judiciary Act's provision giving the Court this power was itself a violation of the Constitution.

As Marshall was expanding the power of the Court, he was careful not to claim too much. "The province of the court is, solely," he wrote, "to decide on the rights of individuals, not to inquire how the executive, or executive officers, perform duties in which they have a discretion. Questions in their nature political, or which are, by the constitution and laws, submitted to the executive, can never be made in this court." Yet the Constitution, Marshall argued, stated explicitly in what actions the Supreme Court had original jurisdiction, and Marbury's complaint was not among them. That being so, Marshall continued, the provision in the Judiciary Act of 1789 that granted the Supreme Court the authority to issue such a writ as Marbury sought was unconstitutional.

Marshall's decision did not set a precedent. In 1792, a United States circuit court in Pennsylvania had declared a federal law unconstitutional. But *Marbury v. Madison* became memorable because Marshall firmly and effectively established the supremacy of the Constitution over ordinary congressional statutes, as well as the power of the Supreme Court to decide when the two conflicted. "It is a proposition too plain to be contested, that the constitution controls any legislative act repugnant to it. . . ." And "it is, emphatically, the province and duty of the judicial department, to say what the law is." In a ringing and politically tactful summation, Marshall declared that all branches of the federal government had to conform to the nation's most fundamental law:

Thus the particular phraseology of the constitution of the United States confirms and strengthens the principle, supposed to be essential to all written constitutions, that a law repugnant to the constitution is void; and that courts, as well as other departments, are bound by that instrument.

Marbury never got his commission. More important, this was the only time for more than fifty years that the Supreme Court declared an act of Congress unconstitutional.

Despite certain ambiguities in his decision, Marshall's pronouncements have stood the test of time. But that the power of judicial review should be assigned to the Supreme Court by a Federalist justice so early in the first Republican administration made Jefferson furious. If Federalist judges could negate legislation simply by declaring it unconstitutional, the legislature must have some means to counteract them. Congress, some Republicans claimed, had these means in the power of impeachment. The most conspicuous victim of the resultant impeachment program was Supreme Court Justice Samuel Chase, who had a habit of lecturing juries with anti-Republican speeches before sentencing Republican victims. Chase had become especially outrageous in cases involving the Sedition Act. The House impeached him for misconduct in 1805, but the Senate voted not to convict him.

The Republicans were unable to convict Chase because they were not united. The so-called Old Republicans, led by John Randolph of Virginia, made up what they thought of as the "democratic" wing of the party. They distrusted executive and judicial power in particular, and the federal government in general. The moderate wing of the Republican party, led by the more nationally minded Madison, was less willing to let government be led by the "whims" of the people. On the issue of Chase's impeachment—and on many other issues, as things turned out—the moderates were usually able to defeat the more radical members of their own party, both at the national and the state levels. Sometimes they had the help of moderate Federalists, and they generally enjoyed Jefferson's support.

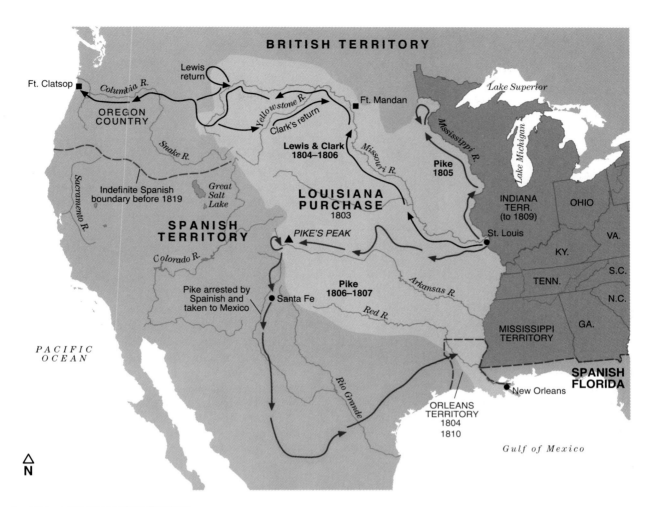

BRITISH TERRITORY

Lewis return

Ft. Clatsop

Columbia R.

OREGON COUNTRY

Snake R.

Yellowstone R.

Clark's return

Ft. Mandan

Lewis & Clark 1804–1806

Missouri R.

Mississippi R.

Pike 1805

Lake Superior

Lake Michigan

INDIANA TERR. (to 1809)

OHIO

VA.

Indefinite Spanish boundary before 1819

Great Salt Lake

LOUISIANA PURCHASE 1803

St. Louis

KY.

Sacramento R.

SPANISH TERRITORY

PIKE'S PEAK

Colorado R.

Pike 1806–1807

Arkansas R.

TENN.

S.C.

N.C.

Pike arrested by Spanish and taken to Mexico

Santa Fe

Red R.

GA.

MISSISSIPPI TERRITORY

PACIFIC OCEAN

Rio Grande

ORLEANS TERRITORY 1804 1810

New Orleans

SPANISH FLORIDA

Gulf of Mexico

N

American explorations of the Far West

Jefferson and the West

In 1801, though other Europeans were not challenging the Americans' right to settle the region east of the Mississippi River, the land was not vacant. Indians had lived there for centuries and continued to do so. Yet over the next forty years these original Americans were systematically driven from their homelands by means of one-sided "treaties" and naked force.

To encourage white settlement of the "public" lands, Congress in 1796 and 1800 had lowered both the minimum acreage pioneers had to buy and the amount of actual cash they had to put down. In 1804 Jefferson got Congress to reduce requirements to the point where, for a down payment of only eighty dollars, white settlers could gain title to a "quarter section" of land—

that is, 160 acres. These measures encouraged westward migration by farmers into the Northwest Territory. In 1803 this rapid growth resulted in Ohio's admission as a state of the Union.

Jefferson also promoted settlement in the Southwest. After much confusion and quarreling about Georgia's western land claims, two new states were eventually carved out of the lands along the Gulf coast between Georgia and the Mississippi River. By that time Jefferson had retired from office, but he had been instrumental in the eventual admission of the states of Mississippi (1817) and Alabama (1819), both of which included a county named after him.

As president, Jefferson had even larger plans for the West. Early in 1803, he persuaded Congress to secretly appropriate money for sending Meriwether Lewis and William Clark on an

Meriwether Lewis. *(Library of Congress)*

expedition to the Pacific coast. As one of the United States' leading scientists, Jefferson instructed them to keep careful journals about the plants, minerals, and animals they found. They were also told to record all information about Indian tribes, trading opportunities, and possible routes for overland migration. Jefferson's scientific interest was genuine, but his explanation to Spain's ambassador was less than honest. He told the Spanish minister that the expedition "would have no other view than the advancement of geography."

The Lewis and Clark expedition took more than two years, but it was a stunning success. In 1804 Lewis and Clark set out with nearly fifty white men, and at times Indian men and women, northwestward along the Missouri River. In the spring of 1805 they left Fort Mandan in what is now North Dakota, guided by an extraordinarily knowledgeable interpreter, a Shoshoni woman named Sacagawea (variously translated as "Bird Woman" or "Canoe Launcher"). The explorers crossed the Rockies, and descended along the Columbia River to the Pacific Ocean. By Septem-

ber 1806 they had arrived back at St. Louis. The expedition added greatly to knowledge of the West and showed that overland travel was possible in those enormous expanses. It also strengthened the claims of the United States to the vaguely defined "Oregon country" on the Pacific Ocean's northeastern coast, called by white Americans (because of their own geographic orientation) "the Northwest."

Jefferson spurred two other expeditions, both led by Zebulon Pike, to find the source of the Mississippi River and to explore the Southwest. Pike's second expedition found an awesome mountain (Pike's Peak), but traveled through territory that by international law belonged to Spain.

The Louisiana Purchase

Lewis and Clark had also thought that they would be traversing foreign territory. But before they left, an extraordinary series of events had placed much of the central portion of the continent in American hands.

Spain, with Jefferson's blessing, had held the vast Louisiana territory—or New Orleans, as the whole area was often called—since 1763. "Till our population can be sufficiently advanced [in numbers] to gain it from them piece by piece," it could not "be in better hands," Jefferson thought, implying his own judgment of Spain's lack of power on the international scene. But in October 1800, Napoleon retrieved Louisiana for France through a secret treaty. Napoleon intended to develop Louisiana as a breadbasket for the French West Indies, thereby ending those islands' dependence on the United States for food. But he could not proceed with this plan until his position in Europe was secure, since France was being pressed by several hostile nations.

In western Santo Domingo (Haiti), an overwhelming slave insurrection led by the black general Toussaint L'Ouverture threatened Napoleon's proposed new French-American empire. Upon achieving a temporary truce in Europe by the Peace of Amiens in 1802, Napoleon ordered some twenty thousand men to sail to the West Indies, crush Toussaint, and then occupy the port of New Orleans near the mouth of the Mississippi River. His campaign in Haiti failed disastrously. His troops lost to the Haitian former slaves and died by the thousands of yellow fever and other tropical diseases.

Sketch from the journal of Sergeant Patrick Gass, who accompanied Lewis and Clark in their travels; (left) Clark and his men hunt bears; (right) Captain Lewis shooting an Indian. *(Library of Congress)*

That same year, Jefferson learned about Napoleon's secret deal with Spain. The president grew concerned; he warned the French that their action might "completely reverse all . . . political relations" and drive the United States into the arms of England. In May 1802, Jefferson instructed Robert Livingston in Paris to try to persuade France to put a price on the city of New Orleans. Before Livingston could make much progress, Jefferson learned that the Spanish official still in charge at New Orleans had suspended the American right (under Pinckney's Treaty) to deposit cargoes there. Nothing could have more strongly confirmed American suspicions of both the Spanish and the French.

Yet Jefferson was determined to avoid war. He obtained from Congress an appropriation of $2 million to be used by James Monroe, who sailed to Paris in March 1803, to aid Livingston. Monroe's instructions were to buy the city of New Orleans. If France refused to sell and kept New Orleans closed to American commerce, Monroe and Livingston were to suggest to Britain that it join the United States in the expected event of renewed war against Napoleonic France. By the time Monroe arrived in Paris, however, he found his instructions obsolete. Napoleon needed money, and he offered the entire Louisiana territory to the United States. Livingston and Monroe almost immediately closed the deal for $15 million.

To negotiate such a "bargain" was one thing; to get the money for it, quite another. One difficulty was that the Constitution did not give the federal government power to purchase territory. Jefferson was so worried about this fact that he at first suggested a constitutional amendment to authorize such agreements with foreign powers. But a delay might have caused Napoleon to change his mind, so Jefferson pushed the treaty through, despite his scruples about the Constitution. As he stated to one of the French

JEFFERSON ON NEW ORLEANS

Although he was a friend of France, Jefferson opposed French acquisition of New Orleans. Such a move, he thought, would force the United States to ally with France's traditional enemy.

The cession of Louisiana and the Floridas by Spain to France works most sorely on the U.S. . . . There is on the globe one single spot, the possessor of which is our natural and habitual enemy. It is New Orleans, through which the produce of three-eighths of our territory must pass *to market, and from its fertility it will ere long yield more than half of our whole produce and contain more than half of our inhabitants. France placing herself in that door assumes to us the attitude of defiance. . . . The day France takes possession of N. Orleans . . . seals the union of two nations who in conjunction can maintain exclusive possession of the ocean. From that moment we must marry ourselves to the British fleet and nation.*

philosophes, "Your government has wisely removed what certainly endangered collision between us."

The Senate ratified the treaty, 26 to 5, and the House appropriated the money, 90 to 25. On December 20, 1803, the United States formally took possession of the heartland of the North American continent. On a price-per-acre basis, the Dutch purchase of Manhattan Island from Indians for a supposed twenty four dollars was downright expensive.

The next year, two territories were carved out of the purchase, to be administered under the terms of the Northwest Ordinance of 1787. Louisiana, with its present boundaries, became a state in 1812, leaving the rest of the Purchase as the Missouri Territory. Florida had not been included in the arrangement, since Spain had never actually turned it over to France. But Jefferson remained enthralled about the nation's continental destiny: Speaking of Spain, he wrote that "if we push them strongly with one hand, holding out a price in the other, we shall certainly obtain the Floridas, and all in good time."

THE WESTERN WORLD AT WAR

John Randolph, reflecting in his old age on the first three years of Jefferson's presidency, declared: "Never was there an administration more brilliant than that of Mr. Jefferson up to this period. We were indeed in the 'full tide of successful experiment.' Taxes repealed; the public debt amply provided for . . . ; sinecures abolished; Louisiana acquired; public confidence unbounded." Even in the New England states, the congressional elections of 1802–1803 favored the Republicans. (In the early years of the nation, elections for Congress were held on various days set by the individual states.) The next fall, Jefferson carried every state except Connecticut and Delaware in his bid for reelection.

Jefferson's first administration coincided roughly with the first years of peace in Europe since the French Revolution, and he had made the best of this brief interlude. His second administration had hardly begun when the country was buffeted once more by renewed war in Europe. In 1805 Napoleon's victory over combined Austrian and Russian armies at Austerlitz in eastern Europe gave France control of much of the European continent. The same year, Admiral Nelson's victory over French and Spanish naval forces off the southwest Spanish coast at Cape Trafalgar gave Britain control of the seas. This stalemate between Napoleon's armies on the Continent and British naval supremacy became "a war between the lion and the whale."

Freedom of the Seas

The conflict had disastrous results for neutral carriers, especially the United States. Between 1804 and 1807, hundreds of American ships were confiscated by the British. A more emotional issue was the impressment of American seamen. The British navy was always short of men, and British policy held that anyone who had ever been a subject of His Majesty could be forced to serve aboard any of His Majesty's naval vessels. There were many British subjects sailing aboard American ships. Given these circumstances, British officers were not fussy about citizenship papers when boarding an American ship in search of "British deserters."

There was bound to be an incident. In June 1807, the new U.S. frigate *Chesapeake* was cruising just outside the traditional three-mile limit off the coast of Virginia. When H.M.S. *Leopard* ordered her to heave to and permit search for a named deserter, *Chesapeake's* captain refused. *Leopard* opened fire. *Chesapeake*, her new guns poorly mounted and her decks still cluttered with gear, suffered twenty-one casualties before being boarded by *Leopard's* officers. They found their deserter and also took three Americans who had served in the British navy.

To most Americans, this attack meant war. But Jefferson insisted on a policy of "peaceful coercion." To save ships and men from capture and thereby save the country from provocation, he decided to keep American ships off the high seas. He thought withholding American goods and carriers would force the warring European nations to respect the rights of neutral countries. Congress went along. The famous Embargo Act passed easily on December 27, 1807.

The Embargo Act resulted in ruin for American commerce and American ports. Despite ship losses, commerce had doubled between 1803 and 1807. Under the embargo it came to a standstill, and the northern industries associated with it, such as shipbuilding and sailmaking, had to close shop. There were immediate protests from the people directly affected. Merchants, seamen, rope makers—everyone whose livelihood came from international trade—saw Jefferson's policy as weak-kneed, unworthy of the Republic, and subservient to agrarian interests.

Though in the long run agricultural exporters would have been drastically affected, the immediate effect of the embargo was to worsen sectional feelings. It appeared to many people that the cities and New England would suffer most, while agricultural interests—Virginia, in particular—would suffer hardly at all. The embargo did, in fact, throw thousands of urban laborers out of work.

It also temporarily resurrected the Federalist party for the national election of 1808. James Madison, Jefferson's handpicked successor, seemed for a time to face an uphill fight for the presidency. By the summer of 1808, every Republican governor in New England had been turned out of office in favor of a Federalist. That party's representation in the House doubled between 1807 and 1809. For the presidential campaign of 1808, the Federalists advanced their old ticket of 1804—Charles C. Pinckney of South Carolina and Rufus King of New York. They carried Maryland, North Carolina, and Delaware, as well as the New England states except Vermont. Yet the results of the election made clear how dominant the Jeffersonian Republicans had become since the election of 1800. Despite diplomatic reverses, Madison won by a considerable margin.

Jefferson was happy to retire. He believed deeply that "the earth belongs to the living not to the dead," that each generation must make its own laws. One of his last acts as president was to sign an act repealing the embargo.

Madison, the Speakership, and War

James Madison proved to be temperamentally unsuited for the crisis he inherited. Some men have clearly grown in the presidency. Madison, more than any president in American history, seemed to shrink. "Our President," a young congressman observed during Madison's first term, "tho a man of amiable manners and great talents, has not I fear those commanding talents which are necessary to control those about him." In congresses, conferences, and conversations, Madison's mind had been telling. He was much less effective at political infighting. At the very beginning, he lost control of his cabinet and of his appointments.

As for the national economy, northern businessmen, driven from the sea by Jefferson's embargo after 1807, began to take greater interest in manufacturing, especially textiles. In the South, cotton was booming. These changes in American economic life, which were to have such great effects at home in later decades (see Chapter 10), were not lost on British manufacturers. They sensed the rise of a rival industrial power.

WORDS AND NAMES IN AMERICAN HISTORY

The verb *gerrymander* is peculiarly American and is scarcely known outside this country. It refers to forming an electoral district for some political office by drawing boundaries that will virtually ensure that one political party (the one in control of the legislature doing the mapping) has its own candidate elected from that district. When the voting districts of a state or even county are drawn with this aim in mind, the result can be weirdly shaped districts. The name of this practice, which has been common in American politics, comes from Elbridge Gerry, who was not really personally responsible for starting it. Gerry was an enthusiastic supporter of the American cause during the Revolution. He was also one of the few delegates to the Constitutional Convention in Philadelphia to end up opposing its ratification. Later he became a Jeffersonian Republican. When he was governor of Massachusetts in 1812, the legislature redrew all the electoral districts in the hope of maintaining Republican control. One result was a district in easter Massachusetts so oddly shaped on the map that some people thought it looked like the small amphibian called the salamander. It rapidly became known as *Gerrymander*, and the practice became so common in most states that the word is no longer capitalized. Most historians have concluded that Mr. Gerry would have preferred to have his name immortalized in some other way.

At the same time, many people in Britain still had not forgiven the Americans. They were happy to see the American flag stripped from the seas. British policy was to continue the impressments and captures that had forced Jefferson to resort to the embargo. Napoleon and his minister Talleyrand played their own game with Madison and Congress: In 1811 they tricked them into cutting off commerce with Great Britain.

Popular disgust with administration fumbling in foreign affairs showed itself in the elections of 1810 and 1811, in which the voters unseated most of the Eleventh Congress (the greatest turnover in the House of Representatives ever). The replacements arriving in Washington in November 1811 included many political newcomers. Madison had to deal with a new and very sectionally oriented generation in Congress: dynamic men such as Henry Clay, the idol of the West; John C. Calhoun, the idol of the South; and Daniel Webster, the idol of New England. All these men were young enough never to have been subjects of the British crown. Little concerned with European attacks on American shipping, they hoped to take advantage of the warfare in Europe by expanding American territory.

On the southern frontier, Spain still held the Floridas, long a bastion for runaway slaves, marauding pirates, and hostile Indians. By this time, many permanent settlers in West Florida were American whites, and they asked to be annexed by the United States. Madison approved. Early in 1812 he sent an armed American expedition to take East Florida as well. But when Spain threatened war and New England threatened secession if war came, Madison recalled the troops.

On the frontier in the Ohio and Mississippi valleys, developments seemed even more ominous. In this region, between 1801 and 1810, more than a dozen crushed Indian tribes were forced to make treaties by which they granted upwards of 100 million acres of prime land to the United States. They were soon being driven off their old grounds.

In 1811, the great Shawnee leader Tecumseh determined to make a stand. He attempted to organize an alliance of all the Indian nations from Florida to the upper Missouri, with the goal of establishing the Ohio River as a permanent Indian borderline against continued invasion. The plan was ruined by a premature military attack ordered by Tecumseh's brother, known as the Prophet. In response, Governor William Henry Harrison, one of the hardest negotiators of Indian treaties, attacked Tecumseh's headquarters at Tippecanoe while Tecumseh was away mobilizing other tribes. The Prophet ordered defense of the village, which resulted in a disastrous defeat for the Indians. Tecumseh vowed revenge.

The Battle of Tippecanoe signaled the beginning of the end of Tecumseh's power. White settlers on the frontier had long believed that the British had been arming Tecumseh and egging him on. They saw Tippecanoe as a victory over the British as well as the Indians. They began calling for the conquest of all Canada, the expulsion of the British from "Our Continent," and the acquisition of all Florida.

Among the people who brought these goals to Congress in November 1811 were such men as John Calhoun of South Carolina, whose grandmother had been scalped by Cherokees; Felix Grundy of Tennessee, who had lost three brothers in Indian raids; and their eloquent leader, Henry Clay of Kentucky. The aggressive views of these upstarts about the British Canadians and Indians caused established easterners to label them War Hawks.

Taking advantage of political quarrels among older members of the Republican party, Clay's

Tecumseh. *(Library of Congress)*

TO KEEP IT EXCITING, MAJOR LEAGUE BASEBALL EACH WEEK WILL

strange new body parts to themselves. A

friends had elected him Speaker of the House on the same day he took office. The Speakership was provided for in the Constitution, but the duties and powers of the office depended greatly on custom originating in the colonial assemblies and Parliament. Apart from the first Congress, Clay was one of only two men ever elected Speaker upon his first term in the House. He did much more than merely preside over that body's proceedings; he used his power to name his friends chairmen of major committees. Soon Clay and his allies were presenting the House with bills for an enlarged army and navy. Madison found it difficult to withstand this pressure from the War Hawks, coming as it did on top of the failure of his foreign diplomacy and more incidents at sea.

Two events in particular played into the hands of the War Hawks. One was the encounter in May 1811 between the American frigate *President* and the British corvette *Little Belt*. The *President's* captain mistook the *Little Belt* for the much more formidable British *Guerrière*, known to be active in impressment raids off New York harbor. Believing she had spotted *Guerrière* off Sandy Hook, New Jersey, *President* gave chase. When the other ship refused to identify herself, *President's* captain gave the order to fire. Nine British seamen were killed and twenty-three wounded. *President* suffered no casualties.

At home, the pounding of *Little Belt* was hailed as a great triumph. A few months later, public disclosure of the "Henry Letters" further inflamed American public opinion. John Henry was a British Canadian secret agent. His letters included reports on widespread disunion feeling in New England. British interest in this subject enraged many Americans, and brought pressure on Madison to a peak.

On June 1, 1812, the president reluctantly sent a message to Congress asking for a declaration of war against Great Britain. Many members of the House and Senate backed him with great enthusiasm. "I verily believe that the militia of Kentucky are alone competent to place Montreal and Upper Canada at your feet," boasted Henry Clay during the House debate. Congress must have believed him, for when it adjourned it had voted no new taxes and only a few additional men to carry on the war it had officially declared.

Representatives of the maritime interests in the Middle States as well as in New England voted against the "War of 1812," mainly because they knew their shipping would suffer. For the most part, the southern states supported it, partly because the struggle still raging in Europe had depressed their markets for tobacco and cotton. Except in upper New York State and part of upper Vermont, where relations with Canada were close and trade across the border profitable, the war had strong support from people in regions not close to the sea.

In his request for a declaration of war, Madison claimed that impressment was the most important issue. He said nothing about Canada and Florida and little about the Indians. Yet all these matters were tied together, as was made clear in a letter written the previous March by Andrew Jackson, a rising political figure in Tennessee:

We are going to fight for the reestablishment of our national character, . . . for the protection of our maritime citizens impressed on board British ships of war, . . . to vindicate our right to a free trade, and open markets for the productions of our soil, . . . to seek some indemnity for past injuries, some security against future aggression, by the conquest of all the British dominions upon the continent of North America.

The Second War for American Independence

Confusion over the nature and objectives of the war muddied American preparations and strategy. Money, men, ships, and supplies had somehow to be obtained. Yet early in 1811, Congress had allowed the Bank of the United States to die at the expiration of its twenty-year charter, just when it was to be needed most. Despite the urging of Secretary of the Treasury Gallatin, Congress put off new taxes until 1813. Throughout the war, taxes were voted reluctantly and evaded expertly. Loans were authorized but hard to float.

Congress appropriated no money to enlarge the navy until six months after war had been declared. The army faced a different problem. Early in 1812 President Madison was authorized to accept 50,000 volunteers for one year's service, but during the next six months only 5000 signed up. Later the president was given power to call out 100,000 state militia, but few of the men would follow their officers across the borders of their own states. The army probably was no worse than its generals deserved. "The old officers," observed Winfield Scott at the beginning of hostilities, "had very generally sunk into either sloth, ignorance, or habits of intemperate drinking."

Canada, it was agreed, was the place to engage the British. But New England, the logical base for an invasion of Canada, opposed the war. The South seemed less and less enthusiastic. Slave-holders feared that acquisition of Canada would place the slave states in a minority. Popular opinion in the West was much more favorable, but would not tolerate withdrawal of troops from the garrisons guarding against feared attacks by Indians.

At the opening of the war, the United States tried three timid forays against Canada, scattered over almost a thousand miles of border. In the first of these, in July 1812, General William Hull not only failed to penetrate Canada, but was forced to yield Detroit to the brilliant Canadian general Isaac Brock. American forces attempted a second attack early in October. Captain John Wool led an American detachment across the Niagara River and took Queenston Heights, where New York militia were to join him and push on. But New York's militiamen refused to cross their state line and stood by while Canadian reinforcements mowed down Wool's men.

The third foray in November was directed against Montreal from Plattsburgh on Lake Champlain between New York and Vermont. Here, militia under General Henry Dearborn

marched twenty miles, decided that was far enough from home, and marched back. Before the year 1812 was over, a new American force under General William Henry Harrison was frustrated in its efforts to regain Detroit. Capturing Canada had proved somewhat less easy than anyone had supposed. Far from occupying it, the Americans after six months of fighting found their own frontier pushed back to Ohio.

Things went better at sea. The United States Navy was no match for the enemy in numbers. In the opening months of hostilities several American vessels won dramatic victories over British men-of-war in single-ship engagements. Yet the winter of 1812–1813 found most of the American fleet back in harbor, where the British bottled it up for the rest of the war. But even the British navy failed to control American privateers. All told, these ships captured more than 800 British merchant vessels.

In the November election of 1812, DeWitt Clinton of New York, named by the "peace party" among the Republicans and supported by the Federalists, carried every northern state except Pennsylvania and Vermont. Madison, however, with the support of the South and West, was reelected.

Perhaps the war party's political victory inspired more successful efforts in the field. The first step seemed to be to regain Detroit. General

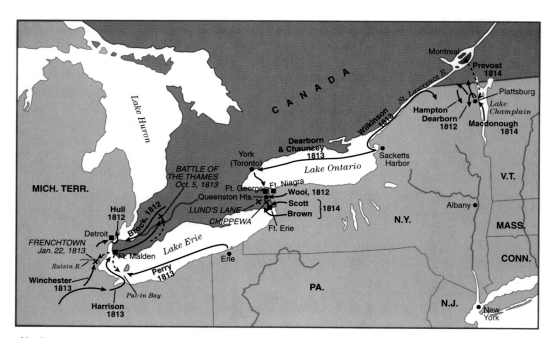

Northern campaigns, 1812–1814

CHAPTER 9   JEFFERSON, THE CONTINENT, AND WAR

Harrison and others agreed that control of Lake Erie was essential to success in such an effort. The task of clearing out the Canadians was given to young captain Oliver Hazard Perry. By August 1813 Perry's little fleet was ready, and on September 10 he found the British squadron in Put-in-Bay at the western end of the lake. At the end of the engagement Perry reported to Harrison, "We have met the enemy and they are ours."

Harrison followed immediately by leading American troops to victory at the Thames River in Canada. Tecumseh, who had earlier gone over to the British, was killed in this engagement, and his Indian forces ceased to be important participants in the war. To the east, on Lake Ontario, United States troops raided York (now Toronto), burned the Parliament houses, and fled.

In April 1814, Napoleon abdicated. Britain was eager for a general peace, but not before putting the Americans in their place. In May the British extended their blockade of Atlantic ports to northern New England and strengthened it farther south. A force of British regulars supported by a British fleet began a march from Chesapeake Bay toward Washington. The hastily mobilized defenders, led by the incompetent general William H. Winder, were defeated at Bladensburg, Maryland, leaving Washington open. On August 24, in revenge for the burning of York, the British set fire to the Capitol and the White House. But the next month, an unsuccessful assault against Baltimore and Fort McHenry (of "Star-Spangled Banner" fame) caused them to withdraw.

More important than the burning of Washington was a three-pronged attack the British directed against Niagara, Lake Champlain, and New Orleans, starting in the summer of 1814. All three phases of this offensive failed. At Niagara, new American commanders—General Jacob Brown and his subordinate, Winfield Scott—fought the British to a standstill. A month later, ten thousand veterans of Wellington's Napoleonic campaigns arrived at Montreal ready to march south toward Lake Champlain. Their objective may have been to detach northern New York and New England and bring them back into the British empire. Whatever their purpose, they were foiled at the battle of Plattsburgh Bay, the last armed clash of the war before the Treaty of Ghent officially ended hostilities on Christmas eve 1814.

But it was not the last battle, for the Americans won a stunning victory at New Orleans without either side knowing that the peace

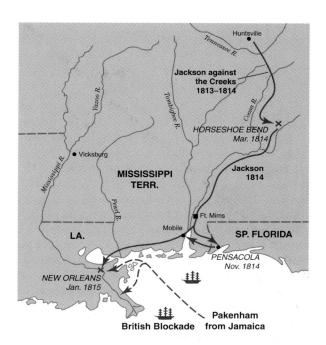

Southwest campaigns, 1813–1815

treaty had just been signed. In the Southwest, Andrew Jackson had been advancing his own more or less private campaign against Indians. After defeating Creek warriors at the battle of Horseshoe Bend in Alabama in March 1814, he forced them to sign a treaty giving up huge tracts of land. Jackson's actions brought him full command in the southwestern theater and the responsibility for checking any British attack in that sector. As it turned out, he faced the third prong of a supposedly comprehensive assault. On learning that the British might use Pensacola in Spanish Florida as a base, Jackson highhandedly invaded this foreign colony and burned the town. Then he directed his men to New Orleans and prepared to confront regiments of British redcoats.

The battle between General Sir Edward Pakenham's 8000 veterans of the Napoleonic Wars and the collection of militiamen, black men, sailors, and pirates under the command of General Andrew Jackson took place two weeks after the Treaty of Ghent had been signed, but more than a month before news of the signing reached Washington. The British lost more than 2000 men; American casualties numbered 21. Jackson became the Hero of New Orleans, the country's most conspicuous political man since George Washington.

The Hartford Convention

If the British were trying to detach New England from the United States, many New Englanders would have wished them luck. As early as January 1811, during the opening stages of the debate over the admission of Louisiana as a state, Josiah Quincy of Massachusetts told the House of Representatives that favorable action would make it "the duty of some to prepare definitely for a separation—amicably if they can, violently if they must." His remarks suggested secession by the "eastern states" from the new Union. When "Mr. Madison's War" began, most New Englanders decided to have as little to do with it as possible, except to make a profit. Some New England farmers and manufacturers grew rich selling supplies to the army their sons refused to serve in.

The Hartford Convention of December 1814–January 1815 marked the climax of this discontent. Many of this convention's organizers hoped that New England and possibly New York would secede. The Hartford meeting was originally called by the Massachusetts legislature, but when the participants assembled they found that only Massachusetts, Rhode Island, and Connecticut had sent formal delegations. There were none from New Hampshire and Vermont. And there were enough moderates among the delegates to outvote the hotheads. Secession was postponed.

Yet even the demands of the New England moderates exposed the workings of sectionalism. One amendment proposed by the convention would have eliminated the "three-fifths" clause of the Constitution, depriving the southern states of the portion of their representation in Congress based on slaves. Another proposal would have limited the presidency to one term and prohibited the election of successive presidents from the same state—a resolution clearly aimed at Virginia, which had produced Washington, Jefferson, and Madison. Other resolves suggested a two-thirds majority in each house for the admission of new states, for the cessation of commerce with foreign nations, and for declarations of war. The members of the Hartford Convention threatened to meet again if Congress rejected these proposals. They were saved from themselves by the ending of the war.

The Treaty of Ghent

Britain had launched its military offensive in the summer of 1814 partly to gain a better position from which to dictate terms at the war's end. When peace commissioners from both sides met in the Belgian town of Ghent in August 1814, the British stalled because they expected reports of new victories. They also presented Madison's negotiations with sweeping demands. Their terms created much conflict among the American negotiators, especially between Henry Clay of Kentucky and John Quincy Adams of Massachusetts, whose temperamental differences sharpened their sectional ones.

The British opened by demanding western territory to provide for an Indian buffer state between the United States and Canada and to give Canada access to the Mississippi. They seemed determined to concede nothing on maritime matters, including New England's privilege (granted in 1783 but withdrawn in 1812) to fish in Newfoundland and Labrador waters.

Britain's claims to the American West angered Clay, but not nearly so much as Adams's willingness to acknowledge them if necessary to recover fishing rights. Clay was ready to trade away those privileges for territorial demands of his own. As often happens in diplomatic situations, personal differences became crucial. Adams hated the smell of Clay's cigars. Another member of the American mission, Albert Gallatin, kept the negotiations from breaking down by arranging personal truces among the American delegates.

At the same time, however, Britain's expected victories in America did not take place. Gradually, the British negotiators backed down. On Christmas Eve, both sides at last agreed. The Treaty of Ghent, ratified by the Senate in February 1815, left most issues just as they had stood at the war's start. It provided for commissions to settle questions of boundaries, fisheries, and commerce. Few people were optimistic about the future. Adams called the treaty an "armistice." Clay declared that "we are destined to have war after war with Great Britain, until, if one of the two nations be not crushed, all grounds of collision shall have ceased between us.

Although without funds, Congress voted in March 1815 to establish a standing army of ten thousand men, to enlarge appropriations for the West Point training college for military officers, and to spend $8 million for more warships. As things turned out, new wars against European powers were avoided for nearly a century, but many "grounds of collision" kept the threat of such warfare immediately alive.

POSTWAR FOREIGN RELATIONS

The coming of peace did not end all conflict between the United States and Great Britain. British businessmen adopted a policy of dumping manufactured goods in the United States at bargain prices. They did so, as one member of Parliament declared, "to stifle in the cradle those rising manufactures in the United "States which the war has forced into being." Henry Clay had this rivalry in mind when he spoke of Britain's determination to crush America. When petitions poured into Congress demanding that these British practices be stopped, Clay led the fight for the first protective tariff in the nation's history, the tariff of 1816.

Trade and Territory

The tariff of 1816 had solid support in all parts of the country. When it failed to stop the flood of imports, Clay denounced Britain's "mean, barefaced, cheating, by fraudulent invoices and false denominations." Also, the Americans still resented being excluded from trade with their long-standing markets in the British West Indies.

Despite friction over economic matters and widespread expectations of more armed conflict, the original "mother country" and the newly independent and united former colonies never again went to war against each other. No one at the time thought the "armistice" of Ghent would last. Yet diplomatic negotiations, with concessions offered freely by both sides, preserved peace, until in the twentieth century the two nations became the firmest of allies.

The first successful negotiations came shortly after the War of 1812. The Rush-Bagot Treaty of 1817 (named after the two negotiators) amounted to a disarmament agreement on the Great Lakes.

At the time, that string of enormous lakes made up nearly half the border between the United States and Canada. Both sides agreed to maintain no more than four small armed vessels on the lakes. Except for technical changes, the Rush-Bagot agreement is still in force. With westward expansion, the U.S.–Canadian border has become what has rightly been called the longest undefended international border in the world.

This demilitarization of the Great Lakes was a good omen for the settlement of the boundary issues left to commissions by the Treaty of Ghent. By 1818 four separate commissions had worked out a permanent boundary between the United States and Canada as far west as the "Great Stony [Rocky] Mountains." Despite the Lewis and Clark expedition, knowledge of the topography beyond the Rockies was still vague, and Britain and the United States agreed upon "joint" occupation of the Oregon country. When large numbers of Americans began to settle in this region in the 1840s, the "continental destiny" of the United States had become an obsession, and joint occupation became intolerable enough to inspire new talk of war (see Chapter 15).

Spanish and Indians

The apparent improvement in Anglo-American relations that resulted from peaceful negotiations over the Canadian boundary was endangered by events on the Spanish and Indian frontiers even before those negotiations were over. The first trouble occurred in the area between American West Florida and Spanish East Florida. When Indian–white violence in this region seemed to endanger settlers moving into western Georgia after the war, Georgia asked the federal government for help. Early in 1817, General Andrew Jackson got instructions, or so he believed, to perform this service. In his usual manner he performed it ruthlessly, burning Indian villages and hanging Indian chiefs.

Jackson also arrested, court-martialed, and executed two British citizens—an old Scottish trader, Alexander Arbuthnot, and a young adventurer, Robert Ambrister—who, he believed, had turned Indians against white Americans. He then marched on Spanish colonists in Florida and on the Seminoles who had found refuge with them. He ejected the governor, installed his own garrisons, and claimed the territory for the

United States, as he had promised he would do "in sixty days."

Many people in Britain demanded war over the execution of Ambrister and Arbuthnot. The Spanish, outraged over the invasion of their territory, also made angry gestures. Peace was kept, but Jackson's adventure gave Spain just the push Jefferson believed the Spanish needed to make them sell Florida to the United States before the Americans simply took it.

In the Adams-Onís Treaty of 1819, Spain ceded both West and East Florida. In exchange, the United States agreed to assume, up to $5 million, the claims of American merchants who had lost ships and cargoes to Spain during the Napoleonic Wars. The Adams-Onís Treaty also established the boundary between the United States and Mexico all the way west to the Pacific.

Secretary of State John Quincy Adams was disappointed in not gaining Texas as well. The absorption of all North America by the United States, he said in 1819, was "as much a law of nature . . . as that the Mississippi should flow to the sea." But American interest in Texas was only just awakening. Adams, finding little support, did not press the issue.

The boundary agreements with Britain and Spain sharpened the definition of the United

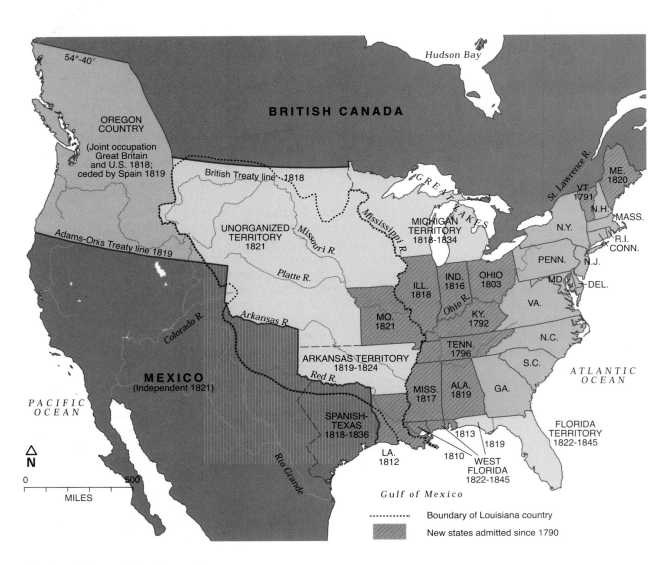

New boundaries established by treaties

States' vast inland empire. But this "empire" was the homeland of hundreds of thousands of Indians. Land-hungry whites could not settle there without, they thought, dealing with those original settlers. Tecumseh's death had taken away the leader of the northern tribes, and Britain's retirement from the Great Lakes area had created a power vacuum. The situation encouraged the United States to embark on an ambitious fort-building program.

To discourage Indians from seeking any new allegiance to Canada, the United States government established a string of fortified trading posts where Indians could buy goods below cost. This stick-and-carrot policy gradually pressured the Indians in the Northwest Territory to agree, in a series of new treaties, to move westward beyond the Mississippi.

In the Southwest, the Indians had been overawed by Jackson's wartime victories. Now the government offered them (in what was regarded by most whites as a humane move) the choice of taking up agriculture on the lands where they lived or moving west. To the disappointment of many whites, most of the Indians preferred farming to abandoning their homes. Not until Jackson became president in 1829 were they forcibly removed from their lands.

Latin America and the Monroe Doctrine

In 1800, Spain had yielded its claim to the Oregon country to Britain and Russia, and its vast territory of Louisiana to France. But the Spanish crown still claimed an immense New World empire that ranged from Upper California to Cape Horn. Portugal dominated Brazil, a vast land populated by huge numbers of African slaves.

Twenty-five years later, Spain's New World empire had been shrunk to the Caribbean islands of Cuba and Puerto Rico; Portugal's, to nothing. The immediate cause of this shattering collapse was Napoleon's invasion of Portugal and Spain in 1807–1808. The Spanish empire in America had been an almost personal possession of the monarchs of that kingdom. When they fell to Napoleon, revolutions began throughout Hispanic America, starting about 1810, led by such patriots as Simón de Bolívar, José de San Martín, and Bernardo O'Higgins. By 1824, most of Latin America had achieved independence from Spain.

After Napoleon's downfall in 1814 and the restoration of the monarchy in France, Spanish authorities made a serious effort to regain what they regarded as their lands in the New World. But they had little success.

Ironically, two other nations took a deep interest in the revolutions in Latin America: Great Britain and the United States. Britain was developing a profitable trade with the new republics there. In 1823 Britain's foreign secretary, George Canning, "unofficially and confidentially" suggested to Richard Rush, the American minister in London, that their countries declare to the world that "we conceive the recovery of the [American] colonies by Spain to be hopeless." Canning also suggested that the two English-speaking nations jointly announce "we could not see any portion of them transferred to any other Power [meaning especially France] with indifference."

Canning's proposal was sailed to Washington, where it immediately became the subject of debate in the cabinet and of consideration by two elder statesmen, Jefferson and Madison. Jefferson, acknowledging that "Great Britain is the nation which can do us the most harm of any one," advised that "with her on our side we need not fear the whole world." He recommended accepting Canning's proposal. Madison agreed.

Secretary of State John Quincy Adams feared that the British proposal for joint protection of the revolutionary countries was an attempt to head off future acquisition by the United States of any territory still held by Spain, especially the island of Cuba. He urged that the United States act alone in the Western Hemisphere. President Monroe yielded to Adams's arguments, and in his annual address to Congress in December 1823 used the words later called the Monroe Doctrine:

The political system of the allied powers [of Europe] is essentially different . . . from that of America. . . . We owe it, therefore, to candor and to the amicable relations existing between the United States and those powers to declare that we should consider any attempt on their part to extend their system to any portion of this hemisphere as dangerous to our peace and safety. . . . With the governments who have declared their independence and maintained it, and whose independence we have . . . acknowledged, we could not view any interposition . . . by any European power in any other light than as . . . an unfriendly disposition towards the United States.

Latin America was not the only area of the Western Hemisphere in which European aggression worried Monroe's administration. The Russians had been in Alaska since the 1740s. Few in number, they had been chiefly interested in fur trading, but they had built a fort as far south as the coast of northern California. In 1821, the ambitious Czar Alexander I decreed that "the pursuit of commerce, whaling and fishing, and of all other industry on all islands, posts, and gulfs, including the whole of the northwest coast of America, beginning from the Bering straits to fifty-one degrees north latitude . . . is exclusively granted to Russian subjects."

Nothing could have aroused Secretary Adams more. He immediately advised the American minister in Russia that "the United States can admit no part of these claims." Monroe in turn added "as a principle" in his message to Congress that the American continents "are henceforth not to be considered as subjects for future colonization by any European powers." The following April the president learned that the czar had agreed on 54°40' north latitude as Russia's southern boundary in North America. With this development, the United States entered a period of thirty years of freedom from serious involvement with foreign powers other than Great Britain.

SUMMARY

Thomas Jefferson came to the presidency determined to move the country in a Republican rather than a Federalist direction. He nullified the Alien and Sedition Acts, and also cut the armed forces. His aim was financial economy and a simple style of government.

Toward this end, Jefferson tried to thwart the Federalist Supreme Court, where Chief Justice John Marshall continued to hand down decisions based on a broad interpretation of the Constitution. But in his landmark decision in *Marbury V. Madison* (1803), Marshall crafted an important victory for the Court's right to declare an act of Congress unconstitutional.

Although a Republican, Jefferson was a strong nationalist. He sent the navy to the coast of North Africa to battle the Barbary pirates who were harassing American shipping. And he believed it was America's destiny to expand over the North American continent. In 1803, he got Congress to sponsor the Lewis and Clark expedition to the Pacific coast and the two Pike expeditions to find the source of the Mississippi and explore the Spanish/French Southwest. His most ambitious undertaking was the Louisiana Purchase of 1803. For $15 million, Napoleon sold the United States the Louisiana territory, the whole middle of the continent.

Jefferson's second administration saw the beginnings of international problems caused by the Napoleonic Wars in Europe. American hostility was directed against the British over the issues of the rights of neutrals, freedom of the seas, and the impressment of American seamen into the British navy. An Embargo Act keeping American ships off the seas passed Congress

at the end of 1807. It resulted not in keeping the United States out of war but in ruining American commerce and American ports.

It also brought the revival of the Federalist party, sectional conflict, and eventually war with England. After Jefferson's retirement, Madison tried unsuccessfully to maintain peace. The War of 1812 ended in 1814 with the Treaty of Ghent, which left most issues—boundaries, fishing rights, and the terms of commerce—to be settled by commissions. The war also made a national figure of Andrew Jackson, the hero of New Orleans.

American-British hostilities continued in the form of trade wars. But relations eventually improved, and a Canadian boundary dispute was settled peacefully. In the South, the issue of Spanish Florida was settled in 1819 after another military adventure by General Andrew Jackson. The Adams-Onís Treaty established the boundary between the United States and Mexico all the way to the Pacific. The United States was forced to come to terms with the great wave of independence movements in Latin America which resulted in the establishment of many new republics. In 1823, the Monroe Doctrine set forth the principle that in the Western Hemisphere the United States would act alone rather than concede in demands from European powers. The settlement of Russia's southern limit in 1822 ended American boundary problems for the time being and gave the United States thirty years of freedom from trouble with foreign powers. The troubles now were to be growing pains at home.

TIME LINE

1801–1805	Barbary War	1812–1813	Warfare at sea and along U.S.–Canadian border
1803	Louisiana Purchase	1814–1815	Hartford Convention
1803	*Marbury v. Madison*	1814	Jackson defeats Creeks at Horseshoe Bend
1803–1806	Louis and Clark Expedition		
1807	Congress passes Embargo after years of impressment of U.S. seamen	1814	British fail in attacks from Canada, but burn Washington
1810	Outbreak of revolutions in Spanish America	1814	Peace of Ghent
1811	War Hawks in Congress elect Clay as Speaker	1815	Jackson's victory at New Orleans
		1815	End of Napoleonic Wars in Europe
1811	Tecumseh's power ebbs after defeat at Tippecanoe	1817	Rush-Bagot Agreement
		1819	Adams-Onís Treaty
1812	Madison asks for declaration of war against Great Britain	1823	Monroe Doctrine

Suggested Readings

Much the best approach to Jefferson is to read his own writings. The great modern edition, J. Boyd (ed.), *The Papers of Thomas Jefferson*, is not yet complete and will not be in our lifetimes. For the period of his administration, one must rely on the far less satisfactory edition by P. Ford (10 Vols., 1892–1899). L. Cappon (ed.), *The Adams–Jefferson Letters* (2 vols., 1959), furnishes one of the great correspondences of American history, especially after 1812, when the two political foes reconciled.

The standard multivolume biography is D. Malone, *Jefferson and His Time* (5 vols., 1948–1974). See also M. Peterson, *Thomas Jefferson and the New Nation: A Biography* (1970); and M. Peterson (ed.), *Thomas Jefferson: A Reference Biography* (1986). For insights into his personality, A. Nock, *Thomas Jefferson* (1926), remains unsupplanted. A fine short biography is N. Cunningham, Jr., *In Pursuit of Reason: The Life of Thomas Jefferson* (1987). D. Boorstin, *The Lost World of Thomas Jefferson* (1948), is a brilliant re-creation of the Jeffersonian world view. W. Jordan, *White over Black: American Attitudes toward the Negro, 1550–1812* (1968), analyzes his views on race.

M. Cunliffe, *The Nation Takes Shape, 1789–1837* (1959), offers a good summary and analysis of the period. For the rise of the Republican party, see N. Cunningham, Jr., *The Jeffersonian Republicans in Power, 1801–1809* (1963). These should be read in light of R. Ellis, *The Jeffersonian Crisis: Courts and Politics in the Young Republic* (1971), which emphasizes divisions in the Jeffersonian ranks between "radicals" and "moderates," especially on judicial issues.

On the Federalists in this era, see J. Banner, *To the Hartford Convention: The Federalists and the Origins of Party Politics in Massachusetts* (1970); D. Fischer, *The Revolution of American Conservatism* (1965); S. Livermore, Jr., *The Twilight of Federalism: The Disintegration of the Federalist Party, 1815–1830* (1962); and L. Kerber, *Federalists in Dissent: Imagery and Ideology in Jeffersonian America* (1970).

Physical and social conditions in the new federal city get lively treatment in J. Young, *The Washington Community, 1800–1829* (1966). Another good account is C. Green, *Washington: Village and Capital, 1800–1878* (1962). Two other aspects of the social history of the new capital are discussed in L. Brown, *Free Negroes in the District of Columbia, 1790–1846* (1972); and M. Smith (ed.), *The First Forty Years of Washington Society* (1906), a woman's account of the political and social scene.

On the war with the judiciary, see C. Miller, *The Supreme Court and the Uses of History* (1969). For American expansionism in general, A. Weinberg, *Manifest Destiny: A Study of National Expansionism in American History* (1935), is still useful. For the Louisiana Purchase in particular, see C. Dangerfield's superb biography, *Chancellor Robert Livingston of New York, 1746–1813* (1960); and I. Brant, James *Madison and American Nationalism* (1968). On the people, animals, and geography of this territory, B. De Voto (ed.), *The Journals of Lewis and Clark* (1953), makes fascinating reading. Another important episode during Jefferson's administration is covered in T. Abernethy, *The Burr Conspiracy* (1954).

Major issues of Anglo-American diplomatic relations are best handled in a fine series by B. Perians: *The First Rapprochement: England and the United States, 1795–1805* (1955); *Prologue to War: . . . 1805–1812* (1961); and *Castlereagh and Adams: . . . 1812–1823* (1964). National prestige as a factor in bringing on the war is examined in H. Brown, *The Republic in Peril: 1812* (1964). H. Coles, *The War of 1812* (1965), surveys the war itself. On the diplomacy of the war and the peace, see S. Bemis, *John Quincy Adams and the Foundations of American Foreign Policy* (1949). F. Engleman, *The Peace of Christmas Eve* (1962), focuses on the Treaty of Ghent. J. Stagg, *Mr. Madison's War: Politics, Diplomacy, and Warfare in the Early American Republic, 1783–1830* (1983), places the War of 1812 in a much broader context.

The Hartford Convention is discussed in Banner, mentioned above; see also S. Morison, *Harrison Cray Otis* (1969). The latter and C. Dangerfield's *The Awakening of American Nationalism, 1815–1828* (1965) are perceptive treatments of the postwar period.

Various aspects of the postwar years are examined in H. Ammon, *James Monroe* (1971); and D. Perkins, *A History of the Monroe Doctrine* (1955). The rise of West Point and militaristic ambitions among Americans, especially after 1815, are discussed in M. Cunliffe, *Soldiers and Civilians: The Martial Spirit in America, 1775–1865* (1973). H. A. Humphreys and J. Lynch, *The Origins of the Latin American Revolutions, 1808–1826* (1965), is a good introduction.

The completion of the Pacific Railroad. A meeting of locomotives of the Union and Central Pacific lines: the engineers shake hands.
(Library of Congress)

CHAPTER 10

INTERNAL DEVELOPMENT

The War of 1812 has often been called America's "second war of independence." The coming of peace in 1815 set the stage for important developments in the American political system and the American economy. The two-party system fell apart, largely because the Federalists had opposed the war and the Republicans had adopted so many Federalist programs. The nation's economy boomed—and then went bust. John Marshall produced an impressive series of court decisions, many of which had as much to do with economic matters as with federal supremacy. And the issue the Founding Fathers had tried to avoid came spilling out into the open: Slavery suddenly emerged, exposing deep sectional hostili-

ties. An aging and alarmed Thomas Jefferson called it "a firebell in the night."

Slavery was the main issue in renewed sectional division, but economic differences also contributed to the split. Alexis de Tocqueville, in his famous *Democracy in America* (1835) and in his letters home during his visit to the United States, made the usual observations about the free North ("everything is activity, industry; labor is honored") and the slave South ("you think yourself on the other side of the world; the enterprising spirit is gone"). Yet the South also enjoyed a strong westward and economic surge. And like that of the North, it added to the strength of the union.

THE ERA OF GOOD FEELINGS

With Madison's support, James Monroe became the Republican candidate for the 1816 election. His Federalist opponent was Rufus King, a New Yorker chosen by the New Englanders who still dominated the Federalist party to make it appear less sectional than it actually was. In the election, King carried only Massachusetts, Connecticut, and Delaware. He was the last Federalist candidate.

Monroe had been an admirer of Jefferson. Later on, he thought himself a competitor to Madison. But he lacked their imagination and intellect and was slow to shed his narrow localism. Monroe had served twice as governor of Virginia. On the national scene, American military activity in the last phases of the War of 1812 reflected favorably on his performance in the War Department and helped him win the nomination and the election in 1816. Sixty-one years old at the time of his election, he seemed a solid link with the old revolutionary generation. He was the last president to wear a powdered wig.

Unlike many men jealous of power, Monroe felt strong enough to surround himself with able associates. His cabinet was probably the strongest since Washington's first administration. Shortly before his inauguration in March 1817, he made a triumphal journey through the northeastern states. His visit was capped by a cordial reception in Boston. There, soon after, the *Columbia Sentinel* published an article called "Era of Good Feelings," in which it hailed a new era of political peace. By then, the Republicans had shown so much concern for manufacturing and a protective tariff, for an army and a navy, even for chartering a national bank, that the old issues seemed no longer to stand in the way of national unity. Virginia and Massachusetts appeared to have made peace at last. Monroe was reelected in 1820 with only one electoral vote cast against him.

Boom, Bank, and Bust

The War of 1812 had apparently converted Republicans to the support of American commercial, industrial, and financial growth. Jefferson himself acknowledged that "manufactures are as necessary to our independence as to our comforts." But once the war ended, most of the "war babies" among American factories lost out to British competition, despite efforts at tariff protection.

Britain's own postwar boom soon caused another kind of boom in the United States. The spurt in British textile manufacturing brought an enormous demand for southern cotton. The end of the war also reopened European markets for southern tobacco. Poor European harvests in 1816 and 1817 added to the demand for American grain. Agricultural exports helped provide the hard money Americans needed to pay for postwar imports.

The boom in agriculture quickly inspired an outburst of land speculation, especially in the West, where population soared. By 1820, Ohio had more people than Massachusetts, and the entire West had more people than New England. Settlers and speculators bought and sold land with the aid of several hundred state and private banks that had been established after the first Bank of the United States went out of existence (by terms of its charter) in 1811. The newer, smaller banks had issued $100 million in paper money by 1817, much of it nonnegotiable even in neighboring communities.

Congress established a Second Bank of the United States in 1816. Like the first national bank, the Second Bank was chartered for twenty years as the sole depository for government funds. Its capital was set at three and a half times that of the earlier bank. Of this amount, the government was to subscribe one-fifth and private capitalists the rest. Five of the bank's twenty-five directors were to be appointed by the president of the United States, the rest by American stockholders. Foreign stockholders were to have no say in the bank's affairs.

The Second Bank had the right to establish branches in different parts of the country. But influential local bankers had persuaded some states to write into their constitutions provisions against "foreign banks"—that is, branches of the national bank doing business within their borders. The Second Bank proceeded to justify local fears by outdoing even the state banks with enormous loans. These loans, made in the form of national bank notes, were more acceptable as currency than the notes of most local banks. Injured local bankers soon got their states to try to tax out of existence both the national bank's branches and its notes.

In the summer of 1818, when the postwar boom was at its height, the Second Bank decided

Boys loading and firing pistols, blowing horns, and setting off firecrackers on the Fourth of July. *(Library of Congress)*

to try deflationary measures to control speculation. But the sudden contraction of credit prevented many people from keeping up payments on their debts. For this and other reasons, the whole boom collapsed before 1819 was over. The Second Bank became as unpopular with the public as it had always been with local financiers. The country was gripped by its first major economic depression.

Actually, the economic collapse was worldwide. The revival of European agriculture after the Napoleonic Wars and the weakening of the postwar textile boom created a glut both of wheat and cotton in world markets. But the depression was most severe in the United States and most devastating in the West. The crisis prompted a number of states to abolish the practice of punishing debtors with imprisonment and to pass liberal bankruptcy laws. Congress also came to the aid of the West with a new land act in 1820, which permitted a settler to buy an eighty-acre homestead for a hundred dollars in cash. The next year it added a relief act to assist

land purchasers who had run into trouble with the credit provisions of earlier land acts.

The Marshall Court

Against this background of local self-assertion, economic crisis, and conflict between debtors and creditors, John Marshall issued a series of historic Supreme Court decisions. Already he had sustained the Court's power to declare acts of Congress unconstitutional (*Marbury v. Madison*, 1803), and he had upheld the obligation of contracts against state interference (*Fletcher v. Peck*, 1810).

The question of contracts gave Marshall the chance for two decisions in 1819 that alarmed states'-rights advocates. The first issue arose in *Dartmouth College v. Woodward*. Could the royal charter granted to the college in 1769 and later acknowledged by the New Hampshire legislature be altered by the legislature without the college's consent? In a decision that interested business corporations chartered by state legislatures more than colleges, Marshall decided that a charter was a contract between two parties, neither one of whom alone could change it. In a second decision in 1819, *Sturges v. Crowninshield*, Marshall declared a New York bankruptcy law unconstitutional for seeking to relieve a debtor of his contractual debts. He held that the legislature could not constitutionally interfere with private contracts.

In several important cases not involving contracts, the Marshall court set aside state laws that it determined to be contrary to the federal Constitution. One of the most far-reaching of these cases was *McCulloch v. Maryland*, also decided in 1819. The state of Maryland had attempted to tax the Baltimore branch of the Second Bank of the United States out of existence. But, said Marshall in finding the Maryland tax law unconstitutional, "the power to tax involves the power to destroy. " If the states were permitted to nullify acts of Congress by attacking its agencies, they could "defeat and render useless the power to create." In broad language, Marshall asserted the constitutionality of the act creating the bank. His decision strengthened the foundation for a broad interpretation of the implied powers of Congress.

Finally, in *Gibbons v. Ogden* (1824), Marshall spoke out on the power of Congress to regulate commerce. New York had granted Robert Fulton and Robert R. Livingston a monopoly of steam navigation in state waters, and Aaron Ogden had bought from them the right to operate a ferry between New York and New Jersey. When Thomas Gibbons set up a competing ferry under a federal coasting license, Ogden tried to use the state-sanctioned monopoly to stop him from running it. Marshall held that the original grant by New York interfered with the exclusive right of Congress to regulate interstate commerce. But he was not content with throwing out the New York monopoly. He went on to interpret the term *commerce* to include commerce "among the several states" that extended into the interior of any state. No state could act on such commerce when its acts intruded on the powers of Congress.

It is often said that Marshall handed down Federalist law from the fortress he held for thirty-four years in the Supreme Court. But it is closer to the truth to say that once his battle with Jefferson had ended, Marshall gave all his energies to extending national power, just as Jefferson gave his to extending the national domain. Both were expansionists; the work of one complemented that of the other. Together they gave Americans geographic and legal room for an expanding economy.

The Missouri Compromise

One notable feature of the constitutional and economic growth of the country was the orderly admission of new states to the Union. After Vermont (1791), Kentucky (1792), Tennessee (1796), and Ohio in 1803 and Louisiana in 1812, in the four years after the war came the admissions of Indiana, Mississippi, and Illinois. This easy procession was suddenly interrupted by a controversy over the admission of Missouri, which reopened the issue of the extension of slavery.

Slavery had been forbidden in the Northwest Territory by the Northwest Ordinance of 1787.

MARSHALL ON FEDERAL POWER

In his vigorous decision in *McCulloch v. Maryland* (1819), John Marshall set forth a powerful case for the broad exercise of national powers under the Constitution:

We admit, as all must admit, that the powers of the government are limited, and that its limits are not to be transcended. But we think the sound construction of the Constitution must allow to the national legislature that discretion, with respect to the means by which the powers it confers are to be carried into execution, which will enable that body to perform the high duties assigned to it, in the manner most beneficial to the people. Let the end be legitimate, let it be within the scope of the Constitution, and all means which are appropriate, which are plainly adapted to that end, which are not prohibited, but consist with the letter and spirit of the Constitution, are constitutional.

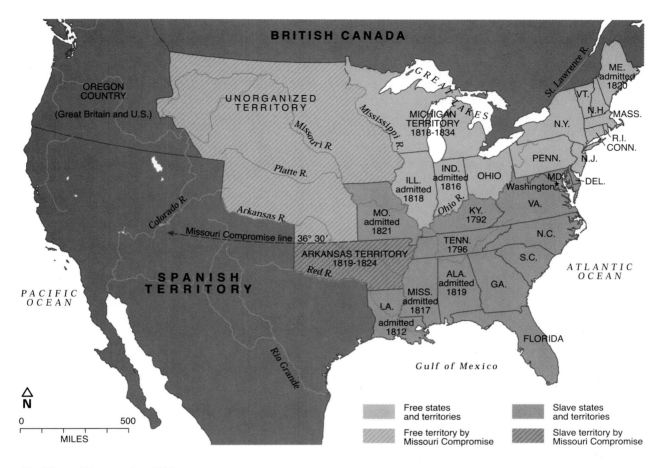

The Missouri Compromise, 1820

The first real conflict over the issue occurred just beyond, in the so-called Upper Louisiana Territory, whose settlers first applied for admission to the Union under the name of Missouri in 1818. There was no problem until Representative James Tallmadge of New York shocked the South by offering an amendment to the Missouri enabling act to prohibit the introduction of additional slaves into the new state. He also proposed that all children born of slaves in that region be freed when they reached the age of twenty-five.

The Tallmadge Amendment passed the House by a narrow margin, reflecting the populous North's strength there. The story in the Senate was different. Even though the free states outnumbered the slave states eleven to ten at the time, a number of northern senators who had been born and brought up in the South voted with southern senators and helped defeat the amendment.

The deadlock carried over to the next session of Congress, which opened in December 1819. Now, along with Missouri's petition for admission as a slave state came Alabama's as well. There was no issue about admitting Alabama as a slave state. It became the twenty-second state and established a balance between slave and free states at eleven each. Admission of Missouri would give the South a virtual veto in the Senate of all legislation enacted by the House. The northern majority in the House insisted on keeping Missouri closed to slavery. When the detached northeastern part of Massachusetts applied for admission to the Union as the state of Maine, some members of Congress, led by Henry Clay, seized the chance to break the deadlock.

The series of measures known as the Missouri Compromise arranged for the temporary preservation of the balance of power in the Senate by admitting Missouri as a slave state and Maine as a free one. The most significant part of the compromise permitted slavery in Missouri, but prohibited it "forever... in all territory ceded by France to the United States... which lies north of 36°30'... not included within the limits of [that] state." President Monroe signed the compromise measures on March 6, 1820.

There the slavery issue rested for a generation. But the Missouri controversy intensified sectionalism and threatened the spirit of nationalism. At the same time, a booming economy was making fundamental changes in the lives of many Americans.

AN EXPANDING ECONOMY

In 1815, and for several decades thereafter, the majority of white Americans in the South as well as in the North still lived on family farms. These people or their forebears had come to America in search of personal freedom based on economic independence. Isolated on their farms, they were not fully aware that new technology and expanding business enterprise were fundamentally altering American life.

Fishing and Lumbering

Some Americans continued to make their living from fishing long after the Revolution. In 1821, Timothy Dwight, reporting on his travels through New England, said of the fishing ports south of Boston: "The whole region wears remarkably the appearance of stillness and retirement; and the inhabitants seem to be separated in a great measure, from all active intercourse with their country."

Fishermen in these ports went out, like farmers, only for the day. Each had his own boat and brought back his catch for his family and for buying grain, clothing, and equipment. At more active fishing centers, such as Newburyport and Beverly, and on Cape Cod, voyages were longer and better organized. But here too, the rule was that each man supplied his own gear and provisions in return for a share of the catch. The fisherman always preferred going out "on his own hook," a phrase that originated with these Yankees.

One specialized occupation—whaling—remained important until kerosene supplanted whale oil for lighting after the Civil War. Until the War of 1812, just about every New England port had its whaling fleet. Afterward, Nantucket and New Bedford, Massachusetts, nearly monopolized the industry, with New Bedford having perhaps a third of the international fleet.

The concentration of whaling activities in New Bedford added to the efficiency of operations. Yet whaling remained a conservative industry. The only significant changes since colonial times were that voyages grew longer and that crews—paid, like fishermen, with a share of the catch—were more ruthlessly exploited. Rebellious hands, when they did not mutiny or desert, often were abandoned on some foreign shore by a captain who thus avoided paying them their shares. On return voyages, crews were often made up of men from a dozen different lands. Even Fiji Islanders and Polynesians, like the harpooner Queequeg in Melville's *Moby Dick*, could be seen walking the streets of New Bedford after a whaler had put in.

In lumbering, as in farming, fishing, and whaling, few changes were made in the first third of the nineteenth century. The industry grew, of course, but until the railroads brought a huge demand for wood for fuel, ties, and rolling stock, lumbering remained the occupation of individual loggers, who supplied timber to widely scattered and independently owned sawmills.

The Indians had taught the first settlers how to grow corn, harpoon whales, and bring down trees. For more than two centuries, these basic techniques of farming, fishing, and lumbering spread unchanged as the country gradually expanded. Commodities such as flour, leather goods, and ironware were made according to the old methods, generation after generation in the same family. It was a living, and a way of life. Until vast new markets were opened up by improved transportation, this traditional system continued to characterize the American economy.

Expansion: The Fur and China Trades

No one in early-nineteenth-century America was more isolated than the fur trapper and trader.

But unlike the other primary occupations, the fur trade soon gave a new direction to American life, a new method to American business, and a new spirit to the American economy. Fur—mink, otter, lynx, fox, and beaver, as well as bear, wolf, deer, rabbit, muskrat, "coon," and "possum"—had been one of the first staples exported by the colonies. The finer pelts were used for hats, cloaks, and robes; the coarser ones, in blankets. The Indians, who did most of the actual trapping, traded furs for guns, ironware, and liquor.

From the start, profits had been large and competition keen. As early as 1700, overtrapping had depleted the fur-bearing animals on lands along the Atlantic seaboard. In the next fifty years, French traders from Canada and Spanish traders from Mexico, as well as the English colonists, forced their way a thousand miles inland, far in advance of European settlement.

Two thousand miles beyond even the farthest inland fur-trading post in the Mississippi Valley, the waters off the Oregon coast were rich with sea otter. Sea captains from New England and New York in the China trade discovered a market for the beautiful otter skins (as well as for other domestic furs) among the wealthy of North China. New Englanders were attracted to the sea otter because it gave them a commodity to export in exchange for the tea, silk, spices, willowware china, and cheap cottons of the Orient.

By the early 1800s, the sea otter was nearly extinct. Profits from Chinese imports, however, had proved even greater than those from the sale of furs in China. When the sea otter supply failed, around the outbreak of the War of 1812, ship captains began to carry Hawaiian sandalwood to the Orient, where it was used for incense. Upright Yankee traders also began to smuggle opium from the Dutch East Indies and neighboring islands into China. But the American opium traffic always remained a small fraction of the trade carried on by the British East India Company, which used cannon and bayonets to force immense quantities of Indian opium into China.

The fur market in China had attracted land trappers and traders as well as sea captains. After Lewis and Clark returned from their expedition across the continent in 1806, trappers began to exploit the upper Missouri, the Yellowstone, the Green and other northwestern river valleys, and the Colorado and the Gila in the southwestern desert. The farther trappers and traders went from their Mississippi base at St. Louis, however, the harder it was to carry on business. One reason was the hostility of the Plains Indians. Of greater importance was the cost: Only well-financed organizations could send trappers and traders into far-off regions for a year or more.

It was the New Yorker John Jacob Astor, by 1800 the city's leading fur merchant and one of its most creative businessmen, who most successfully met the new conditions. His instrument was the American Fur Company. In 1810 Astor sent out two expeditions, one by sea and another by land, to set up a trading post (named Astoria) at the mouth of the Columbia River in Oregon. With the outbreak of the War of 1812, Astor's men were forced to sell out to the Canadian fur traders of the Oregon country. But this setback did not stop him. In 1816 he persuaded Congress to prohibit foreigners from the fur trade on United States soil except as licensed employees of American traders. He then persuaded the governor of Michigan Territory, which rivaled the Oregon Country in its fur-trading potential, to issue licenses almost exclusively to employees of the American Fur Company.

Until the 1830s, when European hat styles changed from fur to silk, Astor's company averaged an annual profit of $5 million. Astor became the first American millionaire. But he was not the last to make a fortune out of a dwindling natural resource, or the last to obtain the assistance of the government in doing so.

The Santa Fe Trail

Less dramatic than the fur trade, and involving far fewer men and far less capital, was the trade along the Santa Fe Trail. Spain had established the isolated outpost of Santa Fe in the desert of New Mexico early in the seventeenth century and had supplied it from Vera Cruz, 1500 miles away. Early American efforts to trade at Santa Fe were frustrated by Spain's rigid colonial policy, which excluded foreigners. Soon after Mexico won its independence from Spain in 1821, however, it opened Santa Fe to its northern neighbor, a step it later regretted and reversed.

In 1825, the United States Army surveyed the Santa Fe Trail westward from Independence,

Missouri. Thereafter, for twenty years, caravans of American farm wagons trekked across it, hauling all sorts of goods from the East and from Europe and exchanging them for Spanish gold and silver.

The arrival of the caravan each year was a great event in the Spanish town. Gradually, some Americans settled in Santa Fe. Others, attracted by the land bordering the eastern part of the trail, staked out farms along the way. When Santa Anna, the Mexican leader, closed the trail in 1844, Americans viewed his act as interference with their rights and "destiny."

The Santa Fe trade never involved more than a few hundred persons a year. But like the fur trade, it opened a new path across the continent, lured American business into new country, and led to a political and territorial claim that eventually would be enforced by war (see Chapter 15).

The Rise of the Middle West

Well to the east of fur trappers and traders, traveling over trails they had marked through the wilderness, thousands of settlers moved onto the lands of the Middle West. Some were new immigrants from Europe. Many more were second-, third-, and fourth-generation Americans who moved westward in successive steps of a few dozen or a few hundred miles. The wealthier ones had wagons, usually pulled by oxen. Other women and men walked, often pushing all their possessions in handcarts. Many of these families suffered from periodic bouts of "ague," as malaria was then called.

In 1810 only one-seventh of the American population of 7.2 million lived west of the Alleghenies; by 1840 more than a third of 17.2 million Americans lived there. Production of corn and wheat rose, but not dramatically. Yet the new lands were more fertile than those in the East, which had been worn out by years of continuous planting. The result was that many unproductive farms in New England were simply abandoned.

Until settlers reached the more open prairie country in Indiana and Illinois, the supply of trees seemed unlimited. Farmers wanted wood for fuel, fences, tool handles, and house construction. But they also regarded standing trees as a barrier to farming. Piles of fallen dead trees were burned outdoors simply to get them out of the way.

One symbol of this wastefulness was the log-cabin method of constructing houses. Introduced in the seventeenth century by Swedes and Finns along the Delaware River, this technique was adopted by westward-moving pioneers. It was probably the most labor-efficient way of turning trees into housing; it wasted a lot of wood, but it saved a lot of work. Since wood was far more plentiful than labor, Americans did not think twice about wasting it; when it ran out, settlers could always move on to where there was more. This attitude was part of a general assumption that the abundant natural supplies of the continent would exist forever.

LIFE ON THE FRONTIER

The lives of these westward-moving pioneers consisted mostly of hard work and sickness. When they moved, they traveled mostly on foot, carrying their possessions in a wheelbarrow or pushcart or strapped to the backs of a few scrawny cows. When they settled, they had to clear land and build shelter. Many of them suffered from the "ague."

Thomas Lincoln's experience was typical of these pioneers of the early nineteenth century. Part backwoodsman, part farmer, part handyman-carpenter, Thomas was a native of the western Virginia hills but grew up in Kentucky. "A wandering laboring boy," without schooling, he married the illiterate Nancy Hanks, who bore their son Abe in 1809. The Lincolns and the Hankses rarely stayed put for long. By 1816 the whole tribe had reached Indiana, where they "squatted" the first year.

"We lived the same as the Indians," one of the Hankses said years later, "ceptin' we took an interest in politics and religion." They managed to build a log cabin, without floor, door, or windows. A roof stuffed with mud and dry grass was the only protection from the rain. This cabin remained their home for a decade before they pushed on to Illinois.

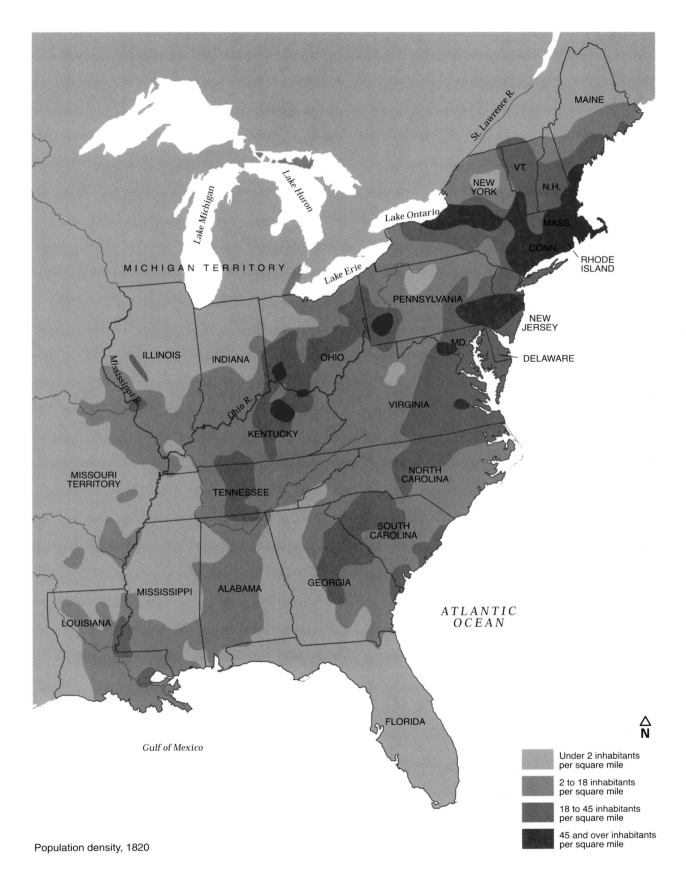

Population density, 1820

Under 2 inhabitants
per square mile

2 to 18 inhabitants
per square mile

18 to 45 inhabitants
per square mile

45 and over inhabitants
per square mile

The New Cotton Empire

In the Southwest, westward settlement was encouraged by the expansion of upland cotton. Commercial cotton growing had made great strides in the South after 1790, when British East Indian indigo destroyed American growers' market for that product. For two generations, indigo had been a staple of the South Carolina and Georgia planters. Between 1790 and 1793, the indigo planters turned their land to cotton. Most of this cotton was of the fragile long-staple variety—the finest kind, and the only kind that could be separated from its oily black seed at reasonable cost.

In America, however, the climate and soil requirements of long-staple cotton limited it to the South Carolina and Georgia sea islands and the coastal plain extending into Spanish Florida. The other type of cotton, the coarser, short-staple, green-seed boll, could be grown on almost any soil, provided the warm season was long enough. Its single drawback was the difficulty of removing the seed: One worker could clean only a single pound in a day.

A young man from Massachusetts solved this problem and at the same time brought about an economic revolution in the American South. In 1793 Eli Whitney, in Georgia tutoring a planter's family, invented an engine for cleaning the greenseed plant. His cotton gin was so simple that he soon became involved in patent suits in order to try to make money on his invention.

By 1794, the production of short-staple cotton was spreading rapidly. One worker operating a single gin by hand could clean fifty pounds a day. Rapid improvements in Whitney's and other gins and the eventual application of animal and steam power multiplied its capacity. In 1800 about 75,000 bales of cotton went to market, most of it the short-staple kind. By the eve of the War of 1812, this figure had soared to over 175,000 bales annually, nearly three-fourths from South Carolina and Georgia.

Within a few years, however, the Piedmont land was used up, as the Tidewater land had been earlier. The Piedmont, a traveler said in 1820, presented a scene of "dreary and uncultivated wastes . . . half-clothed negroes, lean and hungry stock, houses falling to decay, and fences wind-shaken and dilapidated." Cotton planters pushed west into Alabama and Mississippi. By 1830, the combined population of these states exceeded 400,000, even though the large planters had bought up many small farms in the best cotton areas. Sections of Tennessee, Arkansas, and Florida suitable for cotton planting also became heavily settled, as did the Louisiana sugar country.

The traffic at New Orleans reflected the rapid growth of the new regions. In 1816, only 37,000 bales of cotton were shipped from this port; by 1822, the figure was 161,000 bales; by 1830, it was 428,000. Most of this cotton went to English textile factories, though some fed the mills of New England.

The Cotton Kingdom's growing need for food and work animals gave northwesterners an opportunity. As markets and prices improved, northwestern farmers went into debt to acquire more land. They were thus forced to concentrate on cash crops to meet their financial obligations.

HOW AMERICA GREW

The last French governor of Louisiana offered this description of the thousands of Americans pouring into the Old Southwest:

They set up their huts, cut and burn the timber, kill the savages or are killed by them, and disappear from the country either by dying or ceding to some steadfast cultivator the land they have already begun to clear. When a score of new colonists are thus gathered in a certain spot, they are followed by two printers, one a federalist and the other an antifederalist, then by doctors, lawyers and adventurers; they propose toasts and nominate a speaker; they erect a city; they beget children without end; they vainly advertise vast territories for sale; they attract and deceive as many buyers as possible; they increase the figures of the population till they reach a total of 60,000 souls, at which time they are able to form an independent state and send a representative to Congress . . . and there is one more star in the United States flag.

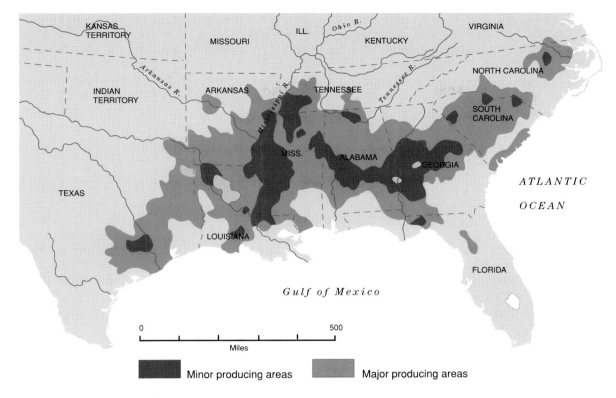

Cotton-growing areas

Southern specialization in cotton brought north-western specialization in grain and meat and mules. The marvelous Mississippi River system tied the two sections together, and the steamboat tightened the knot.

TRANSPORTATION AND TRADE

In colonial America, the ocean was the easiest means of communication and trade. As farms and plantations spread inland, the eastern rivers also began to carry their share of people and goods. Settlement in the West brought the Mississippi River system into the transportation network, and the steamboat made it the foremost inland carrier of all.

The Steamboat

The first steamboat on the western waters was the *New Orleans*, built in 1811 by Robert Fulton,

four years after his success with *North River* (usually and erroneously called *Clermont*) on the Hudson.

As he had in New York, Fulton won a supposed monopoly of the carrying trade in the West, but it began to collapse rapidly as other inventors turned to high-pressure engines. In 1824 John Marshall, in *Gibbons v. Ogden*, dealt a death blow to monopolies on interstate waters. By 1830, there were nearly two hundred steamboats on the western rivers.

Keelboat rates between Louisville and New Orleans had been about five dollars per hundred pounds of freight. By 1820, steamboat rates for this trip had fallen to two dollars per hundred pounds. By 1842, competition had driven them down to twenty-five cents. Western staples now moved down to New Orleans for shipment overseas or for distribution to the rest of the South and Southwest and even to the Northeast. Commodities from abroad or from the Northeast also were funneled into New Orleans for transshipment inland.

The Mississippi system, however, was less ideal than it appeared on a map. The river itself and most of its tributaries were filled with snags, shifting sandbars, floating trees, and unpredictable eddies. Pirates infested the entire system. Summer droughts pinched the river channels into narrow ribbons, stranding many vessels in shallow water.

New Roads

The difficulties of road transportation presented even greater challenges. From the earliest times, many Americans chose to settle far from neighbors on land several miles from water routes. And yet somehow they had to travel to grist mills, tobacco warehouses, cotton gins, forges, country stores, and county courts, and to the rivers themselves. As time went on, a crude network of roads spread across the countryside, often following old Indian trails and the paths of trappers and traders. Only a few such roads had been made wide enough for wagons or carts. Rains transformed them into muddy pools, and winter cold froze them into ruts.

As early as 1806, Congress had chartered a National Highway to he built with federal funds. Not until 1811, however, did the first crews begin to cut the road westward from Cumberland, Maryland. By 1818 it had been pushed to Wheeling, Virginia, on the Ohio River. The failure of Congress to provide additional money stopped construction there. But work was resumed in 1825, and by midcentury the road had reached Vandalia, Illinois, its western terminus. The National Highway, paved with stone over much of its length, became an efficient carrier, "the path of empire" for hundreds of thousands of Americans on the move westward.

Another useful road was the privately financed Lancaster Turnpike, built in 1794 across the sixty-two-mile stretch from Philadelphia to Lancaster, Pennsylvania. At first only a dirt road, the Lancaster pike was reconstructed, after many accidents, on the principles worked out by the Scottish engineer John L. McAdam. These principles ruled road building in America and England until asphalt began to be used in the automobile age.

"It is the native soil," McAdam wrote, "which really supports the weight of traffic." But the soil had to be kept dry by a covering impenetrable to rain. This covering was made of small stones carefully broken into the right sizes. Tolls collected along the Lancaster pike more than paid for its cost, and the idea proved profitable enough to encourage the construction of similar roads elsewhere.

By 1825, private companies, mostly in New England and the Middle Atlantic states, had built more than ten thousand miles of turnpike. State and local governments often helped with the cost by buying the stock of these companies and granting them proceeds from the sale of government bonds. Most turnpikes, however, remained modest enterprises, and the short stretches of toll roads did little to improve the network of country paths. High tolls for the transportation of heavy agricultural goods discouraged shippers. By the 1830s, management and maintenance of privately operated turnpikes had become so costly, and the return so little, that thousand of miles of such roads were abandoned or turned over to the states.

WORDS AND NAMES IN AMERICAN HISTORY

The word *snag* has many meanings. It is both a noun and a verb, originally deriving from a medieval Norwegian word meaning peninsula. It is not all clear how it came to have such a variety of meanings in modern English. It can mean to catch on something, as a fishing line on a rock at the bottom of a stream. A related usage is a *snag* (or "run") in a woman"s stocking, often resulting from the stocking catching on some rough object. The word is also used to mean "catch" in sports, especially in baseball, as when an outfielder *snags* a fly ball. In pre–Civil War days, the term had a different and often terrifying meaning on the steamboat waters of the Mississippi. A *snag* was a floating or partially submerged log or even a whole tree that could pierce the hull of a boat and sink it. On the Mississippi itself and on many of its tributaries, specially designed "snagboats" were worked full time to keep the channels clear. Even today we say that our plans or hopes have "hit a snag."

The Canal Boom

New York, Philadelphia, Boston, and the other eastern seaports turned to canals to link the great waterways of the American continent. But canals were far more expensive than turnpikes, and they took not a year or two but seven to ten years to build. They presented new problems in finance and management as well as in engineering.

In 1816, the country had only a hundred miles of canals. As early as 1810, however, the New York State legislature had appointed a committee to investigate the possibility of digging a canal to the west, and in 1816 DeWitt Clinton again raised the issue. His arguments were so convincing that even his political opponents voted for his project—a canal to connect the Hudson River with Lake Erie, a breathtaking 363 miles.

Construction of the Erie Canal began in 1817. By 1823, a 280-mile stretch was in operation from Albany to Rochester. The tolls that came pouring in from traffic helped finance the final leg to Buffalo, completed in 1825. In 1823, New York had also opened the Champlain Canal, connecting the Hudson River and Lake Champlain to the north. Two figures tell the story of the Erie's success: It reduced freight rates between Albany and Buffalo from a hundred dollars to fifteen dollars a ton, and travel time from twenty to eight days, even though the canal vessels moved only at the walking pace of the towpath animals that pulled them.

In 1825, Boston persuaded the Massachusetts legislature to consider building a canal into the interior, but the hilly Massachusetts terrain discouraged the project. When Boston did finally gain entry to the West in 1842, it was by way of railroads across Massachusetts to the eastern terminal of the Erie Canal at Albany. In 1826, Philadelphia won state approval for still another scheme to tap the West, a project even bigger than the one Boston had abandoned. This system included both a canal as its main artery and railroad track. It was completed to Pittsburgh in 1834 at a cost of more than $10 million, all of it supplied by the state.

In 1827, Baltimore joined the race for western business by announcing plans for the Chesapeake and Ohio Canal. Maryland's legislature refused to finance the project, but work began with private and federal funds. The state legislators turned out to be right, for construction of the canal stopped at the mountains. In 1828, a private corporation began to lay track for the Baltimore and Ohio Railroad, the first successful line in America. But many years passed before the B & O reached the Ohio River in the 1850s.

Internal Improvements

Westerners became as energetic as easterners in seeking ways to promote trade. They soon discovered that their rich soil could produce more wheat and corn, and their corn could fatten more hogs, than southern markets could absorb. In the 1820s westerners turned a sympathetic ear to Henry Clay's program for high tariffs and "internal improvements." The tariffs were designed to promote the growth of eastern factory towns; the improvements were to provide the means for opening towns to western produce. "Internal improvements" would also mean that manufactured goods could be shipped more cheaply from the East than through New Orleans.

Congress never adopted Clay's program. But even without federal assistance, Ohio and other western states started ambitious canal and railroad projects. By 1840, some 3326 miles of canals, most of them in the North and West, had been built in the United States. Private investors supplied only a small part of this money. Federal and state subscriptions to the securities of private canal companies accounted for some of the balance, but more than half the total was provided directly by the states out of revenues or through the sale of state bonds abroad, mainly in England.

The canals, the first enterprises to receive large-scale public financial backing, proved as beneficial as expected. The South remained a valuable, growing customer of the West, and the Ohio and Mississippi river systems continued to be heavily used. But the West's connection with the North and East became stronger as the canal system developed. Without that connection, the history of American sectional conflict would have been very different.

Travel was much cheaper over canals than over turnpikes, but for about four months of the year the northern canals were frozen solid, since they were customarily only about four feet deep. Railroads soon freed shippers from the weather

Principal canals and roads

and from the medieval pace of oxen, mules, and tow horses. By 1840, the United States had 3328 miles of railroad, almost exactly equal to the canal mileage. But only 200 of these railroad miles were in the West. For some time after 1840, rivers, canals, and turnpikes remained the principal channels of inland commerce.

New York City's Spectacular Rise

From this discussion and a glance at a map of the physical geography of the northeastern United States, it is clear why New York City suddenly became so prominent. Until the Revolution, New York had remained the second or third largest of the Atlantic cities of North America. Situated as it was at the gateway to the only gap through the Appalachian Mountains, it was bound to grow. As people and commerce moved westward, and as technological innovations began to transform this route, the settlement that had once been New Amsterdam rapidly became one of the world's largest metropolitan centers. Its population of about 150,000 in 1830 dwarfed other American cities.

New York won its eventual supremacy through the enterprise of its businessmen. The promotion and construction of the Erie Canal, of course, was the most rewarding accomplishment. But even before canal digging began, New Yorkers had developed attractive innovations in business practices. One was a modified auction system for disposing of imports. Most American ports held auctions at which traders customarily offered imports for sale and then withdrew them if the bids were too low. In New York City, after 1817, merchants decided to guarantee that the highest bid would be accepted and that purchases would be delivered promptly at the price named.

This change drew merchants to New York from all over the country. And where merchants gathered, shippers were bound to bring their goods. Another New York innovation was a trans-atlantic packet service with vessels running on regular schedules, "full or not full." Before, ocean commerce had depended on the weather and the convenience of ship captains. New

Peter Cooper's Tom Thumb. The first American built steam locomotive to be operated on a common area railroad. It was built around 1829 and was used to convince owners of the Baltimore and Ohio railroad that they should use locomotives rather than horses. (Library of Congress)

York's Black Ball Line, first in the world to operate on the new basis, sent the ship *James Monroe* from New York on January 5, 1818, in a snowstorm that would have been regarded as a valid excuse for delay by any ordinary vessel.

Even after the Black Ball Line began operations, irregular sailings continued to characterize most ocean shipping. The American merchant marine carried cargo around the world to the Middle East, the Baltic states, Africa, and the East Indies, as well as to the West Indies, South America, western Europe, China, and India. In an age without wireless communication, shipowners could not tell when a vessel might return to its home port, what it might be carrying, or where it might have been.

The shipowners of New England thrived on this old-fashioned worldwide carrying trade. Nevertheless, the so-called Atlantic shuttle grew in importance as cotton exports soared and American markets for manufactured goods expanded. And New York became the most important shuttle port. By 1828, New York's share of the American merchant marine almost equaled that of Philadelphia, Boston, and Baltimore combined.

Since dependable auctions and scheduled sailings brought business and goods into New York, the city needed an export staple to balance its trade. Western produce pouring in over the Erie Canal helped. But in the 1820s New York's shippers began to sail directly to New Orleans, Mobile, and other southern ports to pick up cot-

Broadway and Canal Street, New York *(Library of Congress)*

ton to carry to Britain and the Continent. At European ports they exchanged the cotton for other goods, which they brought back to New York for distribution in the city and the interior.

The New York merchants were so successful that by 1830 an estimated forty cents of every dollar paid for raw cotton went north—almost exclusively to New York—to cover freight charges, insurance, commissions, and interest. In 1837, at a convention in the South called to promote the revival of direct trade with Europe, southern merchants were reminded: "You hold the element from which [the New York merchant] draws his strength. You have but to speak the word, and his empire is transferred to your own soil." But words were not enough. Two years later, a participant at a similar convention declared that "the importing merchants of the South [had become] an almost extinct race, and her direct trade, once so great, flourishing, and rich, [had] dwindled down to insignificance." The South had become an economic colony of the North, where New York City was the economic capital.

THE INDUSTRIAL REVOLUTION

The expansion of commercial agriculture in the West, the rapid growth of population, and access to western markets all encouraged the development of eastern industry. Concentration on cotton in the South made that region a market for the coarse textiles and shoes worn by slaves, and for other manufactures. Until western and southern markets were opened, however, factory industry had difficulty getting started in America.

First Factories

Back in 1791, in his *Report on Manufactures* to Congress, Alexander Hamilton had written, "The expediency of encouraging manufactures in the United States . . . appears at this time to be pretty generally admitted." He was too optimistic. In its first decades, America had neither surplus capital to invest in factories nor surplus labor to work in them. In 1791, Hamilton himself had helped organize the Society for Establishing Useful Manufactures. In the next few years, this corporation founded the city of Paterson, New Jersey, where there was a large waterfall. It built

numerous buildings to house its works, smuggled in skilled British mechanics, and began manufacturing yarn, cloth, hats, and other commodities. By 1796, however, both the works and the town were dead.

Other undertakings suffered the same fate. Cautious financiers at that time chose to keep their money in trade, shipping, and land. Federalist businessmen in northern cities and Republican planters in the South, both with English commercial connections, had no interest in manufacturing at home. They wanted imported English woolens, linens, china, cutlery, furniture, and tools.

The first successful full-time factory in America was the cotton-spinning plant of Almy & Brown, Providence merchants. Under the direction of an experienced Englishman, Samuel Slater, this factory began operations at Pawtucket in 1791. As Hamilton had suggested, this early factory employed only children at twelve to twenty-five cents a day—wages unacceptable to adult males. After the outbreak of the Napoleonic Wars in Europe, Americans found it more and more difficult to get British products. To supply their needs, Slater's mill expanded operations, and many hopeful imitators started up.

The Entry of Big Capital

The first textile mills were small operations rarely capitalized at more than $10,000—perhaps something like $120,000 in terms of today's dollar. Since their managers had little experience in keeping accounts, handling money and workers, and supplying markets, conservative banks would have nothing to do with them. But in 1813 a group of wealthy Boston investors headed by Francis Cabot Lowell organized the Boston Manufacturing Company. This firm built the first cotton manufacturing plant in the world in which all operations were under one roof, from the unbaling of raw cotton to the dyeing and printing of finished cloth. Lowell's group even established its own selling agencies instead of depending on local jobbers.

After the depression of 1819, the opening of the West and the expansion of cotton in the South brought a general business upturn. The revolutions against Spain in Latin America opened new foreign markets for American manufactured goods. More and more such goods found their way to China to help pay for the tea Americans were drinking in ever larger quantities.

All these changes were reflected in the expansion of firms that had survived the depression and in the great numbers of new textile corporations that set up business during the 1820s and 1830s. Some of these new companies were organized and chartered by the same group that had started the Boston Manufacturing Company. Between 1821 and 1835, these men, often called the Boston Associates, opened nine new companies in Massachusetts and southern New Hampshire. Each specialized in a particular textile or other product on a large scale.

More important, during and after the depression, these men founded insurance companies and banks to maintain and concentrate their supply of capital. They established real estate companies to take over the best factory sites. They formed companies to control dams and dam sites for harnessing the power of the rivers. The fifteen families of the Boston Associates directed much of Massachusetts's economic, political, and cultural life. By the 1840s they controlled 20 percent of the state's railroad mileage, 39 percent of its insurance capital, and 40 percent of Boston's banking resources.

These financial enterprises were aided by the development of the corporation, a legal device whereby capitalists accumulate large amounts of money through the sale of shares to subscribers. By the time the canal and railroad companies were being formed in the 1810s and 1820s, the idea of limited liability had also become well established in law and finance. It meant that owners of corporation stock were liable for the obligations of the company only to the extent of their own investment, regardless of how large their personal fortune might be. This protection helped to attract the capital required for costly, long-term projects. Since corporate securities could be disposed of more easily than investments in partnerships or single-owner businesses, corporations also could look forward to a long life. In most cases, they would not be affected by the death or withdrawal of an individual investor.

Repairing power-driven textile machine. *(Library of Congress)*

Lowell Girls, as they were called, operate looms in one of the town's mills. The young women, most of whom came from local farm families, were very closely chaperoned off the job. *(Museum of American Textile History)*

Women and Industrial Labor

Many of the new textile mills found a cheap and eager source of labor in young women from surrounding rural areas. A major reason was that rural New England had a shortage of men. Many young males had headed west—to upper New York State and beyond—for better and more plentiful farmland. Like many human migrations, the westward movement from the New England states was heavily male. The first census of 1790 showed that New England was the

---

THE WOMEN IN THE MILLS

Early in the 1840s a radical American reformer, Orestes Brownson, described the situation of Lowell women who had gone to work just long enough to accumulate a dowry, add to the family income, or send a brother to school. He offered a dissenting view of the frequently praised Lowell mills, whose young women were said to be so well and carefully treated. This picture of "well-dressed" and "healthy and happy" workers, he wrote, was

the fair side of the picture; the side exhibited to distinguished visitors. There is a dark side, *moral as well as physical. Of the common operatives, few, if any, by their wages, acquire a competence.... The great mass wear out their health, spirits, and morals, without becoming one whit better off than when they commenced labor. The bills of mortality in these factory villages are not striking, we admit, for the poor girls when they can toil no longer go home to die. The average life—working life, we mean—of the girls that come to Lowell... is only about three years. What becomes of them then? Few of them ever marry, fewer still ever return to their native places with reputations unimpaired."*

---

only major section of the new nation to have significantly more women than men. Young women in Massachusetts and the other New England states found husbands in short supply.

Thus in the early nineteenth century, unmarried farm girls flocked to such new mill towns as Lowell, Waltham, Lawrence, and Dover (all of which contained Boston Associates factories). There they endured long and difficult hours on the job and a completely controlled environment in boardinghouses off the job. All their visitors were screened and their hours carefully restricted by matrons. They were required to attend church and forbidden to discuss grievances, even among themselves. At the mills, their wages were kept low and they were subject to fines for the slightest infringements of company rules. Many of the women were forced to sign contracts agreeing not to form any sort of alliance, at the risk of losing their wages. Since most factories paid workers only two to four times a year, this threat carried considerable weight.

At first the "dormitory factories" drew considerable admiration from foreign visitors. Here were young ladies industriously earning their own dowries in hopes of eventual marriage. As time went by, however, factory work became more onerous and less respectable. Increasingly, "nice" young ladies shunned it. The poorest of New England women and children were joined by women just off the boat from Ireland and other European countries.

Conditions for these women textile workers as well as other industrial workers worsened during the frequent and severe economic crises in the United States. When demand lagged behind expanding production, shops and factories closed. Workers were laid off, and many small businesses were swallowed up by bigger ones that were able to absorb the losses.

In the seventy years before the Civil War, American workers slowly came to learn that their interests were best served by joint action. Skilled male artisans first broke away from their employers in the 1790s by joining mutual aid societies. By the beginning of the nineteenth century, improvements in transportation had opened larger markets to master artisans, some of whom gave up their handwork to become merchant capitalists—that is, businessmen who gathered up larger orders than one artisan and a few helpers could fill and who employed others to work for them. Those who had never been artisans also entered various crafts as merchant capitalists. By the 1820s, as competition became keen, wages were cut. Artisans were further embittered by the loss of their independent status. Worse still, the integrity of their work and their product was being destroyed as skills were broken down into simpler tasks to be performed by lower-paid apprentices.

The first unions in America were formed in protest against these conditions. From the start, big business, with the aid of the government, made it hazardous for workers to join these al-

CHILD LABOR

Small textile factories employed women and children drawn from the poorest farm families in an area. They could be paid less, and they were thought to be more obedient than men. Children were especially cheap to hire, and their small, thin hands could fit easily into the narrow slots of the machines. But the mill children had to be swift and careful, or the machines would grab their fingers or their hair and a bit of scalp. The children worked twelve and thirteen hours a day, rarely seeing their families, much less the sun. The older ones had to watch over the younger ones to make sure they did not fall asleep on the job.

Such miserable conditions were pointed to with pride by the mill owners. They were keeping the children out of trouble, teaching them the value of money and the virtue of hard work. This "educational" program actually provided high profits for the new entrepreneurs and abject poverty for many New England families, whose sole support became the scanty wages of their children. Cheap child labor in many cases put the father out of a job. In 1820, half the factory workers in America were children, earning thirty-three to sixty-seven cents a week.

liances. Until 1842 labor unions were frequently declared by the courts to be "conspiratorial combinations." In a trial of Pittsburgh cordwainers in 1815, the artisans were found guilty of "combining to raise wages." The court recorder wrote of the verdict: "It is most important to the manufacturing interests of the community for it puts an end to these associations which have been so prejudicial to the successful enterprise of the capitalist in the western country."

Neither court decisions nor coercion could prevent laborers from organizing. Economic depressions, however, slowed the labor movement considerably during the first half of the nineteenth century. In the 1819–1822 depression, forty thousand laborers were thrown out of work in Philadelphia and New York alone. Budding labor unions were crushed, and no relief for the unemployed was offered by the government. It was not until the late 1820s that labor revived, with the movement for a ten-hour day.

In Philadelphia the first citywide federation of labor, the Mechanics Union, emerged out of this struggle for shorter hours. Carpenters, masons, stonecutters, hatters, tailors, riggers, stevedores, cabinetmakers, cordwainers, and other workers joined to secure their "right, derived from their creator, to have sufficient time in each day for the cultivation of their minds and for self-improvement." Through strikes and labor solidarity among the different trades, the ten-hour day was eventually won by workers in most eastern cities.

The first recorded strike of factory workers was conducted by children in 1828. The mill owners in Paterson, New Jersey, tried to change the dinner hour from twelve to one. The children went out on strike, "for fear," said one observer, "if they assented to this, the next thing would be to deprive them of eating at all." The militia was called in to break the strike. Soon after, the other large group in the textile mills, working women, went on strike; four hundred of them paraded through the streets of Dover, New Hampshire. For Yankee "young ladies" to take to the streets required courage in a period when any kind of public activity was thought to disgrace a woman.

From 1833 to 1837, labor organizations, particularly those of artisans, grew at a rate not to be matched again in the century. Trade unions grew from 26,000 members to 300,000 during that period. In New York City nearly two-thirds of the workers were organized, and unions were beginning to move west to Buffalo, St. Louis, and Pittsburgh. During these four years there were over 170 strikes. Wage earners who had never before been organized—including seamstresses, tailors, bookbinders, and shoemakers—formed unions and went on strike.

Women textile workers were again in the forefront of the labor struggle. In 1834 a thousand or more Lowell Girls walked out in protest against a 15 percent wage cut. "One of the leaders," reported the *Boston Transcript*, "mounted a stump, and made a flaming . . . speech on the rights of women and the iniquities of the 'monied aristocracy' which produced a powerful effect on her auditors, and they determined to 'have their way, if they died for it.'" The strike was broken, and many of the women went home.

Those who stayed, however, continued to fight back, forming a Factory Girls' Association in 1836, with a membership of 2500. They declared: "As our fathers resisted unto blood the lordly avarice of the British ministry, so we, their daughters, never will wear the yoke which has been prepared for us." When they went out on strike they were evicted from the company-owned boardinghouses and starved into defeat. But the struggle inspired other women textile workers, whose strikes were later successful.

The business collapse of 1837, when unemployment threatened all workers, crushed the early labor movement. Layoffs were becoming harsher for industrial workers. Women, children, and men had moved off their farms and had become dependent on the factory for a living. Many European immigrants were also tied to the factories. Having arrived penniless, they had to remain in the cities. Industrialization did provide jobs for these new Americans, as well as for many poor farming families. But the cost in the quality of life was great. Farm work did not disrupt families and subject individuals to lonely, alienating, and dangerous jobs.

These changes in the lives of Americans were not so obvious then as they are now. Many people were conscious that something was going on, but they were not sure what. They welcomed what they called the "age of improvement." But they grew vaguely anxious about the direction of social change. There was an inherent tension between these reactions, a tension that easily spilled over into politics.

SUMMARY

America experienced a boom after the War of 1812, and then a bust in 1819. The Second Bank of the United States was chartered for twenty years. Federal power and the national economy were strengthened by a series of Supreme Court decisions by Chief Justice John Marshall.

The problem of admitting new states that allowed slavery and those that forbade it was settled for a time by the Missouri Compromise of 1820. Slavery was permitted in Missouri; Maine was admitted as a free state; and slavery was prohibited "forever" in the entire Louisiana Territory north of a line drawn westward from Missouri's southern border—36°30'.

The economy began to grow and change. Farming, fishing, and lumbering remained traditional ways of earning a living. But now the fur trade in the West and the China trade in the Pacific began to expand American horizons. So did the trade on the Santa Fe Trail in the Mexican Southwest. Meanwhile, thousands of settlers poured onto the lands of the Middle West and mid-South. The lives of these western settlers were hard, but it was clear the land was fertile and could be a source of agricultural wealth. The demand for cotton in world markets, especially Britain, led the southern plantation system to expand westward into Alabama and Mississippi. Eli Whitney's cotton gin, invented late in the eighteenth century, greatly expanded production. The new Cotton Kingdom provided a market for the agricultural products of the West. Southern specialization in cotton brought western specialization in grain and meat and mules.

Trade and regional specialization fostered the growth of a national transportation system. The steamboat revolutionized inland water transport. So did the many miles of canals built to link the inland waterways. The longest and biggest was the Erie Canal in New York, completed in 1825. On land, a national highway was built from Cumberland, Maryland, to Vandalia, Illinois. Private turnpikes were built in other areas, mostly in New England and the middle states. But by the 1830s most of these roads had been turned over to the states. They now formed the basis for a national system of public roads.

Henry Clay in the 1820s tried to advance his American System, a program for high tariffs and "internal improvements." The tariff was to promote eastern factory towns; the internal improvements were to open towns to western products. By 1840, the United States had about 3000 miles of canals and an equal amount of railroad track.

TIME LINE

1790s	Skilled artisans begin to separate from their employers	1818	National Highway reaches Wheeling
1791	First U.S. textile mill built by Samuel Slater	1819	Onset of major economic depression
1793	Whitney invents cotton gin	1819	*Dartmouth College* case; *McCulloch v. Maryland*
1810s	Women and children begin to form the bulk of textile employees	1820	Missouri Compromise
1811	First steamboat, the *New Orleans*, on western rivers	1824	*Gibbons v. Ogden*
1813	Organization of Boston Manufacturing Company	1825	Completion of the Erie Canal
1816	Astor wins monopoly for his American Fur Company	1825	Survey of Santa Fe Trail
1816	Establishment of Second Bank of the United States	1834	Women textile workers strike in Lowell
1818	First packet ship sails from New York City	1837	Business collapse undermines union movements
		1840	Miles of railroads equal miles of canals

In the East, New York suddenly rose to dominance as a port and a trading center. Its merchants pioneered a modified auction system and the idea of running ships on a regular schedule, full or not full, in all kinds of weather. These merchants helped make the South an economic colony of the North.

The North was also helped by the fact that the Industrial Revolution in America took root in New England. The first successful full-time factory in America was a textile mill in Rhode Island. Most of the early factories were small, but in 1813 a group of wealthy Boston investors organized the Boston Manufacturing Company. The holdings of this group grew to include not only textile plants, but insurance companies and banks to maintain and concentrate capital, real estate companies to buy factory sites, and companies to control sources of waterpower.

Women and children of both sexes began to work in the new textile factories. Especially in New England, a surplus of women contributed to this development.

Children and women could be paid much less than men. Many of these new industrial workers suffered on their jobs from long hours, harsh discipline, and dangerous machinery. All kinds of working people, including skilled male artisans as well as women and children in the factories, took part in the first steps toward organizing in unions and even in strikes for better working conditions. These efforts at first had some success, but were crushed by the economic depression that struck in 1837.

Americans generally began to realize that economic progress could have disastrous costs, but for the most part they welcomed the "improvements" that were bringing prosperity to the nation. This twin sense of improvement and suffering spilled over into the realm of politics.

Suggested Readings

A brief survey is D. Hawke, *Nuts and Bolts of the Past: A History of American Technology, 1776–1860* (1988). G.Taylor, *The Transportation Revolution, 1815–1860* (1951), is still important. Two books by D. North, *Economic Growth of the United States, 1790–1860* (1961) and *Growth and Welfare in the American Past: A New Economic History* (2nd ed., 1974), should be compared with the appraisal of causation by S. Bruchey, *The Roots of American Economic Growth, 1607–1861* (1965).

For agricultural history, see P. Gates, *The Farmers' Age: Agriculture, 1815-1860* (1960); C. Danhof, *Change in Agriculture: The Northern United States, 1820–1870* (1969); and J. Faragher, *Sugar Creek: Life on the Illinois Prairie* (1986). An older work that still contains information on production and slave populations not found elsewhere is L. Gray, *History of Agriculture in the Southern United States to 1860* (2 vols., 1933). S. Bruchey (ed.), *Cotton and the Growth of the American Economy, 1790–1860* (1967), deals with that extraordinary expansion. J. Mirsky and A. Nevins, *The World of Eli Whitney* (1952), describes not only the invention of the cotton gin, but also the development of interchangeable parts in the manufacture of furs.

One of the most authoritative descriptions of whaling is contained in Herman Melville's great novel, *Moby Dick* (1851). Also very readable is the scholarly work by S. Morison, *The Maritime History of Massachusetts, 1783–1860* (1921). T. Karamanski, *Fur Trade and Exploration: Opening the Far Northwest, 1821–1852* (1983), emphasizes exploration. Race relations are stressed in L. Saum, *The Fur Trader and the Indian* (1965).

River transportation before the age of steam is discussed in L. Baldwin, *The Keelboat Age on Western Waters* (1941); the later period is covered by L. Hunter, *Steamboats on the Western Rivers* (1939). See Also O. Holmes and P. Rohrbach, *Stagecoach East: Stagecoach Days in the East from the Colonial Period to the Civil War* (1893).

A lifetime of study is reflected in C. Goodrich, *Government Promotion of American Canals and Railroads, 1800–1890* (1960). Two more recent works bear on important canals: R. Shaw, *Erie Water West: A History of the Erie Canal, 1792–1854* (1966); and H. Scheiber, *The Ohio Canal Era: A Case Study of Government and the Economy, 1820–1861* (1968). M. Reed, *New Orleans and the Railroads: The Struggle for Commercial Empire, 1830–1860* (1966) is an interesting study of the South's greatest city, which was a river and an ocean port as well as a railroad terminal. For more on railroads, see the citations in Chapter 13 and Volume 2 of J. Doriman, *The Economic Mind in American Civilization* (5 vols., 1946–1959).

R. Albion, *The Rise of New York Port, 1815–1860* (1939), is a stunning work. S. Warner, *The Urban Wilderness: A History of the American City* (1972), contains a section covering 1820 to 1870 that discusses transportation, technology, land use, and social problems. See also J. Machor, *Pastoral Cities: Urban Ideals and the Symbolic Landscape of America* (1987).

All phases of America's first modern industry are presented in C. Ware, *The Early New England Cotton Manufacture* (1931): and H. Josephson, *The Golden*

Threads: New England's Mill Girls and Magnates (1949). On business more generally, see E. Dodd, *American Business Corporations until 1860* (1954); R. Dalzell, *Enterprising Elite: The Boston Associates and the World They Made* (1987); and T. Cochran, *Business in American Life: A History* (1972), a magnificent and broadly interpretive work. There is much information but virtually no interpretation in V. Clark, *History of Manufactures in the United States* (3 vols., 1928). M. Smith, *Harpers Ferry Armory and the New Technology: The Challenge of Change* (1977), is a marvelously comprehensive account of the development of the machine-tool industry and its social impact. On technology and the enterprising spirit, see the widely ranging J. Ellul, *The Technological Society* (1967).

The history of labor in the early years of the United States has not received the treatment it deserves. A beginning may be made with N. Ware, *The Industrial Worker, 1840–1860* (1924); L. Ulman, *The Rise of the National Trade Union* (1955); and Volume 1 of P. Foner, *History of the Labor Movement in the United States* (3 vols., 1947–1964). B. Wertheimer, *We Were There: The Story of Working Women in America* (1977), treats the early years of women's unionization particularly well.

Major General Andrew Jackson, President of the United States, painted by Thomas Sully. *(Library of Congress)*

CHAPTER 11

NEW POLITICS FOR A NEW AGE

When James Monroe left the White House in 1825, the age of the Founding Fathers had clearly ended. The nation was free from foreign entanglements. Monroe himself was the last president of the Virginia dynasty and the revolutionary generation. His successor was in many ways a transitional figure. John Quincy Adams inherited his own position in diplomacy and politics from his distinguished father. He himself was the last president until the twentieth century who could possibly be called an intellectual. His famous father was still alive in Quincy, busily corresponding with Thomas Jefferson about statecraft, religion, and the nature of man. The two elder statesmen died on the same day during the presidency of the younger Adams. The symbolism of their passing was not lost on Americans, for the date was July 4, 1826, the fiftieth anniversary of the Declaration of Independence. Surely God's providence was guiding the American nation.

The resulting outburst of oratory and self-congratulation was very brief. Americans returned to political bickering in an extremely nasty campaign for the presidency in 1828. The outlines of two new political parties were beginning to emerge, and the next few years saw the development of what has been called the second political party system. In 1828 the voters rejected the incumbent president, who was the last ever to look upon political parties as basically harmful to the nation. They elected an old war hero who enjoyed having political opposition because he could fight against it.

President Jackson dominated the political scene, and the 1830s are often called the Age of Jackson. He greatly enlarged the power of the presidency and in doing so aroused controversy that cast a shadow over American politics long after his death. Both he and his opponents adapted their styles to a changed society. Neither would have put the matter that way; rather, they talked about "democracy" and "the common man." Exactly what these words meant was not clear.

It *is* clear, however, that the American people were in a changed mood. They no longer turned for leadership to gentlemen of wealth and breeding. Many of them praised the virtues of the common people, even while they admired those who forged ahead in the world of business. They welcomed the new age, yet grew nostalgic for the simpler days of the early Republic. They hailed the achievements of the nation, and at the same time, as we will see in the next chapter, they denounced its failings. We can sense in these self-assessments a response to profound changes they knew were taking place but did not fully understand.

Yet there was more to Jacksonian politics than a change in mood and style. Economic transformations presented Americans with very real issues, including banking and the tariff. Westward expansion raised problems of how to treat Indians and whether to construct "internal improvements." These matters often involved important questions about the proper interpretation of the Constitution. At the center of these controversies stood the figure of Andrew Jackson, who stamped the era with his iron will and vigorous style.

THE BEGINNINGS OF THE NEW POLITICS

The Age of Jackson may be said to have begun in 1824, when he won the popular vote but lost the election. During the entire administration of John Quincy Adams, Jackson had friends pushing him for the presidency. One important development often associated with Jackson actually took place before he was a political candidate and owed nothing to his ideas or actions. This was the extension of the franchise through elimination of property requirements, and oddly enough, it was one of the few important political developments that did *not* arouse debate about constitutional issues.

Expanding the Electorate

During the first quarter of the nineteenth century most states quietly eliminated property qualifications for voting, thus opening up the franchise to almost all adult white males. In Europe, particularly in Great Britain, broadening the suffrage was a major public issue throughout much of the nineteenth century. The United States escaped major quarrels on this matter largely because the Founding Fathers had left suffrage requirements to the states: Americans did not have to deal with the matter as a national issue. Nonetheless, it is clear that public feeling was in favor of giving the vote to "all men."

The Vermont constitution of 1777 put some restrictions on voting, but it was the first to remove property-holding and tax-paying qualifications. This constitution was intact when Vermont entered the Union in 1791. Kentucky, New Jersey, Maryland, and Connecticut then widened the franchise. Connecticut became a model for northern states such as Maine, Massachusetts, and New York. Between 1816 and 1821, six new states entered the Union with constitutions that required no property qualifications for voting.

The South generally lagged behind. Virginia, despite the Jeffersonian tradition, was the last state to abolish the property test. Only a few years earlier, Louisiana broadened the franchise by reducing its heavy tax-paying qualification. Elsewhere in the slave states, the more liberal example of Maryland had been followed. "We ought," said a Virginia senator in 1829, "to spread wide the foundation of our government, that all white men have a direct interest in its protection." What he meant especially was protection against slave revolts.

Restricting Blacks in the North

The democratic spirit failed to carry over to one significant class of the population—free blacks. As late as 1820, they were permitted by law to vote equally with whites in northern New England, New York, Pennsylvania, and even Tennessee and North Carolina. This right, however, usually came from omissions in the law and was denied in practice until the law itself was tightened. As a delegate to the Pennsylvania constitutional convention of 1837 said on his way to the meeting that would disenfranchise free blacks: "The people of this state are for continuing this commonwealth, what it always has been, a political community of white persons."

By 1837, free blacks could vote only in those New England states from Massachusetts northward. In Connecticut, after 1818, blacks who had voted previously could continue to vote, but newly freed slaves were disfranchised. In the other states, free blacks who had once voted were now deprived of the vote, usually by the very same article that for the first time provided full manhood suffrage for whites. No state entering the Union between 1819 and the Civil War permitted free blacks to vote.

Loss of the right to vote was only one of the lengthening list of restrictions on blacks in the free states. They were cooped up in miserable slums, confined by curfews, placed outside the judicial and educational systems, and increasingly barred from all but the most menial occupations and from the land as well. An Oregonian said that the free black was "cast upon the world," even in his own distant commonwealth in the 1850s, "with no defense; his life, liberty, his property, his all, are dependent on the caprice, the passion, and the inveterate prejudices of not only the community at large but of every felon who may happen to cover an inhuman heart with a white face." By then, many western states would not allow free blacks even to enter.

National Elections

For the "political community of white persons," on the other hand, even more important than the right of suffrage was the exercising of that right on the national level. Earlier, up to 70 percent of the electorate had voted in hot local contests, but presidential elections before 1828 seem to have left most voters cold. Even in 1824, when Jackson first was a candidate, only 27 percent of those eligible voted, compared with 56 percent in 1828. Popular enthusiasm for presidential elections peaked in 1840, after Jackson had retired, when 78 percent of the eligible voters went to the polls.

That proportion was new in American politics and has never been equaled in any presidential election since. One reason for the new interest was the gradual emergence of a new two-party system after 1824 and sharper party differences on issues. Another was voter participation in actually naming the candidates.

Presidential candidates had formerly been nominated by a caucus, or meeting, of congressmen in Washington, a system that kept cliques in power. The success of the caucus system was prolonged by the availability of strong candidates from populous Virginia, who defeated opponents put forward by scattered factions in other states. Rising politicians hated the caucus, and in 1831, as we shall see, they brought about the first real break in the system.

Still another institution gave way before the rising demand to bring government closer to the people. In most states, presidential electors had been chosen by the legislatures. But by 1828, every state except Delaware and South Carolina had provided for popular election of members of the electoral college. This change forced presidential candidates to appeal to the people rather than to a small group of politicians. After 1828 Jackson, as he often reminded his opponents, was the first president who could claim to have been elected directly by the voters. (The claim was not altogether justified, since members of the electoral college technically still had, as they do today, personal discretion in casting ballots.) Governors also began to be popularly elected, and property qualifications for that office and others were swept away. Finally, by the 1840s many state judges were being elected rather than appointed.

This trend toward popular participation did not, of course, bring many lumberjacks, fishermen, artisans, backwoodsmen in coonskin caps, or even farmers into high political office. A man still needed standing in the community, conspicuous achievement, or at least persuasive eloquence to win office. But popular participation in politics was more broadly based in the United States than in any other major nation in the world. It would not be long before some reformers would at least consider the possibility that women too should be included in the political process.

The Election of 1824

Everyone assumed that Monroe would not run for a third term, chiefly because of the precedent established by Washington. But the Republicans had lost their unity and were unable to replace him with a single candidate. Four contenders for the presidency emerged in 1824, all of them rather vaguely claiming to be "Republicans." One was Andrew Jackson, who had little government experience but a towering reputation as an Indian fighter and especially as the Hero of New Orleans. In 1822 his supporters in Tennessee had pushed him into the United

States Senate because they wanted to nominate the somewhat reluctant general for president two years later. Another candidate was John Quincy Adams of Massachusetts, the heir apparent because by this time it was assumed that the secretary of state would succeed to the presidency. Adams could legitimately present himself as a skillful, hardworking diplomat, a committed American nationalist, and a man of incorruptible honor. William Crawford of Georgia was a personally attractive man who presented himself as the true heir of Thomas Jefferson. He would have polled more votes had he not suffered a stroke during the campaign. Finally, Kentucky's Henry Clay had built a strong power base as Speaker of the House, as well as a broad popular following for his American System.

Jackson ended up winning a large plurality of the popular vote. In the electoral college, however, his ninety-nine votes fell short of the required majority, so the contest was thrown into

Henry Clay. *(Library of Congress)*

the House of Representatives, as required by the Constitution. Here Clay, having polled the lowest electoral total, was eliminated. Of the top three, Crawford was ill. The contest was left to Jackson and Adams.

Clay, a power in the House, did not admire Jackson. "I cannot believe," he said, "that killing 2500 Englishmen at New Orleans qualifies [him] for the various difficult and complicated duties of the Chief Magistracy." After a private talk with Adams, Clay swung his supporters to him. Clay's influence was largely responsible for Adams's election. One of Adams's first presidential acts was to name Clay as secretary of state. As far as the public was concerned, this was like naming him as his successor.

The Jackson men lost little time in charging that a "corrupt bargain" had been made. The charge was not really fair, since Clay and Adams agreed on most matters. But "bargain and corruption" became the Jacksonians' slogan for the 1828 campaign, which opened as soon as they learned of their defeat in 1824.

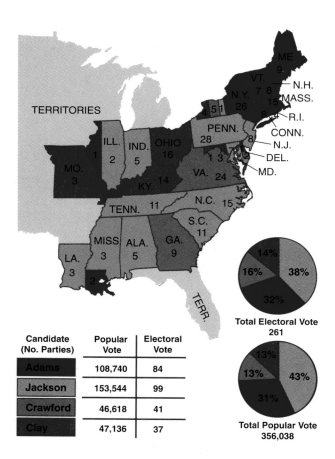

Candidate (No. Parties)	Popular Vote	Electoral Vote
Adams	108,740	84
Jackson	153,544	99
Crawford	46,618	41
Clay	47,136	37

Total Electoral Vote 261

Total Popular Vote 356,038

The election of 1824

John Quincy Adams as President

The alleged "deal" was not the only issue that haunted Adams in the White House. A sensitive and high-minded man, he regretted having to accept the presidency with, as he said, "perhaps two-thirds of the whole people adverse to the actual result." Popular opinion, however, did not stop Adams from launching a program he considered right for the country. With stubborn courage and political ineptitude, he argued for an active national government and for internal improvements.

He was warned by Clay and most of his cabinet that, at a time when states'-rights feelings were rising and sectional jealousies were strong, it was all but suicidal for a president—and a minority president at that—to urge such a policy. Adams himself agreed that his program was a "perilous experiment."

Under the Constitution, Adams argued in his first message to Congress, the federal government had the power to "provide for the common defense and general welfare." The "common defense" seemed a clear enough obligation; the "general welfare," not nearly so. Adams proposed to stretch the latter to justify establishing a national university, financing scientific expeditions, building astronomical observatories, reforming the patent system, and developing a national transportation system.

A dozen years later, Adams explained that "the great effort of my administration" was to put "all the superfluous revenue of the Union into internal improvement." He continued with an analysis of the defeat of his program: "When I came to the Presidency this principle of internal improvement was swelling the tide of public prosperity." However, he went on, "the South saw the signs of its own inevitable downfall in the unparalleled progress of the general welfare in the North, and fell to cursing the tariff and internal improvements, and raised the standard of free trade, nullification, and state rights." In fact, many people in the middle states and the Midwest, with their own "mass of local jealousies," joined the South in rejecting the Adams program. At the same time, many "self-made" men (Clay coined this term to describe the rising manufacturers of Kentucky) were on Adams's side.

Adams's comprehensive program for centralized economic and cultural development, and

John Quincy Adams, the sixth president of the United States, seated in the library. *(Library of Congress)*

his inability to push it through, encouraged states' rights opponents everywhere to mobilize their own machines behind Jackson. An especially humiliating outcome resulted from the president's efforts to preserve the lands of the Creek and Cherokee Indians in Georgia against outraged opposition from the state, its speculators, and potential frontier settlers.

Jackson Elected

By the time of the congressional elections of 1826, Adams's program had gained for his followers the name of National Republicans. His opponents became known as Democratic Republicans. In these elections, for the first time in the history of the country, a president lost his majority in Congress after two years in office. On convening under Jacksonian leadership, the new Congress made its single purpose the advancement of the general's presidential prospects in 1828.

The Jacksonian strategy was to win support in all key or questionable states by means of legislative handouts. Beyond that, the Jacksonian press blackened Adams's name. The attacks continued during the 1828 campaign, when Jackson's supporters also introduced a carnival spirit into the presidential contest. They paraded with hickory sticks to symbolize the toughness of Old Hickory and waved hickory brooms to signify the need for sweeping the rascals out. Adams's supporters replied with similar tactics, but Adams himself characteristically tried to remain aloof from such a campaign. Said he: "If my country wants my services, she must ask for them."

Apart from personalities, the major issue in 1828 was the protective tariff on manufactured goods, adopted in 1824. The act had gained the support of the industrial middle states and the Old Northwest, which continued to look to eastern cities for markets for its agricultural surpluses. New England, with large manufacturers of its own, was still heavily committed to commerce, and had split on the measure. The South, which had nearly given up its hopes for manufacturing, overwhelmingly opposed it.

Jackson's lieutenants hoped to profit politically from this alignment. Their means was the Tariff of 1828. Its object, said one political observer, was to encourage "manufactures of no sort but the manufacture of a president of the United States." But the scheme backfired. Because it raised the general level of duties, southerners called it "the tariff of abominations." And because it failed to protect woolen manufactures while it raised duties on raw wool and other raw materials, the tariff also angered certain northern industrialists.

Yet Jackson's candidacy survived—with the help of his supporters in Congress, who made large grants of federal lands to politically doubtful states. In 1828, the Hero of New Orleans, the supposed victim of the Adams-Clay "corrupt bargain," the most visible old soldier in the country for four solid years, polled 647,000 votes. The surprise, if any, was that Adams received 508,000. Several other U.S. presidents have won election by a wider margin.

OLD HICKORY IN THE WHITE HOUSE

Jackson's inauguration attracted an immense crowd to Washington. People surged through the unpaved streets, pressed into the White House, stood on sofas in muddy boots, smashed glassware, and generally convinced observers that the presidency had somehow been brought home to the real people. Jackson himself did nothing to discourage this mood. He thought of himself as a man of humble background. In fact, he had been born in poverty in the Carolina backcountry, the son of Scotch-Irish immigrants, and both he and his supporters made a great deal of this. He was the first American president since Washington to have had no college education.

At the time of his election at the age of sixty-one, however, he was scarcely one of the common people. He had built a highly successful career in Tennessee in law, politics, land speculation, cotton planting, and soldiering. His home, the Hermitage, was a mansion, not a log cabin. Anyone who owned more than a hundred slaves, as Jackson did, was a very wealthy man.

He was also a man of strong convictions. As president, he saw himself as the one government

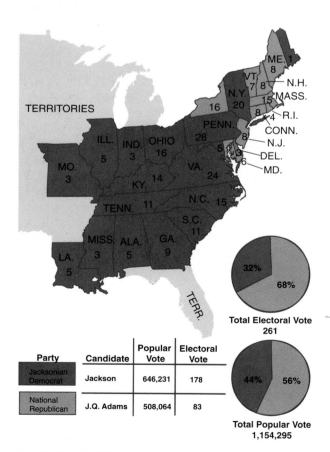

Party	Candidate	Popular Vote	Electoral Vote
Jacksonian Democrat	Jackson	646,231	178
National Republican	J.Q. Adams	508,064	83

Total Electoral Vote 261

Total Popular Vote 1,154,295

The election of 1828

official who had been elected by all the people, and he therefore regarded himself as representing the national interest. Always suspicious, Jackson disliked special-interest groups and men whose power came from special privilege. Lurking just beneath the surface of his iron will was a deep streak of anger. When crossed, he lashed back, whether it was at the British army, Indians, Spanish officials, judges, bank officers, or political opponents. He was the least forgiving of men. He was the only president ever to have killed a man in a duel.

In sheer physical presence, he was more commanding than any public figure since George Washington. Yet whereas Washington had commanded widespread respect, Jackson commanded widespread popularity. He seemed to symbolize the virtues of the new American—a common man successfully on the make, ready to tackle and destroy aristocratic privilege wherever he found it. His opponents sensed that he had all the qualities of a democratic emperor. The National Republicans soon began calling themselves Whigs to symbolize their resistance to "King Andrew I." As president, Jackson moved quickly to defend the political spoils system, to exercise his veto power, and to challenge the Supreme Court.

Andrew Jackson. *(Library of Congress)*

The Spoils System

When the new chief executive set about to name his major department heads, his most important appointment went to Martin Van Buren of New York as secretary of state. But Jackson liked to rely on the advice of personal friends. His administration was marked by the rise to power of a category of men who became known as the Kitchen Cabinet—a small group of what today we would call White House advisers. Three were trusted western newspaper editors. Whatever these men or Jackson may have thought about the new issues in national politics—the tariff, internal improvements, the national bank, land, and Indian policy—they all shared his feeling about the need for a strong presidency.

Jackson's policy toward the executive civil service was consistent with his independent view of his high office. He shocked the Adams men by firing about 900 federal jobholders from among the 10,000 he found on the payroll. Actually, his party chiefs, having made many commitments in two campaigns, wanted even more

heads to roll, but Jackson restrained them. The Adams press protested against this new "reign of terror," this grim "purge" that was bloodying the federal bureaucracy. But in the long run it was the president's defense of the spoils system, rather than his particular replacements, that so firmly associated his name with it. Earlier presidents had removed political opponents from office without raising many eyebrows.

Jackson was the first to make the spoils system seem a social and moral as well as a political "reform." In his first annual message to Congress in December 1829, he defended "that rotation [in office] which constitutes a leading principle in the republican creed." Such rotation, he continued, would nullify the prevailing idea that "office is . . . a species of property, and government . . . a means of promoting individual interest, . . . an engine for the support of the few at the expense of the many." Jackson was ready to exclude judges, cabinet officers, and high-ranking diplomats from this rule. Otherwise, "the duties of public offices" are "plain and simple," and plain and simple men could best perform them in the people's interest.

The Rights of the States

In his relations with Congress and the courts, the new chief executive proved equally aggressive. Earlier presidents had been content to administer the laws passed by Congress. But Jackson took the constitutional power given the executive to participate in making (or unmaking) the law as well as executing it. In his two terms, Jackson vetoed more legislation than all former presidents combined.

Such actions appear remarkable in a man so openly attached to popular government. But Jackson, especially after losing the election of 1824 in the House, had come to regard Congress as the home of "aristocratical establishments" such as the national bank. He saw his own office as the only popular defense against such "interests" as the new industrialists.

One of his most outstanding vetoes killed the Maysville Road Bill of 1830, which would have required the federal government to buy stock in a private corporation. The company was to build an internal improvement, a road in Clay's home state of Kentucky. Because the road would lie within a single state, Jackson's stand was easy to justify. He was well aware that he would be strongly supported in such states as New York and Pennsylvania, for they had helped his election and had developed transportation systems at their own expense. He knew he would also find support from the South Atlantic states, committed as they were to slavery and states' rights. These states were also becoming opposed to protective tariffs, which supplied most of the federal money for internal improvements.

But throughout his presidency, Jackson approved large appropriations for river- and harbor-improvement bills and similar pork-barrel legislation sponsored by worthy Democrats, in return for local election support. Yet he told Congress: "The great mass of legislation relating to our internal affairs was intended to be left where the Federal Convention found it—in the State governments. . . . I can not . . . too strongly or too earnestly . . . warn you against all encroachments upon the legitimate sphere of State sovereignties." Jackson viewed the presidency as the only direct reflection of the people's will. Almost inevitably this view resulted in a clash with the Supreme Court as well as Congress. Once again, he based his stand on the rights of the states.

The Cherokee Indians

In 1803, after Georgia had ceded its western lands to the United States, the federal government agreed to settle Creek and Cherokee claims to the region. Federal action, however, was slow, and as cotton growing spread in the state, the planters' patience ran out. Georgia's militant governor, George M. Troup, ordered a state survey of Creek lands in 1826. When President Adams threatened to stop the survey with federal forces, Governor Troup said he would resist force with force. Conflict was avoided only by the surrender of the Creeks and their removal beyond the Mississippi.

Far more than most Indian ethnic groups, the Cherokee, like the Creek, had embraced the white man's ways. They had established farms and factories, built schools, and begun a newspaper. They also adopted a constitution. In 1827 they decided to form an independent state on the United States model. Georgia responded by nullifying all federal Indian laws and ordering seizure of Cherokee lands.

When Georgia courts convicted a Cherokee of murder, the Supreme Court of the United States ordered that conviction set aside. Governor Troup and the state legislature ignored the federal government's "interference" and executed the prisoner. By then, Jackson had become president. His malice toward Indians was well known. The Cherokee sought an injunction in the Supreme Court prohibiting the extension of Georgia law to Indian residents and Georgia's seizure of Indian lands.

In 1831 John Marshall rejected the idea that Indian tribes were like "foreign nations" with whom the United States made treaties. The Indians, he said, were "domestic dependent nations" who could not sue in United States courts. He denied the injunction, but he asserted that the United States alone, and no single state, had sovereignty over Indians and their lands.

In 1832 Marshall strengthened this opinion. In *Worcester v. Georgia* he declared that the Cherokee nation was a legitimate political community, with clearly defined territories, where "the laws of Georgia can have no force, and which the citizens of Georgia have no right to enter" without Cherokee consent. In effect, Marshall was saying that the Cherokee nation would exist or not at the pleasure of the federal government, not that of any single state. The state ignored the Court's decision.

JACKSON AND THE INDIANS

In a formal message to Congress, President Jackson stated his views about removing the southern Indians:

The consequences of a speedy removal will be important to the United States, to individual States, and the Indians themselves. The pecuniary advantages which it promises to the Government are the least of its recommendations. It puts an end to all possible danger of collision between the authorities of the General and State Governments on account of the Indians. It will place a dense and civilized population in large tracts of country now occupied by a few savage hunters. By opening the whole territory between Tennessee on the north and Louisiana on the south to the settlement of the whites it will incalculably

strengthen the southwestern frontier and render the adjacent States strong enough to repel future invasions without remote aid. It will relieve the whole State of Mississippi and the western part of Alabama of Indian occupancy, and enable those States to advance rapidly in population, wealth, and power. It will separate the Indians from immediate contact with settlements of whites; free them from the power of the States; enable them to pursue happiness in their own way and under their own rude institutions; will retard the progress of decay, which is lessening their numbers, and perhaps cause them gradually, under the protection of the Government and through the influence of good counsels, to cast off their savage habits and become an interesting, civilized, and Christian community.

The Jackson-dominated House of Representatives tabled the enforcement order to restrain Georgia from evicting the Cherokee. This meant that no federal troops would be made available to support Marshall's decision, and the takeover of the Indian lands continued. By 1835, only a few southwestern Indians retained their lands. After the subjugation of the Florida Seminoles and their black allies (1835–1842), millions of acres were thrown open to white settlement.

The Indians, meanwhile, were forced onto a westward trek that became known as the Trail of Tears. Many of these men, women, and children died on the journey and were hastily buried on the wayside. Officials overseeing them robbed them of their money. Of the Cherokee removal, one critic cried that "such a dereliction of all faith and virtue, such a denial of justice, and such deafness to screams for mercy were never heard of in time of peace . . . since the earth was made."

The Webster-Hayne Debate

While the head of the federal government was asserting his leadership, congressional leaders of various geographical regions were arguing about sectional differences. Many issues divided slave from free states, and the free West from the free East. Although the Missouri Compromise of 1820 seemed to have settled the question of slavery in the West, new developments in the

rapidly expanding country once again aroused sectional quarrels. Two of the most persistently disruptive issues were public-land policies and protective tariffs. The Webster-Hayne debate in 1830 revealed the extent of both.

For a generation, pioneers had been calling for cheap government land and for protection of squatters who staked out such land before it was surveyed and put on the market. Squatters who had improved their land during their illegal tenures demanded the right to buy it at the minimum rate of $1.25 an acre when it came up for sale. This right became known as *preemption*. It was permitted for short periods in the 1830s, but not until 1841 was it enacted for an unlimited period for male citizens (meaning whites only) and for aliens having declared their intention of becoming citizens.

Many westerners, for whom Senator Thomas Hart Benton of Missouri became the spokesman, went further. As early as 1824 Benton had proposed that the price of unsold government land be gradually reduced to $.75 an acre and then to $.50. If no buyers appeared at that price, the land should be given away. This proposal came to be known as *graduation*. For the first time, a senator formally proposed that the work of pioneers opening the country was more valuable to the nation than money from the sale of land would be to the national treasury.

Easterners saw Benton's plan as a scheme to tap their labor supply and raise their wage costs.

They also saw development of the West as a threat to their political strength. On the other hand, it was obvious that land sales at the established prices would flood the Treasury with money. And a wealthy Treasury would destroy the most respectable argument for high tariffs—the need for revenue to pay off the national debt and support government services.

In an effort to eat their cake and have it too, some easterners offered the policy of *distribution:* Keep up the price of land and the tariff, and distribute the surplus revenue among the states to help them improve public education and business morality. When this proposal went nowhere, the easterners turned to the rather desperate (and completely unworkable) idea that the West be closed to settlement altogether.

In December 1829, Senator Samuel A. Foot of Connecticut offered a resolution that public land surveys be stopped for a time and that future sales be limited to lands already on the market. Senator Benton, speaking for the West, called Foot's resolution a manufacturers' plot. Spokesmen for the slave South supported Benton in hopes that they could aggravate the growing differences between the free East and the free West. The South's most pointed purpose was to undermine the West's support of the protective tariff.

Senator Robert Y. Hayne of South Carolina presented the South's case. His most divisive remarks were derived from an antitariff essay published anonymously by Vice-President John Calhoun back in 1828. According to Calhoun, the Tariff of 1828 made southerners serfs to northern manufacturers. "The tariff is unconstitutional and must be repealed," Calhoun wrote. "The rights of the South have been destroyed, and must be restored, . . . the Union is in danger, and must be saved." No free government, Calhoun argued, would permit the transfer of "power and property from one class or section to another." The tyranny of the majority could be met by the constitutional right of each state to nullify an unconstitutional act of Congress.

In an address for many years regarded as a model of eloquence (and therefore parts of it memorized by several generations of northern schoolchildren), Daniel Webster of Massachusetts replied that the Union was no mere compact among state legislatures; it was "the creature of the people." They had erected it, and therefore they alone were sovereign. It was for the Supreme Court, not the states, to decide whether laws passed by Congress conformed to the Constitution. If a single state had that right of nullifying federal laws, the Union would be dissolved. Webster closed his four-hour speech with what Senator Benton ridiculed as "a fine piece of rhetoric misplaced," a vision of two Americas. One was a land "rent with civil feuds, or drenched . . . in fratricidal blood"; the other, a republic "now known and honored throughout the earth, still full high advanced, its arms and trophies streaming in their original lustre." He ended with the famous words: "Liberty and Union, now and forever, one and inseparable."

Once the debate ended, the first question everyone asked was where Jackson stood. There was a long delay before he spoke out. When he finally decided to do so he confronted not the spokesman, Hayne, but the political theorist, his own vice-president.

Nullification

The doctrine of nullification was clearly not a logical way of gaining western support. Beyond the coastal tier of the thirteen original states, all the new ones had come into being as additions to the single nation known as the United States of America. None had ever known full independence, and they had no grounds for claiming to have been participants in an original compact among sovereign republics. Jackson was fully aware of this fact. He was for states' rights, but he was for the rights of states *within* the Union.

A few months after the Webster-Hayne debate, when Democratic party leaders gathered at a dinner to celebrate Jefferson's birthday, Old Hickory painfully raised himself to his feet and, looking Calhoun straight in the eye, proposed this toast: "Our Union—it must be preserved!" (Before news of Jackson's toast was released, Hayne got the president to soften it by inserting the word *federal* before *Union.)* But federal or not, Calhoun refused to back down. In response to Jackson's pointed words, he immediately rose to reply: "The Union—next to our liberty, the most dear."

In the months following the famous dinner toasts in Washington, Jackson and Calhoun came to a complete break. The grounds for the split were both personal and political. A complicated scandal involving the reputation of a cabinet member's wife placed Jackson on one side of the controversy and Calhoun on the other. Politically, Calhoun's enemies let Jackson know that Calhoun, as secretary of war in 1818, had severely criticized Jackson in a cabinet meeting for his aggressive actions against the British and Indians in Florida.

The vice-president tried to explain away these reports, but Jackson remained unforgiving. The break was nearly out in the open when in 1832 Jackson urged Congress to consider a tariff reduction. Calhoun found this an insult to his constituency. The president had thought a reduction in duties would please the South, but the most immediate result of his proposal was to send Calhoun into a huff. He resigned the vice-presidency and went home to South Carolina to rally support.

The Tariff of 1832 passed, and Calhoun immediately responded with his doctrine of nullification. This time, South Carolina moved to put Calhoun's theories into action. Despite strong opposition within the state, the legislature (following the precedent of 1787–1788 for adoption of the Constitution) ordered the election of delegates to a special state convention in November 1832. That body adopted an ordinance of nullification that pronounced the tariffs of 1828 and 1832 "unauthorized by the Constitution" and therefore "null, void, and no law, nor binding upon this state."

The convention also demanded that the legislature prohibit collection of customs duties in state ports after February 1, 1833. If federal troops were used to collect the duties, the con-

vention declared, South Carolina would secede from the federal union.

Jackson was furious. He replied with his ringing Nullification Proclamation:

I consider . . . the power to annul a law of the United States assumed by one State, incompatible with the existence of the Union, contradicted expressly by the letter of the Constitution, unauthorized by its spirit, inconsistent with every principle on which it was founded, and destructive of the great object for which it was formed.

Jackson warned that the Constitution, the "supreme law" of the land, compelled him to meet such defiance with force.

In February 1833 the Senate passed a Force Bill empowering the president to use the army and navy if South Carolina resisted federal customs officials. While the Force Bill was being debated in the House, Henry Clay introduced a compromise tariff bill that would gradually reduce the 1832 duties. South Carolina leaders also learned that other southern states would not go along with nullification and that a strong Unionist faction inside their own borders would continue to fight it. Jackson signed both Clay's tariff bill and the Force Bill on the same day in March 1833—a carrot and a stick.

Faced with these twin measures, South Carolina withdrew its nullification ordinance. But to save face, the state also adopted a new ordinance nullifying the Force Act. Jackson was wise enough to disregard this closing defiance. Both sides claimed victory, but most Americans welcomed the fact that the Union had weathered a major constitutional crisis. Outright conflict had been avoided, and the idea of nullification appeared to be dead.

THE BANK WAR

Not long before his reelection in 1832, Jackson settled into brooding hostility toward the Bank of the United States. Rechartering was not due for another four years, but the question of the bank's continuation came up during the election campaign. Although real and serious financial issues were involved, the fact that Jackson carried on a war against "the monster" bank, even after he had won the election, suggests that his opposition came as much from what the bank symbolized as from what it actually did. Many of the political developments of the 1830s had this same symbolic quality.

The Anti-Masonic Party

It was this atmosphere of symbolic politics that partly explains the rapid rise of an unexpected third party during the 1832 campaign. It was at this time that the Jacksonians formally adopted the name Democrats. The National Republicans would soon adopt the label Whig. The Anti-Masonic party, like the Whigs, also seized upon something it was against, rather than for.

The Masons were a national fraternal order with local lodges. Little was known about the organization, except that its members were sworn to secrecy, practiced mysterious rituals, and on occasion dressed in odd costumes. In fact, Masonry was an international fraternity, much more interested in its own internal affairs than anything else. Yet Masonry's secrecy became the source of suspicion and hostility.

The rise of the Anti-Masonic party was triggered by a mysterious murder in upper New York State. The new party became strong enough in a number of states to hold a national political convention in 1832, at which Anti-Masons talked about the "horrid, oath-binding system" that threatened American Christianity and the openness of a democratic society. Jackson himself had once been a Mason, and for that reason alone the Anti-Masons opposed him.

The new party had no permanent impact on American politics, though at the time its exis-

Nicholas Biddle. *(New York Public Library)*

tence and ideas worried many politicians. Anti-Masonic candidates carried only one state in the 1832 election and then disappeared from the political scene. Most supporters went over to the Whigs because they opposed the president. But this brief comet across the political skies strongly suggested how much Americans wanted to find a villain responsible for a changing world they did not fully understand.

Jackson versus Biddle

For ten years prior to the 1832 election, the Second Bank of the United States had been managed by Nicholas Biddle of Philadelphia. A former Federalist, Biddle was appointed a director of the bank by President Monroe. In 1824 and 1828 he voted for Jackson. On becoming president of the bank, Biddle intensified the deflationary policies his predecessor had introduced during the panic of 1819.

Biddle was careful about issuing notes on his own bank. By refusing to accept at face value the notes of state and local banks that had issued more paper than their reserves warranted, he forced them into more cautious policies. They resented it, and so did their clients.

In addition, the Second Bank was an enormous institution with far-reaching powers. It had considerable control over the private economy as well as custody of government funds. Its enemies were apparently justified in denouncing it as a monopoly. Whether it really was a "monster" was a matter of opinion.

Nobody attacked the bank more vigorously than the Democratic senator from Missouri, Thomas Hart Benton. In February 1831 Benton introduced a resolution against rechartering the bank and spoke for several hours on its threat to democracy. He exploited feelings against the bank: "It tends to aggravate the inequality of fortunes; to make the rich richer and the poor poorer; to multiply nabobs and paupers."

The Senate rejected Benton's resolution, but he had helped antibank sentiment. His fear that the bank was "too great and powerful" reflected a widespread conviction that the bank was corrupting the nation's virtue. In fact, the bank did grant financial favors to senators, congressmen, and newspapermen. Many of the old Republican school, moreover, had never accepted the bank's constitutionality.

Jackson grew increasingly upset about the bank. It began to take on personal importance. When urged by one of his advisers to say nothing, he said, "My friend, I am pledged against the bank." When the time came to submit his message to Congress in December, Jackson remained silent almost to the end. Then he said it was not too soon for the issue of rechartering the bank in 1836 to be submitted "to the deliberate consideration of the Legislature and the people." With words that made his own position clear, he added: "Both the constitutionality and the expedience of the law creating this bank are well questioned by a large portion of our fellow-citizens."

Jackson would have preferred to keep the Second Bank out of the 1832 campaign. His secretary of State and secretary of the Treasury were busy talking to Biddle's friends about renewal after the election. But Webster and Clay, grossly overestimating public support for the bank, urged Biddle to take the offensive. Biddle, increasingly confused, gave in to their advice. On July 3, 1832, as forecast, the recharter bill passed both houses of Congress.

Jackson, bedridden for the moment, grimly observed to his heir apparent: "The Bank, Mr. Van Buren, is trying to kill me, but I will kill it." In his veto message of July 10, Jackson noted at the start that the recharter bill had come to him on the Fourth of July and that he had considered it "with that solemn regard to the principles of the Constitution which the day was calculated to inspire." His closing remarks were well suited to the coming election:

Distinctions in society will always exist under every just government. Equality of talents, of education, or of wealth cannot be produced by human institutions . . . .but when the laws undertake to add to these natural and just advantages artificial distinctions . . . to make the rich richer, and the potent more powerful, the humble members of the society—the farmers, mechanics, and laborers—who have neither the time nor the means of securing like favors to themselves, have a right to complain of the injustice of their government.

To the Panic of 1837

Jackson's victory over Clay in the election of 1832 caused him to interpret his triumph as a mandate for his war against Biddle's "hydra of corruption." The president's opening shot was to order the removal of government deposits from the Second Bank's branches. His reason: Biddle's policies no longer insured the safety of public funds. He then ordered that these deposits and all new government revenue be placed in selected state institutions, which became known as Jackson's "pet banks."

His orders were more easily issued than carried out, however, for the secretary of the Treasury alone had legal power to withdraw government deposits, and Jackson's secretary was a friend of the bank. Such obstacles did not stop Old Hickory. He fired two secretaries of the Treasury until he found in Roger B. Taney of Maryland someone who would do as he wished. Late in 1833, Taney began the removal of the deposits. By the end of the year, twenty-three state banks had been named to receive federal funds.

Even though his bid for a new charter had been defeated, Biddle refused to accept this assault on his bank. If the bank was to be forced to close, it must begin to call in loans and limit new business. After the federal deposits had been removed, Biddle embarked on this policy. His object was to create a business panic so widespread that public opinion would force Jackson to reverse his stand. For some months in 1833 and 1834, a panic indeed seemed imminent. But once again Biddle miscalculated the political situation. To those who began to press Jackson for help, the president replied, "Go to Nicholas Biddle."

In time, segments of the conservative business community, alienated by Jackson's high-handed political maneuvers, appealed to Biddle to relent. And finally he gave in. Relief turned the near panic into a boom, especially in the South and West. Speculation was further stimulated by the inflationary practices of the pet banks, which used the federal deposits as reserves for many bad loans. By throwing millions of acres of public land on the market, the administration itself encouraged wholesale borrowing.

The land boom quickly heightened the demand for internal improvements, leading to reckless investments in turnpikes, canals, and railroads. Many projects were financed in part by foreign capitalists who would not risk their money in private American corporations. They were willing to purchase the bonds, backed by state revenues, that many states issued to support internal improvement.

The optimistic state programs got a boost in the summer of 1836 when it became clear that the federal government was about to distribute to the states most of the $35 million surplus that had accumulated in the Treasury from tariff revenues and public-land sales. Distribution began in time to sustain the boom.

Before payments could be completed, however, the surplus evaporated. Responsibility for this rested largely on another administration measure, Jackson's Specie Circular. Issued on July 11, 1836, this regulation required that all land purchased from the federal government after August 15 be paid for in silver or gold. Settlers were allowed to use bank notes for an additional four months, provided their purchases were under 320 acres.

This drastic reversal of policy slowed land sales and sent prices plunging. In the spring of 1837, after Jackson had left office, stock and commodity prices also broke. Soon the panic of 1837 was on in earnest. Like other such panics, that of 1837 was worldwide and had international as well as American causes and effects. British banks that were engaged in financing American trade, mainly in cotton and the new railroads, called in their loans and forced many American merchants to the wall. The failure of Biddle's bank, which had been operating since 1836 under a Pennsylvania charter, helped deepen the depression that followed the panic. After suspending activities twice, the bank went out of business in 1841. Biddle was charged with fraud, though subsequently acquitted.

After a brief economic recovery in 1839, the country sank into a severe depression that lasted until the mid-1840s. Banks and businesses folded. Farms and plantations were lost by people who had borrowed more than they could repay. Men, women, and children were thrown out of work. City streets became crowded with a new class not seen before in the United States— hungry, frightened people who wanted work but could find none. Many state governments had to stop paying interest on their bonds; a few states announced they could not even pay back the face amount they had borrowed. British financiers, who themselves were under strain, were outraged as they saw their loans go down the drain.

They blamed the Americans. Americans, in turn, blamed everyone. They blamed British capitalists, American bankers, their state governments, the federal government, President Van Buren, former president Jackson, Nicholas Biddle, the Whig party, the Democratic party,

WORDS AND NAMES IN AMERICAN HISTORY

In this country, few words as simple as *stump* have such eloquent histories. The phrase *to be up a stump* goes back to the eighteenth century and indicates a state of helplessness and frustration. It came from the fact that wagons and coaches traveling on the incredibly crude roads of the time sometimes caught their axles or even their floorboards on the stumps of trees left between the two ruts that formed the road. In the antebellum era, in the days of popular electioneering and political oratory, candidates often stood on tree stumps to address the crowd. hence we have the phrase *stump speeches*. Even today, without ever actually standing on one, political candidates *stump* their district or state or even the entire nation in search of votes. And the phrase *to stump* someone—to ask a question the person cannot answer—comes from that same political tradition, where candidates often debated each other by asking difficult questions.

alcohol, misguided social reformers, medical doctors, their food, and the moral fiber of the American people. When a man worked hard and then lost his farm, his business, his job, his plantation, who else was there to blame? When people could no longer support their children or even themselves, who could explain it?

No American fully realized that large, impersonal, international market forces were at work. Van Buren himself could only suggest that the depression was caused by "overbanking" and "overtrading." He was not altogether wrong, but the dimensions and nature of the problem were not well understood.

The national and international market economy had become far more complex and interwoven than it had been a generation before, but it was not easy to see the relationships. It was not yet obvious that a bank failure in New Orleans might be connected with the failures of a New York cotton merchant, a bank in Boston, and a cotton factory in Manchester, England. It was even more difficult to see the relevance of a rise in silver exports from Mexico or a temporary interruption of the opium trade in China. Such developments, in fact, could affect a farmer in Illinois or Alabama. It was easier to find the cause of one's own difficulties closer to home. It is no wonder that many Americans in this era turned inward to reform their own society without realizing that it was rapidly becoming part of a much larger and more impersonal economic world.

JACKSONIAN POLITICS WITHOUT JACKSON

President Jackson barely escaped the economic storm and its political consequences. The election of 1836 took place before financial panic set in, and Van Buren's nomination was ensured by Jackson's support. Having failed four years earlier with Henry Clay, the Whigs were unable to decide on a candidate. At their national convention, they tried to resolve matters by running four regional candidates in the hope of depriving Van Buren of a majority and throwing the election into the House of Representatives.

With national prosperity at its height, Van Buren won. But his popular and electoral majorities were far smaller than his predecessor's. In the election of 1840, he paid the political price of presiding over a depression. The Whigs outballyhooed the Democrats and finally won control of the presidency—only to lose it a month later because their candidate caught a chill at his inauguration.

Critics of the Jackson Presidency

President Jackson's enlargement of presidential power cast a long shadow over American politics. Not for another generation would an American president use the office with such vigor. In part this was because no successor until Lincoln had Jackson's force of personality. But it was also because Jackson himself had aroused fears about a strong president.

The principal complaint against Jackson was that of "executive usurpation." After Jackson had fired two Treasury secretaries who would not do what he wanted, Henry Clay bitterly attacked the "revolution, hitherto bloodless, but rapidly tending toward . . . the concentration of all power in the hands of one man." In 1834, the Senate gave Jackson a taste of his own medicine by adopting, twenty-six to twenty, the following unprecedented resolution:

Resolved, That the President, in the late Executive proceedings in relation to the public revenue, has assumed upon himself authority and power not conferred by the Constitution and laws, but in derogation of both.

Jackson responded with an eloquent protest, which the Senate refused to enter in the journal of its proceedings. Jackson's supporters in the Senate fought for almost three years to have the censure resolution removed from the record, and at last they had their way. During the debate, Clay again expressed the resentment of many senators over what they regarded as Jackson's enlargement of the executive's rights:

The Senate has no army, no navy, no patronage, no lucrative offices, nor glittering honors to bestow. . . . How is it with the President? . . . By means of principles which he has introduced, and innovations which he has made in our institutions, alas! but too much countenanced by Congress and a confiding people, he exercises uncontrolled power of the state. In one hand he holds the purse and in the other brandishes the sword of the country! . . . He has swept over the government like a tropical tornado.

Others voiced similar judgments. "I look upon Jackson," wrote Chancellor Kent of New York, "as a detestable, ignorant, reckless, vain and malignant tyrant. . . . This American elective monarchy frightens me. The experiment, with its foundations laid on universal suffrage and our unfettered press, is of too violent a nature for our excitable people." In the Senate, Webster roared out this protest: "The President carries on the government; all the rest are subcontractors."

Jackson's Successor

Martin Van Buren stepped into the much criticized shoes of his predecessor and almost immediately stumbled into an economic depression. He was a capable politician. He made his career in politics, first in New York State and then at the national level, and his cleverness at landing on his feet earned him the nickname of the Little Magician. A man of honesty and instinctive sympathy with the common people, he lacked the forcefulness of Jackson, the charm of Clay, the eloquence of Webster, the subtle and complicated mind of Calhoun.

Martin Van Buren. *(Library of Congress)*

The new president spent much of his administration trying to deal with the vacuum left by the disappearance of the "monster" bank. Van Buren was convinced that banks in general were a threat to the working man. He pressed for what he called an Independent Treasury, a "divorce of bank and state." The government would deposit its temporary surplus funds in vaults in various cities. They would not be tied in any way to state banks or to a central federal financial institution.

Whig leaders were not happy with the proposed system, but they had no better alternative. In 1840, in the darkest year of the depression, Congress finally went along with Van Buren's plan.

The Election of 1840

The Independent Treasury did little for economic recovery, and as the election of 1840 drew near, Whig leaders scented victory. Clay, defeated in the election on the bank issue in 1832 and bypassed in 1836 for strategic reasons, now hoped to win. This time, however, he received no support from Webster, who looked upon him as a rival. With little hope of winning the nomination himself, Webster backed General William Henry Harrison, who had made his name during the War of 1812.

At the Whig convention Old Tippecanoe was nominated. John Tyler of Virginia was picked as the general's running mate to strengthen Whig chances in the South. The Democrats renominated Van Buren. But since Jackson's retirement, they had become so divided that they were not able to agree on a candidate for vice-president and were forced to leave that choice to the states.

The presidential campaign of 1840 was one of the most dramatic in American history. The Whig campaigners lashed out at the hard times under the Democrats. They focused on the president's supposedly luxurious tastes. A campaign document, "Royal Splendor of the President's Palace," pictured Van Buren in the White House as an Oriental potentate eating French cookery from golden plates and resting on a "Turkish divan." By contrast, the Whigs stressed the stern simplicity of Old Tippecanoe. When a Baltimore newspaper taunted the Whigs by saying that Harrison would be perfectly satisfied with a log cabin and a good supply of cider, his managers picked up the log cabin as a party symbol. "It tells of

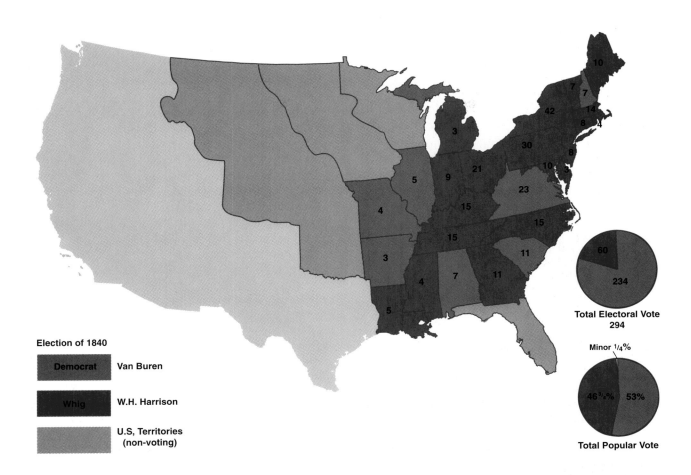

Election of 1840

Democrat — Van Buren

Whig — W.H. Harrison

U.S, Territories
(non-voting)

Total Electoral Vote
294

Minor ¼%

Total Popular Vote

The election of 1840

virtues," New York's Thurlow Weed declared, "that dwell in obscurity, of the privations of the poor, of toil and danger." The log cabin, this "emblem of simplicity," was as foreign to Harrison's gentlemanly origins and living habits as Van Buren's supposed Turkish divan, but the symbol helped elect him. Seventy-eight percent of eligible voters went to the polls, by far the highest percentage ever in the history of the nation.

Having given over the nomination to a popular hero for the sake of winning the presidency, such Whig leaders as Clay and Webster planned to run the administration once he took office. In fact, during his single month as president, Harrison yielded to them. Of Clay, a New York newspaper correspondent reported: "He predominates over the Whig Party with despotic sway. Old Hickory himself never lorded it over his followers with authority more undisputed, or more supreme. But Harrison died on April 4, 1841, having established two presidential records: the shortest

presidency (one month) and the longest inaugural address (a mere one and three-quarter hours). Tyler became president, and the political atmosphere changed drastically.

Tyler was a Whig only because he had followed Calhoun out of the Democratic party after the break with Jackson. A veteran of the Virginia legislature and of both houses of Congress, he had had many opportunities to disclose his strong antitariff views, his antagonism to Biddle's bank, his dislike of federal aid for internal improvements. Beyond these issues, he sided with Calhoun on nullification. The Whigs had named him for the vice-presidency in order to attract southern anti-Jackson support, despite his enthusiasm for states' rights. They soon wished they had made another choice.

Tyler's presidency was less than successful. Henry Clay thought the time had come for putting his American System into full effect. As a states' rights man, Tyler thought otherwise. He vetoed bills for internal improvements and agreed only reluctantly to the repeal of Van Buren's Independent Treasury. But when the Whigs tried to reestablish another national bank, Tyler vetoed one proposal after another. The government continued to use state banks.

Gradual economic recovery made the issue of a national bank seem less and less important. As politicians turned to other matters in the 1840s, the banking issue slid underground as a major factor in American politics for more than twenty years.

Tyler's vetoes outraged Whig leaders, but they lacked enough votes in Congress to override them. National domestic legislation came almost to a standstill. Angry Whig congressmen issued a formal statement reading Tyler out of the party. The entire cabinet resigned except for Webster, who stayed on as secretary of state to complete certain diplomatic negotiations.

The victory of 1840 turned out to be a nearly empty one, and Whig leaders began falling out among themselves. They lost their majority in the House in the 1842 congressional elections. Clay resigned his Senate seat to try once again for the presidency.

The Jacksonian Legacy

The sheer force of Andrew Jackson's personality did a great deal to bring about the second party system. During the 1830s, two distinct parties emerged, each with considerable strength in every section of the nation and each with a large core of loyal followers who identified themselves as lifetime Whigs or Democrats. The Anti-Masonic party disappeared as quickly as it arose. By this time almost all Americans accepted parties as a fact of political life. Once regarded as an evil, political parties—especially *two* political parties—were now seen as beneficial and even necessary to the functioning of national government.

The style of politics had changed drastically. Politicians appealed more to passions and less to reason. They courted popularity in a way that John Quincy Adams and his predecessors could never have brought themselves to do. Far more Americans than ever before were involved, often quite emotionally, in the political process. In an age lacking visual mass media, long political speeches became a form of popular entertainment.

Jackson himself set a precedent for a strong, activist presidency—the kind we are accustomed to now. Few men could fill that role as well as he, though some would attempt to do so. Jackson was not the last president to remind other politicians that he alone was elected by all the people and represented them in all their majestic power. He thought (incorrectly, as things turned out) that he had settled the question of the relationship of the states and the federal government. But he had considerable justification at the time for thinking he had helped strengthen the permanence of the Union.

Both Jackson and his opponents had to wrestle with problems created by the new economy. They did their best in a new world that in many ways was confusing and mysterious. For ten years, the major issue in American politics was banking, or rather The Bank. The rapid disappearance of this issue suggests that it was in large measure symbolic. Yet there was another issue both Jackson and the Whigs managed to keep off center stage, and it was both symbolic and very real. Already in the 1830s a small but noisy band of men and women were trying to bring it to the nation's attention. They insisted that American democracy contained a serious flaw. If Americans were a free and democratic people, why were some Americans slaves?

That issue came to dominate American politics in the years after John Tyler's presidency. But in order to understand why, it is necessary to turn away from politics to examine important changes in the minds of Americans as they stepped onto the slippery slope that eventually led to a civil war.

SUMMARY

The political tone of the Age of Jackson began even before Andrew Jackson became president in 1828. During the first quarter of the nineteenth century, most states opened up the vote to almost all adult white males. And interest in national politics grew as government seemed to become more accessible to the people. A new two-party system gradually emerged after 1824, and voters began to participate in naming the candidates in national conventions. By 1828, most states allowed voters rather than legislators to choose members of the electoral college, and governors were being popularly elected.

The election of 1824 brought John Quincy Adams to the presidency, with Henry Clay as secretary of state. But Adams's program for national economic and cultural development failed, and he lost his congressional majority in the midterm elections. In 1828 Andrew Jackson—Old Hickory and the Hero of New Orleans—became president.

Jackson greatly enlarged the power of the presidency. His administration was marked by the rise to power of the Kitchen Cabinet—a small group of advisers who were also personal friends. Jackson's name also became linked with the spoils system, the right of a president to put his own people in the executive branch upon election. He clashed with Congress and with the Supreme Court, and warred on the Second Bank of the United States.

During his administration, the heads of the various geographical sections in Congress solidified their positions. They lashed out at one another on various issues: The Webster-Hayne debate of 1830 was one instance; South Carolina's nullification effort was another.

The campaign of 1832 brought a third party to national prominence for the first time. The Anti-Masonic party had no permanent effect on American politics, but it showed that a single issue could generate political force.

Almost immediately after his reelection, Jackson continued his war with the Second Bank of the United States. He had vetoed the bill for rechartering before the election, and saw his victory as a sign that the public approved. Jackson succeeded in removing the government's money from the bank and placing it in selected state banks, known as "pet banks." President Biddle of the national bank responded by calling in loans and limiting new business. He relented finally, but the shaky economic boom became a panic in 1837. After a brief recovery in 1839, the country went into a severe depression that lasted until the mid-1840s.

Andrew Jackson cast a long shadow over American politics. His enlargement of presidential power aroused fears of a strong executive. His successor, Martin Van Buren, had to cope with an economic depression and with the vacuum left by the disappearance of the Bank

TIME LINE

1820	New York broadens white suffrage but restricts blacks
1824	Presidential election thrown into House of Representatives; John Quincy Adams wins
1825	Adams attacked for appointing Clay secretary of state
1825	Adams proposes nationalist program, which is eventually defeated
1830	Webster-Hayne debate
1830	Jackson vetoes Maysville Road Bill
1832	Anti-Masons hold the first political-party convention
1832	Veto of renewal of national bank charter
1832	Nullification controversy
1832	Jackson defies Supreme Court on Indian policy
1833–1834	Biddle's maneuvers bring financial instability
1836	Jackson's Specie Circular
1837	Financial panic and long ensuing depression
1840	Congress enacts Van Buren's Independent Treasury plan
1840	Proportion of eligible men voting in presidential elections peaks at 78 percent
1840	Whigs defeat Democrats in Log Cabin and Cider campaign
1841	Harrison dies in office; succeeded by Vice-President Tyler
1841–1843	Tyler in conflict with Congress and his own cabinet

of the United States. As a result, though renominated, he lost the election of 1840 to a Whig, William Henry Harrison. When Harrison died within a month of his inauguration, John Tyler of Virginia became president. Tyler, nominated only in order to attract southern support, was a supporter of nullification and states' rights. He vetoed the legislation of his own party, and Congress came almost to a standstill; his entire cabinet resigned except for the secretary of state.

Jackson's presidency did a great deal to create a second two-party system. During the 1830s the Whigs and the Democrats emerged as two distinct groups, and the idea of a two-party system came to be seen as beneficial to the functioning of national government. Both parties had to deal with economic problems they did not fully understand, and with social changes that seemed to come from nowhere.

Suggested Readings

R. McCormick, *The Second American Party System: Party Formation in the Jacksonian Era* (1966), is an impressive state-by-state electoral analysis. More oriented toward prevailing thought than simple voting behavior is R. Hofstadter, *The Idea of a Party System: The Rise of Legitimate Opposition in the United States, 1780–1840* (1969).

C. Williamson, *American Suffrage: From Property to Democracy, 1760–1860* (1960), is the standard account of the suffrage. A comprehensive anthology of contemporary accounts on the subject is M. Peterson (ed.), *Democracy, Liberty, and Property: The State Constitutional Conventions of the 1820s* (1966). The developing exclusion of blacks from the franchise is dealt with by L. Litwack, *North of Slavery: The Negro in the Free States, 1790–1860* (1961). L. Benson, *The Concept of Jacksonian Democracy: New York as a Test Case* (1961), remains a controversial work that stresses the correlation between ethnic affiliation and party alignment. C. Sellers, *James K. Polk, Jacksonian, 1795–1843* (2 vols., 1957–1966), is a first-rate biography and reveals much about political practices in the Jacksonian era.

Several other studies bear more directly on the machinery of the Jacksonian party: J. Curtis, *The Fox at Bay: Martin Van Buren and the Presidency, 1837–1841* (1970); R. Remini's fine *Life of Andrew Jackson* (1988); and L. White, *The Jacksonians: A Study in Administrative History, 1829–1861* (1954), which is especially informative on the spoils system. The types of men appointed to high office in the early Republic are discussed in S. Aronson, *Status and Kinship in the Higher Civil Service: Standards of Selection in the Administrations of John Adams, Thomas Jefferson, and Andrew Jackson* (1964).

G. Dangerfield, *The Era of Good Feelings* (1952) and *The Awakening of American Nationalism, 1815–1828* (1965), are smoothly written analyses of American life and politics leading to the election of Jackson. S. Bemis, *John Quincy Adams and the Union* (1956), is the second volume of a compelling biography. For clashing views, see the piece on Jackson in R. Hofstadter, *The American Political Tradition* (1948), which contains essays on various political figures throughout American history; J. Dorfman, *The Economic Mind in American Civilization, 1606–1865* (5 vols., 1946–1959); M. Meyers, *The Jacksonian Persuasion: Politics and Belief* (1957), a brilliant study stressing the nostalgic yearning of Jacksonians for the supposedly golden years of the founding of the Republic; and J. Ward, *Andrew Jackson, Symbol for an Age* (1962), which relates key events in Jackson's life to the historical period and discusses his reputation as a popular leader. For a rich portrait of the habits and attitudes of ordinary Americans in this period, see the famous work by the French traveler Alexis de Tocqueville, *Democracy in America* (1835), available in many editions.

For other key figures in that era of senatorial giants, the most embrasive work is M. Peterson, *The Great Triumvirate: Webster, Clay, and Calhoun* (1987). But also see C. Eaton, *Henry Clay and the Art of American Politics* (1957); S. Nathans, *Daniel Webster and Jacksonian Democracy* (1973), dealing with the period 1828-1844; and C. Wiltse, *John C. Calhoun, Nullifier, 1829–1839* (1949). The latter should be balanced against the brilliant essay on Calhoun, "The Marx of the Master Class," in the Hofstadter volume cited in the previous paragraph. W. Freebling, *Prelude to Civil War: The Nullification Controversy in South Carolina, 1816–1836* (1966), presents a masterly analysis that stresses the profound impact of slavery on South Carolina politics. For President Tyler, there is R. Seager II, *And Tyler Too* (1963).

It has become clear only fairly recently that Indian policy is crucial to an understanding of the Jacksonian age. Prevailing ideas about the Indian are discussed with a literary emphasis in R. Pearce, *The Savages of America: A Study of the Indian and the Idea of Civilization* (rev. ed., 1965). See also T. Wilkins, *Cherokee Tragedy: The Story of the Ridge Family and the Decimation of a People* (1970); and W. McLoughlin, *Cherokee Renascence in the New Republic* (1986). The political rationale for these national tragedies is covered in F. Prucha, *American Indian Policy in the Formative Years: The Indian Trade and Intercourse Acts, 1790–1834* (1962). M. Rogin, *Fathers and Children: Andrew Jackson and* the Subjugation of the American Indian (1975), is an important and fascinating study, though many readers may find it overly psychoanalytic.

A short introduction to the bank war (a subject also treated in many of the works cited earlier) is found in G. Taylor (ed.), *Jackson versus Biddle* (1949). More recent studies are B. Hammond's sweeping *Banks and Politics in America: From the Revo-lution to the Civil War* (1957); T. Govan, *Nicholas Biddle, Nationalist and Public Banker, 1786–1844* (1959), which is pro-Biddle; and J. McFaul, *The Politics of Jacksonian Finance* (1972), which disagrees with Hammond. J. Sharp, *The Jacksonians versus the Banks: Politics in the States after the Panic of 1837* (1970), covers the years following the great financial crash.

Edgar Allan Poe. *(Library of Congress)*

CHAPTER 12

THE SPIRIT OF ANTEBELLUM AMERICA

The United States was a far more complex society in its antebellum period (from roughly 1815 to the Civil War) than it had been in the eighteenth century. It was becoming one of the world's most prosperous nations, in terms of both agriculture and industry. The variety of its occupations and lifestyles, and the pace of life, had increased greatly. Families of all kinds—farming, industrial, professional, commercial, planting, and slave—were less isolated than ever before from the wider world of neighborhood, town, city, state, the nation, and the entire globe. The mood of Americans was also changed; a new spirit was abroad in the land. Perhaps we ought to say spirits, for Americans exhibited many qualities, some of which seemed downright inconsistent with others.

Historians have a remarkably full picture of Americans in this period, thanks in large part to the hundreds of curious Europeans who came to the United States to observe and report on this astounding and often disturbing new phenomenon among nations. And Americans themselves were acutely conscious of living in a new and changing society; they too commented on their characteristics and examined themselves and their lives.

It is therefore possible for historians to generalize about the mood and mind of antebellum America. One central difficulty, however, arises from the need to disentangle two interwoven facts. Granted, the United States was different from other Western countries. Yet while the United States was changing in many ways, becoming more "modern," so were other Western nations. It is easy to call such attributes as optimism and egalitarianism peculiarly American, but in fact those attributes were part of the modernization of Western culture.

It was during this period that a truly American literature was born, that the fine arts became more than an aristocratic pastime, that a movement for free public education gained strength, and that reformers began to try to achieve social justice. These activities reflected contradictions and inconsistencies that touched many Americans. The drive for material success resulted in increasingly unequal wealth, a fact that contradicted the widespread belief in social equality. Religious principles offered some Americans a justification for slavery but led many others to denounce it as an institution.

AMERICAN QUALITIES

Most Americans agreed about certain distinguishing qualities in their society. They were quite willing to admit that they were a restless people, constantly moving, forever chasing the dollar or a new style of life. They regarded themselves as committed to progress, whether progress came in the form of making money, eradicating violence, inventing things, establishing new forms of entertainment, or finding new zeal in religion.

Restlessness, Money, and Violence

All observers agreed that Americans worked harder, ate faster, spat tobacco juice farther, moved around more, and relaxed less than Europeans. People seemed to be perpetually on the move, always in transit, going from here to somewhere better. Much of this restlessness came from a sense of unlimited possibilities on what seemed an empty continent.

In 1832 an anonymous writer listed some of the reasons for America's glorious prospects: "an extensive seacoast, abundantly providing the means for a lucrative internal trade"; a tremendous waterpower potential; "every variety of soil and climate"; "a capacity for raising cotton to supply the demand of the whole world"; a population "active, energetic, enterprising, and ingenious"; the most liberal, and most cheaply administered government in the world; the absence of a nobility; and "abundant room for all the superfluous population of Europe." What more could anyone want? Faith in the American future had been strong before the Revolution. But after 1820 all signs seemed to confirm the prospects of "indefinite perfectibility."

What seemed to drive the country was the dynamic "engine" of business enterprise. Even while Jacksonian Americans lashed out at the national bank, they praised their business-oriented society. They acclaimed the fact that "the resources of this country are controlled chiefly by the class which, in our own peculiar phraseology, we term 'business community'— embracing all those who are engaged in the great occupation of buying, selling, exchanging, importing, and exporting merchandise." As Americans saw it, moneymaking motivated the commercial class; indeed, "it . . . constitutes the great business of our people." Even America's severest critics usually agreed there was some-

thing great and even heroic in this pursuit of wealth. Many people regarded making money as both a source of and evidence of virtue. Merchants and financiers who shared this view supported humanitarian and cultural enterprises. Wealthy men had always had influence in America, but now wealth itself was honored. By the 1840s, in several cities people could buy privately published directories of the wealthiest citizens, complete with their names and addresses and the estimated sizes of their fortunes.

More hostile foreign critics pointed to the American liking for the gun and the Bowie knife. Stories from the frontier and the cities told of stabbings and shootings, of ambushes, river piracy, deadly feuds, and ordinary fights that included eye gouging and noses and ears bitten off. By the 1830s, violence in the cities had become a public issue. Prostitutes, thieves, and murderers were usually explained as the inevitable consequences of social injustices or of human wickedness.

Yet many people refused to condemn the law of "Judge Lynch." The motives behind lynchings and mobbings in northern cities and in the South and West were much the same. Mobs were sometimes composed of solid middle-class citizens who demanded conformity in public behavior. It was during the Age of Jackson that so many American men banded into crowds that whipped, burned, hanged, shot, or exiled people they thought dangerous or subversive— gamblers, murderers, rapists, horse thieves, Mormons, abolitionists, Roman Catholics, and especially blacks.

Equality, Individualism, and Cooperation

Despite their admiration for wealth, Americans also championed social and political equality. Many new immigrants were particularly impressed by American egalitarianism. A new citizen wrote old friends in Germany in the late 1830s: "Our President walks across the street the same as I do—no Royal Highness or Majesty would ever do that. They do not even call him 'Mister.' . . . When talking to the President you say simply: 'How are you, President?' and he answers: 'Thank you, how are you?'"

There was a special irony in the growth of the ideal that in the United States every person was as good as every other. That ideology began to flourish at a time when economic forces were actually causing differences in wealth to widen. The distribution of wealth among Americans was becoming less equal rather than more.

There are probably several reasons for this lack of fit between belief and fact. For one thing, the egalitarian ideal was so attractive that it tended to override reality. Also, observers of American society tended to talk with people who were relatively well off and expecting to do better, not with the downtrodden. Further, the economic distinctions among Americans were still much less obvious—and much less real—than they were in the older societies of Europe. Finally, the economic and social environment in the United States was open and fluid enough to allow some people to rise from rags to riches, and so give the ideal convincing support.

It was partly the opportunities afforded by an expanding economy that gave Americans a strong sense of the power of the individual. Many foreign observers commented on this quality of individualism, on the common American belief that what a person did was what counted, rather than who he or she was. Without realizing it, they too came from societies that gave individual concerns priority over group interests. If the observers had come from, for example, traditional societies in Africa or Asia, they would have been appalled that the interests of individual Americans were allowed to override the claims of the general welfare.

Paradoxically once again, these same outside commentators found Americans engaged in an orgy of "association." They found businessmen joining in clubs, which should not have been a surprise, but they also found "clubbiness" everywhere. Immigrants formed mutual aid associations. Citizens set up libraries, art associations, and "societies for mutual improvement." The charitable, reform, fraternal, and benefit organizations that were being established flowered in an atmosphere in which there seemed to be no ruling class with a tradition of social responsibility.

Religious Fervor and Diversity

If Americans poured their energies into organizations pulling in many directions at once, what was it that held their society together? Many observers during the 1830s and 1840s were disturbed by the diffuseness of American activity, by the "lack of a common skeleton."

One major unifying bond was religious revivalism. There was no burst of revivalism such as had swept the colonies during the Great Awakening, although a massive outdoor camp meeting at Cane Ridge, Kentucky, in 1800 led some people to speak hopefully of a "second great awakening." Yet revivals recurred at various times and places. Outdoor camp meetings, often lasting for days, attracted people from hundreds of miles away. At these gatherings audiences could listen to a dozen different preachers of nearly as many denominations.

Revivals could take place in unexpected places: Letters from students at the University of North Carolina, for example, indicate that outbreaks of religious enthusiasm sometimes swept that school. It is less surprising that upper New York State, settled largely by New Englanders, was frequently swept by the fires of religious passion—so much so that it became known as the "burned-over district." Revivals were not confined to rural areas: In 1857 there was an outbreak in several eastern cities.

Perhaps the most astute comment on revivalism was made by Alexis de Tocqueville, the famous French analyst of American society in the early 1830s. Tocqueville found a "fanatical and almost wild spiritualism" in America. He decided that religious enthusiasm was probably a kind of compensation for the worldliness of a society "exclusively bent upon the pursuit of material objects."

Americans seemed to be the most religious of people, and yet the most torn by denominational conflict. The country had always provided a fertile soil for new sects. But in the 1830s and 1840s the splintering of dissenting churches, with each group claiming the true faith, reached a new peak. Baptists and Methodists, the fastest-growing denominations, were susceptible to schisms. So were Presbyterians, Congregationalists, and even Quakers. New sects sprang up everywhere, and the competition for the souls of immigrants pouring into the Mississippi Valley was often uncharitable. Doctrinal differences created a good deal of friction, and different denominations catered to different social classes. Presbyterians, Congregationalists, Episcopalians, and Unitarians differed in theology and in church organization, but drew their membership especially from the well-to-do. Baptists, Methodists, Campbellites, and Universalists were held to be a cut lower socially. Immigrant Catholics and blacks stood, so people thought, at the bottom.

Most Protestants shared an enmity toward the Roman Catholic church. Even to sophisticated ministers such as Lyman Beecher, president of Lane Seminary in Cincinnati, Catholicism still meant the torturing of Protestants and dictatorship by the pope. Gullible Americans swallowed stories about Catholic plots against American liberties and sensational "exposés" of Catholic depravities such as priests fathering babies in convents.

Anti-Catholic prejudice deepened after 1830, when immigration began to rise. In the following twenty years, 2.5 million newcomers arrived, many of them Catholics from Ireland and Germany. In 1830, there were 500 priests in the United States and about 500,000 Catholics. Twenty years later, 1500 priests served 1,750,000 of their faith. In addition, the Roman Catholic church had established seminaries, schools, colleges, monasteries, convents, hospitals, and other institutions. A Catholic press had come into being in 1822 with the publication of the *United States Catholic Miscellany*, and the Catholic Tract Society was founded in Philadelphia in 1827 to combat Protestantism and to propagate the Roman faith.

Yet the general acceptance of democracy, private property, and Christianity seemed somehow to give a national character to American society. Even in religion, powerful clergymen such as the great revivalist Charles Grandison Finney had begun in the 1820s to preach a "social gospel." The idea was to redeem entire communities, not just individuals. Many clergy equated sin with social selfishness. Indifference toward enterprises such as Sunday schools, home missions, and temperance crusades was a sign of a "backslidden heart." Not all religious leaders went along with Finney's ideas, but his Christianity gave religion a social relevance.

MEDICINE AND PUBLIC HEALTH

Like all people, Americans had to struggle with their physical as well as their spiritual health. They faced a general environment of disease and suffering that dwarfs even such modern scourges as AIDS. Since no one knew anything about germs, people dug outdoor privies near outdoor drinking wells, and "doctors" proceeded with the best of intentions to kill more people than they cured. The average life ex-

pectancy of Americans at birth remained where it had been for two hundred years—roughly thirty to forty, about half what it is today.

Public Health

For centuries, sickness had been associated with God's inevitable striking down of individuals or with the widespread devastations that we would call epidemics. In the colonies, smallpox had been the most feared disease, partly because it struck so unexpectedly and scarred the victims it did not kill. Authorities in most ports had long-standing policies of holding newly arrived suspected vessels in quarantine. Malaria ("the ague") became so common that it was often regarded as something people eventually "got." Diphtheria ("the sore-throat distemper") tended to strike children and by doing so tested their parents' religious faith. Yellow fever came in quick but devastating epidemics. In antebellum cities cholera did the same.

Even in an age accustomed to early death, these plagues terrified people. On occasion whole cities were evacuated. Everyone but the most courageous, foolhardy, and poor fled— a wholesale public-health "remedy" that may actually have saved many lives. There was nowhere else to turn—no health authorities, no hospitals, no trained nurses, few trained and virtually no trusted physicians. People simply died, in ways and numbers that today are hard to comprehend.

The Practice of Medicine

Medical doctors had little knowledge, not much prestige or income, few agreed-upon standards, and usually nothing they could do to help their patients. They bled the sick, so as to adjust the body's supposed imbalance. They had few effective weapons. Quinine, "the Peruvian bark," worked against malaria. Mercury worked against syphilis, but killed minds and bodies along with the disease. The most common "drugs" were emetics and purgatives. Aspirin (and of course its new cousins) was unknown.

Yet in the 1840s there was one major medical breakthrough—the development of ether and chloroform. These gases blocked pain during surgical procedures, almost magically relieving the patient of torment, as well as the necessity of being held down by numerous attendants. These anesthetics enabled surgeons to abandon speed as their chief skill, in favor of greater precision and increasing knowledge of human anatomy. At the same time, however, opium became an increasingly popular pain-killing drug. After the Civil War it became very widely used by both men and women without anyone realizing its addictive and mind-killing effects.

Because conventional medicine was so ineffective and medical schools as we know them nonexistent, there were political quarrels in many states about the licensing of physicians. It is equally no surprise that many people were drawn to such medical movements as Thompsonianism and homeopathy. Samuel Thompson of New Hampshire sparked an enormously successful movement that favored herbal medicines and the use of cold and heat. His method took on the dimensions of a religious and political crusade. Homeopathy came to the U.S. from Germany; its practitioners contended that illness was best treated by doses of medication 1/500,000 their customary strength. Both these movements may well have saved many lives.

At the same time that the practice of medicine was in chaos, the country experienced an extraordinary outburst of literary creativity.

A NATIONAL LITERATURE

In the four decades before the Civil War, the United States experienced a literary flowering. In 1802, when Washington Irving began to write, America had produced no literature except for sermons and political tracts. When Irving died, a year before the Civil War began, Emerson, Thoreau, Hawthorne, Poe, Melville, and Whitman had already written masterpieces.

The achievements of these writers seem all the more remarkable when we consider the environment from which they came. Besides the prevailing hostility to intellectual activity in general, there was specific hostility to literature, and particularly to American literature. After the Revolution, some people had called for a national literature that would reflect the greatness of the new nation. But American poets such as Timothy Dwight and Joel Barlow, who planned mighty epics, turned out only pale and unreadable imitations of English literary forms. Among the writers of this period, only the poet Philip Freneau and the Philadelphia novelist Charles Brockden Brown had more than minor talent. Most American readers found the works of British authors such as Sir Walter Scott and Charles Dickens much more interesting. For a time it seemed that there would in fact be no new national literature.

American writers at first tended to look toward Europe. Besides being conscious of living in a materialistic, unromantic society, they had to contend with religiously inspired distrust of literature; some Protestant sects regarded fiction as dangerous to the mind and to morals.

Irving, Cooper, and Longfellow

Washington Irving, an urbane New Yorker, was the first professional man of letters to win wide popularity at home and applause abroad. Irving spent a good deal of time in Europe and wrote his best books about it. While still in his twenties, however, he wrote and published in America his *History of New York* (1809), a burlesque of the early Dutch and the later backwoods Democrats. It had the whole country laughing. Even more popular was *The Sketch Book* (1819–1820), which had immediate success in Britain and the United States. It made unforgettable American characters of Rip Van Winkle and Ichabod Crane, two products of the rural and village setting of Irving's native state.

An even more illustrious New Yorker was the novelist and moralist James Fenimore Cooper. In Europe, where he lived and wrote for a number of years, Cooper defended the government and institutions of his native land. In America, he scolded Americans for bad manners, chauvinism, contempt for privacy, and slavish submission to public opinion. Cooper's upbringing among the landed gentry of rural New York did not prevent him from having sympathy with Jacksonian America. His thoughtful depiction of republican government, *The American Democrat* (1838), remains one of the best political essays ever written by an American.

A prolific writer, Cooper remains best known for his Leatherstocking series, the romance of the white hunter Natty Bumppo among the Indians of the woods, lakes, and open country: *The Pioneers* (1823), *The Last of the Mohicans* (1826), *The Prairie* (1827), *The Pathfinder* (1840), and

The Deerslayer (1841). Natty, in his first incarnation, was only a composite of some of the types Cooper had known during his boyhood in New York. He grew into a kind of forest philosopher-king mediating between white men and red, a mythic figure who was immune to the viciousness of civilization and the barbarism of the frontier.

A surer sign of American taste in this early period was the phenomenal success of the New England poet Henry Wadsworth Longfellow. Like Irving and Cooper, Longfellow spent some years in Europe. He later became a professor of modern languages, first at Bowdoin and later at Harvard. Sitting in his Cambridge study, Longfellow composed volume after volume of flowing verse that made him famous throughout the world. *Hyperion* (1839), *Evangeline* (1847), *Hiawatha* (1855), and *The Courtship of Miles Standish* (1858) delighted the largest audience, perhaps, that any American poet ever commanded. His sentimentality, his moralistic tone, his optimism, and his sense of the past satisfied popular taste. If his Hiawatha smacked more of Cambridge, Massachusetts, than of the shores of Gitchie Gumee, and if the brawny "Village Blacksmith" was a dream of the docile and respectful worker, poems such as "A Psalm of Life" expressed without irony the aspirations of middle-class America:

> *Let us, then, be up and doing*
> *With a heart for any fate;*
> *Still achieving, still pursuing,*
> *Learn to labor and to wait.*

Longfellow and his Boston and Cambridge associates belonged to a group of writers who contributed to what one critic has called "the flowering of New England." The emphasis placed by historians on this regional renaissance has partially hidden the intellectual and artistic activity of other sections, notably New York. Yet New England's "golden day" was real enough. The output of New England between 1830 and 1850 remains impressive, and the great names live on: Francis Parkman and William H. Prescott, historians; James Russell Lowell, Oliver Wendell Holmes, John Greenleaf Whittier, Ralph Waldo Emerson, and Henry David Thoreau, essayists and poets; Nathaniel Hawthorne, writer of romances and tales.

Edgar Allan Poe. *(Library of Congress)*

Poe

One Bostonian who did not agree with Boston's appreciation of itself was Edgar Allan Poe. Although born in the "hub of the universe," a city he sarcastically referred to in later life as Frogpond, Poe regarded himself as a Virginian. He spent much of his short life writing and editing brilliantly for inferior men, publishing poems, stories, and critical essays that brought him little money or recognition. In his most productive year, 1843, Poe earned three hundred dollars.

In 1836 he had married his thirteen-year-old cousin, Virginia Clemm. "I became insane," he wrote after her death ten years later, "with long intervals of horrible sanity." In 1849, at the age of forty, Poe was found lying unconscious in a Baltimore street; he died in delirium.

Poe was no apostle of progress. He disliked middle-class democracy. As a literary critic, he wrote cruel reviews of bad books and performed a tremendous service by attacking American provincialism. His own poetry and fiction contained most of the weaknesses he detected in his inferiors—theatricality, bombast, and sentimentality. But stories such as "The Fall of the House of Usher," "The Imp of the Perverse," "The Black Cat," "The Man in the Crowd," and "The Premature Burial"—tales of murderers, neurotics, the near-insane—were redeemed by an extraordinary intelligence and intensity. The owner who sorrowfully cuts out the eyes of his pet, the brother who entombs his sister alive, the lover who pulls out the teeth of his mistress while she sleeps in a cataleptic trance—all live in a tormented world far removed from Emerson's optimistic America. Yet Poe's works profoundly influenced later poets and critics in Europe and America. And in "The Gold Bug" Poe helped lay the foundation for modern detective fiction.

Emerson and Transcendentalism

The most compelling literary figure of his generation was Ralph Waldo Emerson. Boston-born and Harvard-educated, he entered the ministry, as his father and grandfather had. But he resigned his pastorate in 1832, finding Unitarian church formality meaningless, and devoted himself to writing and lecturing. *Nature* (1836), which presented in condensed form most of the themes of his later books, was followed by two volumes of essays and then by *Poems* (1847), *Representative Men* (1850), and several other works.

Emerson contained within himself the warring tendencies of his age. Part of him belonged to the practical American world of banks and railroads. No one more enthusiastically celebrated the deeds of powerful individuals (in his essays "Wealth," "Power," and "Napoleon"). At the same time, Emerson was a mystic and idealist who looked upon the external world as a passing show and detected an unchanging reality behind it. He wanted to revive old-time Puritan fervor without the rigidity of Puritan theology.

Quakerism, with its doctrine of the inner light, its gentleness, and its humanitarianism, moved him deeply. He was drawn to any philosophy that broke down the barriers between mind and matter, and he found support for his idealism in the works of certain European and Scottish philosophers, Oriental poets and sages, and English romantic poets.

Transcendentalism, the philosophy associated with Emerson and his sympathizers, was not a systematic faith. It had no creed and could not easily be defined. To Emerson, transcendentalists were "all those who contend for perfect freedom, who look for progress in philosophy and theology, and who sympathize with each other in the hope that the future will not always be as the past."

Although vague in its outlines, transcendental doctrine was clearly formulated in Emerson's essays and lectures, in which he announced to Americans that they too could speak to God directly without churches and creeds. He urged them to be self-reliant, to get their experience at first hand. Every object in the physical world had a spiritual meaning, and those capable of seeing that material things were the symbols of spiritual truths would best understand nature's purpose. The ability to communicate with God, the "Over Soul," was everyone's gift. But only a few poets, scholars, and philosophers develop this capacity. From them, others might learn that only the idea is real, that evil is negative (the mere absence of good), and that a kindly destiny awaited them.

Emerson expressed these thoughts in bold and fresh language. Even in his most abstract utterances, he used simple, concrete words and homely illustrations, just as Puritan ministers had done in their sermons. In urging every person to maintain his or her own views, he wrote: "Let him not quit his belief that a popgun is a popgun, though the ancient and honorable of the earth affirm it to be the crack of doom." Each person, Emerson insisted, should stand up against the tyranny of public opinion, must be, in short, an individual: "What I must do is all that concerns me, not what the people think. . . . It is easy in the world to live after the world's opinion, it is easy in solitude to live after our own; but the great man is he who in the midst of the crowd keeps with perfect sweetness the independence of solitude."

Thoreau

Like Emerson, Henry David Thoreau was a graduate of Harvard and a resident of Concord,

Massachusetts. "He declined," Emerson later wrote of him, "to give up his large ambition of knowledge and action for any narrow craft or profession, aiming at a much more comprehensive calling, the art of living well." Thoreau gave all his time to self-cultivation and self-exploration. He entered the results in his literary medium, a diary-like record of his experiences. As he once wrote, "I have traveled much in Concord."

In *Civil Disobedience* (1849) and especially, *Walden; or, Life in the Woods* (1854), Thoreau expressed his unconventional conclusions about literature, religion, government, and social relations.

Like most transcendentalists, Thoreau was a forthright egoist. He wrote about himself, he said, because he knew no one else so well. His accounts of how he discovered the miraculous in the commonplace contained suggestions for those who led "lives of quiet desperation." The wealth of the world, he said, is a lesser reward than one true vision: "The ways by which you may get money almost without exception lead downward. . . . There is no more fatal blunderer than he who consumes the great part of his life getting his living. . . . you must get your living by loving."

Thoreau advised Americans to simplify their private lives and their government. He regarded the state as a threat to independence. Abolitionist, naturalist, poet, rebel, and a down-to-earth but subtle writer, he attracted little notice while he lived. Yet in our day, *Walden* is considered a literary masterpiece, and its author—who discovered a universe in Concord—is regarded as one of the most original minds of New England's flowering.

Whitman

In 1842 Emerson had written: "We have yet had no genius in America. . . . Our log-rolling, our stumps and their politics, our fisheries, our Negroes and Indians . . . the northern trade, the southern planting, the western clearing, Oregon and Texas, are yet unsung. Yet America is a poem in our eyes; its ample geography dazzles the imagination, and it will not wait long for metres."

Walt Whitman of New York proved to be that genius. Whitman worked as a schoolteacher, printer, carpenter, journalist, publisher, and editor. When *Leaves of Grass*, his first volume of poems, appeared in 1855, its open references to the body and sex caused people to attack him as the "dirtiest beast of his age." The most friendly review, except for three he wrote himself, described his verse as "a sort of excited compound of New England transcendentalism and New York rowdy." Emerson was the only eminent writer who instantly recognized Whitman's freshness and found (as he wrote to the poet) "incomparable things, said incomparably well."

Whitman's poems, like Emerson's essays, embody the idea of progress, celebrate the innate goodness of humankind, and idealize nature. They insist on the spiritual reality underlying the material world. But Whitman looked more to the people than to his own soul for inspiration. Both poets and scholars, he said, have tried to "form classes by themselves, above the people, and more refined than the people." But he was not ashamed to embrace "what is vulgar." He wrote poems about blacks and Indians, carpenters,

Walt Whitman. *(Library of Congress)*

coach drivers, sailors and trappers, felons and prostitutes, and above all himself:

> *I celebrate myself;*
> *And what I assume you shall assume;*
> *For every atom belonging to me, as good belongs*
> *to you.*

In his poems, Whitman imagined ranks, races, and civilizations mingling together. It was to be America's mission, he thought, to promote this joining of peoples. His optimism was severely tested by the Civil War, and his faith in America's destiny was shaken by the events after 1865. But he did not despair:

> *Do I contradict myself?*
> *Very well, then, I contradict myself;*
> *(I am large, I contain multitudes.)*

Whitman died believing that his people still possessed "a miraculous wealth of latent power and capacity."

Hawthorne and Melville

Emerson and Whitman made many criticisms of American society, but their optimism never flagged. Some other writers, however, were less sure.

Nathaniel Hawthorne was one who could not shake off the pessimistic doctrines of his Puritan ancestors. The son of a Massachusetts shipmaster, Hawthorne held government jobs and enjoyed human contacts. But his ideas went against the grain of his age. In his tales, sketches, and novels—notably *The Scarlet Letter* (1850)—Hawthorne painted a somber moral landscape where men and women were devoured by vices they were forced to keep secret. These terrible facts of life mocked the claims of progress. In Hawthorne's hands, schemes for human reform came to nothing, and reformers changed into monstrous villains thwarted in their search for perfection.

Hawthorne's New York friend Herman Melville was also haunted by the idea of original sin. After his father's bankruptcy, Melville endured the humiliations of genteel poverty. In 1841 he quit city life and sailed to the South Pacific on a whaling ship. Three years of adventure there

Nathaniel Hawthorne. *(Library of Congress)*

provided materials for his two best-selling books, *Typee* (1846) and *Omoo* (1847).

His reputation declined after he stopped writing sketches of Polynesian life and turned to public as well as to private conflicts. An ardent nationalist and celebrator of "the great democratic God," Melville pronounced slavery "a blot, foul as the craterpool of hell," and predicted that the southern states "may yet prove battlefields." A saddened observer of the conflict he predicted, he wrote in *Battle-Pieces* (1866) some of the noblest poetry on the Civil War.

In rejecting transcendental optimism, Melville reacted even more strongly than Hawthorne to Emerson's bland optimism. Evil, for Melville, resided not merely in the tainted heart; it hung over the world like a curtain. In *Moby Dick* (1851), perhaps this country's finest novel, Melville pierced the "pasteboard mask" of life to confront this eternal menace. Ahab, a Yankee whaling captain, the doomed hero of this great book, exhausts himself in pursuit of Moby Dick, a gigantic white whale that symbolized the beauty, evil, and mystery of nature and of life. The pursuit fails; Ahab dies. If humans were half divine, as the transcendentalists insisted, they still faced a tragic destiny. God remained unknowable, progress an illusion.

FORMAL CULTURE AND EDUCATION

To many Americans of the Jacksonian age, the fine arts, even more than literature, seemed particularly aristocratic; painting and sculpture were associated with the "corrupt and despotic courts" of Europe. In an environment in which few people found much usefulness in the arts, it is not surprising that someone like Samuel F. B. Morse turned to mechanical inventions after spending half his life struggling as an artist.

Fine Arts in the Jacksonian Age

Many American artists began their careers as artisans and mechanics. The sculptor Hiram Powers worked in a Cincinnati organ factory and made wax statues before turning to art as a career. Powers's work pleased the critics of the 1830s, who praised only art that was "uplifting." Artists were invited to contemplate native forests, rivers, and sunsets, which "inspired the soul of man with visions of the ideal, the beautiful, the immortal." Those of the Hudson River School painted scenic wonders on a grand scale. By 1860, a realistic school of landscape painters had emerged. They caught the character of the horses, buffalo, Indians, and white settlers on the Great Plains, the real flavor of the frontier. Among the best were George Catlin and Alfred Jacob Miller.

A change in the national attitude toward the fine arts could be observed after 1840, when wealthy patrons in the larger cities began to support talented painters, sculptors, and architects. In the two decades before the Civil War, New York City, Philadelphia, and Boston competed in establishing "academies" and "athenaeums." Artists began to exhibit their work in private and public galleries. New schools of design appeared, along with magazines devoted to the fine arts. The Gothic style of architecture was the most popular.

The ordinary citizen, meanwhile, continued to derive more enjoyment from "a carnival of wild beast" and from huge painted panoramas, unwound from rollers, that presented the Mississippi River or historical scenes such as George Washington crossing the Delaware. The depiction of native scenes sometimes attained lasting artistic merit, as in the work of John James Audubon and the famous team of Currier and Ives. By fusing science and art, Audubon produced meticulous studies of American bird and animal life. Currier and Ives flooded the country with carefree lithographs of forest and farm, railroads, sleigh rides, and skating and boating.

Some moralists had stern reservations about literature and the plastic arts, and they felt even more strongly about the theater. Dramatic productions, as one of them declared, "lead the minds of youth from serious reflection." Lay preachers attacked the "vagabond profession" and the indecency of "displays of half-clad females." Despite these objections, the theater flourished. Audiences applauded everything from Shakespeare to the broadest farces. Shakespeare was popular rather than highbrow entertainment, and rowdy audiences were astonishingly familiar with the great bard's plays. New York was the center, but cities in every region supported theaters, and stars such as Edwin Forrest, Eddie Ellsler, and Fanny Kemble won national popularity. Traveling theatrical companies brought Shakespeare and other plays even to small towns.

In the 1820s a peculiarly American form of entertainment, the blackface minstrel show, began to draw enthusiastic crowds in northern cities. The performers were white men masquerading as blacks by means of burnt-cork makeup. They caricatured the songs and dances of the African American slave quarters in the South, mixing old English tunes with imitations of what they supposed was the peculiar pronunciation of blacks. They popularized the banjo—an instrument that had in fact originated in Africa. The supposedly happy "dancing darky" was portrayed in a way that suggested blacks had scarcely a care in the world. Both the performers and the characters they played were always male. Because these minstrel shows appealed to popular prejudices about blacks, they gained wide popularity. As one of the new small group of entertainment promoters said, "I've got only one method, and that is to find out what the people want and then give them that thing. . . . There's no use trying to force the public into a theater."

The Age of Oratory

For Americans of the 1990s it is especially difficult to appreciate the importance of public speaking, of formal oratory, in pre–Civil War America. As we look back now, it seems astonishing that huge audiences should have sat and stood in rapt attention to listen to speeches that lasted two, three, even four hours. Politicians such as Daniel Webster spoke that long without notes, although only after hours of hard preparation. When Webster or another prominent senator spoke, the Senate gallery was crowded with attentive listeners. Abraham Lincoln's two-minute Gettysburg Address was preceded by Edward Everett's two-hour oration, and many people at the time thought Everett's effort the centerpiece of that occasion. Many years earlier, after he left the presidency, John Quincy Adams had acquired the nickname Old Man Eloquent by speaking to the House of Representatives on a topic that is now nearly forgotten. The popularity of public speaking was most evident on the Fourth of July, when in cities and towns all across the country speakers carried on for an hour or more about the magnificent past and future of the nation.

These public performances reflected several aspects of the growing society. For one thing, people were accustomed to and expected long sermons in church and at camp meetings. For another, there was little other popular entertainment: no sports on TV (let alone professional games to attend) or "news" on the radio. Speechmaking provided an open door for talented men and even a few women—a door to fame as masters of the spoken word. Most Americans could name more popular orators than musicians, actors and actresses, or even authors. Speeches drew people together in enormous crowds, without electronic help, and provided opportunities for sociability and communal sharing in "uplifting" experiences.

The Popular Press

"The influence and circulation of newspapers," wrote an astonished visitor to the United States in about 1830, "is great beyond anything known in Europe. . . . Every village, nay, almost every hamlet, has its press." Even today, despite the recent tendency toward consolidation of American newspapers, the American press remains much more diversified than that of European countries.

During the first third of the nineteenth century, the number of newspapers rose from 200 to 1200. Most were weeklies. The larger cities had many daily papers, and competition was ferocious. New York City in 1830 had 47 papers, and only one daily among them claimed as many as 4000 subscribers. Enterprising editors reduced the price of their papers to a penny. They were able to produce them faster and cheaper by

---

WEBSTER ON THE UNION

The following is an example of the kind of flowery oratory that made Daniel Webster's speeches so famous.

When my eyes shall be turned to behold, for the last time, the sun in heaven, may I not see him shining on the broken and dishonored fragments of a once glorious Union; on States dissevered, discordant, belligerent; on a land rent with civil feuds, or drenched, it may be, in fraternal blood! Let their last feeble and lingering glance, rather, behold the gorgeous ensign of the republic, now known and honored throughout the earth, still *full high advanced, its arms and trophies streaming in their original lustre, not a stripe erased or polluted, nor a single star obscured, bearing for its motto no such miserable interrogatory as, What is all this worth? Nor those other words of delusion and folly, Liberty first, and Union afterwards: but every where, spread all over in characters of living light, blazing on all its ample folds, as they float over the sea and over the land, and in every wind under the whole heavens, that other sentiment, dear to every true American heart—Liberty and Union, now and forever, one and inseparable!*

means of the new steam-driven rotary press. Newspapers lured more readers by featuring "robberies, thefts, murders, awful catastrophes and wonderful escapes."

Benjamin Day's *New York Sun* pioneered the new sensationalism. Day's rival, James Gordon Bennett of the *Herald*, rapidly surpassed him. Bennett played up New York "society" (he headlined his own marriage) and developed circulation techniques that were quickly copied throughout the country.

Some newspapers were sponsored by business groups and others by religious organizations, but many more were devoted to the interests of a political party. People expected that many newspapers were "Democratic" or "Whig" or else the organ of some other political party. No one expected neutrality in news about national politics. The ideal of "objective" reporting was entirely foreign to nineteenth-century editors and their readers.

Magazines also sprang up by the dozen, but few survived for long. Having no generally accepted literary standards to draw on, always in danger of offending the prudish, yet aware of the "vulgar" preferences of their public, harassed magazine editors scarcely knew which way to turn. Many subscribers failed to pay their bills. The penny newspapers and cheap editions of pirated English books also reduced the potential audience. A few metropolitan monthlies or quarterlies gained national audiences—the *North American Review* (Boston), the *Knickerbocker Magazine* (New York), *Graham's Magazine* (Philadelphia), and the *Southern Literary Messenger* (Richmond). They printed pieces by such authors as Cooper, Poe, Bryant, Hawthorne, and Longfellow. Yet monthly agricultural journals such as the *Southern Cultivator* probably had wider circulations.

Perhaps the most significant change in popular writing—in novels as well as magazines—was its increasing orientation toward women. After about 1820, more than half the novels published in the United States were written by women, often prefaced with apologies for "imposing upon the reading public a product of the weaker sex." Not only were more women writing for the general public, women themselves were becoming an identifiable group of reading consumers. New magazines were published for a specifically female audience. The two that circulated most widely were the *Ladies' Magazine* and *Godey's Lady's Book*, which merged under the editorship of Sarah Josepha Hale in 1836.

Sarah Hale's career was one of the most remarkable in the history of American magazine publishing. She was born in 1788, the year the Constitution was adopted. Widowed just before the birth of her fifth child, she ran a millinery shop and wrote a competent novel, *Northwood* (1827), "literally with my baby in my arms." The next year she began editing the *Ladies' Magazine*. In her first issue she pledged that her magazine would "mark the progress of female improvement, and cherish the effusions of female intellect." She firmly believed that women had no proper role in politics or public affairs, yet she strenuously backed the struggling new movement for higher education for women. Intensely patriotic, she urged construction of the Bunker Hill Monument and the renovation of Washington's old home at Mount Vernon. She also campaigned successfully for recognition of Thanksgiving Day as a national holiday. In addition, she wrote poems for children, including the

WORDS AND NAMES IN AMERICAN HISTORY

Sometimes a person's name becomes attached to an invention or new product, or to a new way of producing a product. Unlike, say, the Ford motorcar, some of these names have become extinct. When Robert Fulton designed the first commercially successful steamboats in the early 1800s, one of the first was called Fulton's Folly, because many people thought the strange thing would never work. Because of DeWitt Clinton's years of advocating and sponsoring the canal that came to be known as the Erie, skeptics called it Clinton's Ditch. And Amelia Bloomer, a temperance and women's-rights advocate beginning in the 1840s, was immortalized by her call for reforms in women's dress, especially for the long, loose trousers worn under a short dress that became known and ridiculed as "bloomers."

Bloomers. *(Library of Congress)*

now classic "Mary Had a Little Lamb." Although *Godey's Lady's Book* declined in quality and influence after the Civil War, in its heyday it had a circulation of 150,000, a figure that dwarfed most other American magazines. Sarah Hale finally retired at the age of seventy-nine and then, as so often happens with energetic people, died within the year.

Public Schools

During this same period there were important accomplishments in the field of education. Most Americans favored Bible teaching in the schools because, as the famous evangelical minister Lyman Beecher expressed it, the Bible gave no sanction "to civil broils, or resistance to lawful authority, but commands all men to follow peace, and to obey magistrates that are set over them, whatever the form of government may be."

Despite the lip service paid to Christian, democratic, and practical education, crusades for free schools faced an apathetic and often hostile public. Parents who could afford to educate their children in private academies saw no reason why they should be taxed to educate the children of the poor. They saw education as a benefit to their own children rather than to society in general. Administrators of private and parochial schools, farmers, and non-English-speaking groups joined in fighting the free school movement.

But the advocates of free public schools had strong arguments. Everyone would benefit, said one publicist in 1832: "The man who is poor must see that this is the only way he can secure education for his children. The man in moderate circumstances . . . will have his children taught for a less sum than he pays at present. The rich man, who will be heavily taxed, must see that his course secures to the rising generation the only means of perpetuating our institutions."

The leaders of the free school movement—Horace Mann in Massachusetts, Henry Barnard in Connecticut, and Calvin Stowe in Ohio—hammered away in widely circulated reports and articles based on thorough investigation. They began to win their battle. By 1860, most northern states had a tax-supported school program. One motive behind this movement was the itch on the part of many working-class Americans for education as a means of personal advancement. Another was the hope that free public schools would help assimilate the large number of immigrants coming to America. These European immigrants often joined the ranks of the urban poor, whose children could not afford to stop working to attend school.

Even after the establishment of free public schools, it was chiefly the middle class and not the poorer workers or farmers whose children benefited. Education on all levels continued to suffer from rigid teaching methods, large classes, a short school year, and the low salaries paid teachers. The one-room schoolhouse really did exist, but whether youngsters suffered or benefited from being taught in the same room with students ten years younger or older is not at all clear. Reformers suggested a variety of schemes to raise the educational level, but these usually met opposition. Yet the quality of education remained high enough to cause foreign visitors to comment on the exceptional literacy of the American public—which was in fact the most literate in the world.

Schools began to be "graded" by age and accomplishment, and the curriculum was pushed further and further from the classical languages and toward the three Rs: reading, writing, and 'rithmetic. Formal teacher training came about largely through the work of Horace Mann, who established the first "normal schools" for the preparation of teachers, and Henry Barnard, one of the founders of the American Association for the Advancement of Education (1855) and editor of the *American Journal of Education*. Public high schools were rare until 1840, but during the next two decades the number increased, especially in Massachusetts, New York, and Ohio. Such schools offered a more practical kind of education than private schools and were open to girls as well as boys.

Education for Girls and Women

As opportunities for formal education broadened, young women were included—gradually and reluctantly. This was a new and radical development. Before the Revolution, formal education of girls and young women had been regarded as an entirely subsidiary matter—parsley, as it were, on the steak of providing young men with the essentials of the ancient languages, moral philosophy, and arithmetic. Yet many young women had always been taught how to read, since the ability to read the Bible had been thought vital, especially in New England and Pennsylvania.

The success of the American Revolution provided a new reason for educating women. The new republic would require an educated and virtuous citizenry. Young men would, of course, be nurtured by their mothers. How could women raise up the next generation of young men to support the new republican experiment if they themselves were ignorant? Thus, the education of future mothers was crucial. Dr. Benjamin Rush, among others, insisted that the educators themselves be educated according to true republican principles.

More than a generation after the Revolution, such ideas began to have an effect on formal education for young ladies. Most secondary academies did not admit girls, largely because they assumed that sufficient education would be provided at home. Emma Willard was raised on a small Connecticut farm, but her father adopted the unusual view that she was qualified to read

John Locke and philosophical essays. When she was only twenty-two, she published *An Address to the Public . . . Proposing a Plan for Improving Female Education*, a pamphlet that was vigorously argued and received considerable favorable attention. In 1821 she opened the Troy (New York) Female Seminary, which proved a great and long-lasting success.

Young ladies there learned some polite accomplishments, but they also studied many subjects that were normally restricted to the better men's colleges. One of her pupils reported in the 1830s: "We had reading, writing, spelling, arithmetic, grammar, geometry, trigonometry, astronomy, natural philosophy, chemistry, botany, physiology, mineralogy, geology, and zoology in the morning; and dancing, drawing, painting, French, Italian, Spanish, and German in the afternoon. Greek and the higher branches of mathematics were only studied by the tall girls [i.e., the oldest ones]." Altogether, Mrs. Willard aimed at producing polished young ladies who could hold their own in the supposedly masculine intellectual world. Many of her pupils came from families with domestic servants, but at the school the girls made their own beds.

Mary Lyon, who came from a background similar to Emma Willard's, also founded an academy for girls. She had had the quite unusual experience of attending one of the new academies that admitted girls as well as boys. Her Mt. Holyoke Female Seminary later became a college, one with a good claim to being the oldest women's college in the country.

Coeducational colleges seemed to some a logical next step. Oberlin College in Ohio admitted women as well as men from its start in 1837, although its women students were given an essentially second-class status, since most of them were not permitted to take Latin and none were allowed to be valedictorians. Several of the new state colleges in the West began to admit women: Michigan was the first to do so on paper (1837), but Iowa was the first to do so in fact (1858).

These developments in formal schooling for girls and women took place largely in the North, especially in New England and in parts of the upper West that were settled by New Englanders. Clearly the old Puritan emphasis on literacy and education was having long-term effects. Yet even in the South the winds of change were blowing. One of the country's most challenging female seminaries was in Hunstville, Alabama, and the first women's college to require both classical languages and a full four years of study was Mary Sharp College, founded in 1851 in Winchester, Tennessee.

Colleges and Lyceums

The number of so-called colleges grew from 16 in 1799 to 182 in 1860. In those same years, 412 others started and died. Colleges, said a prominent educator in 1848, "rise up like mushrooms on our luxuriant soil. They are duly lauded and puffed for a day; and then they sink to be heard of no more." The multiplication of colleges resulted in part from the difficulties and expenses of travel. But sectarian rivalry and local pride were probably the major causes.

Each important denomination and many minor ones supported one or more colleges. Most of them were hardly more than dressed-up academies that students might enter at fourteen or fifteen; so-called universities were hardly more than large colleges. Most professional schools in this period, law and medical schools in particular, were separate institutions.

College and university curriculums varied little throughout the country. Latin, Greek, mathematics, science, political economy, and moral philosophy offered a solid enough program. Teaching by rote memory was as popular at upper levels as in lower schools. Before the Civil War, a few professors found time to write and experiment, but in general the college atmosphere offered little stimulation.

Franklin, Jefferson, and other philosophers of democracy had insisted that only an educated electorate could maintain a republican government. Many people, too busy or too old to go to school, continued to believe them. The most popular informal educational institution was the lyceum, which grew out of the proposals of an Englishman, Lord Henry Brougham. Admirers in America, spurred on by a New Englander, Josiah Holbrook, put his ideas into practice.

By 1835, lyceums could be found in fifteen states, their activities coordinated by a national lyceum organization. By 1860 more than three thousand lyceums had been set up, mainly in New England, New York, and the upper Mississippi Valley, where public school sentiment was strong. The lyceums sponsored public lectures on every conceivable topic, with scientific and practical subjects arousing greatest interest.

Eminent personages such as Emerson addressed lyceum audiences (women as well as men) on such themes as "Wealth" and "Power." The education that the lyceums offered was often superficial and remote from the interests of those for whom it was theoretically designed. Yet lyceums helped bridge the gulf between the learned minority and the community, and they fostered some intellectual ideals in a predominantly commercial society.

AMBIGUITY

The inclusion of young women in formal education and the beginnings of "free," tax-supported schools were in fact revolutionary. Yet historians often treat these educational developments as reflections of the new spirit of reform that swept the northern states especially, beginning about 1820 and blossoming in the 1830s and 1840s. The very term *reform* suggests going back to better days, remedying evils that have crept into an essentially sound system. Yet the label Age of Reform has fastened itself on this period for good reason. Even changes in education were meant to broaden participation in institutions regarded as crucial to the young Republic, institutions and practices that needed improvement—perhaps even a little repair—but not overthrowing. The same may be said of many other reforming movements of this era, movements that sought to eliminate flaws in American society. These flaws seemed more and more in need of reformation as Americans congratulated themselves on the progress of democratic government and the expanding prosperity of their young nation.

The more the country seemed to improve, the more its remaining faults stood out and cried for elimination. The prevailing spirit of optimism and mastery could also cry out for innovations (such as we have just seen in education) that would further improve an already improving society. Thus the impulses of this age of reform had a dual quality: the elimination of evil and the advancement of good. Obviously both aims pointed in the same direction.

Temperance

The first specific reform movement—and the one that enlisted by far the largest number of people—was "temperance" with alcohol, and then its prohibition. This movement was partly a response to a very real need, since the consumption of alcohol was on the rise. It has recently been shown, in fact, that the American people (mostly men) were on a binge during the period 1790–1830. They drank more alcohol than ever before or since—not in the form of "cocktails," but as hard cider, corn whiskey, wheat whiskey, rum, beer, and (for the wealthy) wine. They gulped it down in all sorts of places and on all sorts of occasions, the hard stuff often without the benefit of dilution with "branch water."

It is hard to say why this national binge took place. The causes most frequently pointed to are the increasing mobility of the American population, the breakup of families and disruption of community life, the loneliness and fatigue of the farmer, and the long hours of the industrial worker. The 1810 census claimed that there were 14,000 distilleries in the United States. In 1820, census takers would not list distilling as a separate industry, since almost everyone in rural areas engaged in it. In some cities, saloons numbered in the thousands.

The agitation against drinking was first given strong support by the publication in 1805 of Dr. Benjamin Rush's *Inquiry into the Effect of Ardent Spirits upon the Human Mind and Body*. As a physician, Rush attacked drinking for its bad effects on health. Increasingly, however, religious revivalists dominated the campaign against "demon rum." The younger temperance reformers stressed its moral viciousness. Lyman Beecher and other evangelical preachers—with the support of Bible and Tract Societies and missionary boards—persuaded millions to take the pledge as "teetotalers." Beecher claimed: "Intemperance is a sin upon our land and with boundless prosperity is coming in upon us like a flood."

In 1826 the American Temperance Society was organized in Boston to coordinate the activities of hundreds of local groups. The crusaders went beyond persuasion to legislation, and from advocating moderation to insisting on abstinence. The first prohibition law was enacted in Maine in 1846, and within five years twelve other states, all in the North, had adopted some kind of liquor-control law. Many people who supported such legislation were opposed to total prohibition, and their quarrels with the teetotalers weakened the movement. Yet the campaign against "ardent spirits" actually helped reduce the consumption of alcohol. The movement had enlisted "cold-water armies" of children, women, and men, who marched and sang in support of abstinence. The crusade against alcohol marked the first instance in America of the private organization of large groups in the cause of righteousness for the entire society.

A One-Woman Crusade

Most reform movements involved organizations. One cause, however, the treatment of the insane and feebleminded, was dominated by a single

---

AMERICAN HUMANITARIANISM

The typical American fusion of humanitarian benevolence and missionary zeal is evident in the following appeal by Samuel Gridley Howe, a leader in education for the blind.

The advantage, nay the necessity, of printing the Gospel in raised letters for the use of the blind will be apparent to every thinking Christian. Here is a large number of our fellow creatures within our reach, who might be supplied with the New Testament at small expense, compared with that laid out in sending it among distant heathens. It may be said indeed, that the blind can hear the Bible read by their friends, while the heathen cannot; but, on the other hand, let one consider what a precious treasure a copy of the Testament in raised letters would be to a blind man; he would pore over it, read and reread it, until every word became familiar; and how much greater probability there would be of its producing a good effect than in the hands of those who have a thousand other things to occupy their thoughts. . . . In fine, let any pious Christian put the case to himself and say, whether he could be content with having the Scriptures read by another.

The nine steps of the drunkard's progress, beginning with "a glass with a friend" and ending with "death by suicide." *(Library of Congress)*

person. Dorothea Dix taught school for a time in her native Massachusetts, but a chance experience led her to challenge the widespread abuses of such "unfortunate" people. For the most part, she operated alone, though she had backing from a number of prominent New England reformers.

When she was about forty years old, Dorothea Dix undertook a personal survey of nearly every jail and almshouse in Massachusetts. It took her eighteen months. Her notebook recorded the awful conditions in which she found "lunatics" and "idiots": "confined . . . in cages, closets, cellars, stalls, pens! Chained, naked, beaten with rods, and lashed into obedience." She published her data in a Memorial to the Legislature of Massachusetts (1843). It was a powerful and elo-

quent document that began with a simple statement: "I come to place before the Legislature the . . . condition of the miserable, the desolate, the outcast." It was also effective, for after much debate the Massachusetts General Court voted substantial funds for improved facilities and treatment for mentally ill and retarded people.

Heartened by this success, Dorothea Dix used the same strategy in other states. In three years she traveled thirty thousand miles, as far west and south as Illinois and Mississippi. She investigated conditions, then sent her increasingly famous "memorials" to one state legislature after another. Her only major defeat was at the hands of the U.S. Congress, which thought care of the insane a matter for the states. All together she was principally responsible for the founding of thirty-two state mental institutions, and her work inspired many more in the United States and in Europe.

Unlike so many reformers, Dorothea Dix remained largely devoted to a single cause. It may have been this very singlemindedness that made her one of the most directly effective humanitarian reformers of all time.

Communitarians

In the early stages of the Industrial Revolution in America, as in Britain and France, the condition of the workers often seemed so terrible that even some leading industrialists thought there ought to be an alternative. Cooperatives—even entire new cooperative communities—were one idea. Before the militant abolitionism of William Lloyd Garrison heightened feelings and hopes on the slave issue in the 1830s, the idea of black communities as an alternative to slavery also attracted followers. Of the scores of different communitarian experiments in this period, we may take three of the most controversial sorts as examples. Many of these communities were started by Americans, but two Scots and a Frenchman provided considerable inspiration. Robert Owen was a successful manufacturer and industrial reformer from New Lanark, Scotland. He helped inspire a young Scotswoman, Frances Wright, who wrote an enthusiastic account of her travels in America (1821) that was widely read and (for the most part) well received in Great Britain as well as in the United States. Charles Fourier was much more a library person, a theorist who developed a somewhat eccentric proposal for a socialist society.

Robert Owen came to America in 1825 to found a community at New Harmony, Indiana, on a site he had purchased from a group of German communitarians. A number of gifted European scholars came to Owen's utopia, and for a time the community offered the best education in the country. But the rank and file had more than their share of human frailties. According to one observer, New Harmony attracted "the indolent, the unprincipled, men of desperate fortunes, moon-worshippers, romantic young men . . . those who had dreamed about earthly Elysiums, a great many honest aspirants after a better order of things, poor men simply desiring an education for their children."

Owen's experiment failed after two years, hastened to its end more by its founder's intolerance of established social norms than by its main purpose: the establishment of a rational system of society. Owen's attack on "marriage, . . . private or individual property, . . . [and] absurd and irrational systems of religion" as a "trinity of the most monstrous evils that could be combined to inflict mental and physical evil" got him into the most trouble. Owen was classed by his critics with "whores and whoremongers," and his community was called "one great brothel."

The collapse of New Harmony in 1827 speeded the end of Nashoba, the black community set up by Frances Wright in 1826 in Shelby County, Tennessee. Ironically, Nashoba was situated on three hundred acres seized from the Chickasaw Indians some time before. From 50 to 100 slaves were to be taken there to earn enough money to purchase their freedom while learning the attitudes and skills thought necessary to sustain it.

Wright, however, soon imposed on Nashoba a full-scale communitarian scheme open to whites as well as blacks. She also went further than

Frances Wright. *(National Portrait Gallery, Smithsonian Institution)*

Owen in attacking marriage and religion. One of her lieutenants proceeded to publish in a popular magazine accounts of the free sexual relationships there. Frances Wright defended these. If "the possession of the right of free action," she said, "inspire not the courage to exercise the right, liberty has done but little for us." Nashoba did not survive long. Yet its end was happier than that of many other cooperative communities. Frances Wright sailed with Nashoba's slaves to Haiti, where they were emancipated.

Owenism had threatened middle-class Americans with free thought and free love. The doctrines of Charles Fourier seemed less dangerous, and during the 1840s were advocated by a number of "respectable" people. The Fourierists regarded private capitalism as wasteful and degrading. If people would only abandon the ethic of competition and gather in "phalanxes," or associated groups, they could transform the world into a paradise. What particularly appealed to the Fourierists, many of whom were New England transcendentalists, was the emphasis Fourier placed on practical idealism and the dignity of the worker.

Between 1840 and 1850, Fourier's followers organized more than forty phalanxes in the United States. All had been abandoned by 1860, but one at least became a lasting legend, the subject of Hawthorne's *The Blithedale Romance*. This was Brook Farm in Massachusetts, organized by a group of transcendentalist intellectuals in 1841 and converted to Fourierism a few years later. The Brook Farmers decided to demonstrate the possibility of combining the life of the mind with manual labor.

"After breakfast," Nathaniel Hawthorne noted in his diary, "Mr. Ripley put a four-pronged instrument into my hands, which he gave me to understand was called a pitch-fork; and he and Mr. Farley being armed with similar weapons, we all commenced a gallant attack upon a heap of manure." The community, never more than 100 people, attracted about 4000 visitors a year. But its practical side proved less successful. In 1847 a fire ruined the already failing enterprise, and it was abandoned. Secular communities such as Owen's, Wright's, and Fourier's may have failed partly because of the personalities of their promoters. In any case, Americans as a rule proved too individualistic to trust their glowing private prospects to collective undertakings.

Abolition

From the early 1830s on, slavery attracted more and more attention until it overshadowed all other issues. The origins of antislavery sentiment lay in the mid-eighteenth century, when Quakers denounced the buying and selling of slaves. Many political leaders in revolutionary and postrevolutionary America deplored slavery. They also deplored the presence of blacks. This conviction inspired the American Colonization Society, founded in 1817 with private, state, and federal support, to establish Liberia in 1822 as an African colony for ex-slaves.

Despite the hopes of many whites, the idea of ridding the United States of black people by sending them to Africa never worked. By 1860 no more than fifteen thousand American blacks had been settled in Liberia, most of them former slaves who had been freed on condition that they go there. This number was far less than the natural increase of the American black population. The failure of the colonization plan and the ineffectiveness of those who backed gradual liberation encouraged radical abolitionists to start their campaign for immediate emancipation.

In 1831, William Lloyd Garrison began publishing *The Liberator*, an abolitionist periodical that described slavery as a hideous evil and a terrible sin. Its appearance marked the beginning of a great antislavery offensive. Garrison was a Massachusetts journalist, a gentle but somewhat neurotic man with a hatred of injustice. As with many of his followers, abolition was only one of Garrison's causes. He was an ardent worker for women's rights and international peace, an opponent of capital punishment and imprisonment for debt. But after 1830 he focused primarily on slavery.

Garrison attacked slavery not because it was inefficient or undemocratic or unjust, but because it was sinful. Slaveholders must give up their slaves immediately, he shouted, since no one could give up sin by gradual methods. He called the Constitution, which "guaranteed" slavery by not interfering with it and by including a fugitive-slave clause, "the most bloody and heaven-daring arrangement ever made by men for the continuance and protection of a system of the most atrocious villainy ever exhibited on earth." Garrison's attacks on the "Southern oppressors" did much to intensify antiabolition sentiment in the South. His fanaticism frightened moderate antislavery people everywhere. A majority of subscribers to *The Liberator* were northern free blacks. Garrison's refusal to resort to political action also reduced his effectiveness.

A different approach was taken by Theodore Dwight Weld of Ohio, who preferred patient organization to dramatic pronouncements. His followers, well versed in the techniques of revival meetings, converted thousands to the abolitionist cause. Throughout the North, thousands of women organized women's antislavery societies and raised money by holding "antislavery fairs," where they sold such articles as handkerchiefs embroidered with a picture of a chained, kneeling slave and the motto (borrowed from the British antislavery movement) "Am I Not a Man and Brother?" By 1850, almost two thousand societies had been formed with a membership close to 200,000.

Although it was always a minority movement in the North, abolition had the backing of many prominent intellectuals and reformers. John Greenleaf Whittier of Massachusetts became the poet of abolition; Emerson, Thoreau, Whitman, Longfellow, and Melville all condemned slavery. Boston's Wendell Phillips thundered against it, as did ministers such as Theodore Parker, William Ellery Channing, and the Quaker Lucretia Mott. Southerners such as James G. Birney and the Grimké sisters renounced their slave property and joined the antislavery forces. Many blacks who moved north—Frederick Douglass and Sojourner Truth were the most famous—worked as speakers for the cause.

Abolitionist strength lay in the movement's unselfish dedication to Christian principles. Its weakness lay in not realizing the social barriers blacks had to overcome once they were free. Practically all abolitionists opposed the idea of violent revolution by the slaves. They did not want a civil war over slavery. But in the mid-1830s, even in the North, public opinion saw the abolitionists as a band of misguided bigots whose activities on behalf of a hopelessly inferior people would destroy the nation. Many northern cities were swept by antiabolitionist riots in defiance, or with the approval, of local authorities. Garrison was dragged through the streets of Boston by an angry mob, and then briefly jailed for his own safety. George Thompson, an English abolitionist, was howled down and threatened with bodily harm. Elijah Lovejoy, an antislavery editor in Alton, Illinois, was murdered by a mob in 1837.

The issue of abolition was thrust onto the floor of Congress. By the mid-1830s petitions against the trade in slaves in the nation's capital were pouring into that body, often signed by thousands of northern men and women. The petitions raised constitutional issues. Clearly Congress had jurisdiction over the District of Columbia. Yet some petitions called for abolition of slavery in the states, even though few people thought Congress had any such power. Southern congressmen, with considerable northern support, passed a resolution in 1836 ordering that petitions relating "in any way" to slavery be immediately tabled and thus ignored.

This was the famous Gag Rule, which became the target of eight years of attack by the only former president to sit in the House of Representatives. John Quincy Adams, representing his home district in Massachusetts, carried on an eloquent and for a time nearly solitary war against the Gag Rule. His case had great force, since it was based on the First Amendment provision that Congress could not deny "the right of the people . . . to petition the government for a redress of grievances." Adams was not an abolitionist, although he detested slavery. As an old son of the American Revolution, however, he thought the Gag Rule itself smelled of tyranny. Finally, in 1844, Adams's campaign succeeded. The resolution was repealed.

All these petitions, in addition to more flagrant abolitionist activities, made white southerners more and more uneasy and angry. They demanded laws against antislavery activists. Southern postmasters confiscated suspected abolitionist literature. Fear of slave insurrections and resentment against atrocity stories in abolitionist propaganda caused the South to overestimate the strength of the antislavery movement in the North. And of course this southern response only increased northern feeling. As the sectional conflict deepened, the dream of peace and justice that had stirred the hearts of the reformers in the 1830s and 1840s began to fade.

Yet the issue would not go away. It continued to reverberate. Slavery as a practice and antislavery as an ideal continued to affect all Americans, both black and white, northern and southern. As we will see, the question of slaveholding eventually came to dominate American politics.

Even sooner, though, it became intertwined with other issues in American culture, especially the role of another subordinate group—women. Yet the position of women, and the roles of their fathers, mothers, daughters, and sons, was undergoing change that had more to do with the nation's demographic patterns, its economy, and its social values than its formal politics.

SUMMARY

Antebellum America was a changing society, one in which ideals, tradition, and material progress battled for the attention and loyalty of the public. It was also a time when Americans became conscious of themselves as different—as a restless people forever chasing the dollar or a new style of life, as a people more tolerant of violence than others. Americans were also an idealistic people: Equality, individualism, and opportunity remained strong ideals, even though economic forces were causing the distribution of wealth to become less equal rather than more.

Religion was still an active force in American life, but religion also had its contradictions: Along with tolerance there was intolerance, and along with the unifying bond of revivalism there was sectarianism. Yet the general acceptance of democracy, private property, and Christian faith seemed somehow to give American society a national character.

In the four decades before the Civil War, the United States experienced an intellectual flowering. In New England and New York, writers such as Washington Irving, James Fenimore Cooper, and the poet Henry Wadsworth Longfellow became world figures. Edgar Allan Poe's short stories influenced later generations of poets, critics, and writers. Two compelling figures of this period were Ralph Waldo Emerson and Henry David Thoreau. Walt Whitman's poetry celebrated the new America in language that shocked his generation but foretold and influenced the work of those to come. And in the work of Nathaniel Hawthorne and Herman Melville, Americans had treasures of world literature.

The fine arts began to grow in America as well. After 1840 there was a change in the traditional distrust of the arts. Wealthy patrons in the larger cities began to support talented painters, sculptors, and architects. The theater flourished, from Shakespeare to blackface

TIME LINE			
1800	Huge revival at Cane Ridge, Kentucky	1837	Mary Lyon founds Mt. Holyoke Female Seminary
1819–1820	Irving's *The Sketch Book*	1840s	Fourierists organize dozens of communitarian "phalanxes"
1820s	Beginnings of blackface minstrel shows		
1822	Liberia founded as African colony for American blacks	1841	Last of Cooper's Leatherstocking series, *The Deerslayer*
1822	Beginnings of Roman Catholic periodical press	1843	Dorothea Dix's first Memorial on treatment of the insane
1826	Organization of the American Temperance Society	1844	J. Q. Adams finally wins repeal of Gag Rule in Congress
1826	Josiah Holbrook initiates lyceum movement	1849	Death of Edgar Allan Poe
1830	Webster's "Reply to Hayne" speech	1850	Number of Roman Catholics in U.S. reaches 1.75 million
1831	First issues of Garrison's *The Liberator*	1850	Hawthorne's *The Scarlet Letter*
1833	Day's *New York Sun*, first successful penny newspaper	1851	Melville's *Moby Dick*
		1854	Thoreau's *Walden*
1836	Emersons' *Nature*	1855	Longfellow's *Hiawatha;* Whitman's *Leaves of Grass*
1837	Horace Mann heads new Massachusetts Board of Education	1857	Extensive religious revivals, especially in cities

minstrel shows. Newspapers boomed, and magazines sprang up by the dozen, including some edited by and for women. In addition, hundreds of public speakers—political, patriotic, and religious—held thousands of Americans spellbound in this "age of oratory."

Free public education began to spread, although its advocates had a difficult time persuading the taxpayers that it was a worthwhile investment. Horace Mann established the first normal schools. Schools began to be graded, and the curriculum to focus not on classical languages but on the three Rs. Colleges and lyceums grew in number as well. For the first time, some institutions sought to meet the growing demand for better educational opportunities for women.

The free school and lyceum movements were reflections of another new spirit in society, that of reform.

During the 1830s and 1840s, many men and women devoted their lives to stamping out social evils or supporting social innovations: temperance with alcohol; education for the deaf, dumb, and blind; world peace; and the abolition of slavery. Dorothea Dix waged a successful one-woman campaign for better treatment of the insane and feeble-minded.

The activities of abolitionists made the South uneasy and deepened sectional conflict. When hundreds of anti-slavery petitions poured into Congress, the House of Representatives refused to receive them. Former president John Quincy Adams fought a long and lonely battle against this Gag Rule. Finally he succeeded, but soon afterward the issue of whether slavery should be allowed to expand westward into newly acquired territories came to dominate American politics and national life.

Suggested Readings

R. Nye, *Society and Culture in America, 1830–1860* (1974), is an excellent introduction. E. Branch, *The Sentimental Years, 1836–1860* (1934), is a neglected classic. A fine general treatment is L. Perry, *Intellectual Life in America: A History* (1984).

D. Davis, *Homicide in American Fiction, 1798–1860* (1967); and F. Somkin, *Unquiet Eagle: Memory and Desire in the Idea of American Freedom, 1815–1860* (1967), are analytical studies. Some important writers are covered by the following: K. House, *Cooper's Americans* (1965); A. Quinn, *Edgar Allan Poe* (1941); M. Van Doren, *Nathaniel Hawthorne* (1949); C. Olson, *Call Me Ishmael: Herman Melville, Moby Dick and America* (1968); J. Parte, *Emerson and Thoreau: Transcendentalists in Conflict* (1966); R. Richardson, Jr., *Henry Thoreau: A Life of the Mind* (1986); and G. Allen, *The Solitary Singer: A Critical Biography of Walt Whitman* (1955). D. Lawrence, *Studies in Classic American Literature* (1923), is available, along with other penetrating literary studies, in a superb anthology edited by E. Wilson, *The Shock of Recognition* (2nd ed., 1955). F. Matthiessen, *American Renaissance: Art and Expression in the Age of Emerson and Whitman* (1941), is a brilliant interpretation of America's literary flowering; and L. Marx, *The Machine in the Garden* (1964), of innocence under pressure.

O. Larkin, *Art and Life in America* (1949), covers the history of painting and sculpture. See also R. McLanathan, *The American Tradition in the Arts* (1968), which emphasizes the antebellum period. N. Harris, *The Artist in American Society: The Formative Years, 1790–1860* (1968), presents a searching analysis. J. McCoubray's illustrated essay *American Tradition in Painting* (1963) suggests the American ambivalence toward their vast landscape. R. Toll,

Blacking Up: The Minstrel Show in Nineteenth-Century America (1974), deals with a popular American "art" form. Public entertainment (especially Shakespeare) is discussed by L. Levine, *Highbrow/Lowbrow: The Emergence of Cultural Hierarchy in America* (1988). For the relationship between newspapers and the government, see C. Smith, *The Press, Politics, and Patronage: The American Government's Use of Newspapers, 1789–1875* (1977). For oratory, see B. Baskerville, *The People's Voice: The Orator in American Society* (1979).

Probably the best place to start on medicine is J. Duffy, *The Healers: A History of American Medicine* (1979). Also useful are J. Cassedy, *Medicine and American Growth, 1800–1860* (1986); R. Shryock, *Medicine in America: Historical Essays* (1966); and S. Cayleff, *Wash and Be Healed: The Water-Cure Movement and Women's Health* (1987).

P. Cohen, *A Calculating People: The Spread of Numeracy in Early America* (1983), is a fine, sweeping study. C. Kaestle, *The Evolution of an Urban School System: New York City, 1750–1850* (1973), describes the shift away from reliance on the family, church, and apprenticeship for socializing children. M. Katz, *The Irony of Early School Reform: Educational Innovations in Mid-Nineteenth-Century Massachusetts* (1968), contends that early reforms served the interests of the middle class while programming working-class youngsters for industrial work. B. Wishy, *The Child and the Republic: The Dawn of Modern American Nurture* (1968), deals with tensions that arose from training children for an increasingly competitive society. Higher education is treated in F. Rudolph, *The American College and University* (1962), and in R. Hofstadter and W. Metzger, *The Development of Academic Freedom in the United States* (1955).

For a sense of the variety of antebellum reform movements, see L. Ratnor, *Pre–Civil War Reforms:*

The Variety of Principle and Programs (1967). Two books are much broader in scope than their titles suggest: D. Rothman, *The Discovery of the Asylum: Social Order and Disorder in the New Republic* (1971); and G. Grob, *Mental Institutions in America: Social Policy to 1875* (1973). R. Walters, *American Reformers, 1815–1860* (1978), gives a fine overview. Perhaps the best place to start on the communitarians is a collection of original documents: R. Fogarty (ed.), *American Utopianism* (1972). See also W. and J. Pease, *Black Utopia: Negro Communal Experiments in America* (1963).

For revivalism, the best introduction is W. McLoughlin, *Revivals, Awakenings, and Reform: An Essay on Religion and Social Change in America, 1607–1977* (1980). The first section of P. Miller, *The Life of the Mind in America, from the Revolution to the Civil War* (1966), is a brilliant study of evangelical impulses. T. Smith, *Revivalism and Social Reform in Mid-Nineteenth-Century America* (1957), emphasizes the cities. C. Griffin, *Their Brother's Keepers: Moral Stewardship in the United States, 1800–1865* (1960), deals with the rise of a benefactor class.

Two good studies on drinking and the temperance movement are W. Rorabaugh, *The Alcoholic Republic: An American Tradition* (1981); and I. Tyrrell, *Sobering Up: From Temperance to Prohibition in Antebellum America, 1800–1860* (1979).

The best introduction to abolitionism is R. Walters, *The Antislavery Appeal: American Abolitionism after 1830* (1976). Different viewpoints are contained in M. Duberman (ed.), *The Antislavery Vanguard: New Essays on the Abolitionists* (1965); J. Stewart, *Holy Warriors: The Abolitionists and American Slavery* (1976); and L. Perry and M. Feilman (eds.), *Antislavery Reconsidered: New Perspectives on the Abolitionists* (1979). Important biographies are J. Thomas, *The Liberator, William Lloyd Garrison* (1963); G. Lewis, *The Grimké Sisters from South Carolina: Pioneers for Women's Rights and Abolition* (1971); and B. Wyatt-Brown, *Lewis Tappan and the Evangelical War against Slavery* (1969). Some of the best perspectives on abolition have resulted from study of its opponents—see L. Richards, *"Gentlemen of Property and Standing": Anti-Abolition Mobs in Jacksonian America* (1970)—and from works on the struggles of northern African Americans—B. Quarles, *Black Abolitionists* (1969); and J. and W. Pease, *They Who Would Be Free: Blacks' Search for Freedom, 1830–1861* (1974).

Immigrants landing at Castle Garden. (*Library of Congress*)

CHAPTER 13

SOCIETY IN THE NORTH

Most of the developments described in the previous chapter took place in the northern states that had gradually done away with slavery. From about 1820 to the outbreak of the Civil War in 1861, the slave states south of the Mason-Dixon line began to take a separate road. There, the notion of reform and change was smothered by devotion to the status quo. James Madison and several others among the Founding Fathers had suggested that the slave/agricultural southern states had different interests from those of the free/commercial states of the North, and Madison predicted that the two regions might have difficulty in maintaining a stable union. His fears about an eventual rift proved well founded. But neither he nor any of his contemporaries foresaw how different the two regions would become.

The northern states became increasingly prosperous, expansive, and committed to manufacturing, efficient transportation, new technology, and even the mechanization of agriculture. The southern states became increasingly defensive about slavery, while people in the North became convinced that free wage labor and the family farm were the proper foundations for the young Republic. Yet the tendencies that prevailed in the North also existed in the South. No one in either section fully understood that fundamental demographic changes were taking place in American society. There were several such changes, and they affected American society in different ways.

DEMOGRAPHIC CHANGE

The Growth of Cities

Before the Revolution, the largest urban areas were, by modern standards, nothing more than small towns. The subsequent growth of those settlements was astounding. This explosion may be seen in the following table. If we take the U.S. Census Bureau's traditional definition of an urban center as a population center of 2500 or more, then in the year 1790, 5 percent of the U.S. population was urban. By 1860, that figure had risen to 25 percent.

Although tables and percentages give us information about the actual and relative growth of cities, they say nothing about what it was like to live in them. Because cities such as New York grew so rapidly, they were unable to keep up with the need for adequate supplies of unspoiled food; the disposal of garbage and of human and animal waste; drinkable water; public transportation; adequate housing; and protection against crime—services that many of us today take for granted. At the same time, the pattern of settlement in cities began to reflect differences in wealth. Poor people began to crowd into certain areas. The wealthier enjoyed far more space in their own neighborhoods.

This pattern of settlement had prevailed in urban areas for centuries, but the sheer size of the new cities emphasized the distinctions between wealthy and poor neighborhoods. Wealthy families got the new urban services first: Their garbage and trash were carried away and fresh water brought in by pipes from the new pumping stations. The poor—many of whom were recent immigrants from Europe—had their garbage and refuse left in the street, used outdoor privies, and got fresh water from a single public pump a block or more away from their tiny tenement apartments. Public transportation, which consisted of horse-drawn trolleys and, later, steam railways, became a necessity because of the long distances in these sprouting cities. Police protection, such as it was, was expanded and regularized, but the streets of New York and other large cities were probably no safer at night than they are in the 1990s.

The Dynamics of Population Growth

The growth of American cities was startling, but no more so than the growth of the American population as a whole. Nothing is more important to an understanding of American culture in this period than an appreciation of this astonishing expansion. Nothing like it had ever occurred in historic times in Europe—or, probably, in Africa and Asia. On the eve of the American Revolution, the population of the thirteen colonies was less than 2.5 million—a figure considerably smaller than the total number of people today sitting in college stadiums across the country on any given Saturday afternoon during football season. By 1790, the first year of the national census required by the Constitution, the U.S. population had risen to 4 million. By 1830s, during Jackson's first administration, it has more than tripled to 13 million. On the eve of the Civil War it was 32 mil-

POPULATION OF LARGEST U.S. CITIES, 1820 AND 1860

1820		1860	
New York and Brooklyn	130,000	New York and Brooklyn	1,079,000
Philadelphia	112,000	Philadelphia	565,000
Baltimore	62,000	Baltimore	212,000
Boston	43,000	Boston	177,000
New Orleans	27,000	New Orleans	168,000
Charleston	24,000	Cincinnati	161,000
		St. Louis	160,000

(If this table were to be expanded to include somewhat smaller cities, the concentration of urbanization in the free North would be even more apparent.)

lion, making the United States roughly as populous as Great Britain and even France, although of course smaller than Russia and especially India and China.

Sheer numbers do not tell us very much, but a little common sense will suggest certain powerful effects that this growth had on all Americans. An exploding population contributed to westward expansion. It fueled economic growth by providing an expanding work force that served a growing number of consumers. It created mounting demands for transportation, housing, food, education, consumer goods, banking and other financial services, and means of communication.

Today, of course, we are well aware that an exploding population can result in economic stagnation, poverty, and famine. Such situations are tragically common in many parts of the world. But the United States was then blessed with an enormous abundance of natural resources that made for a rising rather than falling standard of living. The principal resource was land, staggering amounts of it. Americans were able to extract enormous wealth from the land, partly by means of technological innovation (as we shall see), but partly because there were so many people, year after year, to work it and consume its bounty.

An expanding population had other effects, more subtle but no less important. It lay at the base of the kind of "mass politics" that emerged in the Jacksonian era, most conspicuously in the Log Cabin campaign of 1840. It complicated people's lives by creating the loneliness and anonymity that characterize so much of modern life. At the same time, it generated a general mood of exhilaration: America was growing in wealth, power, and maturity. And by analogy with budding crops, suckling calves, and squalling babies, who could doubt that growth was anything but improvement?

Another effect of this expansion has often gone unnoticed: The American population was beginning to age, though not nearly so fast as it has recently. In 1790 half of the American people were younger than sixteen. On the eve of the Civil War, the median age (the age at which half the people are younger and half older) was between nineteen and twenty. This was the beginning of a trend that has accelerated dramatically in recent years: Today the median age of Americans is about thirty-two and is still rising.

What generated this rapid growth of the American population? Two obvious possible causes may be ruled out. Although the birth rate remained high, it was (as we will see shortly) actually dropping steadily during this period, and it continued to do so long after the Civil War. The death rate remained roughly constant, and infant mortality still hovered at a level that was ten times today's. Second, as we saw in the previous chapter, there were no notable advances in medical practices and care, other than the development of anesthetics. Sanitation problems and overcrowding made the cities less healthy than rural areas—as had been true throughout human history. The driving engine behind the nation's population was the arrival of massive numbers of people from northwestern and central Europe.

WORDS AND NAMES IN AMERICAN HISTORY

There are numerous American folktales about frontier boatmen and woodsmen who called themselves *half-horse, half-alligator*. These were men who bragged about their toughness and bragged about bragging about it in exaggerated terms. The phrase *half-horse, half-alligator* came to be a kind of shorthand for frontiersmen in general, but particularly those of Kentucky and Tennessee. Davy Crockett was one. He was born in Tennessee and died at the Battle of Alamo in 1836. The standard reference work, the *Dictionary of American Biography*, begins all its entries with the occupations of the person whose biography is being sketched: Crockett's entry gives his sole occupation as "frontiersman," even though he served in the U.S. Congress. One of his contemporaries claimed that Crockett said the following: "I'm that same David Crockett, fresh from the backwoods, half horse, half alligator,—a little touched with the snapping turtle; can wade the Mississippi, leap the Ohio, ride upon a streak of lightning, and . . . whip my weight in wildcats, and if any gentleman pleases, for a ten dollar bill, he may throw in a panther,—"hug a bear too close for comfort, and eat any man opposed to Jackson." Historians have difficulty with such legendary quotations, because Crockett ran for office on a specifically anti-Jackson program.

Immigration

The rate of European immigration had picked up after the wars in Europe and America that ended in 1815. Immigration from Africa had been slowed to an illegal trickle after 1808, when the federal ban on the Atlantic slave trade went into effect. After 1830 immigrants arrived at an increasing rate until the depression that began with the panic of 1837. Then, in the mid-1840s, Europeans poured into northern ports and New Orleans in unprecedented numbers. The return of prosperity in the United States combined with an agricultural disaster and political persecution in parts of Europe to provide the classic pull-and-push that so often accounts for major human migrations.

In 1845 Catholic Irish peasants were devastated by a blight that struck the potato crop, the mainstay of their miserable diets. The blight brought famine that was only partly relieved by massive emigration to America. In the following decade, about 1.3 million Irish fled to the United States. Though bred to the land rather than urban life, they were usually too poor to move inland from the coastal cities where they landed, though some traveled west as laborers with canal and railroad building crews. An only slightly smaller wave of immigrants came from Germany, driven by religious and political persecution and by poverty. Some 940,000 Germans arrived, many of whom settled in midwestern cities such as Cincinnati, St. Louis, and Milwaukee. During that same decade, immigrants from Britain numbered about 375,000. Thousands of Scandinavians also came, along with smaller groups of Dutch, Swiss, Belgians, French, and Czechs.

All told, between 1844 and 1854 almost 3 million immigrants braved the Atlantic crossing. That figure amounted to three-fifths of the total immigration into the United States between 1815 and the beginning of the Civil War in 1861. The great majority of the newcomers avoided the South. Many were young, unmarried adults, which helps account for the rising age of the American population. Others came in family groups, among them independent, outspoken middle-class businessmen, lawyers, doctors, scientists, and journalists. They brought new skills, new learning, and new styles of leadership. The majority, however, were peasant families. Irish Roman Catholics usually remained in northeastern cities, especially Boston and New York. In 1855, more than half the population of New York City was foreign-born. The Germans, often led by their old-country pastors, tended to settle in the Midwest, though some established communities in the western parts of the South, especially in Texas. By 1860, 30 percent of the population of Wisconsin and Minnesota was foreign-born.

Because so many people participated in this migration, it is hard to generalize about their experiences. Most of them endured a voyage across the Atlantic that normally lasted more than a month. They slept and ate below decks in foul weather, though when the wind and seas were fair they could stand on lurching decks,

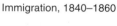

Immigration, 1840–1860

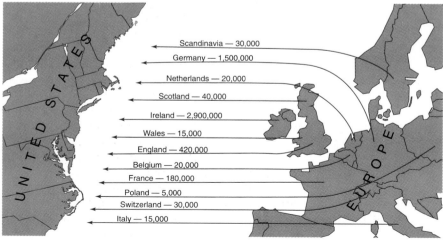

bracing themselves on the rails, and watch the white tassels of the endless waves that accompanied their passage from a familiar way of life toward one of unknown promise.

What they found in America usually differed from their expectations. On the wharves, as they got their shore legs back, they were often victimized by hucksters of all kinds who gave false promises of immediate food, housing, jobs, and hundreds of acres of farming land somewhere in the West—all for a price. It is scarcely surprising that the newcomers were confused and found it hard to make their way. It is no wonder that these European peasants huddled into city tenements, trying to reestablish their old communal ties, or banded together in the rural West, where they had better luck and better leadership.

In the cities especially, they were greeted with outright hostility. They found it hard to get jobs. Often they saw the notice "No Irish Need Apply." In turn, the Irish came to look down on free blacks. The new immigrants actually squeezed out many blacks, even from the dirtiest and lowest-paying jobs. And the Irish were not segregated or refused transportation on public streetcars, as free African Americans often were.

In large part the Irish met hostility because they were Roman Catholic. The United States was becoming a nation of even greater religious and ethnic diversity than ever before. But despite their traditional tolerance of such diversity, native-born Americans had long prided themselves on being a Protestant Christian people. Hostility to Roman Catholicism was so widespread that it eventually formed, as we will see later, the basis of a major political movement.

AMERICAN WOMEN

The Declining Birth Rate

In the early 1800s, American women began to bear fewer and fewer children. The birth rate began to drop slowly but steadily until well into the twentieth century. Without immigration, the rate of population growth would have slowed appreciably. This dropping birth rate partially accounts for the rising median age of the population, though the immigration of so many people in their late teens and early twenties also contributed.

The birth rate dropped fastest in the cities, but it dropped in rural areas as well, in the South as

well as the North. It declined faster among native-born than immigrant Americans. There seems to have been no marked increase in completely childless families, though there was a slight rise in the proportion of "old maids"—women who never married at all. But that statistical creature, the average mother, was having fewer children: six in 1800, five in 1860, and four in 1900.

In themselves, these facts do not do much to explain the causes of this new and obviously important social development. Those causes appear to have been linked with changes in the economy and especially with changing roles, expectations, and values among American mothers. These changes seem to have affected middle- and upper-class women more than poor ones. Though historians have only recently taken an interest in the matter and are not in complete agreement about it, the evidence suggests that American women felt pressure to limit the number of their children and, with or without cooperation from their husbands, were taking deliberate steps to do so.

One important source of pressure was the changing economic role of the family. In the more crowded eastern rural areas, large numbers of children were more a burden than a benefit if there was not enough land to divide among them as they grew to maturity. This was especially the case in New England, though the use of children in the cotton mills helped offset rural overcrowding. In the larger cities, children could not contribute to the productive chores that normally went with farming. Indeed those of school age could easily become an economic burden, especially as the school year lengthened. In the society as a whole, westward migration played a part in making young children seem a drag on a family's fortunes. Pulling up stakes for months of hard traveling did not make two- and four-year-olds seem much of a welcome asset.

Prevailing new ideas and values about motherhood also played a part in the declining birth rate. During the Revolution there was a perceptible shift toward a popular view that motherhood was a domestic, hearth side role, that "the Mother" of a family carried the heavy burden of shaping the early educational, religious, and moral development of the children in order to prepare them for their roles as citizens of a virtuous republic. Here, as they so often do, economic changes dovetailed with changing values. In an increasingly complex and commercial economy, the father's work was more often separated from the home. If Father was more often away, whether marketing the products of his farm or working at the shop, then Mother's role at home took on added importance.

A growing body of popular literature emphasized what has been called a "cult of domesticity" for women. Writers such as Lydia Maria Child churned out books of advice for homemakers. Male physicians published manuals warning of the dangers of repeated childbirth. In fact, these dangers were not new and were very real. What was new, was the suggestion that wives avoid having too many children, as was the suggestion to husbands that frequent intercourse would sap the energies of the male body and mind.

We may accept as a basic fact of nature that a fairly persistent pattern of sexual intercourse between fertile men and women usually results in frequent pregnancies—unless, of course, there are human attempts at intervention, reduction in frequency, or attempts at monthly timing. Although historians know much more about what went on in the halls of Congress than in American bedrooms, they have been able to show that all three means of reducing pregnancies were going on at the same time.

The term *birth control* had not yet come into use. The phrase would have shocked most Americans of this era, but in fact various means toward that end were being practiced. Probably the one most commonly used was male withdrawal before ejaculation, a practice supposedly dignified and disguised by the Latin words *coitus interruptus*. It worked to reduce pregnancies statistically, though it often failed (as it still does) in individual cases. Condoms were sometimes used, though they were hard to make, expensive, and unattractive, since they were usually fashioned from materials such as sheep and pig bladders. Vaginal tents, the forerunners of the diaphragm, were made from similar materials and were less frequently employed. Probably douching with vinegar or some other acidic substance was used more commonly than any other method of physical or chemical intervention.

What is especially striking is that deliberate "birth control" came before—and not as the result of—either public advocacy of the practice or any technological or medical innovations. The first little books that suggested and talked around, more than about, the practice were published in the early 1830s. Dr. Charles Knowlton, an English physician, published *Fruits of Philosophy* in 1831. Its appearance in the United States is often cited as the first American publication of a birth control manual. But it was not until Charles Goodyear's invention of usable rubber in 1844 that technological change began to influence the prevention of pregnancy. "Rubber" condoms came into quite widespread use in the 1850s.

Two other methods of reducing pregnancies involved no interventions. There is a bit of evidence that some couples tried timing the wife's monthly cycle, but knowledge about it and ways of detecting its occurrence were so uncertain that what is now called the rhythm method was probably nearly totally ineffective. Another method—if indeed it may be called a method—was very simply less frequent sexual activity. On this matter, there is no clear proof. Yet there are many indications that some couples were starting to fear the consequences of sexual intercourse and to engage in it less frequently. At the same time that women were being placed on a pedestal by the hearth there was an indisputable rise in the use of prostitutes by middle-class men, despite the warnings of physicians that sexual activity—with wives or whores or by masturbation—would drain a man's finite lifetime supply of energy. Of course, the prostitutes themselves had much more knowledge of longstanding lore about douching and other birth control methods than middle-class women.

Finally, it seems that abortion was becoming more common, both through crude home methods and through actual "operations" by physicians. The practice was becoming sufficiently common and recognized that several states for the first time passed laws against it, though the matter received nothing like the national attention it has had in very recent years.

Woman's Proper Sphere

The cult of motherhood and domesticity was a powerful one. Many women accepted the prevailing value that "woman" was endowed with weaker intellect than "man," even though blessed with special talents for religious piety and moral purity. Yet just when this valuation of women was being advanced most fulsomely in press and pulpit, there were signs of dissent and even outright revolt.

At the same time that woman's place was being so widely defined as "in the home," many women, especially in the North, were getting out of the home. This fact suggests that the prevailing ethic reflected anxiety about what was actually going on. During the first three decades of the nineteenth century, middle-class women in the North began to form church auxiliary groups. They met together in pious causes. The temperance movement also attracted women, who formed their own organizations to advance that good work. In the larger cities, women started Magdalene Societies with the purpose of rescuing their unfortunate sisters who had fallen into lives of prostitution. In addition, more and more women were becoming schoolteachers. All these activities reflected the prevailing view that woman's sphere was essentially moral and nurturing, but the fact remained that influential women were taking jobs and forming organizations on their own, away from the family hearth.

This quiet process went almost unnoticed until abolition burst on the scene in the 1830s. Some women enthusiastically joined that cause and then quite rapidly began to see similarities between the condition of the slave and their own. Virtually all the women who became famous in the crusade for women's rights began their careers in the abolitionist movement. As Abby Kelly Foster said: "We have good cause to be grateful to the slave for the benefit we have received ourselves, in working for him. In striving to strike his irons off, we found most surely, that we were manacled ourselves."

At first, in the 1830s, the women's movement took aim against laws that reflected prevailing ideas about male dominance and superiority. As an eminent judge accurately described such laws in 1860:

A married woman cannot sue for her services, as all she earns legally belongs to the husband, whereas his earnings belong to himself and the wife legally has no interest in them. Where children have property and both parents are living, the father is the guardian. In case of the wife's death without a will, the husband is entitled to all her personal property and to a life interest in the whole of her real estate to the entire exclusion of her children, even though this property may have come to her through a former husband and the children of that marriage still be living. If a husband die without a will, the widow is entitled to one-third only of the real estate. In case a wife be personally injured, either in reputation by slander, or in body by accident, compensation must be recovered in the joint name of herself and her husband, and when recovered it belongs to him. . . . The father may by deed or will appoint a guardian for the minor children, who may thus be taken entirely away from the jurisdiction of the mother at his death. . . .

The women's rights movement at first focused on these disadvantages much more than on the radical notion of women's right to vote. The cause of abolition triggered women's awareness that they suffered from social and legal discriminations that had nothing to do with electoral politics. Thus the abolition movement raised the issue of whether women could properly participate in what were called "promiscuous assemblies"—public meetings attended by both sexes.

Angelina and Sarah Grimké were probably the best-known of such public speakers. Both sisters moved north from South Carolina because of their unpopular antislavery views. Their outspokenness in the cause of abolition drew fire from northern clergymen who thought women ought to remain silent on matters of public interest and policy. A large group of New England ministers mounted a direct attack on their efforts in 1838:

We appreciate the unostentatious prayers of women advancing the cause of religion at home and abroad; in Sabbath-schools . . . and in all such associated efforts as become the modesty of her sex. . . . But when she assumes the place and tone of a man as a public reformer . . . she yields the power which God has given her for her protection, and her character becomes unnatural.

Such opposition was widespread; the number of men willing to back the cause of women's rights was very small. Those who did, such as Garrison and James Mott, risked ridicule. It was left to a small but growing number of women to speak out on their own behalf. They did so with vigor and eloquence. Sarah Grimké declared in 1838:

[Man] has done all he could to debase and enslave [woman's] mind; now he looks triumphantly on the ruin he has wrought and says, the being he has thus deeply injured is his inferior. . . . I ask no favors for my sex. I surrender not our claim to equality. All I ask of our brethren is that they will take their feet from off our necks, and permit us to stand upright on the ground which God has designed us to occupy.

Elizabeth Cady Stanton holding her daughter Harriot. *(Library of Congress)*

As time went on, women's rights became a campaign in its own right, independent of, yet still connected with, the abolition movement. In 1848 Lucretia Mott and Elizabeth Cady Stanton organized a Woman's Rights Convention at Seneca Falls, New York. The resulting Declaration of Sentiments was deliberately modeled on an earlier declaration: "We hold these truths to be self-evident: that all men and women are created equal . . . ." The convention was attended by sixty-eight women and thirty-two men. It was characteristic of the movement as a whole that the only resolution not passed unanimously was a demand for women's suffrage.

These middle-class women were bucking not only active opposition, but common cultural assumptions about their proper place in society. During no other period of American history was so much written about woman's proper character and sphere of influence. Her place was in the home, where she was supreme. In this prevailing view, her naturally refined nature made her first duty the moral nurture of her children and the gentle encouragement of her husband, who was said to be overly busy at the countinghouse or even, alas, at the tavern. Most women accepted this role. But the demands of a vocal minority suggested that there was growing discontent on the pedestal.

For working-class women, the issues were very different. A grueling fourteen-hour day in a factory was an issue in itself. In 1844 five women workers organized the Lowell Female Labor Reform Association, which joined with male workers in the growing movement for the ten-hour day. Within a year, six hundred women in Lowell alone had joined the association. It was in the 1840s too that Sarah Bagley became the editor of the *Voice of Industry*, the most widely read labor newspaper of the time.

Perhaps the most remarkable perspective on the problems faced by women was provided by Sojourner Truth, a former slave who became a popular speaker for abolition and women's rights. She told a women's rights convention in 1851:

That man over there says that women need to be helped into carriages, and lifted over ditches, and to have the best place everywhere. Nobody ever helps me into carriages, or over mud-puddles, or gives me any best place! And ain't I a woman? . . . .I have borne thirteen children, and seen them most all sold off to slavery, and when I cried out with my mother's grief none but Jesus heard me! And ain't I a woman?

THE AGRICULTURAL REVOLUTION

Westward Expansion

Accompanying all these social developments were economic forces that were changing the pattern of work in both sections of the nation. In the North, agriculture was becoming hitched to the machine, especially in the western portions of the free states. Mechanized agriculture first became widespread in the United States on the free family farms of the northern prairies and the eastern edges of the Great Plains. This enormously fertile country stretched from upper Indiana and Illinois north to central Wisconsin and Minnesota, then westward through Iowa and upper Missouri to the townships of eastern Kansas and Nebraska. Even more than the southern coastal plains, this lush, flat, nearly treeless terrain invited the large-scale farming that characterizes the twentieth century.

Most settlers in this region were independent small farmers front the British Isles and continental Europe or from neighboring eastern

WHAT DO WOMEN WANT?

In 1849 Lucretia Mott delivered a speech in Philadelphia that was published as "Discourse on Women." In answer to a man who had ridiculed the idea of female equality, she declared:

The question is often asked, "What does woman want more than she enjoys? What is she seeking to obtain? Of what rights is she deprived? What privileges are withheld from her?" I answer, she asks nothing as favor, but as right; she wants to be acknowledged a moral, responsible being. She is seeking not to be governed by laws, in the making of which she has no voice. She is deprived of almost every right in civil society, and is a cipher in the nation, except in the right of presenting a petition. In religious society her disabilities ... have greatly retarded her progress. Her exclusion from the pulpit or ministry—her duties marked out for her by her equal brother man, subject to creeds, rules, and disciplines made for her by his—this is unworthy of her true dignity. In marriage there is assumed superiority, on the part of the husband, and admitted inferiority, with a promise of obedience, on the part of the wife. This subject calls loudly for examination, in order that the wrong may be redressed.

Lucretia Mott. *(Library of Congress)*

states. in the mid-1840s, new settlement blossomed. Germans especially moved directly into the Middle West. Technical innovations helped the development of large-scale farming. Soon farmers found themselves dealing with the profits and problems of producing for distant markets. In the East, the continued rapid growth of the urban population also affected agricultural practices.

Tens of thousands of farm families in the Ohio Valley and on the borders of Lake Erie and Lake Michigan had been struck by the worldwide depression of the early 1840s. Debts forced them to sell their cleared and cultivated homesteads to newcomers. The government's liberal land policy encouraged them to try again farther west. They migrated in such numbers that Iowa became a state in 1846, Wisconsin in 1848, and Minnesota in 1858. Admission of Kansas was delayed until 1861 for political reasons.

Groups of families sometimes settled a particular region. But even here, the territory being so vast, farms often were a day's travel or more apart. One reason for choosing isolated

sites was the settlers' suspicion of intruders. Yet the diaries of women in this migration reveal a profound sense of loneliness. Many settlers plunked themselves down far apart because they hoped to add more land to the quarter section with which they usually started.

For most of the fifteen years before the Civil War, many of these pioneer families traveled on foot, hauling or pushing handcarts piled with their few possessions. Those who could afford the expense made the journey in wagons pulled by oxen and crowded onto barges on the Erie Canal or boats on the western rivers and the Great Lakes. Many of them suffered from "the ague," as the intermittent attacks of malaria were called.

Having picked out their land and registered it at the nearest land office, farming families built a one-room log cabin or, in treeless country, a hut made of slabs of sod. Then came a barn of the same material. They turned out a few sheep, cows, and oxen to graze on the wild buffalo grass, and fenced them off as best they could from the vegetable garden. Once he had fenced

Abraham Lincoln showing Sojourner Truth the Bible presented by African-Americans of Baltimore. *(Library of Congress)*

furniture and a touch of color in a table covering, a window curtain, or a picture on the wall.

Growing Markets and Production

These pioneer farmers were in fact the vanguard and support of a worldwide business surge. The increasingly industrial nations of Europe were no longer able to feed their growing urban populations, and they were beginning to lower tariffs on agricultural produce and to simplify the procedures of international monetary exchange. It began to dawn upon observers on both sides of the Atlantic that the United States could serve as Europe's granary, with profit for everyone.

Nor was the business ferment restricted to Europe. After 1844, American ships and the vessels of other nations gained new concessions in the treaty ports of China. In 1854, Commodore Matthew Perry, with a show of American naval power, opened up Japan to American trade. In 1856, Siam (modern Thailand) broadened the privileges given twenty years before to United States exporters. And all this stirring in the Pacific warmed American interest in Hawaii.

in his main fields, at a cash outlay of $1 or $1.25 an acre, a farmer could begin cultivation. His first discovery was that his plow could hardly scratch the heavily matted virgin soil. So at a further cost of $1.75 to $2.50 per acre, he hired professional "breakers," teams of men with huge iron plows drawn by oxen, to cut the first shallow furrows on the prairie.

In the following seasons, the farmer and his family would be able to plow and plant the land broken by the professionals. But the pioneers could hope to cultivate no more than an acre and a half a day; there was no possibility of one family fully cultivating an entire 160-acre section. Nonetheless, men who had moved their families with the idea of reestablishing an independent way of life based on self-help and Christian zeal were quite satisfied. The sheer fertility of the soil soon inundated the pioneers with surplus crops. Many of them welcomed the opportunity to market their produce for cash and to buy more land. Every farming family seemed to want to move on from the crude log cabin or musty sod hut to a neat frame house with proper

Settlement of the Middle West

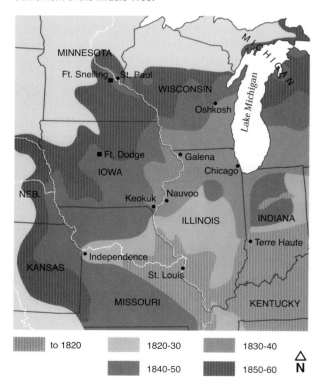

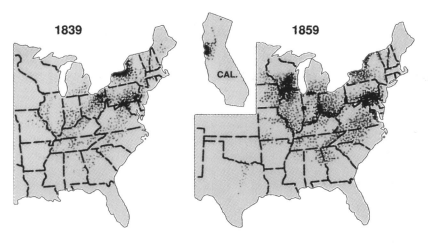

1839   **1859**

CAL.

Each dot equals 1,000,000 bushels

Wheat production, 1839 and 1859

The Orient did not become a market for American farms or for more than a fraction of the products of American factories. Yet trade with Asia contributed to American aspirations toward world power. It helped transform the American merchant marine into the world's largest fleet and its home ports into booming metropolises where, as in the great cities of Europe, millions clamored to be fed.

In the West itself farmers were finding markets at frontier forts. They sold to the loggers who had recently opened up the north woods of Wisconsin and Minnesota and to the lead miners who, after the 1830s, had extended their operations from Illinois into Wisconsin and Iowa. Gold-mining camps farther west had also begun to look to nearby farmers for flour and meal.

From the beginning of the westward movement, corn was the frontier farmer's first marketable crop. Easily converted into fattened hogs (which were commonly turned loose in the cornfields to "hog down" the ripened ears), corn could be made to walk to market. Corn also served as winter feed for beef cattle. For human consumption, corn was distilled into "likker," eaten off the cob, baked into bread, and prepared in many other ways.

Wheat was far more selective than corn in terms of soil and climate. Even in suitable latitudes, it grew best on land that had already produced a corn crop. In 1849, Pennsylvania, Ohio, and New York were the leading wheat states. Ten years later, the country's total wheat produc-

tion had soared 75 percent, and Illinois, Indiana, and Wisconsin had taken the lead. In succeeding decades, reflecting the momentum of the westward surge of wheat growing, first Iowa, then Minnesota, then Kansas, and then the Dakotas became the leaders.

Acre for acre, wheat paid better than corn, over which it had advantages in both marketing and production. Unlike corn, wheat was eaten all over the world. Less bulky than corn in relation to value, it could bear high transportation costs more easily. It also withstood shipment more successfully. Finally, on the open prairies and plains, where land was plentiful but labor scarce, wheat production responded to improved tools and laborsaving machinery.

The Business of Mechanized Farming

In 1837, John Deere, an Illinois blacksmith, produced the first American steel plow. By 1858, after making many improvements on his original design, he was manufacturing thirteen thousand a year. Light enough for a strong man to sling over his shoulder, the Deere plow could cut deep, clean furrows in the prairie sod. Nor did it take oxen to draw it. The weaker but faster-moving horse began to replace the ox on western farms.

So great was interest in plow improvement that by the time of the Civil War 150 varieties of plows were on the market. Experimenters were working on steam-powered "plowing engines" that could cut as many as six furrows at once.

Even more striking improvements were being made in machines designed for wheat growing. Cyrus McCormick of Virginia and Obed Hussey of Ohio both patented practical steel-tooth reapers in the early 1830s. With McCormick's horse-drawn machine a single man could do the work of five men equipped with scythes. Sales lagged until McCormick moved his plant to Chicago in 1848. Ten years later, by means of interchangeable parts, McCormick was producing five hundred reapers a month and still not meeting the demand.

The standardized parts were packed and shipped directly to the farmer, along with printed instructions on how to assemble them. At first, entire neighborhoods had to be mobilized to gather the vast quantities of wheat the new reapers could cut down. But in the 1850s progress was being made in the design of mechanical wheat binders, and mechanical threshers were already in use. In 1800, the average American farmer had spent about $15 to $20 for tools. By 1857, *Scientific American* was recommending that every farmer with a hundred acres of land have machinery worth about $600.

Once the farmer had committed himself to machinery, his life was greatly changed. He rapidly discovered that he was suddenly in the grip of forces over which he had little control. His principal machines, for example, such as reapers and threshers, could speed the production of wheat. But they could be used for little else when the wheat market fell off. The fact that he usually purchased these machines on credit further narrowed the farmer's range of choice.

Debts eventually had to be paid in cash, and wheat—the specialty of the new machines—was also the best cash crop. Falling wheat prices forced farmers to grow more wheat than ever, to get as great a cash return as at higher prices. But increasing wheat production often meant breaking or buying new land, which plunged them still more deeply into debt.

The continuous round of specialization, mechanization, and expansion in the free West gave a momentum to wheat production that was a priceless boon to the world. Other aspects of wheat growing, however, were hardly good for the farmer. In some years, frost, hail, and windstorms far more severe than in the East destroyed the crop before it could be harvested. Even in the best growing seasons, the servicing of distant new markets seemed to involve an endless spiral of new charges.

The steps between the wheat grower and the ultimate urban consumer, for example, seemed to multiply with distance. All along the line, weighers, graders, storage-elevator operators, rail and water carriers, warehouses, local haulers, insurers, moneylenders, and speculators—the whole apparatus of finance and distribution—mysteriously placed hands on the farmer's fate and in his pocket. The worldwide collapse of prices in 1857 staggered the wheat farmer. In 1858, western farmers began attending protest meetings. The farmer's special place in God's plan received publicity, and farmers were urged to "assert not only their independence but their supremacy" in society. Vague proposals also began to be made for farm cooperatives and for state and federal control of railroads and other big businesses.

Out of it all came a stronger demand for two specific programs. One, a favorite among reformers, was for agricultural colleges to educate farm youth in the science of agriculture and to give them broader educational opportunities as well. These colleges were to be encouraged by the federal government and financed by federal land grants. The second demand, with far broader backing among farmers, was for free homesteads—free of payment and free of slaves—on the remainder of the public domain.

Over southern opposition, Congress in 1859 enacted a bill for land-grant colleges, only to have President Buchanan veto it. Then in June 1860 he vetoed a homestead bill that would have made western lands available at twenty five cents an acre. In the elections later that year, the farmers of the West, with the slogan "Vote Yourself a Farm," helped carry the country for Lincoln.

Agricultural Revolution in the East

Right up to the outbreak of the Civil War, southern planters remained active customers of the western farmers. But the great bulk of western grain and meat flowed to the swelling population of the Northeast. So great did this volume become that the agricultural revolution in the West forced upon the East an agricultural revolution of its own.

Let the West "supply our cities with grain," said a Massachusetts man in 1838. "We will manufacture their cloth and their shoes." But he went on to point out that eastern farms could supply "what cannot so well be transported from a distance," products such as meat, butter, and vegetables. What he had foreseen developed with a rush in the following twenty years, not only in New England but also on the more friendly soil of other northeastern states. Two foodstuffs he did not list became the most profitable of all—milk and fruit.

Dairying, once a routine chore in most households, had become big business by 1850. In that year, the Harlem Railroad brought about 25 million quarts of milk into New York City. Every other sizable city in the East had developed its own "milk shed," a nearby expanse of pastureland where carefully bred and carefully tended herds of cows were reared for milk production.

Fruit orchards in the East were as common as pastures. Strawberries, blackberries, and many varieties of melons added interest to the urban American's diet. The tin can, an English invention for packaging perishables, became widely used by American fruit and vegetable merchants in the late 1840s, greatly enlarging their markets.

A revival of scientific farming in the East furthered the agricultural revolution in that section. With success depending more and more on special knowledge and the latest processes, eastern farmers took a keen interest in information about climate, soils, fertilizers, methods of cultivation, and the differences among crops. Agricultural associations, fairs, magazines, books, and schools multiplied. Thus the Northeast joined the Northwest in a spurt of agricultural innovation that placed the United States in a position of world leadership in the production of food.

TRANSPORTATION AND TRADE

The agricultural revolution helped the nation's position in the international marketplace; it also contributed to the growth of domestic trade. The huge territory of the United States was turning into a giant common market, its development free of the customs duties the various nations of Europe used to protect their own markets and products.

Foreign Trade

One of the most important commercial developments of the 1840s and 1850s was the revitalization of America's overseas trade. During the depression that followed the crash of 1837, foreign trade had fallen to a point well below the level of the early years of the Republic. In 1843, combined imports and exports were only $125 million. Then began an almost continuous rise to a record $687 million in 1860.

In almost every year during this period, imports exceeded exports. Eighty percent of the half-billion dollars in gold taken from the California mines before 1857 was sent abroad to make up the difference. The increasing export of western wheat and flour helped keep the imbalance within reasonable limits.

The revival of foreign trade greatly affected the pace of immigration. Without the vast fleets that sailed the Atlantic between Europe and America, millions of newcomers to the United States in those years could never have found passage to the New World. Seventy-five percent of American commerce and an even greater proportion of the immigrant traffic was carried in American sailing ships.

The average westward crossing by sail from Liverpool, England to New York took about thirty-five days. Ocean-going steamships, which had been used since 1838, could make this crossing in the 1850s in ten to fifteen days. But the steam vessels remained undependable and excessively costly to operate. As late as 1899, ocean steamships carried sails for auxiliary or emergency power.

Domestic Commerce

In the fifteen years before the Civil War, American domestic commerce outdid even the record foreign trade in volume and rate of growth. The vitality of foreign trading contributed to this development. The mere collection at American ports of commodities for export generated business for home carriers. Similarly, the need to distribute imports added to the demand for domestic transportation.

But domestic commerce was far more than a part of foreign trade. As the American population grew, the home market expanded. As different regions began to specialize in particular commodities, the need for exchange increased. Exchange was made easier by the gold being mined in California and by the improved credit facilities of the expanding banking system. Between 1851 and 1860, money in circulation in the

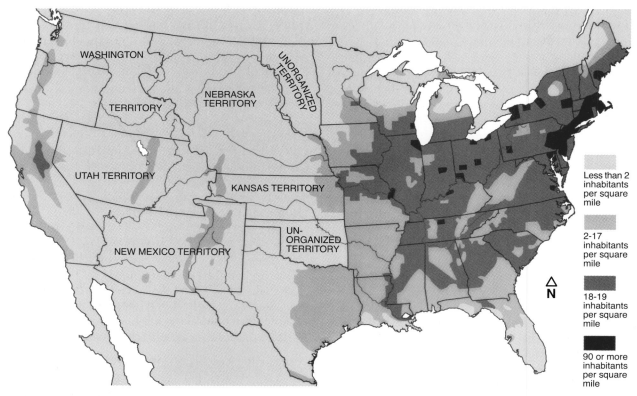

Population density, 1860

Legend:
- Less than 2 inhabitants per square mile
- 2-17 inhabitants per square mile
- 18-19 inhabitants per square mile
- 90 or more inhabitants per square mile

United States, including specie and bank notes, rose 9 percent per capita.

The importance of this increase was even greater than this figure indicates, for the telegraph and the railroads were now speeding up transactions and the collection of bills. Money in circulation could be used many more times in a single year than before. And since the amount of money itself was rising, the whole pace of domestic commerce quickened. Between 1843 and 1860, while American foreign trade grew 5.5 times, domestic trade grew 10 times.

The Clipper Ship Era

Before the railroad boom of the 1850s, domestic commerce was almost monopolized by water carriers. Of these, the oldest—and for a long time the most successful—were the coastal sailing ships. In 1852, the value of goods carried by American coastal vessels was three times the combined value of goods hauled by the railroads and on canals.

The most glamorous period of ocean commerce was the era of the clipper ship, the boldest commercial sailing vessel ever built. Designers of the clippers, among whom Donald McKay in East Boston, Massachusetts, was the master, lengthened the ordinary three-masted packet ships and drastically narrowed the ratio of beam to length. The result was the fastest and most graceful hull that ever took to the sea. The tallest masts available, spread with an enormous amount of canvas, challenged the courage of both seamen and shipmasters.

The first clippers were built early in the 1840s, in an attempt to shorten the voyage to the Orient. But they really came into their own with the discovery of gold in California. Since the clippers' designers had to sacrifice cargo space for speed, their owners had to charge higher rates for their limited cargoes than most shippers could afford. To the California adventurers, however, speed was all-important. Conventional sailing ships arriving at San Francisco in the summer of 1850 from Boston and New York averaged 159 days for the journey around the Horn. The next summer, the clipper *Flying Cloud* arrived from New York after a voyage of 89 days, 21 hours—a record not broken by a sailing vessel until 1989.

The clippers were beaten at their own game, however, just when they seemed to have perfected it. Even before the gold rush, New York steamship operators had organized an alternate route to the West Coast that took five weeks or less. This route involved an Atlantic run to Panama, portage of the cargo across the isthmus, and then a Pacific run north in another steamship.

The Great Lakes versus the Great Rivers

When the canals between east and west first were built, rivermen hoped that the artificial waterways would serve as feeders to river craft, just as the rivers fed the coastal carriers. In many eastern states, the canals did perform this function. None, of course, performed it better than the Erie Canal in New York. Yet in the long run, the Erie, along with the Ohio Canal and others completed in the West before 1837, actually took trade away from the western rivers.

By 1838, Buffalo, at the Erie's western end, was receiving more grain and flour annually than New Orleans. And once western canal construction began in the 1840s, almost every project was aimed at swinging more and more of the western trade away from the Mississippi River system and toward the North and the East. Perhaps the most dramatic shift was brought by the completion in 1848 of the Illinois and Michigan Canal, linking Chicago on Lake Michigan with La Salle on the Illinois River. The Illinois, which joined the Mississippi north of St. Louis, quickly siphoned off so much traffic that by 1850 Chicago had become a great port even though the city was still without a single railroad connection.

During the fifteen years before the Civil War, there was a struggle for control of western commerce between the Mississippi River system and the Great Lakes. The struggle paralleled the rivalry between the free and slave states for control of the West itself. By reversing the direction of southbound traffic on the Ohio, Illinois, and northern Mississippi rivers, the canals transformed these arteries into mere feeder streams. By midcentury, the canals had swung the victory to the Great Lakes.

Triumph of the Railroad

The extension of the canal system should remind us that the railroad was not so obvious an improvement over other means of inland

Clipper ship *Challenge. (Library of Congress)*

transportation as we might suppose. Practical steam locomotives had been invented in England and the United States long before 1829, when their commercial feasibility was first established. But problems of roadbed construction, track scheduling, and safety continued to harass railroad operators. Nevertheless, by 1860 Americans had built a railroad network of thirty thousand miles that was one of the marvels of the world.

Passenger trains sped along at more than twenty miles per hour. Freight trains averaged about eleven miles an hour. Almost all the 3328 miles of railroad track in the United States in 1840 lay in the Northeast and the Old South. No railroad linked the two sections, and none extended across the Appalachians to the Ohio or Mississippi valleys.

Pennsylvania, with about one-third of all the northern mileage at this time, was the nation's leader. The state government was so determined to protect its canal system that when it chartered the privately financed Pennsylvania Rail Road in 1846 for a line from Harrisburg to Pittsburgh, it required the new company to pay the state's canal administration three cents for each ton-mile of freight hauled. Second to Pennsylvania in 1840 was New York, where most of the lines lay near the eastern end of the Erie Canal or stretched westward roughly parallel to the canal itself.

Until 1851, New York, as eager as Pennsylvania to protect its canals, forbade railroads to carry freight except when the Erie Canal was frozen or otherwise closed to navigation. In 1840, New York City had only one tiny railroad, the New York and Harlem, which connected the metropolis with the independent town of Harlem, seven miles to the north.

Boston's thriving entrepreneurs, always on the lookout for new investment opportunities, tried not to allow Massachusetts to lag in railroad construction. By 1850 almost every town in the state with two thousand persons or more was served by trains. Boston became the hub of the New England railroad network. More important, rail connections with the Erie Canal now made the city a competitor for western trade. Bostonians, under the leadership of John Murray Forbes, began investing in railroads in the West, successfully transferring much of their capital from seagoing ventures to what they foresaw as a new boom in the West.

Like Boston, Baltimore was unhampered by a canal system's prior claims to western traffic, and railroad promoters were free to build. The

Baltimore and Ohio Railroad completed a route from Baltimore to Wheeling, Virginia, in 1853. Enterprising Massachusetts and Maryland jolted Pennsylvania and New York out of confidence in canals. In 1857 the Pennsylvania Rail Road bought the state canal system and the short railroad lines the state had built to feed the canals. From that time, the Pennsylvania Rail Road dominated the transportation structure of the commonwealth and much of its economic and political life. In similar fashion, the New York Central and the Erie Railroad rose to dominance in New York.

During the 1850s, the national rail network was expanded dramatically, especially within a 500-mile radius of Chicago. These roads faced more difficult conditions than those in the East, for private investment capital was scarce, distances were great, and population was sparse. By 1860 Congress had granted 18 million acres in ten states for the benefit of forty-five different railroads. With these lands as collateral, the roads were able to market bonds through Wall Street investment bankers to American and foreign investors.

During the 1850s, issues of such bonds grew so much that many New York business firms, especially those with connections abroad, gave up handling goods and became investment bankers specializing in the distribution of railroad securities. Development of the first-mortgage bond and the growth of investment banking were as important as iron and steel in the development of the western railroads.

All over the West, railroad construction knocked out canal systems and decimated river traffic. Railroad trains were faster than barges or steamboats, and railroad spurs could be laid to factory doors and warehouses. The competitive practices of railroad managers also helped. Where they encountered water rivals, the railroads cut rates to capture the available traffic. They got back their losses by charging all that the traffic would bear at noncompetitive terminals.

Two waterways survived railroad competition. One was the Great Lakes route, over which heavy freight such as wheat and iron ore could still be carried more efficiently by barge. The second was the Erie Canal. The continued use of these two waterways reflected the massive volume of the east–west trade, which needed every carrier available to meet the demands of the rising population of the western farms and the eastern cities.

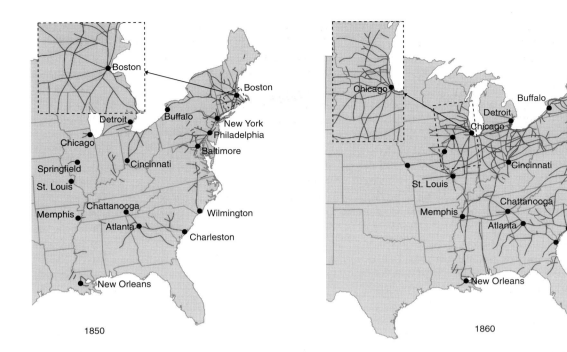

The railroad network, 1850 and 1860

As for the east–west railroads, the census of 1860 reported. "So great are their benefit that, if the entire cost of railroads between the Atlantic and the western States had been levied on the farmers of the central west, their proprietors could have paid it and been immensely the gainers." As things turned out, farmers thought otherwise.

NORTHERN INDUSTRY

In the 1850s, southern businessmen—merchants, land speculators, manufacturers, and railroad promoters—sometimes saw that their section's future lay in joining the "truly national" development of the country. Wealthy planters sometimes invested in northern land, mines, and railroads. But these men, some of whom were among the last to yield to secessionist agitators, remained a tiny minority. Northern businessmen, on their part, valued their southern connections. Almost without exception they deplored the abolitionists in their own section. Yet few of them wished to restore to New Orleans or St. Louis the commerce New York and Chicago had captured. Fewer still were willing to grant the "slavocracy" the first transcontinental railroad or the western lands it would cross.

The New Economy

As late as 1860, the richest northerners were merchants rather than industrialists. Among them was H. B. Claflin, who had built up an enormous wholesale dry-goods business on the modern principle of mass sales at low unit profits; A. T. Stewart, one of the creators of the American department store; and Charles L. Tiffany, who had made a fortune selling jewelry and silverware to other merchants. Former China traders such as John Murray Forbes supplied much of the early enterprise and capital for railroad building and for eastern manufacturing.

The first reasonably accurate census of American manufactures was taken in 1850. Its results were dramatic, for they showed that the annual output of American industry had just surpassed the value of all agricultural products, including cotton. The growth of manufacturing and of agriculture reinforced each other. As the industrial cities grew, their landless people needed to be fed. And as the number of farms increased, farm families provided an expanding market for domestic manufactures. Urban and rural communities remained intertwined. Neither could do without the other.

What characterized the new economy was its organization. Lumber mills, for example, began to specialize in the production of barrel staves or shingles or railroad ties, and to use single-purpose machines for the work. Specialization and mechanization appeared in other industries as well. In meat-packing, for example, the hams and shoulders of hogs were packed for eating and the rest of the flesh was rendered into oil for lubricants and shortening. The hog's bristles went into brushes, the blood into chemicals, the hooves into glue. What remained was ground into fertilizer. It is no wonder that Americans thought of themselves as being on the edge of a "newly efficient" age.

Another modern feature of meat-packing was the use of inclined tables, down which each carcass would slide past a stationary worker responsible for removing a particular part. This "continuous-flow" method was the beginning of modern assembly-line techniques.

A Spirit of Invention

At the 1851 fair at the Crystal Palace in London, few exhibits drew greater admiration than the display of American farm devices. Everything from road scrapers and sausage stuffers to currycombs and hayracks won acclaim for ingenuity, utility, and cheapness. Few of these inventions were ever patented, and we know hardly any of the inventors' names. Nonagricultural inventions remained far fewer than agricultural ones. But

they helped swell the number of patents issued by the United States Patent Office, which had opened in 1790. In 1835, a record number of patents (752) were issued. More than six times that number were issued fifteen years later.

One of the great inventions of the nineteenth century was the electric telegraph, for which the talented painter Samuel F. B. Morse received the first American patent in 1840. In fact, Morse borrowed heavily from previous inventors, and he did not construct the code that has since been given his name. He did, however, convince Congress to contribute money to the telegraph's development. With federal money, Morse staged the famous scene in the Supreme Court chambers in Washington in which he asked "What hath God wrought?" of a correspondent in Baltimore and got an answer.

In England, the telegraph was first used to control railroad traffic. Americans first used the telegraph for transmission of business messages and public information. Its effect on the newspaper business was immediate. The "penny press" already dominated American journalism, and printing machinery could produce 1000 newspapers an hour. With telegraphy, the demand for newspapers rose so sharply that presses needed to turn out at least 10,000 papers an hour. This volume was achieved in 1847 by a cylindrical press developed by Richard March Hoe. Other improvements in printing equipment enabled publishers to keep pace with the public's appetite for "hot news," advertising, and entertainment.

To most Americans, and to Europeans also, there seemed to be no end to Yankee inventiveness. Vulcanization of rubber was one of the most widely utilized processes. "India" rubber (most of which came from South America) had always seemed to have a unique imperviousness to rain, snow, and mud. But when exposed to heat, it melted, grew sticky, and collapsed. After years of effort, Charles Goodyear, a stubborn, impoverished New Englander, hit upon just the right mixture of raw rubber, chemicals, and heat that would yield a stable product at all ordinary temperatures. Until the automobile, Goodyear's rubber was used mainly in the boot and shoe industry.

A less dramatic but equally important invention was Elias Howe's sewing machine. I. M. Singer's long-term success lay in his innovative marketing. He tried the novel idea of installment selling, backed by advertising. Having worked up an impressive demand for his sewing machines, Singer proceeded to mass-produce them by as-

The ten leading American industries as listed in the 1860 census of manufactures are ranked here by the value of product. *(John A. Garraty,* The American Nation, *fourth edition, p. 291. Copyright © 1966, 1971, 1979 by Harper & Row, Publishers, Inc. Reprinted by permission of the publisher.)*

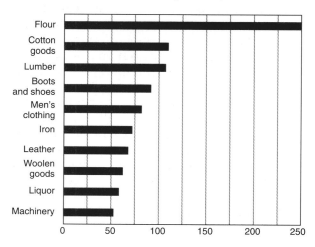

sembly-line methods. In doing so, he made possible mass manufacture of shoes and clothing.

The perfection of new machines often led to the development of entirely new industries. In older industries, such as the manufacture of cotton and woolen goods, spectacular new inventions were no longer looked for. Yet a continual round of inventions greatly speeded production and turnover. New dyes and new machines (such as the Crompton loom, which could weave patterns) added to the variety of factory-made cloth.

An Age of Iron

The whole cycle of invention—from the simple steel plow to the sewing machine—gave the American iron industry a great boost. Most of the new agricultural machinery was made from iron and steel. When the Civil War started, about 3500 steamboats had been built for the western rivers. All required iron for their boilers—and for replacement boilers after the first ones blew up. The hulls of clipper ships were reinforced with iron forms. The telegraph was strung entirely with iron wire until copper began to replace it in the 1860s. In 1850 the world's first completely cast-iron building was built in New York City. It was shortly after that, with the discovery of the far greater tensile strength of wrought iron, that the possibility of scraping the sky with a building became a reality.

By far the biggest single user of iron in the 1850s was the railroad—for rails, locomotives, wheels, axles, and hundreds of other parts. Railroads ran the most extensive machine shops in the country, making parts and repairs and their own iron and steel tools and machinery.

One of the fundamental changes in iron manufacture after 1840 was the rapid shift in fuel from wood and charcoal (half-burned wood) to anthracite (hard coal) and coke (half-burned soft coal). Much higher temperatures could be attained with these new fuels, and the rate of production was boosted to ever higher levels. Another great change was the widespread use of rolling mills in place of the hand forge for shaping iron forms. Improvements in iron working were reflected in a fourfold increase in the production of pig iron between 1842 and 1860.

Dramatic as all these steps were, the American iron industry in the 1850s developed very slowly in comparison with progress abroad. In 1860, the United States mined less iron ore and manufactured less pig iron than Britain had twenty years earlier. Britain's coal production in 1860 was five times that of the United States.

It is difficult for us today to recapture the sense of exhilaration that this new metal provided. To the industrial peoples of the world, iron was the staff of life. America's leading iron manufacturer observed: "The consumption of iron is a social barometer by which to estimate the relative height of civilization among nations." Certain scattered incidents, as we see them now, underline the immaturity of that industrial spirit. In 1829, drillers had brought in an oil gusher in Kentucky. It only terrified and angered the workmen, who had been looking for salt. Two years later, Joseph Henry worked out the essentials of the electric dynamo. But many decades were to pass before his "philosophical toy," as he called his electromagnetic machine, found practical use. It was not until after the Civil War that Englishman Henry Bessemer successfully worked out both the process and the machinery for mass steel production.

By 1860, invention and industry had just begun to transform the face of America and the character of its people. Nobody knew exactly what was taking place, but everyone was aware that the world was being rapidly transformed. By and large, people were delighted by the opening horizons. It seemed to many Americans in mid-century that the generous promise of their continent was being realized. Others were able to see only the seamy underside of the process. Even when fully employed and receiving regular wages, the members of the new industrial working class had the worst working and living conditions yet found in white America.

Thus Americans in the northern states began to realize they had important problems on their hands, problems that stemmed from a new kind of agriculture and new ways of making things. They did not fully see their difficulties, partly because new developments of this sort are hard to understand and partly because their attention became riveted on sectional tensions between the North and the South. The driving, dynamic power of economic development in the North made the South seem like another world. The South's relative lack of prosperity and its commitment to slavery caused most whites in that region to think of the northern states as an enemy. Many northerners thought that aggression was on the other side.

SUMMARY

During the pre–Civil War, or antebellum, years the United States underwent fundamental changes in its population. After 1800, and especially after 1815, the size of American cities swelled dramatically. The growth of cities created numerous urban problems that were only partially solved. The nation's total population continued to expand at a much more rapid rate than Europe's. This expansion was caused chiefly by an enormous flood of immigrants from Ireland, Germany, and Great Britain, an influx of people that reached its height in the decade after 1845.

At the same time, the American birth rate was actually dropping. This new development reflected important changes that were taking place in the role of women in American culture—in the way women were regarded by men, in the functions of women in the economy, and especially in the values and ideas women held about themselves. Through various methods of what we would now call birth control, women seem to have begun deliberately reducing the number of children they bore. At the same time, middle-class women began getting out of their homes to form women's organizations. As they worked for various pious causes and social reforms, their growing commitment to the abolition of southern slavery resulted directly in the movement for women's rights in northern states and throughout the nation. Their poorer sisters had little time for such activities, but women in factories also began to show discontent with their lives.

Even as these changes took place, another revolution was under way, this one on traditional family farms. Expansion of settlement onto the treeless lands of the western free states resulted in a new kind of farming. Growing markets for grain in the East and in Europe created an enormous demand for corn and wheat. Production of wheat, especially, helped encourage the use of newly invented farm machinery. The mechanization of farming and the longer distance from markets stimulated demand for cheap transportation, but placed farmers increasingly at the mercy of middlemen. in the northeastern states, farmers turned to fruits, vegetables, and dairy products to help feed the cities.

The new stretches of sheer distance in the expanding economy generated a pressing need for efficient transportation. Rivers, canals, and eventually railroads helped meet this demand. Coastal shipping grew in importance, and swift clipper ships added to the nation's effectiveness in international trade. For a time, there was a sectional tug in transportation developments, but eventually the new states around and west of the Great Lakes grew more tightly tied to the northeastern part of the country than to the South.

Especially during the thirty years before the Civil War, the northeastern states sprouted with new and old manufacturing enterprises. Textiles continued to be central to this development, but so did new industries that were helped by such inventions as the sewing machine

---

TIME LINE

1810	Approximate beginning of decline in the U.S. birth rate	1847	Hoe develops cylindrical steam printing press
1820	N.Y. and Brooklyn form largest city, with 130,000 people	1848	Seneca Falls Convention appeals for women's rights
1830	U.S. population of 13 million more than triples 1790 figure	1848	McCormick moves his reaper manufacturing plant to Chicago
1830s	Emergence of the women's rights movement	1850	World's first cast-iron building, in New York City
1837	Deere's first American steel plow	1851	Clipper *Flying Cloud* sets speed record, New York to San Francisco
1840	Morse patents telegraph		
1844	Formation of Lowell Female Labor Reform Association	1853	Baltimore and Ohio Railroad completed to Wheeling, Virginia
1845–1854	Massive immigration from Ireland and Germany	1857	Brief worldwide depression
1846	Howe patents sewing machine	1860	U.S. population roughly equal to those of Britain and France
1846	Admission of Iowa to statehood		

and the vulcanization of rubber. Above all, iron production lay at the base of a new industrial economy and the values that accompanied it. By 1860, industrialization had proceeded so much further in the North than in the South that the free and slave states seem almost to have become two different societies.

Suggested Readings

Demographic statistics are available in *Historical Statistics of the United States: Colonial Times to 1970* (2 vols., 1975); P. McClelland and R. Zeckbauser, *Demographic Dimensions of the New* Republic: *American Inter-regional Migration, Vital Statistics, and Manumissions, 1800–1860* (1982); and R. Wells, *Uncle Sam's Family: Issues in and Perspectives on American Demographic History* (1985).

Different and extremely interesting perspectives are offered in N. Cott, *The Bonds of Womanhood: "Woman's Sphere" in New England, 1780–1835* (1977); C. Degler, *At Odds: Women and the Family from the Revolution to the Present* (1980); F. Dudden, *Serving Women: Household Service in Nineteenth-Century America* (1983); C. Smith-Rosenberg, *Disorderly Conduct: Visions of Gender in Victorian America* (1986); J. Boydston, M. Kelley, and A. Margolis, *The Limits of Sisterhood: The Beecher Sisters on Women's Rights and Woman's Sphere* (1988); and J. Jensen, *Loosening the Bonds: Mid-Atlantic Farm Women, 1750–1850* (1986). Family limitation is considered by L. Gordon, *Women's Body, Women's Rights: A Social History of Birth Control in America* (1976); J. Molir, *Abortion in America: The Origins and Evolution of National Policy, 1800–1900* (1978); and J. Reed, *From Private Vice to Public Virtue: The Birth Control Movement and American Society* (1978). See also J. D'Emilio and E. Freedman, *Intimate Matters: A History of Sexuality in America* (1988).

Women's rights and abolition were closely connected: O. Cromwell, *Lucretia Mott* (1958), and K. Lumpkin, *The Emancipation of Angelina Grimké* (1974), discuss two women who were strong bridges between the movements.

Most of the books on economic history suggested for Chapter 10 are also important for this later period. See, in addition, C. Danhof, *Change in Agriculture: The Northern United States, 1820–1870* (1969); and the early chapters of A. Bouge, *From Prairie to Corn Belt: Farming on the Illinois and Iowa Prairies in the Nineteenth Century* (1963).

Immigration (in this and later periods, mostly to the northern states) is discussed by M. Jones, *American Immigration* (1960); and C. Wittke, *We Who Built America* (1967). An important group is presented in M. Walker, *Germany and the Emigration, 1816–1885* (1964). For the more numerous Irish , see G. Potter, *To the Golden Door* (1960); and C. Wood-ham-Smith, *The Great Hunger* (1962). For a numerically important group sometimes not thought of as immigrants, see R. Berthoff, *British Immigrants in Industrial America* (1953). O. Handlin, *Boston's Immigrants: A Study of Acculturation* (rev. ed., 1959), is an evocative recreation.

Specialized aspects of American commerce in this period are covered in R. Pineau (ed.), *The Japan Expedition, 1852–1854: The Personal Journal of Commodore Matthew C. Perry* (1969); and J. Fairbank, *Trade and Diplomacy on the China Coast* (1953), a fine account of the subtle mixture of force and diplomacy. The still stirring saga of the clipper ships is in C. Cutler, *Greyhounds of the Sea* (1930). The experience of sailing on a vessel built for the California trade was vividly recounted by R. Dana, *Two Years before the Mast* (1840). Inland water transportation is discussed in L. Hunter, *Steamboats on the Western Rivers* (1949).

In this period, railroads were beginning to take over the task of linking goods and people. See A. Fishlow, *American Railroads and the Transformation of the Ante-Bellum Economy* (1965). One of the best regional studies of railroading focused on New England: E. Kirkland, *Men, Cities, and Transportation, 1820–1900* (2 vols., 1948). The crucial importance of railroad financing appears in such works as I. Neu, *Erastus Corning, Merchant and Financier, 1794–1872* (1960); A. Johnston and B. Supple, *Boston Capitalists and Western Railroads* (1967); and S. Salisbury, *The State, the Investor and the Railroad: Boston and Albany, 1825–1867* (1967).

American society remains so locked into technological change that there is still no satisfactory overall assessment of our technological history. A great deal of suggestive information is offered in W. Kaempifert (ed.), *A Popular History of American Invention* (2 vols., 1924). The illustrations in M. Wilson, *American Science and Invention: A Pictorial History* (1954), add to an understanding of the newly technological world. R. Thompson, *Wiring a Continent: The History of the Telegraph Industry in the United States, 1832–1866* (1947), focuses on the shrinking of the continent.

On labor and banking, see the studies cited in Chapters 10 and 11. In addition, M. Walsh, *The Manufacturing Frontier: Pioneer Industry in Ante-Bellum Wisconsin, 1830–1860* (1972), presents a specialized regional study with implications for early manufacturing practices in all outlying areas.

Large group of slaves standing in front of buildings on Smith's Plantation, Beaufort, South Carolina. *(Library of Congress)*

A SOUTHERN NATION

After 1830, white southerners began increasingly to feel that they were a separate people with their own peculiar destiny. It is of course impossible to place the beginnings of southern nationalism at any exact date, but certainly by the 1850s it was apparent to many southerners, including some slaves, that their society was on a collision course with the North.

All southerners knew, however vaguely, that their region was different from the rest of the nation: different by reason of slavery, a large number of African Americans, fewer immigrants from Europe, fewer Roman Catholics, and a less rapidly expanding population. Some were also conscious that their economy was tied to cotton and other agricultural staples and that they lagged behind the North and Great Britain and France.

Many southern Americans, of both races, developed a deep attachment to their localities in the countryside—a commitment to home ground and to the way the sky looked and the land smelled. Sometimes knowing it and sometimes not, they grew defensive about their accomplishments. For purposes of analysis, it is useful and necessary to consider various separate aspects of southern culture in the antebellum period. But when we speak of "southerness"—of slavery, race, monoculture, economic dependency and intellectual stagnation, intolerance and violence, hospitality and gallantry—we risk taking apart a culture and not being able to get it back together again. In fact, it had great coherence, even though racial antagonisms were a fatal flaw. That coherence became evident in the 1850s and the war that followed.

WHITE PEOPLE OF THE SOUTH

Richard Hildreth, a New England historian, visited the South in the 1830s and then published a book, *Despotism in America; or, An Inquiry into the Nature and Results of the Slave-Holding System in the United States.* Within the "great social experiment of Democracy" in America, he found the South to be "another experiment," less talked about, less celebrated, but not the less real or important. It was "the experiment of Despotism." The southern states, he wrote, "are Aristocracies; and aristocracies of the sternest and most odious kind."

Hildreth saw only two classes in the South: the privileged planters and all lesser whites, on the one hand, and their "hereditary subjects, servants and bondsmen," on the other. "Extremes meet," he added. "Ferocity of temper, idleness, improvidence, drunkenness, gambling—these are vices for which the masters are distinguished, and these same vices are conspicuous traits in the character and conduct of slaves"

This was the image of Dixie in many of the abolitionist tracts of the day. Some southerners tried to expose the excessive simplicity of the image and thereby discredit it. The section's aggressive defenders, following the lead of Calhoun, preferred an equally simple approach, a meeting of extreme with extreme, the better to convey an alternative image of their own. Calhoun told Congress:

This agitation [against the slave system] has produced one happy effect at least; it has compelled us in the South to look into the nature and character of this great institution, and to correct many false impressions that even we had entertained in relation to it. Many in the South once believed that it was a moral and political evil; that folly and delusion are gone; we see it now in its true light, and regard it as the most safe and stable basis for free institutions in the world.

Southern Farmers

Southern society was actually far more complex than the simple pictures sketched by Hildreth and Calhoun. There were wealthy and aristocratic planters, but not many. Easily the largest group of whites were simple farmers who labored with their families on their own land to produce their own food and clothing and the small amount of extra produce necessary for a little cash. A smaller but important group of whites owned one or several slaves. On their somewhat larger farms, blacks and whites labored and lived together. The "poor white trash," disease-ridden folk reduced to scratching subsistence from marginal lands or no land at all, were a minority of southern whites.

The farms of the plain people of the South were sometimes tucked away among the large plantations in the cotton and tobacco country, but they predominated in the upland South—in eastern Tennessee, western North Carolina, northern Georgia, Alabama, and Mississippi. There, while some produced the southern staples, most grew subsistence crops—corn, squash, greens, beans, sweet potatoes—and raised livestock and cut lumber. The plain people also included the storekeepers, the mechanics, and other artisans in southern villages and towns.

Seen through the perceptive eyes of Frederick Law Olmsted, a Connecticut Yankee who traveled through the South in the early 1850s, living standards seemed distinctly below those of northern farmers. And yet, though Olmsted complained of wretched cooking, vermin-filled beds, and rough manners, he also noted that these people were hospitable. "If you want to fare well in this country," he was told in northern Alabama, "you stop to poor folks' houses; they try to enjoy what they've got while they ken, but these yer big planters they don' care for nothing but to save."

Riding through an area of thin, sandy soil, Olmsted reported:

The majority of dwellings are small log cabins of one room, with another separate cabin for a kitchen; each house has a well, and a garden enclosed with palings. Cows, goats, mules and swine, fowls and doves are abundant. The people are more social than those of the lower country, falling readily into friendly conversation . . . They are very ignorant; the agriculture is wretched and the work hard. I have seen white women hoeing field crops today. A spinning-wheel is heard in every house . . . every one wears home-spun. The negroes have much more individual freedom than in the rich cotton country, and are not infrequently heard singing or whistling at their work.

Among such farmers, as one who grew up in Mississippi reported, "people who lived miles apart, counted themselves as neighbors, . . . and

Unlike the wealthy aristocrats, the majority of southern white farmers lived in humble homes, like this one drawn in 1838 by the French naturalist Francis Comte de Castelnau in his travels through the backcountry. *(Library of Congress)*

in case of sorrow or sickness, or need of any kind, there was no limit to the ready service" they gave to one another.

Among the white population there was also considerable cultural diversity. There were the French Creoles and Cajuns in Louisiana, fiercely independent hill folk in the Ozarks and Appalachia, and Irish and German wage laborers. Though it was overwhelmingly rural, the South also had business and professional men—doctors, lawyers, editors, ministers, and industrial and commercial entrepreneurs—as well as artisans and industrial laborers.

In many parts of the South the growing season was too short for cotton, too cold for rice and sugar. It snowed every winter, and even animals needed sheltering barns. Yet the characteristic and distinguishing feature of the southern climate was the prevailing heat. If the weather drew the southerner outdoors, the terrain and what it held helped keep him there. All across the Cotton Kingdom stood dense forests that rewarded the hunter with game. As late as 1860, a large part of the slave's labor was clearing new land for cultivation. Thousands of creeks and ponds provided a choice of fish. The region was also well endowed with navigable streams to carry cotton and other staples to export centers.

Despite the popularity of hunting, trapping, and fishing in the South, the region also had men who strove just as hard as any Jacksonian busi-nessman to make their way up in the world. The Cotton Kingdom was not extended in a single generation from South Carolina to Texas by men content to loaf and dream at home. A typical Red River planter, asked to buy a "Bible Defence of Slavery," shouted: "Now you go to hell! I've told you three times I didn't want your book. . . . I own niggers; and I calculate to own more of 'em, if I can get 'em, but I don't want any damn'd preachin' about it."

The violence of white southern life has perhaps been exaggerated, but the "Arkansas toothpick" (as the Bowie knife was sometimes called) became one of the principal instruments for settling differences in the rougher sections. Even in the older and more settled regions, the dueling code prevailed.

The Planter Class

In 1860, three-fourths of southern whites owned no slaves at all. Almost half the slaveholding families owned fewer than six slaves, and only 12 percent of all slave owners possessed twenty or more. The real "planting class" was actually a very small minority. A mere eight thousand planters owned fifty or more slaves.

There were, in addition, important regional differences in slaveholdings. In the six states of the lower South (except Texas), between one-third and one-half of the white families owned slaves. Elsewhere the proportions ranged from only one-thirteenth to one-fourth. Within each state, large plantations were concentrated in areas with the most fertile soil and the best access to water transportation.

Some large planters lived the high life of saber-rattling, fire-breathing "cavaliers." In their youth, sons of the well-to-do were often sent West with the hope that they might settle down on plantations of their own. Many did. But many more found room for recklessness and violence. Those who were determined to develop their lands spent many years in crude surroundings. The sawmill came late to Alabama, Mississippi, and Louisiana. Even in the 1840s and 1850s, some planters continued to live in "two-pen" log houses with crevices between the unhewn logs that let in the light, wind, and rain.

In the older South many of the gentry lived well—some extravagantly. Most were devoted to the simple pleasures of rustic society: hunting, horse racing, card playing, visiting, and perhaps an annual summer pilgrimage to the mountains or the sea to escape the heat. Many men found time for politics, and the planting class dominated southern political life, just as it dominated the southern economy.

Susan Dabney Smedes's account of her father conveys many of the ideals of the highest class of whites. Humane, upright, generous, and courteous, Mr. Dabney was deeply concerned with sick slaves, the price of cotton, and unreliable overseers. "Managing a plantation," Mrs. Smedes observed, "was something like managing a kingdom. The ruler had need of great store, not only of wisdom, but of tact and patience as well." Nor did the planter's wife escape the domestic duties of supervising and sometimes nursing slaves.

BLACK PEOPLE OF THE SOUTH

Negro slavery had taken root in the South because Africans provided a cheap and readily available labor force to cultivate staple crops. Prior to the cotton gin (1794), slaves were concentrated in eastern Virginia and in lowland South Carolina and Georgia. With the westward expansion of upland cotton and with the federal prohibition of the Atlantic slave trade in 1808, there began a massive forced movement of slaves into Alabama, Mississippi, Louisiana, and beyond.

This domestic slave trade meant that hundreds of thousands of African Americans were uprooted from their homes in Virginia and elsewhere in the East and forced into the role of land-clearing western pioneers. Some were carried on ships to ports such as Mobile, Alabama, and New Orleans and to river towns farther up the Mississippi and its tributaries. Probably more were forced by slave traders to walk the entire distance on the dusty trails of southern meadows and forests.

Most of these uprooted people were thrown onto large cotton and sugar plantations. Indeed, the slaves (unlike whites) typically lived on factory-like plantations. On the eve of the Civil War, more than half the slave population lived in units with more than twenty slaves, about one-quarter in units of more than fifty. Slaves were concentrated in the richest agricultural regions. In some counties of the lower South, they greatly outnumbered whites. Only about 10 percent lived in cities and towns. Slaves were also employed in factories and in river commerce.

In fact, just before the Civil War, about 6 percent of the blacks in the South were technically not chattel slaves at all. These "free negroes" were concentrated in the upper South and to a

WORDS AND NAMES IN AMERICAN HISTORY

Hoecake was a common dish in the eighteenth and nineteenth centuries. It was commonly associated with blacks, because hoecake was sometimes all that slaves had to eat at a hasty meal. Hoecakes were flat "cakes" of ground corn, which the Algonkian Indians and later many other Americans called *hominy*. Rather than cooked on a pan, or grill, like our pancakes, they were spread on the business end of a hoe and held over a fire of hot coals. White people in the South also ate hoecakes. Sometimes, more commonly in the North, this food was called *johnnycake*. Some scholars think this term was a corruption of *journey cake*, since there are literary references to the use of this dish by travelers. A modern book on the diet of slaves is aptly entitled *Hog Meat and Hoe Cake*.

lesser extent in the cities of the lower cotton areas. While they were technically free, they lived in a world of legal, social, and economic marginality.

These circumstances profoundly affected the lives of both blacks and whites. The predominance of large plantations meant that the principal social contacts of many African Americans were with other African Americans. And it meant that the families of the wealthy planting class, more than other whites, had direct contact with masses of slaves. Many blacks grew up somewhat isolated in their own Afro-American subculture. And the South's ruling class was raised in intimate contact with the actual workings of the slave system, with all its ambiguities of friendship, distrust, hostility, and fear.

Another characteristic of the black population immediately preceding the Civil War also had important implications for both peoples. By 1860, despite some smuggling of slaves from Africa, the overwhelming majority of American slaves were native-born, as had not been the case a century earlier. The black population was Afro-American, not African. From birth, for example, slaves spoke English, though in their own dialects. All this meant that the cultural distance between blacks and whites had narrowed.

The Slave's Outer World

Frederick Douglass was born and bred a slave in Maryland. He had various masters and mistresses, both kind and brutal. Of one especially harsh master Douglass recalled in his autobiography:

Frederick Douglass. *(Library of Congress)*

If at any one time of my life more than another, I was made to drink the bitterest dregs of slavery, that time was during the first six months of my stay with Mr. Covey. We were worked in all weathers. It was never too hot or too cold: it could never rain, blow, hail, or snow, too hard for us to work in the field. Work, work, work, was scarcely more the order of the day than of the night. The longest days were too short for him and the shortest nights too long for

---

DOUGLASS ON SLAVERY

As a young slave in Maryland, Frederick Douglass had several different masters. One of them, a man named Covey, had a reputation of being a "slave breaker." In his autobiography, Douglass admitted that Covey had temporarily broken his spirit. But then he went on to generalize about the effects of his being owned by a less brutal master.

Not withstanding all the improvement in my . . . home and my new master, I was still restless and discontented. . . . When entombed at Covey's and shrouded in darkness and physical wretchedness, temporal well-being was the grand desideratum, but, temporal wants supplied, the spirit

put in its claims. Beat and cuff the slave, keep him hungry and spiritless, and he will follow the chain of his master like a dog, but feed and clothe him well, work him moderately and surround him with physical comfort, and dreams of freedom will intrude. Give him a bad master and he aspires to a good master; give him a good master, and he wishes to become his own master. Such is human nature. You may hurl a man so low beneath the level of his kind, that he loses all just ideas of his natural position, but elevate him a little, and the clear conception of rights rises to life and power, and leads him onward.

him. I was somewhat unmanageable when I first went there, hut a few months of this discipline tamed me. Mr. Covey succeeded in breaking me.

Yet in actuality Douglass was never completely broken. His early life was unusual in its variety of owners and experiences, and with some help from whites he learned to read and write. He was also an enormously talented man. Eventually he escaped from slavery and went on to become the most famous black abolitionist and champion of racial equality.

Although his life as a slave was far from typical, he and millions of others would have appreciated the later words of Paul Lawrence Dunbar, son of another fugitive slave:

A crust of bread and a corner to sleep in,
A minute to smile and an hour to weep in,
A pint of joy to a peck of trouble,
And never a laugh but the moans come double:
*   And that is life!*

Douglass's own recollection caught the essence of life for slaves on most plantations: unremitting toil. On the characteristic Black Belt plantation, as elsewhere, the field hand's routine varied little from day to day, year to year. The day's work lasted, as the saying went, from "can see, 'til can't," with short breaks for breakfast and lunch, which were brought to the men and women in the fields. Physically, the heaviest work was clearing the land, or "rolling logs"; anyone who has ever chopped down a tree knows that the real work has just begun.

But plowing behind a stubborn mule, weeding or "chopping" the endless rows, and finally picking the bolls of their white fiber without including in one's bag too much in the way of brown leaves and stalks—this routine, twelve to sixteen hours a day, was the slave's life. And whether the master or overseer was brutal or kindly, this labor was forced. One of the commonest causes for a whipping was picking underweight or "trashy" cotton.

A slave and his home. *(Library of Congress)*

The treatment of slaves ranged all the way from hideous sadism to gentle paternalism. On some plantations, slaves found themselves continually beaten; on others, never. Some slaves were always hungry; others ate nearly as well as the white folks. Some slaves were so poorly clad and housed that they drew sympathy from neighboring whites and blacks. Others lived so well that they were envied by poor whites and exhibited as model specimens to visiting foreigners. The major cause of this variation in treatment was not so much the region or plantation size, as the personalities involved.

On large plantations, the slave's principal contact with authority was usually with the overseer, whose personality made a great difference. But at least in the long run, the owner and the slaves decided what kind of overseer they would tolerate. The size of the crop depended on a subtle and complicated balance among slave drivers, field hands, artisans, house servants, hired white laborers, overseers, and slave masters and their wives and children. Any person involved in this human equation had at least some power to alter its dynamics. The weight of power, of course, lay with whites. But they were rarely in full control.

Generalizations about "the slave experience" keep breaking down along these lines. But it is possible to make certain summary statements. Slaves were treated with greater severity in the frontier Southwest than in the older South. Slaves on large plantations were confronted with more impersonal, though not necessarily more severe, discipline than slaves on small plantations. There were greater class and occupational distinctions among slaves on large plantations than on small ones.

The distinction between house servants and field hands was never absolute. But as time went on, there was a tendency for slave children to inherit the skills and status of their parents. Slaves in the old upper South and on small farms were more likely than others to have their lives disrupted by sale away from homes and families.

The family life of slaves has been a matter of debate among historians. In the eyes of the law there was no such thing as binding marriage between slaves, and slave children might be sold away from their parents. In practice, however, although a great many families were broken up, a far larger number managed to survive as much intact as other nineteenth-century families. Slaves wanted, and many masters actively en-

Wash Wilson, slave. *(Library of Congress)*

couraged, a stable family life with children raised by their parents, all under the same roof. On large plantations, this was the usual pattern. On smaller units, the husband was likely to live on a neighboring plantation, able to see his family once or twice a week, under protection of a written pass from his owner. So despite the absence of legal protection and the informality of marriage ceremonies—which often consisted of "jumping over the broomstick"—many slaves were able to maintain loving and nurturing family relationships.

Many of these families lived under the threat of disruption because of sexual advances by white men. Sometimes it was a matter of outright rape. Sometimes there developed long-standing, affectionate relationships between white men and black women. Undoubtedly the most common situation was simply some variety of the sexual exploitation that takes place when men are powerful and women are helpless.

African American men could do little, of course, to defend their sexual interests, and they knew better than to approach white women. The

Slave family in front of their wooden house. *(Library of Congress)*

restrictions on white women were equally clear: They had all the advantages and disadvantages of being confined to the top of a pedestal.

The Slaves' Inner World

Hemmed in as they were on so many sides, slaves struggled to create a measure of independence. Some took fierce pride in productivity; others took an equal satisfaction in malingering. Some boasted of their capacity for bearing punishment; others claimed skill at avoiding it. A great many sought the comforts of religion. It was an ambiguous refuge. Christianity could be used as a handbook for revolutionary action. For the most part, though, slaves adopted their own kind of Christianity to make their own communities partially independent of the white world.

Here again they were under pressure. After 1830, whites began to push upon slaves a brand of Christianity that supposedly would keep them docile. White preachers told slaves to serve their masters obediently, and that it was their Christian duty to do so. Left to themselves, however, slaves heard a very different message, one that fused eternal salvation with earthly freedom.

Music was frequently used by slaves to heighten shared feelings within the community.

In no other arena of activity was their common West African background more obvious. Sometimes the occasion was religious, as at a wake described by an elderly former slave:

When a nigger died, we had a wake an' dat was diffrunt too from what 'tis today. At de wake we clapped our han's an' kep' time wid our feet—Walking Egypt, day call hit—an' we chant an' hum all night til de nigger was funeralized.

Singing and dancing were part of a wide variety of activities: prayer meetings, quilting bees, corn shuckings. There were ax songs, boat songs, and children's ring dance games. What is perhaps most remarkable about the words of these songs is that there was no clear dividing line between sacred and secular concerns. One common theme runs through a great many of the songs: a resigned desire for a better life.

I know moon-rise, I know star-rise,
  Lay dis body down.
I walk in de moonlight, I walk in de starlight,
  To lay dis body down.
I'll walk in de graveyard, I'll walk through de graveyard
  To lay dis body down.
I'll lie in de grave and stretch out my arms;
  Lay dis body down.

A FORMER SLAVE ON RELIGION

In the 1930s an elderly ex-slave recalled religious practices on his old plantation:

Dey did allow us to go to church on Sunday about two miles down de public road, and dey hired a white preacher to preach to us. He never did tell us nothing but "Be good servants, pick up old marse and old misses' things about de place, don't steal no chickens or pigs, and don't lie about nothing." Den dey baptize you and call dat you got religion. Never did say nothing about a slave dying and going to Heaven. When we die, dey bury us next day and you is just like any of *the other cattle dying on de place . . . We used to slip off in de woods in de old days on Sunday evening way down in de swamps to sing and pray to our liking. We prayed for dis day of freedom. We come from four and five miles to pray together to God dat if we don't live to see it, to please let our chillen live to see a better day and be free. . . . And we'd sing "our little meetin's about to break, chillen, and we must part. We got to part in body, but hope not in mind. Our little meetin's bound to break." Den we used to sing "We walk about and shake hands, fare you well my sisters, I am going home."*

"Never," said a northern officer when he first heard those words in an army camp of black troops during the Civil War, "since man first lived and suffered, was his infinite longing for peace uttered more plaintively than in that line."

Slave Resistance and White Response

Slaves also dealt with the circumstances of their lives by actively resisting the system. Throughout two centuries of slavery, slaves malingered, broke tools, abused farm animals, feigned illness, and otherwise struck out at the principal requirements of the system: hard work and productivity. There were instances of slave women remaining "pregnant" for eleven months without producing a child. Slaveholders responded with a combination of punishments and rewards, although planters disagreed about which was more effective.

From the planters' point of view, the worst problem was running away. After about 1800, slaves in the upper South sometimes headed for freedom in the northern states. A far more common pattern involved slaves running off for a few days or weeks in the woods and then returning to face a whipping. Many runaways did not run "away" at all; they left their owner's plantation in an attempt to rejoin a spouse or other relative.

Slavery rested on a base of violence, and slaves sometimes responded in kind. There were just enough instances to keep the white population thoroughly on edge. Two of the most effec-

tive and drastic means at the slaves' disposal were arson and poisoning. Probably more common were the many instances when a slave suddenly and simply decided that he would rather fight and die than be whipped.

Some paid with their lives for their courage, but a surprising number fought their overseers to a physical and psychological standoff. Sometimes a slave might be pressed beyond the brink of rational judgment and turn upon an oppressor with a hoe or an ax and split his head open. The penalty for such "murder" was, of course, death.

Despite the overwhelming odds against them, slaves also conspired in armed rebellions. Most of these uprisings involved half a dozen to twenty-five slaves, and most were stopped when whites were told ahead of time by a slave unwilling to go along with the rebels. The most important rebellions (as opposed to panics and rumors among whites) occurred during a forty-year period following the example of the successful slave uprising in Haiti.

A flurry of conspiracies in the 1790s led up to the Gabriel plot outside Richmond in 1800. Slaves armed themselves and gathered to march on the city, but the plot was ruined by informers and a violent rainstorm. Gabriel, "the mainspring and chief mover," and about thirty others were hanged as examples. White Virginians were badly shaken. In 1822, a Charleston freedman, Denmark Vesey, organized another large rebellion. It was also betrayed and followed by some forty public hangings.

Nat Turner, a Virginia slave preacher, led the most drastic slave revolt. He took his followers on a route of killings through Southampton County in 1831 and left some sixty white people dead. Terrified whites, who regarded Turner as a fanatic, lashed back by tracking down the rebels and killing many on the spot. In the process, one or two hundred blacks who had no connection with the rebellion were slaughtered. Turner himself remained at large for a month but was finally caught, tried, and hanged.

The impact of Turner's revolt was immediate and long-lasting. The reports of suppression and bloody reprisals carried a disheartening message across the black South. The white South sharpened its defenses as abolitionist propaganda spread. Even planters rode night patrols, whiskey often giving them courage against the terrors of darkness. In the towns and cities, police costs "for the purpose of 'keeping down the niggers,'" as one traveler reported, made up the largest item in municipal budgets. Olmsted wrote that in nearly every southern city he visited, "you come to police machinery such as you never find in towns under free governments: citadels, sentries, passports, grapeshotted cannon, and daily public whippings . . . for accidental infractions of public ceremonies."

"Free people of color," along with abolitionists, came increasingly under suspicion in the South. Many black preachers among the slaves were silenced. Indeed, the religious language in which slave rebels exhorted their followers convinced many planters that Bible reading—in fact any reading—was downright dangerous. Many states outlawed teaching slaves to read and write. Yet many slaves persisted in study and in individual strikes for freedom, despite the hostility of their environment.

THE PLANTATION ECONOMY

Everyone in the South, of whatever color, age, sex, or status, was affected by the workings of the plantation economy. Cotton, of course, was by far the most important crop, but in certain regions other staples predominated. In the South Carolina–Georgia low country, long-staple cotton surpassed rice as the most important crop. Upland cotton held sway in the lower tier of southern states, except in southern Louisiana, where sugar cane was the dominant staple. In the upper South the growing season was normally too short for cotton. Very little

was grown, and states such as Virginia and Kentucky relied on tobacco and hemp along with fruits and grains.

Secondary Staples

Of course the first southern agricultural staple had been tobacco in the Maryland and Virginia tidewater region. After 1800, tobacco culture spread westward across the upper South. By midcentury, more tobacco was being grown there than on the older plantations. Yet after 1850 Virginia, North Carolina, and Maryland made a spectacular comeback in tobacco production. A slave who was an overseer and blacksmith on a North Carolina plantation discovered a method of curing a type of "bright yellow" tobacco that grew better on the poor, sandy soil of the Roanoke Valley and inland Maryland than on the worn-out soil of the Tidewater. Large plantations once again flourished in the Old Dominion and in neighboring states. Yet compared with cotton, tobacco remained a minor southern crop.

The boom in tobacco benefited both large and small farmers. The latter were most successful with hemp, another source of profit, especially in Kentucky and Missouri. Only the wealthier planters, however, could successfully produce rice or sugar, the South's two other lesser staples. Both crops required gang labor, easily drawn from the dense slave populations of South Carolina and Georgia. These plantations were unmatched in scale even by those of the Gulf states of the Cotton Kingdom. In 1860, the only estate with more than a thousand slaves was in the South Carolina rice country.

Cane-sugar planting made great headway after 1822, when steam engines were introduced to crush the cane. Only large plantations could support the cost of the machinery, and the cane required an exceptionally long growing season. Both conditions were fulfilled in the warm, rich lands of southern Louisiana. It was in this area that French influence was still strong. An unusual ethnic intermixture combined with the climate to create a special cultural subregion for both blacks and whites.

Harvesting and grinding the cane demanded intensive periods of the hardest labor by slave gangs and white and African American craftsmen. During the late autumn and early winter "grinding season," the vats were kept fired

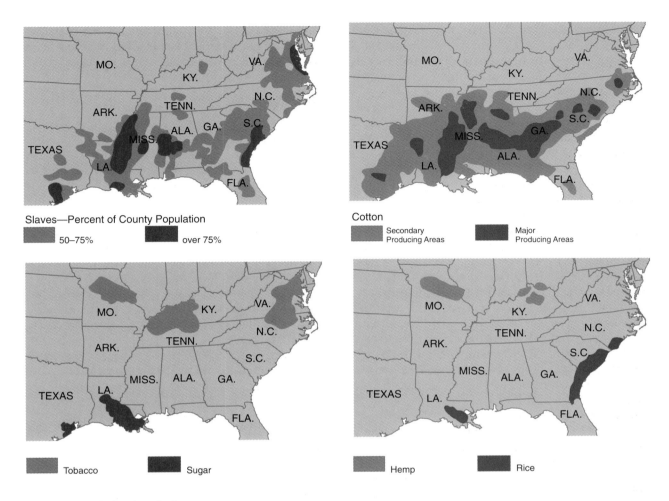

Slaves—Percent of County Population

■ 50–75% ■ over 75%

Cotton

■ Secondary Producing Areas ■ Major Producing Areas

■ Tobacco ■ Sugar

■ Hemp ■ Rice

Slavery and agricultural production

twenty-four hours a day, and slaves worked nearly around the clock. (Even today, sugar mill workers put in twelve-hour shifts.) At the same time, the complicated process of sugar refining provided exceptional opportunities for slaves to acquire mechanical skills and the self-respect that went with them.

King Cotton

As early as 1820, the South's cotton crop had become more valuable than all its other crops combined. By 1835 the Cotton Kingdom had spread more than a thousand miles from South Carolina and Georgia into Texas and some seven hundred miles up the Mississippi Valley. Just before the Civil War, cotton accounted for two-thirds of the nation's exports.

With a little capital, small acreage, and a few slaves, a cotton farmer could still make a profit. Cotton could survive rough handling during shipping, and it did not spoil when stored. These were important considerations where poor transportation and warehousing caused marketing delays. Some of the American cotton crop, even on the frontier, was grown by small farmers. Yet cotton, with its huge market and great adaptability to gang labor, was the ideal staple for the big planters who spread over the virgin lands of the Southwest.

By 1860, slave gangs were growing more than 90 percent of the Mississippi crop. Where land was plentiful and cheap but labor was not, the essence of good plantation management was high production per slave rather than per acre. Under effective overseers and slave drivers, the more slaves a planter had, the greater his margin of success with cotton.

Large-scale operations gave large planters other advantages as well. They could purchase necessities they could not grow or make on the plantation in large quantities at wholesale rates. They could also market their crops more efficiently. Wealthier planters, moreover, were more likely to be interested in conserving the soil and more willing to experiment with new agricultural techniques.

White southerners were familiar with the contrasts drawn even by their own spokesmen between the busy North—enterprising, public-spirited, prosperous—and the indolent, poverty-stricken South. But many of them still feared the impact of factories on an agrarian slave society. Some felt that slaves working in a factory were already half-free. Despite much evidence to the contrary, others believed that blacks were incapable of mastering machinery. Many still harbored the distrust of cities that Jefferson had expressed so vividly a half-century earlier.

Despite such doubts and apprehensions, a favorable attitude toward manufacturing developed during the 1820s and early 1830s, when tariff debates made the South conscious of its dependence on the North. Factories, it was said, would furnish employment for unproductive poor whites and help keep southern wealth at home.

Yet while there were some attempts at establishing cotton mills, the South remained overwhelmingly agricultural. Between 1850 and 1860, the number of industrial workers in the South rose only from 165,000 to 190,000. On the eve of the Civil War, the South was producing less than 10 percent of the nation's manufactured goods. In 1860, the Lowell mills alone operated more spindles than all the cotton-spinning factories of the South.

The region showed even greater aversion to commerce. At the numerous commercial conven-

Large group of slaves standing in front of buildings on Smith's Plantation, Beaufort, South Carolina. *(Library of Congress)*

tions held in the South between 1830 and 1860, the southern imagination was fired with visions of teeming cities, happy artisans, and bustling markets—all to be the reward of recapturing the cotton-carrying trade from the North. But financial control of cotton marketing remained in the hands of outsiders. It was not southerners who held the reins of insurance, shipping, brokerage, and banking; the capital of the Cotton Kingdom was actually New York City.

THE VALUES OF SOUTHERN WHITES

Slavery discouraged diversity in agriculture. It also accelerated the migration of southern farmers from the upper South into the western free states and gave rise to a false prosperity based on long-term credit, declining fertility of the soil, and expensive slaves. Yet after 1830 the allegiance of the vast majority of white southerners to the slave plantation system deepened. Their attachment varied according to class, region, and occupation, but a general consensus emerged. It depended heavily on economic self-interest, racial hostility, and the realization that slavery was under attack.

Commitment to White Domination

The consensus that supported slavery was in turn supported by certain important beliefs. The high concentration of slaves in certain parts of the South generated deep-seated fears among whites who found themselves in a minority. In response to northern abolitionists, southern spokesmen replied that people living in the North, where blacks made up only a small fraction of the population, could not possibly know what things were like in South Carolina or Mississippi communities.

Many whites in the South really thought that slaves would be harmed by abolition. This belief was strengthened by reports about the condition of free blacks in the North. Everywhere in the free states, African Americans were abused and discriminated against politically, economically, and socially—and then blamed for their situation. The evidence of abuse and discrimination was so plentiful that abolitionists found it very difficult to refute.

White workers in southern cities and factories, like most northern working men and women, did not want to work alongside blacks, slave or free. They shared the common human tendency to exclude identifiable groups of "other" people from the labor market so as to reserve it for themselves. At the same time, small planters, linked to the planting class by kinship or common interest, felt that their chances of rising in the world would be crippled by abolition. They, and many farmers too poor to own slaves, shared the common assumptions of the Jacksonian era. They hoped they might rise in the world and one day become masters of larger plantations.

Impoverished southern whites supported slavery as a way of preserving what little status they had. Olmsted commented on this class of whites: "They are said to 'corrupt' the negroes and to encourage them to steal, or to work for them at night on Sundays, and to pay them with liquor, and to constantly associate licentiously with them. They seem, nevertheless, more than any other portion of the community, to hate and despise the negroes." When the crisis came in 1861, these men fought for slave property and a slave-owning class, although the planters often held them in contempt.

Limitations of the Reform Spirit

Many southern writers claimed that the South had built a superior civilization on a solid base of slavery. But the claim itself stood on shaky ground. New ideas were not welcome in the antebellum South. In education, literacy, and the arts, the region lagged behind the North. In the southern mind, all "isms"—feminism, transcendentalism, Fourierism—quickly became tinged with abolitionism. Actually, there was good reason for this attitude, since northern abolitionists such as Garrison, Theodore Parker, Theodore Weld, Lucretia Mott, Sarah and Angelina Grimké, and Lydia Maria Child were drawn to the whole range of reform programs.

Like many people under attack, southern writers developed code words to describe the opposition, phrases such as "misguided philanthropy" and "northern fanaticism." Feminism in particular outraged the southern ideal of womanhood. Southern mavericks—notably the aristocratic Grimkés of Charleston—turned abolitionist or gave in to other "enthusiasms." Such nonconformists were made to suffer for their independence and were driven North.

Yet the spirit of humanitarianism and reform that flooded the North in the 1830s and 1840s did not leave the South untouched. A number of southern states moderated their harsh criminal codes, improved their prisons, and humanized the treatment of the insane. Dorothea Dix was welcomed in the South for her work on behalf of the mentally ill. During the same period, schools for the deaf were patterned after northern models. The crusade against alcohol was the most enthusiastically supported reform movement in the prewar South. Backed by religious and political leaders, temperance societies sprang up everywhere.

The Proslavery Argument

In the revolutionary period, many leaders in the upper South had seen the contradiction of slavery in a republic dedicated to the principles of the Declaration of Independence. They did little about it, except for scattered individuals who privately freed their own slaves. A later generation of southerners dominated the American Colonization Society, founded in 1817 with the unrealistic hope of getting rid of slavery by freeing blacks on condition that they emigrate to Africa.

The personal penalties that slavery imposed on the consciences of slave owners just after the Revolution could be considerable. The following extract from the will of a North Carolinian who emancipated his slaves makes this clear. He gave four reasons for his actions:

Reason the first. Agreeably to the rights of man, every human being, be his or her colour what it may, is entitled to freedom . . . Reason the second. My conscience, the great criterion, condemns me for keeping them in slavery. Reason the third. The golden rule directs us to do unto every human creature, as we would wish to be done unto. . . . Reason the fourth and last. I wish to die with a clear conscience, that I may not be ashamed to appear before my master in a future World.

In this man's case, which was not unusual in the revolutionary era, two independent traditions merged: a devotion to natural rights and a commitment to Christian principles.

This way of thinking never completely died out in the South. But at the beginning of the 1830s a number of events caused a crisis in southern thinking about slavery. In 1829 David Walker, a free black man in Boston, published a fiery *Appeal* to southern slaves for a full-scale revolt. A shudder of horror and outrage ripped through the white South. Walker was later found mysteriously murdered. In January 1831, also in Boston, William Lloyd Garrison brought out the first issue of the *Liberator*, in which he began his attack on southern slavery. Abolitionism seemed to shift into high gear, and soon a price had been placed upon Garrison's head.

Late that summer, Nat Turner's rebellion horrified the nation. The following winter the Virginia legislature not only debated gradual emancipation bills, but came close to passing one. At the same time the nation was in the midst of the nullification controversy with South Carolina, which itself ultimately revolved around the issue of slavery.

The response to these events was immediate and drastic. Whereas southerners had previously claimed that slavery was a "necessary evil," they now eagerly took up the proposition that it was a "positive good." The first full-blown defense of slavery on this basis was written in 1832 by Thomas R. Dew, a professor of legal philosophy at the College of William and Mary. Dew's argument was somewhat ambiguous, but as the case was elaborated over the next generation, southern spokesmen used many authorities in support it: the Bible, the Constitution, the history of Greece and Rome, the science of political economy, and the "facts" of biology. Slavery, southern writers claimed, fostered the classical form of democracy with all the ancient Greek virtues, as distinct from the tyranny of "wage slavery" in the North.

George Fitzhugh's *Sociology for the South; or, The Failure of Free Society* (1854) and *Cannibals All! or, Slaves without Masters* (1857) brought together many of the familiar arguments in favor of slavery. Following Calhoun's lead, Fitzhugh claimed that in the South capital and labor were not divorced. The fierce exploitation of one class by another, as in the laissez-faire economy of the North, was absent here. Northern capitalism, Fitzhugh declared, led to the impoverishment of the masses and to social revolution, not to liberty and democracy.

His arguments constituted a telling and sophisticated critique of the northern industrial economy. But they failed to deal with weaknesses in southern society. These weaknesses were causing many southerners to declare their society perfect in the face of the general assessment of Western civilization that it was backward and even sinful.

Education and Literature

Southern society possessed many characteristics of Jacksonian America, but it lacked certain dynamic elements that proved to be the cutting edges of a more modern world. Public education remained almost nonexistent in the South. In thinly populated rural areas, rich planters resisted taxation for public schools. Those who would have benefited from schools felt that such institutions bore the stigma of charity. Some 2700 private academies could be found in the South by 1850, more than in New England and the middle states combined. But students were few and the quality of education was lower than in the North. The 1850 census showed that illiterate whites constituted 20 percent of the population in the South, 2 percent in the middle states, and 1 percent in New England.

Southern higher education compared more favorably. Some wealthy southern families continued to send their sons to Yale, Princeton, Harvard, and the University of Pennsylvania, rather than to their own new state universities and denominational colleges. At the same time, the percentage of southerners attending college was higher than that of northerners. In 1860, for example, when the northern population was 2.5 times that of the white population of the South, each section had about 26,000 college students.

Most southern colleges were less richly endowed than those in the North. Such schools as the University of Virginia, South Carolina College, and the University of North Carolina struggled to keep up with the institutions above the Mason-Dixon line. In addition, southern colleges were dependent on the North for much of their reading material, since virtually all textbooks were published in the North. Most were also written by northern authors. One text, for example, described slavery as a "stain on the human race, which corrupts the master as much as it debases the slave"—a statement white southerners could scarcely accept.

The political and religious liberalism of the Jeffersonian South began to dissolve in the early years of the nineteenth century. Enlightenment ideas began to give way before the sweep of religious fundamentalism and the necessity of defending slavery. The religious revivals of the antebellum period converted thousands of people to the Methodist and Baptist churches, and ministers of these and smaller denominations gained great influence.

These ministers tended to endorse the status quo. They thundered against the evils of infidelity, alcohol, and the ideas and "isms" of the North. They denounced atheists, deists, Unitarians, and "nothingarians" as enemies of God and social order. In 1835, a North Carolina constitutional convention voted to exclude Jews and atheists from public office.

A spirit of intellectual repression was by no means confined to the South. Heresy hunts and anti-infidel crusades also flickered through the North and West. But in the South the skeptical minority was much more thoroughly pressured into silence by those who felt called upon to denounce what they saw as the works of "profane sinners, downright skeptics, and God-defying wretches."

Even though a number of talented southern writers published fiction, poetry, and essays during the antebellum period, there was no literary flowering comparable to New England's. John Pendleton Kennedy's novels, such as *Swallow Barn* (1832), were colored by defensiveness about slavery. No southern author treated slavery or slaves meaningfully. William Gilmore Simms, the section's most prolific novelist, offered heroes whose lips curled and eyes flashed, along with doll-like heroines who spoke in stilted phrases. His low-life characters, his traders, tavern keepers, and poor whites, were much more real. He was the only southern novelist before the Civil War who wrote convincingly about ordinary farmers and poor whites.

Too much energy was going into defending the South's special culture to permit either writers or readers a broader outlook. The most popular writer in the South was Sir Walter Scott, a Scottish author who filled his novels with dauntless cavaliers of an earlier age. His gallant knights seemed an appropriate model for southern chivalry. It was only later, in the twentieth century, when America's southland was partially released from the pain of slavery that southern authors such as William Faulkner could fully portray their own world. In doing so, they would produce some of the nation's finest literature.

Southern Women, White and Black

In many ways the burden of this thinking fell especially on southern women. The practice and defense of slavery led to habits of mind that affected white women in different ways than men. And of course black women were affected in ways that were distinctive to both their social condition and their cultural heritage.

While black women were sometimes the sexual victims of white men, they were less likely to become the victims of destructive racial stereotyping than black males. White southern literature and folklore turned adult black males into "boys" and tried to shape them into fawning, irresponsible buffoons. This dehumanizing, infantilizing stereotype was applied much less to slave women, who were often thought of in terms of the loving "Mammy." As one foreign observer wrote:

"Field hands"—"Force"—"Hands"—"People" and "Niggers" are terms applied to the purchased laborers of a plantation: but "Slaves"—never. "Boys" is the general term for the men, and "women," for females. It is common to address a Negroe forty years of age as "boy." If much older he is called "daddy," or "uncle"; but "mister," or "man"—never. The females, in old age, become "aunty," "granny," or "old lady."

Then, too, black women were rarely seen as physically threatening, whereas black men (despite being thought of as childlike) were often considered potential murderers and lustful rapists.

The wives and daughters of nonslaveholders lived lives much like those of their northern counterparts, though they were more likely to be truly poor and to have fewer opportunities to visit with one another in little towns. For white women of the planting class, slavery and its defense imposed a rigid orthodoxy. Unlike many of their northern sisters, they were confined to their homes and to rounds of parties, entertaining, and social visits. Many of them found the supervision of the household slaves more a burden than a privilege. They were expected by their husbands and other male relatives to be decorative, charming, but most certainly not learned. The diaries kept by these women reveal that at least some of them felt confined and even maimed by the system of chattel slavery. They resented especially the miscegenation their men were involved in. One woman lashed out at the destructiveness of illicit interracial sex in a famous passage:

God forgive us, but ours is a monstrous system, a wrong and an iniquity! Like the patriarchs of old, our men live all in one house with their wives and concubines; and the mulattoes one sees in every family partly resemble the white children. Any lady is ready to tell you who is the father of all the mulatto children in everybody's household but her own. Those, she seems to think, drop from the clouds. My disgust sometimes is boiling over. Thank God for my country women, but alas for the men!

It is no wonder that few southern women became involved in reform causes. They had major grievances at home, but the growing orthodoxy concerning slavery prevented their even discussing them in public. That orthodoxy was increasingly making the South something of a closed society. It tightened its grip as national expansion in the West made slavery more and more the dominant issue between the sections.

SUMMARY

The South was different from the North, and in the decades before the Civil War it became more and more conscious that is was.

Among the white people of the South, the largest group were not planters or poor whites, but simple farmers who owned no slaves. The real planting class was a very small minority; only eight thousand planters owned fifty or more slaves, and almost half of all slave-owning families had fewer than six slaves. Yet most of the blacks of the South were on the large plantations. More than half lived on plantations with more than twenty slaves; only about 10 percent lived in cities and towns. The principal social contact of many blacks was with other blacks; they lived somewhat isolated in their own subculture that was no longer African, because by 1860 most slaves were American-born.

The treatment of slaves varied from sadism to gentle paternalism. In general, slaves were treated more severely in the frontier Southwest than in the older South. But everywhere the white man was dominant. So the slaves created an inner world of their own, especially through religion and music. There was also resistance, both passive and active, in the form of arson or rebellion.

The southern economy was largely a plantation economy. Cotton was the most important crop, but tobacco, rice, and sugar were also grown. As early as 1520, cotton had become more valuable than all the other crops combined. Despite some interest in the 1820s and 1830s in establishing the factory system in the South and in making the South a commercial center, the region remained overwhelmingly agricultural.

As northern pressure over slavery mounted, the allegiance of the vast majority of southern whites to the slave plantation system deepened. So did the southern belief in the rightness of white domination and the superiority of southern civilization. After 1830 there were proslavery arguments, not just the defensive attitude that slavery was a "necessary evil." White southerners contended that slavery was a "positive good" for both whites and blacks. Yet the South continued to lag behind in education. Intellectual repression became another characteristic of a society that felt itself under siege.

The women of the South, both black and white, felt the impact of the slave system in special ways. After the mid-1840s that impact grew stronger and stronger, as national expansion in the West sharpened political issues between the country's two sections, slave and free.

TIME LINE

1740s– 1860s	Slaves adopt their own forms of Christianity	1829	David Walker's *Appeal*
1791	Outbreak of Haitian Revolution in French St. Domingue	1830	White churches sponsor first formal missions to slaves
1793	Whitney invents new cotton gin	1831	Nat Turner's revolt
1800	Gabriel plot	1831	First issues of Garrison's *Liberator*
1803	New Orleans takes off as major city and slave mart	1832	Kennedy's *Swallow Barn*
1808	Federal ban nearly halts forced immigration from Africa	1845	First of three editions of Frederick Douglass's autobiography
1820	Cotton's value surpasses all other southern crops combined	1850s	Record cotton production and slave prices
1822	Vesey conspiracy	1850s	Olmsted publishes accounts of three trips through the South
1822	Introduction of steam engines for sugar mills	1857	Fitzhugh's *Cannibals All!*
		1860	About 6 percent of southern blacks are legally not slaves

Suggested Readings

Two different overviews are C. Sydnor, *The Development of Southern Sectionalism, 1819–1848* (1948); and A. Craven, *The Growth of Southern Nationalism, 1848–1861* (1953). E. Genovese, *The Political Economy of Slavery* (1965), is a provocative analysis of the southern economy and its social dimensions; see also his *The World the Slaveholders Made* (1970). L. Gray, *History of Agriculture in the Southern United States to 1860* (2 vols., 1933) is still valuable. A newer approach is offered by H. Woodman, *Slavery and the Southern Economy* (1966); and A. Cowdrey, *This Land, This South: An Environmental History* (1983).

Frederick Olmsted was the most astute northern observer. Some of his travel accounts are available in A. Schlesinger (ed.), *The Cotton Kingdom* (1953). Five works focus on important aspects of southern white society: J. Franklin, *The Militant South, 1800–1861* (1956), a description of the strain of violence and militarism; E. Dick, *The Dixie Frontier* (1938); F. Owsley, *Plain Folk of the Old South* (1949); J. Oakes, *The Ruling Race: A History of American Slaveholders* (1982); and S. Stowe, *Intimacy and Power in the Old South: Ritual in the Lives of the Planters* (1987). White southern women are discussed in A. Scott, *The Southern Lady: From Pedestal to Politics* (1970); and C. Clinton, *The Plantation Mistress:*

Woman's World in the Old Sooth (1982). See also S. Lebsock, *The Free Women of Petersburg: Status and Culture in a Southern Town, 1784–1860* (1984).

The most balanced history of Afro-Americans is J. Franklin and A. Moss, Jr., *From Slavery to Freedom: A History of Negro Americans* (6th ed., 1988); see also P. Foner, *History of Black Americans: From the Emergence of the Cotton Kingdom to the Eve of the Compromise of 1950* (1983). A. Weinstein and F. Gatell (eds.), *American Negro Slavery: A Modern Reader* (3rd ed., 1979), is an excellent collection of various modern views. U. Phillips, *American Negro Slavery* (1918), will repel many readers because of the author's views on blacks, but it contains useful information. K. Stampp, *The Peculiar Institution: Slavery in the Ante-Bellum South* (1956), is a modern classic, but it should be read in light of a different view of the slave's culture presented in J. Blassingame, *The Slave Community: Plantation Life in the Antebellum South* (1972). W. L. Rose, *Slavery and Freedom*, ed. W. Freehling (1982), convincingly stresses how different slavery was in the antebellum years than it was earlier.

E. Genovese, *Roll, Jordan, Roll: The World the Slaves Made* (1974), is a richly detailed discussion of the strength of black culture. In this connection, see also: D. Epstein, *Sinful Tones and Spirituals: Black Folk Music to the Civil War* (1977); and L. Levine, *Black Culture and Black Consciousness: Afro-American Folk Thought from Slavery to Freedom* (1977). An account of slavery by the victims is R. Starobin (ed.), *Blacks in Bondage: Letters of American Slaves* (1974). One book that is not about slavery sheds much light on it: E. Ayers, *Vengeance and Justice: Crime and Punishment in the Nineteenth Century American South* (1984).

These general studies may be supplemented by important monographs such as Starobin's *Industrial Slavery in the Old South* (1970); R. Wade, *Slavery in the Cities: The South, 1820–1860* (1972); W. Scarborough, *The Overseer: Plantation Management in the Old South* (1966); and C. Joyner, *Down by the River-*

side: A South Carolina Slave Community* (1984). There are many works comparing slavery regionally in the New World. S. Elkins, *Slavery: A Problem in American Institutional and Intellectual Life* (2nd ed., 1968), a controversial study, should be read along with A. Lane (ed.), *The Debate over Slavery: Stanley Elkins and His Critics* (1971). A more balanced view is presented in C. Degler, *Neither Black nor White: Slavery and Race Relations in Brazil and the United States* (1971). For a fascinating comparison, see P. Kolchin, *Unfree Labor: American Slavery and Russian Serfdom* (1987). Try also J. Boles, *Masters and Slaves in the House of the Lord: Race and Religion in the American South, 1740–1870* (1988); and E. Fox-Genovese, *Within the Plantation Household: Black and White Women of the Old South* (1988).

H. Aptheker, *American Negro Slave Revolts* (1943), first made an extended case for the inherent rebelliousness of American slaves. N. Yetman (ed.), *Voices from Slavery* (1970), is a fascinating collection of interviews with elderly former slaves done in 1937; G. Rawick has written a fine account based on those interviews, *The American Slave: A Composite Autobiography* (1972).

W. Cash, *The Mind of the South* (1941), is a penetrating study of illusion and reality. W. Taylor, *Cavalier and Yankee: The Old South and American National Character* (1961), probes regional differences. E. McKitrick (ed.), *Slavery Defended: The Views of the Old South* (1963), is an anthology of proslavery writings. D. Bailey, *Shadow on the Church: Southwestern Evangelical Religion and the Issue of Slavery*, 1783-1860 (1985), illuminates conflicting values in the South. An important turning point is covered in A. Freehling, *Drift toward Dissolution: The Virginia Slavery Debate of 1831–1832* (1982).

Racial attitudes are explored in G. Frederickson, *The Black Image in the White Mind: The Debate on Afro-American Character and Destiny, 1817–1914* (1971); J. Kovel, *White Racism: A Psychohistory* (1970); and W. Stanton, *The Leopard's Spots: Scientific Attitudes toward Race in America, 1815–1859* (1960).

Landing of emigrants at the Battery, New York. Photo is outside of the barge office. *(Library of Congress)*

MANIFEST DESTINY AND SLAVERY

Throughout the 1820s and 1830s, Americans were very much on the move—not only into the new states created from the Louisiana Purchase, but all the way to the Pacific coast and even beyond to islands in the Pacific Ocean. Within little more than a quarter of a century, the unbroken expanse of the United States had been extended to its present limits, the annexation of Hawaii had been proposed, and the purchase of Alaska completed. Canada, Mexico, and Cuba still looked tempting to those who thought the United States was destined to rule the entire North American continent.

The phrase "manifest destiny" became identified with American expansionism about 1845, but the idea of a divine mission was much older. This notion, which had begun to tempt colonial Americans when they had captured Louisburg a century before, suggested that God had set aside the American continent and nearby islands as reservations "for the free development of our yearly multiplying millions." No physical barrier, no foreign force, could stop the American people from expanding their territory and their system of free government.

Practical politicians in charge of the country's day-to-day policies in the 1840s promoted more tangible objectives. They hoped to dominate northern Pacific waters and trade to the Orient, which they saw as a legitimate extension of the American West. They also turned their eyes to Canada, where for a time they kept running into serious border conflicts. They had to deal with the question of the Oregon country, an area claimed by both Great Britain and the United States. In the Southwest, a new republic emerged as the result of American westward settlement. For a time Texas remained independent, but there was strong sentiment for annexing it to the United States.

In the mid-1840s an aggressive American president provoked a war with Mexico. That conflict brought great territorial gains for the United States. But it also raised the question of whether those territories should be open to slavery. That issue came close to tearing the nation apart, but it was patched over by a complex compromise in 1850. As the compromise went into effect, it produced both relief and anger. Many people began to doubt it would last.

THE CANADIAN BORDER

The westward surge of the American people and some star-spangled predictions that their flag would wave from Cape Horn to the North Pole strengthened suspicions in Europe. The British (along with the rest of Europe) saw the Yankees as a people to be watched. These opinions were based partly on the reports of British travelers who made quick tours of America. Many people in Britain were greatly angered by the American states' repudiating their debts to British creditors after the panic of 1837.

They also disliked the boastful spirit of American democracy, which the popular author Charles Dickens mimicked: "We are a model of wisdom, and an example to the world, and the perfection of human reason." Britain had led the world by emancipating blacks in its colonies in 1833, and thereafter the British scoffed at the peculiar American brand of liberty which defended slavery and assaulted abolitionists. Underlying each nineteenth-century conflict between Britain and the United States was the growing commercial and industrial rivalry of the two nations.

There were more practical reasons to be watchful of the Americans. The British had very low expectations of Canada as a paying colony. But Canada had its uses—"above all," wrote a future colonial secretary, "in case of war with the United States." In such an event, he added, Canada "furnishes ample assistance in men, timber and harbours for carrying on the war, and that on the enemy's frontier." How seriously Britain took the American menace was made clear by its spending millions of pounds to build the Rideau Canal as an alternative to the St. Lawrence River in case control of the latter ever fell to American invaders. The British spent millions more rebuilding the strategic citadel of Quebec. In the late 1830s and early 1840s, three confrontations gave the British and Americans excuses for war: the *Caroline* affair, the Maine border, and the *Creole* incident.

The *Caroline* Affair

In 1837, inspired in part by the "great experiment" below the border, insurrections flared up in Canada. Loyal forces quickly suppressed these uprisings, but not before some Americans had come to the rebels' aid. One night the *Caroline*, a small American steamer ferrying supplies to the insurgents, lay moored off the New York shore of the Niagara River. A party of loyal Canadian volunteers rowed across, threw out the *Caroline*'s crew, set her afire, and watched her sink. During the scuffle one American was killed.

The United States promptly demanded an apology. But the British replied that the *Caroline*, by aiding the criminal conspiracy in Canada, had become fair game. New York authorities arrested Alexander McLeod, one of the Canadian participants in the raid on the vessel, and charged him with murder and arson. The British foreign secretary, Lord Palmerston, admitted that the raid had been officially planned to prevent American aid to the insurrectionists. He went on to demand McLeod's release on grounds that any actions he may have taken were done under orders. McLeod's execution, Palmerston warned, would mean war. New York's governor, William H. Seward, insisted that McLeod would be pardoned. Fortunately for both countries, he was acquitted.

The Aroostook "War"

The winter freeze on the St. Lawrence had hampered the movement of the troops putting down the Canadian revolts of 1837. The next year the British decided to build a road from St. John on the Bay of Fundy in New Brunswick to Quebec and Montreal. In February 1839 they began work in the rich Aroostook River valley, where conflicting claims of the state of Maine and the province of New Brunswick had grown sharper as the value of the timber in the valley rose. When "foreign" lumberjacks entered the area and began clearing trees for the road, the Maine militia chased them out.

The Aroostook "war" was a bloodless affair, but an angry Congress appropriated $10 million and authorized President Van Buren to enlist fifty thousand volunteers. As it turned out, neither money nor men were needed. General Winfield Scott, the president's negotiator, succeeded in smoothing things over at the scene. Scott was not able to eliminate the source of the trouble, however, which lay in the vagueness of the frontier line. Not until the Webster-Ashburton Treaty of 1842 was Maine's northern boundary firmly established.

The *Creole* Incident

The *Creole* case of 1841 strained Anglo-American relations on another touchy subject, and made Canadian border issues more difficult to settle. In its attempts to stop the Atlantic slave traffic on the high seas, Britain had made treaties with many nations in which its navy was given the right even in peacetime to stop and search suspected ships under all flags. Palmerston boasted that Britain had enlisted in the fight against the slave trade "every state in Christendom which has a flag that sails on the ocean, with the single exception of the United States of North America." This was not entirely true. France, like the United States, had resisted Britain's assumption of authority. But it suited Palmerston to point his finger at the United States—with some justice, for slave ships of various nations often escaped search and seizure simply by running up the Stars and Stripes.

The American brig *Creole* was carrying about 130 slaves from Virginia to New Orleans in 1841 when the blacks, led by a man named Madison Washington, revolted and took over the vessel. It was the most successful slave insurrection in American history. They sailed her to the British port of Nassau in the Bahamas and went ashore, knowing that reaching British territory would mean freedom. Only one white passenger had been killed in the revolt. The *Creole's* owners and American officials tried to reclaim the slaves. The British insisted the slaves were freed by their own action in successfully reaching a British port. The blacks remained in Nassau as free people, while white Americans fumed in indignation.

The Webster-Ashburton Treaty

Palmerston's attitude made him sufficiently unpopular to evoke sighs of relief on both sides of the Atlantic when a change of ministers threw him out of office in 1841. The new foreign secretary was far more agreeable, and he appointed as special envoy to the United States Lord Ashburton, the husband of an American heiress.

The principal point of the talks between Ashburton and Secretary of State Daniel Webster was the Canadian-American border. The talks took place in an atmosphere dominated by assumptions on both sides of the Atlantic that at some point or another, a third war between Great Britain and the United States was nearly inevitable. Ultimately, the two diplomats compromised on the Maine boundary; they also agreed on the inaccurately surveyed boundary along northern Vermont and New York and westward to Minnesota and Ontario. They smoothed over the *Caroline* and the *Creole* affairs with such skillful language that both sides were made to seem in the right.

The results did much for their historical reputations, though not their popularity at the time. Extremists in both countries protested that their country had suffered a diplomatic defeat. But the Webster-Ashburton Treaty, signed in 1842,

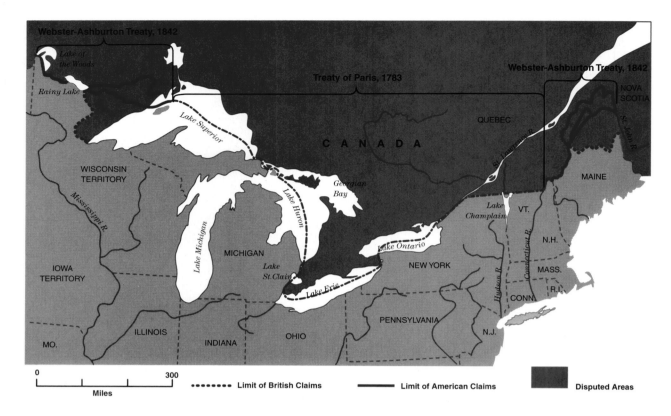

Webster-Ashburton Treaty and Treaty of Paris Boundaries

was a model of compromise that paved the way for other peaceful settlements during the next two decades.

TEXAS

In the North, after forcible removal of the Sauk and Fox tribes in 1833, white emigrants from Illinois, Indiana, Ohio, and Kentucky began to spill into the newly opened Iowa and Wisconsin country. By 1840, some 75,000 settlers had established themselves on the rich farmlands there. Smaller numbers, including lumbermen and trappers, pushed into Minnesota. Southern farmers as well as planters had no land like this at their disposal. By 1840, much of the best land on the southern Gulf plains was occupied by large planters and slaves. After the admission of Arkansas in 1836, the only remaining prospective slave state under the provisions of the Missouri Compromise was the territory of Florida.

Immediately to the west of the last southern settlements lay the "permanent Indian frontier,"

established in the 1820s in much of present-day Oklahoma and Kansas. That land was set aside forever, it was said, for the displaced woodland Indians of the East as well as the tribes native to the region. South and west of this "Indian territory" stretched Texas, only recently independent of Mexico. Beyond Texas lay Mexico's vaguely defined California empire.

The Lone Star Republic

American claims to the Mexican province of Texas were based on the carefree geography of the Louisiana Purchase treaty. When the United States obtained Florida from Spain in 1819, it surrendered those claims. American traders and military adventurers continued the illegal commercial relations they had already established with the Mexicans, despite Spain's many warnings. When Mexico, with the assistance of these traders and fighters, won its independence from Spain in 1821, the Mexican government placed commerce with the Americans on a legitimate footing and invited them to settle in Texas. Connecticut-born Moses Austin, who obtained a land grant from the Mexican government in 1820, pioneered American colonization there. He died before developing his Texas tract, but Mexico validated the grant for his son Stephen, who carried through the first colonization program.

Mexican officials had hoped that the settlement of Texas by Anglo-Americans would protect their sparsely settled borderland outposts from Indian raids. They soon realized they had miscalculated the results of immigration from the United States. Between 1820 and 1830, about twenty thousand Americans with approximately two thousand slaves had crossed into Texas, largely from the lower Mississippi frontier. Most were law-abiding people. But rougher elements made the Mexicans agree with John Jay's old complaint that white frontiersmen were more dangerous than Indians. Texas Americans, on their part, soon began to complain about lack of self-government.

Offers by the United States to purchase Texas only served to deepen Mexico's anxiety. Furthermore, American settlers in Mexico had failed to become Catholics, as they were required to do by the terms of their invitation. They ignored a Mexican prohibition on bringing in slaves by substituting a thinly disguised indenture system. Some Americans, moreover, slipped into territory reserved by law for Mexicans.

In 1830 the Mexican government sent troops to occupy Texas, stopped further American immigration, and passed other restrictive measures, including the abolition of slavery. Shortly thereafter, General A. L. de Santa Anna, Mexico's strongman, instituted a centralist program and abolished all local rights of self-government in his distant province. Early in 1836 he led an army of six thousand into Texas. Confronted with this threat, Americans there declared their independence on March 2, 1836. They set up a provisional government under a constitution that allowed slavery, and appointed Sam Houston commander in chief of a Texas army.

Santa Anna already had the Alamo mission in San Antonio under siege. For ten days, 187 Americans held off a much larger number of Mexican troops, taking a heavy toll. Finally, on March 6, Mexican cannons opened holes in the walls. The Mexicans poured through and killed the Americans, including the wounded and such legendary figures as Davy Crockett and James Bowie, threw oil on the bodies, and burned

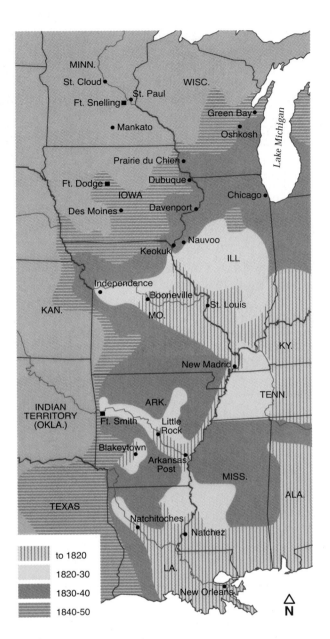

Settlement of the Mississippi Valley

them. It proved to be a costly victory, for it aroused the anger of Texas Americans, who went into later battles crying "Remember the Alamo." Three weeks later, more than 300 Americans died at Goliad after surrendering to troops led by General José Urrea.

These defeats forced Houston to retreat east until he reached the vicinity of San Jacinto creek. There, on April 21, 1836, his troops suddenly turned on the unprepared pursuers, defeated Santa Anna's army, and took the general captive. Santa Anna signed a treaty giving Texas independence and fixing a vague boundary between Mexico and Texas. Although the Mexican Congress promptly disallowed the treaty, it seemed powerless to reverse it.

Annexation

Sympathy for the Texas rebels had been strong in the South and also in the Northwest, where their cause was identified with the struggles of all frontiersmen. There was far less support in the Northeast. Whig leaders viewed the Texans' request to enter the Union as a slave owners' plot. Anywhere from five to seven states, they pointed out, might be carved from the huge

Texas domain, thus ensuring southern control of Congress. Opponents of annexation protested so strongly that President Jackson waited to give diplomatic recognition to the Lone Star Republic until just before he left office in 1837. Van Buren also withstood growing annexationist pressure, a policy that was to cost him his political future during the next presidential election and administration.

Denied admission to the United States and menaced by a hostile Mexico, the Lone Star Republic turned elsewhere for protection. Britain welcomed an independent Texas that would export cotton and import British manufactured goods. Britain also opposed slavery, and Foreign Secretary Aberdeen declared that "with regard to Texas, we avow that we wish to see slavery

The Texas revolution

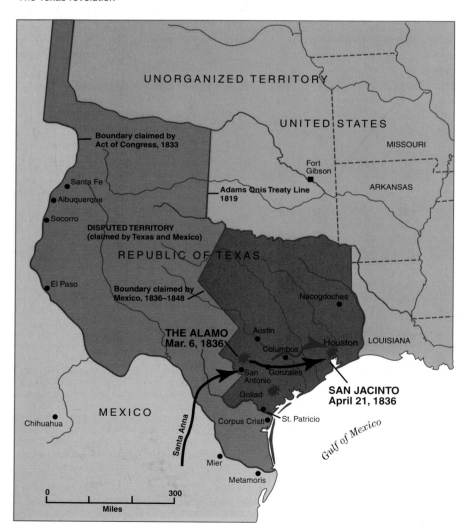

abolished, as elsewhere." But the presence of slavery did not keep Britain from wanting to recognize and support Texas as an independent republic that would serve as an obstacle to continued United States expansion.

President Tyler worked tirelessly to gain credit for annexation before his successor took office. In April 1844 he submitted to the Senate a Texas statehood treaty drawn up by Calhoun, his newly appointed secretary of state. But with characteristic tactlessness, Calhoun attached a little essay on the virtues of slavery in response to Aberdeen's vow to abolish it. These remarks ensured the Senate's rejection of the arrangement, thirty six to sixteen. But Tyler was not finished.

In February 1845, after President Polk's election on an expansionist platform, Tyler persuaded Congress to annex Texas by passing a joint resolution that required only a majority vote, not the two-thirds needed for treaties. In October Texas accepted the terms of the resolution, which explicitly permitted slavery under the Missouri Compromise. On December 29, 1845, Texas became the twenty-eighth state. Mexico recalled its minister from Washington.

THE FAR WEST

The grand but forbidding Pacific coastline of North America had only three first-rate natural harbors: Puget Sound, the gateway to the Oregon country; San Francisco Bay, inside Mexico's California; and the San Diego Bay, farther south. American spokesmen from all sections of the country were in agreement on taking these fine anchorages and keeping out rival powers, especially Britain. Americans also learned about the beauty and fertility of the Willamette Valley in the Oregon country and the stunning expanses of California.

The Oregon County

The future of Oregon as well as the future of Texas had reached a critical point when the presidential campaign of 1844 began. Distant though it was from the mainstream of European and American politics and business, the Oregon country had long been the scene of competition among France, Spain, Russia, Britain, and the United States. Early in the nineteenth century, France and Spain had surrendered their claims. The Russians had agreed to fix their own southern boundary at 54°40'. This left Britain and the United States free to contest ownership of the remainder of "Oregon."

After John Jacob Astor's Pacific Fur Company was forced out in 1812, American interest in the region was quiet until the 1830s. Then Nathaniel J. Wyeth, an enterprising Massachusetts merchant,

PIONEER WOMEN

Many pioneer women found that the way west was difficult emotionally as well as physically. Lavinia Porter recalled the inner pain of her move to California:

I never recall that sad parting from my dear sister on the plains of Kansas without the tears flowing fast and free. . . . We were the eldest of a large family, and the bond of affection and love that existed between us was strong indeed . . . as she with the other friends turned to leave me for the ferry which was to take them back to home and civilization, I stood alone on that wild prairie. Looking westward I saw my husband driving slowly over the plain; turning my face once more to the east, my dear sister's footsteps were fast widening the distance between us. For the time I knew not which way to go, nor whom to follow. But in a few moments I rallied my

forces . . . and soon overtook the slowly moving oxen who were bearing my husband and child over the green prairie. . . . the unbidden tears would flow in spite of my brave resolve to be the courageous and valiant frontiers—woman.

On the trail, Mrs. Porter began to have serious doubts about the entire enterprise:

I would make a brave effort to be cheerful and patient until the camp work was done. Then starting out ahead of the team and my men folks, when I thought I had gone beyond hearing distance, I would throw myself down on the unfriendly desert and give way like a child to sobs and tears, wishing myself back home with my friends and chiding myself for consenting to take this wild goose chase.

sent out several expeditions. Though financially unsuccessful, they called attention to the overland route that had first been explored by Lewis and Clark. Accompanying Wyeth to Oregon was a band of Methodist missionaries. The fertility and beauty of Oregon's Willamette Valley captivated this group, and they quickly became more interested in farming than in converting the Indians.

The home church in the East soon washed its hands of the enterprise, but settlement flourished. Letters from missionaries continued to praise Oregon's agricultural possibilities. By 1843 "Oregon fever" had swept across the Mississippi Valley frontier. In May of that year, more than a thousand settlers started out on the nearly two-thousand-mile Oregon Trail from Independence, Missouri. As anyone who has traveled the Great Plains knows, a wagon train journey over those endless miles was a harrowing experience.

While American leaders in Oregon struggled to organize a provisional government, expansionists back east began to thunder about America's right to the territory. They rejected the old boundary at the forty-ninth parallel, the limit of American claims in earlier discussions with Britain. The Democrats' campaign slogan for 1844 was "Fifty-four Forty or Fight!" No other presidential election was so clearly fought over the issue of national expansion.

By opposing the annexation of Texas, Van Buren had forfeited his chance of renomination by the Democrats, and Calhoun seemed too closely tied to his sectional interests. The Democratic convention finally settled on a single-minded Jacksonian planter from Tennessee—an expansionist named James K. Polk—who endorsed "the reoccupation of Oregon and the reannexation of Texas."

Having in previous years passed him over, the Whigs were almost forced to choose Henry Clay. But Clay had openly opposed the annexation of Texas, on which the Whig platform remained silent. The more he hedged during the campaign, the worse off he became. Polk won by an electoral margin of 170 to 105.

Yet the popular vote was extremely close, and Clay would have won the election if he had carried New York. There, despite its failure nationwide, the new Liberty party—which was

America's Progress by artist John Gast (1872). As the Indians flee westward, the advance of civilization is headed by the trapper and the miner, followed by the settler, the farmer, and the railroad. (Library of Congress)

CHAPTER 15   MANIFEST DESTINY AND SLAVERY

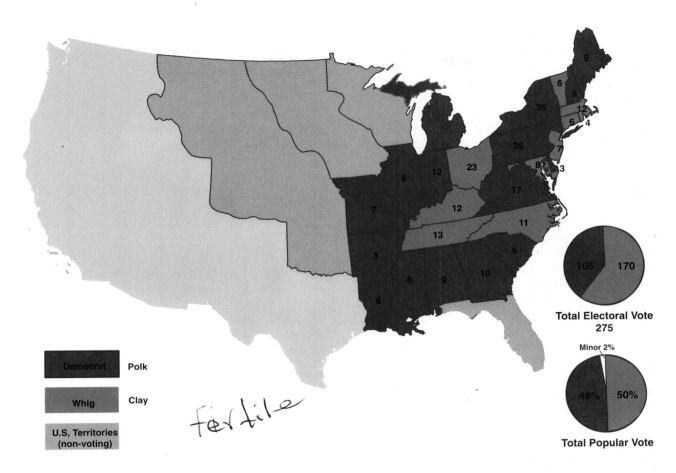

Democrat — Polk

Whig — Clay

U.S. Territories (non-voting)

fertile

Total Electoral Vote
275

Minor 2%

48% 50%

Total Popular Vote

The election of 1844

pledged to oppose the expansion of slavery—drained enough votes away from Clay to throw that state into the Democratic column. Its showing here indicated for the first time that a small third party could have an important impact on American politics. But antislavery enthusiasts could take no delight in the outcome. Polk was a slaveholder, and his fellow Democrats enlarged their House majority and gained a majority in the Senate. In fact, the election results were widely interpreted, especially by Polk himself, as a mandate for expansion.

A Peaceful Solution

Polk was not so obscure as his Whig opponents tried to suggest. A veteran of state politics in Tennessee before his elevation to the White House, Polk had served fourteen years in the House of Representatives in Washington, the last

four as Speaker. As president, Polk remained the solid Democrat he had always been

He opposed protection, and in 1846 signed the Walker Tariff, which put the country back on low duties for revenue only. He opposed a national debt and meant to keep it low enough to pay the interest (and reduce the principal if possible) with current taxes. He opposed banks and restored Van Buren's Independent Treasury system for handling federal funds. He gave nullifiers no comfort. Above all, he was fully as expansionist and isolationist as Jefferson.

In his inaugural address, Polk asserted "the right of the United States to that portion of our territory which lies beyond the Rocky Mountains. American title to the country of the Oregon," he said, "is 'clear and unquestionable,' and already are our people preparing to perfect that title by occupying it with their wives and children." In his first annual message to Congress in 1845, Polk stretched the Monroe Doctrine by

James Polk. *(Library of Congress)*

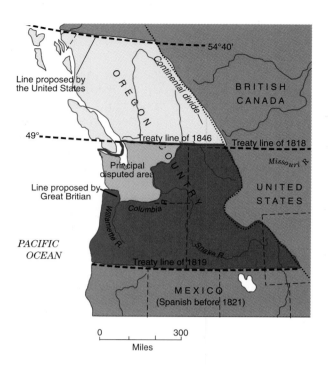

The Oregon controversy

making two statements that are sometimes called the Polk Doctrine: first, that "the people of this continent alone have the right to decide their own destiny"; second, that the United States cannot allow European nations to prevent an independent state from entering the American union.

While war with Mexico over Texas still threatened, a war against Britain over Oregon seemed foolish. After the election was over and the "Fifty-four Forty" slogan had served its purpose Polk found a way to back down. He had been advised that Oregon above the forty-ninth parallel was not suited to agriculture. Below that latitude, he said, lay "the entrance of the Straits of [Juan de] Fuca, Admiralty Inlet, and Puget's Sound, with their fine harbors and rich surrounding soils." Britain was also beginning to think of compromise. British Canadian authorities were finding it difficult to keep Americans out of Oregon. At the same time, depletion of fur-bearing animals along the Columbia River gave them good reason for pulling out.

After long negotiations, both sides were able to agree by treaty in 1846 to extend the old line of 1818 along the forty-ninth parallel westward to Puget Sound and from there to the Pacific through the Strait of Juan de Fuca. Some territory north of the Columbia River, though clearly British by right of settlement, fell into American hands. Britain retained Vancouver Island and navigation rights on the Columbia. Running the former border westward across two-thirds of the continent had finally been accomplished without war.

THE MORMONS IN UTAH

While thousands of Americans from the North and South were moving west to "perfect," as Polk said, American title to North America, one group moved west to escape the American government. In 1823, Joseph Smith, a visionary from Vermont, claimed to have been led by angels to a hill near Manchester, New York, where "there was a book deposited, written upon gold plates," and "two stones in silver bows." As God's helper, Smith used these stones to translate the book from its mysterious language. What was revealed was the Book of Mormon, a composite of mythology and prophecy that recalled the old legend that the Indians were descendants of the lost tribes of Israel and that directed Smith's followers to convert them. Given this revelation, Smith founded the Church of Jesus Christ of Latter-day Saints.

Scorned as heretics, the Mormons were harried to Nauvoo, Illinois, on the bank of the Mississippi River. There they found peace until Joseph Smith's practice of plural marriages began to gather notoriety. To most Victorian Americans, one wife was enough. The Nauvoo settlement was mobbed, and Smith was killed in jail by men who saw him as a threat to domestic order and their own domestic tranquillity. Smith's murder almost killed the Mormon movement. But it provided the Mormon church with a martyr in whose name a new leader might rally its forces.

Such an leader appeared in the person of Brigham Young, who became the new "Lion of the Lord." Forced out of Illinois after the Prophet's assassination, Young led the Mormons westward in the winter of 1846. Eventually they found in the Salt Lake Valley a Zion isolated on a barren Mexican plateau remote from the lands of the Gentiles. There, encircled by dusty mountains and a smoking desert, the Mormon leaders created a theocracy superbly organized for survival.

Because of both geography and theology, the Salt Lake community was cooperative rather than competitive. Its very existence depended on control of a limited supply of fresh water. Young and his followers laid out numerous tightly regulated communities. The Mormon desert state (eventually named Utah) was probably the most successful communitarian project ever established in the United States. Despite the Mormon state's original reputation as a gigantic brothel, the rigid sobriety and fruitful labor of its inhabitants gradually won the Mormon community respect from other Americans. One of the few religious denominations with exclusively American roots, the Mormons thought of themselves as a chosen people—a familiar claim in American history.

On to California

The present state of California had first been opened to European expansion by Spanish Franciscan missions protected by small garrisons. The purpose had been to convert Indians and to prevent British and Russian penetration of the California coast. In theory, these missions were temporary; they were set up to teach the Indians agriculture and household arts and to Christianize them. But gradually mission lands fell into private hands, and ranching became the prevailing way of life. The California Indians died rapidly from European diseases. By the time of the Mexican-American War in 1846, the various tribes were tragically dependent remnants. Few active missions remained.

During the preceding twenty-five years, Yankee whalers from Nantucket and New Bedford had begun stopping at Monterey and San Francisco, leaving behind them deserters and adventurers. They were joined by people from the Oregon and Mississippi frontiers. Anglo-American immigration completely disrupted the lives of the Mexican and Indian residents. Bitter conflicts arose over land, religion, and living habits. A comment from a letter by an American soldier reflected one view of this clash of cultures: "The Mexican, like the poor Indian, is doomed to retire before the more enterprising Anglo-Americans."

Although California had not been an issue in the 1844 campaign, it soon became identified with Oregon. San Francisco was the great prize—twenty times more valuable, thought Daniel Webster, than the whole of Texas. San Diego harbor, according to many observers, would outweigh Oregon. The United States had no claim to California except desire. During Jackson's and Tyler's administrations, government efforts to buy California merely deepened Mexican hostility. Anglo-Californians waited cautiously until they learned of the outbreak of war with Mexico in 1846. Then they raised a standard for a Bear Flag Republic, which they hoped would be annexed to the United States.

WAR AGAINST MEXICO

In one of the most obviously aggressive wars in American history, in 1846 President Polk ordered General Zachary Taylor to occupy disputed territory on the southern boundary of Texas, between the Nueces River and the Rio Grande. Taylor had carried out his orders by the end of March. That show of force, thought Polk, might push the Mexicans into reconsidering their refusal to negotiate a purchase. Or it might cause an incident to serve as an excuse for war. Almost inevitably there was a clash of troops at the disputed border. Polk had already prepared a war message for Congress, which did as he asked.

Trails of the Old West

The shedding of American blood on what the United States claimed to be its own soil put the legislators in a mood to act without much debate.

A Divided People

The size of his congressional majorities may have raised Polk's hopes for bipartisan support of the war, but these hopes were soon dashed. His refusal to declare his war aims openly (the seizure of New Mexico and California) encouraged southern as well as northern Whigs to attack his Mexican policy.

By forcing an unwilling people into war, said northern Whigs, Polk was simply "attempting to consummate a scheme for the extension and strengthening of slavery and the Slave Power." Some southern Whigs feared that the acquisition

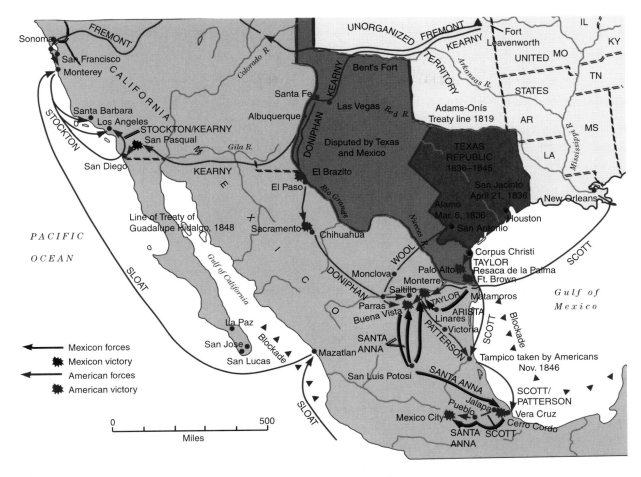

Mexican War campaigns

of new territories would intensify sectional rivalries and destroy their party. But if the Whigs publicly attacked Polk, most of them quickly made all the political capital they could out of the triumphs of two Whig generals, Zachary Taylor and Winfield Scott.

Moral and political dissatisfaction with the war was greatest in the Northeast, where New England Whigs and antislavery spokesmen such as Emerson, Parker, James Russell Lowell, and Robert C. Winthrop denounced Polk's adventurism. The populous Northeast supplied only 7900 recruits for the army; some 20,000 southerners and 40,000 westerners enlisted.

The Fruits of Victory

General Taylor captured Monterrey, Mexico, on September 24, 1846, and defeated a Mexican force of 15,000 men at Buena Vista early in 1847.

General Scott, appointed next to lead an expedition against Mexico City, overcame tough resistance on the coast at Vera Cruz and took Mexico City on September 14, 1847. Troops commanded by Colonel Stephen W. Kearny captured Santa Fe and pushed through to California. Commodore Robert F. Stockton and a battalion under General John C. Fremont had already proclaimed the annexation of California in August 1846.

When news of the victories at Buena Vista and Vera Cruz reached Washington, Polk thought he would be able to arrange an immediate peace. When the negotiations were taken out of his hands by envoys operating on their own, Polk was outraged. He considered several angry and probably impossible alternatives: that northern Mexico and all California be annexed; that Mexico be forced to pay all costs of the war; that all of Mexico be annexed. At last better sense prevailed; on February 2, 1848, Polk signed the Treaty of Guadalupe Hidalgo.

Polk secured the Rio Grande boundary, Upper California, including the ports of San Diego and San Francisco, as well as "New Mexico"—in other words, all the territory north and westward from the Rio Grande River. In return for this vast territory, Polk agreed on a payment of some $13 million to Mexico. Several years later, when southern Americans became interested in a railroad to the Pacific coast, the United States negotiated the purchase of 54,000 square miles along the southern New Mexico border for $10 million—the Gadsden Purchase of 1853.

THE QUESTION OF SLAVERY

As American soldiers stormed into Mexico, Ralph Waldo Emerson wrote in his journal: "The United States will conquer Mexico, but it will be as the man who swallows the arsenic, which brings him down in turn. Mexico will poison us."

Slavery in the Territories

The symptoms of poisoning appeared almost immediately. As early as August 1846, David Wilmot, a Free Soil Democrat from Pennsylvania, offered an amendment to an appropriation bill in the House: "Neither slavery nor involuntary servitude shall ever exist in any part" of the territory that might be acquired from Mexico. The heavily northern House adopted the amendment; the Senate defeated it. But that was not the end of the matter. The Wilmot Proviso was added to bill after bill in Congress and was hotly debated there and in the country generally.

At the same time, admission of Iowa and Wisconsin to the Union was pending; Minnesota was soon to apply for statehood; and even the Oregon Territory was getting ready. For all these free states to enter the Union while the South was to be deprived of slave states in the new southern territory was intolerable for many southerners. And growing numbers of northerners saw slavery as an evil that must be contained.

Did Congress have authority to determine whether or not slavery could exist in territory obtained by the United States? Southerners who first raised this question replied that since the Constitution recognized and protected property in slaves, owners of such property could not lawfully be prohibited from carrying that property wherever they went, even across the Missouri Compromise line.

Antislavery northerners pointed out that the Constitution plainly gave Congress jurisdiction over the territories and that the Confederation Congress had exercised those rights by excluding slavery from the Northwest Territory in 1785. Then the federal Congress had adopted the Missouri Compromise, in 1820, which had excluded slavery north of a westward line running from the southern border of Missouri.

A third position on slavery in the territories was possible. Usually called *squatter sovereignty* or *popular sovereignty*, this interpretation was set forth by Lewis Cass of Michigan and Stephen A. Douglas of Illinois. They argued that there was a long-established precedent in America for communities to act as the best judges of their own interests. Let the new territories be set up with the question of slavery left open, and then permit the people to decide for themselves.

It sounded sensible, but this doctrine was disastrously vague on the crucial matter of timing. Just when should a territory decide—after slaves had been brought in or before? By leaving resolution of this question open to zealots of both camps, popular sovereignty also left it open to violence.

The Election of 1848

By 1848 the issue of the extension of slavery to new territories had become so poisonous that both major parties tried to avoid it while preparing for the presidential campaign. On taking office, Polk had pledged himself to a single term. "Regular" Democrats, at their convention in Baltimore, nominated Cass on a platform that ignored slavery. The "regular" Whigs, at their convention in Philadelphia, hoped to silence talk on all issues by nominating the "hero of Buena Vista," General Taylor.

The watchword of the regulars in both parties was "party harmony." But they reckoned without antislavery northern Democrats. In New York and New England they became known as Barnburners, because they were said to be willing to burn down the Democratic "barn" in order to get rid of the proslavery "rats." The regulars also reckoned without the "conscience" Whigs. In August 1848 these antislavery Democrats and Whigs, who had left their regular party conventions, met in Buffalo with other antislavery leaders and formed the Free Soil party. Its slogan was "Free soil, Free speech, Free labor, and Free men." They nominated Martin Van Buren, who had won their favor by his stand against the annexation of Texas.

The 1848 election itself aroused little popular enthusiasm. Neither Taylor nor Cass had much popular appeal, and Van Buren—despite his antislavery position—could not live down his reputation as a slippery fox. Moreover, he had no nationwide machine behind him. When the votes came in, Taylor had 1,360,000 popular votes to Cass's 1,220,000. The Free Soilers polled only 291,000, but they absorbed enough Democratic support in New York to give that state's electoral vote to Taylor, and enough Whig votes in Ohio and Indiana to throw those states to Cass.

The Free Soil party also elected nine congressmen to a closely divided House, where they might hold the balance of power. Most important, the Free Soilers had demonstrated the potential strength and disruptive power of a purely sectional party. Now there could be no glossing over the slavery issue. Southern extremists had fresh reasons with which to convince moderates in their states that the South must unite to protect slavery.

The Compromise of 1850

Sectional tensions relaxed for a moment in 1848 when news of gold in California spread across the nation. Americans of every class and occupation headed for the Pacific Coast. Men from all over the world rushed to join them. By 1849, California had an unruly and heavily male population of over 100,000—and an inadequate military government. Polk had retired before a deeply divided Congress could decide California's future. President Taylor recommended that California (and New Mexico and Utah as well) draw up constitutions and decide without congressional direction whether or not slavery should be excluded. Congress, however, was in no mood to let the new president decide such an important matter on his own.

The fears of proslavery spokesmen were soon confirmed. The constitutions of all three territories banned slavery. Many southern congressmen then took an uncompromising stand on all sectional issues. Should the sale of slaves be

banned in the District of Columbia? Should the 1793 law on fugitive slaves be tightened? Must Texas, a slave state, give part of its western lands to the proposed free territory of New Mexico? Southern unity in defense of slavery had never been so strong. Some politicians in the South began talking about the slave states seceding—withdrawing from the Union.

Everyone knew a crisis was coming except President Taylor; his reaction was to ask Congress to avoid "exciting topics of sectional character." At a time when senators and representatives carried Bowie knives and Colt revolvers, Taylor's request seemed rather less forceful than it might have been. Clearly the South had no intention of allowing California to enter the Union as a free state unless it received important concessions. And it was becoming clear that the South might secede rather than accept the Wilmot Proviso.

Yet Congress was still controlled by older men who loved the Union more than their section. They were shocked by the possibility that the Union might fail. Henry Clay, at seventy-three, remained a powerful and persuasive orator who understood the desperate mood of the South. He consulted his old rival, Daniel Webster of Massachusetts, and got his backing. In his last and finest hour, Clay rose to present the Senate with eight resolutions that carefully balanced the interests of the free and slave states. No more momentous package of compromises had ever been presented in the federal legislature—and none have equaled it since for comprehensiveness, good will, and ultimate failure.

The Compromise of 1850, as adopted, amounted to the following eight propositions: (1) California was to be admitted as a free state; (2) two separate territorial governments in Utah and New Mexico would decide for themselves whether to permit or abolish slavery; (3) the disputed land between Texas and New Mexico was to be assigned to New Mexico; (4) the United States would pay debts Texas had contracted before annexation; (5) slavery in the District of Columbia would not be abolished without the consent of its residents and Maryland's and not without compensation to owners; (6) the slave trade would be prohibited in the District of Columbia; (7) a stricter fugitive slave law was to be adopted; (8) Congress would declare its own lack of jurisdiction over the domestic, interstate slave trade.

Forging the Compromise of 1850 involved one of the most hotly contested battles in congressional history. Against Clay were an angry, suspicious president, secessionists, outright antislavery men, and Free Soilers. President Taylor was firm in his conviction that California must be admitted to the Union without any reservations. Secessionists such as Jefferson Davis (Mississippi), Barnwell Rhett (South Carolina), and Louis T. Wigfall (Texas) were contemptuous of compromise. Antislavery extremists and radical Free Soilers such as William H. Seward (New York), Salmon P. Chase and Joshua Giddings (both of Ohio), and Charles Sumner (Massachusetts) stood firm for the Wilmot Proviso and spoke of a "higher law" than the Constitution—the law of God—under which slavery could never be justified.

But Clay's resolutions were sufficiently broad and conciliatory to win over the many moderates in both sections. Among the staunchest was Webster, whose moving speech in the Senate supported the entire compromise, even Clay's severe new fugitive slave law. There was an immediate, angry outcry against Webster. He had underestimated northern revulsion against returning fugitive slaves, as well as northern hatred of the whole plantation system. For the moment, however, his efforts strengthened the Unionist position, to which others rallied.

Outstanding among them was Stephen A. Douglas, who brought many in Congress around to the view that the Southwest was geographically unsuitable for slave labor. After the exhausted Clay retired from the battle, Douglas whipped through the measures that made up the Compromise of 1850. He was helped by the sudden death of President Taylor early in July and the succession of Vice-President Millard Fillmore, a Free Soiler who supported the compromise.

Several northern states soon virtually nullified the fugitive slave law through "personal liberty" laws that allowed alleged fugitives to have legal counsel, jury trials, and other means of defending their freedom. Northern blacks also took up the defense of fugitives. Americans of African ancestry, they said, had too long been characterized as meek and yielding. "This reproach must be wiped out," declared the escaped slave Frederick Douglass, "and nothing short of resistance on the part of the colored man can wipe it out. Every slave-hunter who meets a bloody death in his infernal business is an argument in favor of the manhood of our race."

The Election of 1852

The nation as a whole rejoiced when news of the compromise became known. In the presidential election of 1852, the national desire for tranquillity and moderation seemed to persist. Franklin Pierce, the Democratic candidate, easily defeated General Winfield Scott, the Whig candidate, by a margin of 254 to 42 in the electoral college. The Free Soil party was mauled in the election: Its candidate, John P. Hale of New Hampshire, won only half the number of votes Van Buren had received just four years earlier.

In the long run, the issue of slavery and its extension could not be so easily settled. An ominous sign of trouble ahead was the breakup of the Whig party following the deaths of Webster and Clay in 1852. The party, said one commentator, "seems almost annihilated by the recent elections." Southern Whigs felt this was precisely what any party that accepted the guidance of antislavery men such as Seward deserved. The Democrats still stood as a great national party, to which many southern Whigs were now drawn.

Northern Whigs found nowhere to go. Having lost the presidential election, with their foremost

Daniel Webster. *(Library of Congress)*

traditional leaders dead, with many of their southern followers defecting to the Democrats, and with their own adherents divided by the issues of slavery and Catholic immigration, northern Whigs seemed to have no political home. One of the two great national political parties simply fell apart almost overnight, and its disintegration left a vacuum in the nation's traditional system of politics.

In the few years since 1846, the nation had taken a new fork in the road. The cry for Manifest Destiny and an aggressive president brought the vast Northwest under United States control and commenced a war against Mexico which ended with even larger stretches of territory seized from that neighboring republic. Whatever the justification or lack of it, this addition of territory set the United States on a perilous experiment. Could the national government take control of such a huge amount of land and incorporate it into the nation without controversy? Clearly the answer was no.

The essential problem was that the expansion of slavery in the south and its previous abolition in the northern states made for a fundamental conflict of interest. That conflict came to settle on a single important issue: How would slavery be handled in the newly incorporated territories? That issue nearly took the nation apart after the Mexican-American War. It was patched over in a dazzling feat of political compromise in 1850. Yet it was by no means clear that the nation had settled the question on a permanent basis.

The United States in 1850

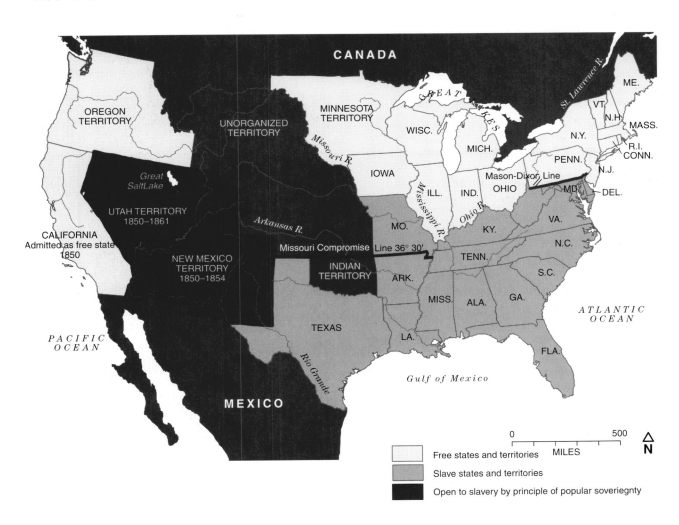

CHAPTER 15   MANIFEST DESTINY AND SLAVERY

SUMMARY

Along with slavery the issue that dominated American politics during the 1840s was manifest destiny—the idea that America was destined to rule the entire continent. By the end of the decade, the United States had gone a long way toward reaching this goal.

The Canadian border conflict with Britain, aggravated during this period by incidents such as the *Caroline* affair, the Aroostook "war," and the *Creole* incident, was settled peacefully by the Webster-Ashburton Treaty of 1842, which fixed the boundary as far west as Minnesota and Ontario.

In the Southwest, Texas became an independent republic in 1836 and a new state in 1845. In the Far West, Americans looked to the Oregon country and to California, which was then part of Mexico.

The election of James Polk in 1844 was a victory for expansionists. Polk promptly settled the Oregon boundary with Britain, since war with Mexico over Texas seemed a real possibility. By treaty in 1846, the Canadian–United States border was finally fixed to the Pacific.

In the same year, Americans who had settled in California declared themselves independent of Mexico as the Bear Flag Republic. Polk provoked war against Mexico, with the aim of winning New Mexico and California. Though the United States handily defeated Mexican armies, the war aroused great opposition, especially among northern Whigs. The Treaty of Guadalupe Hidalgo in 1848 established the Rio Grande boundary and obtained Upper California and the Utah and New Mexico territories for a payment of $13 million to Mexico.

The joy over these new territories was marred by the urgency of the slavery issue. The questions now were whether the new states to be carved out of the territories would be slave or free, and who would decide—Congress or the people who settled the newly acquired region. The issue of the extension of slavery became poisonous. In the election of 1848, it led to the formation of a new third party, with Van Buren as its candidate. The Whig candidate, General Taylor, won, but the Free Soilers elected enough representatives to a closely divided House of Representatives to threaten the balance of political and sectional power.

Open conflict was postponed another ten years with the Compromise of 1850, by which California entered the Union as a free state, and the western boundary of Texas was fixed. In two new territories—New Mexico and Utah—the question of slavery was left to the people to decide. Slave trading, but not slavery, was prohibited in the District of Columbia. A strong fugitive slave law was passed to satisfy the South.

The fugitive slave law deeply angered many northerners. Yet for a few years politics went on as usual, and in 1852 the Democratic candidate, Franklin Pierce, was elected president. Almost immediately the Whig party began to disintegrate. Its collapse resulted in the end of the nation's second party system (of Whigs and Democrats) and left a political vacuum.

TIME LINE

1821	Mexico wins independence from Spain	1845	Texas admitted to Union by joint resolution of Congress
1833	Sauk and Fox forced from Iowa and Wisconsin territories	1846	Border of Oregon country settled by treaty with Britain
1836	Anglo-Americans declare Texas independent	1846	U.S. declares war against Mexico
		1846	Wilmot Proviso
1836	Santa Anna overwhelms Americans at the Alamo	1847	Led by Brigham Young, Mormons found Salt Lake City
1836	Houston defeats and captures Santa Anna at San Jacinto	1847	Americans capture Mexico City
		1848	Treaty of Guadalupe Hidalgo
1837	*Caroline* affair	1849	California gold rush
1839	Aroostook "war"	1850	Compromise of 1850
1841	Successful slave revolt aboard the *Creole*	1852	Electoral defeat signals drastic decline of Whig party
1842	Webster-Ashburton Treaty		
1844	Expansionist Polk elected president		

Suggested Readings

R. Slotkin, *Regeneration through Violence: The Mythology of the American Frontier* (1973), focuses on Indian–white relations. R. Berkhoffer, *Salvation and the Savage: An Analysis of Protestant Missions and American Indian Response, 1787–1862* (1965), should be balanced by R. Pearce, *The Savages of America: A Study of the Indian and the Idea of Civilization* (rev. ed., 1965). The link between western expansion and militarism may be approached through F. Prucha, *The Sword of the Republic: The United States Army on the Frontier, 1783–1846* (1969). A. Moore, *The Frontier Mind* (1957), portrays the pioneer experience as a brutalizing one that turned sensitive people into unthinking toilers.

The impact of westward expansion on American society as a whole is discussed in R. Billington, *America's Frontier Heritage* (1966), which has a fine bibliography. D. Boorstin, *The Americans: The National Experience* (1965), is full of fascinating trivia on, as well as provocative analyses of the material culture of antebellum America. See also W. Goetzmann, *Exploration and Empire: The Explorer and the Scientist in the Winning of the American West, 1805–1900* (1973). The physical devastation of Indian lands, first by the fur trade and later by land speculation and governmental policies, is described in V. Vogel, *This Country Was Ours: A Documentary History of the American Indian* (1972).

A special perspective on an important region is D. Weber, *The Mexican Frontier, 1821–1846: The American Southwest under Mexico* (1982). In addition, see W. Binkley, *The Texas Revolution* (1952); S. Siegel, *A Political History of the Texas Republic, 1836–1845* (1956); A. Bill, *Rehearsal for Conflict: The War with Mexico, 1846–1848* (1947); and P. Bergeron, *The Presidency of James K. Polk* (1987). In addition, there is an interesting study by R. Johannsen, *To the Halls of the Montezumas: The Mexican War in the American Imagination* (1985). Diplomatic complications are explored in D. Pletcher, *The Diplomacy of the Annexation of Texas, Oregon, and the Mexican War (1973)*.

United States expansion into the Far West in this period is treated in C. Gates, *Empire of the Pacific: A History of the Pacific Northwest* (1957); J. Rawls, *Indians of California: The Changing Image* (1984);

and the relevant portion of J. Caughey, *California* (1970). In addition, C. Drury, *Marcus Whitman, Pioneer and Martyr* (1937), supplies information on the importance of the missionary impulse. See D. Morgan, *Jedediah Smith and the Opening of the West* (1964), for the fur trade in the Rockies and farther west. Francis Parkman's personal and evocative account, *The California and Oregon Trail* (1849), better known as *The Oregon Trail*, is available in several modern editions.

There is interesting and often controversial material on the Mormons in L. Arrington, *Great Basin Kingdom: An Economic History of the Latterday Saints, 1830–1900* (1958). F. McKiernan et al. (eds.), *The Restoration Movement: Essays on Mormon History* (1973), is a comprehensive account of church history with a particularly strong analysis of the relationship between two major branches, the Brighamites and the "Reorganization." Two of the great Mormon leaders have received perceptive biographical treatments: F. Brodie, *No Man Knows My History: The Life of Joseph Smith* (1945); and N. Bringhurst, *Brigham Young and the Expanding American Frontier* (1986).

An excellent account of domestic politics in this period contains considerable detail but is nonetheless highly readable: A. Nevins, *Ordeal of the Union* (2 vols., 1947). J. Silbey (ed.), *The Transformation of American Politics, 1840–1860* (1967), is a well-chosen anthology, especially revealing on the forces behind the restructuring of party alignments. H. Hamilton, *The Compromise of 1850* (1964), offers a fine analysis of events that seemed to contemporaries to be a turning point in the course of the nation. The very strong reaction of African Americans to the compromise and to the events preceding it can be found in H. Aptheker (ed.), *A Documentary History of the Negro People in the United States* (1951).

This was an age dominated by struggles among towering personalities in the political arena; hence the studies of Calhoun, Clay, and Webster cited in Chapter 11 are of particular importance. In addition, see M. Baxter, *One and Inseparable: Daniel Webster and the Union* (1984). For a fascinating look at the personal writings of ordinary women who crossed the country in the mid-nineteenth century, see J. Jeffrey, *Frontier Women: The Trans-Mississippi West, 1840–1880* (1979).

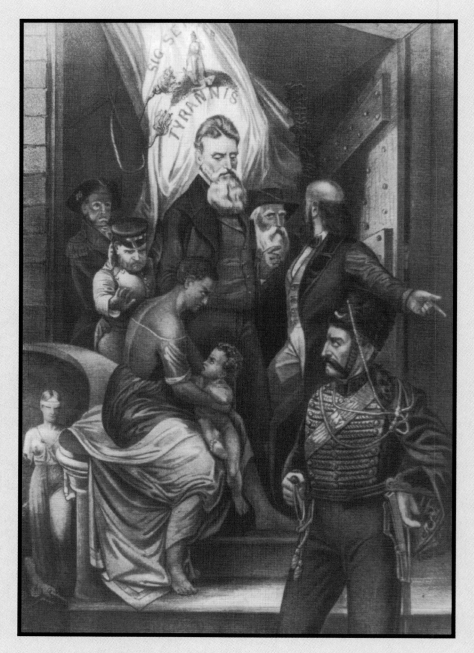

John Brown meeting the slave-mother and her child on the steps of Charlestown jail on his way to execution. *(Library of Congress)*

CHAPTER 16

THE UNION COMES APART

For two months, from December 1859 through February 1860, the House of Representatives was locked in struggle over the election of its own Speaker. Southern Democrats and northern Republicans attacked each other in fiery language. At one point a pistol fell onto the floor from the pocket of a New York congressman. Some members thought he had drawn to shoot, and hands were seen quickly reaching for pockets. The tension remained at a fever pitch. One senator commented: "The only persons who do not have a revolver and a knife are those who have two revolvers." Another wrote: "The members on both sides are mostly armed with deadly weapons, and it is said that the friends of each are armed in the galleries." The atmosphere even affected the much quieter world of women. In 1857, the wife of a new cabinet member wrote to a friend: "I avoid making myself acquainted with politics lest in an unguarded moment something slip from my lips that evil minded listeners can seize upon . . . for the newspapers." Finally, after forty-two ballots, the House elected an obscure Whig from New Jersey. William Pennington was the first (and last) freshman congressman to serve as Speaker since Henry Clay in 1811.

The cause of this tension was slavery, especially slavery in the territories. In the early 1850s, slavery was brought home to northerners who had previously regarded it as a distant problem. First of all, the new fugitive slave law created widespread anger in the North. A second factor was, of all things, publication of a novel. *Uncle Tom's Cabin* had an enormous impact on northern public opinion.

Yet it was slavery in the territories that became the central and most divisive issue. The Democrats in Congress pushed through the Kansas-Nebraska Act, which repealed the Missouri Compromise and put the future of the "free" territories in doubt. The question became cancerous. A small-scale civil war broke out between Free Soilers and proslavery elements in Kansas. When the Supreme Court was asked to settle the question in the *Dred Scott* case, it decided in favor of the South. Many northerners concluded that there really was a "slave-power conspiracy" to extend slavery throughout the West and perhaps eventually to the free state as well.

That decision flew directly in the face of the principal plank of the new Republican party. The collapse of the Whig party after

1852 left a political vacuum that at first was filled by the rise of the Know-Nothings, a party dedicated to countering the great wave of Roman Catholic immigration. But dedication to free soil proved even stronger, and the Republicans emerged as the major counterweight to the Democrats almost overnight.

The principles of the two parties were given a thorough airing in 1858, when the Democrat Stephen A. Douglas debated a rising lawyer, Abraham Lincoln, in a contest for a Senate seat from Illinois. By insisting that slavery must expand no farther, the Republicans made themselves a purely sectional party. Not only did the South see itself under attack from Republican victories in the North, but an antislavery zealot, John Brown, mounted a raid on a federal arsenal in Virginia, hoping to spark a general slave rebellion. John Brown confirmed the South's worst suspicions. A year later, in 1860, many southern spokesmen made it clear that the election of a Republican president would mean secession.

Upon Lincoln's election as a minority president in a four-way contest, the states of the lower South began to secede and organize a government of their own. The upper South remained on the fence until Lincoln maneuvered South Carolina authorities into firing the first shot, at the federal Fort Sumter in Charleston harbor. That action forced the states of the upper South to a decision. They split evenly, four joining the Confederacy and four remaining with the Union. Lincoln moved to suppress the "rebellion," and southerners rallied to the cause of their newly independent nation. The United States had finally come apart on the one issue the Founding Fathers had tried so hard to avoid.

THE FAILURE OF COMPROMISE

The Democrat Franklin Pierce of New Hampshire took office as president on March 4, 1853. A contemporary described him as a "vain, showy, and pliant man." Unfortunately, the description was close to being correct. Most Americans, including the president, still hoped that the Compromise of 1850 would end the agitation over slavery once and for all. In the Senate, Stephen A. Douglas grandly announced: "I have determined never to make another speech on the slavery question." He urged senators to "drop the subject." But the subject would not "drop."

The weakness of the president did not help matters, but even a much stronger man would probably have been overwhelmed. Enforcement of the fugitive slave law and Harriet Beecher Stowe's vivid fictional account of slavery gave northerners a view of slavery they had never had before. Douglas's Kansas-Nebraska Act unraveled the agreements of the Missouri Compromise. And the disintegration of the Whig party, so badly rotted by sectional division and the loss of its leaders, resulted in a new political alignment.

Slavery Comes Home to the North

The fugitive slave law of 1850 provided southern slaveholders with considerable powers for recovering runaways. Its provisions were so broad that it made some free northern blacks move to Canada in fear of being legally kidnapped into slavery. Any slaveholder or his or her hired agent was empowered to seize a "runaway" slave, to demand assistance from any federal marshal in the process, and then to go before a federal magistrate. These judges received $10 if they ruled that a Negro was a slave, $5 if they ruled that the person was free. The law also provided for a fine of $1000 and six months in jail for anyone convicted of assisting a fugitive slave.

All these provisions outraged abolitionists. They also angered a good many people in the North who had been hostile to abolition. African American leaders such as Frederick Douglass called upon the black community to resist with force. Many northern states passed "personal liberty" laws that attempted to nullify the effects of the new federal statute. Then a series of incidents brought state and federal officials into conflict.

In Ohio, for example, a crowd of students from Oberlin College—long a hotbed of abolition sentiment—forcibly rescued a fugitive from a slave catcher. Several members of that crowd were convicted by a federal jury under terms of the Fugitive Slave Act. Then a state court ordered the arrest of the slave catcher and all federal officials who had cooperated with him. Eventually a compromise was worked out, but it had become clear that enforcement of the act would create problems.

Other dramatic incidents inflamed public opinion. A black man named Frederick Wilkins was working quietly as a waiter in a Boston coffeehouse when he was suddenly seized by a Virginia slave catcher who knew him as Shadrach, a runaway slave. While Wilkins was being held for return to Virginia, a crowd of blacks burst in and took him away. In New York City, James Hamlet was grabbed and packed off to Maryland so fast that his wife and children had no chance to say goodbye to him. As things turned out, Hamlet was lucky. His African American friends and a few sympathetic whites raised eight hundred dollars to purchase his freedom.

A more publicized incident occurred at Christiana, Pennsylvania. A Maryland slave owner tried to recapture his runaway slave, the slave escaped, and the owner and his son were badly wounded in the ensuing gun battle. Several blacks and whites were indicted for murder and treason, but all were acquitted by a local jury. Only a few years later, the streets of Boston were lined with federal troops and marshals when the fugitive Anthony Burns was marched from the courthouse down to the ship waiting to carry him back to slavery in Virginia. That federal force held back a crowd, estimated at fifty thousand, that hissed, booed, and shouted in protest. The throng was three times larger than the entire population of Boston at the time of the Stamp Act crisis.

It cost the federal government the enormous sum of $100,000 to return Anthony Burns to slavery. The expense, and much more the injustice, was widely publicized throughout the North. About three hundred blacks were dragged back to slavery under terms of the Fugitive Slave Act. For every slave returned, however, thousands of northerners changed their minds about the South's peculiar institution. It had often seemed remote, but a glimpse of Anthony Burns in chains was far more vivid than the most awful tales in abolitionist literature.

Harriet Beecher Stowe, Uncle Tom's cabin, Topsy dancing, and Little Eva and Uncle Tom. *(Library of Congress)*

There was one exception—*Uncle Tom's Cabin,* probably the most influential novel ever published in the United States. Harriet Beecher Stowe grew up in New England. As a daughter of the famous preacher Lyman Beecher, she lived for some time in Cincinnati, just across the river from slave cabins in Kentucky. She wrote *Uncle Tom's Cabin* as a series of magazine articles. Then, in the spring of 1852, the publisher brought out her story in book form. He printed only 5000 copies because he had no great expectations for heavy sales.

The first printing sold out in two days. Within another week, 10,000 copies were swept up in the North. Within a year, the novel sold 300,000 copies. In order to meet demand, the publisher kept eight of the new rotary steam presses going around the clock and bought the entire stock of three paper mills. Throughout the North, Mrs. Stowe was hailed for lifting the veil of the peculiar institution. In the South, she was denounced for having painted it in false colors.

Such widespread readership clearly indicated that *Uncle Tom's Cabin* told many people what they wanted to hear. The story focused on Uncle Tom, a loyal and deeply Christian slave who grew to manhood in Kentucky. Tom's benevolent master got into financial trouble and was forced to sell him. The forgiving slave had to leave his wife and his "Old Kentucky Home" for the long trip "down the river" to New Orleans.

While Tom is carried off by a vicious slave trader, his daughter, her baby, and her husband flee to Ohio. (The book's description of that flight provided stage producers with a fine challenge to meet the public's taste for melodrama: Eliza was represented as darting across ice in the Ohio River, babe in arms, bloodhounds baying at her heels. Finally, to everyone's relief, she found herself nearly safe in the warm home of kindly Quakers.)

In New Orleans, Tom is purchased by a kindly, genteel family. But once again fate intervenes just when his new owner is about to free him. He is sold again, this time to an unfeeling slave master who takes him to a desolate plantation in Arkansas. His new owner, Simon Legree, grew up in New England but is thoroughly heartless. In the end, Tom is beaten to death at Legree's orders. As he dies, Tom forgives the two black overseers who had been ordered to lash him.

Mrs. Stowe's story was more complicated than this. For modern tastes it is almost unbearably sentimental, and its characters and situations downright unbelievable. It has been criticized as a third- or even tenth-rate novel. But at the time it deeply touched many Americans. It had a good story. It made a strong case that slavery was evil even when good people were involved. And it showed that the institution itself damaged families and homes, both white and black. This demonstration, as much as anything, gave the novel its powerful appeal.

The Kansas-Nebraska Act

Northern incitement and protection of runaways led the planters to seek countermeasures. A minority demanded nothing less than the reopening of the African slave trade. A more influential group, supported by Pierce himself, urged acquisition of the Spanish colony of Cuba, where slavery was flourishing during a boom in sugar production. There might have been enough public support for seizing Cuba if Congress, in 1854, had not passed a law that, in the words of a New York newspaper, "has forever rendered annexation impossible." This was the Kansas-Nebraska Act. By reopening the question of slavery in the western territories, it strengthened northern determination to stop the spread of slavery everywhere.

The Nebraska country was a vast empire ranging west of the ninety-fifth meridian all the way to the Oregon Territory and north to the Canadian border. Its southeastern portion bordered the slave state of Missouri. But slaveholders were forbidden to extend slavery there by the Missouri Compromise of 1820, which had banned slavery "forever" north of a line drawn westward from the southern border of Missouri. This same portion of the Nebraska country and the area north of it to the Great Bend of the Missouri River (which now forms the northeastern boundary of the state of Nebraska) also lay just beyond the "permanent" Indian frontier. Here, in the words of Stephen A. Douglas (the italics are his), the Indians, by treaty, had been guaranteed "perpetual occupancy, *with an express condition that* [the land] *should never be incorporated within the limits of a territory or state of the Union.*"

As early as the congressional session of 1843-1844, Douglas, then a freshman member of the House of Representatives from Illinois, had introduced the first bill to break the Indian treaties and organize the Territory of Nebraska. Others, meanwhile, led by Senator David R. Atchison of Missouri, vowed that they would see Nebraska "sink in hell" before allowing it to be organized as a free territory. The sectional conflict was intensified by the rivalry between North and South for the first transcontinental railroad. Douglas became the leading spokesman for its construction over a northern route that would link the Pacific coast with Chicago, where he owned considerable real estate. He offered a grand vision:

No man can keep up with the spirit of this age who travels on anything slower than the locomotive, and fails to receive intelligence by lightning. We must therefore have Rail Roads and Telegraphs from the Atlantic to the Pacific, through our own territory. Not one line only, but many lines. . . . The removal of the Indian barrier and the extension of the laws of the United States in the form of Territorial governments are the first steps toward the accomplishment of each and all of those objects.

Douglas reported his fateful Nebraska bill in the Senate on January 4, 1854. His initial report was deliberately vague. He specifically undertook to apply in Nebraska that part of the Louisiana Purchase north of 36°30'—the "popular sovereignty" provisions of the Compromise of 1850, which allowed Utah and New Mexico to make their own decisions about slavery. Once he had enlarged the area of application of the principle of popular sovereignty, Douglas was forced to concede that the Missouri Compromise was henceforth to be "inoperative and void."

Still another concession by Douglas revolved around the railroad issue. It was clear to most people at this time that Congress would help build only one transcontinental line. That route, according to a government-sponsored survey, would meet the fewest physical obstacles along the Mexican border. In fact, the purpose of the Gadsden Purchase from Mexico had been to provide a route for such a railroad.

Atchison's prosouthern group in Missouri advocated a central route originating in St. Louis. But they would not even consider supporting any transcontinental line, including their own, if it passed through territory closed to slavery. Fearful of their strength, and fearful that the southern part of Nebraska bordering Missouri would fall to slavery, a group of Iowa congressmen urged Douglas to divide Nebraska into two territories—north and south. This, they thought, would ensure the passage of the transcontinental trains through the the Platte River valley, which had been settled by free soilers, in the northerly territory. Although skeptical of the Iowans' fears concerning slavery in the Nebraska country, Douglas felt he had to agree to their request as well. His bill was altered so as to propose the division of Nebraska into two territories,

The United States in 1854

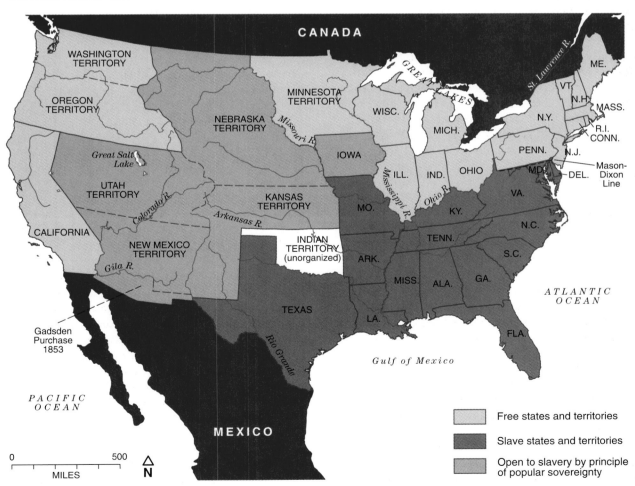

Free states and territories

Slave states and territories

Open to slavery by principle of popular sovereignty

Nebraska and Kansas. The southerly territory of Kansas was immediately marked for slavery by the South.

It took southerners outside Congress a little time to realize what they had won. One newspaper declared that the Kansas-Nebraska Act was "barren of practical benefit." But once northerners began to attack the measure, southern opinion began to rally in its favor. For their part, northerners were particularly angered by repeal of the Missouri Compromise. Lincoln wrote in his third-person autobiographical sketch that "the repeal of the Missouri Compromise aroused him as he had never been before."

While Douglas's draft of the bill was being revised, Senators Salmon P. Chase of Ohio and Charles Sumner of Massachusetts were writing an Appeal of the Independent Democrats in Congress to the People of the United States. Their words helped stimulate formation of a new Republican party and became the most influential attack on the Kansas-Nebraska Act.

They were determined to block passage of a "criminal betrayal of precious rights; . . . part and parcel of an atrocious plot to exclude from a vast unoccupied region immigrants from the Old World and free laborers from our own States, and convert it into a dreary region of despotism, inhabited by masters and slaves." Douglas tried to defend his legislation. Members of his own party, at his home base in Chicago, hooted him off the platform, and crowds menaced him in the streets.

"Bleeding Kansas"

The Kansas-Nebraska Act failed its test in the new Territory of Kansas. Did a new territory under "popular sovereignty" have the power to prohibit or legalize slavery before framing its constitution and seeking statehood? Douglas said yes; southern spokesmen said no. Only a state could decide this question, southerners maintained; a territory could not keep slaves out. As settlers moved into Kansas, the issue moved beyond debate. Most of the newcomers were nonslaveholding farmers from nearby states. But as in all frontier settlements, there were hustlers out to bleed the new arrivals. To draw attention away from their activities, the schemers kept the slavery controversy boiling. Other people also helped turn Kansas into a battleground. The New England Emigrant Aid Company and other northern associations financed

Stephen Arnold Douglas. (*Library of Congress*)

the migration of more than a thousand "right-thinking" northerners to Kansas to vote against slavery and to see that everyone else did also. When they got there, they found boxes from home—filled with rifles.

Henry Ward Beecher, Mrs. Stowe's brother and an antislavery clergyman, preached that guns, rather than Bibles, would be most persuasive against slavery. So firearms known as "Beecher's Bibles" turned up in Kansas. Missourians moved into the territory to counter this invasion. Other southerners came, determined to pack the first Kansas territorial legislature with "right-thinking" proslavery men.

On election day in March 1855, slightly more than 2000 Kansans were registered to vote. Over 6000 ballots were cast, most of them by Missourians who had crossed their western border into Kansas for the day. The governor of the Kansas Territory tried to disqualify eight of the thirty-one members who had been elected irregularly. President Pierce refused to back the governor and eventually recalled him. The new legislature adopted a series of repressive laws that, among other punishments, prescribed the death penalty for aiding a fugitive slave. But Free Soilers in Kansas remained unintimidated. In the fall of 1855 they gathered in Topeka and drew up their own constitution. In January 1856, they elected their own legislature and governor. Kansas now had two rival administrations and was ripe for war.

While Pierce delayed, war came. A force of hard-drinking proslavery men raided Lawrence in search of some Free Soil leaders the proslavery legislature had indicted for treason. The raiders burned the hotel, destroyed homes, and smashed Free Soil printing presses. The "Sack of Lawrence," which was of course exaggerated by northern newspapers, brought a bloodier sequel. John Brown of Osawatomie, Kansas, a fanatical abolitionist who was soon to become better known, gathered six followers, rode into the proslavery settlement at Pottawatomie Creek, and hacked five men to death. He acted, so he said, under God's authority. But his sacred

---

SOUTHERN REACTION TO THE BEATING OF SUMNER

A southern newspaper, the *Richmond Enquirer*, offered the following commentary on Brooks's beating of Sumner in the Senate:

In the main, the press of the South applaud the conduct of Mr. Brooks, without condition or limitation. Our approbation, at least, is entire and unreserved. We consider the act good in conception, better in execution, and best of all in consequence. The vulgar Abolitionists in the Senate are getting above themselves. They have been humored until they forget their position. They have grown saucy, and dare to be impudent to gentlemen! Now, they are a low, mean, scurvy set, with some little book-learning, but as utterly devoid of spirit or honor as a pack of curs. In-

trenched behind "privilege," they fancy they can slander the South and insult its representatives with impunity. The truth is, they have been suffered to run too long without collars. They must be lashed into submission. Sumner, in particular, ought to have nine-and-thirty early every morning. He is a great strapping fellow, and could stand the cowhide beautifully. Brooks frightened him, and at the first blow of the cane he bellowed like a bullcalf. . . . Mr. Brooks has initiated this salutary discipline, and he deserves applause for the bold, judicious manner in which he chastised the scamp Sumner. It was a proper act, done at the proper time, and in the proper place.

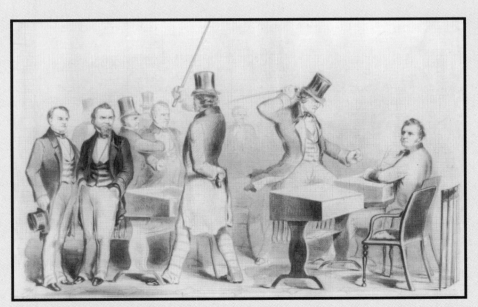

A depiction of the enraged Preston S. Brooks standing over Charles Sumner in the senate chamber about to land him a heavy blow of his cane. *(Library of Congress)*

AN ANTI-IRISH RIOT

Nativist sentiment resulted in a short-lived political party in the 1850s, but hostility toward foreign Catholics was considerably older. In Boston in 1837 a group of firemen pushed some mourners in an Irish funeral procession. The results were described by a man whose sympathies were with the Yankee firemen.

The ranks of the Irish were gradually thinned by the arrest of some of their more prominent members, who were carried off to jail amid loud shouts. . . .

Finally the Irish gave up the contest just in time to save themselves from the bayonets of the [militia], several companies of which were ordered to the scene. . . .

During the conflict the firemen demolished several tenements, throwing furniture, provisions and children into the street. Featherbeds were ripped open . . . The east wind wafted the feathers all over the city, causing such a shower as might have been taken, at a little distance, for a snow-storm. A large number of persons were badly injured on both sides, but the Irish suffered most severely. . . . There is not the least doubt that the riot originated in the assault upon the firemen. . . .

Much prejudice and ill blood had, for several years, existed between the fire department and the Irish. . . . It cannot be expected that the members of the fire department will look passively on and see their brethren assaulted, or their "machines" overturned.

The riot on St. Patrick's Day showing the attack on the police at the corner of Grand and Pitt Streets, New York City. *(Library of Congress)*

mission started a guerrilla war in which over two hundred were killed.

Violence over Kansas spread to Congress. Charles Sumner of Massachusetts, speaking in the Senate, railed for two days at the "harlot slavery," but aimed his sharpest barbs at Senator Andrew P. Butler of South Carolina. Two days later, Butler's nephew, a congressman, marched onto the floor of the Senate and beat Sumner over the head with a cane, making him an invalid for several years. The assault on Sumner by South Carolina's "Bully" Brooks, together with the news from Kansas, came as preparations were being made for the presidential campaign of 1856.

A New Party Alignment

The breakup of the Whig party had by this time become obvious to all political observers. The sectional strife of Pierce's administration had weakened but not destroyed the other great national party, the Democrats, and had sent politicians searching for new political homes.

The first of the new parties, the American party, raised its standard in 1852. It took its name from its opposition to Catholic immigrants. Politicians in both sections were drawn to it partly because they thought the issue of immigration might deflect attention from slavery. They were soon proved wrong.

The American party was so concerned over its "Americanist" purity that it adopted secret regulations requiring members to pretend they "knew nothing" when asked for information. They soon became known as the Know-Nothings. Secret handclasps and passwords attracted many people to the party, but its anti-immigrant/Catholic stance antagonized many others. One of them was Abraham Lincoln. Slower than most to disown his Whig allegiance, Lincoln wrote in 1855:

I am not a Know-Nothing. That is certain. How could I be? . . . Our progress in degeneracy appears to me to be pretty rapid. As a nation, we began by declaring that "all men are created equal." We now practically read it "all men are created equal except Negroes." When the Know-Nothings get control, it will read "all men are created equal except Negroes and foreigners and Catholics." When it comes to this I should prefer emigrating to some country where they make no pretense of loving liberty. . . .

Despite such objections, the new party won astounding victories in the state elections of 1854. But when the American party's national convention voted to support the Kansas-Nebraska Act, most of its southern following joined the Democrats. Many northeastern Know-Nothings moved to the new Republican party.

That party came into being almost spontaneously in 1854. No single leader or group could claim credit for its organization. Two central and firm beliefs brought its adherents together: the determination to keep slavery out of the territories and the conviction that Congress had the right to do so. Besides northern Know-Nothings, Free Soilers flocked to the Republicans. So did "conscience Whigs"—those whose dislike of slavery was so strong they had refused to join their party's condemnation of the Wilmot Proviso. Northern Democrats who rejected all further compromise with the South also joined, as did abolitionists and a considerable number of German immigrants. Although the Republicans opposed the extension of slavery, no more than a small minority had any interest in the well-being of African Americans. North or South, blacks remained outside the land of opportunity. Most Republicans wanted free soil—not freed slaves—and the advancement of the common white man rather than the betterment of the black.

BUCHANAN'S ORDEAL

Franklin Pierce's support of southern interests in Kansas cost him renomination in 1856. The Democrats won that election, but the most important political development was the surprisingly strong showing of the Republican party in the North. The new president, James Buchanan, encouraged the Supreme Court to settle the question of slavery in the territories once and for all. The Court tackled the matter and decided that the Missouri Compromise was unconstitutional, that Congress could not keep slavery out of the territories.

Northerners were infuriated. The entire question was publicly aired in the extraordinary debates between Stephen A. Douglas and Abraham Lincoln, which first brought Lincoln to national attention. Not along afterward, the country was thrown into an uproar by one old man who decided to attack slavery directly where it already existed.

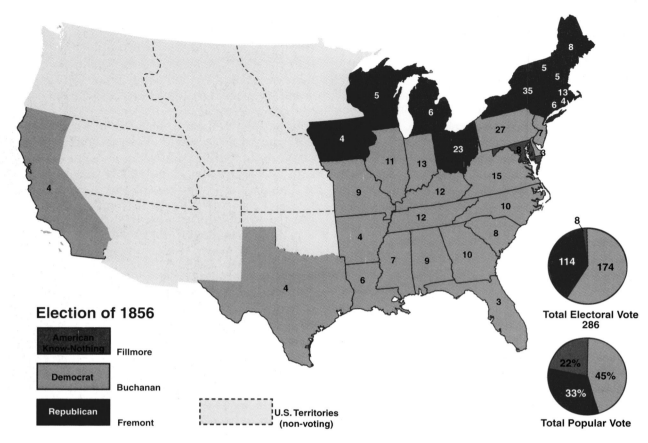

Election of 1856

American Know-Nothing — Fillmore

Democrat — Buchanan

Republican — Fremont

U.S. Territories (non-voting)

Total Electoral Vote 286

8 114 174

Total Popular Vote

22% 33% 45%

The election of 1856

The Election of 1856

National Democratic leaders did not dare back Douglas for the presidency. His successes, as in the adoption of the Kansas-Nebraska Act, proved even more damaging to the party than Pierce's failures. Instead, they turned to a veteran of forty years in politics, the conservative Pennsylvanian James Buchanan. As ambassador to Britain, Buchanan had the advantage of having been out of the country during Pierce's administration. For their first presidential campaign, Republicans placed their hopes on a military hero—General John C. Fremont, the glamorous Georgia-born son-in-law of the Jacksonian Democrat Senator Thomas Hart Benton of Missouri. The American party named former president Millard Fillmore.

Although "Old Buck" Buchanan soon came to be despised as a "northern man with southern principles," this combination of characteristics helped the efficient Democratic machine put him across with 174 votes in the electoral college to Fremont's 114 and Fillmore's 8. Buchanan's popular vote came to only 45 percent of the ballots cast. The sectional character of the balloting was scarcely a good omen. New England voted overwhelmingly for Fremont, who also won New York. Had he taken Pennsylvania and Illinois, the Republicans would have won the election. What comfort the South found in the victory hardly made up for the Republican show of strength.

Dred Scott

Buchanan took office only a few days before the first great crisis of his administration. The trouble came over the Supreme Court decision in *Dred Scott v. Sandford* (1857). Dred Scott, a slave, had been taken by his master in 1834 from Missouri to the free state of Illinois, and from there to the Wisconsin Territory, where he stayed until his return to Missouri several years later. The antislavery group who backed his suit for freedom hoped to prove that Dred Scott's living in a free state and in a territory where slavery was illegal under the Missouri Compromise had made him a free man.

The Supreme Court might simply have dismissed this case on the grounds that Scott was not a citizen of Missouri or of the United States and so not entitled to sue in a federal court. Or, falling back on an earlier Supreme Court decision, it might have ruled that Scott's residence in a free state suspended his slave status only temporarily. But the Court knew that Buchanan was expecting the judiciary to resolve the issue of slavery in the territories, especially in Kansas.

No fewer than eight of the nine justices on the Supreme Court wrote opinions on different aspects of the *Dred Scott* case. In speaking for the Court for more than two hours, Chief Justice Roger B. Taney spent half his time arguing that since blacks had been viewed as inferior beings at the time the Constitution was adopted, its framers did not intend to include them within the meaning of the term *citizen*. Therefore, the right of citizens of different states to sue in the federal courts could never apply to a former slave or a descendant of a slave.

Only two justices agreed with Taney's racial concepts and his history. But these two and four others joined Taney in a majority finding that Scott, even had he become free, had reverted to slavery on his return to the slave state of Missouri and had no right to sue in a federal court. Five justices, conforming to the president's wishes, joined the Chief Justice in plunging further. The slave, they explained, is property, pure and simple. According to the Fifth Amendment to the Constitution, "No person shall be . . . deprived of life, liberty, or property without due process of law." It was a violation of this clause, they said, to prohibit anyone from taking slaves into the territories.

"No word can be found in the Constitution," Taney observed about slaves, ". . . which entitles property of that kind to less protection than property of any other description." Thus Congress had no right under the Constitution to exclude slavery from the territories, and the Missouri Compromise was, and always had been, unconstitutional.

The Kansas-Nebraska Act had already declared the Missouri Compromise "inoperative and void." If, as the Court now held, the attempt of the compromise to legislate slavery out of the territories was also unconstitutional, the objec-

Chief Justice Roger B. Taney. *(Library of Congress)*

tive for which the Republican party had been formed was unconstitutional. Even the Douglas Democrats were troubled by the decision. For if slaves were property untouchable by law under the federal constitution, Douglas's program for popular sovereignty on slavery in the territories was dead.

In June 1857, as part of his continuing campaign against Douglas's popular-sovereignty position, Lincoln said of the *Dred Scott* decision:

If this important decision had been made by the unanimous concurrence of the judges, and without any partisan bias, and . . . had been in no part, based on assumed historical facts which are not really true; or, if . . . it had been before the court more than once, and had there been affirmed and reaffirmed through a course of years, it then might be, perhaps would be, factious, nay, even revolutionary, to not acquiesce in it as a precedent.

But when, as it is true, we find it wanting in all these claims to the public confidence, it is not resistance, it is not factious, it is not even disrespectful, to treat it as not having yet quite established a settled doctrine for the country.

The Lincoln–Douglas Debates

The troublesome issue of slavery in the territories was most thoroughly examined during the contest for the Illinois senatorial seat in 1858. The rising Republican candidate, Abraham Lincoln, challenged his Democratic opponent, Stephen A. Douglas, "the Little Giant," to a series of debates. Before the debates began, however, two events dashed southern hopes that had been raised by the *Dred Scott* decision.

The first was the business panic of August 1857. The depression that followed gave antislavery Republicans strong allies among two groups in the free economy. Both businessmen and their employees favored the Republican plank for high tariffs to stimulate free industry and industrial employment. Farmers liked the Republican plank for free homesteads. The sudden collapse of the economy did allow southern spokesmen to point with pride to the comparative stability and success of the slave system. But southerners were as fearful of high tariffs and free land as of the Republican party itself They grew more determined to preserve for their section, if only for political advantage, all the western territories not yet lost to slavery.

The second event was the state constitutional convention at Lecompton, Kansas, in October 1857. Proslavery delegates named in a rigged election wrote a constitution guaranteeing slavery. When the proposed constitution came up for popular approval, the dominant antislavery voters boycotted the balloting, and the proslavery party carried the vote. After considerable maneuvering, Congress offered Kansas statehood immediately, with a federal land grant, if in a second balloting its voters accepted the Lecompton Constitution. The alternative was continuing territorial status if they rejected it. Given the chance, Kansas voters overwhelmingly turned down the Lecompton Constitution. Here the matter rested until 1861, when Kansas entered the Union as a free state.

The Illinois Republican convention that was to nominate Lincoln to run against Douglas for the Senate met in Springfield in June 1858. Lincoln was not so well known as he soon would be. But in Illinois he was a popular figure, a prosperous lawyer, and a Whig leader who had served a term in the United States House of Representatives. In his speech accepting the nomination, he observed that the slavery issue had grown worse each year. "In my opinion," he said, "it will not cease until a crisis shall have been reached and passed. 'A house divided against itself cannot stand.'"

This "house divided" speech was studied carefully by Douglas and furnished the basis for his attacks on Lincoln in the seven debates that followed. Douglas, who admired Lincoln personally, attacked him during the debates as a sectionalist whose philosophy would end in "a war of extermination." Why, Douglas asked, did the Republicans say that slavery and freedom could not coexist? Lincoln replied that his party did not propose to interfere with slavery where it existed, nor did he wish to enforce social equality between blacks and whites, as Douglas charged. In keeping with the Republican program, he merely opposed any extension of slavery.

WORDS AND NAMES IN HISTORY

The *Mason-Dixon line* is named after two English surveyors, Charles Mason and Jeremiah Dixon, who surveyed part of the border between the two colonies of Maryland and Pennsylvania in 1763–1767. The original proprietary grants to the Calvert family and to William Penn overlapped, resulting in a boundary dispute that was finally settled by this survey on behalf of the descendants of the Calverts and Penn. At the time, shortly before the American Revolution, slavery existed in both Maryland and Pennsylvania (as well as Delaware). During that war, Pennsylvania became the first state to adopt a gradual emancipation law. As time went on, the *Mason-Dixon line* came to mean the dividing line between the slave and the free states. It became a kind of shorthand way of describing the line of division between the North and the South.

In the debate at Freeport, Illinois, Lincoln asked Douglas a momentous question: "Can the people of a United States territory, in any lawful way, against the wish of any citizen of the United States, exclude slavery from its limits prior to the formation of a State constitution?" In order to answer, Douglas had to abandon popular sovereignty or defy the *Dred Scott* decision. If the people could not exclude slavery, popular sovereignty meant little. If they could exclude it, popular sovereignty was as much in conflict with the *Dred Scott* decision as the Republican principle of congressional exclusion.

Douglas answered that the people of a territory could take this step, in spite of the *Dred Scott* decision. Slavery could not exist for a day, he explained, if the local legislature did not pass the necessary laws to protect and police slave property. Therefore, merely by failing to arrange for slavery, a territorial legislature, without formally barring it, could make its existence impossible. Douglas's realistic answer—his "Freeport doctrine"—broadened the opposition to him in the South and widened the split in the Democratic party, as Lincoln anticipated. Douglas won the senatorial election in the Illinois state legislature, but the Democratic party and the Union were more divided than ever.

Lithograph of John Brown by Charles W. White, 1949. *Library of Congress)*

John Brown's Raid

The most emotional event in the sectional struggle was John Brown's raid on the federal arsenal at Harpers Ferry, Virginia, in 1859. Brown and his seventeen black and white men captured the arsenal and its millions of dollars worth of arms. That night he sent a detachment to seize nearby planters and some of their slaves as hostages. This mission accomplished, he awaited news of the slave uprisings he hoped would follow. "When I strike, the bees will swarm," Brown had privately told Frederick Douglass and other prominent abolitionists.

By dawn the next day, news of his exploit had spread across the countryside, and a hastily gathered militia counterattacked. Dangerfield Newby, a free black—his wife and seven children still slaves in Virginia—was the first of Brown's raiders to die. Brown's two sons were also mortally wounded that day, along with others. Before the day ended, Brown and the other survivors had been trapped in the arsenal. Exag-

gerated stories of the adventure had by now reached Washington.

Buchanan quickly ordered the nearest federal troops to the scene. He also sent Colonel Robert E. Lee and Lieutenant Jeb Stuart from the capital to take charge. Having rejected Brown's truce terms, Stuart led the attack on the arsenal and soon regained it. He captured Brown and five others, leaving the rest of Brown's men dead.

Several eminent abolitionists, although they did not support violence, had known of Brown's project and provided him with money and weapons, supposedly for antislavery partisans in Kansas. News of this support aggravated the reaction in the South, where vigilante groups assaulted anyone suspected of antislavery sympathies and concerned citizens publicly burned dangerous books. In New York, Boston, and elsewhere, huge meetings organized by northern conservatives attacked Brown and his methods. Lincoln, Douglas, and men of all parties joined in the condemnation. But when Virginia's governor rejected the plea of Brown's relatives and friends that the raider was insane and ordered him hanged, he ensured Brown's martyrdom.

Brown's bravery and dignity on the scaffold touched millions who condemned his deeds. "One's faith in anything is terribly shaken," a conservative New Yorker confided in his journal, "by anybody who is ready to go to the gallows condemning and denouncing it." The deification of John Brown that followed was partly the work of writers such as Emerson and Thoreau, who converted a brave monomaniac into an "angel of light." "A fervid Union man" of North Carolina, as he described himself, reflected the southern response in these words: "I confess the endorsement of the Harpers Ferry outrage . . . has shaken my fidelity and . . . I am willing to take the chances of every probable evil that may rise from disunion, sooner than submit any longer to Northern insolence and Northern outrage."

TOWARD SEPARATION

Four major candidates ran in the election of 1860. The Republican party nominated Lincoln. The Democrats were so divided along sectional lines that they ran two separate candidates, ensuring Lincoln's election. The states of the lower South took his victory as a signal that they must leave the Union and establish their own government. In Washington, some politicians tried to patch up another compromise during the long months between the November election and the inauguration in March.

Lincoln's Election

In April 1860 the Democratic national convention assembled at Charleston, South Carolina, the heartland of secession sentiment. Southern extremists insisted on a plank in the party platform declaring that neither Congress nor a territorial government could outlaw slavery or impair the right to own slaves. Northern Democrats, hoping to nominate Douglas without alienating the southerners, expressed willingness to accept the *Dred Scott* ruling. Yet they stood equally firm for popular sovereignty. "We cannot recede from this doctrine," a Douglas spokesman insisted, "without personal dishonor."

When it became clear that the extremists' plank would fail, most delegates from eight southern states withdrew. Their departure made it impossible for Douglas to obtain the necessary two-thirds of the ballots, and the convention adjourned. In June, Democrats reconvened in Baltimore. When the southern delegates bolted once again, the convention nominated Douglas on a popular-sovereignty platform. Ten days later, the southern Democrats met independently in Baltimore and chose John C. Breckinridge of Kentucky, a moderate, to represent their position on slavery in the territories. With two Democrats in the field, the last Unionist bond— a great political party with support in the North and the South—had broken.

The Republicans met in Chicago. Their front-runner was William H. Seward of New York. But Seward had a reputation as an irreconcilable because he once had spoken of the "irrepressible conflict" between North and South. The character of his backer, political boss Thurlow Weed, and the pushy behavior of Weed's henchmen at the convention also handicapped him. The way was open for Lincoln, who was strongly supported by the Illinois and Indiana delegations and acceptable to both East and West.

Six weeks before the convention Lincoln had reviewed his chances in a letter to a friend: "My name is now in the field; and I suppose I am not the first choice of a very great many. Our policy, then, is to give no offense to others—leave them in a mood to come to us, if they shall be impelled to give up their first love." This strategy paid off when Pennsylvania and Ohio switched from Seward, and Lincoln was nominated.

The Republican platform, while making a shrewd appeal to powerful economic interests, also sounded a high moral tone. It included planks for a protective tariff, free homesteads, a Pacific railroad, and the rights of immigrants. "The normal condition of all the territory of the United States," it said, "is that of freedom, . . . and we deny the authority of Congress, of a territorial legislature, or of any individuals, to give legal existence to slavery in any territory of the United States."

The campaign was further complicated by the nomination of John Bell of Tennessee, a fourth candidate, by the new Constitutional Union party, composed largely of Whigs in the border states. His platform tactfully called upon the people "to recognize no political principle other than the Constitution of the country, the Union of the states, and the enforcement of the laws."

The 1860 election presented the remarkable picture of a divided nation simultaneously carrying out two separate contests for the presidency: one between Breckinridge and Bell in the South, the second between Lincoln and Douglas in the North. The slave states did not even put Lincoln on the ballot. Only 1.4 percent of his popular votes came from the South. Douglas, although acknowledged as a candidate, also ran poorly there. In the North, at the same time, neither Breckinridge nor Bell found support.

Although sectional loyalties were decisive in the election, the considerable Unionist vote in the South should not be overlooked. Bell won Kentucky, Tennessee, and Virginia, and only barely lost Maryland and Missouri. Although Lincoln had a decisive majority in the electoral college, he carried less than 40 percent of the popular vote. A sectional candidate had been elected president of the United States.

The Deep South Moves Out

After Lincoln's nomination, southern leaders had repeatedly warned that a Republican victory would mean secession. The governor of South Carolina forecast that the election of a sectional northern candidate would "ultimately reduce the southern states to mere provinces of a consolidated despotism." Such expectations perhaps best answer the question Why did the South move out?

To understand secession, we must also realize that few people in the South anticipated the results. It was by no means certain that the North would go to war to keep the South in the Union. And if war came, why should not the South win,

The election of 1860

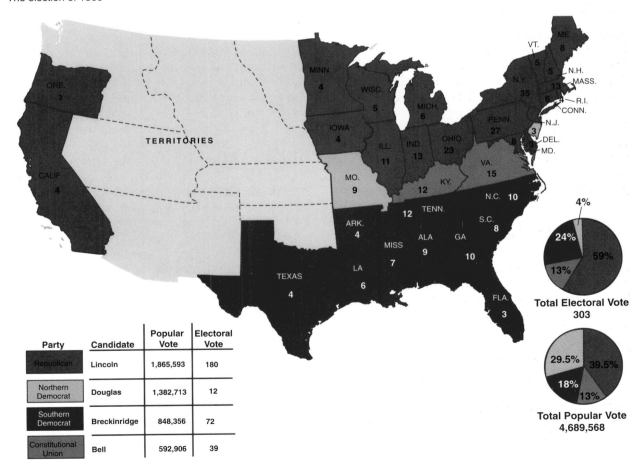

Party	Candidate	Popular Vote	Electoral Vote
Republican	Lincoln	1,865,593	180
Northern Democrat	Douglas	1,382,713	12
Southern Democrat	Breckinridge	848,356	72
Constitutional Union	Bell	592,906	39

Total Electoral Vote 303

Total Popular Vote 4,689,568

and quickly? Many southerners imagined that the will to fight was weak in the North. They also looked to the sympathy of foreign aristocrats, the commercial power of King Cotton, and the help of the many prosoutherners in the North.

Secession also had a positive side. No longer would the South be drained of its resources by northern banking and shipping interests and by taxes and tariffs that chiefly benefited the North. Perhaps the slave trade would be reopened. Cuba, Santo Domingo, Mexico, and even territories in Central America might become available to enterprising planters.

On December 20, 1860, South Carolina took the initiative. A special convention formally repealed the state's ratification of the Constitution and withdrew from the Union. By February 1, 1861, six other states—Mississippi, Florida, Alabama, Georgia, Louisiana, and Texas—had followed its example. But the urge to secede proved far from universal even in the Deep South. In almost every case, the step was taken over opposition. There were people ready to give Lincoln a chance to show whether he would really enforce the Fugitive Slave Act and meet other southern demands. But the tactics of the extremists overwhelmed the "cooperationists," as southern moderates were called. Pockets of unionism persisted in the lower South. Texas Germans, Alabama and Georgia mountaineers, and small farmers in Louisiana parishes clung to their federal loyalties.

Yet the majority of white southerners of all classes were ready to leave. On February 4, 1861, with seven states having seceded, but with Texas absent, delegates from six states met at Montgomery, Alabama, to form a new government. They called it the Confederate States of America, adopted a new flag, the "Stars and Bars," and wrote a new constitution.

A Federal Vacuum

Secession, having begun with Lincoln's victory, took place while Buchanan still occupied the White House. At such a moment the country had a lame-duck president, one without the will or the power to make commitments. Although Buchanan declared that secession was unconstitutional, he also claimed that Congress had no power under the Constitution to prevent it.

While Buchanan delayed, border state leaders in particular, aware that if secession resulted in

war their land would become a battleground, tried to avert disaster. The most seriously considered proposals were those put forward by Senator John J. Crittenden of Kentucky, two days before South Carolina's formal withdrawal from the Union. Crittenden offered these constitutional amendments: (1) slavery was to be barred in the territories north of the Missouri Compromise line, 36°30'; (2) it was to be permitted and protected south of that line. (3) future states were to enter as they wished, slave or free. (4) the fugitive slave law was to be enforced, and compensation paid by the federal government when enforcement failed because of the action of northerners; (5) the Constitution was never to be amended to authorize Congress to interfere with slavery in any state or the District of Columbia.

Crittenden's compromise failed to win support from either side. Southern leaders would not accept it unless it was endorsed by the Republican party. Lincoln favored enforcement of the fugitive slave law and would accept an amendment protecting slavery where it then existed. But he opposed any compromise on excluding slavery from the territories. To a friend in Congress he wrote: "Entertain no proposition for a compromise in regard to the extension of slavery. The instant you do they have us under again: all our labor is lost, and sooner or later must be done over."

FINAL FAILURE

When Abraham Lincoln stood up to take the oath of office on March 4, 1861, secession was a fact. A southern Confederacy had been formed, and important federal properties had fallen into rebel hands. Yet a far greater territory than the existing Confederacy remained very much at issue. The upper South—Virginia, Maryland, North Carolina, even Delaware—was torn by conflict as individuals, families, and neighborhoods wrestled with their alternatives. Farther west, in Tennessee, Kentucky, Arkansas, and Missouri, actual battles were fought before allegiance to North or South could be established.

Lincoln's Inaugural

In all these states, the president's inaugural address had been long awaited. Early in his

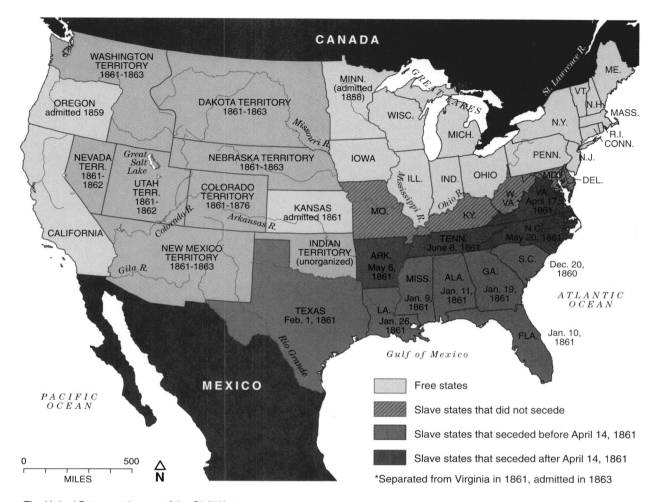

The United States on the eve of the Civil War

Legend:
- Free states
- Slave states that did not secede
- Slave states that seceded before April 14, 1861
- Slave states that seceded after April 14, 1861

*Separated from Virginia in 1861, admitted in 1863

speech, Lincoln stressed the perpetuity of "the more perfect Union" established by the Constitution. Then followed his sharpest words to the rebels: "No State upon its mere motion can lawfully get out of the Union; . . . acts of violence . . . against the authority of the United States, are insurrectionary or revolutionary, according to circumstance. . . . The mails, unless repelled," Lincoln added, "will continue to be furnished in all parts of the Union."

The president was as conciliatory as his office and his nature allowed. As chief executive, he said, he was bound to enforce federal regulations, including those requiring the return of fugitive slaves, in all the states. He even went so far as to say he had no objections to a proposed constitutional amendment guaranteeing that "the Federal Government shall never interfere

with the domestic institutions of the States"— including slavery. Other constitutional obligations, on the other hand, required that he "hold, occupy, and possess the property and places belonging to the Government, and to collect the duties and imposts" in every American port. But in performing these acts "there needs be no bloodshed or violence; and there shall be none, unless it be forced upon the national authority."

Near the end of his address, Lincoln reminded the South: "In your hands, my dissatisfied fellow-countrymen, and not in mine is the momentous issue of civil war." Characteristically, Lincoln did not close on a hard note; he added this eloquent paragraph:

I am loath to close. We are not enemies, but friends. We must not be enemies. Though passion may have strained, it must not break, our bonds of affection. The mystic chords of memory, stretching from every battlefield and patriot grave to every living heart and hearthstone all over this broad land, will yet swell the chorus of the Union when again touched, as surely they will be, by the better angels of our nature.

Few inaugural orations in United States history bore the burden of Lincoln's first. Few if any played so deliberately for time. In the terrible economic crisis of 1933, Franklin D. Roosevelt caught the public mood when he declared in his inaugural address: "In their need [the people of the United States] have registered a mandate that they want direct, vigorous action." But Lincoln, though pressed by those of every political creed, electrified the nation by putting action off: "My countrymen, one and all, think calmly and well upon this whole subject. Nothing valuable can be lost by taking time."

Fort Sumter Falls

And yet action was required of the president himself. In defiance of Buchanan's threat to meet force with force, the Confederacy in the early months of 1861 had seized federal forts, post offices, and customhouses throughout the South. Only Fort Sumter in Charleston harbor and three forts off the coast of Florida remained in federal hands. The day after his inauguration, Lincoln was handed a letter from Major Robert Anderson, the commander at Sumter, reporting that he could hold the fort only with the immediate aid of twenty thousand men, a large naval force, and supplies.

Anderson, in effect, recommended evacuation. If Lincoln retreated, as his advisers urged, he would have taken the first step toward recognizing the power of the Confederacy. If, on the other hand, he attempted to strengthen Sumter, he would be made to appear the aggressor. Lincoln cautiously steered a middle course. He notified South Carolina authorities that he would attempt to supply Sumter peacefully. "If such attempt be not resisted," he wrote the governor, "no effort to throw in men, arms, or ammunition will be made."

Lincoln's decision shifted the burden to Confederate authorities. If they permitted the supplying of Sumter, the fort would remain indefinitely in the mouth of their best harbor, a reproach to their prestige throughout the world. If they attacked a peaceful expedition bringing food, they would have fired the first shot.

When requested by Confederate authorities to surrender Sumter before the supply ships arrived, Major Anderson promised to evacuate by April 15, unless relieved or ordered to remain. But the Confederacy could not risk such a delay. On April 12 the batteries on the Charleston shore began a thirty-four-hour bombardment. When Anderson at last ran down the flag, Sumter was burning, its ammunition gone. Remarkably, not a man had been hit on either side during the engagement. But a war that was to take more casualties than even Napoleon's campaigns had in fact begun.

Before Sumter, northern opinion had divided sharply on the proper response to secession. Abolitionists such as Garrison thought it pointless to enforce union "where one section is pinned to the residue by bayonets." For once, the business community, still suffering the effects of the panic of 1857 and concerned over collecting southern debts and holding southern markets, agreed with abolitionist policy to let the "erring sisters go in peace." But warlike voices also spoke out. "If South Carolina is determined upon secession," warned *The New York Times*, "she should take the plunge with her eyes open. She must face the consequences—and among them all, the most unquestionable is war."

Disunion was especially opposed by the Northwest, where freedom for white men on the land was the very watchword of the Lord. No section uttered "Amen" more appreciatively to Lincoln's March 4 statement, "Physically speaking, we cannot separate." After Sumter, peace partisans still were heard here and there in the North. But with the Confederacy branded as the aggressor, it became easier to portray hostilities as a defense of the Union. Lincoln's call on April 15 for 75,000 three-month volunteers met with an overwhelming response everywhere. Walt Whitman in Manhattan, whose *Drum Taps* established him as the Union poet of the war, caught the new surge of spirit:

*From the houses then and the workshops, and
    through all the doorways
Leapt they tumultuous, and lo! Manhattan
    arming.*

The Upper South and the Border States Decide

It is sometimes said that South Carolinians, aware that a Confederacy without Virginia would be nothing, bombarded Fort Sumter to force that state to join the Confederacy. Yet three months after Virginia's "secession convention" was called, it still refused to vote. Then, on April 15, Lincoln issued the fateful proclamation declaring that "combinations too powerful to be suppressed" by ordinary means existed in the seven Confederate states; he called forth "the militia of the several States of the Union, to the aggregate number of seventy-five thousand, in order to suppress such combinations."

His proclamation was received with approval throughout the North. Throughout the upper South and the border states, it came like a death knell. Should Virginia and the rest answer the president's call and give their men to the Union cause? Should they stand by while the South was invaded by northern men and arms?

More than his election, more than his inaugural, more even than the attempt to provision Sumter, Lincoln's proclamation of April 15 sealed the issue of war and peace. Two days later, the Virginia convention passed its ordinance of secession, eighty-eight to fifty-five. The provisional Confederate government named Richmond its permanent capital and prepared to move from Montgomery. At the end of May a referendum in Virginia approved secession, though people in the western portion of the state disagreed so strongly that they began to organize to secede from the new Confederate state. Only then did the president acknowledge that all hope was gone: "The people of Virginia have thus allowed this giant insurrection to make its nest within her borders; and this government has no choice left but to deal with it where it finds it."

Lincoln had supplemented his proclamation calling out the militia with an order to the navy to blockade the ports of the first seven Confederate commonwealths. Later he extended the blockade to Virginia and North Carolina. The Supreme Court was eventually to rule that the war legally began with these blockage orders, which officially recognized that a state of "belligerency" existed between two powers. Lincoln himself never accepted this idea. He never recognized the Confederacy as a nation, or secession as anything but "insurrection."

Other states soon followed Virginia's example. In March an Arkansas convention had rejected secession, but in May it approved. In North Carolina a convention called by the legislature voted unanimously to secede. In Tennessee, the governor and legislature took the state into the Confederacy even before the people ratified their decision. Unionist regions, nevertheless, could still be found in the upper South and on the border. Like the western Virginians, the people of eastern Tennessee would probably have rejoined the Union had Confederate troops not prevented them. Four indecisive slave states—Kentucky, Missouri, Maryland, and Delaware—remained in the Union.

Maryland's strategic position forced Lincoln to take strong unconstitutional measures against agitators there. With a show of federal force, the secessionist spirit in Maryland subsided. Rich and populous Kentucky maintained neutrality until September 1861, when the legislature voted to remain loyal to the Union. Kentucky volunteers for the Confederates numbered only half as many as those who fought with the Federals. In Missouri, the division between southern and northern supporters flared into a small civil war, though only one-fifth of Missouri's fighting men were with the South. And no one on either side thought the war would last long.

SUMMARY

By the late 1850s, tension over slavery had led to violence and threats of violence in Congress itself. The crisis came over the extension of slavery to the new territories as earlier compromises fell apart. Enforcement of the fugitive slave law resulting from the Compromise of 1850, and Harriet Beecher Stowe's fictional account of slavery, *Uncle Tom's Cabin,* gave northern-

ers a view of slavery they had never had before. Dramatic incidents when "runaways" were seized led thousands to change their attitude toward slavery.

Northern incitement and protection of runaways led the planters to react. In 1854, Congress passed the Kansas-Nebraska Act, which reopened the question of slavery in the western territories and nullified the Missouri

Compromise. Iowa congressmen wishing a northern route for the proposed transcontinental railroad obtained the division of Nebraska into two territories, Nebraska and Kansas. Kansas was marked for slavery by the South, but not by the North. The territory was turned into a battleground, and for a period civil war raged there.

After 1852, the Whig party fell apart. The election of 1856 brought new political parties: the Know-Nothings, opposed to Catholic immigrants, and the Republicans, who opposed the extension of slavery to the western territories. The Democrats were now largely the party of the South and slavery. Their candidate, James Buchanan, won, but the Republican party ran strongly in the North.

Buchanan hoped the Supreme Court would settle the question of slavery in the territories. The Court, in the *Dred Scott* decision, decided the Missouri Compromise was unconstitutional. The issue then became the focus of the Lincoln-Douglas debates of 1858, which made Abraham Lincoln a national figure. Lincoln lost the Illinois senatorial election, but Douglas's treatment of the issue widened the split in the Democratic party. The next year John Brown's raid on the federal arsenal at Harper's Ferry, Virginia, shocked the entire country.

Brown, a fervent abolitionist, was hanged—but then became a legend in the North.

Four candidates ran in the election of 1860. The winner was Abraham Lincoln of the sectional Republican party. The South took his election as a signal. By February 1, 1861, even before Lincoln's inauguration, seven states—South Carolina, Mississippi, Florida, Alabama, Georgia, Louisiana, and Texas—had seceded from the Union. On February 4, delegates from six states met at Montgomery, Alabama, to form a new government, the Confederate States of America. Buchanan, the outgoing president, hesitated; senators from the border states tried a last attempt at compromise, but it failed. When Lincoln took the oath of office on March 4, secession was a fact.

The firing on Fort Sumter in Charleston harbor on April 12 began the war. On April 15, by proclamation, Lincoln issued a call for 75,000 three-month volunteers to "suppress" the rebellion. At that point the upper South and the border states were forced to make a decision: Virginia, Arkansas, North Carolina, and Tennessee seceded; Kentucky, Missouri, Maryland, and Delaware remained in the Union. And both sides prepared for what neither thought would be a long war.

TIME LINE

1851	Frederick Wilkins ("Shadrach") rescued from slave catchers	1858	Lincoln-Douglas debates
1852	Emergence of Know-Nothing party	1859	John Brown's raid
		1860	Election of Lincoln
1852	Harriet Beecher Stowe's *Uncle Tom's Cabin*	1860	South Carolina secedes, followed by the rest of the lower South
1854	Emergence of new Republican party	1861	
1854	Kansas-Nebraska Act	February	Confederate States of America formed at Montgomery
1855	Two rival governments set up in Kansas Territory	March	Lincoln inaugurated
1856	Brooks's beating of Sumner in the Senate	April	Fort Sumter falls
		April	Lincoln calls for troops
1856	Civil war in Kansas	April–May	Four upper South states join the Confederacy
1857	*Dred Scott* decision		
1857	Business panic		Four border states and western
1857	Lecompton Constitution		Virginia remain in the Union

Suggested Readings

With very few exceptions, general historical treatments of the 1850s have focused on the approach of the Civil War. Historians have been divided not only by sectional sympathies, hut also by the factors they think led to conflict. The ambitious account by A.

Nevins, *Ordeal of the Union* (2 vols., 1947) and *The Emergence of Lincoln* (2 vols., 1950), is widely admired. The humane perceptions in D. Potter, *The South and the Sectional Conflict* (1968), have also commanded great respect. See also Potter's *The Impending Crisis, 1848–1861* (1976), a skillful account of the road to war.

Several books deal with important specific issues: S. Campbell, *The Slave Catchers: Enforcement of the Fugitive Slave Law, 1850–1860* (1970); G. Wolff, *The Kansas-Nebraska Bill: Party, Section, and the Origin of the Civil War* (1980); R. May, *The Southern Dream of a Caribbean Empire, 1854–1861(1973);* and D. Fehrenbacher, *The Dred Scott Case: Its Significance in American Law and Politics* (1978). R. Takaki, *A Pro-Slavery Crusade: The Agitation to Reopen the African Slave Trade* (1971), focuses on a rather small group. U. Davis, *The Slave Power Conspiracy and the Paranoid Style* (1969), discusses the North's mounting fear of the South's intentions.

The first outbreak of violence is dealt with in P. Gates, *Fifty Million Acres: Conflicts over Kansas Land Policy, 1854–1890* (1954); J. Rawley, *Race and Politics* (1969); a biography of John Brown by S. Oates, *To Purge This Land with Blood* (1970); and a brief, perceptive essay by C. Vann Woodward in U. Aaron (ed.), *America in Crisis* (1952). E. Stone (ed.), *Incident at Harpers Ferry* (1956), has contemporary material on the Brown raid.

The rise and the role of the Republican party are described in many of the books cited thus far. Increasingly, the tendency among historians has been to concentrate on the issue of race. E. Foner, *Free Soil, Free Labor, Free Men: The Ideology of the Republican Party before the Civil War* (1970), and E. Berwanger, *The Frontier against Slavery: Western Anti-Negro Prejudice and the Slavery Extension Controversy* (1967), both stress that issue. So does H. Trefousse, *The Radical Republicans: Lincoln's Vanguard for Racial Justice* (1969). Two other studies, a biography and a study of voting behavior, are among the most illuminating about the coming conflict: R. Durden, *James Shepherd Pike: Republicanism and the American Negro, 1850–1882* (1957); and M. Holt, *Forging a Majority: The Formation of the Republican Party in Pittsburgh, 1848–1860* (1969).

The rapid political realignment in this period is dealt with by T. Alexander, *Sectional Stress and Party Strength* (1967), an examination of congressional roll calls; and more broadly in M. Holt, *The Political Crisis of the 1850s* (1978). J. Silbey's introduction to a short collection of documents, *The Transformation of American Politics, 1840–1860* (1967), offers a good guide to politics in this period. Two more recent books add a great deal: R. Sewall, *A House Divided: Sectionalism and Civil War, 1848–1865* (1988); and M. Summers, *The Plundering Generation: Corruption and the Crisis of the Union, 1849–1861* (1987). See also U. Knobel, *Paddy and the Republic: Ethnicity and Nationality in Antebellum America* (1986). Several biographies also stand out: G. van Deusen, *William Henry Seward* (1967), dealing with a puzzling and neglected figure; U. Donald, *Charles Sumner and the Coming of the Civil War* (1981), a psychological study of great value; and the long but first-rate R. Johannsen, *Stephen A. Douglas* (1973). Four unfortunate presidents have been treated in E. Smith, *The Presidencies of Zachary Taylor and Millard Fillmore* (1988); R. Nichols, *Franklin Pierce: Young Hickory of the Granite Hills* (2nd ed., 1958); and P. Klein, *President James Buchanan: A Biography* (1962).

The early career of Abraham Lincoln may be studied in C. Sandburg, *Abraham Lincoln, The Prairie Years* (abridged ed., 1929), a classic study; U. Fehrenbacher, *Prelude to Greatness: Lincoln in the 1850's* (1962); and J. Randall, *Lincoln, the President: Springfield to Gettysburg* (2 vols., 1945), part of a full-scale biography. The Lincoln–Douglas debates are printed in full in P. Angle (ed.), *Created Equal* (1958).

Of the many books on secession, state studies stand out—for example, W. Barney, *The Secessionist Impulse: Alabama and Mississippi in 1860* (1974). P. Rainwater, *Mississippi: Storm Center of Secession, 1856–1861* (1938), is still impressive. S. Channing, *Crisis of Fear: Secession in South Carolina* (1970), is a dramatic account of the background as well as the final act. An extremely interesting triangular view of the secession crisis may be had by reading the following three works: U. Potter, *Lincoln and His Party in the Secession Crisis, 1860–1861(1942);* K. Stampp, *And the War Came: The North and the Secession Crisis, 1860–1861* (1950); and R. Current, *Lincoln and the First Shot* (1963).

The gallant charge of the Fifty-Fourth Massachusetts Regiment on Fort Wagner. *(Library of Congress)*

CHAPTER 17

CIVIL WAR

Secession led directly to war: It was not so easy to break the Union as southern leaders supposed. At the start, both sides seemed paralyzed. Both fervently wished that the fighting would soon be over. The Civil War became the deadliest ever fought on this continent, yet it was very slow in gathering momentum. And when it was finally over, little seemed to have been accomplished by the slaughter. Not that it was in vain. Lincoln made that clear in his Gettysburg Address: "From these honored dead we take increased devotion to that cause for which they gave the last full measure of devotion—that . . . this nation, under God, shall have a new birth of freedom—and that government of the people, by the people, for the people, shall not perish from the earth." The war pointed the way "for us the living," as Lincoln said, to dedicate themselves to "the unfinished work which they who fought here have thus far so nobly advanced."

For Lincoln, the unfinished task was restoration of the Union. But in the back of his mind he knew very well that the condition of black people was fundamental to the entire conflict. Their future was altered but scarcely settled by the war in which roughly one white man died in battle for every six slaves "freed."

ENEMIES FACE TO FACE

On paper the North was far stronger than the South. It had two and a half times as many people, and it possessed far more ships, miles of railroad, and manufacturing enterprises. Southerners, however, had the advantage of fighting on home ground with better military leadership. Civilian authority was another matter. The new Confederate government ran into trouble because of one of the principles it was fighting for—states' rights. In the North, moreover, Abraham Lincoln was self-confident enough to assemble a cabinet of exceptionally strong and able men. He himself assumed powers that made him the closest thing to a dictator that the United States had ever had.

Soldiers and Supplies

At the beginning of the conflict, about 22 million persons lived in loyal states and territories; there was in addition an unknown number of Indians in the West. Nine million (5.5 million whites and 3.5 million blacks) lived in the South. But Union superiority in manpower was not so great as the gross figures suggest. Half a million people, scattered from Dakota to California, could make no substantial contribution to Union strength. And every year during the Civil War, Union regiments were sent to the West to fight Indians. Hundreds of thousands of Americans in loyal border states and in southern Ohio, Indiana, and Illinois worked or fought for southern independence. Many southerners, of course, remained loyal to the Union. Indeed, every state furnished men for the other side. But there is little doubt that more Federals than Confederates "crossed over."

Certain other considerations favored the Confederacy. One was the South's superior officer personnel. For twenty years before Lincoln's inauguration, southern officers had dominated the U.S. Army. Many northern West Pointers, including William T. Sherman and Ulysses S. Grant, found little opportunity for advancement and resigned their commissions early in life in favor of civilian careers. Another source of southern confidence was cotton. Secession leaders expected to exchange that staple for the foreign manufactured goods they needed.

Probably the South's most important advantage was that it had only to defend relatively short interior lines against invaders who had to deal with long lines of communication and to attack on a broad front. The Confederacy also had no need to divert fighting men to tasks such as garrisoning captured cities and holding conquered territory.

The South's armies contained a considerably larger proportion of the region's white men than the North's. Taking the two white populations as separate wholes, it is clear that the war was more widely supported in the South. In addition, thousands of slaves were made to perform fatigue duty and construct fortifications. Wealthy planters and their sons took favorite slaves into the field as personal servants. On the other side, blacks were not welcomed as soldiers at first. After 1862, however, abolitionists succeeded in gaining approval for black regiments, staffed by white officers. Some of these units were recruited from the free black population in the North; others came directly from slavery in border states or in areas captured by Union forces. They suffered discrimination in pay and quarters, but their performance in battle encouraged those—black and white—who hoped to disprove the presumption that blacks could not become good fighting men.

In a short war, northern numerical superiority would not have made much of a difference. As the war continued, however, numerical strength became a psychological as well as a physical weapon. During the closing years of the conflict, Union armies, massed at last against critical strongholds, suffered terrible casualties but seemed to grow stronger with every defeat. Any staggering Confederate losses sapped the southern will to fight.

The fact that the Civil War stretched over years instead of months magnified every material advantage of the North—money and credit, factories, food production, transport. It took time to redirect the economy to the requirements of war, especially because these requirements, like the length of the war, were underestimated.

The South found it even more difficult to convert to a war footing. As the war lengthened, southern troops suffered from short rations, ragged clothing, and no boots. Until the end, though, the Confederacy had the basic materials of war—small armies, artillery, ammunition, and horses. Every rural home in the South had weapons. Large quantities of munitions were also taken from captured Federal forts, seized after battles, and imported on ships that were

CIVIL WAR SUPPLY PROBLEMS

Both armies spent a great deal of time worrying about problems of supply, problems that inevitably involved contact with the local civilian populace as well as possible brushes with armed men of the opposing side. A colonel in a Union cavalry division gave the following report.

COLONEL: I have the honor to report that I left Germantown on the morning of the 16th instant with 250 men and two howitzers of the Ninth.

I learned that within a few days 150 wagons loaded with ordnance stores for Kirby Smith had been ferried across at this point to the Louisiana shore, and that beef-cattle in large numbers were constantly being driven across through this point, as previously reported to General Grant, and pastured between Natchez and the Mississippi Central Railroad, and that a portion of them were still in the county, a few miles east of me.

By 3 A.M. of the 14th, I succeeded in mounting 200 infantry, from the citizens of the place, and by daylight had expeditions to the country on both sides of the river. The expedition on this side of the river captured a drove of 5,000 Texas beef-cattle, in excellent order, about 4 miles out of the city. A small guard of rebel cavalry fled at our approach. I have secured the cattle, and am loading them on transports.

The expedition on the Louisiana shore returned at sunset, having captured a lieutenant (with the inclosed order marked A on his person) and rear guard with a portion of Kirby Smith's ordnance train, which had been delayed 15 miles out on the road to Trinity, bringing back with them 312 new Austrian muskets, 203,000 rounds musket cartridges, and 11 boxes of artillery ammunition, and destroying 268,000 rounds of ammunition, which could not be moved. The rest of the train had pressed on beyond our reach.

Kirby Smith is said to be fortifying at Trinity, on the Big Black River, and that a division of his troops are in that vicinity. I hear of no other force of the enemy in this region.

I detained the transports designed for General Banks and am loading them with beef-cattle. Two were loaded yesterday, and convoyed down by the gunboat Arizona. I will get 2,000 of the cattle embarked tomorrow. I have sent 100 mounted men and a regiment of infantry this morning to Quitman's Landing, 10 miles up the river, to intercept a drove of cattle reported to be crossing at that point. The store-houses in the city contain large quantities of sugar liable to fall into the hands of the rebel army in case this post is abandoned. I have detailed a commission to inquire into its ownership, and desire instructions as to whether it shall be seized, if it is private property, as it will probably appear at least to be. There is also an immense quantity of lumber here, about the disposition of which I desire instructions. Will it be shipped, destroyed, or allowed to remain.

I am disarming the citizens, and will have a large quantity of assorted fire-arms on my hands.

The country about Natchez abounds in fine horses, mules, cattle, and other stock. All the plantations are planted with heavy crops of corn. Old corn is not abundant. Is it not desirable to seize enough artillery horses at least to supply the batteries in the Army of the Tennessee? If this is not done soon, the best stock will be run out of the country, and probably be used against us by the rebel army. I also desire some instructions as to what policy I shall pursue with regard to the negroes. They flock in by thousands (about 1 able-bodied man to 6 women and children). I am feeding about 500, and working the able-bodied men among them. I can send you any number encumbered with families. I cannot take care of them. What shall I do with them? They are all anxious to go; they do not know where or what for.

My troops have worked hard—frequently forty-eight hours on duty—and have behaved admirably. Hardly a case of pillaging, or even of disrespectful treatment of a citizen, has occurred.

able to run the Federal blockade. Under the brilliant administration of its chief of ordnance, the Confederacy also developed its own munitions plants to supplement the output of the giant Tredegar Iron Works in Richmond.

The Confederate Government

Delegates from the first seceding states met at Montgomery, Alabama, in February 1861 to draft a frame of government. By not departing too greatly from the familiar federal document, they hoped to attract their neighbors in the upper South. Because they were so committed to states' rights, however, they wrote in certain weaknesses that had been kept out of the Constitution in 1787. Their preamble declared that the Confederacy was established not by "we the people," but by "the people of the Confederate states, each state acting in its sovereign and independent character." Of course the new constitution "recognized and protected . . . the right of property in negro slaves."

While the Confederate Congress was granted power "to . . . provide for the common defense," no mention was made of promoting the "general welfare." " The judicial power of the Confederate States" was placed in a Supreme Court and certain lower tribunals. But no Supreme Court was ever established. The old federal district courts continued to sit, often under their old judges, who applied the old rules and precedents inherited from English common law. The president's term was extended to six years. Whatever advantage in stability this brought may have been lost by the provision barring his reelection.

The Montgomery constitutional convention named Jefferson Davis of Mississippi and Alexander H. Stephens of Georgia as provisional president and vice-president, respectively. Neither man wanted his job, but in the first elections in November 1861, voters confirmed the convention's choices.

A West Pointer of the class of 1828, Jeff Davis longed to be a soldier. At the time of the war against Mexico he resigned his seat as a Democratic congressman to lead his regiment of Mississippi Rifles in a grand stand at the battle of Buena Vista. Devoted to the South, he never became an extremist. But when the question came in 1861, he backed secession. Convinced he had been born to be a general, he proved to be a mediocre military strategist. Always well meaning, but proud, aloof, and not in good health, he often quarreled with his subordinates.

Vice-President Stephens, who stayed home in Georgia most of the time, was a scholar devoted to his studies and racked by ill health. A stickler for states' rights, he complained constantly that Davis was becoming a despot. His pessimism about the Confederate cause became contagious. And Davis's cabinet was not much more help. Fourteen different men filled six cabinet posts during the life of the Confederacy.

Judah P. Benjamin, a brilliant New Orleans lawyer who served through the whole administration, first as attorney general, then as secretary of war, and finally as secretary of state, was by far the ablest. His determination to make the Confederacy face up to the grim realities of its financial, economic, and diplomatic problems led people to call him "the hated Jew," and he was frequently slandered by newspapers and legislatures.

Davis was especially hard-pressed by states' rights enthusiasts who saw almost no justification for central government. His military strategy came under harsh and constant criticism. Reverses on the battlefield made his life increasingly miserable. More and more the Confederacy looked to its military leaders, particularly to Robert E. Lee of Virginia.

Lincoln and the Divided Nation

Lincoln was temperamentally far better suited for a long struggle than Davis. Patient, tolerant, flexible, and crafty to the point of deviousness, Lincoln had a genius for giving men enough rope to hang themselves. Throughout the war, he was savagely abused in the press. Many people thought him not dignified enough for high office, a bungler as commander in chief, devious and spineless, yet out for himself As wartime president, Lincoln absorbed the abuse quietly, often with wry self-satisfaction. Regarded by many people at the time as petty and oafish, he now seems much more an embodiment of both the narrowness and greatness of the Puritan ethic.

His reputation rests largely on his talent at statecraft, his decent magnanimity, and his stunning mastery of English prose. Even to men who knew him longest he remained something of a mystery. He enlivened cabinet meetings with his stories, yet was melancholy and aloof. His law partner, William H. Herndon, considered him a "sphinx . . . incommunicative—silent—reticent—secretive—having profound policies—and well laid—deeply studied plans."

Lincoln seldom acted until he felt public opinion would sustain him. His delay in getting on with the fighting encouraged the ambitious egotists around him—Secretary of State Seward, for example, and Secretary of the Treasury Chase—to strive for "a sort of dictatorship for the national defense." They all learned sooner or later, as Seward acknowledged after a brush with

Abraham Lincoln. *(Library of Congress)*

He was tested early from all sides. In 1861 the federal government was filled with secessionists. Lincoln fired a great many federal employees, but he chose replacements with care. Outside his administration he faced two principal groups of opponents. Some abolitionists were pacifists, and in the early years of the war they argued that the Union would be better off without the slave South. As the conflict continued, however, many abolitionists became Lincoln's most enthusiastic supporters.

"Peace" was also the goal of many northern Democrats, often called Copperheads, who thought the war needless. To them, the Union seemed nothing in comparison with the thriving North. In their debating arsenal they carried a heavy weapon.. "Why fight?" They underestimated popular devotion to that almost mystical entity "the Union."

As the war continued, many abolitionists began to sense an end to slavery. At the same time, Copperheads in the North pressed their demands for compromise and became more active in obstructing enlistments. As abolitionists gradually came around to conceding the rightness of the fighting, they threw their support to those within the Republican party most in sympathy with emancipation as a war objective. This faction became known as the Radicals. The Regulars, or Conservatives, wanted only to suppress the "insurrection" and to restore the Union.

The Radicals had a formidable array of talent in both houses of Congress, led in the Senate by Charles Sumner of Massachusetts and Benjamin Wade of Ohio, and in the House by Thaddeus Stevens of Pennsylvania, chairman of the Ways

Lincoln, that "the President is the best of us. There is only one vote in the Cabinet and it belongs to him. Executive ability and vigor are rare qualities, but he has them both."

LINCOLN ON SELF-GOVERNMENT

Probably Abraham Lincoln's major political theme was his insistence on the importance of the American experiment in self-government. He regarded the United States as a crucial example for the entire world. In his first message to Congress after the fall of Fort Sumter, Lincoln argued that the contest between the North and the South

presents to the whole family of man, the question of whether a constitutional republic, or a democracy—a government of the people, by the same people—can, or cannot, maintain its territorial integrity, against its own domestic foes.

He brought this theme to a great climax in his address at Gettysburg, concluding with the famous words:

That from these honored dead we take increased devotion to that cause for which they gave the last full measure of devotion—that we here highly resolve that these dead shall not have died in vain—that this nation, under God, shall have a new birth of freedom—and that government of the people, by the people, for the people, shall not perish from the earth.

and Means Committee. Stevens regarded slavery as "a curse, a shame, and a crime." As a lawyer and businessman, he had defended fugitive slaves without fee.

Lincoln allowed nearly a whole year to pass after the first act of secession before he would even acknowledge that the gulf between the two sections could be closed only by mutual slaughter. He hated bloodshed. But he lost no time in getting the Union ready for survival. In doing so, he earned the labels "despot," "tyrant," and "dictator" more deservingly than any other president. On May 3, without precedent or legislative authority, Lincoln issued a call for forty regiments of three-year United States volunteers to supplement the state militia he had called out in April. On no firmer constitutional grounds, he ordered a rapid expansion of the fleet for blockade service. The Constitution had stated: "No money shall be drawn from the Treasury, but in Consequence of Appropriations made by Law." Without any such law, Lincoln ordered Chase to get funds to pay for the new army and navy. Chase obliged.

More widely opposed than these military and monetary moves was Lincoln's trampling of traditional safeguards of personal rights. Neither private letters nor telegrams were safe from prying federal eyes. Military commanders were empowered to make arrests without warrants and "in the extremist necessity," in Lincoln's words, to suspend the writ of habeas corpus. Eventually, at least fifteen thousand Americans were jailed. Despite his gestures of clemency, many remained in prison until the war's end without trial or even accusation.

Lincoln's high-handed tactics fell most heavily on citizens of the border states, which had immense strategic importance. Maryland virtually surrounded Washington and could make the national capital captive. Baltimore, Maryland's leading port and railroad center, was also Washington's main link with the outside world. Kentucky controlled the traffic on the Ohio River. Missouri, with Kentucky, controlled the use of the Mississippi.

THE STRUGGLE FOR RICHMOND

The North's strategy was to strangle the South with a naval blockade, gain control of the Mississippi River, and capture the Confederate capital. Few people anticipated that it would take four years of bloody war before all these aims were accomplished. The North lost many of the important battles, but finally, at Antietam, Union forces produced a victory that had important nonmilitary consequences.

Early Battles

Lincoln's principal military adviser during the early months was a holdover from the Mexican War, General in Chief of the U.S. Army Winfield Scott. Born in 1786, Scott was a year older than the Constitution. But he was one of the few men who realized the Union must prepare for a long struggle. His strategy was that the North should clamp a vise of steel on the border states, take the entire length of the Mississippi, and tighten the blockade on every rebel port. This would gain time for raising and equipping armies for the final blows. Lincoln's early success in the border states provided a favorable start. The early success of Navy Secretary Gideon Welles in making Lincoln's "paper blockade" effective

The Spirit of 1861, by Currier and Ives. *(Library of Congress)*

further improved prospects. In a few months, most rebel seaports were almost shut down. The South's foreign trade had been cut at least 80 percent.

Jefferson Davis, also reluctant to abandon the fantasy that the South would be permitted to leave peacefully, had a war plan of his own that played right into Scott's hands. The South, Davis said, had seceded to get away from, not to conquer, the North. He saw a "natural frontier" stretching from the line between Maryland and Pennsylvania to the Dakota Territory. Along this border he proposed to plant a line of forts, and then to look for help from cotton-hungry Britain and France.

Almost a month before the bombardment of Fort Sumter, Davis sent three commissioners to Europe to carry out his "cotton diplomacy." Their initial goal was to arrange for massive amounts of munitions and supplies. But his assumption that King Cotton would win the war was badly misplaced. Britain had filled its warehouses in anticipation of the war and in 1861 needed wheat; The Union's ability to trade massive wheat exports for munitions and supplies made it difficult for Davis's agents to do business.

While Davis opted for a defensive strategy, many other Confederate leaders urged an offensive, without delay. They presumed that southern troops would prove superior on the battlefield, and they sensed that if the South did not win quickly, it was not likely to win at all. In June 1861 the main rebel army under General P. G. T. de Beauregard was stationed at Manassas Junction in Virginia, a critical railroad crossing between Washington and Richmond. On the other side, Radical Republican congressmen and newspapers were demanding "crushing . . . overwhelming" action.

A touch of hysteria was in the air. The Confederacy, everyone said, was gathering for an assault on Washington. "Why don't they come?" was the anxious question. At last, in mid-July, with the "three-months men" nearing the end of their service, Lincoln ordered General Irvin McDowell to move.

With little training and no experience in battle, McDowell's 30,000 men were green and untested. But so was Beauregard's force, estimated at 24,000. As McDowell's men marched south, Beauregard's moved north to meet him. His troops dug in on the southern side of the little stream of Bull Run; there, the next morning, the Federals found him. By noon a Union

triumph seemed certain. Then General Thomas J. Jackson's "stonewall" stand in one sector, followed by a succession of counterattacks, halted the Union offensive. The southern army received reinforcements that afternoon.

McDowell, disappointed at not receiving reinforcements of his own, soon thought it better to retire. Some of his men, their three months' service over, kept going all the way home to New York, New Hampshire, and Maine, where they first had volunteered. "Give me 10,000 fresh troops, and I will be in Washington tomorrow," Stonewall Jackson is reported to have said after Bull Run. But President Davis remained devoted to his defensive plan.

"All Quiet on the Potomac"

The defeat of its forces made Congress jump. Radicals pushed through a measure that Lincoln, afraid of driving the South to revenge, said he "had some difficulty in consenting to approve." This was the so-called First Confiscation Act, making it the duty of the president to seize all property used in aiding the insurrection. Though the Radicals had hesitated to identify blacks as property, this act made slaves subject to forfeit if they were used in building fortifications and in other military and naval work. Also in the wake of the Bull Run disaster, Lincoln relieved McDowell, created a new Division of the Potomac, and placed General George McClellan, then thirty-four years old, at its head.

First Battle of Bull Run (1861)

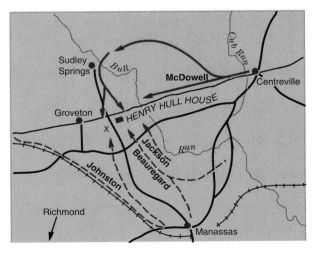

Great battle at Bull Run between the Federal Army, commanded by Major-General McDowell, and the Rebel army under Jefferson Davis, General Beauregard and General Johnston, Sunday, July 21, 1861. *(Library of Congress)*

"All tell me that I am held responsible for the fate of the nation," the new commander wrote to his wife. A few days later, with characteristic flourish, he told her of his plan: "I shall . . . crush the rebels in one campaign." McClellan was, in fact, a masterly organizer. His failings were his pride in smart execution on parade grounds and his reluctance to risk his well-drilled troops in battle. By the time Congress reconvened for its regular session in December 1861, McClellan was still grandly housed in Washington, still marching his men on parade, and beginning to try even Lincoln's patience. "Forward to Richmond!" was forgotten by the press and the people; "All Quiet on the Potomac" became the sarcastic slogan of the day.

Little more than two weeks after Congress assembled, the Radicals succeeded in establishing a Joint Committee on the Conduct of the War, with wide powers of investigation. It was the "bounden duty" of Congress, they said, to watch "executive agents," including generals who made a practice of returning fugitive slaves to their owners and who were otherwise soft on "the Negro question." McClellan, known for his "softness" on slavery, soon became the committee's pet target. Radicals began to suspect that McClellan was unwilling to fight the rebels.

The president, though still dreading a war to the finish, shared this view but kept his own counsel. Then, his patience gone, Lincoln issued General Order Number One, naming Washington's Birthday, February 22, as "the day for a general movement of the land and naval forces of the United States against the insurgent forces." But even this sharp command failed to move McClellan. "In ten days I shall be in Richmond," the general boasted on February 13, 1862. As things turned out, Union soldiers did not strike into Richmond until more than three years of carnage had gone by.

War in the West

While the federal city remained preoccupied with the long silence on the Potomac, the war was far from quiet in the West. There subordinate Union officers took things more or less into their own hands. Early in 1862, Commodore Andrew H.

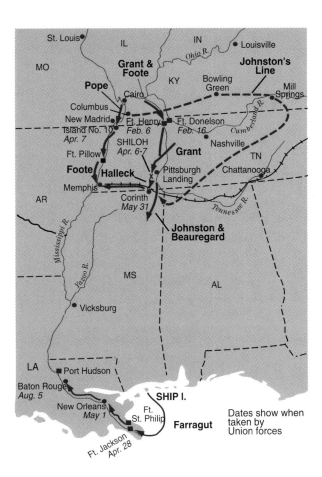

War in the West (1862)

Rebels, now led by Beauregard. General Henry W. Halleck, recently placed in command of the Department of the West, took charge of pressing the Union counteroffensive on to Corinth. But he delayed for weeks, and the Rebels got away with their army intact.

Shiloh was the first battle of the Civil War to make people on both sides realize how many men could be killed and maimed in this new kind of massive warfare. A total of 23,000 men were dead or wounded, and of course many of the wounded later died. When Grant saw that the Rebels here "not only attempted to hold a line farther south, . . . but assumed the offensive and made such a gallant effort to regain what had been lost, then, indeed," he wrote in his *Memoirs*, "I gave up all idea of saving the Union except by complete conquest." Robert E. Lee, still sitting in Richmond as a presidential adviser, warned Davis that unless he held the lower Mississippi and kept the Confederacy from being split, Grant's "complete conquest" would not be far off.

Lee's warning was underscored soon after Shiloh by more decisive Union operations farther west. At the end of April, a Union fleet led by Captain David G. Farragut smashed through Confederate fortifications below New Orleans and forced the great Mississippi port to surrender. Baton Rouge fell soon after to a force under General Benjamin F. Butler. In the meantime, Foote's gunboats had pressed down the Mississippi to Memphis, where it destroyed a Confederate fleet. Between Memphis and New Orleans only Vicksburg, Mississippi, and Port Hudson, Louisiana, now blocked Union control of the entire river.

The Peninsular Campaign

Union operations in the West early in 1862 received only the barest notice in Washington, where protection of the capital and preparation of the grand assault on Richmond were the main concerns. Lincoln, who had taken to studying books on military strategy, had formed definite opinions about how Richmond might be taken. He was for a new frontal attack, which would have the advantage of keeping the Army of the Potomac between the Confederates and Washington itself.

Largely because he had not been consulted about it, McClellan opposed the plan. The Confederate capital, the general successfully argued,

Foote, commanding a small fleet of gunboats under Ulysses S. Grant's supervision, captured Fort Henry on the Tennessee River, and then took nearby Fort Donelson on the Cumberland. During the following month, Confederate general Albert Sidney Johnston was left to lead his men across Tennessee to the strategic railroad center of Corinth, Mississippi. On April 6, Johnston ordered an attack back across the Tennessee border at the little crossroads of Shiloh. He was killed the first day of the ensuing battle, which the Federals called the Battle of Pittsburgh's Landing. (Perhaps because they were defending their homeland, southerners tended to name battles after towns, whereas the invading northerners chose the names of geographical features, as in this case and that of Manassas/Bull Run.)

With the advantage of surprise, Johnston's forces pushed the Federals back the first day. On the next, the Union armies drove off the should be approached by way of the peninsula formed by the York River on the north and the James River on the south. The peninsular plan involved a dangerous amphibious operation. The Confederates controlled the Norfolk navy yard at the mouth of the James. At Norfolk, moreover, was the Confederate ironclad ship *Virginia*, formerly the United States frigate *Merrimac*, which only a month before McClellan began his campaign had fought to a standstill the Union's new ironclad, *Monitor*.

The first contingents of McClellan's force—all told, 110,000 strong—landed on the peninsula on April 4, 1862. Yorktown, the first Confederate stronghold on the way to Richmond, might have been overrun in a day. But McClellan, afraid of another Bull Run, took a month to enter the town. Almost another month was lost while the general, awaiting expected reinforcements, advanced at a snail's pace up the peninsula. What kept McClellan's reinforcements away was Stonewall Jackson's brilliant foray up the Shenandoah Valley. As Lincoln had anticipated, he menaced Washington from the rear.

Having unnerved the Union capital sufficiently to force Lincoln to keep an even stronger army there than he had planned, Jackson dashed back to confront McClellan. Before Jackson arrived, McClellan's men had forced their way to within five miles of Richmond. There, on May 31, McClellan narrowly averted disaster at Seven Pines. McClellan might have taken advantage of the Confederates' confusion and the wounding of General Joseph Johnston. Instead, he left 25,000 men under General Fitz-John Porter in the vicinity of Richmond and withdrew the rest to his base at the town of White House, some twenty miles to the east. He waited once again for additional men to oppose the vast horde he imagined stood between his army and the Confederate capital. While McClellan dawdled, Robert E. Lee took command of "the Army of Northern Virginia."

Lee possessed the abilities as well as the appearance of a hero. His many admirers regarded him as the greatest military genius of the war. His soldiers came to look upon him as a man who "communed with the angels of Heaven."

CIVIL WAR MISCELLANEOUS "ACTIONS"

The military history of the Civil War is usually told in terms of major battles, but many soldiers spent most of their time walking and camping. The following official report by a Union officer gives some idea of the kind of miscellaneous "actions" so many soldiers on both sides found themselves involved in.

Report of Col. Fielding Hurst,
First West Tennessee Cavalry.

LA GRANGE, TENN., July 20, 1863.

Sir: I have the honor of submitting the following report:

In compliance with your order bearing date Jackson, Tenn., July 15, 1863, I proceeded with the regiment of Montezuma; thence to Purdy and Camden, where I ascertained the bridge across Big Hatchie River, near Bolivar, was destroyed. I then moved to this place, by way of Pocahontas. On leaving Jackson I marched up the Forked Deer 8 miles, and found the trail of 1,500 to 1,800 rebels, under Biffle, Forrest, and Newsom. They fled before us in great haste, destroying all the bridges they crossed on, giving me such difficulty

in crossing streams in 40 miles travel that I found myself 10 or 12 miles in their rear without any hope of overtaking them this side of our lines.

We took about 20 prisoners; paroled 8 and brought in 7. Some 5 or 6 fell back and made their escape, my rear guard being worn out with fatigue from hard marching and crossing streams by fording, swimming, &c.

I beg leave to state it as my belief that the entire rebel force which we met at Jackson fled by way of Shiloh in a badly torn up and demoralized condition, and could have been easily captured by a small force if thrown out from Corinth.

The prisoners all concur in stating that they were out of ammunition and low-spirited.

I am, sir, your very obedient servant.

FIELDING HURST,
Colonel, Commanding Regiment.

Col. EDWARD HATCH,
Commanding Second Cavalry Brigade.

Some military historians have argued that Lee was so concerned with defending his native state that he never developed a coordinated overall strategy. But for most of the war the Virginia front was his only command. He used it, with forays into the North itself, as the most effective means of relieving Union pressure elsewhere.

Other writers point to Lee's failure to provide adequate supplies for his armies, his habit of giving too much independence to his generals in the field, and his practice of taking on staff work he should have delegated to subordinates. As long as he could draw on brilliant corps commanders, however, Lee's confidence was rarely misplaced; it was only in the later stages of the war that the caliber of his junior officers declined.

On learning how McClellan had split his army, Lee immediately formed a plan to send a small force "looking numerous and aggressive" to intimidate the general, while he himself moved in to crush Porter. McClellan and Porter, however, were prepared. Lee's "eye" in spying out McClellan's position was his cavalry chief, Jeb Stuart. It was Stuart's nature to use any opportunity for showmanship. In a marvelous display of contempt for the enemy—and of foolish disregard of risk for his own cause—he had his cavalry circle about the Federals for three days and

Robert E. Lee. *(Library of Congress)*

Peninsular campaign (1862)

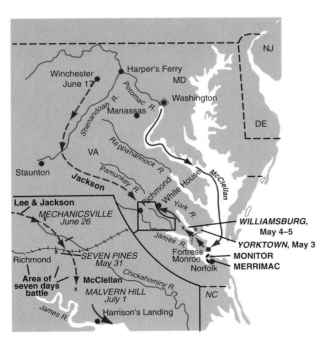

brought Lee the wanted information. His exploit also alerted the Union invaders.

McClellan regrouped his forces and surprised the Confederates with his mobilized strength. Having done this much, however, he turned again to the strategy of retreat. In the Seven Days Battle, between June 26 and July 2, McClellan inflicted heavy losses on Lee's advancing troops. But his own objective was merely Harrison's Landing on the James River, where the Union navy, if necessary, could evacuate his men.

Second Bull Run and Antietam

Lincoln visited McClellan at Harrison's Landing on July 9 and called off the whole peninsular campaign. He also named "Harry" Halleck commander of all the Union armies. In McClellan's place as commander of the Army of the Potomac, Halleck placed the rash and boastful

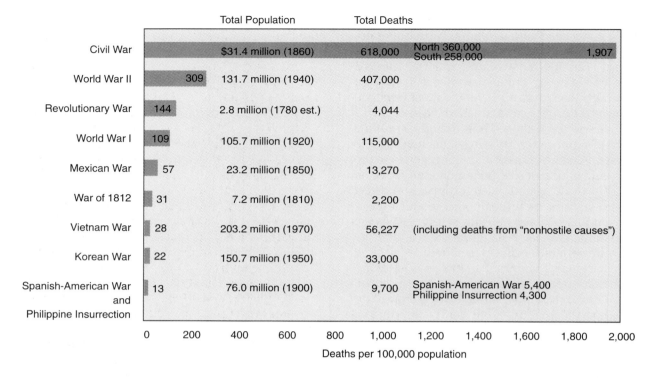

Battle deaths in the Civil War compared with battle deaths in other wars. The battle death total for American soldiers was considerably higher in the Civil War than in any other war in which the United States has taken part. The proportion of battle deaths to contemporary population, as shown in the chart, gives a truer conception of the seriousness of the losses in each war than do the absolute figures. *(Richard Current, T. Harry Williams, and Frank Freidel,* American History: A Survey, *third edition, Volume II, p. 393. Copyright © 1979 by Richard Current, T. Harry Williams, and Frank Freidel. Reprinted by permission of McGraw-Hill, Inc.)*

WAR DEATHS

After wars, it is often surprisingly difficult for even the winners to count the number of dead with any accuracy. Different historical sources give different figures, and the ones in the chart above should be regarded as approximations. In addition, these figures vastly underestimate the number of deaths caused by these wars, especially for those before World War II. Until that time, military deaths from disease greatly outnumbered deaths caused by action on the battlefield, as has been true throughout human history until the mid-twentieth century. Thus it has been only quite recently that modern medicine and sanitation have already reduced the toll of disease. Previously, the gathering of large numbers of men in army camps helped cause the rapid spread of a variety of deadly diseases. Some of these people would have died if they had remained at home, but the mere concentration of armies resulted in epidemics sweeping through them like a wildfire. Men previously not exposed to living in crowded conditions were especially vulnerable, which explains why Union deaths from disease during the Civil War occurred at a higher rate among men from the rural Middle West than among those from the more urban northeastern states. In both Union and Confederate armies, deaths from disease outnumbered deaths caused by battle at a ratio of about two to one. Thus, the figures in the chart represent only about one-third of the deaths caused by American wars before the twentieth century. The figures also do not reflect the very large numbers of men who were permanently disabled. Ironically, modern medicine has raised the proportion of wounded men who became disabled and thus has caused much suffering as well as relieving it. Earlier, men with serious wounds were much more likely to die.

John Pope. The president ordered these men to take Richmond. But Lee routed Pope in the momentous Second Battle of Bull Run (Second Manassas), August 29–30, 1862. This fresh setback left Union soldiers bitter and discouraged. "So long as the interests of our country are entrusted to a lying braggart like Pope," one of them wrote home, "we have little reason to hope successfully to compete with an army led by Lee, Johnston, and old Stonewall Jackson."

In June 1862 McClellan had been close to Richmond. Three strong Union armies appeared to have control of the Shenandoah Valley, and western Virginia was in Union hands. Now, at the end of August, one historian has written, "the only Federals closer than 100 miles to Richmond were prisoners . . . and men . . . preparing to retreat." In desperation, Lincoln again entrusted McClellan with temporary command of the disorganized army in the east. "If he can't fight," Lincoln said, "he excels in making others ready to fight."

Meanwhile, Lee pressed the attack, hoping to penetrate the North. Across his path lay the refurbished federal arsenal at Harpers Ferry, Virginia, with 10,000 men and munitions and supplies much needed by his own men. If he could take the arsenal and move from there into Maryland, he might win new recruits in the border states. Strengthened, he could move on to Pennsylvania. France and Britain then might recognize the Confederacy and intervene actively on its behalf And McClellan would be driven to the defensive with a demoralized force backed by a disheartened citizenry. But Lee's plans did not work.

On September 15, 1862, Stonewall Jackson with 25,000 men did take Harpers Ferry and everything they wanted there. The Confederates also learned that McClellan had found out about this adventure in time to have smashed the diminished force that remained with Lee. For two days, McClellan did nothing. When he did attack Lee on September 17 at Antietam Creek, his men almost overwhelmed the Rebels. By then, Jackson had returned to help stop the Federal momentum, and Lee's battered army was permitted to slip away.

Antietam has been called a defeat for both armies. But the North, at least, had repulsed an invasion on which the South had spent too much. "Our maximum strength has been mobilized," Jefferson Davis told his secretary of war

Second Battle of Bull Run. *(Library of Congress)*

The Battle of Antietam, September 17th, 1862. *(Library of Congress)*

after the battle, "while the enemy is just beginning to put forth his might."

WAR ON THE HOME FRONTS

The brutal, inconclusive engagement at Antietam was an appropriate symbol of the entire war. The seemingly aimless slaughter badly damaged civilian morale on both sides. As the war dragged on, its effects were felt far behind the battle lines. The South tried desperately to win aid and recognition from Great Britain; the North made every effort to keep that country neutral. And Lincoln had an important card to play in the war of nerves between the two sections—the Emancipation Proclamation.

The Confederacy in Wartime

To check criticism, Davis persuaded his Congress to enact the first Confederate law allowing the executive to suspend the writ of habeas corpus and impose martial law. But so intense had states'-rights feeling become in the South that no sooner were Davis's critics locked up under Confederate authority than state authorities released them.

The military stalemate was even more acutely felt by those who had to maintain the resources and manpower of the fighting forces. As early as April 1862, the Confederate Congress had to enact the first conscription act in American history, calling up for three years' service all white men eighteen to thirty-five. Later acts raised the age limit to fifty. But anyone could escape the draft by paying for a substitute, and there were occupational exemptions for such people as ministers and overseers. Evasion had the support of some states'-rights governors.

Statistics show that the draft in the South brought in few soldiers. But the figures veil the real effects of conscription. *Conscript* became such a dirty word that many young men volunteered before their age group was called. They, more than the conscripts themselves, maintained Confederate military manpower. On the other hand, the purchasing of substitutes seemed to confirm the slogan "a rich man's war and a poor man's fight." Desertions soared to well over 100,000—only a third, perhaps, of Union desertions, but much more keenly felt.

Symptoms of economic difficulties could be detected in the South even during the first year of the war. Loans in money were virtually impossible in a country where wealth was tied up in land and slaves. By 1862 the Confederacy was trying to "produce loans" by having planters buy Confederate bonds with cotton and other commodities. These loans had two drawbacks. Many planters would not surrender their commodities for government paper, and when they did, it was as difficult for the government as for citizens to transform commodities into cash.

The Confederacy had little better luck with taxes. Like other frustrated governments, it began to print paper money. By 1864 a Confederate paper dollar was worth, on average, 1.5 cents in specie. Prices soared; speculation and hoarding spread. An angry clerk in the War Department in Richmond described the situation in his diary:

In these times of privation and destitution, I see many men, who were never prominent secessionists, enjoying comfortable positions, and seeking investments for their surplus funds. . . . The true patriots . . . have sacrificed everything, and still labor in subordinate positions, with faith and patient suffering. These men and their families go in rags, and upon half rations, while the others fare most sumptuously.

The suffering was also caused by geographic maldistribution. The same clerk explained:

These evils might be remedied by the government, for there is no great scarcity of any of the substantials and necessities of life in the country, if they were only equally distributed. The difficulty is in procuring transportation, and the government monopolizes the railroads and canals. . . .

The gaunt form of wretched famine still approaches with rapid strides. Meal is now selling at $12 per bushel, and potatoes at $16. Meats have almost disappeared from the market, and none but the opulent can afford to pay $3.50 per pound for butter. . . . I am spading up my little garden, and hope to raise a few vegetables to eke out a miserable subsistence for my family.

Difficulties at home were aggravated by the collapse of diplomacy abroad. There had been some early successes. The ruling classes in Europe had no liking for slavery, but as aristocrats they would have been pleased with the failure of the "American experiment" in democratic government. Their attitude was reflected in the decision of Britain and France early in 1861 to recognize the Confederacy as a belligerent power though not as a sovereign government. Britain, moreover, threatened Lincoln's administration with war in November 1861 after a Union cruiser stopped the British mail steamer *Trent* on the high seas and removed Mason and Slidell, two Confederate diplomats, on their way to London and Paris. War was averted when Secretary of State Seward released the two Rebels.

Confederate hopes for foreign military assistance, high after the *Trent* affair, died a year later with military failure at Antietam. When Lincoln took this occasion to announce his Emancipation Proclamation, the surge of Union sentiment among foreign middle- and working-class groups made it even more unlikely that foreign nations would risk discontent at home by backing the wrong side in America.

Britain's willingness to build sea raiders for the Confederacy, however, seemed contrary to its official policy of nonintervention. International law permitted neutrals to build non-naval craft for belligerents. But it forbade such craft to be "equipped, fitted out, or armed" for fighting. British shipbuilders evaded this restriction by allowing apparently inoffensive hulls to "escape" to obscure ports, there to take on guns and munitions. All told, eighteen such "brigands of the sea" preyed on northern shipping. Union threats in 1863 to loose a "flood of privateers" against Britain's neutral trade had the desired effect; no more Confederate raiders were launched.

By 1863 an air of caution had taken hold in France as well, where Napoleon II had dreams of reinstating a monarchy in Mexico, to which the Confederates might look for help. Maximilian of Austria, a puppet of Napoleon, actually was placed at the head of Mexico's government soon after French army units had taken over Mexico City in 1863. Thereafter he received little French support. When Maximilian was captured and executed by Mexican rebels in 1867, the French agreed quietly to the end of their hopes.

The North in Wartime

Some of the important measures enacted by the Republican Congress had little to do with the war and a great deal to do with economic goals of the

Republican party. In 1861 the Morrill Tariff raised duties to their 1846 levels, from which they soared during and after the war. The next year Congress voted to build the transcontinental railroad over a central route and to help finance it with huge grants of public lands and generous cash loans. In 1863 Congress created a national banking system agreeable to northern capitalists.

Nor did Republican leaders neglect their Free Soil supporters. The Homestead Act of 1862 made available to adult "citizens of the United States" (meaning whites only), and to those who declared their intention of becoming citizens, 160 acres of the public domain. The land itself was free, but only if it received "settlement and cultivation." Only men who had borne arms against the United States were excluded. Farmers also benefited from the Morrill Land Grant Act of 1862. This act donated public lands to the states and territories to support colleges where agriculture, mechanical arts, and military science became the core of the curriculum.

After a short depression in 1861–1862, caused by the loss of $300 million in uncollectible southern debts and uncertainty about the war, the northern economy enjoyed a substantial boom. The splurge of government war buying helped the expansion and mechanization of agriculture, the production of shoes and other apparel, and the manufacture of munitions. Some profiteers made fortunes by selling the government huge amounts of cheap and nearly useless material, such as uniforms that fell apart in the rain. Other millionaires of the future—Rockefeller, Carnegie, Mellon, Morgan—laid the foundations of their huge fortunes in wartime activity.

But wartime prosperity hurt some people very badly. Industrial wages, for example, rose far more slowly than living costs, causing great hardship in cities where food speculators flourished. Families on fixed incomes were especially hard hit. Yet few northerners suffered the deprivation that became almost universal in the Confederacy.

Despite the boom, Lincoln's government had a difficult time financing the war, partly because it failed to realize how long the war would last. Secretary of the Treasury Chase's monetary policies did not help. Chase distrusted debt and paper money. He got Congress to approve excise taxes and even a new experiment, an income tax. But these measures failed to provide the needed revenue. Before long he had to use deficit financing. After a shaky start, he sold

bonds to a million persons. In 1862 he was forced to begin printing paper money. That year and the next, the Treasury issued certificates, soon known as *greenbacks*, to the amount of $450 million. Unsupported by gold, greenbacks were legal tender for domestic debts. By the summer of 1864, they had fallen to their low of thirty nine cents on the gold dollar.

Despite the Union's much greater population, shortages of manpower hurt its military effort at certain points. Large numbers of European immigrants arrived during the war, and many of them served in the northern army. So did a growing number of blacks. Yet eventually, in 1863, Congress was forced to vote the first Union draft, almost a full year after the Confederacy did so.

Far from helping the situation, the wording of the act added to social discontent. One of its provisions permitted a man to escape service simply by paying three hundred dollars to the authorities, leaving them with the responsibility of finding substitutes. Clearly the poor were to be saddled with the rich man's duty in a struggle that seemed to benefit only black laborers.

Riots protesting this law occurred in many towns. In Boston several rioters were shot dead after stoning troops. Democratic governor Horatio Seymour of New York helped turn the protest in New York City into a violent disturbance of major proportions. On the eve of the first drawing of names, he publicly questioned the wisdom and constitutionality of the draft. For three days, huge mobs terrorized the city. Federal troops had to be withdrawn from the battlefield to stop the violence.

The outburst of anger was aimed as much against blacks as against the draft. The leaders of the mobs were poor Irish American workingmen, themselves discriminated against. Some were striking longshoremen whose jobs the city's free blacks had filled. African American homes and churches became the principal targets of the rioters. Fires roared out of control. At least a dozen people were killed, and hundreds wounded.

Women in a Semimodern War

Even more than during the American Revolution, the Civil War left grown women alone at home to manage farming, finances, and children as best they could. On both sides they suffered the wrenches that go with sending loved ones to distant battlefields. Everyone assumed that the shooting part of war was men's work. Yet the Civil War saw more women closer to the actual fighting fronts than ever before. But while a handful of women became involved in the conflict as spies and even as double agents, most American women remained at home.

In the South, many white women did most of the work on southern farms, including tasks that had usually been taken care of by men. Wives of slaveholders were left with the new and difficult role of supervising overseers and slaves. Many of them found the job taxing and discouraging. Yet many women of the planting class were exercising independent authority for the first time in their lives.

In the North, wives (and widows) of farmers in the army found their work similarly broadened, except that wealthier ones supervised other women, boys, and old men as hired hands rather than slaves. Many women entered factories for the first time. The proportion of women in the manufacturing labor force rose from one-quarter to one-third. Women had always dominated numerically in textiles and garment making, but these fields were themselves expanding to meet the mounting demand for military uniforms.

In both South and North, women became nurses in far greater numbers than ever before. At first, most of the female nurses in the South were slaves, since it was felt that genteel ladies were unsuited and unsuitable for the raw, physical, and masculine atmosphere of army hospitals. As time went on and the numbers of wounded mounted, however, ladies were used as nurses in increasing numbers. In the North, nursing was better organized. In June 1861 Dorothea Dix was appointed superintendent of nurses. Dix angered some nursing applicants because she insisted that her nurses be over thirty years old and "plain in appearance"; she thought young, pretty, unmarried nurses would prove distracting and perhaps be distracted in hospitals filled with young men. Even Dix's nurses had to overcome male prejudice against women in army hospitals. One male army surgeon complained that every northern preacher "would recommend the most troublesome old maid in his congregation as an experienced nurse."

Most women nurses worked in hospitals away from the fighting front, but some served in the crude and sometimes dangerous field hospitals.

Clara Barton, who later founded the American Red Cross, worked in several battlefield units. Another woman, Mary Ann Bickerdyke, served with Grant's army in Tennessee, where she won the affection and gratitude of many soldiers and the lifelong respect of that crusty general.

Women also dominated numerically in the United States Sanitary Commission, a private aid and relief organization that received recognition from the government. The commission helped provide food and medical supplies, even ambulance service, for Union soldiers. As its name implied, it inspected army camps with an eye for clean food and water and safe latrines. Not only were many of the commission's nurses women, but women on the home front did much of the fund raising by holding "Sanitary Fairs."

Altogether, in both the North and the South, the Civil War gave or forced upon women new roles outside the home, roles that gave many of them unaccustomed measures of independence and a sense of accomplishment on their own.

The Emancipation Proclamation

While Lee tried to end the slaughter by breaking the North's morale through invasion, Lincoln attempted to break the stalemate through political action.

From the day he took office, Lincoln had "struggled," as he said, against every kind of pressure—religious, journalistic, political, personal—to declare the slaves free without compensating their owners and without undertaking to "colonize" freed blacks outside the country. Even if he had sympathized with such demands, the sensitivity of slaveholding border states within the Union, and northern sentiment in general, would have made him hold back. "On the news of General Fremont having actually issued deeds of manumission" in Missouri in 1861, Lincoln declared, "a whole company of our volunteers threw down their arms and disbanded."

At first, as the fighting spread and slaves sought security behind Union lines, generals in the field were left to their own discretion in dealing with them. Then in March 1862 Congress adopted "an additional article of war" forbidding the army to return fugitive slaves to their owners. Shortly thereafter, the War Department issued specific authorization for recruitment of fugitive slaves as soldiers. The authorization was accompanied by

A group of "contrabands." *(Library of Congress)*

an admonition that it "must never see daylight because it is so much in advance of public opinion."

Congress added more rungs to the ladder of freedom. In April 1862 it passed and Lincoln signed a measure abolishing slavery in the District of Columbia. Former owners were to be paid, on average, three hundred dollars per slave, not much below the going price on the eve of the war. Two months later, another act abolished slavery in United States territories, with no financial compensation. Congress then adopted the so-called Second Confiscation Act, which declared all persons engaged in rebellion, "or who shall in any way give aid . . . thereto," guilty of treason, and included among its penalties the stipulation that "all slaves" of such persons "shall be forever free of their servitude."

In the meantime, Lincoln mounted his own effort to use emancipation to end the war and restore the Union. He cautiously awaited good news from the battlefield before taking public action. On September 22, after indecisive Antietam, he read to the cabinet a draft of a proclamation that the papers published the next day. Lincoln declared that at the next meeting of Congress in December he would recommend enactment "of a practical measure" offering "pecuniary aid" to all slave states not then in rebellion against the

United States and having "voluntarily adopt[ed] immediate, or gradual abolishment of slavery within their limits." He also promised to continue his efforts to "colonize persons of African descent, with their consent."

On January 1, 1863, the September proclamation went on, he would designate which states still were in rebellion, and in them, "all persons held as slaves . . . shall be then, henceforward, and forever free," with no compensation whatever. Moreover, "the military and naval authority" of the United States would make no effort to suppress any attempts slaves might make to gain freedom; on the contrary, these authorities would do whatever necessary to shelter them.

Conservatives in the North, sick of the military stalemate and afraid that any tampering with slavery would only prolong the South's resistance, registered their disapproval in the fall elections of 1862. The Democrats cut deeply into the Republican majority in the House. The Radicals, on the other hand, attacked Lincoln's maneuverings and demanded that he get on with the "revolutionary struggle." Lincoln held to his plan. After the November elections, in accordance with his announcements, he urged Congress in his second annual message to adopt an amendment to the Constitution providing that each slave state that abolished slavery "any time before the 1st day of January, 1900, shall receive compensation from the United States." But only those not in rebellion against the United States on January 1, 1863, might participate in this offer.

On January 1, the "full period of one hundred days" of grace since his September announcement having expired with no takers among the rebellious states, Lincoln issued his final Emancipation Proclamation:

I, Abraham Lincoln, . . . in time of actual armed rebellion against the . . . United States, and as a fit and necessary war measure for suppressing said rebellion, do. . . order and declare that all persons held as slaves within . . . states and parts of states wherein the people . . . are . . . in rebellion . . . are and henceforward shall be free. . . . And I hereby enjoin upon the people so declared to be free to abstain from all violence, unless in necessary self-defense. . . . And I further declare . . . that such persons . . . will be received into the armed service of the United States.

The proclamation neither freed any slaves nor shortened the war. But it ensured the death of slavery when the war was won. In fact, many slaves had already seized their own freedom, especially in parts of the South where Federal troops were active.

TO APPOMATTOX

No matter how great the difficulties on the home fronts, the two armies staggered from battle to battle in the field. Men died in horrifying numbers, more than in any war of the nineteenth century except the Taiping Rebellion against the Manchu rulers of far more populous China. As was true of all major wars until the twentieth century, many more men died of disease than in battle. For the first time, women worked near the front lines in army hospitals, nursing wounded and dying men amid the screaming and the stench of body filth, blood, and gangrene.

The Long Road to Gettysburg

After Antietam, observing that McClellan had the "slows," Lincoln replaced him with General Ambrose E. Burnside. The new commander soon showed, at the battle of Fredericksburg in December 1862, that he was far worse than his predecessor. Lincoln replaced Burnside with General Joseph Hooker. "My plans are perfect," announced "Fighting Joe" in the spring of 1863, "and when I start to carry them out, may God have mercy on General Lee, for I will have none." Hooker decided to fake a movement of troops that would draw Lee's from their dug-in positions outside Fredericksburg. His tactic nearly worked, but early in May, when Hooker caught up with Lee at Chancellorsville, he, like so many of his predecessors, lost his nerve and almost lost his army.

Victory at Chancellorsville cost Lee 12,000 men and the life of Stonewall Jackson, who was shot by mistake in the dark by a Confederate soldier. But Lee now thought he saw the path open to an invasion of the North and to final victory. When Davis refused to pull men from the western theater in support of a grand assault, Lee decided to go ahead with the nearly 75,000 men in his Virginia command. "General Lee," one of his lieutenants said at this time, "believed that the Army of Northern Virginia, as it then existed, could accomplish anything." He was wrong.

Lee's army headed toward Harrisburg, Pennsylvania, on the strategic Susquehanna River. Hooker thought he saw in Lee's departure yet one more chance to move on Richmond. But Lincoln, grown wiser with the years, undertook to set him straight: "Lee's army, not Richmond, is your true objective point. If he comes toward the upper Potomac, follow on his flank and on his inside track, shortening your lines while he lengthens his." By June 29 Lee's advance corps had reached a point ten miles from Harrisburg— their deepest northern thrust of the war. Concerned now about the lengthening of his communications, Lee began to look for favorable terrain onto which to lure and confront the "Yanks." By then, Hooker had been replaced by "the old snapping turtle," General George Gordon Meade, who was making his own plans to invite attack on favorable ground. Both generals were to be disappointed.

On June 30, some of Lee's cavalry, searching for shoes, accidentally bumped into a Union patrol at the crossroads town of Gettysburg, Pennsylvania. They exchanged shots and attracted more troops from both sides. General Meade ordered Union troops to occupy a long north-south ridge outside the little town, with each end anchored on a hilltop. Lee instructed his forces to take up positions on a parallel ridge about a mile to the west. In between the two armies lay an open field, and the scene was set for a fight to the finish.

On July 2 the air thundered with the heaviest artillery exchange of the entire war. Wave after wave of Confederate soldiers charged across that field and up the slope of what is now known as Cemetery Ridge. Neither side gave way, but the Confederates suffered more casualties. The next day, July 3, Lee ordered the men under the command of General George Pickett to mount a frontal assault on the center of the Union line. Raked by artillery and rifle fire, they charged up the hill and for a moment broke through. But superior numbers forced them to fall back, leaving behind three-quarters of the men who on that day had sought to win independence for the Confederacy.

Lincoln telegraphed Meade, "Call no council of war. . . . Do not let the enemy escape." But Meade hesitated. He called his general officers together, and the guns were silent throughout the Fourth of July. The next morning Lee's battered army limped off toward Virginia. Lincoln was stunned. As he said later, "Our army held the war in the hollow of its hand and would not close it."

As for the battle itself, a seasoned Union officer described the awful slaughter, which characterized so many battles of the war:

We see the poor fellows hobbling back from the crest or unable to do so, pale and weak, lying on the ground with the mangled stump of an arm or leg, dripping their life-blood away; or with a cheek torn open, or a shoulder mashed. And many, alas! hear not the roar as they stretch upon the ground with upturned faces and open eyes, though a shell should burst at their very ears. Their ears and their bodies this instant are only mud.

Many months afterward the bodies of thousands who there gave their lives still lay unburied. The degrading spectacle led to a call for a national cemetery in their honor. It was at the dedication of this cemetery that Lincoln delivered the Gettysburg Address, promising "that these dead shall not have died in vain.

Grant Takes Command

On July 4, 1863, on the heels of the victory at Gettysburg, came the report of a great Union triumph in the west. After a year of struggle, Grant had taken Vicksburg, "the Gibraltar of the Mississippi." Four days later, Port Hudson, the last Confederate stronghold on the river, surrendered. Grant's victory in the western theater focused the attention of the entire nation on this West Point graduate, a veteran of the Mexican War who had resigned his captaincy in 1854 so that he could better support his family. Grant was not glamorous, but he eventually proved to be the Union's best general. His "art of war" best sums up his military theory: "The art of war is simple enough. Find out where your enemy is. Get him as soon as you can. Strike at him as hard as you can and keep moving on."

Fredericksburg to Gettysburg, 1862–63

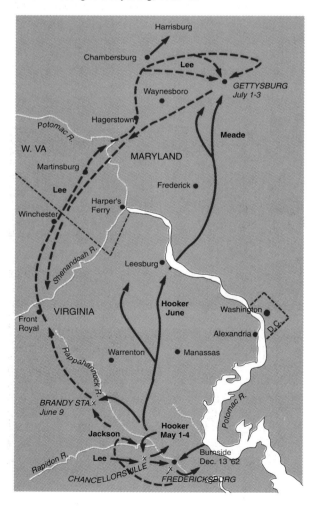

Pursuit of Lee's army on the road near Emmitsburg, July 7, 1863. *(Library of Congress)*

After Vicksburg, one Confederate army and part of the Confederacy itself were isolated west of the Mississippi. But another Confederate army commanded by General Braxton Bragg was still operating in central Tennessee. In September 1863, under Grant's orders, General William Rosencrans began to pursue Bragg in earnest. But after being outmaneuvered at Chickamauga, Rosencrans's army found itself bottled up in nearby Chattanooga.

To raise the siege, Grant called on armies from the east and west. He received them because of northern railroad efficiency. On November 25 these combined forces won a spectacular victory at Chattanooga, splitting the Confederacy north and south as well as east and west.

In the spring of 1864 Lincoln rewarded Grant by appointing him supreme commander of all Union armies. Grant quickly set to work on his victory program. His plan was for the Army of the Potomac to keep Lee's army so busy that it could not link up with any other rebel force—and to bleed it daily in the bargain. At the same time, General William T. Sherman's army was to push eastward from Tennessee into Georgia and take Atlanta, thereby striking into the heart of Rebel territory.

The first reports were disheartening. Throughout May 1864, the Army of the Potomac, under Meade and Grant himself, engaged Lee's forces in murderous but indecisive battles north of Richmond. Enormous Federal casualties in the Wilderness and at Cold Harbor—Grant is said to have lost 55,000 men in this first month—aroused strong resentment in the North. Newspapers began to call Grant "the butcher." But Lincoln stood by him. "I have just read your dispatch," he wrote to Grant after Cold Harbor. "I begin to see it. You will succeed. God bless you all."

Grant himself, however, began to have second thoughts. He decided to swing down to the peninsula to get at Richmond once more from

Ulysses S. Grant. *(Library of Congress)*

CIVIL WAR FIGHTING

The first of these two views of the fighting came from a perceptive novelist, Stephen Crane, in *The Red Badge of Courage:*

There was a consciousness always of the presence of his comrades about him. He felt a subtle battle brotherhood more potent even than the cause for which they were fighting. It was the mysterious fraternity born of the smoke and danger of death. The rifles, once loaded, were jerked to the shoulder and fired without aim into the smoke, or at one of the blurred and shifting forms which, upon the field before the regiment, had been growing larger and larger like puppets under a magician's hand. . . .

The second is from a report by a Union general after the battle of Fredericksburg:

The dead were swollen to twice their natural size, black as Negroes in most cases. They sprawled in every conceivable position, some on their backs with gaping jaws, some with eyes as large as walnuts, protruding from glassy stares; some doubled up like a contortionist . . . here lay one without a head, there's one without legs, yonder a head and legs, without a trunk; everywhere horrible expressions, fear, rage, agony, madness, torture; lying in pools of blood, lying with heads half-buried in mud, with fragments of shell sticking in oozing brain, with bullet holes all over puffed limbs.

---

the south and to send General Philip Sheridan to stop Confederate thrusts northward in the Shenandoah Valley. For nearly a year there was continual slaughter and devastation in the valley and in the tidewater of Virginia. Sheridan executed Grant's order to leave the Shenandoah Valley "a barren waste." He reported: "A crow would have had to carry its rations if it had flown across the valley." Sheridan then joined Grant for a final thrust at Richmond.

The tide of war in the Deep South was much clearer. Starting in Tennessee, Sherman's army pushed through Georgia against weakening Confederate resistance. Sherman, announcing that "war is hell," pursued a policy of devastating the countryside, of deliberately aiming at the civilian as well as the military morale of his opponents. His famous "march to the sea" was in fact a major turning point in the modern history of warfare. It was a new strategy to aim not only at an opposing army, but at the society supporting it.

The chaos was complicated by the enormous number of slaves suddenly set free from ruined plantations. On September 3, Sherman wired Washington: "So Atlanta is ours, and fairly won." Having left Atlanta "smouldering and in ruins," Sherman's "bummers" thrust toward Savannah. "To realize what war is," Sherman said, "one should follow in our tracks."

The End in Sight

Sherman's capture of Atlanta in September 1864 had more than military significance. Early in the year, politicians had begun to prepare for the presidential elections in November. Lincoln, for the good of the Republican party, had been urged not to seek renomination. By the time of the party convention at Baltimore in June, however, his Radical opponents had failed to agree on a candidate, and his loyal backers put him across. To bolster the ticket, they nominated the War Democrat Andrew Johnson of Tennessee for vice-president. Lincoln and Johnson ran under a Union party label.

The Democrats chose General McClellan. The "war failure" plank in the Democratic platform declared that hostilities should cease and that the "Federal Union of the States" should be reestablished on the old basis. This was nothing less than an armistice offer. McClellan, after serious soul-searching, decided to reject the plank and to commit himself to continuing the war. At the same time, some of Lincoln's advisers had begun to press him to make overtures to Richmond. Then came the news of Atlanta's fall.

There was a revival of confidence not only in Lincoln's generals, but in the president himself. In November, Lincoln won a smashing victory.

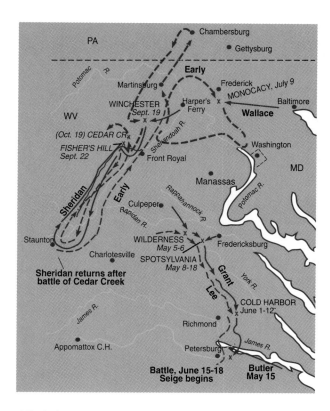

War in the east, 1864

knowledged that "two thirds of our men are absent . . . most of them absent without leave."

In March 1865, the Confederacy took the fateful step of recruiting men "irrespective of color," slaves "who might volunteer to fight for their freedom." It was a signal of desperation. By then, Grant's 115,000 "blues" outnumbered Lee's 54,000 "grays" in Virginia. The time had come for Lee to pull out of his trenches while he still had troops and to try to join up with Johnston in North Carolina. Under cover of darkness and while Davis and his government fled, contingents of Grant's army poured into Richmond.

On April 7, his path to North Carolina sealed off, Lee asked for terms. On April 9, standing stiffly in a new uniform, he met the mud-spattered Grant at the McClean farmhouse at Appomattox Court House, a village some ninety-five miles west of Richmond. "Give them the most liberal terms," Lincoln had ordered Grant. "Let them have their horses to plow with, and, if you like, their guns to shoot crows with. I want no one punished."

As defeat loomed that terrifying spring, a patriotic and sensitive southern matron confided in her diary: "Such a hue and cry, everybody blamed by somebody else. Only the dead heroes left stiff and stark on the battle field escape. I cry: 'Blame every man who stayed at home and did not fight, but not one word against those who stood out until the bitter end, and stacked

A defender of the Confederacy. *(Library of Congress)*

With 55 percent of the popular vote, he outdistanced McClellan in the electoral college, 212 to 21. Victory, not negotiated peace, became the military theme as well.

From Savannah, in February 1865, Sherman headed north toward the "hellhole of secession," South Carolina, where, as he said, "the devil himself could not restrain his men." The "pitiless march" brought him to Columbia, South Carolina's capital. Soon, whether by accident or design, one of the most beautiful cities in the country was consumed in flames. Charleston, outflanked, was occupied the next day by Union forces blockading the harbor after the defending Rebels had fled.

Sherman, meanwhile, pounded on into North Carolina. Gettysburg, Vicksburg, Atlanta, the humiliating failure of cotton diplomacy, the bruising wall of the blockade—none of these had quite managed to kill the Confederacy's capacity for war. But after Sherman's march, southern spirits drooped. As early as September 1864, Davis ac-

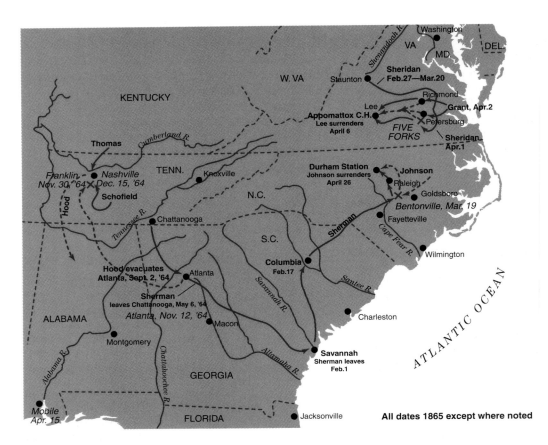

Final campaigns of the Civil War, 1864–1865

muskets at Appomattox.'" On April 26, Johnson surrendered his army to Sherman at Durham Station, in north central North Carolina. On May 10, Davis was caught in Georgia and imprisoned for two years.

Lincoln's Death

When news of Richmond's fall reached Washington on April 3, the city exploded with joy. Then, on April 14, a fanatic actor, John Wilkes Booth,

---

WORDS AND NAMES IN AMERICAN HISTORY

Platform, in its original and literal meaning, meant an object formed like a plate (the word has the same root as *plateau*.) That is, a platform was something flat. It came to mean something a person could stand on above the ground. Platforms were useful for outdoor public performances, since an indoor platform set before an audience is usually called a *stage*. Revivalist speakers used them out-of-doors. So did politicians, especially in the early years of the nineteenth century, when outdoor platforms came to be the usual place for people to gather to hear speeches. By the middle of the nineteenth century, when so many politicians were speechifying from these raised plat-

forms, the very term had come to denote their political beliefs. This was an almost inevitable development, because political candidates announced their programs and then thundered forth at the end: "I stand upon this platform." Political parties started to adopt specific programs, or "platforms," after they began in the 1830s to hold national conventions. Almost inevitably, individual proposals in a party's platform began to be known as a *plank*. Thus some candidates could claim to endorse the whole platform except for the plant on such-and-such an issue. Never before has ordinary carpentry contributed so much to political discourse.

shot Lincoln as the president sat in his box at Ford's Theatre in Washington, watching a performance of *Our American Cousin*. At seven-twenty the next morning Lincoln died. It was the first assassination of a United States president.

The victorious president had charged the nation to act "with malice towards none, with charity for all." He had acknowledged the guilt of the North as well as the South for slavery. At first Robert E. Lee would not believe the news of Lincoln's death. Then, on that Sunday, he told a visitor that he had "surrendered as much to [Lincoln's] goodness as to Grant's artillery." Now Lincoln and "goodness" were removed, with consequences Herman Melville foretold when he wrote in "The Martyr":

> He lieth in his blood—
> The father in his face;
> They have killed him, the Forgiver—
> The Avenger takes his place. . . .

SUMMARY

The Civil War became the deadliest war Americans have ever fought. It lasted tour years, killed a generation of young men, and left the South devastated.

It began slowly. At first it was thought that the war would be quick, that the South, fighting on its home ground and led by talented officers, would win. But in the long war that ensued, the North's advantages in numerical strength and industrial resources proved overwhelming. The North had other advantages—in its government, which was strong and centralized, and in its political leader, Abraham Lincoln. The South, dedicated to states' rights, had difficulty with even the idea of strong central government.

Lincoln immediately prepared for war, but let nearly a year go by before he acknowledged that it would be a fight to the finish. The North's strategy was to strangle the South with a naval blockade, gain control of the Mississippi, and take Richmond, the Confederate capital. The first two steps went well; the third did not. In July 1861, Union forces were beaten at Bull Run in Virginia. But Confederate military commanders anxious to push on to Washington were overruled, and the Union armies were commanded by generals whose main talents seemed to be inaction and delay.

Even with direct orders from Lincoln, the army did not move in the east and the campaign for Richmond went nowhere. Under more vigorous commanders, Union forces in the west gained control of the Mississippi except for Vicksburg and Port Hudson. The grand assault on Richmond in the spring and summer of 1862 failed utterly because of the generals' incompetence. The North was again defeated, in the second battle of Bull Run in August. But at Antietam in September, the Confederate attempt to penetrate the North failed.

This was to be the turning point, for now the South's resources were being used up, and victory was still nowhere in sight. In its brutality and inconclusiveness, Antietam also symbolized a war that seemed to produce only aimless mutual slaughter.

By this time, there were clear signs of economic difficulties in the South. The frustrated Confederate government had begun to print paper money in 1861; by 1864 a Confederate paper dollar was worth 1.5 cents. Prices soared. Cotton diplomacy failed because the British during those years needed wheat more than cotton. In the North, there was an economic boom and wartime prosperity as mechanized agriculture and expanding factories poured out huge amounts of food and supplies. The federal government also printed paper money—greenbacks—which fell in value to 39 cents on the gold dollar by the summer of 1864. While the war brought hardship to many women, especially in the South, it also brought some of them opportunities for self-assertion and independent activities. North and South, many women had no choice when their husbands and sons went off to war: They had to undertake farming chores and supervision of free and slave laborers to an extent they had never before experienced. Many women on both sides seized the opportunity to help in the war effort by taking jobs in factories, raising funds for the relief of soldiers in difficulty, and becoming nurses in army hospitals.

By 1862, Lincoln was ready to put in motion a plan to end the military stalemate by a bold political action—freeing the slaves. In September he issued a proclamation whose terms were to take effect on January 1,1863. On that day, he issued the final Emancipation Proclamation. It did not shorten the war or free any slaves, but it ensured the death of slavery when the war was over.

After Antietam, the military pace of the war picked up. The North lost at Chancellorsville in May of 1863, but then came Gettysburg, July 1–4, and the end of Confederate hopes. On the same day the battle at Gettysburg ended, news came of Grant's victory at Vicksburg. In September, Union forces won a spectacular victory at Chattanooga in Tennessee that split the Confederacy north and south as well as east and west. Grant was made supreme commander of the Union armies in the spring of 1864, but another year of terrible fighting followed as Union armies advanced toward Richmond in a great pincer movement. Sherman's army, starting in Tennessee, moved relentlessly toward the sea, laying waste the area over which it traveled and burning Atlanta in September 1864.

In November Lincoln was reelected on the strength of the military victories and the clear signs that the end was in sight. By the end of March 1865, Grant's army was ready to enter Richmond. On April 9, General Robert E. Lee surrendered for the Confederacy at the village of Appomattox Court House. But then on April 14, Lincoln was shot in Washington and died the next day. The war was over. It had cost the life of an American president, in addition to more American lives lost than in any other war before or since.

TIME LINE

1861		
April	Lincoln proclaims blockade of rebel ports	
June	Dorothea Dix appointed superintendent of Union nurses	
July	First battle of Bull Run/Manassas	
Nov.	General Scott retires; McClellan promoted	
Nov.	*Trent* affair	
1862		
Feb.	Federals capture Forts Henry and Donelson	
Mar.–June	McClellan's peninsula campaign; Jackson in Shenandoah Valley	
Apr.	Enormous casualties at Shiloh	
Apr.	Davis pushes through first Confederate military draft	
Aug., Sept.	Second Bull Run and Antietam	
1863		
Jan.	Emancipation Proclamation goes into effect	
May	Lee's costly victory at Chancellorsville	
July	Battle of Gettysburg	
July	Grant's siege finally takes Vicksburg	
July	Draft/race rioting in New York City	
Sept.–Nov.	Battles of Chickamauga and Chattanooga	
1864		
May, June	The Wilderness and Cold Harbor	
May–Dec.	Sherman marches from Tennessee through Georgia to the sea	
June–Dec.	Lee versus Grant: continued warfare in Virginia	
July	Union greenbacks fall to thirty-nine cents on the dollar	
Nov.	Lincoln outpolls Democratic and Copperhead opponents	
1865		
Apr.	Grant takes Richmond; Lee surrenders at Appomattox	
Apr.	Lincoln assassinated	

Suggested Readings

A superb survey of the coming of the war and the struggle itself is J. McPherson, *Battle Cry of Freedom: The Civil War Era* (1988). Allan Nevins has written magnificent accounts: *The War for the Union: The Improvised War, 1861–1862* (1959), *War Becomes Revolution, 1862–1863* (1960), and *The Organized War, 1863–1864* (1971). A shorter study is J. Randall and D. Donald, *The Civil War and Reconstruction* (rev. ed., 1961). A good overall military history is H. Hattaway and A. Jones, *How the North Won* (1983).

Strong national feeling is emphasized in G. Frederickson, *The Inner Civil War: Northern Intellectuals and the Crisis of the Union* (1965); see also E. Hess, *Liberty, Virtue, and Progress: Northerners and Their War for the Union* (1988). There are many insights in D. Aaron, *The Unwritten War: American Writers and the Civil War* (1973).

The relationship of the war to economic developments has long been debated by historians. A crucial development is covered by T. Weber, *The Northern Railroads in the Civil War, 1861–1865* (1952); and R. Black, *The Railroads of the Confederacy* (1952). Stimulating essays on the war and industrial growth may be found in D. Gilchrist and W. Lewis (eds.), *Economic Change in the Civil War Era* (1965). R. Sharkey, *Money, Class and Party: An Economic*

Study of the Civil War and Reconstruction (1959), offers a more general financial analysis. Key developments in military technology are discussed in R. Bruce, *Lincoln and the Tools of War* (1956).

C. Eaton, *A History of the Southern Confederacy* (1952), is the best general survey. For the Confederacy's president and his administration, see the over-enthusiastic study by H. Strode, *Jefferson Davis* (2 vols., 1955, 1959). R. Durden, *The Gray and the Black: The Confederate Debate on Emancipation* (1973), reproduces portions of the 1860s debates and gives narrative commentary.

Of the enormous number of biographies of Lincoln, a relatively brief one stands out: B. Thomas, *Abraham Lincoln* (1952). D. Donald, *Lincoln Reconsidered* (1956), offers insights on the man; see also R. Current, *The Lincoln Nobody Knows* (1958). Also good is S. Oates, *Abraham Lincoln: The Man behind the Myth* (1984). For Lincoln's fascinating relationships with his cabinet, see B. Thomas and J. Hyman, *Stanton: The Life and Times of Lincoln's Secretary of War* (1962); and H. Beale and A. Brownsword (eds.), *Diary of Gideon Welles, Secretary of the Navy under Lincoln and Johnson* (1960).

The strong feeling behind the Democratic opposition in the North is evident in F. Klement, *The Copperheads in the Middle West* (1960). For antiblack sentiment in the Midwest, see V. Voegeli, *Free but Not Equal: The Midwest and the Negro during the Civil War* (1967). The role of the abolitionists during the war is presented in J. McPherson, *The Struggle for Equality: Abolitionists and the Negro in the Civil War and Reconstruction* (1964). Outstanding biographies of important Radical Republicans include F. Brodie, *Thaddeus Stevens* (1959); and two books by D. Donald, *Charles Sumner and the Coming of the Civil War* (2nd ed., 1981) and *Charles Sumner and the Rights of Man* (1976). A famous and frequently misunderstood document is placed in context in J. Franklin, *The Emancipation Proclamation* (1963).

The diplomatic aspects of the war are treated in all general histories. Additional insight is contained in M. Duberman, *Charles Francis Adams* (1961), who was the Union minister in London. There is a huge literature on military aspects, enough to fill several hundred feet of shelf space. One of the best overall surveys is B. Catton, *Centennial History of the War* (3 vols., 1961–1965). Moving accounts of the Union army in the East are offered in Catton's *Mr. Lincoln's Army*

(1951), *Glory Road* (1952), *A Stillness at Appomattox* (1954), and *This Hallowed Ground* (1956). There are superb photographs in W. Frassanito, *Grant and Lee: The Virginia Campaigns, 1864–1865* (1983). The Union president's agonized search for the right man is chronicled in T. Williams, *Lincoln and His Generals* (1952). Another important aspect is treated in R. West, Jr., *Mr. Lincoln's Navy* (1957). Greatness of leadership in the South lay with a general: See D. Freeman, *R. E. Lee: A Biography* (4 vols., 1934–1935). An outstanding one-volume life is C. Dowdey, *Lee* (1965).

Many other biographies celebrate generals on both sides. For the ordinary man's role in the war, consult H. Commager (ed.), *The Blue and the Gray: The Story of the Civil War as Told by Participants* (2 vols., 1950); and B. Wiley, *The Life of Johnny Reb* (1943) and *The Life of Billy Yank* (1952). The role of blacks is discussed by B. Quarles, *The Negro in the Civil War* (1953); and the importance of black Union troops by D. Cornish, *The Sable Arm: Negro Troops in the Union Army, 1861–1865* (1958). Magnificent documents and commentary may be found in I. Berlin et al. (eds.), *Freedom: A Documentary History of Emancipation, 1861–1867*, Ser. 1, Vol.1(1985). J. McPherson, *The Negro's Civil War* (1965), is a superb combination of original documents and commentary; and A. Cook, *The Armies of the Streets: The New York City Draft Riots of 1863* (1974), provides a complete analysis of that subject. The dramatic confrontation between northern troops, accompanying abolitionists, and liberated slaves in the South Carolina-Georgia Sea Islands is vividly recreated in W. Rose, *Rehearsal for Reconstruction* (1964). L. Litwack, *Been in the Storm So Long: The Aftermath of Slavery* (1979), is a sweeping account about the coming of freedom both during and after the war.

For southern civilian life, see B. Wiley, *The Plain People of the Confederacy* (1943). For women, see Wiley's *Confederate Women* (1975); and M. E. Massey, *Bonnet Brigades* (1966).

There are powerful literary treatments of the war: W. Whitman's *Drum Taps* (1865) and *Specimen Days* (1882), the latter a wrenching account of the horrors of the Union "hospitals." H. Melville, *Battle Pieces and Other Aspects of the War* (1964 ed.), is also fine. S. Crane's *The Red Badge of Courage* (1895) is one of the few novels in the English language to catch the real feelings of the ordinary soldier under fire.

From the plantation to the Senate. *(Library of Congress)*

CHAPTER 18

AFTER THE WAR: RECONSTRUCTION AND RESTORATION

After four years of warfare, the Union had withstood its most serious challenge. Measured in physical devastation and human lives, the Civil War remains the costliest war in the experience of the American people. When it ended, in April 1865, 620,000 men (in a nation of 35 million) had been killed, at least that many more had been wounded, and portions of the Confederacy lay in ruins. Two questions were firmly settled: the right of a state to secede and the right to own slaves. But new problems soon surfaced that would plunge the nation into still another period of turmoil and uncertainty.

Having won the war, the victors had no rules to guide them in how to reconstruct the South and ensure its future loyalty. Under what conditions should the former Confederate states be permitted to return? What if any punishment should be meted out to those southerners who had led their states out of the Union? Were the nearly 4 million freed slaves entitled to the same rights as white citizens? Finally, where did the responsibility lie for resolving these difficult questions—with the president or with Congress?

Lincoln's view of reconstruction was consistent with his theory of secession and re-

bellion. He held from the outset that states could not break away from the Union. The Civil War, then, had been an illegal rebellion waged by disloyal men. Now that the rebellion was over, the task of reconstruction consisted simply of restoring loyal governments to the former Confederate states. The rebels themselves could be quickly reinstated as citizens by presidential pardon, and they could then take part in the establishment of the new governments. Although this became known as the "moderate" approach to reconstruction, stressing the president's generous spirit and statesmanship, the meaning of Lincoln's "moderation" should be clearly understood: After agreeing to repudiate secession and to recognize the abolition of slavery, the newly restored southern states would retain the same powers of decision enjoyed by all states, including the right to determine the status of their black residents.

The Radical Republicans, a faction within the party, believed Lincoln's program would hamper their objective; they wanted to rebuild southern society around the equality of newly freed slaves and whites. The rebel states, they argued, had been reduced to the status of territories because of their "rebellion." In seeking statehood once again, they came under the jurisdiction not of the president but of Congress, which governed territorial affairs. This was not simply an argument over the respective powers of the legislative and executive branches of government; it was a battle over the very objectives and content of southern reconstruction.

By his policy, President Lincoln hoped to build a Republican party in the South based on the votes of white men and on the leadership of those who had initially opposed secession. His successor, Andrew Johnson, also advocated a "moderate" approach, based on his strict reading of the Constitution and on his belief in white supremacy. The Radicals, on the other hand, viewed the southern black vote as the only means of winning that section of the country for the Republicans and ensuring the party's national strength. Lincoln and Johnson were willing to entrust the fate of the newly freed slaves to the defeated whites. The Radicals tried to develop a program of civil rights and education that would protect the freed blacks from the defeated whites.

Despite the war and emancipation, the white South's attitude toward blacks remained the same. The "corner-stone" of the Confederacy, Vice-President Alexander Stephens had declared in 1861, "rests upon the great truth, that the negro is not equal to the white man; that slavery—subordination to the superior race—is his natural and normal condition." Even as they acknowledged emancipation, few whites surrendered their justifications for having held black men and women as slaves. A planter in South Car-

olina gave voice to that sentiment in the questions he asked after the war: "Can not freedmen be organized and disciplined as well as slaves? Is not the dollar as potent as the lash? The belly as tender as the back?"

Neither military defeat nor the collapse of slavery suggested to whites the need to re-examine their racial relationships or assumptions. If anything, the need to maintain white supremacy took on an even greater urgency now that the slaves had been freed. The repression of the newly freed slaves made a shambles of "moderate" or presidential Reconstruction. By refusing to grant blacks minimal civil rights and educational opportunities, the white South succeeded only in alienating northern public opinion, strengthening the Radical position, and helping to make possible Radical or congressional Reconstruction.

Radical rule in the South ended in 1877 (much sooner in most states), having failed to achieve the objective of a democratic, biracial society. That failure does not mean Lincoln's or Johnson's programs would have worked any better. Whatever its shortcomings, Radical Reconstruction transformed the lives of southern blacks and raised black expectations and aspirations. This remarkable but brief experiment in biracial government enabled blacks to gain political experience as voters and officeholders, it brought badly needed reforms to southern society, and it laid the legal foundations for a "second reconstruction" in the 1950s and 1960s, when black leaders and movements would seek to complete the work of emancipation.

THE DEFEATED SOUTH

The Civil War took a heavy toll of families in the North as well as the South, among both whites and blacks. But the physical devastation was largely limited to the South, where almost all the fighting had taken place. Large sections of Richmond, Charleston, Atlanta, Mobile, and Vicksburg had burned to the ground. The countryside through which the armies had passed

was littered with gutted plantation houses and barns, burned bridges, and uprooted railroad lines. Many crops had been destroyed or confiscated, and much of the livestock had been slain. To rebuild the devastated areas and to restore agricultural production required outlays of capital and labor that were not readily available.

In the North, the $4 billion in direct wartime expenditures had provided huge profits. But only a few southerners managed to accumulate capital during the war—some by running cotton through the northern blockade; others by demanding gold or goods instead of Confederate paper money in payment for food, clothing, and farm supplies. Most southerners were now poor.

The planters' land, worth $1.5 billion in 1860, was evaluated at half that amount ten years later. The South's $1 billion in banking capital had been wiped out, and its credit system was paralyzed. The money invested in Confederate bonds and currency was lost. Finally, and most critically, the planters' $2.5 billion investment in slaves had vanished, along with many of the slaves.

Aftermath of Slavery

After Appomattox, most planters assembled what blacks were left, acknowledged their freedom, and asked them to work for wages or shares of the crop. Having lived for years in close daily contact with the "white folks," and facing an uncertain future with a vaguely defined freedom, the emancipated slaves had to make some difficult decisions. If they remained on the farms and plantations, what relations would they now have with those who had once owned them? How adequately would they be paid for their labor? If they left, where would they go, and how would they support themselves?

For some, the first need was to take some kind of action to prove to themselves that they were really free. The quickest and most direct test was to leave the plantation. As one newly freed slave explained to his former master, "I must go, for if I stay here I'll never know I am free." By leaving, many expected to improve their economic prospects; others hoped to locate family members from whom they had been separated during slavery; and some expected greater freedom by settling in the nearest town.

To throw off a lifetime of bondage, black men and women adopted different priorities, ranging from dramatic breaks with the past to subtle though no less significant changes in demeanor and behavior. Many did not move at all, at least not in the first postwar year, choosing to remain in familiar surroundings and to find ways of exercising their freedom even as they worked in the same fields and kitchens. "Henney is still with me," a South Carolina white woman said of her former slave, "but she is not the same person that she was."

Family members who had been sold away during slavery sought each other out after emancipation—an effort that spanned several decades for some and ended for many in failure, tragedy, and disappointment. New emotional ties had sometimes replaced the old; husbands and wives who had given up any hope of seeing each other again had remarried, and children sold away from their parents had been raised by other black women or by the white mistress, creating complications. The question facing some freedmen and freedwomen was not whether to formalize their slave marriages, as so many did in the postwar years, but which marriage should take precedence. And that often proved to be a difficult and agonizing decision.

After emancipation, many black women opted to stop working in the fields and kitchens in order to spend more time tending to their own households and children. If the women themselves did not initiate such moves, the men sometimes insisted, as a way of reinforcing their position as head of the family. "When I married my wife," a Tennessee freedman told his employer, in rejecting his request for her services, "I married her to wait on me and she has got all

---

WORDS AND NAMES IN AMERICAN HISTORY

The word *miscegenation* refers to interracial sexual contact, with or without resulting children. It was made by combining the Latin *miscere*—to mix—and *genus*—race, people, or even species. The word was minted in 1863, during the Civil War, by two New York newspapermen, David Croly and George Wakeman, who were both antiblack and antiabolitionist. They raised the matter of interracial sex in order to appeal to widely held prejudices against it. Their purposes were primarily political, yet the term has endured, superseding the more common words then in use, *amalgamation*. Perhaps because the word is long and so many Americans feel so awkward about the matter, *miscegenation* is commonly mispronounced: the accents are on the first and fourth syllables.

THE LEGACY OF SLAVERY

Several years after their forced separation during slavery, the husband of Laura Spicer remarried in the belief that his wife had died. When he learned after the war that she was still alive, the news stung him. He dictated a letter to her:

I want to see you and I don't want to see you. I love you just as well as I did the last day I saw you, and it will not do for you and I to meet. I am married, and my wife have two children. . . . You know it never was our wishes to be separated from each other, and it never was our fault. Oh, I can see you so plain, at any-time. I had rather anything to had happened to me most that ever have been parted from you and the children. As I am, I do not know which I love best, you or

Anna. If I was to die, today or tomorrow, I do not think I would die satisfied till you tell me you will try and marry some good, smart man that will take good care of you and the children; and do it because you love me; and not because I think more of the wife I have got than I do of you. The woman is not born that feels as near to me as you do. Tell them [the children] they must remember they have a good father and one that cares for them and one that thinks about them every day.

Source: Henry L. Swint (ed.) *Dear Ones at Home: Letters from Contraband Camps* (Nashville: Vanderbilt University Press, 1966), pp. 242–43.

she can do right here for me and the children." But not all black women agreed to such a narrow definition of their roles. And even if they wanted to leave the labor force, they could seldom afford to do so. Many continued to work in the fields alongside their men, in the white family's kitchen, and at other tasks that would supplement the family income. "They do double duty," a black Mississippi woman observed—"a man's share in the field, and a woman's part at home. They do any kind of field work, even ploughing, and at home the cooking, washing, milking and gardening."

That many freedmen and freedwomen changed their lives, displayed feelings of independence, deserted their former owners, seized the land of absentee owners, engaged in work stoppages, sat where they pleased in public places and vehicles, and no longer felt the need to humble themselves in the presence of whites should not obscure the extent to which life went on very much as it had before the war. As long as whites had political and economic dominance, they were in a position to control the very content of black freedom. "The Master he say we are all free," a former South Carolina slave recalled, "but it don't mean we is white. And it don't mean we is equal. Just equal for to work and earn our living and not depend on him for no more meats and clothes."

During the war, various plans were advanced to help blacks who sought shelter and freedom behind Union lines. With federal approval,

blacks in portions of the occupied South—as on the Sea Islands along the South Carolina coast and on the land in Mississippi that had belonged to Jefferson Davis and his brother—were permitted to work on the plantations with the expectation of dividing the crops and carving out plots of land for themselves. Some abandoned lands were offered on easy terms to former slaves, and many of them did well as independent farmers. But most of the land was ultimately returned to its original owners, and the freedmen's goal of becoming landowning farmers remained unrealized.

To ease the transition from slavery to freedom, Congress in March 1865 created the Freedmen's Bureau. It was authorized to furnish food, clothing, and transportation to refugees and freed blacks, to oversee labor contracts, and to settle freedmen on abandoned or confiscated lands. Although the bureau provided relief, tried to ensure the fairness of labor contracts, and helped to maintain schools for black children, it never fulfilled its promise or potential.

Oliver Otis Howard, the bureau's commissioner and a founder of Howard University, was well meaning and sympathetic, as were a number of the field agents. But many of the regional and local officers were more concerned with gaining the approval of the white communities in which they worked. Too often, bureau officers thought their main responsibility was to get the ex-slaves to accept contracts with their former masters and to prevent them from drifting into the towns. Some of the more dedicated officers who identified with the freed blacks' cause found themselves quickly removed under President Johnson.

With capital and even food in short supply, white farmers and planters often did little better than the blacks. Famine struck many parts of the South in the middle of the war. Afterward, wartime systems of relief collapsed in the general ruin of the Confederacy. In the first four years after the war, the Freedmen's Bureau fed thousands of starving whites as well as blacks. In several instances, the ex-slaves themselves came to the assistance of their former masters and mistresses, some by making small contributions for their welfare, others by agreeing to stay with those who seemed incapable of running the plantations without them.

Perhaps the heaviest blow to the white South was the moral and psychic cost of war and defeat. Purpose, morale, and aspiration declined. The losses in youth and talent hurt beyond measure. And it had all been in vain—the suffering, the self-sacrifice, the devastation. That was the most difficult fact to accept. "Now we belong to Negroes and Yankees," a South Carolina woman cried in despair. Emancipation, moreover, forcibly reminded former slaveholding families of how dependent they remained on their black laborers, of how helpless they were. "They need us all the time," a black domestic recalled.

They don't want no food unless a nigger cooks it. They want niggers to do all their washing and ironing. They want niggers to do their sweeping and cleaning and everything around their houses. The niggers handle everything they wears and hands them everything they eat and drink. Ain't nobody can get closer to a white person than a colored person. If we'd a wanted to kill 'em, they'd all done been dead.

With equal frankness, a Virginia planter conceded his dependence on black labor: "I must have niggers to work for me. I can't do nothin' on my place without 'em. If they send all the niggers to Africa, I'll have to go thar, too."

The former slaveholding class seemed less equipped, mentally and physically, to make the transition from slave to free labor than their former slaves. No matter how hard a few of them tried, they seemed incapable of learning new ways and shaking off old attitudes. That failure was demonstrated during presidential Reconstruction, when the white South was given the opportunity to reconstruct itself with a minimum of federal interference.

Lincoln's Plan

The Civil War began as a war with limited objectives. The Crittenden Resolution, adopted by the House of Representatives on July 22, 1861, with only two dissenting votes, made those objectives abundantly clear:

This war is not waged . . . for any purpose . . . but to defend and maintain the supremacy of the Constitution and to preserve the Union, with all the dignity, equality, and rights of the several States unimpaired; and . . . as soon as these objects are accomplished the war ought to cease.

Three days later, the Senate adopted an almost identical resolution. Although the Emancipation Proclamation broadened the objectives of the war, President Lincoln remained faithful to the spirit of the resolution.

When in 1862 much of Tennessee, Louisiana, and North Carolina had fallen, Lincoln appointed military governors to bring these states into conformity with the Constitution. On December 8, 1863, with still other rebel states on the verge of surrender, the president issued his Proclamation of Amnesty and Reconstruction, which became known as the "10 percent plan" and set forth the terms by which the southern states would be restored to the Union.

Except for high military and civil officers of the Confederacy, any southern citizen would be granted amnesty by the president after taking an oath of loyalty to the Constitution and the laws of the Union. Confiscated property other than slaves would be restored. As soon as 10 percent of those who had voted in the presidential election of 1860 had taken the oath and sworn allegiance to the Union, that state could proceed to write a new constitution, elect new state officers, and send members to the United States Congress. The House and Senate, of course, retained their constitutional privilege of seating or rejecting such members.

The president failed to confront the social realities of emancipation. Lincoln assured the states to which his proclamation applied that he would not object to "any provision" they might wish to make regarding the freed slaves "which may yet be consistent with their present condition as a laboring, landless, and homeless class." This was nothing short of an invitation to the former Confederate states to adopt the inflammatory Black Codes they enacted in 1865 and 1866.

Until late in the war, Lincoln still held that the best way to deal with "the Negro problem" was to persuade blacks to leave the country. "There is an unwillingness on the part of our people, harsh as it may be, for you free colored people to remain with us," he told a black delegation in August 1862. "It is better for us both, therefore, to be separated." But black leaders rejected Lincoln's colonization scheme, even as Radical Republicans would reject his "moderate" reconstruction program. In his last public address, on April 11, 1865, Lincoln made no mention of colonizing freed blacks. In defending his reconstruction plan, he suggested that the states might wish to extend the suffrage to "the very intelligent" blacks and to "those who serve our cause as soldiers." That was for the states to decide, however, and it soon became apparent that none of them thought the president's suggestion worthy of serious consideration.

The Radical Plan

In treating the former Confederate states, Lincoln had urged a minimum of federal interference. The Radical Republicans called for a more thorough reconstruction of southern society. Under their program, the power of the old planter class would be destroyed, and the freedom of the emancipated blacks fully protected. Thaddeus Stevens of Pennsylvania, a Radical leader in the House, stated this position most forcefully. To make the Confederacy "a safe republic," he insisted, "the whole fabric of southern society must be changed."

To Stevens, this meant the confiscation of the estates of the southern ruling class and their distribution to the very people who had made the land productive—the freed slaves. In the Senate, Charles Sumner added his voice to that of Stevens; to preserve the gains of the war, the Union must extend the vote to blacks, he insisted.

Practical political considerations also encouraged Republicans to favor a tougher program. With the abolition of slavery, all freedmen

(rather than three-fifths of them) would be counted for purposes of representation. And the reconstructed South would regain its seats in Congress, even if it denied the vote to blacks. That latter fact won over many conservative Republicans, who feared that northern and southern Democrats would again close ranks and overturn Republican economic legislation.

The Wade-Davis bill, adopted by Congress a few days before it adjourned in July 1864, set forth the first Radical response to Lincoln's program. It required a majority of the citizens of a state, not just 10 percent, to swear loyalty to the Union before a provisional governor could call an election for a state constitutional convention. Only those southerners able to swear that they had *always* been loyal to the Union and had not "voluntarily borne arms against the United States" were entitled to vote for delegates to the constitutional conventions. The bill also prescribed that new state constitutions in the South must abolish slavery, repudiate state debts, and deprive former Confederate leaders of the right to vote.

Radical strategists hoped to commit the Republican party to their program in the 1864 presidential campaign. Lincoln attempted to stop them by permitting the Wade-Davis bill to die by a pocket veto. Defending his action, Lincoln said rebel states might follow the Wade-Davis provisions if they wished, but he refused to make them mandatory. Most Radical leaders supported Lincoln in the 1864 campaign because they did not want to disrupt the party and endanger the war effort.

Once the election was over, the Radicals pressed again for their program. In January 1865 they adopted the Thirteenth Amendment, passed by Congress and submitted to the states, which would abolish slavery throughout the United States. (It was ratified in December of that year by the required three-fourths of the states, including eight formerly of the Confederacy, which Congress for other purposes did not even recognize as states.) In February, Congress refused to admit members from Louisiana, which Lincoln had declared "reconstructed" under the 10 percent plan. In March, Congress created the Freedmen's Bureau. With these measures, Congress adjourned. When it reconvened, in December, it would have to deal with a new president and with a South that had been "reconstructed" under the president's plan.

Johnsonian Restoration

When Lincoln died on April 15, 1865, the victim of an assassin's bullet, Andrew Johnson of Tennessee became president. Like Lincoln, he was born in poverty. Uneducated, he was ultimately taught to read by his wife. Unlike Lincoln, he was tactless and inflexible, possessing neither humility nor the capacity for compromise. He rose to political power in nonslaveholding eastern Tennessee. When he told poor farmers of his dislike for rich cotton planters, they rallied to his support. But even though Johnson delighted his constituents with attacks on special privilege and the planter aristocracy, he never became a vocal opponent of slavery, and he held traditional southern views on race relations. "I wish to God," he said on one occasion, "every head of a family in the United States had one slave to take the drudgery and menial service off his family."

He refused, however, to give up his seat in the Senate after Tennessee left the Union. In 1864, as a demonstration of wartime unity, the Republican party nominated Johnson for the vice-presidency even though he had been a Democrat all his life. During the campaign, Johnson made himself attractive to Radicals by his fierce denunciations of rebel leaders as "traitors." But the enthusiasm with which Johnson appeared to have embraced the Radical cause proved to be short-lived.

With Congress still in recess, the new president set out to complete Lincoln's restoration of the South to the Union. Early in May 1865, he recognized Lincoln's "10 percent" governments in Louisiana, Tennessee, Arkansas, and Virginia. He next appointed military governors in the seven states that had not yet complied. On May 29 he offered executive amnesty to all citizens of these states except high Confederate military and civil officers and others owning more than $20,000 worth of property. These people had to apply for amnesty to the president.

The "whitewashed" electorate—that is, those who benefited by the amnesty offer—was then

While Thaddeus Stevens (left), House leader of the Radical Republicans, sought to alter "the whole fabric of southern society" and provide a legal and economic underpinning for black freedom, President Johnson (right) proceeded with a restoration of the former Confederate states to the Union that would have permitted southern whites to determine the status of blacks. *(Library of Congress)*

to elect members to a constitutional convention in each state. They were to abolish slavery, rescind the state's secession ordinance, adopt the Thirteenth Amendment, repudiate the war debt, and call an election for a new state government. The suffrage for this election was to be determined by each state rather than by Congress, and that clearly meant blacks would be denied participation in southern political life.

By the winter of 1865, all the seceding states but Texas had complied with Johnson's terms. Given the opportunity to reconstruct themselves, the former Confederate states moved quickly to restore the old planter class to political power. The president cooperated in this move. For all his dislike of the southern Old Guard, Johnson's personal grants of amnesty exceeded all bounds. He pardoned the heroes of the "Lost Cause," whom the whitewashed voters proceeded to elect to national, state, and local offices. None other than Alexander Stephens, for example, the former vice-president of the Confederacy, became Georgia's duly elected United States senator.

The spirit that dominated the former Confederate states was apparent not only in the individuals elected to office, but in the decisions made by the new governments. Widespread reluctance to renounce the war debt was accompanied in some states by determination to resist taxation for redemption of the Union debt. That was bound to provoke northern public opinion, as was the legislation adopted to deal with the emancipated slaves.

While ratifying the Thirteenth Amendment as required, the reconstructed states, almost as a unit, warned Congress to leave the status of the freedmen to those who knew them best—the white southerners. And when the new governments confronted the question of what to do with the former slaves, they used the old slave codes and their previous experience with free blacks.

In the Black Codes adopted in 1865 and 1866, the new southern governments recognized the fact of emancipation in some of the rights accorded to blacks for the first time. Although still universally forbidden to serve on juries, even in cases involving blacks, freedmen could now swear out affidavits in criminal cases, sue and be sued in civil actions, appear as witnesses, and otherwise give testimony. Marriages between blacks were to be sanctified under law, but interracial marriages carried sentences of up to life

imprisonment for both parties. Blacks could make wills and pass on personal property. Their children could go to school and were to be protected from abuse if they were apprenticed.

But nowhere could blacks bear arms, vote, hold public office, or assemble freely. In some states they could work at any jobs and quit jobs freely. Most states, however, forbade them to leave their jobs except under stated conditions. Nor in some states could they work as artisans, mechanics, or in other capacities in which they competed with white labor. The Mississippi code forbade freedmen to rent or lease land or houses.

The idea behind these codes was that blacks would not work except under compulsion and proper supervision, and with the vigorous enforcement of contracts and vagrancy laws. The vagrancy provisions were the worst. In Georgia, for example, the law said that "all persons wandering or strolling about in idleness, who are able to work and who have no property to support them," could be picked up and tried. If convicted, they could be set to work on state chain gangs or contracted out to planters and other employers who would pay their fines and their upkeep for a stated period.

The Johnson governments confirmed the worst fears and predictions of the Radicals and shocked many moderates. The rapid return to power of the Confederate leadership suggested an unwillingness by the South to accept defeat. By defining the freedman's role in a way that was bound to keep him propertyless and voteless, the Black Codes attempted to deny the fact of black freedom. In the North, the conviction grew that the white South was preparing to regain what it had lost on the battlefield. By their actions, the South and President Johnson had set the stage for Congress to act.

THE RADICAL CONGRESS

When Congress met in December 1865, it was faced with Johnson's actions and the South's responses. As their first countermove, Radicals set up the Joint Committee of Fifteen—six senators and nine representatives—to review the work of presidential reconstruction and the qualifications of those elected by the southern states to serve in Congress. Exercising its constitutional power, Congress refused to seat the southerners. Early in 1866, it enacted a bill continuing the Freedmen's Bureau; Johnson vetoed the bill because he believed that care and protection of the freedmen should be left to the states.

In March 1866 Johnson also vetoed a civil rights bill that forbade states to discriminate among citizens on the basis of color or race, as they had in the Black Codes. By now a sufficient number of conservative senators were ready to join the Radicals in defense of congressional power, if not of Radical principles, and both houses overrode the president. A few months later, in July 1866, Radicals pushed through a second Freedmen's Bureau bill over Johnson's veto.

Even if many Republicans, like their constituents, remained divided over the proper place of blacks in American society, they could agree that the newly freed slaves should be protected in their basic rights and given the opportunity to advance themselves economically. The actions of the southern governments and the president's vetoes undermined those possibilities. With growing unanimity, Republicans now moved to provide a constitutional basis for black freedom.

The Fourteenth Amendment

When Radicals introduced the Fourteenth Amendment in June 1866, they were concerned about the constitutionality of the Civil Rights Act and the danger that another Congress might repeal it. A civil rights amendment would end the constitutional issue and make repeal more difficult. It was perhaps the most far-reaching amendment ever added to the Constitution, but its importance rested largely on how it was later interpreted.

The Fourteenth Amendment, for the first time, defined citizenship in the United States as distinct from citizenship in a state. By identifying as citizens "all persons born or naturalized in the United States," it automatically extended citizenship to American-born blacks. It also forbade any state to abridge "the privileges and immunities" of United States citizens, to "deprive any person of life, liberty, or property, without due process of law," and to "deny to any person within its jurisdiction the equal protection of the laws."

The second section of the amendment did not give blacks the vote, as many Radicals hoped it would, but penalized any state for withholding it. (The penalty was never imposed and was replaced by the Fifteenth Amendment.) The third section disqualified from federal or state office all Confederates who before the war had taken a federal oath of office, unless Congress specifically lifted the disqualification by a two-thirds vote. Finally, the amendment guaranteed the Union debt but outlawed redemption of the Confederate debt and any claims for compensation for loss of slaves.

The Fourteenth Amendment had a stormy history before it was finally ratified in July 1868. Many years later, the use of the word "person" in the first section of the amendment was interpreted by the federal courts as applying to "legal persons" such as business corporations as well as to blacks, who were the only persons the framers of the amendment had in mind. It thus supplied legal grounds for the courts to declare unconstitutional state regulation of railroads and trusts. Still later, the phrase in Section 1 prohibiting the denial of "equal protection of the laws" supplied legal grounds for the Supreme Court's school desegregation decision in 1954.

As far-reaching as it would become through subsequent interpretation, the Fourteenth Amendment failed to satisfy the Radicals as a final condition for the reconstruction of the southern states. They thought it too full of compromises, and hoped in time to stiffen its provisions. Dissatisfaction with the amendment was also voiced by Susan B. Anthony, Elizabeth Cady Stanton, and other agitators for women's suffrage who had hoped to win the franchise because of women's contributions to victory in the Civil War. They fought to delete the word *male* from the voting provisions of the Fourteenth Amendment and later to add the word *sex* to "race, color, or previous condition of servitude" in the Fifteenth Amendment. But Radical leaders and black activists believed that merging women's rights with blacks' rights would imperil passage of both amendments. Although an abolitionist and an advocate of civil rights, Stanton became so furious over the failure of women to win the vote that she denounced poor, uneducated blacks as a "liability to the electorate and a danger to women."

Radicals demanded that the southern states ratify the Fourteenth Amendment as a condition for regaining representation in Congress. Johnson advised them not to. By mid-February 1867, all but Tennessee—that is, ten of the eleven former Confederate states—had followed his advice. Without the required three-fourths majority of the states, the amendment was dead. But the rejection of the amendment, along with the president's defiance, only reinforced in the minds of

Republicans—Radicals and moderates alike—the need to take over southern reconstruction.

The Reconstruction Acts and Impeachment

The Fourteenth Amendment had drawn the issue clearly between president and Congress. In the congressional campaign of 1866, Johnson visited key cities on behalf of candidates who favored his policy. The more the president talked, however, the more he antagonized northern voters. At the same time, racial clashes in New Orleans and Memphis appeared to confirm Radical warnings about the consequences of Johnson's southern policy.

The Democrats tried to exploit northern fears of racial equality, warning that Republican rule would not only Africanize the nation but encourage cheap black labor from the South to compete with northern workers. The Republicans responded with their own appeal, called "waving the bloody shirt," which exploited wartime passions and identified the Democrats with treason. "In short," cried Oliver P. Morton, the Radical governor of Indiana, "the Democratic party may be described as a common sewer and loathsome receptacle, into which is emptied every element of inhumanity and barbarism which has dishonored the age." The strategy worked, and the Radicals won a sweeping electoral victory. With a two-thirds majority in Congress, they would be able to impose even sterner measures and carry them over presidential vetoes.

The Radicals began with the First Reconstruction Act, passed over Johnson's veto on March 2, 1867. Tennessee had been accepted back into the Union in 1866, but all other southern state governments were declared illegal. The South was organized into five military districts, each under a general to be named by the president. The general's main task was to call a new constitutional convention in each state, its delegates to be elected by universal adult male suffrage, black and white, excluding those deprived of the vote under the proposed Fourteenth Amendment. The new conventions would establish state governments in which blacks could vote and hold office. These governments were to ratify the Fourteenth Amendment as a condition for their return to the Union and the acceptance of their representatives by Congress.

By June 1868 all but three states—Mississippi, Texas, and Virginia—had complied with these requirements, and in July the ratification of the Fourteenth Amendment was completed. The three reluctant states were readmitted in 1870, as was Georgia, whose earlier readmittance had been suspended because of the expulsion of black members from its legislature.

The Radicals' next step was to protect their program from the Supreme Court. In the case of *ex parte Milligan* (1866), which arose over Lincoln's suspension of habeas corpus in Indiana during the war, the Supreme Court had held that any military rule persisting after the regular courts were reinstated would constitute "a gross usurpation of power." That is exactly what happened when the First Reconstruction Act was passed. Southern courts were open, but by establishing military rule, the act usurped their power.

The constitutionality of the act was challenged in *ex parte McCardle*, but the Supreme Court yielded to Radical pressure and elected not to hear the case. The First Reconstruction Act survived.

Having checked the Supreme Court, the Radicals next set about defending their program from presidential sabotage. The Tenure of Office Act, passed along with the First Reconstruction Act, declared that the president could not remove federal officers who had been appointed with the consent of the Senate unless the Senate agreed. The second, the Command of the Army Act, forbade the president to issue orders to the army except through the General of the Army (Ulysses S. Grant). These measures were designed to prevent the president from using patronage or control of the army to undermine the Radical program.

The conflict between Congress and Johnson ended in a move to impeach the president. Radicals held that as long as he remained in office, their reconstruction program could never be fully or fairly implemented. Although Johnson had no real choice but to enforce the acts of Congress, he had used his executive powers to weaken them. As commander in chief, for example, he had removed district commanders who were overly sympathetic to Radical policies and to the cause of the freedmen. He had also helped to restore the vote to southerners of doubtful loyalty. But there was no evidence directly implicating the president in any "high crimes and misdemeanors"—the only constitutional grounds for impeachment.

After almost a year of investigation, the House Judiciary Committee in 1867 voted by a narrow majority to recommend that the president be impeached. It charged him with attempting to reconstruct the former Confederate states "in accordance with his own will, in the interests of the great criminals who carried them into rebellion." This charge proved too vague for the whole House to accept, and it rejected the recommendation. But by attempting to remove Secretary of War Stanton, the remaining Radical in his cabinet, in apparent violation of the Tenure of Office Act, Johnson provided new grounds for impeachment. On February 21, 1868, Stanton was formally removed. Three days later, a new impeachment resolution came before the House. This time the House voted for impeachment 126 to 47. All but one of the charges ("particular articles") referred to the Tenure of Office Act. (Johnson's lawyers would contend that the Tenure of Office Act was unconstitutional and that it could not be applied to Stanton in any case, since he was a Lincoln appointee.) The tenth article charged that Johnson had been "unmindful of the high duties of his office" and had attempted to bring Congress into "disgrace, ridicule, hatred, contempt and reproach." This proved to be the major thrust of the impeachment move.

To convict Johnson, two-thirds of the Senate would have to be convinced that the charges against him amounted to "high crimes and misdemeanors" or that impeachment could be broadened to include political conduct that rendered a president unfit to hold office. But seven Republicans could not be persuaded, and that was enough. By the barest possible margin—only one vote—the Senate refused to remove the president.

The Election of 1868: Grant

Although they had done everything possible to block the president before the election of 1868, the Radicals were determined to secure the office for themselves that year. Their choice was General Grant, who had no known political allegiances—or, for that matter, any known political ambitions. He had served the Radicals in the controversy over Stanton's removal, and his war record appeared to make him a certain winner.

At the Republican convention, Grant was nominated on the first ballot. Johnson sought the Democratic nomination. But after twenty-two ballots, the Democratic convention chose former New York governor Horatio Seymour.

In the campaign, the Democrats sought to divert attention from their reconstruction record by making an issue of cheap money. In 1866 Congress had passed a measure providing for the gradual retirement of the wartime greenbacks, whose dollar value had always remained below that of gold. In the next two years, almost $100 million worth were withdrawn from circulation, much to the disappointment of businessmen as well as farmers.

Western farmers, although emotionally attached to the Republican party for its liberal land policy, wanted cheap money to meet mortgage obligations and other debts. The Democrats' platform made a bid for their support by advocating the reissue of greenbacks to retire war bonds that did not specifically require repayment in gold. The leading proponent of this "soft money" plank was an early aspirant for the 1868 Democratic nomination, George H. Pendleton of Ohio. The plank became the Ohio Idea.

The Republicans had another idea. War bonds, they said, should be redeemed in gold; anything else would be a repudiation of a sacred debt. At the same time, they promised businessmen they would extend redemption "over a fair period," so as not to disturb the credit structure. When the time came, all bondholders would be paid in gold.

The Radicals kept the main political issue before the voters—Radical Reconstruction versus Democratic dishonor. The "bloody shirt," which had done such service in the 1866 campaign, was waved again. The Democratic party, cried Republicans, was the standard-bearer of rebellion, repression of blacks, and financial repudiation.

But the campaign did not overwhelm the opposition. In 1868, against a weak opponent, Grant was elected with a popular plurality of only 310,000 (about 52.7 percent of the popular vote). If not for the seven reconstructed southern states and the black vote, he might have lost.

The part blacks played in winning the election—or rather the fact that blacks in states such as Louisiana and Georgia had been prevented from casting what might have been much-needed Republican votes—led Radicals to

"Yes, yes, we are ignorant. We know it. I am ignorant for one, and they say all niggers is. They say we don't know what the word constitution means. But if we don't know enough to know what the Constitution is, we know enough to know what Justice is. I can see for myself down at my own court-house. If they makes a white man pay five dollars for doing something today, and makes a nigger pay ten dollars for doing that thing tomorrow, don't I know that ain't justice? They've got a figure of a woman with a sword hung up thar, sir; Mr. President, I don't know what you call it—["Justice," "Justice,"

several delegates shouted]—well, she's got a handkercher over her eyes, and the sword is in one hand and a pair o' scales in the other. When a white man and a nigger gets into the scales, don't I know the nigger is always mighty light? Don't we all see it? Ain't it so at your court-house, Mr. President?" (Delegate to a freedmen's convention, Raleigh, North Carolina, 1865)

Source: John R. Dennett, *The South as It Is*, 1865–1866, ed. Henry M. Christman (New York: Viking, 1965), pp. 150–51.

attempt to strengthen the Fourteenth Amendment's protection of black suffrage. When Congress convened early in 1869, it promptly passed the Fifteenth Amendment: "The right of citizens of the United States to vote shall not be denied or abridged by the United States or by any State on account of race, color, or previous condition of servitude." This amendment was ratified in March 1870. By then, blacks had already made their influence known in the newly established southern governments.

RADICAL RECONSTRUCTION: LEGEND AND REALITY

With the passage of the First Reconstruction Act in 1867, Congress began a new era in southern political history. The new state governments were the first to be organized on the basis of universal male suffrage and to operate on the premise that all men, white and black, were entitled to equal legal protection. For whites, as well as for the blacks themselves, this proved to be an extraordinary experience—black voters, black officeholders, black jurors, black sheriffs, black militias. Here was a society, remarked one observer, "suddenly turned bottom-side up." That statement captured the spirit of Radical rule in several of the states, even though it exaggerated black strength and influence in most of them.

Contrary to legend, blacks did not dominate any of the new governments; federal military occupation was never extensive; and only in South Carolina, Florida, and Louisiana did Radical rule

last as long as eight years. The impressions that survived Reconstruction, however, impressions that generations of Americans would believe, added up to a "tragic era" in which corrupt carpetbaggers, poor white scalawags, and illiterate blacks ran wild in an unprecedented and outrageous orgy of misrule. The historians later supplied the footnotes, the novelists embroidered the plots, and finally the motion picture industry (in films such as *The Birth of a Nation* and *Gone with the Wind*) depicted this version of Reconstruction for millions of believing spectators. For nearly a century, this distorted image of Reconstruction helped to freeze the white southern mind in opposition to any challenge to the racial status quo.

Few periods of American history have produced a worse collection of villains—white and black. The very names by which the white South came to know them suggested deceit, treachery, and alien rule. The carpetbaggers were "those Yankees who came South like buzzards after the surrender with all their worldly possessions in one carpetbag." The scalawags were "southerners who had turned Republican very profitably" and in doing so betrayed their own people. And the misled former slaves, as Woodrow Wilson would later write of them, had been nothing more than "a host of dusky children untimely put out of school."

Like most stereotypes, this picture is simplified, distorted, and falsified. The carpetbaggers were northerners who moved to the South after the Civil War and supported or participated in the Radical state governments. Their reasons for settling in the South were as varied as their personal character. For some, legitimate business opportunities and the availability of land and natural resources provided the incentive. Others were Union veterans who had found the South an attractive place in which to live. Still others were teachers, clergy, and agents of charitable societies who had committed themselves to the tasks of educating and converting the former slaves. Finally, there were political adventurers, but their numbers were small. To the white South, however, the fact that some carpetbaggers aided black voting and officeholding was enough to make the rest guilty by association.

Like the carpetbaggers, the scalawags—native white Republicans who supported Radical rule—were a varied lot. In no state were they a majority of southern whites. They were not necessarily poor whites, nor did they all welcome or support black participation in political life. To those who had been Whigs before the war, the Republican party appeared to offer the best hope for promoting the industrial and economic interests of a new South. To those who had opposed secession, the Radical program was a way to neutralize the dominant planters and gain political power. And some felt it important to participate in order to retain some control.

But whatever their individual motives, the scalawags faced ostracism in their communities. Some found it impossible to withstand the pressure, and few had any enthusiasm for racial equality. When blacks demanded a more substantial share of political power, many whites deserted the party.

Although carpetbaggers and scalawags aroused white hatred, black voters and officeholders symbolized the changes in postwar southern society far more dramatically. To find black men, many of them only recently slaves, now voting and holding public office was a change so drastic and so fearful in its implications that few white southerners could accept it; "If the negro is fit to make laws for the control of our conduct and property," a southern educator warned, "he is certainly fit to eat with us at our tables, to sleep in our beds, to be invited into our parlors, and to do all acts and things which a white man may do."

No matter how competently carpetbaggers, scalawags, and blacks might have carried out their political responsibilities, they would have been denounced by a majority of white southerners. Their very presence in the government and their commitment to black voting and officeholding was enough to condemn them.

Radical Rule in the South

Although blacks voted in large numbers, they did not in fact dominate any of the southern states. At the beginning of Radical Reconstruction, of the 1.35 million citizens qualified to vote in the former Confederate states, about half were black. In Alabama, Florida, Louisiana, Mississippi, and South Carolina, black voters were a majority. Only in South Carolina, however, did black legislators outnumber whites (eighty-eight to sixty-seven). In other state legislatures, blacks made up sizable minorities. But in no state did blacks control the executive mansion.

There were black lieutenant governors, secretaries of state, state treasurers, speakers of the house, and superintendents of education. Fourteen blacks were elected to the United States House of Representatives between 1869 and 1877, and two (Hiram Revels and Blanche K. Bruce of Mississippi) to the United States Senate. The majority of black officeholders had

---

THE FIRST VOTE

"Mr. Judge [a northern visitor], we always knows who's our friends and who isn't. We knows the difference between the Union ticket and the Rebel ticket. We may not know all about all the men that's on it; but we knows the difference between the Union and the Rebel parties. Yes sir; we knows that much better than you do!

Because, sir, some of our people stand behind these men at the table, and hear 'em talk; we see 'em in the house and by the wayside; and we know 'em from skin to core, better than you do or can do, till you live among 'em as long, and see as much of 'em as we have." (a black preacher in Georgia)

Robert Smalls, South Carolina legislator and U.S. congress-man. *(Library of Congress)*

local positions, such as justice of the peace, sheriff, and county supervisor, which were important at a time of much local decision-making.

Most were young men, generally in their twenties and thirties at the outset of Reconstruction. Some were illiterate, some were self-educated, and a few were graduates of northern colleges. Many were ministers, teachers, artisans, and farmers who had managed to accumulate small landholdings. Before the war, a number of them had been members of the class of free blacks in the South. Still others, either northern-born or self-imposed "exiles" from their homeland, had resided in the North. Most impressive, however, were those who had only recently been slaves. The skills they had gained from learning how to survive as slaves may explain why many of them proved to be successful politicians.

The Radical governments operated on the principle that all men, black and white, were entitled to equal political and civil liberties. Both races, in fact, made impressive political and social advances. Many of the gains grew out of the new state constitutions, written by conventions in which blacks and whites participated. These constitutions eliminated property qualifications for voting and holding office, for whites as well as blacks. They apportioned representation in state legislatures and in Congress more fairly. Judicial systems were revised, and juries were opened to blacks. Imprisonment for debt was abolished, along with other archaic social legislation. Above all, for the first time in many southern states, the constitutions provided for public schools for whites and blacks.

Next to giving blacks the vote, nothing offended the white South more than Radical efforts to give blacks schooling at public expense. Even the segregation of black and white pupils did not satisfy critics. It had long been an article of faith among white southerners that education spoiled blacks as laborers, developing in them wants that could never be satisfied and expectations that could never be realized. Invariably, then, an educated black person could be expected to be discontented, frustrated, and troublesome. That was reason enough for whites to burn black schools and to threaten and harass teachers and students. Yet blacks persisted in their quest for education, and by 1877 southern schools had enrolled 600,000 blacks.

Several colleges and universities, including Fisk, Howard, Atlanta, and the Hampton Institute in Virginia, had been established by the Freedmen's Bureau and northern philanthropic agencies. Night schools for adults flourished. But despite the commitment of the Radical governments to education, the financial resources of the states were often not sufficient to support a dual school system. It was the private efforts of various northern groups, such as the American Missionary Association, that enabled many blacks to obtain an education.

The Radical governments displayed restraint when dealing with economic matters. Even black legislators refused to interfere with the rights of private property, though land ownership remained the principal goal of their black constituents. Rather than experiment with land redistribution, most black leaders urged the familiar mid-nineteenth-century self-help creed: be thrifty and industrious and buy property. (These leaders assumed that whites would welcome evidence of black economic success and independence—a mistaken assumption.) Like their white colleagues, most black legislators accepted the idea of individual responsibility for one's own material well-being. In their overriding concern for realizing the same rights to life, liberty, and property enjoyed by whites, black leaders did not wish to undermine their own position by advocating anything as un-American as confiscation. Nor did they want to alienate native whites, with whom they expected to share political power.

Black sharecroppers and tenants knew only too well, however, that legal equality and the vote could not feed hungry mouths or end economic hardship. They needed land of their own and the means to farm that land. "Give us our own land," said one freedman, "and we take care of ourselves; but widout land, de ole massas can hire or starve us, as dey please." But neither the Radical legislatures nor Congress, even while giving liberally to railroads, were willing to make that kind of commitment to the former slaves—even as a token payment for years of unpaid labor.

The black officeholder gained experience in governing during an era in which corruption marked much of American political life. Although corruption in the Radical governments was not as bad as painted, there was enough to tarnish them and to confirm the skepticism in the North about the entire experiment. Between 1868 and 1874, the bonded debt of the eleven ex-Confederate states grew by over $100 million. This enormous sum was not itself evidence of corruption. To raise money, the southern states had to sell bonds in the North, where southern credit was so poor that investors often demanded a 75 percent discount from a bond's face value. Thus, for every $100 worth of bonds sold, a southern state might actually realize only $25.

Many of the social and humanitarian reforms of the Reconstruction legislatures were costly, as was the relief extended to the starving and homeless of both races. Taxes to pay for such expenditures, including new "luxuries" such as public schools, fell heavily on the planters, who before the war had been able to pass taxes on to other groups.

Still, much of the debt was incurred corruptly, though carpetbaggers, scalawags, and blacks were not necessarily the principal beneficiaries. Like the rest of the nation, the South suffered at the hands of railroad interests, business speculators, and contractors who sought legislative favors and were willing to pay for them. Corruption in the South, as elsewhere, tended to be

bipartisan, involving men of both races and all classes, and it included some of the most distinguished names of the South. It had been under way before Radical rule, and it lasted long after the overthrow of Reconstruction.

A black legislator might quickly learn from white colleagues of both parties that payoffs were a natural part of the political process and often a necessary supplement to an otherwise meager income. After accepting a bribe, one black legislator, a former slave, offered this perspective: "I've been sold in my life eleven times. And this is the first time I ever got the money." For most black leaders, however, political participation entailed personal sacrifice rather than financial gain. Henry Johnson of South Carolina, for example, was a former slave, a bricklayer and plasterer by trade, and an active participant in Republican politics. "I always had plenty of work before I went into politics," he noted, "but I have never got a job since. I suppose they do it merely because they think they will break me down and keep me from interfering with politics." Jefferson Long, a Macon tailor elected to Congress, found that his political position "ruined his business with the whites who had been his patrons chiefly." But black leaders faced more serious dangers than the loss of business—and that was the loss of their lives.

The ability of black officeholders varied considerably; most important, blacks were learning the uses of political power and gaining confidence in their ability to rule. As they did, and as they began to demand political power on a par with their electoral strength, the shaky alliance on which Radical rule rested began to fall apart. When blacks made startling gains in Mississippi and South Carolina in the early 1870s, for example, they vividly demonstrated their new independence and self-confidence. At the same time, they may have sealed their own doom.

The idea of black success, independence, and power drove numerous whites out of the party, accelerated internal divisions, and gave the Democrats the opportunity for which they had carefully prepared. If anything about "black reconstruction" truly alarmed the white South, it was not so much the evidence of corruption, but the very real possibility that this unique experiment in biracial government might succeed! As W. E. B. Du Bois wrote: "There was one thing that the white South feared more than negro dishonesty, ignorance, and incompetency, and that was negro honesty, knowledge, and efficiency."

Influential African American men involved in the radical reconstruction of the South. *(Library of Congress)*

The End of Reconstruction: The Shotgun Policy

From the beginning of Radical rule, before any evidence of corruption had come to light, the white South was determined to use every method at its disposal to maintain control of black labor and black lives. To overthrow Radical rule and the black vote on which it rested, thousands of even the most respectable people in the South banded together in the Ku Klux Klan, the Knights of the White Camellia, and other secret groups. Between 1867 and 1879, hooded or otherwise disguised, they roamed the land, shot, flogged, and terrorized blacks and their supporters, burned homes and public buildings, and assaulted Reconstruction officials. To suppress this violence, Congress responded with the Force Act of 1870 and the Ku Klux Klan Act of 1871. These laws imposed heavy fines and jail sentences for offenses under the Fourteenth and Fifteenth amendments and gave Republican-controlled federal courts, rather than southern state courts, jurisdiction in all cases arising under the amendments or out of conspiracies or terrorism against freedmen. The president was empowered to suspend habeas corpus in any terrorized community, to declare martial law, and to send troops to maintain order. In October 1871, President Grant invoked that authority in nine South Carolina counties where the Klan was especially active.

Federal intervention in South Carolina marked the peak of forceful repression of southern violence. Except for the passage of the Civil Rights Act of 1875—a seldom-enforced law that guaranteed blacks equal access to public accommodations—the Republican party began to retreat from its commitment to civil rights and black voting. In May 1872 Congress passed an Amnesty Act that restored voting and officeholding privileges to all white southerners except a few hundred of the highest Confederate dignitaries. In that same year, the Freedmen's Bureau was permitted to expire. By 1877 white terrorism, economic coercion, federal indifference, and factionalism in the Radical governments had brought Radical Reconstruction to an end.

Reconstruction

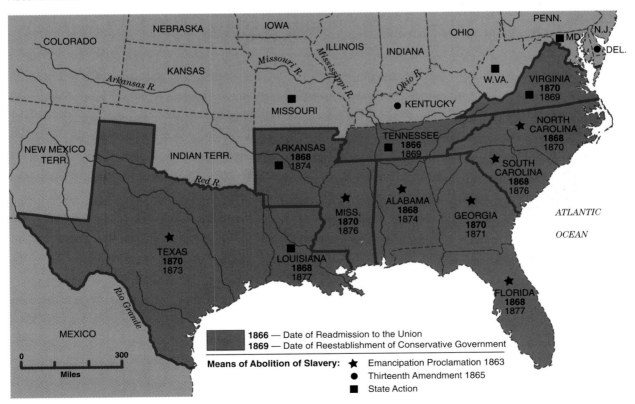

1866 — Date of Readmission to the Union
1869 — Date of Reestablishment of Conservative Government

Means of Abolition of Slavery: ★ Emancipation Proclamation 1863
● Thirteenth Amendment 1865
■ State Action

The Mississippi Plan (sometimes called the "shotgun policy"), by which Democrats regained power in that state in 1875, proved to be a model of repression. It consisted of organized violence and threats, the systematic breakup of Republican gatherings, and the incitement of riots. Its aim was to force all whites into the Democratic party, and at the same time to eliminate black leadership and political participation. "Carry the election peaceably if we can, forcibly if we must," was the way one newspaper described the objective.

In communities where blacks were a majority or nearly so, the plan was carried out with full white support. Where persuasion failed, violence and terrorism were used by well-armed paramilitary units called Rifle Clubs, White Leagues, or Red Shirts. White Republicans who resisted were driven from their homes and their communities. Defiant black sharecroppers were denied credit by southern merchants; they were evicted from the land, denied other employment, assaulted, and murdered.

Even when the governor of Mississippi appealed to President Grant for assistance, claiming he had exhausted all local resources, the president refused to call upon the army to support troubled Republican regimes. Encouraged by Grant's turnabout, southern leaders in states still under Radical rule became more determined than ever to "redeem" their states through their own efforts.

The federal government's refusal to act reflected the North's growing disillusion with the reconstruction experiment. Northern whites were busy with their own economic problems. Traditional racist views persisted, and neither northern whites nor the Republicans were prepared to undertake the massive intervention and federal force necessary to sustain this unique experiment in biracial government. Northern businessmen concluded that only southern Democrats could establish the kind of stability necessary for economic advancement and investment. Alarmed over the persistent turmoil and unwilling to allow federal power to sustain the Reconstruction governments, northerners chose to permit the white South to work out its own solution to "the race problem."

The white southern response to Reconstruction is hardly surprising. Even honest and capable carpetbaggers came to symbolize alien rule, and even if corruption was fashionable, Radical corruption was not. Most important, if blacks were to succeed, politically or economically, they would no longer be content with a lower place in southern society. That was a difficult proposition for whites to accept. Whites wanted a docile, dependent, and productive black laboring class. Blacks acquiring and working their own land posed dangers as great as those of blacks voting or legislating. "The Nigger, when poverty stricken, will work well for you," a Georgia farmer observed, "but as soon as he begins to be prosperous, he becomes impudent and unmanageable." For many in the white South, that observation became an article of faith.

While maintaining that blacks were incapable of becoming their political, social, or economic equals, many whites betrayed the fear that they might. The black person as a buffoon, a menial, a servant was perfectly acceptable; indeed, many whites assumed that irresponsibility, ignorance, and submissiveness were black traits. Consequently, those blacks who failed to fit the stereotype seemed somehow abnormal, even dangerous. "The Negro as a poor ignorant creature," Frederick Douglass observed, "does not contradict the race pride of the white race. He is more a source of amusement to that race than an object of resentment. . . . It is only when he acquires education, property, and influence, only when he attempts to rise and be a man among men that he invites repression." For blacks who aspired to improve themselves, this posed an obvious dilemma.

Within ten years, then, Reconstruction was over. Although the Fourteenth and Fifteenth amendments eventually helped to make a "second reconstruction" possible in the 1950s and 1960s, that may not be enough to judge Radical Reconstruction a success. But what blacks demonstrated in that brief period, even if imperfectly, has too often been ignored. Despite their shortcomings, inexperience, and failure to resolve the most pressing problems of their people, black leaders exercised political responsibility with reasonable competence and gave every indication of learning from their errors. This achievement and the potential it suggested prompted W. E. B. Du Bois to write in *Black Reconstruction* (1935): "The attempt to make black men American citizens was in a certain sense all a failure, but a splendid failure. It did not fail where it was expected to fail."*

---

*W. E. B. Du Bois, *Black Reconstruction in America 1860–1880* (New York: Russell & Russell 1956) p. 708. Copyright 1962, 1935 by W. E. B. Du Bois.

The tragedy of Radical Reconstruction is that it failed to reconstruct southern white racial attitudes. From the very outset, this unique experiment in biracial government rested on a weak base. The commitment of the federal government was limited, and even Republicans did not seek any long-term federal intervention in southern affairs. The commitment of blacks was limited by their economic weakness and dependence. If many of them chose to withdraw from political activism altogether, they did so as a result not only of white intimidation, but of the recognition that politics had not significantly altered the quality of their day-to-day lives.

The end of Reconstruction solidified white supremacy. But this victory entailed serious costs for the South: the corruption of public discourse, political and economic backwardness, high rates of illiteracy and poverty, and continuing racial tension. For blacks, Reconstruction, though short-lived, had been a moment of promise and excitement, a time when they had envisioned a biracial democracy that would revolutionize white–black relations and give substance to abstract notions of freedom. The expectations raised by this promise made the final outcome all the more tragic. The range of choices open to blacks narrowed considerably. The political violence devastated an emerging black leadership class, claiming the lives of many black officeholders and political organizers and driving even more into exile. Nearly a century would pass before southern blacks would be so fully mobilized for political purposes.

THE GRANT PRESIDENCY

When Ulysses S. Grant became president in 1869, the American people expected him to exercise the same qualities of leadership he had shown in the Civil War. He would, many believed, organize a strong government staffed by able aides, much as he had mobilized a victorious army. But the problems Grant faced as president—turmoil in the South, the tariff, falling farm prices, and business speculation—were far different from those he had confronted on the battlefield.

He entered the White House with no political experience and few political convictions; he expected Congress to represent the will of the people and to act on that basis. A failure in business, Grant admired those who had succeeded,

Campaign poster for U.S. Grant and Schuyler Colfax for the National Union Republican nomination. *(Library of Congress)*

accepted their gracious hospitality, and tried to satisfy their needs. Moving in circles far different from those he had known, he turned for advice to people with whom he felt most comfortable. The White House staff—his "kitchen cabinet"—consisted largely of wartime friends. The regular cabinet, with few exceptions, was made up of obscure men.

The First Term: The Great Barbecue

Although personally honest, Grant permitted himself and his office to be used by self-seeking politicians and businessmen. He found it difficult to believe that many of those who befriended him were interested only in personal profit. During his administration, his secretary of war, his private secretary, and officials in the Treasury and navy departments used their positions and influence to enhance their incomes. Even as a disbelieving Grant learned of the

President Ulysses S. Grant delivering his inaugural address on the east portico of the U.S. Capitol, March 4, 1873. *(Library of Congress)*

scandals, he seemed more disturbed by those who made the charges than by the revelations themselves.

Grant, no doubt, was victimized by men whose honesty and loyalty he had never thought to question. If he appointed some of his wealthy friends to cabinet posts, he did so in the conviction that these men had operated in the national interest. Many had made fortunes on war contracts, but in Grant's eyes they had also contributed to winning the war. Some of them were now sustaining the postwar boom. Positions in government were simply a recognition of their achievement and patriotism. To those who expressed alarm over the scandals, moreover, Grant could reply that he had inherited a government already far gone in corruption. The competition for war contracts and the battles for other wartime legislation covering protective tariffs, land grants, and the money system had made

lobbying a full-time occupation. After the war, lobbyists often prowled the floors of the House and Senate to keep their legislators in line.

Few political plums were more valuable than the tariff, which by 1870 had added to the profits of eastern manufacturing and industrial interests. But railroads also shared handsomely in congressional handouts. The last federal land grant for railroad building was made in 1871. By that time, the total distributed to the roads directly or through the states had reached 160 million acres, valued conservatively at $335 million. The railroads also received lavish government loans. Each year after the Union Pacific and Central Pacific railroads obtained their loans, Congress debated legislation that would have provided for repayment. But the railroad owners fought these measures stubbornly and successfully, often distributing company shares among the legislators "where they will do us the most good."

The Union Pacific, for example, was built by the Crédit Mobilier of America, a construction company owned largely by Union Pacific promoters. By awarding themselves large contracts on the most favorable terms, these men were able to realize huge profits. Faced with a congressional inquiry in 1868, the company directors, through Massachusetts congressman Oakes Ames, himself a stockholder in both companies, distributed stock among key members of Congress and government officials. The scandal destroyed some political reputations, including that of Vice-President Schuyler Colfax, but only Representative Ames was censured.

Northern financiers also joined in the Great Barbecue, as Grant's regime has been called. In March 1869, fulfilling campaign promises made the year before, both houses of Congress adopted a resolution pledging the government to redeem the entire war debt in gold or in new gold bonds. This pledge, and the laws soon passed to carry it out, sent the value of war bonds soaring and brought substantial profits to speculators. These laws were also good for the government's credit. Forced during the war to offer interest as high as 6 percent, the victorious national government was soon able to borrow for as little as 2.5 percent.

Grant's Second Term: Disenchantment

In the 1872 presidential campaign, Carl Schurz of Missouri, alienated by Grant's appointments and policies, led a Liberal Republican movement. With a platform stressing civil service reform, the Liberals tried to attract candidates of "superior intelligence and superior virtue." Unfortunately, they were joined by victims of the Radical grafters, political hacks who had lost patronage, and others who were out for revenge. Many northern Democrats also joined the movement, hoping to get rid of the treasonous label of their party and win back power.

At the Liberal convention, the differences among them forced the delegates to name a less-than-inspiring compromise candidate, Horace Greeley, editor for more than thirty years of the *New York Tribune*. The Democrats, seeking to regain national power, gave their support to Greeley. But Grant easily won reelection, carrying all but six states.

The Democrats' hopes were by no means shattered. The scandals of the Grant administration increased public disillusion with the Republican party and those who profited by its corrupt dealings and control of patronage. The first major Grant scandal, the Crédit Mobilier affair, broke while the 1872 campaign was in progress. After the business crash of 1873, each new revelation struck with added force, and once the Democrats captured the House in 1874, the revelations and prosecutions snowballed.

Two scandals hit Grant personally. One was the uncovering in St. Louis of the Whiskey Ring, which had defrauded the government of millions of dollars in internal revenue charges. Deeply involved in this, as in other frauds, was Grant's private secretary, Orville Babcock, whom the president saved from imprisonment only by interfering in his trial. The second affair led to the impeachment of Grant's third secretary of war, W. W. Belknap. Since his appointment in 1870, Belknap had been "kept" by traders in the Indian Territory, which his department administered. When his impeachment appeared imminent, Belknap offered his resignation to the president. Grant, with characteristic loyalty, accepted "with great regret."

Grant deserved a better fate. He had been a great military leader. But he showed little aptitude for the complex machinery of government, politics, and party. His personal honesty, trust, and naiveté made him an easy victim of interests that even the wisest politician found difficult to control. "It was the age of the audacious confidence man," Edmund Wilson has written, "and Grant was the incurable sucker. He easily fell victim to their trickery and allowed them to betray him into compromising his office because he could not believe that such people existed."

The Election of 1876: Hayes

As convention time approached in 1876, Democrats were making an issue of corruption, and Republicans were deeply divided on the best way to answer them. The Grand Old Party, as Republicans were calling themselves, separated into Stalwarts and Half-Breeds. Stalwarts were the hard-core political professionals who put politics first; if business wanted favors, let them pay up. Half-Breeds were Republican reformers who had not deserted to the Liberal Republicans in 1872.

Stalwarts, closest to Grant, wanted him to run for a third term. Half-Breeds lined up behind

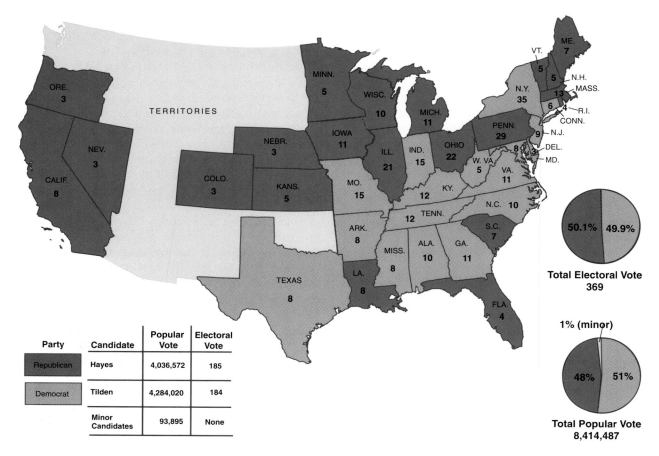

Party	Candidate	Popular Vote	Electoral Vote
Republican	Hayes	4,036,572	185
Democrat	Tilden	4,284,020	184
	Minor Candidates	93,895	None

50.1% 49.9%

Total Electoral Vote 369

1% (minor)

48% 51%

Total Popular Vote 8,414,487

The election of 1876

Congressman James G. Blaine of Maine, despite the dramatic disclosure of his shady relations with the Union Pacific Railroad while serving as Speaker of the House. When the movement to renominate Grant failed to materialize, the nomination went to Rutherford B. Hayes, the reform governor of Ohio.

The Democratic surge in the South, meanwhile, and the vicious repression on which it was based, accented sectional differences in that party on every issue. Hunger for the presidency, long denied them, led the Democrats to close ranks behind Samuel J. Tilden, a rich corporation lawyer and hard-money man who had won a national reputation as a reform governor of New York.

The presidential scandals, the severity of the economic depression of the mid-1870s, and the rising demand for reform all seemed to work to the Democrats' advantage. The campaign they waged stressed the need to end misrule in the South and to weed out corruption in the federal government. On economic issues, little differentiated Tilden from Hayes; both were conservatives who proclaimed their belief in "sound money" and limited government.

First reports of the election results suggested a Democratic victory. Tilden had a plurality of 250,000 votes, and the press proclaimed him the new president. But Republican strategists suddenly awoke to the fact that returns from Louisiana, Florida, and South Carolina, three states still under Radical control, had not yet come in because of election irregularities. Tilden needed only one electoral vote from these states to win; Hayes needed every one. Any accurate count in the disputed states was complicated by the threats, violence, and fraud used by Democrats to keep blacks from voting. Both parties claimed to have won. Congress would have to determine which of the double sets of returns from the three states should be accepted, the Democratic count or the Republican.

The two parties agreed to the extraordinary device of deciding the election by turning the problem over to a commission of five representatives, five senators, and five Supreme Court justices. One of the justices, David Davis, presumably was independent in politics. The remaining fourteen members of the commission were equally divided between Democrats and Republicans. Unfortunately for Tilden, Davis quit the commission before it met and was replaced by a Republican justice. The Republican majority of eight then voted unanimously for Hayes. The Compromise of 1877, by which the South conceded Hayes's election, rested largely on Republican assurances that Hayes "would deal justly and generously with the South." That was understood to mean the withdrawal of the remaining federal troops and no more interference in the restoration of white political supremacy.

In his inaugural speech, Hayes spoke out clearly on the need for a permanent federal civil service beyond the reach of politics and patronage. To show that he meant business, he succeeded in getting rid of some of the party faithful from the New York Customs House, although not for long. In his southern strategy, Hayes chose David M. Key of Tennessee, a high-ranking former Confederate officer and a Democrat, as postmaster general. By the end of April 1877 he had withdrawn the last federal troops from the South; with their departure, the last Radical state governments collapsed.

That autumn he set forth on a good-will tour of the South. He was joined by former Confederate general Wade Hampton, whom "straight-out" Democrats had just elected governor of South Carolina, chiefly by suppressing the black vote. At an enthusiastic meeting in Atlanta, Hayes assured the blacks in the audience that their "rights and interests would be safer if this great mass of intelligent white men were let alone by the general government." On his return to Washington, the president observed of his journey: "Received everywhere heartily. The country is again one and united."

The real losers in the election of 1876 were not the Democrats, but black southerners. Between 1879 and 1881, nearly 50,000 blacks, mostly from rural Texas, Louisiana, Mississippi, and Tennessee, left for Kansas, another 5000 for Iowa and Nebraska. The spirit that pervaded the "great exodus" was largely that of desperation, and the Exodusters, as they were called, appeared to be more refugees than migrants, fleeing from oppression and violence that had become intolerable. A newspaper reporter in Mississippi, observing the daily departures, described families "who seem to think anywhere is better than here." The Exodusters voted with their feet, but another quarter of a century would pass before that vote became overwhelming. Until the early twentieth century, some 90 percent of black Americans spent their whole lives in the South.

THE NEW SOUTH

With the collapse of the remaining Radical governments, politics in the South came to be dominated by a new class of men—industrialists, merchants, bankers, and railroad promoters. Calling themselves Redeemers, for having "redeemed" their states from "carpetbag rule," they envisioned a New South devoted to material progress and based on the profitable use of the region's natural resources and abundant labor supply. The old planter class found its prewar power diminished; the heavy voting strength it commanded in the rural sections, however, particularly the Black Belt, enabled it to exert considerable influence. These two classes were generally able to resolve their differences, ruling by coalition if necessary, and thus maintaining the supremacy of their values.

The new state governments set out to cut spending. The principal victims were the public schools and other state-supported services left over from the Radical years. But the same governments that cut taxes and made a virtue of economy proved to be most generous in their encouragement of economic enterprises, bestowing on them liberal charters and tax exemptions. Corruption was no less widespread under the Redeemer governments than under the previous Radical regimes, but somehow it seemed less offensive when committed by whites.

Although blacks continued to vote, they were able to exert little if any political influence. The race relations of the New South were based on the suppression of black hopes—political, economic, and social. Not even the occasional challenges to Redeemer rule altered that fact of southern life. For most blacks, politics became less important in their daily lives. The need to survive—to grow a crop and to pay their

LABOR RELATIONS IN THE NEW SOUTH

In my condition, and the way I see it for every-body, if you don't make enough to have some left you ain't done nothin, except given the other fel-low your labor. . . . Now it's right for me to pay you for usin' what's yours—your land, stock, plow tools, fertilizer. But how much should I pay? The answer ought to be closely seeked. How much is a man due to pay out? Half his crop? A third part of his crop? And how much is he due to keep

for hisself? You got a right to your part—rent; and I got a right to mine. But who's the man ought to decide how much? The one that owns the property or the one that works it? (Ned Cobb, black cotton farmer, born in Alabama in 1885)

Source: Theodore Rosengarten, *All God's Dangers: The Life of Nate Shaw* (New York: Knopf, 1974), p. 108.

African Americans bringing cotton in from field, Alabama. (*Library of Congress*)

debts—took precedence over a politics that offered them no real choices.

The Economics of Dependency: Agriculture

Even before the overthrow of Radical rule in the South, blacks were economically dependent on whites. Radicals had tried to reconstruct the Union by giving the freed slaves the vote, but po-litical privileges were not backed by economic gains. During their brief hours of joy over free-

dom, the former slaves had talked about owning their own farms and living like "white folks." With few exceptions, however, it never worked out that way. Denied land, dependent on and in debt to the landlord and the merchant (often the same person), who held claims on their unharvested crops, few blacks could achieve the economic independence they coveted. As one former slave recalled:

We thought we was going to be richer than the white folks, 'cause we was stronger and knowed how to work, and the whites didn't, and they didn't have us to work for them any more. But it didn't turn out that way. We soon found out that freedom could make folks proud, but it didn't make 'em rich.

If there was any consolation for the blacks, it would have to be the knowledge that many whites were far from being as independent as they seemed. Before the war, most large southern plantations had been heavily mortgaged. Afterward, hard-pressed creditors began demanding payment of interest and principal. Some southern planters sold off part of their land in order to finance cultivation of the rest. Others leased acreage for money rents. But obviously there was not money enough available to keep this up very long. The result was a continuation of the familiar routine of the prewar South: Planters paid no wages for labor, and their workers paid no rent for land. Instead, each was to share in the forthcoming crop.

In order to get this crop into the ground, both parties had to borrow. Since they had no other security, they had to borrow against the crop they hoped to produce. Only then would the merchants advance the required seed; fertilizer, and equipment, as well as food and clothing. For his own stock, the local merchant had to seek credit from northern suppliers. Risks in the South were so great that these suppliers demanded high prices for the goods and high interest for credit. In addition, oppressive fees were charged for transportation, insurance, and other commercial services. The merchant passed all these charges on to the landlords and sharecroppers. The merchant also added his own profit, and perhaps took a little more to reward himself for his literacy, at the expense of borrowers who could not read his account books. The South became more firmly chained to northern creditors, while the sharecropper was enslaved to the merchant.

The South drifted more and more deeply into sharecropping and crop debts because they offered a solution to the problems of labor and capital. Immediately after the war, many planters had tried to keep their newly freed workers by offering them cash wages. A typical contract stipulated that the planter pay wages of ten to twelve dollars a month, less the cost, determined by the planter, of "quarters, fuel, healthy and substantial rations." In exchange, the freedman agreed to labor faithfully "in the usual way before the War." The wage system failed because there was too little money. Few laborers received the pay they had been promised, and the freedman found little reason to trust his former master.

Sharecropping gradually stabilized labor relations in the cash-poor South. It also helped preserve the plantation system. The plantation was divided into small plots, which the landowner rented to blacks. Typically, the freedman agreed to pay a share of the forthcoming crop, usually one-third, for his use of the land, and still another share, again about one-third, for the necessary tools, seed, and work animals. Once he realized the government was not about to grant him any land, sharecropping seemed better than working in gangs under an overseer or foreman.

But if sharecropping seemed to give blacks some economic independence and the hope of eventually buying the land on which they worked, the financial realities of the postwar South soon turned the arrangement into a form of economic bondage. The sharecropper had to borrow continually on future crops to pay his debts to the planter and supply merchant. He was caught in a web of debt from which there was seldom any escape. Under the sharecropping system, moreover, with its emphasis on the single cash crop, overproduction soon caused cotton prices to fall.

If black southerners sensed an unfairness in their economic lives, it rested in the perception that they worked largely to enrich others—an all too familiar pattern.

> *The old bee makes de honey-comb*
> *The young bee makes de honey.*
> *Colored folks plant de cotton and corn*
> *And de white folks gits de money.*

The devastation of the war also caught up with the small white farmer. He too needed credit from the local merchants to get his land back into production and his home and barns repaired. And as in the case of the sharecroppers, the merchants dictated that the whites grow little but cotton. At first, the white farmer might give the merchant a lien on forthcoming crops. As debts mounted, the merchant demanded a mortgage on the land as well. And as the cotton market deteriorated, the merchant foreclosed. Some white farmers managed to beat the trend and became substantial landowners, even merchants. But by the 1880s, most of them had gone under and become sharecroppers or were left with the poorest land.

The Economics of Dependency: Industry

After the white South had been "redeemed," many people expected it to share in the industrialization that was booming in the North. To achieve self-respect as a region, some argued, the South would need to demonstrate material and financial strength. The idea of a New South was based on industrial development like that of the North, with comparable business institutions and captains of industry, and an end to the dependency that had until now characterized North-South relationships.

The movement to create a New South through industry became a crusade. After 1880, white professionals and retired generals and colonels gave their names and reputations, their energy and their capital, to the mission. The textile industry, already restored, continued to grow rapidly. During the depression of the mid-1880s, southern iron began to compete successfully with Pittsburgh's. The North Carolina tobacco industry responded to the new fad of cigarette smoking, and a bit later the cottonseed-oil industry spurted upward.

Another and more important goal of the crusade was to draw northern capital southward. It was to this goal that Henry Grady, publisher of the powerful *Atlanta Constitution*, devoted the most attention. Invading the North to recruit capital, Grady told a New York audience. "We have sowed towns and cities in the place of theories, and put business in place of politics. We have challenged your spinners in Massachusetts and your ironmakers in Pennsylvania.... We have fallen in love with work."

In the 1880s, northern capital had good reason to look hopefully to the South. The availability of natural resources and abundant waterpower should have been enough. But there was more: the promise of low taxes, legislative favors, and a cheap labor force said to be immune to trade unions and strikes. As late as 1900, however, the so-called industrialized New South actually produced a smaller proportion of American manufactures than had the Old South in 1860. Fewer than 4 percent of the people in the important textile state of South Carolina were engaged in manufacturing, while 70 percent remained in agriculture. The ratios in the rest of the South were the same. Where new industries had estab-

Young woman and girl, working at machine in the Newton Cotton Mills, North Carolina. *(Library of Congress)*

lished themselves, they had done so largely as branches of northern-owned enterprises.

The social price exacted from the southern people proved to be considerable. Champions of the New South expected black laborers to "keep their place," growing staples in the hot sun, while whites found employment in the mills and factories. Industry would redeem the South, and the cotton mills would be the salvation of the poor whites. But when the white farmer gave up his struggle with the land to accept work in the mills, he found that little had changed. He lived in villages that resembled the old slave quarters. He now owed his allegiance to the company store, the company landlord, and the company church. He labored long hours, rarely saw sunlight or breathed fresh air, and fell victim to a variety of diseases. "The harvest was soon at hand," Wilbur Cash writes in *The Mind of the South.*

By 1900 the cotton-mill worker was a pretty distinct type in the South. . . . A dead-white skin, a sunken chest, and stooping shoulders were the earmarks of the breed. Chinless faces, microcephalic foreheads, rabbit teeth, goggling dead-fish eyes, rickety limbs, and stunted bodies abounded—over and beyond the limit of their prevalence in the countryside. The women were characteristically stringy-haired and limp of breast at twenty, and shrunken hags at thirty or forty.

The wages paid to adult male workers varied from forty to fifty cents a day; women and children worked for still lower pay to supplement a meager family income. But there was one compensation: The mill villages were the exclusive domain of whites. And that, said the industrial promoters, lent dignity to their labor. For whites, moreover, the consciousness of race superiority

assumed even greater importance and intensity in the late nineteenth century as the South moved systematically to repress the last vestiges of civil rights.

A Closed Society: Disfranchisement, Jim Crow, and Repression

Although Radical Reconstruction ended in 1877 and white violence at the polls persisted, black voting had not been altogether eliminated. Most blacks remained loyal to the Republicans. But the Redeemers—or Conservatives, as southern Democrats often called themselves—became adept in some regions at making political arrangements with local black leaders whenever black votes were needed to win local elections. And any time the black vote posed a threat, reviving the specter of "Negro domination," whites returned to the tactics of repression, ranging from crude election frauds to threats of loss of land, credit, or jobs. These same tactics might also be employed by the ruling Conservative regimes to thwart the challenge of white independents.

Forced to make political choices that had little or nothing to do with their immediate needs and problems, growing numbers of blacks withdrew from politics altogether or permitted their votes to be bought. What difference did it make who carried the election? "This is a white man's country and government," said one disillusioned black, "and he is proving it North, South, East, and West, democrats and republicans. For my part, I am tired of both parties; the Negro's back is sleek where they have rode him so much."

Despite their traditional allegiance to the Republicans as "the party of emancipation," some blacks were critical of the minimal role they

---

THE LEGACY OF THE NEW SOUTH

When I was a little boy I watched em disfranchise the Negro from votin. . . . Never did hear my daddy say nothin bout losin the vote. But I believe with all my heart he knowed what it meant. . . . the way he handled hisself in this votin business and other colored handled themselves, they had to come under these southern rulins. They thought they did, and the white man said they did, and that's all there was to it . . . Who was behind it? I felt to an extent it was the *rich white man and the poor white man, both of em, workin to take the vote away from the nigger—the big man and a heap of the little ones. The little ones thought they had a voice, but they only had a voice to this extent: they could speak against the nigger and the big man was happy for em to do it. But they didn't have no more voice than a cat against the big man of their own color.* (Ned Cobb, black cotton farmer, born in Alabama in 1885) were permitted to play in party affairs and disappointed by the party's failure to represent the needs of common people. "The colored people are consumers," the chairman of a black meeting in Richmond declared. "The Republicans have deserted them and undertaken to protect the capitalist and manufacturer of the North."

In the late 1880s and early 1890s, agricultural hard times prompted discontented staple farmers to organize in the Populist movement. In some states, it even seemed possible that depressed white and black farmers might be able to challenge the entrenched Conservative regimes. Populist leaders such as Thomas E. Watson of Georgia preached a degree of cooperation among black and white farmers and sharecroppers on the grounds that their economic grievances crossed racial lines. He asked them to recognize their common plight and to subordinate race consciousness to class consciousness. At the same time, Watson made it clear that he did not believe in race mixing, nor would he tolerate "Negro domination." But why should white supremacy be jeopardized by simply telling the black sharecropper that he was "in the same boat as the white tenant; the colored laborer with the white laborer . . . Why cannot the cause of one be made the cause of both?"

In several states, the Populists openly courted the black vote, entered into political coalitions with blacks, and named some blacks to party posts. But the degree of Populist commitment varied considerably, many Populists refused to compromise on white supremacy, and blacks themselves remained skeptical about the motives of white farmers who had been their traditional enemies. Although Populists coveted the votes of blacks, in the end they proved no more committed to equality for blacks than most other southern white men. Only in North Carolina were the Populists able, by joining with the Republicans, to defeat the Conservative Democrats. The triumph proved to be short-lived, however. The Democratic return to power in North Carolina was followed by a race riot in 1898 in the town of Wilmington and by 1900 the Populists were ready to accept an amendment to the North Carolina Constitution eliminating black participation in politics. When Populists succumbed to the rampant racism of this period, they often did so with frightening enthusiasm. Few would be more virulent than Tom Watson himself, who would write of the "hideous, ominous, national menace" of black domination, advocate depriving blacks of the vote, and condone lynching.

Between 1890 and 1915, the white South moved to disfranchise blacks. The issue was not black political power, which no longer posed a serious threat, but how to reconcile racial coexistence with white supremacy. This took on additional urgency as a new generation of blacks—one that had never known the discipline

WORDS AND NAMES IN AMERICAN HISTORY

Originally, *Jim Crow* was the name of a song and dance done on the stage. During the 1820s, a growing number of white performers began blackening their faces and hands with burnt cork and offering to their audiences, mostly in northern cities, versions of what they fancied to be Negro songs and dances. These were the first blackface minstrel shows. One of these popular entertainers, T. D. Rice, copied a routine he had seen done by a crippled old black man. The song went, along with a deliberately awkward dance: "Weel about and turn about and do jus so; Ebery time I weel about, I jump Jim Crow." The word *crow* probably came from the supposed similarity of the bird's and the black man's color. Soon, however, *Jim Crow* took on a broader and more ominous meaning. It became a shorthand phrase for discrimination against and especially segregation of black people. This latter meaning was first applied to railroad cars in Massachusetts in 1841, where blacks were prohibited from sitting in the same sections with whites. Gradually *Jim Crow* came to include all the ways and places that blacks were excluded from public facilities and confined to separate, inferior accommodations throughout the country. It became, for blacks and even for whites, a code word for the entire system of humiliating racial segregation, in public transportation, in schools, in offices of the federal government, in the armed forces, in private industry, and at restaurants, movie theaters, public toilets, and water fountains. By the 1890s Jim Crow in the southern states was rapidly becoming more rigidly applied to all public situations where the two races might come in contact. It was becoming central to the southern way of life.

of slavery—reached maturity. In the white southern mind, black political participation remained linked with social equality. Therefore, if blacks could be made to give up their political aspirations, they would abandon any hope of achieving social equality. And the new generation would learn that there were substantial restraints on their freedom and clear limits to their ambitions.

Mississippi had set the pattern in 1890. Some twenty years later, through such devices as the poll tax, residence requirements, and literacy tests, black voting in the South virtually ceased. In Louisiana, for example, as late as 1896 some 130,000 blacks registered to vote; eight years later only 1342 did so. Because the new laws "did not on their face discriminate between the races," as they were forbidden to do by the Fifteenth Amendment, the Supreme Court, in the case of *Williams v. Mississippi* in 1898, upheld the Mississippi scheme.

Various loopholes were provided for prospective white voters, and Democratic registration boards and "discreet" election officials could make certain that the right people qualified. The effect of the new suffrage laws, however, was to reduce white voting, too. Property qualifications were uniformly high. Poll taxes could be a financial barrier, and literacy clauses could be enforced strictly enough to discourage white illiterates from exposing their limitations.

Throughout the South, small Democratic oligarchies or machines maintained control of politics. The occasional challengers who won office by inflating the racial and class hatreds of the poor whites, "rednecks," and "wool-hat boys" more often than not ended up constructing their own political machines and serving the same business interests they had challenged.

Where southern custom and etiquette had previously set the races apart, in the 1890s and early 1900s the Jim Crow laws made segregation even more systematic and extensive. Few places where the two races might come into social contact were unaffected. When the Supreme Court in 1883 declared the Civil Rights Act of 1875 unconstitutional, it ruled that the federal government had no jurisdiction over discrimination practiced by private persons or organizations. Later on, the Court sanctioned state segregation laws requiring separate public facilities for whites and blacks. In *Plessy v. Ferguson* in 1896, the Court decided that blacks' equal rights under the Fourteenth Amendment were not violated if the separate facilities on railroads (and by impli-

cation, in schools and other public places) were equal. In *Cumming v. County Board of Education* in 1899, the Court formally extended the philosophy of "separate but equal" to schools.

Against this background of growing repression, what remained of black leadership in the 1890s found little comfort in any political party—or in politics. Disillusioned with the failure of black expectations, and fearing still more repressive measures, Bishop Henry M. Turner of the African Methodist Episcopal church, a former black reconstruction leader in Georgia, came to advocate emigration to Africa. Like Marcus Garvey, who would launch a similar movement in the 1920s, Turner urged his people to think differently about themselves, to cease to despise themselves. Rather than "doing nothing day and night but cry: Glory, honor, dominion and greatness to White," the black man must look to himself, for "a man must believe he is somebody before he is acknowledged to be somebody. . . . Neither [the] Republican nor Democratic party can do for the colored race what [it] can do for [itself]. Respect Black!"

Unlike Garvey, Turner never had a mass following; nor did he have any illusions about the realization of his African dream. Some day, though, he felt that his people would realize the true nature of their plight in white America. "They are now sullen, despondent and discontented and sooner or later these feelings will lead to trouble. The Southern whites rely upon the strong arm of power to produce submission, but they are resting upon a slumbering volcano, which sooner or later will cause a fearful eruption."

In 1900 that "fearful eruption" was still more than half a century away. The pattern of race relations established in the aftermath of Reconstruction, reinforced by the triumph of Jim Crow and disfranchisement, persisted until the 1950s and 1960s. The concept of a New South proclaimed by industrialists, promoters, and editors had little meaning for the great mass of southerners—white or black. Sunk in poverty, debt, and ignorance, ravaged by various diseases, many resigned themselves to a dreary and hopeless way of life. The southern white's fear of black domination effectively stifled dissent, class consciousness was subordinated to race consciousness, the Democrats established virtual one-party rule, and race baiting remained a necessary vehicle for every aspiring southern politician. Such was the legacy of the New South.

The Civil War settled two important questions—secession and slavery—but it raised a great many new ones. What was to happen to the South? How were freed blacks to be treated? And who would decide: the president or Congress?

Lincoln's policy of presidential Reconstruction, based on the idea that the southern states had rebelled and now should be restored to the Union, free again to govern themselves like all other states, was one solution. In Congress, Radical Republicans proposed quite another. They considered the South a conquered territory under the jurisdiction of Congress and wanted to create a new southern society based on the equality of blacks and whites.

The South over which the advocates of these policies contended was a ruined land. Its people, both black and white, lacked food and clothing. Buildings, farms, factories were gone. Blacks had the additional problem of learning to deal with their new freedom. Some left to find a new life, but most stayed where they were. And life was much the same, for defeat had in no way changed the beliefs or attitudes of white southerners.

Presidential Reconstruction failed, and not only because of Lincoln's assassination. The new president, Andrew Johnson, believed in white supremacy and followed policies designed to restore the old planter class to power. His liberal pardon policy, plus the sanctioning of Black Codes that kept the freed slaves from participating in economic and political life, brought northern public opinion and the Radicals in Congress to a boil. The war seemed to have been fought for nothing.

By December 1665, the Radicals had begun a legislative counterattack. A bill continuing the Freedmen's Bureau was pushed through Congress over Johnson's veto, and the Fourteenth Amendment was introduced in June 1866. When it was finally ratified in July 1868, the

TIME LINE

1865	Civil War ends		Most southern states comply with reconstruction requirements and are readmitted
	Lincoln assassinated; Johnson becomes president		
	Johnsonian (Presidential) Reconstruction begins		Ulysses S. Grant elected president
	Black Codes	1869	Congress approves Fifteenth Amendment (ratified in 1870)
	Congress refuses to seat newly elected southern representatives	1870–1871	Force Act and Ku Klux Klan Act
	Thirteenth Amendment ratified	1872	Amnesty Act
1866	Freedmen's Bureau extension and Civil Rights Act passed over Johnson's veto		Grant reelected president
	Congress approves Fourteenth Amendment (ratified in 1868)	1875	Civil Rights Act (overturned by Supreme Court in 1883)
	Race riots in New Orleans and Memphis		Mississippi election returns Democrats to power
	Republicans win sweeping victory in Congressional elections	1876	Hayes-Tilden election
1867	Congress passes Reconstruction acts	1877	Federal troops withdrawn from the South; last Radical state governments collapse
	Constitutional conventions convene in the South, launching Radical Reconstruction	1879–1881	Black "exodusters" migrate to Kansas
1868	House votes to impeach Johnson; Senate fails to convict him	1890s	Legal disfranchisement and segregation (Jim Crow) inaugurate new era in race relations in the South, lasting until the 1950s
		1896	*Plessy* v. *Ferguson*

question of civil rights was legally settled, even though it would be another century before its provisions were enforced. The Radical program was written into a series of laws. The First Reconstruction Act was passed over the president's veto in March 1867. It divided the South into five military districts, put each under a general to be named by the president, and directed the generals to call a constitutional convention in each former state. Delegates were to be elected by universal adult male suffrage, black and white, and the conventions were to set up new state governments in which blacks could vote and hold office. Ratification of the Fourteenth Amendment was necessary for readmittance to the Union and acceptance of representatives by Congress.

By 1870, reconstruction under this plan was complete. It was protected by other laws, designed to neutralize the Supreme Court and the president. Johnson had survived an attempt to impeach him, but had lost his bid for renomination. In 1868 Ulysses Grant, Civil War hero, had become the new Republican president, thanks in large part to the black vote.

In the South, Radical Reconstruction, with its carpetbaggers and scalawags, brought blacks into government for the first time and gave them valuable experience. But it also brought corruption, white backlash, and repression fueled by fear that blacks, given education and opportunity, might actually become equal to whites. The "shotgun policy"—terror and violence—brought Radical Reconstruction to an end. By 1877, the federal government had retreated from its commitment to civil rights, and the Republican party in the South was almost destroyed.

The scandals of Grant's presidency had not helped the Republicans. Though a successful general, Grant was a naive and trusting politician and a failure as a businessman. He was reelected in 1872, but the great Crédit Mobilier scandal that broke during the campaign, followed by the crash of 1873 and more revelations of wrongdoing in high places, diminished Republican strength and led to the disputed election of 1876. In return for southern support, the new Republican president, Rutherford B. Hayes, promised to leave the South alone.

The New South that emerged after 1877 was marked by characteristics that have only recently begun to change: white supremacy and repression of blacks; one-party rule; a small and wealthy ruling class holding both blacks and poor whites in economic bondage; and a weak industrial base very much dependent on northern capital.

Suggested Readings

The best introductions to the Reconstruction period are K. M. Stampp, *The Era of Reconstruction 1865–1877* (1965), and E. Foner, *Reconstruction: America's Unfinished Revolution 1863–1877* (1988). W. E. B. Du Bois, *Black Reconstruction in America 1860–1880* (1935), although ignored by historians when it first appeared, remains a classic by a leading black intellectual. K. M. Stampp and L. F. Litwack (eds.), *Reconstruction* (1969), is a collection of revisionist historical interpretations. D. Sterling (ed.), *The Trouble They Seen* (1976), is a collection of black testimony on Reconstruction. For insights into postwar southern white life and attitudes, see R. M. Myers (ed.), *The Children of Pride* (1971).

W. J. Cash, *The Mind of the South* (1941), and B. Wyatt-Brown, *Southern Honor* (1982), are stimulating studies of ethics and behavior in the Old and New South. H. M. Hyman, *A More Perfect Union* (1973), examines legal and constitutional issues during the Civil War and Reconstruction. For a broad and thoughtful examination of white racial attitudes, North and South, see G. M. Fredrickson, *The Black Image in the White Mind* (1971).

The reaction of the former slaves to freedom, in their own words, is exhaustively documented in G. P. Rawick (ed.), *The American Slave: A Composite Autobiography* (41 vols., 1972–79), and in an ongoing documentary history of emancipation edited by I. Berlin and others, *Freedom* (1982–). The transition from slavery to freedom is described in E. Foner, *Nothing but Freedom* (1983), and in L. F. Litwack, *Been in the Storm So Long* (1979). For regional studies, see B. J. Fields on Maryland, *Slavery and Freedom on the Middle Ground* (1985), and C. L. Mohr on Georgia, *On the Threshold of Freedom* (1986). W. S. McFeely, *Yankee Stepfather: General O.O. Howard and the Freedmen* (1968), is a critical study of the Freedmen's Bureau. J. W. De Forest, *A Union Officer in the Reconstruction* (1948), is the personal account of a Freedmen's Bureau agent.

The evolution of Lincoln's commitment to a planter-dominated Reconstruction is examined in P. McCrary, *Abraham Lincoln and Reconstruction: The Louisiana Experiment* (1978). E. L. McKitrick, *Andrew Johnson and Reconstruction* (1960), is highly critical of Johnson. L. Cox and J. H. Cox, *Politics, Principle and Prejudice 1865–1866* (1963), emphasizes Johnson's racial attitudes and his efforts to restore the Democratic party in the North. D. Carter, *When the War Was Over* (1985), assesses the failure of presidential Reconstruction. M. Perman, in *Reunion without Compromise* (1973) and *The Road to Redemption* (1984), examines postwar southern politics in depth.

The Radical Republicans have usually fared badly at the hands of historians. The traditional view is presented in T. H. Williams, *Lincoln and the Radicals* (1941). A sympathetic treatment may be found in H. L. Trefousse, *The Radical Republicans: Lincoln's Vanguard for Radical Justice* (1969). On the economics of Republican rule, see M. W. Summers, *Railroads, Reconstruction, and the Gospel of Prosperity* (1984). J. M. McPherson, in *The Struggle for Equality* (1964) and *The Abolitionist Legacy* (1976), explores the ongoing abolitionist commitment to equal rights. Among the important biographical studies of the Radicals are F.M. Brodie, *Thaddeus Stevens* (1959); D. Donald, *Charles Sumner and the Rights of Man* (1970); and B. P. Thomas and H. M. Hyman, *Stanton* (1962). R. N. Current, *Three Carpetbag Governors* (1967), and O. H. Olsen, *Carpetbaggers' Crusade: The Life of Albion Winegar Tourgee* (1965), examine an equally maligned group.

The best study of Ulysses S. Grant and his presidency is W. S. McFeely, *Grant* (1981). On the abandonment of Radical goals, see R. W. Logan, *The Negro in American Life and Thought: The Nadir 1877–1901* (1954), which focuses on the presidents and their southern strategies.

Two pioneers in exploring the neglected black role in Reconstruction were W. E. B. Du Bois and A. A. Taylor. More recent state studies with the same focus are V. L. Wharton, *The Negro in Mississippi 1865–1890* (1947); J. Williamson, *After Slavery: The Negro in South Carolina during Reconstruction, 1861–1877* (1965); J. M. Richardson, *The Negro in the Reconstruction of Florida, 1865–1877* (1965); E. L. Drago, *Black Politicians and Reconstruction in Georgia: A Splendid Failure* (1982); and T. Tunnell, *Crucible of Reconstruction: War, Radicalism and Race in Louisiana 1862–1877* (1984). Two important local studies are W. M. Evans, *Ballots and Fence Rails: Reconstruction on the Lower Cape Fear* (1966), and O. B. Burton, *In My Father's House Are Many Mansions: Family and Community in Edgefield, South Carolina* (1985). Studies of black leadership include T. Holt, *Black over White: Negro Political Leadership in South Carolina during Reconstruction* (1978); J. H. Franklin (ed.), *Reminiscences of an Active Life: The Autobiography of John Roy Lynch* (1970); H. N. Rabinowitz (ed.), *Southern Black Leaders of the Reconstruction Era* (1982); and W. E. Martin, Jr., *The Mind of Frederick Douglass* (1984).

The violent overthrow of Radical rule is described in A. W. Trelease, *White Terror: The Ku Klux Klan Conspiracy and Southern Reconstruction* (1971). The classic study of the post-Reconstruction South remains C. V. Woodward, *Origins of the New South 1877–1913* (1951). The spirit of the New South is examined in P. Gaston, *The New South Creed: A Study in Southern Mythmaking* (1970). On black labor in the New South, see G. D. Jaynes, *Branches without Roots: Genesis of the Black Working Class in the American South, 1862–1882* (1986). On southern agrarian protest, see C. V. Woodward, *Tom Watson: Agrarian Rebel* (1938); L. Goodwyn, *Democratic Promise: The Populist Movement in America* (1976); S. Hahn, *The Roots of Southern Populism: Yeoman Farmers and the Transformation of the Georgia Upcountry, 1850–1890* (1983); W. I. Hair, *Bourbonism and Agrarian Protest: Louisiana Politics 1877–1900* (1969); and B. C. Shaw, *Wool-Hat Boys: Georgia's Populist Party* (1984).

The most ambitious and far-reaching reinterpretation of race relations in the South since emancipation is J. Williamson, *The Crucible of Race* (1984), which focuses on the post-Reconstruction period. A. Meier, *Negro Thought in America 1880–1915* (1963), and G. B. Tindall, *South Carolina Negroes 1877–1900* (1952), are able examinations of black organization and ideology in the post-Reconstruction South. On the disfranchisement of blacks and poor whites, see J. M. Kousser, *The Shaping of Southern Politics* (1974). On crime and punishment in the New South, see E. L. Ayers, *Vengeance and Justice* (1984). On race relations and the more rigid forms of segregation imposed after 1890, see C. V. Woodward, *The Strange Career of Jim Crow* (1974 ed.); H. N. Rabinowitz, *Race Relations in the Urban South, 1865–1890* (1978); G. M. Fredrickson, *White Supremacy* (1981); J. W. Cell, *The Highest Stage of White Supremacy* (1982); and an outstanding state study by N. R. McMillen, *Dark Journey: Black Mississippians in the Age of Jim Crow* (1989).

How blacks responded to the deterioration of race relations is examined in two works on migration movements: N. I. Painter, *Exodusters: Black Migration to Kansas after Reconstruction* (1977), and E. S. Redkey, *Black Exodus: Black Nationalist and Back-to-Africa Movements, 1890–1910* (1969). See also J. Dittmer, *Black Georgia in the Progressive Era, 1900–1920* (1977), W. I. Hair, *Carnival of Fury: Robert Charles and the New Orleans Race Riot of 1900* (1976), and L. F. Litwack and A. Meier (eds.), *Black Leaders of the Nineteenth Century* (1988). In *Black Culture and Black Consciousness* (1977), a pathbreaking study employing the folklore, music, and humor of Afro-Americans, L. W. Levine illuminates how black southerners perceived themselves, their place in American society, and their relations with whites. Among the most compelling accounts of black life in the South is Theodore Rosengarten, *All God's Dangers: The Life of Nate Shaw* (1974), in which an eighty-five-year-old Alabama cotton farmer recounts his life.

APPENDIX

The Declaration of Independence

When in the course of human events, it becomes necessary for one people to dissolve the political bands which have connected them with another, and to assume among the Powers of the earth, the separate and equal station to which the Laws of Nature and of Nature's God entitle them, a decent respect to the opinions of mankind requires that they should declare the causes which impel them to the separation.

We hold these truths to be self-evident, that all men are created equal, that they are endowed by their Creator with certain unalienable Rights, that among these are Life, Liberty and the pursuit of Happiness. That to secure these rights, Governments are instituted among Men, deriving their just Powers from the consent of the governed, That whenever any Form of Government becomes destructive of these ends, it is the Right of the People to alter or to abolish it, and to institute new Government, laying its foundation on such principles and organizing its Powers in such form, as to them shall seem most likely to effect their Safety and Happiness. Prudence, indeed, will dictate that Governments long established should not be changed for light and transient causes; and accordingly all experience hath shewn, that mankind are more disposed to suffer, while evils are sufferable, than to right themselves by abolishing the forms to which they are accustomed. But when a long train of abuses and usurpations, pursuing invariably the same object evinces a design to reduce them under absolute Despotism, it is their right, it is their duty, to throw off such Government, and to provide new Guards for their future security. Such has been the patient sufferance of these Colonies: and such is now the necessity which constrains them to alter their former Systems of Government. The history of the present King of Great Britain is a history of repeated injuries and usurpations, all having in direct object the Establishment of an absolute Tyranny over these States. To prove this, let Facts be submitted to a candid World:

He has refused his Assent to Laws, the most wholesome and necessary for the public good.

He has forbidden his Governors to pass Laws of immediate and pressing importance, unless suspended in their operation till his Assent should be obtained; and when so suspended, he has utterly neglected to attend to them.

He has refused to pass other Laws for the accommodation of large districts of people, unless those people would relinquish the right of Representation in the Legislature, a right inestimable to them and formidable to tyrants only.

He has called together legislative bodies at places unusual, uncomfortable, and distant from the depository of their Public Records, for the sole purpose of fatiguing them into compliance with his measures.

He has dissolved Representative Houses repeatedly, for opposing with manly firmness his invasions on the rights of the people.

He has refused for a long time, after such dissolutions, to cause others to be elected; whereby the Legislative Powers, incapable of the Annihilation, have returned to the People at large for their exercise; the State remaining in the mean time exposed to all the dangers of invasion from without, and the convulsions within.

He has endeavored to prevent the population of these States; for that purpose obstructing the Laws of Naturalization of Foreigners; refusing to pass others to encourage their migrations hither, and raising the conditions of new Appropriations of Lands.

He has obstructed the Administration of justice, by refusing his Assent to Laws for establishing Judiciary Powers.

He has made judges dependent on his Will alone, for the tenure of their offices, and the amount and payment of their salaries.

He has erected a multitude of New Offices, and sent hither swarms of Officers to harass our People, and eat out their substance.

He has kept among us, in times of peace, Standing Armies, without the consent of our legislature.

He has affected to render the Military independent of and superior to the Civil Power.

He has combined with others to subject us to a jurisdiction foreign to our constitution, and unacknowledged by our laws; giving his Assent to their acts of pretended legislation—

For quartering large bodies of armed troops among us;

For protecting them, by a mock Trial, from Punishment for any Murders which they should commit on the Inhabitants of these States;

For cutting off our Trade with all parts of the world;

For imposing Taxes on us without our Consent;

For depriving us in many cases, of the benefits of Trial by Jury;

For transporting us beyond Seas to be tried for pretended offences;

For abolishing the free System of English Laws in a neighboring Province, establishing therein an Arbitrary government, and enlarging its Boundaries so as to render it at once an example and fit instrument for introducing the same absolute rule into these Colonies;

For taking away our Charters, abolishing our most valuable Laws, and altering fundamentally the Forms of our Governments;

For suspending our own Legislatures, and declaring themselves invested with Power to legislate for us in all cases whatsoever.

He has abdicated Government here, by declaring us out of his Protection, and waging War against us.

He has plundered our seas, ravaged our Coasts, burnt our towns, and destroyed the lives of our people.

He is at this time transporting large armies of foreign mercenaries to compleat the works of death, desolation and tyranny, already begun with circumstances of Cruelty & perfidy, scarcely paralleled in the most barbarous ages, and totally unworthy the Head of a civilized nation.

He has constrained our fellow Citizens taken Captive on the high Seas to bear Arms against their Country, to become the executioners of their friends and Brethren, or to fall themselves by their Hands.

He has excited domestic insurrections amongst us, and has endeavoured to bring on the inhabitants of our frontiers, the merciless Indian Savages, whose known rule of warfare, is an undistinguished destruction of all ages, sexes and conditions.

In every stage of these Oppressions We have Petitioned for Redress in the most humble terms: Our repeated Petitions have been answered only by repeated injury. A Prince, whose character is thus marked by every act which may define a Tyrant, is unfit to be the ruler of a free People.

Nor have We been wanting in attentions to our British brethren. We have warned them from time to time of attempts by their legislature to extend an unwarrantable jurisdiction over us. We have re-minded them of the circumstances of our emigration and settlement here. We have appealed to their native justice and magnanimity, and we have conjured them by the ties of our common kindred to disavow these usurpations, which, would inevitably interrupt our connections and correspondence. They too have been deaf to the voice of justice and of consanguinity. We must, therefore, acquiesce in the necessity, which denounces our Separation, and hold them, as we hold the rest of mankind, Enemies in War, in Peace, Friends.

We, therefore, the Representatives of the United States of America, in General Congress, Assembled, appealing to the Supreme judge of the world for the rectitude of our intentions, do, in the Name, and by Authority of the good People of these Colonies, solemnly publish and declare, That these United Colonies are, and of Right ought to be Free and Independent States; that they are Absolved from all Allegiance to the British Crown, and that all political connection between them and the State of Great Britain, is and ought to be totally dissolved; and that, as Free and Independent States, they have full Power to levy War, conclude Peace, contract Alliances, establish Commerce, and to do all other Acts and Things which in-dependent States may of right do. And for the support of this Declaration, with a firm reliance on the Protection of Divine Providence, we mutually pledge to each other our Lives, our Fortunes and our sacred Honor.

The Constitution of the United States

We the people of the United States, in Order to form a more perfect Union, establish justice, insure domestic Tranquility, provide for the common defense, promote the general Welfare, and secure the Blessings of Liberty to ourselves and our Posterity, do ordain and establish this Constitution for the United States of America.

Article I

SECTION 1. All legislative Powers herein granted shall be vested in a Congress of the United States, which shall consist of a Senate and House of Representatives.

SECTION 2. 1. The House of Representatives shall be composed of Members chosen every second Year by the People of the several States, and the Electors in each State shall have the Qualifications requisite for Electors of the most numerous Branch of the State Legislature.

2. No person shall be a Representative who shall not have attained to the Age of twenty-five Years, and been seven Years a Citizen of the United States, and who shall not, when elected, be an Inhabitant of that State in which he shall be chosen.

3. Representatives and direct Taxes[1] shall be apportioned among the several States which may be included within this Union, according to their respective Numbers, which shall be determined by adding to the whole Number of free Persons, including those bound to Service for a Term of Years, and excluding Indians not taxed, three fifths of all other Persons.[2] The actual Enumeration shall be made within three Years after the first Meeting of the Congress of the United States, and within every subsequent Term of ten Years, in such Manner as they shall by Law direct. The Number of Representatives shall not exceed one for every thirty Thousand, but each State shall have at Least one Representative; and until such enumeration shall be made, the State of New Hampshire shall be entitled to chuse three, Massachusetts eight, Rhode-Island and Providence Plantations one, Connecticut five, New York six, New Jersey four, Pennsylvania eight, Delaware one, Maryland six, Virginia ten, North Carolina five, South Carolina five, and Georgia three.

4. When vacancies happen in the Representation from any State, the Executive Authority thereof shall issue Writs of Election to fill such Vacancies.

5. The House of Representatives shall chuse their Speaker and other officers; and shall have the sole Power of Impeachment.

SECTION 3. 1. The Senate of the United States shall be composed of two Senators from each State, chosen by the Legislature thereof,[3] for six Years; and each Senator shall have one Vote.

2. Immediately after they shall be assembled in Consequence of the first Election, they shall be divided as equally as may be into three Classes. The Seats of the Senators of the first Class shall be vacated at the Expiration of the second Year, of the second Class at the Expiration of the fourth Year, and of the third Class at the Expiration of the sixth Year, so that one-third may be chosen every second Year; and if Vacancies happen by Resignation, or otherwise, during the Recess of the Legislature of any State, the Executive thereof may make temporary Appointments until the next Meeting of the Legislature, which shall then fill such Vacancies.[4]

3. No Person shall be a Senator who shall not have attained to the Age of thirty Years, and been nine Years a Citizen of the United States, and who shall not, when elected, be an Inhabitant of that State for which he shall be chosen.

4. The Vice President of the United States shall be President of the Senate, but shall have no vote, unless they be equally divided.

5. The Senate shall chuse their other Officers, and also a President pro tempore, in the absence of the Vice President, or when he shall exercise the Office of President of the United States.

---

[1] See the Sixteenth Amendment.
[2] See the Fourteenth Amendment.

[3] See the Seventeenth Amendment.
[4] See the Seventeenth Amendment.

6. The Senate shall have the sole Power to try all Impeachments. When sitting for that purpose, they shall be on Oath or Affirmation. When the President of the United States is tried, the Chief justice shall preside: And no person shall be convicted without the Concurrence of two thirds of the Members present.

7. Judgment in Cases of impeachment shall not extend further than to removal from Office, and disqualification to hold and enjoy any Office of honor, Trust, or Profit under the United States: but the Party convicted shall nevertheless be liable and subject to Indictment, Trial, judgment and Punishment, according to Law.

Section 4. 1. The Times, Places and Manner of holding Elections for Senators and Representatives, shall be prescribed in each state by the Legislature thereof; but the Congress may at any time by Law make or alter such Regulations, except as to the Places of Chusing Senators.

2. The Congress shall assemble at least once in every Year, and such Meeting shall be on the first Monday in December, unless they shall by Law appoint a different Day.

Section 5. 1. Each House shall be the judge of the Elections, Returns and Qualifications of its own Members, and a Majority of each shall constitute a Quorum to do Business; but a smaller number may adjourn from day to day, and may be authorized to compel the Attendance of absent Members, in such manner, and under such Penalties, as each House may provide.

2. Each House may determine the Rules of its Proceedings, punish its Members for disorderly Behavior, and, with the Concurrence of two thirds, expel a Member.

3. Each House shall keep a journal of its Proceedings, and from time to time publish the same, excepting such Parts as may in their judgment require Secrecy; and the Yeas and Nays of the Members of either House on any question shall, at the Desire of one fifth of those Present, be entered on the journal.

4. Neither House, during the Session of Congress, shall, without the Consent of the other, adjourn for more than three days, nor to any other Place than that in which the two Houses shall be sitting.

Section 6. 1. The Senators and Representatives shall receive a Compensation for their Services, to be ascertained by Law, and paid out of the Treasury of the United States. They shall in all Cases, except Treason, Felony, and Breach of the Peace, be privileged from arrest during their Attendance at the Session of their respective Houses, and in going to and returning from the same; and for any Speech or Debate in either House, they shall not be questioned in any other Place.

2. No Senator or Representative shall, during the Time for which he was elected, be appointed to any civil office under the Authority of the United States, which shall have been created, or the Emoluments whereof shall have been increased, during such time; and no Person holding any Office under the United States shall be a Member of either House during his continuance in Office.

Section 7. 1. All Bills for raising Revenue shall originate in the House of Representatives; but the Senate may propose or concur with Amendments as on other bills.

2. Every Bill which shall have passed the House of Representatives and the Senate, shall, before it become a Law, be presented to the President of the United States; If he approve he shall sign it, but if not he shall return it, with his Objections, to that House in which it shall have originated, who shall enter the Objections at large on their journal, and proceed to reconsider it. If after such Reconsideration two thirds of that House shall agree to pass the bill, it shall be sent, together with the objections, to the other House, by which it shall likewise be reconsidered, and if approved by two thirds of that House, it shall become a Law. But in all such Cases the Votes of both Houses shall be determined by Yeas and Nays, and the Names of the Persons voting for and against the Bill shall be entered on the journal of each House

respectively. If any Bill shall not be returned by the President within ten Days (Sundays excepted) after it shall have been presented to him, the Same shall be a Law, in like Manner as if he had signed it, unless the Congress by their Adjournment prevent its Return, in which Case it shall not be a Law.

3. Every Order, Resolution, or Vote to which the Concurrence of the Senate and House of Representatives may be necessary (except on a question of Adjournment) shall be presented to the President of the United States; and before the Same shall take Effect, shall be approved by him, or being disapproved by him, shall be repassed by two thirds of the Senate and House of Representatives, according to the Rules and Limitations prescribed in the Case of a Bill.

Section 8. The Congress shall have Power

1. To lay and collect Taxes, Duties, Imposts and Excises, to pay the Debts and provide for the common Defense and general Welfare of the United States; but all Duties, Imposts and Excises shall be uniform throughout the United States;

2. To borrow money on the credit of the United States;

3. To regulate Commerce with foreign Nations, and among the several States, and with the Indian Tribes;

4. To establish an uniform Rule of Naturalization, and uniform Laws on the subject of Bankruptcies through-out the United States;

5. To coin Money, regulate the Value thereof, and of foreign Coin, and fix the Standard of Weights and Measures;

6. To provide for the Punishment of counterfeiting the Securities and current Coin of the United States;

7. To establish Post offices and post Roads;

8. To promote the Progress of Science and useful Arts, by securing for limited Times to Authors and inventors the exclusive Right to their respective Writings and Discoveries;

9. To constitute Tribunals inferior to the Supreme Court;

10. To define and punish Piracies and Felonies committed on the high Seas, and Offences against the Law of Nations;

11. To declare War, grant Letters of Marque and Reprisal, and make Rules concerning Captures on Land and Water;

12. To raise and support Armies, but no Appropriation of Money to that Use shall be for a longer Term than two Years;

13. To provide and maintain a Navy;

14. To make Rules for the Government and Regulation of the land and naval forces;

15. To provide for calling forth the Militia to execute the Laws of the Union, suppress Insurrections and repel invasions;

16. To provide for organizing, arming, and disciplining the Militia, and for governing such Part of them as may be employed in the Service of the United States, reserving to the States respectively, the Appointment of the Officers, and the Authority of training the Militia according to the discipline prescribed by Congress;

17. To exercise exclusive Legislation in all Cases whatsoever, over such District (not exceeding ten Miles square) as may, by Cession of particular States, and the acceptance of Congress, become the Seat of Government of the United States, and to exercise like Authority over all Places purchased by the Consent of the Legislature of the State in which the Same shall be, for the Erection of Forts, Magazines, Arsenals, dock-Yards, and other needful Buildings; And

18. To make all Laws which shall be necessary and proper for carrying into Execution the foregoing Powers, and all other Powers vested by this Constitution in the government of the United States, or in any Department or Officer thereof.

Section 9. 1. The Migration or Importation of such Persons as any of the States now existing shall think proper to admit, shall not be prohibited by the Congress prior to the Year one thousand eight hundred and eight, but a tax or duty may be imposed on such Importation, not exceeding ten dollars for each Person.

2. The Privilege of the Writ of Habeas Corpus shall not be suspended, unless when in Cases of Rebellion or Invasion the public Safety may require it.

3. No Bill of Attainder or ex post facto Law shall be passed.

4. No capitation, or other direct, Tax shall be laid unless in Proportion to the Census or Enumeration herein before directed to be taken.[5]

5. No Tax or Duty shall be laid on Articles exported from any State.

6. No Preference shall be given by any Regulation of commerce or Revenue to the Ports of one State over those of another: nor shall Vessels bound to, or from, one state, be obliged to enter, clear, or pay Duties in another.

7. No Money shall be drawn from the Treasury, but in Consequence of Appropriations made by Law; and a regular Statement and Account of the Receipts and Expenditures of all public Money shall be published from time to time.

8. No Title of Nobility shall be granted by the United States: And no Person holding any Office of Profit or Trust under them, shall, without the Consent of the Congress, accept of any present, Emolument, Office, or Title, of any kind whatever, from any King, Prince, or Foreign State.

SECTION 10. 1. No State shall enter into any Treaty, Alliance, or Confederation; grant Letters of Marque and Reprisal; coin Money; emit Bills of Credit; make any Thing but gold and silver Coin a Tender in Payment of Debts; pass any Bill of Attainder, ex post facto Law, or Law impairing the obligation of Contracts, or grant any Title of Nobility.

2. No State shall, without the Consent of the Congress, lay any Imposts or Duties on Imports or Exports, except what may be absolutely necessary for executing its inspection Laws: and the net Produce of all Duties and Imposts, laid by any State on Imports or Exports, shall be for the Use of the Treasury of the United States; and all such Laws shall be subject to the Revision and Control of the Congress.

3. No State shall, without the Consent of Congress, lay any duty of Tonnage, keep Troops, or Ships of War in time of peace, enter into any Agreement or Compact with another State, or with a foreign Power, or engage in War, unless actually invaded, or in such imminent Danger as will not admit of delay.

Article II

SECTION 1. 1. The executive Power shall be vested in a President of the United States of America. He shall hold his Office during the Term of four Years, and, together with the Vice President, chosen for the same Term, be elected, as follows:

2. Each State shall appoint, in such Manner as the Legislature thereof may direct, a Number of Electors, equal to the whole Number of Senators and Representatives to which the State may be entitled in the Congress; but no Senator or Representative, or Person holding an Office of Trust or Profit under the United States, shall be appointed an Elector.

The Electors shall meet in their respective States, and vote by Ballot for two persons, of whom one at least shall not be an Inhabitant of the same State with themselves. And they shall make a List of all the Persons voted for, and of the Number of Votes for each; which List they shall sign and certify, and transmit sealed to the Seat of the Government of the United States, directed to the President of the Senate. The President of the Senate shall, in the Presence of the Senate and House of Representatives, open all the Certificates, and the Votes shall then be counted. The Person having the greatest Number of Votes shall be the President, if such Number be a Majority of the whole Number of Electors appointed; and if there be more than one who have such Majority, and have an equal Number of Votes,

then the House of Representatives shall immediately chuse by Ballot one of them for President; and if no Person have a Majority, then from the five highest on the List the said House shall in like Manner chuse the President. But in chusing the President, the votes shall be taken by States, the Representation from each State having one Vote; a quorum for this Purpose shall consist of a Member or Members from two-thirds of the States, and a Majority of all the States shall be necessary to a Choice. In every Case, after the Choice of the President, the Person having the greatest Number of Votes of the Electors shall be the Vice President. But if there should remain two or more who have equal votes, the Senate shall chuse from them by Ballot the Vice President.[6]

3. The Congress may determine the time of chusing the Electors, and the Day on which they shall give their Votes; which Day shall be the same throughout the United States.

4. No person except a natural-born Citizen, or a Citizen of the United States, at the time of the Adoption of this Constitution, shall be eligible to the Office of President; neither shall any Person be eligible to that office who shall not have attained to the Age of thirty-five Years, and been fourteen Years a Resident within the United States.

5. In Case of the Removal of the President from Office, or of his Death, Resignation, or Inability to discharge the Powers and Duties of the said Office, the same shall devolve on the Vice President, and the Congress may by Law provide for the Case of Removal, Death, Resignation, or Inability, both of the President and Vice President, declaring what Officer shall then act as President, and such Officer shall act accordingly, until the Disability be removed, or a President shall be elected.

6. The President shall, at stated Times, receive for his Services a Compensation, which shall neither be increased nor diminished during the Period for which he shall have been elected, and he shall not receive within that Period any other Emolument from the United States, or any of them.

7. Before he enter on the execution of his Office, he shall take the following Oath or Affirmation: "I do solemnly swear (or affirm) that I will faithfully execute the Office of President of the United States, and will, to the best of my Ability, preserve, protect, and defend the Constitution of the United States."

SECTION 2. 1. The President shall be Commander in Chief of the Army and Navy of the United States, and of the Militia of the several States, when called into the actual Service of the United States; he may require the Opinion, in writing, of the principal Officer in each of the executive Departments, upon any subject relating to the Duties of their respective Offices, and he shall have Power to Grant Reprieves and Pardons for Offences against the United States, except in Cases of Impeachment.

2. He shall have Power, by and with the Advice and Consent of the Senate, to make Treaties, provided two thirds of the Senators present concur; and he shall nominate, and by and with the Advice and Consent of the Senate, shall appoint Ambassadors, other public Ministers and Consuls, judges of the supreme Court, and all other Officers of the United States, whose Appointments are not herein otherwise provided for, and which shall be established by Law: but the Congress may by Law vest the Appointment of such inferior Officers, as they think proper, in the President alone, in the Courts of Law, or in the Heads of Departments.

3. The President shall have Power to fill up all Vacancies that may happen during the Recess of the Senate, by granting Commissions which shall expire at the End of their next Session.

SECTION 3. He shall from time to time give to the Congress Information of the State of the Union, and recommend to their Consideration such Measures as he shall judge necessary and

---

[5] See the Sixteenth Amendment.

[6] Superseded by the Twelfth Amendment.

expedient; he may, on extraordinary occasions, convene both Houses, or either of them, and in Case of Disagreement between them, with respect to the Time of Adjournment, he may adjourn them to such Time as he shall think proper; he shall receive Ambassadors and other public Ministers; he shall take Care that the Laws be faithfully executed, and shall Commission all the officers of the United States.

SECTION 4. The President, Vice President and all civil Officers of the United States, shall be removed from Office on Impeachment for, and Conviction of, Treason, Bribery, or other high Crimes and Misdemeanors.

Article III

SECTION 1. The judicial Power of the United States, shall be vested in one supreme Court, and in such inferior Courts as the Congress may from time to time ordain and establish. The judges, both of the supreme and inferior Courts, shall hold their Offices during good Behaviour, and shall, at stated Times, receive for their Services, a Compensation, which shall not be diminished during their Continuance in Office.

SECTION 2. 1. The judicial Power shall extend to all Cases, in Law and Equity, arising under this Constitution, the Laws of the United States, and treaties made, or which shall be made, under their Authority;—to all Cases affecting Ambassadors, other public ministers and consuls; to all cases of admiralty and maritime jurisdiction;—to Controversies to which the United States shall be a party;[7]—to Controversies between two or more States; between a State and citizens of another States;—between Citizens of different States;—between Citizens of the same State claiming Lands under Grants of different States, and between a State, or the Citizens thereof, and foreign States, Citizens or Subjects.

2. In all Cases affecting Ambassadors, other public Ministers and Consuls, and those in which a State shall be Party, the supreme Court shall have original Jurisdiction. In all the other Cases before mentioned, the supreme Court shall have appellate jurisdiction, both as to Law and Fact, with such Exceptions, and under such Regulations as the Congress shall make.

3. The trial of all Crimes, except in Cases of Impeachment, shall be by jury; and such Trial shall be held in the State where the said Crimes shall have been committed; but when not committed within any State, the trial shall be at such Place or Places as the Congress may by Law have directed.

SECTION 3. 1. Treason against the United States, shall consist only in levying War against them, or in adhering to their Enemies, giving them Aid and Comfort. No Person shall be convicted of Treason unless on the testimony of two Witnesses to the same overt Act, or on Confession in open Court.

2. The Congress shall have power to declare the Punishment of Treason, but no Attainder of Treason shall work Corruption of Blood, or Forfeiture except during the Life of the Person attainted.

Article IV

SECTION 1. Full Faith and Credit shall be given in each State to the public Acts, Records, and judicial Proceedings of every other State. And the Congress may by general Laws prescribe the Manner in which such Acts, Records and Proceedings shall be proved, and the Effect thereof.

SECTION 2. 1. The Citizens of each State shall be entitled to all Privileges and Immunities of Citizens in the several States.[8]

2. A Person charged in any State with Treason, Felony, or other Crime, who shall flee from justice, and be found in another State, shall on demand of the executive Authority of the State from which he fled, be delivered up, to be removed to the State having jurisdiction of the crime.

3. No Person held to Service or Labour in one State, under the Laws thereof, escaping into another, shall, in Consequence of any Law or Regulation therein, be discharged from such Service or Labour, but shall be delivered up on Claim of the Party to whom such Service or Labour may be due.[9]

SECTION 3. 1. New States may be admitted by the Congress into this Union; but no new State shall be formed or erected within the Jurisdiction of any other State, nor any State be formed by the junction of two or more States, or parts of States, without the Consent of the Legislatures of the States concerned as well as of the Congress.

2. The Congress shall have Power to dispose of and make all needful Rules and Regulations respecting the Territory or other Property belonging to the United States; and nothing in this Constitution shall be so construed as to Prejudice any Claims of the United States, or of any particular State.

SECTION 4. The United States shall guarantee to every State in this Union a Republican Form of Government, and shall protect each of them against Invasion; and on Application of the Legislature, or of the Executive (when the Legislature cannot be convened) against domestic Violence.

Article V

The Congress, whenever two-thirds of both Houses shall deem it necessary, shall propose Amendments to this Constitution, or, on the Application of the Legislatures of two-thirds of the several States, shall call a Convention for proposing Amendments, which, in either Case, shall be valid to all Intents and Purposes, as part of this Constitution, when ratified by the Legislatures of three-fourths of the several States, or by Conventions in three-fourths thereof, as the one or the other Mode of Ratification may be proposed by the Congress; Provided that no Amendment which may be made prior to the Year One thousand eight hundred and eight shall in any Manner affect the first and fourth Clauses in the Ninth Section of the first Article; and that no State, without its Consent, shall be deprived of its equal Suffrage in the Senate.

Article VI

1. All Debts contracted and Engagements entered into, before the Adoption of this Constitution, shall be as valid against the United States under this Constitution, as under the Confederation.[10]

2. This Constitution, and the Laws of the United States which shall be made in Pursuance thereof; and all Treaties made, or which shall be made, under the Authority of the United States, shall be the supreme Law of the Land; and the judges in every State shall be bound thereby, any Thing in the Constitution or Laws of any State to the Contrary notwithstanding.

3. The Senators and Representatives before mentioned, and the Members of the several State Legislatures and all executive and judicial Officers, both of the United States and of the several States, shall be bound by Oath or Affirmation, to support this Constitution; but no religious Test shall ever be required as a qualification to any Office or public Trust under the United States.

Article VII

The Ratification of the Conventions of nine States, shall be sufficient for the Establishment of this Constitution between the States so ratifying the same.

Done in Convention by the Unanimous Consent of the States present the Seventeenth Day of September in the Year of our Lord one thousand seven hundred and Eighty seven, and of the independence of the United States of America the Twelfth. In Witness whereof We have hereunto subscribed our Names.

[Names omitted]

---

[7] See the Eleventh Amendment.
[8] See the Fourteenth Amendment, Sec. 1.

[9] See the Thirteenth Amendment.
[10] See the Fourteenth Amendment, Sec. 4.

Articles in addition to, and amendment of, the Constitution of the United States of America, proposed by Congress, and ratified by the legislatures of the several States, pursuant to the fifth article of the original Constitution.

Amendment I [December 15, 1791]

Congress shall make no law respecting an establishment of religion, or prohibiting the free exercise thereof, or abridging the freedom of speech, or of the press; or the right of the people peaceably to assemble, and to petition the Government for a redress of grievances.

Amendment II [December 15, 1791]

A well regulated Militia, being necessary to the security of a free State, the right of the people to keep and bear Arms shall not be infringed.

Amendment III [December 15, 1791]

No Soldier shall, in time of peace, be quartered in any house, without the consent of the owner, nor in time of war, but in a manner to be prescribed by law.

Amendment IV [December 15, 1791]

The right of the people to be secure in their persons, houses, papers, and effects, against unreasonable searches and seizures, shall not be violated, and no Warrants shall issue, but upon probable cause, supported by Oath or affirmation, and particularly describing the place to be searched, and the persons or things to be seized.

Amendment V [December 15, 1791]

No person shall be held to answer for a capital or otherwise infamous crime, unless on a presentment or indictment of a Grand jury, except in cases arising in the land or naval forces, or in the Militia, when in actual service in time of War or public danger; nor shall any person be subject for the same offence to be twice put in jeopardy of life or limb; nor shall be compelled in any criminal case to be a witness against himself, nor be deprived of life, liberty, or property, without due process of law; nor shall private property be taken for public use, without just compensation.

Amendment VI [December 15, 1791]

In all criminal prosecutions, the accused shall enjoy the right to a speedy and public trial, by an impartial jury of the State and district wherein the crime shall have been committed, which district shall have been previously ascertained by law, and to be informed of the nature and cause of the accusation; to be confronted with the witnesses against him; to have compulsory process for obtaining witnesses in his favor, and to have the Assistance of Counsel for his defense.

Amendment VII [December 15, 1791]

In suits at common law, where the value in controversy shall exceed twenty dollars, the right of trial by jury shall be preserved, and no fact tried by a jury, shall be otherwise reexamined in any Court of the United States, than according to the rules of the common law.

Amendment VIII [December 15, 1791]

Excessive bail shall not be required, nor excessive fines imposed, nor cruel and unusual punishments inflicted.

Amendment IX [December 15, 1791]

The enumeration in the Constitution, of certain rights, shall not be construed to deny or disparage others retained by the people.

Amendment X [December 15, 1791]

The powers not delegated to the United States by the Constitution, nor prohibited by it to the States, are reserved to the States respectively, or to the people.

Amendment XI [January 8, 1798]

The judicial power of the United States shall not be construed to extend to any suit in law or equity, commenced or prosecuted against one of the United States by Citizens of another State, or by Citizens or Subjects of any Foreign State.

Amendment XII [September 25, 1804]

The Electors shall meet in their respective States and vote by ballot for President and Vice-President, one of whom, at least, shall not be an inhabitant of the same State with themselves; they shall name in their ballots the person voted for as President, and in distinct ballots the person voted for as Vice-President, and they shall make distinct lists of all persons voted for as President, and of all persons voted for as Vice-President, and of the number of votes for each, which lists they shall sign and certify, and transmit sealed to the seat of the government of the United States, directed to the President of the Senate; The President of the Senate shall, in the presence of the Senate and House of Representatives, open all the certificates and the votes shall then be counted; The person having the greatest number of votes for President, shall be the President, if such number be a majority of the whole number of Electors appointed; and if no person have such majority, then from the persons having the highest numbers not exceeding three on the list of those voted for as President, the House of Representatives shall choose immediately, by ballot, the President. But in choosing the President, the votes shall be taken by states, the representation from each state having one vote; a quorum for this purpose shall consist of a member or members from two-thirds of the states, and a majority of all the states shall be necessary to a choice. And if the House of Representatives shall not choose a President whenever the right of choice shall devolve upon them, before the fourth day of March next following, then the Vice-President shall act as President, as in the case of the death or other constitutional disability of the President. The person having the greatest number of votes as Vice-President, shall be the Vice-President, if such number be a majority of the whole number of Electors appointed, and if no person have a majority, then from the two highest numbers on the list, the Senate shall choose the Vice-President; a quorum for the purpose shall consist of two-thirds of the whole number of Senators, and a majority of the whole number shall be necessary to a choice. But no person constitutionally ineligible to the office of President shall be eligible to that of Vice-President of the United States.

Amendment XIII [December 18, 1865]

SECTION 1. Neither slavery nor involuntary servitude, except as a punishment for crime whereof the party shall have been duly convicted, shall exist within the United States, or any place subject to their jurisdiction.

SECTION 2. Congress shall have power to enforce this article by appropriate legislation.

Amendment XIV [July 28, 1868]

SECTION 1. All persons born or naturalized in the United States, and subject to the jurisdiction thereof, are citizens of the United States and of the State wherein they reside. No State shall make or enforce any law which shall abridge the privileges or immunities of citizens of the United States; nor shall any State deprive any person of life, liberty, or property, without due process of law; nor deny to any person within its jurisdiction the equal protection of the laws.

SECTION 2. Representatives shall be apportioned among the several States according to their respective numbers, counting the whole number of persons in each State, excluding Indians not taxed. But when the right to vote at any election for the choice of electors for President and Vice-President of the United States, Representatives in Congress, the Executive and Judicial officers of a State, or the members of the Legislature thereof, is denied to any of the male inhabitants of such State, being twenty-one years of age, and citizens of the United States, or in any way abridged, except for participation in rebellion, or other crime, the basis of representation therein shall be reduced in the proportion which the number of such male citizens shall bear to the whole number of male citizens twenty-one years of age in such State.

SECTION 3. No person shall be a Senator or Representative in Congress, or elector of President and Vice-President, or hold any office, civil or military, under the United States, or under any State, who, having previously taken an oath, as a member of Congress, or as an officer of the United States, or as a member of any State legislature, or as an executive or judicial officer of any State, to support the Constitution of the United States, shall have engaged in insurrection or rebellion against the same, or given aid or comfort to the enemies thereof. But Congress may by a vote of two-thirds of each House, remove such disability.

SECTION 4. The validity of the public debt of the United States, authorized by law, including debts incurred for payment of pensions and bounties for services in suppressing insurrection or rebellion, shall not be questioned. But neither the United States nor any State shall assume or pay any debt or obligation incurred in aid of insurrection or rebellion against the United States, or any claim for the loss or emancipation of any slave; but all such debts, obligations, and claims shall be held illegal and void.

SECTION 5. The Congress shall have the power to enforce, by appropriate legislation, the provisions of this article.

Amendment XV [March 30, 1870]

SECTION 1. The right of citizens of the United States to vote shall not be denied or abridged by the United States or by any State on account of race, color, or previous condition of servitude

SECTION 2. The Congress shall have power to enforce this article by appropriate legislation.

Amendment XVI [February 25, 1913]

The Congress shall have power to lay and collect taxes on incomes, from whatever source derived, without apportionment among the several States, and without regard to any census or enumeration.

Amendment XVII [May 31, 1913]

The Senate of the United States shall be composed of two Senators from each State, elected by the people thereof, for six years; and each Senator shall have one vote. The electors in each State shall have the qualifications requisite for electors of the most numerous branch of the State legislatures.

When vacancies happen in the representation of any State in the Senate, the executive authority of such State shall issue writs of election to fill such vacancies: Provided, That the legislature of any State may empower the executive thereof to make temporary appointments until the people fill the vacancies by election as the legislature may direct.

This amendment shall not be so construed as to affect the election or term of any Senator chosen before it becomes valid as part of the Constitution.

Amendment XVIII[11] [January 29, 1919]

SECTION 1. After one year from the ratification of this article the manufacture, sale, or transportation of intoxicating liquors

---

[11] Repealed by the Twenty-first Amendment.

within, the importation thereof into, or the exportation thereof from the United States and all territory subject to the jurisdiction thereof for beverage purposes is hereby prohibited.

SECTION 2. The Congress and the several States shall have concurrent power to enforce this article by appropriate legislation.

SECTION 3. This article shall be inoperative unless it shall have been ratified as an amendment to the Constitution by the legislatures of the several States, as provided in the Constitution, within seven years from the date of the submission hereof to the States by the Congress.

Amendment XIX [August 26, 1920]

The right of citizens of the United States to vote shall not be denied or abridged by the United States or by any State on account of sex.

Congress shall have power to enforce this article by appropriate legislation.

Amendment XX [January 23, 1933]

SECTION 1. The terms of the President and Vice-President shall end at noon on the 20th day of January, and the terms of Senators and Representatives at noon on the 3d day of January, of the years in which such terms would have ended if this article had not been ratified; and the terms of their successors shall then begin.

SECTION 2. The Congress shall assemble at least once in every year, and such meeting shall begin at noon on the 3d day of January, unless they shall by law appoint a different day.

SECTION 3. If, at the time fixed for the beginning of the term of the President, the President elect shall have died, the Vice-President elect shall become President. If a President shall not have been chosen before the time fixed for the beginning of his term, or if the President elect shall have failed to qualify, then the Vice-President elect shall act as President until a President shall have qualified; and the Congress may by law provide for the case wherein neither a President elect nor a Vice-President elect shall have qualified, declaring who shall then act as President, or the manner in which one who is to act shall be selected, and such person shall act accordingly until a President or Vice-President shall have qualified.

SECTION 4. The Congress may by law provide for the case of the death of any of the persons from whom the House of Representatives may choose a President whenever the right of choice shall have devolved upon them, and for the case of the death of any of the persons from whom the Senate may choose a Vice-President whenever the right of choice shall have devolved upon them.

SECTION 5. Sections 1 and 2 shall take effect on the 15th day of October following the ratification of this article.

SECTION 6. This article shall be inoperative unless it shall have been ratified as an amendment to the Constitution by the legislatures of three-fourths of the several States within seven years from the date of its submission.

Amendment XXI [December 5, 1933]

SECTION 1. The eighteenth article of amendment to the Constitution of the United States is hereby repealed.

SECTION 2. The transportation or importation into any State, Territory, or possession of the United States for delivery or use therein of intoxicating liquors, in violation of the laws thereof, is hereby prohibited.

SECTION 3. This article shall be inoperative unless it shall have been ratified as an amendment to the Constitution by conventions in the several States, as provided in the Constitution, within seven years from the date of the submission hereof to the States by the Congress.

Amendment XXII [March 1, 1951]

SECTION 1. No person shall be elected to the office of the President more than twice, and no person who has held the office of President, or acted as President, for more than two years of a term to which some other person was elected President shall be elected to the office of the President more than once.

But this Article shall not apply to any person holding the office of President when this Article was proposed by the Congress, and shall not prevent any person who may be holding the office of President or acting as President, during the term within which this Article becomes operative from holding the office of President or acting as President during the remainder of such term.

SECTION 2. This article shall be inoperative unless it shall have been ratified as an amendment to the Constitution by the legislatures of three-fourths of the several states within seven years from the date of its submission to the states by Congress.

Amendment XXIII [March 29, 1961]

SECTION 1. The District constituting the seat of Government of the United States shall appoint in such manner as the Congress may direct:

A number of electors of President and Vice President equal to the whole number of Senators and Representatives in Congress to which the District would be entitled if it were a State, but in no event more than the least populous State; they shall be in addition to those appointed by the States, but they shall be considered, for the purposes of the election of President and Vice President, to be electors appointed by a State; and they shall meet in the District and perform such duties as provided by the twelfth article of amendment.

SECTION 2. The Congress shall have power to enforce this article by appropriate legislation.

Amendment XXIV [January 23, 1964]

SECTION 1. The right of citizens of the United States to vote in any primary or other election for President or Vice President, for electors for President or Vice President, or for Senator or Representative in Congress, shall not be denied or abridged by the United States or any State by reason of failure to pay any poll tax or other tax.

SECTION 2. The Congress shall have the power to enforce this article by appropriate legislation.

Amendment XXV [February 10, 1967]

SECTION 1. In case of the removal of the President from office or of his death or resignation, the Vice President shall become President.

SECTION 2. Whenever there is a vacancy in the office of the Vice President, the President shall nominate a Vice President who shall take office upon confirmation by a majority vote of both houses of Congress.

SECTION 3. Whenever the President transmits to the President pro tempore of the Senate and the Speaker of the House of Representatives his written declaration that he is unable to discharge the powers and duties of his office, and until he transmits to them a written declaration to the contrary, such powers and duties shall be discharged by the Vice President as Acting President.

SECTION 4. Whenever the Vice President and a majority of either the principal officers of the executive departments, or of such other body as Congress may by law provide, transmit to the President pro tempore of the Senate and the Speaker of the House of Representatives their written declaration that the President is unable to discharge the powers and duties of his office, the Vice President shall immediately assume the powers and duties of the office as Acting President.

Thereafter, when the President transmits to the President pro tempore of the Senate and the Speaker of the House of Representatives his written declaration that no inability exists, he shall resume the powers and duties of his office unless the Vice President and a majority of either the principal officers of the executive departments, or of such other body as Congress may by law provide, transmit within four days to the President pro tempore of the Senate and the Speaker of the House of Representatives their written declaration that the President is unable to discharge the powers and duties of his office. Thereupon Congress shall decide the issue, assembling within forty-eight hours for that purpose if not in session. If the Congress, within twenty-one days after receipt of the latter written declaration, or, if Congress is not in session, within twenty-one days after Congress is required to assemble, determines by two-thirds vote of both houses that the President is unable to discharge the powers and duties of his office, the Vice President shall continue to discharge the same as Acting President; otherwise, the President shall resume the powers and duties of his office.

Amendment XXVI [June 30, 1971]

SECTION 1. The right of citizens of the United States, who are eighteen years of age or older, to vote shall not be denied or abridged by the United States or by any state on account of age.

SECTION 2. The Congress shall have power to enforce this article by appropriate legislation.

Amendment XXVII [1992]

No law varying the compensation for the services of the Senators and Representatives shall take effect, until an election of Representatives shall have intervened.

YEAR	NUMBER OF STATES	CANDIDATES	PARTY	POPULAR VOTE*	ELECTORAL VOTE**	PERCENTAGE OF POPULAR VOTE
1789	11	GEORGE WASHINGTON	No party designations		69	
		John Adams			34	
		Other Candidates			35	
1792	15	GEORGE WASHINGTON	No party designations		132	
		John Adams			77	
		George Clinton			50	
		Other Candidates			5	
1796	16	JOHN ADAMS	Federalist		71	
		Thomas Jefferson	Democratic-Republican		68	
		Thomas Pinckney	Federalist		59	
		Aaron Burr	Democratic-Republican		30	
		Other Candidates			48	
1800	16	THOMAS JEFFERSON	Democratic-Republican		73	
		Aaron Burr	Democratic-Republican		73	
		John Adams	Federalist		65	
		Charles C. Pinckney	Federalist		64	
		John Jay	Federalist			
1804	17	THOMAS JEFFERSON	Democratic-Republican		162	
		Charles C. Pinckney	Federalist		14	
1808	17	JAMES MADISON	Democratic-Republican		122	
		Charles C. Pinckney	Federalist		47	
		George Clinton	Democratic-Republican		6	
1812	18	JAMES MADISON	Democratic-Republican		128	
		DeWitt Clinton	Federalist		89	
1816	19	JAMES MONROE	Democratic-Republican		183	
		Rufus King	Federalist		34	
1820	24	JAMES MONROE	Democratic-Republican		231	
		John Quincy Adams	Independent Republican		1	
1824	24	JOHN QUINCY ADAMS		108,740	84	30.5
		Andrew Jackson		153,544	99	43.1
		William H. Crawford		46,618	41	13.1
		Henry Clay		47,136	37	13.2
1828	24	ANDREW JACKSON	Democrat	647,286	178	56.0
		John Quincy Adams	National Republican	508,064	83	44.0
1832	24	ANDREW JACKSON	Democrat	687,502	219	55.0
		Henry Clay	National Republican	530,189	49	42.4
		William Wirt	Anti-Masonic	33,108	7	2.6
		John Floyd	National Republican		11	
1836	26	MARTIN VAN BUREN	Democrat	765,483	170	50.9
		William H. Harrison	Whig		73	
		Hugh L. White	Whig	739,795	26	49.1
		Daniel Webster	Whig		14	
		W. P. Mangum	Whig		11	
1840	26	WILLIAM H. HARRISON	Whig	1,274,624	234	53.1
		Martin Van Buren	Democrat	1,127,781	60	46.9
1844	26	JAMES K. POLK	Democrat	1,338,464	170	49.6
		Henry Clay	Whig	1,300,097	105	48.1
		James G. Birney	Liberty	62,300		2.3
1848	30	ZACHARY TAYLOR	Whig	1,360,967	163	47.4
		Lewis Cass	Democrat	1,222,342	127	42.5
		Martin Van Buren	Free Soil	291,263		10.1

*Percentage of popular vote given for any election year may not total 100 percent because candidates receiving less than 1 percent of the popular vote have been omitted.

**Prior to the passage of the Twelfth Amendment in 1904, the electoral college voted for two presidential candidates; the runner-up became Vice-President. Data from *Historical Statistics of the United States, Colonial Times to 1957* (1961), pp. 682–883, and *The World Almanac.*

YEAR	NUMBER OF STATES	CANDIDATES	PARTY	POPULAR VOTE	ELECTORAL VOTE	PERCENTAGE OF POPULAR VOTE
1852	31	FRANKLIN PIERCE	Democrat	1,601,117	254	50.9
		Winfield Scott	Whig	1,385,453	42	44.1
		John P. Hale	Free Soil	155,825		5.0
1856	31	JAMES BUCHANAN	Democrat	1,832,955	174	45.3
		John C. Frémont	Republican	1,339,932	114	33.1
		Millard Fillmore	American	871,731	8	21.6
1860	33	ABRAHAM LINCOLN	Republican	1,865,593	180	39.8
		Stephen A. Douglas	Democrat	1,382,713	12	29.5
		John C. Breckinridge	Democrat	848,356	72	18.1
		John Bell	Constitutional Union	592,906	39	12.6
1864	36	ABRAHAM LINCOLN	Republican	2,206,938	212	55.0
		George B. McClellan	Democrat	1,803,787	21	45.0
1868	37	ULYSSES S. GRANT	Republican	3,013,421	214	52.7
		Horatio Seymour	Democrat	2,706,829	80	47.3
1872	37	ULYSSES S. GRANT	Republican	3,596,745	286	55.6
		Horace Greeley	Democrat	2,843,446	*	43.9
1876	38	RUTHERFORD B. HAYES	Republican	4,036,572	185	48.0
		Samuel J. Tilden	Democrat	4,284,020	184	51.0
1880	38	JAMES A. GARFIELD	Republican	4,453,295	214	48.5
		Winfield S. Hancock	Democrat	4,414,082	155	48.1
		James B. Weaver	Greenback-Labor	308,578		3.4
1884	38	GROVER CLEVELAND	Democrat	4,879,507	219	48.5
		James G. Blaine	Republican	4,850,293	182	48.2
		Benjamin F. Butler	Greenback-Labor	175,370		1.8
		John P. St. John	Prohibition	150,369		1.5.
1888	38	BENJAMIN HARRISON	Republican	5,447,129	233	47.9
		Grover Cleveland	Democrat	5,537,857	168	48.6
		Clinton B. Fisk	Prohibition	249,506		2.2
		Anson J. Streeter	Union Labor	146,935		1.3
1892	44	GROVER CLEVELAND	Democrat	5,555,426	277	46.1
		Benjamin Harrison	Republican	5,182,690	145	43.0
		James B. Weaver	People's	1,029,846	22	8.5
		John Bidwell	Prohibition	264,133		2.2
1896	45	WILLIAM MCKINLEY	Republican	7,102,246	271	51.1
		William J. Bryan	Democrat	6,492,559	176	47.7
1900	45	WILLIAM MCKINLEY	Republican	7,218,491	292	51.7
		William J. Bryan	Democrat; Populist	6,356,734	155	45.5
		John C. Woolley	Prohibition	208,914		1.5
1904	45	THEODORE ROOSEVELT	Republican	7,628,461	336	57.4
		Alton B. Parker	Democrat	5,084,223	140	37.6
		Eugene V. Debs	Socialist	402,283		3.0
		Silas C. Swallow	Prohibition	258,536		1.9
1908	46	WILLIAM H. TAFT	Republican	7,675,320	321	51.6
		William J. Bryan	Democrat	6,412,294	162	43.1
		Eugene V. Debs	Socialist	420,793		2.8
		Eugene W. Chafin	Prohibition	253,840		1.7
1912	48	WOODROW WILSON	Democrat	6,296,547	435	41.9
		Theodore Roosevelt	Progressive	4,118,571	88	27.4
		William H. Taft	Republican	3,486,720	8	23.2
		Eugene V. Debs	Socialist	900,672		6.0
		Eugene W. Chafin	Prohibition	206,275		1.4

*Because of the death of Greeley, Democratic electors scattered their votes.

YEAR	NUMBER OF STATES	CANDIDATES	PARTY	POPULAR VOTE	ELECTORAL VOTE	PERCENTAGE OF POPULAR VOTE
1916	48	WOODROW WILSON	Democrat	9,127,695	277	49.4
		Charles E. Hughes	Republican	8,533,507	254	46.2
		A. L. Benson	Socialist	585,113		3.2
		J. Frank Hanly	Prohibition	220,506		1.2
1920	48	WARREN G. HARDING	Republican	16,143,407	404	60.4
		James M. Cox	Democrat	9,130,328	127	34.2
		Eugene V. Debs	Socialist	919,799		3.4
		P. P. Christensen	Farmer-Labor	265,411		1.0
1924	48	CALVIN COOLIDGE	Republican	15,718,211	382	54.0
		John W. Davis	Democrat	8,385,283	136	28.8
		Robert M. La Follette	Progressive	4,831,289	13	16.6
1928	48	HERBERT C. HOOVER	Republican	21,391,993	444	58.2
		Alfred E. Smith	Democrat	15,016,169	87	40.9
1932	48	FRANKLIN D. ROOSEVELT	Democrat	22,809,638	472	57.4
		Herbert C. Hoover	Republican	15,758,901	59	39.7
		Norman Thomas	Socialist	881,951		2.2
1936	48	FRANKLIN D. ROOSEVELT	Democrat	27,752,869	523	60.8
		Alfred M. Landon	Republican	16,674,665	8	36.5
		William Lemke	Union	882,479		1.9
1940	48	FRANKLIN D. ROOSEVELT	Democrat	27,307,819	449	54.8
		Wendell L. Wilkie	Republican	22,321,018	82	44.8
1944	48	FRANKLIN D. ROOSEVELT	Democrat	25,606,585	432	53.5
		Thomas E. Dewey	Republican	22,014,745	99	46.0
1948	48	HARRY S. TRUMAN	Democrat	24,105,812	303	49.5
		Thomas E. Dewey	Republican	21,970,065	189	45.1
		J. Strom Thurmond	States' Rights	1,169,063	39	2.4
		Henry A. Wallace	Progressive	1,157,172		2.4
1952	48	DWIGHT D. EISENHOWER	Republican	33,936,234	442	55.1
		Adlai E. Stevenson	Democrat	27,314,992	89	44.4
1956	48	DWIGHT D. EISENHOWER	Republican	35,590,472	457*	57.6
		Adlai E. Stevenson	Democrat	26,022,752	73	42.1
1960	50	JOHN F. KENNEDY	Democrat	34,227,096	303**	49.9
		Richard M. Nixon	Republican	34,108,546	219	49.6
1964	50	LYNDON B. JOHNSON	Democrat	42,676,220	486	61.3
		Barry M. Goldwater	Republican	26,860,314	52	38.5
1968	50	RICHARD M. NIXON	Republican	31,785,480	301	43.4
		Hubert H. Humphrey	Democrat	31,275,165	191	42.7
		George C. Wallace	American Independent	9,906,473	46	13.5
1972	50	RICHARD M. NIXON***	Republican	47,165,234	520	60.6
		George S. McGovern	Democrat	29,168,110	17	37.5
1976	50	JIMMY CARTER	Democrat	40,828,929	297	50.1
		Gerald R. Ford	Republican	39,148,940	240	47.9
		Eugene McCarthy	Independent	739,256		
1980	50	RONALD REAGAN	Republican	43,201,220	489	50.9
		Jimmy Carter	Democrat	34,913,332	49	41.2
		John B. Anderson	Independent	5,581,379		
1984	50	RONALD REAGAN	Republican	53,428,357	525	59.0
		Walter F. Mondale	Democrat	36,930,923	13	41.0
1988	50	GEORGE BUSH	Republican	48,901,046	426	53.4
		Michael Dukakis	Democrat	41,809,030	111	45.6

*Walter B. Jones received 1 electoral vote.
**Harry F. Byrd received 15 electoral votes.
***Resigned August 9,1974; Vice President Gerald R. Ford became President.

YEAR	NUMBER OF STATES	CANDIDATES	PARTY	POPULAR VOTE	ELECTORAL VOTE	PERCENTAGE OF POPULAR VOTE
1992	50	WILLIAM J. CLINTON	Democrat	44,909,806	370	43.0
		George Bush	Republican	39,104,550	168	37.5
		H. Ross Perot	Independent	19,742,240		18.9
		Andre Marrau	Libertarian	291,631		0.3
1996	50	WILLIAM J. CLINTON	Democrat	47,402,357	379	49.2
		Robert Dole	Republican	39,198,755	159	40.7
		H. Ross Perot	Reform	8,085,402		8.4
		Ralph Nadar	Green	685,128		0.7
		Harry Browne	Libertarian	485,798		0.5
2000	50	GEORGE W. BUSH	Republican	50,459,624	271	47.9
		Albert Gore, Jr.	Democrat	51,003,238	266	48.4
		Ralph Nadar	Green	2,882,985		2.7
		Patric Buchanan	Reform	449,120		0.4
		Harry Browne	Libertarian	384,440		0.4

Index

Georgia Indian pacification, 185
legacy of, 236
presidency of, 224–32
  Bank War, 230–32
  critics of, 233
  Indian policy, 226
  nullification doctrine, 228
  spoils system, 225
  states' rights, 228
  Webster-Hayne debate, 227
Texas republic and, 312
Jackson, James, 155
Jackson, Stonewall, 355, 358, 361
Jacabin reign of terror, 159
James, Duke of York, 33–34
James I, King of England, 20, 24, 49
James II, King of England, 40
James Monroe (ship), 208
James River, 20, 21
Jamestown settlement, 22–23
  Bacon's rebellion, 22–23
Japan, 274
Jarrett, Devereaux, 55
Jay, John, 122, 145, 153
Jay's Treaty (Treaty of London, 1794),
    161–62, 163, 165
Jefferson, Thomas, 114, 124, 139, 156,
    157–59, 163, 166, 172–78, 194, 219
  Barbary War (1801–1805), 173
  Canning proposal and, 188
  drafting of Declaration of Independ-
      ence, 113–15
  election of 1800, 167
  on Federalists, 171
  financial policy, 172–73
  Napoleonic wars and, 178–81
  Neutrality Proclamation and, 160
  on New Orleans (Louisiana terri-
      tory), 176
  Northwest Ordinance and, 136
  opposition to Hamilton, 155
  on property, 115
  as secretary of state, 153
  struggles with judiciary, 173–74
  on Virginia planters' debt, 92
  West, policies on the, 178
Jews, Spanish attempts to expel, 8
Jim Crow laws, 403, 404
Johnnycake, 290
Johnson, Andrew, 370, 372, 377, 381,
    383, 383–95
  impeachment attempt, 386–87
  restoration under, 383–84
Johnson, Edward, 11
Johnson, Henry, 391
Johnston, Albert Sidney, 357
Johnston, Joseph, 358
Joint Committee of Fifteen, 384

Jones, John Paul, 116
Journey cake, 290
Judiary Act (1802), 173
Judicial review, 143, 174
Judiciary, 142
  Jefferson's struggles with, 173–74
Judiciary Act (1789), 152, 153, 174
Judiciary Act (1801), 167
Justice, Department of, 153

K

Kalm, Peter, 59, 77
Kansas, 272
  "bleeding," 332
  constitutional convention (1857), 338
Kansas-Nebraska Act (1854), 330–32
Kearny, Stephen W., 319
"Keel over," source of phrase, 39
Kemble, Fanny, 250
Kennedy, John Pendleton, 301
Kent, Chancellor, 234
Kentucky, 135, 196
Kentucky Resolution (1798), 166
Key, David M., 399
King, Rufus, 144, 179, 194
King George's War, 81–82
King James Bible, 20
King Phillp's War (1675–1676), 28–29
King's College (Columbia University), 77
Knights of the White Camellia, 393
Knowlton, Charles, 270
Know-Nothings (American party), 335
Knox, Henry, 153
Ku Klux Klan, 393
Ku Klux Klan Act (1871), 393

L

Labor
  child, 212, 269
  division of, in colonial farms, 57–58
  movement, 213
  relations in New South, 400, 401
  specialization, 47–48
  women and, 211, 212
Ladies' Magazine, 252
Lafayette, Marquis de, 159
Lake Champlain, Battle of (1814), 182–83
Lancaster Turnpike, 204
Land(s)
  claims, 132
  exploitation of, 59
  graduation policy, 227
  Indian conception of, 4
  of Loyalists, 134
Land act of 1820, 195
Land-grant colleges, 364

Language
  American Indian, 2–3
  creolized, 52
  English, 62
Last names, 72
Last of the Mohicans, The (Cooper), 245
Latin America, Monroe Doctrine and,
    188–89
Law(s)
  common, 61–62
  Jim Crow, 403–4
  women's movement and, 273
"Lawrence, Sack of" (1856), 332
League of the Iroquois. *See* Iroquois
    Confederacy
Leaves of Grass (Whitman), 249
Lecompton Constitution, 338
Lee, Richard Henry, 113
Lee, Robert E., 340, *359*
  in Civil War, 357, 358, 359, 360–61,
      367–68, 371
Legislation, judicial review of, 143,
    174–75
Legislature
  colonial, 34–35
  power to, 130
Leisler, Jacob, 40
L'Enfant, Pierre, 172
*Letters from a Farmer in Pennsylva-
    nia* (Dickinson), 97
Lewis, Meriwether, 176, *176*
Lewis and Clark expedition, 175, 176
Lexington, battle of (1775), 103
Liberator, The, 259–60, 300
Liberia, 259
Liberty incident, 98
Liberty party, 314
Lifestyle in colonies, 45, 53–61
Limited liability, 210
Lincoln, Abraham, 252, 332, 335, 350,
    352, *353*
  Civil War and, 352–59, 367–71
    appointment of Grant, 278–79
    Emancipation Proclamation, 672,
        365–66
    Fort Sumter fall, 344
    Gettysburg Address, 368
  Crittenden's compromise and, 342
  death of, 372
  debates with Douglas, 339–39, *339*
  divided nation and, 352–53
  on *Dred Scott* decision, 337
  election of, 340–41, 380, 382
  inaugural address, 342–43
  on Know-Nothings, 335
  plan for Reconstruction, 378,
      381–82
  on self-government, 353

Portuguese, 7–8
Spanish, 8–11
Milltary, establishment under Constitu-
	tion, 142
Miller, Alfred Jacob, 250
Mills, women in, 211
Mind of the South, The (Cash), 403
Mining, 275
Minnesota, 275, 320
Minutemen, 103
Miscegenation, 379
Mississippi, 176, 197
Mississippi, origin of word, 159
Mississippi Company, 92
Mississippi Plan, 394
Mississippi River, 203, 279
Missouri Compromise (1820), 197–98,
	227, 310, 313, 320
	repeal of, 330, 332, 335
	Supreme Court decision on, 335–36
Missouri Territory, 178
Mittelberger, Gottlieb, 48
Moby Dick (Melville), 249
Moderate Girondist faction, 159
Modernization of Western culture, 241
Mohawk Valley, 80
Molasses Act (1733), 39,93
Monarchies, 7
Monetary policy during Civil War, 364
Money
	American pursuit of, 242
	paper, 63, 136, 142
	political conflict and, 63
Monitor (ironclad), 358
Monroe, James, 165, 171, 176, 177, 194,
	219, 230
Monroe Doctrine, 187–88
Montcalm, Louis Joseph de, 90
Montesquieu, Baron de La Brede et
	de, 139
Montezuma, 10
Montgomery, Richard, 111
Montreal, Canada, 90
Moors, 8
Morgan, Daniel, 161
Morgan, J. P., 374
Mormons, 316–17
Morrill Land Grant Act of 1862, 364
Morrill Tariff (1861), 364
Morris, Gouverneur, 139
Morris, Robert, 134
Morse, Samuel F. B., 250, 282
Morton, Oliver P., 386
Motherhood, ideas and values about, 269
Mott, Garrison, 271
Mott, James, 271
Mott, Lucretia, 262, 272, 273, *274*
Mt. Holyoke Female Seminary, 256

Music, slaves' use of, 294
Muskogean languages, 2
Mutual aid societies, 212

N

Napoleon Bonaparte, 176–77, 178, 180,
	183, 187
Napoleon II, 363
Narragansett Indians, 26, 28
Nashoba community, 258–59
National Gazette (newspaper), 158
National Highway, 204
National Republicans, 223
Nation-states, rise of, 7
Naturalization Act (1798), 166
Natural philosophy, 76
Natural resources, 268
Natural rights, 74,91, 129
Nature, Indian society and, 3–4
Nature (Emerson), 247
Nauvoo settlement, 317
Naval power, mercantllism and, 37–38
Naval stores, 38
Navigation Acts (1660, 1663), 38–39,
	41, 48
Navy
	expansion af (1798–1799), 165
	president as commander in chief
		of, 142
Navy Department, 165
Nebraska country, 330–31
Necessity, Fort, 88
Negroes, 50
Nelson, Horatio, 178
Netherlands
	African slave trade and, 30–31
	migrants from, 12
	naval wars with England (17th c.),
		31, 38
	New Amsterdam colony, 30–31
Neutrality
	Napoleonic wars and, 177
	trade benefits of, 160–61
Neutrality Proclamation (1793), 159–60
New Amsterdam, 30–31
New Brunswick province, 308
Newby, Dangerfield, 339
New England
	colonial. *See also specific* colonies
		classes and lifestyles in, 57
		formal education in, 77–78
		health conditions in, 47
		Molasses Act and, 39–40
		Puritans, 23–30
		royal commissioners and, 39–40
		scientific investigations in, 76
	family role in, 269

flowering of, 246
railroad network, 279
secession threatened by, 184
sex ratio during Industrial
	Revolution, 211
War of 1812 and, 181, 182
New England, Dominion of, 40, 41
New England Emigrant Aid
	Company, 332
Newfoundland, 57
New Hampshire, 135–36
	colony, 27–28, 57
	ratification of Constitution, 144
New Harmony, 258
New Jersey colony, 33–34
	American Revolution in, 115
	classes and lifestyles, 56
New Lights, 70
New Netherland, 38
New Orleans, 202, 203, 269
New Orleans, Battle of (1814), 183
New Orleans (Louisiana
	territory), 176
New Orleans (steamboat), 203
Newport, Christopher, 20, 21
Newport, Rhode Island, 60
New South, 399–405
	labor relations in, 400, 401
Newton, Isaac, *66*, 73
New World, colonization of, 14–15. *See
	also* Migrants
New York, 31
	colonial
		American Revolution in, 115
		classes and lifestyles, 56
		French-English conflict in, 80
		representative government in, 41
		Revolutionary campaigns in,
			117–18, *117*
	immigrants in, 268
	railroads in, 281
	ratification of Constitution, 145
New York and Harlem railroad, 281
New York Central railroad, 281
New York City, 34, 57, 117, 266,
	283, 299
	Civil War draft riot in, 364
	rise of, 207–9
New York Customs House, 399
New York Sun, 250
Niagara, Battle of (1814), 183
Nicholson, Francis, 41
Nina (ship), 9
Nonimportation movement, 97,
	98, 100
Norsemen, 5
North, Frederick Lord, 99, 100–1, 111,
	120, 122

Populist movement, 404
Porter, Fitz-John, 358
Porter, Lavinia, 313
Port Hudson, surrender of (1863), 368
Portugal
    migration from, 7–8
    Napoleon's invasion of
        (1807–1808), 188
Pottawatomie Creek, 333
Poverty in Ireland, 49–50
Power
    to legislatures, 130
    Marshall on federal, 196
    of people, 130
Powers, Hiram, 251
Powhatan (chief), 21
Prairie, The (Cooper), 245
Praying villages, 29
Preachers, itinerant, 69–70
Predestination, doctrine of, 12
Preemption, right of 227–28
Prejudice, 71
    Anti-Catholic, 245
Presbyterians, 70, 72, 244
Prescott, William H., 246
Presidency, activist, 237
President, U.S. *See also specific*
        presidents
    cabinet of, 153
    as commander in chief, 142
    impeachment of, 142
President (U.S. frigate), 181
Press, popular, 251–52
Princeton, battle of (1776), 118
Princeton University, 70
Principal Navigations, Voyages, Traf-
        fiques, and *Discoveries of the*
        English Nation (Hakluyt), 15
Privateers, 165, 182
Proclamation of 1763, 91, 92
Proclamation of Amnesty and Recon-
        struction (1863), 381–82
Production, growth of agricultural,
        274–75
Property, 143
    American Revolution and, 124–25
    Jefferson on, 115
    as natural right, 74
    office holding and, 62–63
    slaves as, 123, 337
    voting and, 62–63, 405
Prophet, the, 180
Proprietary colonies, 31–37, 39
Proprietors, 31
Prostitution, 271
Protestant denominations, 71–72
Protestantism, Calvinist heritage of,
        71–72

Protestant Reformation, 1–2, 12
Protestant Restoration, 20
Providence, 26
"Psalm of Life, A" (poem), 246
Public health, 244
Public office, property requirement
        for, 62
Public schools, 253
Puget Sound, 313
Purgatives, 244
Puritans, 20, 23–30, 39, 41, 68
    formal education among, 77
    ideology of, 23–24
    Indians and, 28
    migration to New Jersey, 33
    New England economy and, 29–30
    Pilgrims in Plymouth, 24–25
    trading in black slavery, 30

Q

Quakers, 34, 48, 115, 243, 247, 259, 260
    Indians and, 35
    intellectual connections abroad, 77
    merchants, 56
    revival in 1750s, 71
Quartering Act (1765), 97,101
Quartering Act (1773), 102
Quebec, Canada, 89, 90, 308
Quebec Act (1773), 101
Quebec Act (1774), 132
Queenston Heights, 182
Quincy, Josiah, 184
Quinine, 249

R

Racism. *See also* Slavery
    northern, 394
    southern, 394, 404
Radical Congress, 384–88
Radical Reconstruction, 388–895
Radical Republicans, 362, 365, 375
Railroads, 207, 281–83, 282, 284,
        377, 385
    federal land grants for, 396
    transcontinental, 330
Raleigh, Walter, 14, *14*
Randolph, Edmund, 40, 139, 140, 145,
        153, 156
Randolph, John, 175, 178
Real estate companies, 210
Reapers, 276
Reason, human, 74
Reconstruction, 377–405
    end of, 393–95
    Grant presidency and, 395–97
    Hayes and, 397–99

Johnsonian Restoration, 383–84
Lincoln's plan for, 377, 378, 381–82
map of, *393*
New South and, 399–405
Radical Congress and, 384–88
Radical Reconstruction, 388–95
slavery, aftermath of, 379–81
South in defeat, 378–83
Red Badge of Courage, The
        (Crane), 370
Redeemers, 399, 403
Redemptioners, 48
Red Shirts, 394
Reformation, 1–2, 12
Reform movements
    abolitionism, 259–60
    communitarians, 259, 316
    temperance movement, 255–56, 270
Reforms, post-Revolutionary War, 126
Regulars (Conservatives) in Civil
        War, 353
Religion, 243–44. *See also specific* reli-
        gions and religious groups
    colonial, 68–72
        church-state separation, 71
        established churches, 68
        Great Awakening, 68–71
        Protestant denominations, 71–72
    freedom of, 35, 72
    revivalism, 70, 243
    slaves' inner world in, 294
    Toleration Act (1649), 32
Religious fundamentalism in
        South, 301
Religious toleration, 32, 41
Rents, colonial, 58
Representation, virtual, 95
Representative assemblies, 129
Representative government, 62
Representative Men (Emerson), 248
Republican clubs, 160
Republican party, 151, 159, 167, 332–33,
        335, 337, 338. *See also* Jefferson,
        Thomas
    1860 platform, 340
    formation of, 338
    Old Republicans, 175
Residence requirements far voting, 405
Resolution of Independence, 113
Restlessness of Americans, 242
Restoration, 20
Revels, Hiram, 389
Revenue Act (Sugar Act), 93–94
Revere, Paul, 99, 99, 100, 104
Revivalism, religious, 70, 243. *See also*
        Great Awakening
    during antebellum period, 303
Revival meeting, 70

West, the
  canal system and, 207
  Civil War in, 356–57, 356
  explorations of, *175*
  Jefferson's policies, 176–78
  railroad construction in, 279
  trails of, 320
West African immigrants, 50–52. *See also* Blacks; Slavery; Slave trade
Western culture, modernization of 241
Western Europe, commercial capitalism in, 1–2
West Indies, 30–31, 36
West Jersey, 34
West Point, 186
Westward expansion. *See* Expansion
Whaling, 198
Wheat binders, 277
Wheat production, 272–73, *272*
Whigs, 324
  breakup of, 327
  decline of power, 237
  disintegration of, 328
  election of 1844 and, 317
  Mexican-American War and, 317–19
Whiskey Rebellion, 156
Whiskey Ring, 397
White, John, 14
Whitefield, George, 68, *68*, 70
White Leagues, 394
Whitman, Walt, 248–49, *248*, 260, 344
Whitney, Eli, 202

Whittier, John Greenleaf, 246, 260
Wigfall, Louis T., 322
Wigwam, 3
Wilkes, John, 96
Wilkins, Frederick, 329
Willard, Emma, 254
William and Mary, 40–41
William and Mary College, 79
William III, King of England, 41
William of Orange (William I), 80–81
Williams, Roger, 26–27
Williams v. Mississippi, 405
Wilmington race riot (1898), 404
Wilmot, David, 320
Wilmot Proviso, 320, 321
Wilson, Edmund, 397
Wilson, James, 138, 141
Wilson, Woodrow, 388
Winder, William H., 183
Winthrop, John, 25, 26, 28
Winthrop, John, 79
Winthrop, John, Jr., 76
Wisconsin, 275, 324
Wise, John, 72
Witchcraft, end of, 73
Wolcott, Oliver, 156–57, 165
Wolfe, James, 90
Woman's Rights Convention at Seneca Falls (1848), 272
Women, 269–72
  in abolitionist movement, 271
  American Revolution and, 125

  black, in aftermath of slavery, 379–80
  in Civil War, 373–74, 367
  declining birth rate and, 269–70
  education for, 254
  formal education among colonial, 78–79
  Industrial Revolution and, 211, 212–14
  pioneer, 312
  proper sphere of, 272–74
  Southern, 304
  suffrage for, 385
Women's rights movement, 269–72
Wool, John, 182
Woolman, John, 71
Worcester v. Georgia, 226
Working-class women, 272
Wright, Frances, 258–59, *258*, 260
Wright, James, 102
Writs of assistance, 91, 97
Wyeth, Nathaniel J., 313

X
XYZ affair, 165

Y
Yale, 78
Yellow fever, 244
York (Toronto), 183
Yorktown, battle of (1781), 121–22
Young, Brigham, 317